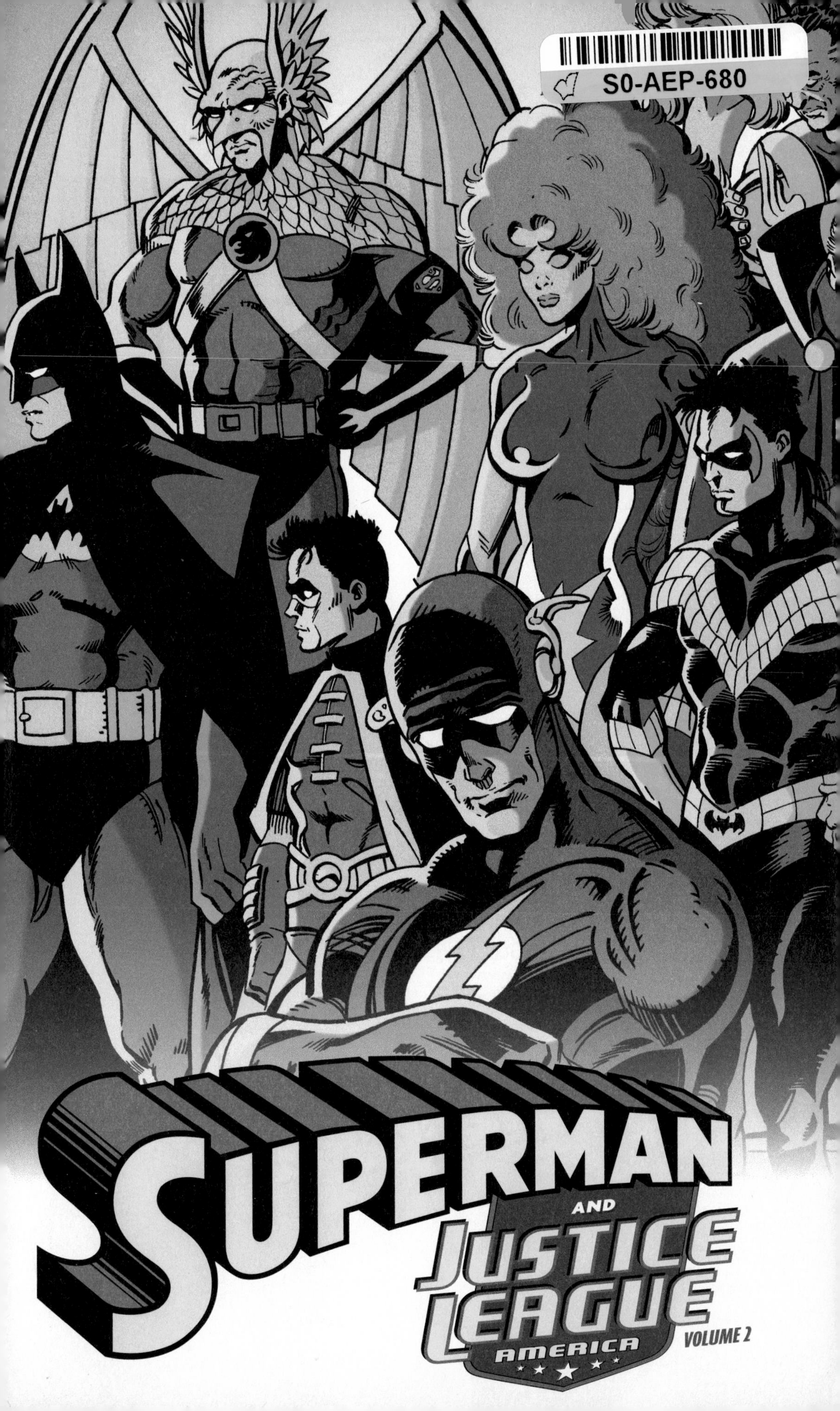
SUPERMAN
AND
JUSTICE LEAGUE AMERICA
VOLUME 2

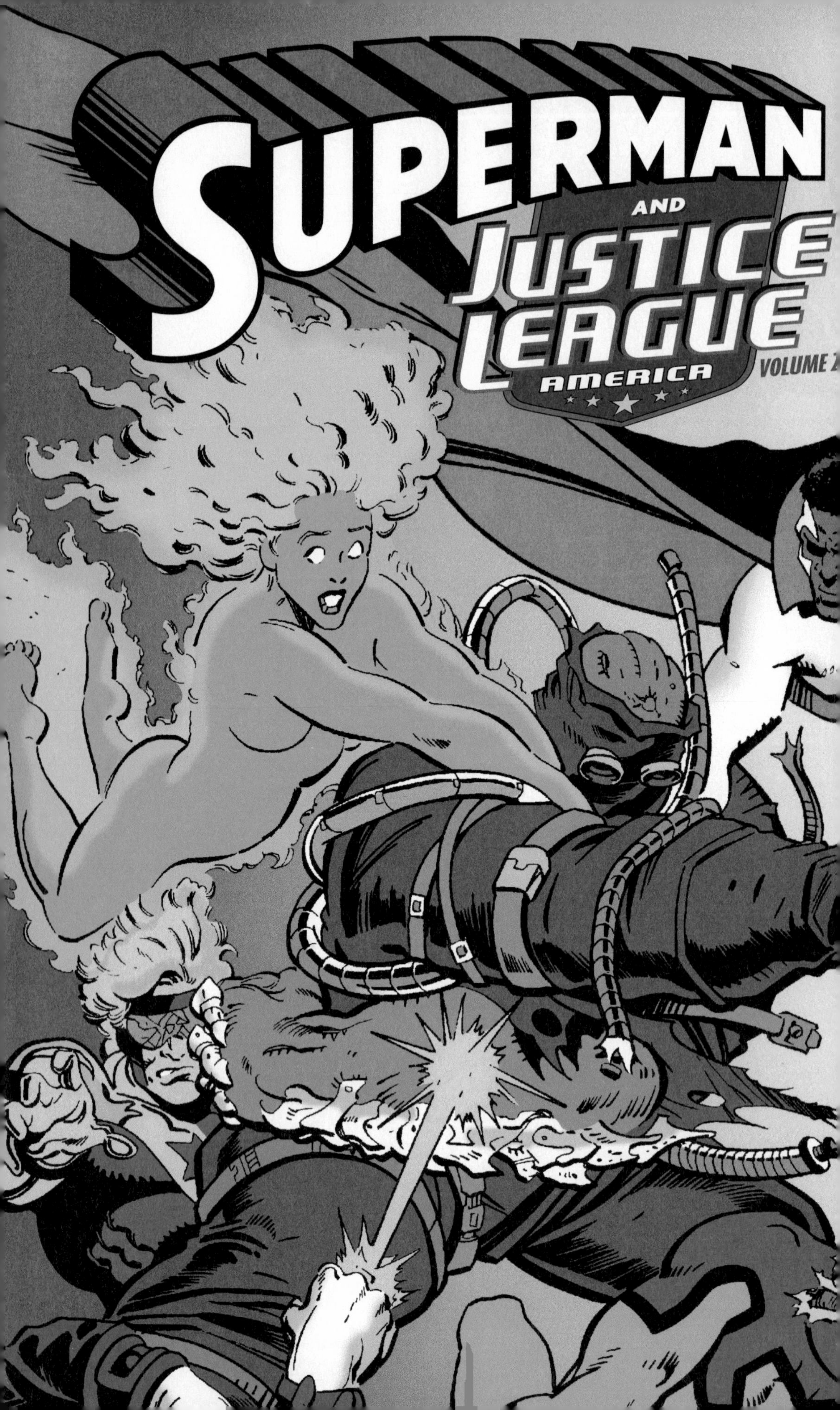
SUPERMAN
AND
JUSTICE LEAGUE
AMERICA
VOLUME 2

DAN JURGENS
DAN MISHKIN
WRITERS

DAN JURGENS
DAVE COCKRUM
RICK BURCHETT
ROMEO TANGHAL
JOSE MARZAN JR
BOB SMITH
SAL VELLUTO
ARTISTS

GENE D'ANGELO
COLORIST

WILLIE SCHUBERT
LETTERERS

DAN JURGENS
RICK BURCHETT
COLLECTION COVER ART

SUPERMAN CREATED BY **JERRY SIEGEL** AND **JOE SHUSTER**.
BY SPECIAL ARRANGEMENT WITH THE JERRY SIEGEL FAMILY.

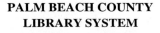

BRIAN AUGUSTYN Editor – Original Series
RUBEN DIAZ Assistant Editor – Original Series
JEB WOODARD Group Editor – Collected Editions
PAUL SANTOS Editor – Collected Edition
STEVE COOK Design Director – Books
CURTIS KING JR. Publication Design
BOB HARRAS Senior VP – Editor-in-Chief, DC Comics

DIANE NELSON President
DAN DIDIO and JIM LEE Co-Publishers
GEOFF JOHNS Chief Creative Officer
AMIT DESAI Senior VP – Marketing & Global Franchise Management
NAIRI GARDINER Senior VP – Finance
SAM ADES VP – Digital Marketing
BOBBIE CHASE VP – Talent Development
MARK CHIARELLO Senior VP – Art, Design & Collected Editions
JOHN CUNNINGHAM VP – Content Strategy
ANNE DEPIES VP – Strategy Planning & Reporting
DON FALLETTI VP – Manufacturing Operations
LAWRENCE GANEM VP – Editorial Administration & Talent Relations
ALISON GILL Senior VP – Manufacturing & Operations
HANK KANALZ Senior VP – Editorial Strategy & Administration
JAY KOGAN VP – Legal Affairs
DEREK MADDALENA Senior VP – Sales & Business Development
JACK MAHAN VP – Business Affairs
DAN MIRON VP – Sales Planning & Trade Development
NICK NAPOLITANO VP – Manufacturing Administration
CAROL ROEDER VP – Marketing
EDDIE SCANNELL VP – Mass Account & Digital Sales
COURTNEY SIMMONS Senior VP – Publicity & Communications
JIM (SKI) SOKOLOWSKI VP – Comic Book Specialty & Newsstand Sales
SANDY YI Senior VP – Global Franchise Management

MIX
Paper from
responsible sources
FSC® C101537
www.fsc.org

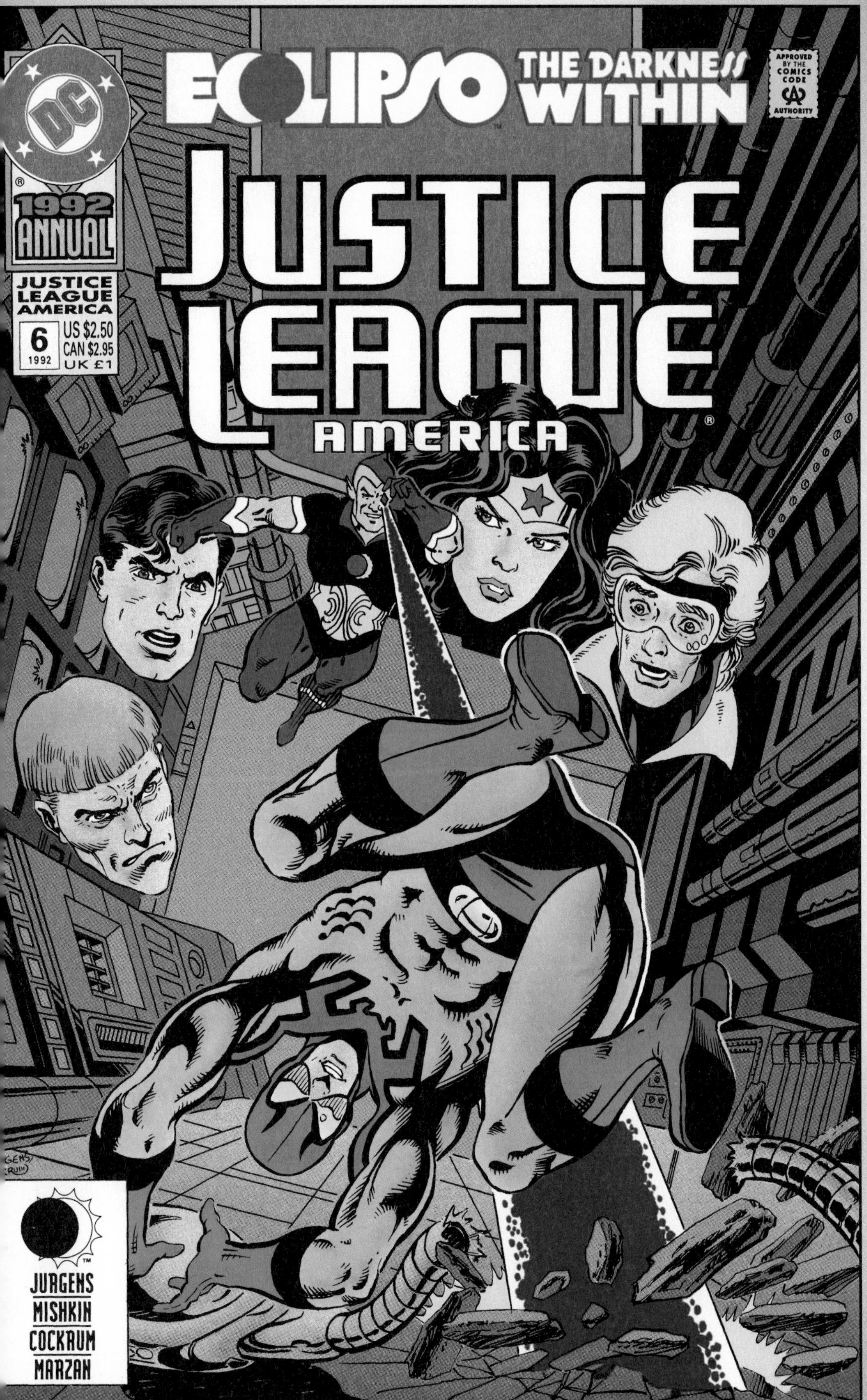
ECLIPSO
THE DARKNESS WITHIN
APPROVED BY THE COMICS CODE AUTHORITY
DC
1992 ANNUAL
JUSTICE LEAGUE AMERICA
6
1992
US $2.50
CAN $2.95
UK £1
JUSTICE LEAGUE AMERICA
JURGENS
MISHKIN
COCKRUM
MARZAN

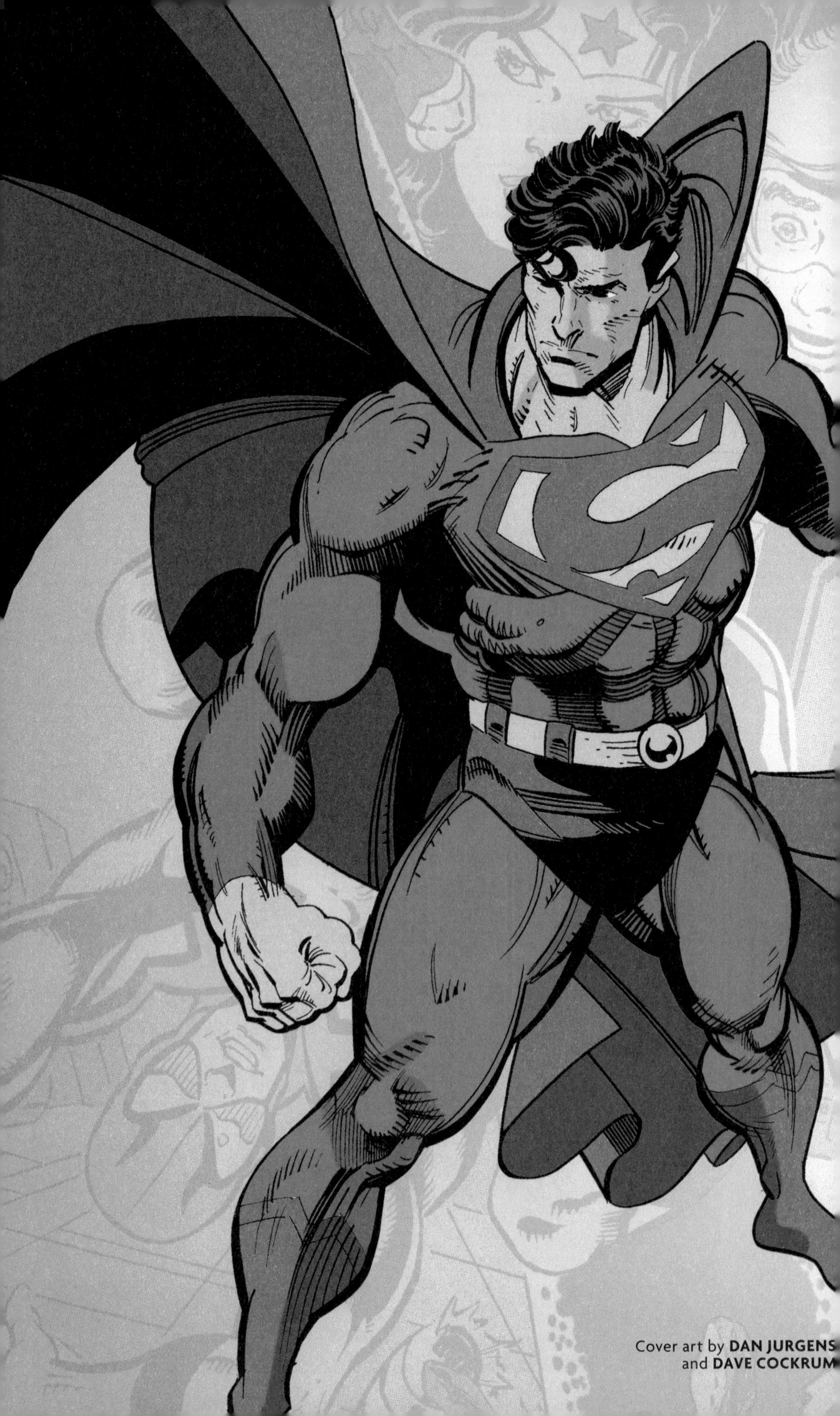

Cover art by **DAN JURGENS**
and **DAVE COCKRUM**

MAXIMUM ECLIPSE

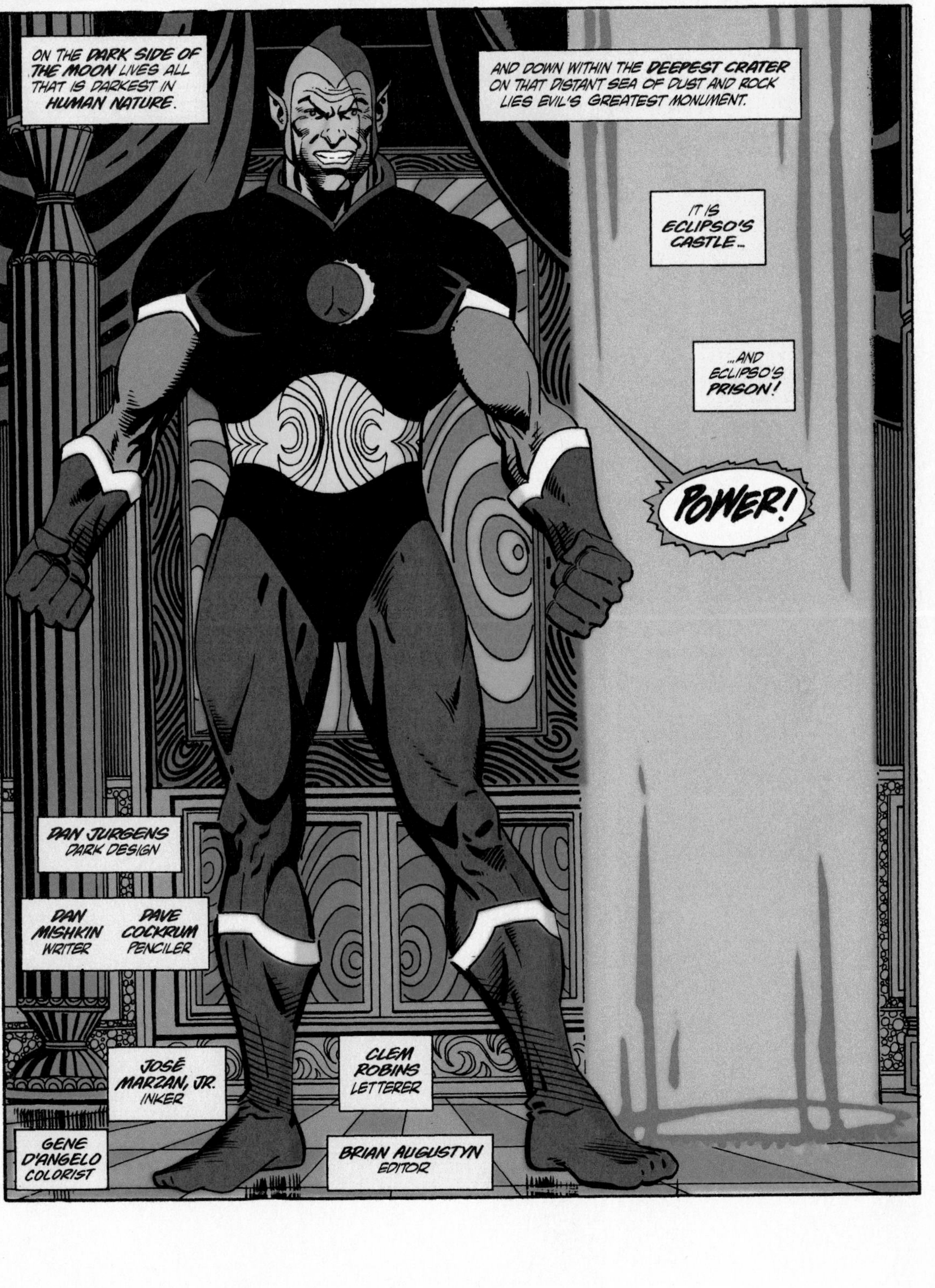

ON THE DARK SIDE OF THE MOON LIVES ALL THAT IS DARKEST IN HUMAN NATURE.
AND DOWN WITHIN THE DEEPEST CRATER ON THAT DISTANT SEA OF DUST AND ROCK LIES EVIL'S GREATEST MONUMENT.
IT IS ECLIPSO'S CASTLE...
...AND ECLIPSO'S PRISON!
POWER!
DAN JURGENS DARK DESIGN
DAN MISHKIN WRITER
DAVE COCKRUM PENCILER
JOSÉ MARZAN, JR. INKER
CLEM ROBINS LETTERER
GENE D'ANGELO COLORIST
BRIAN AUGUSTYN EDITOR

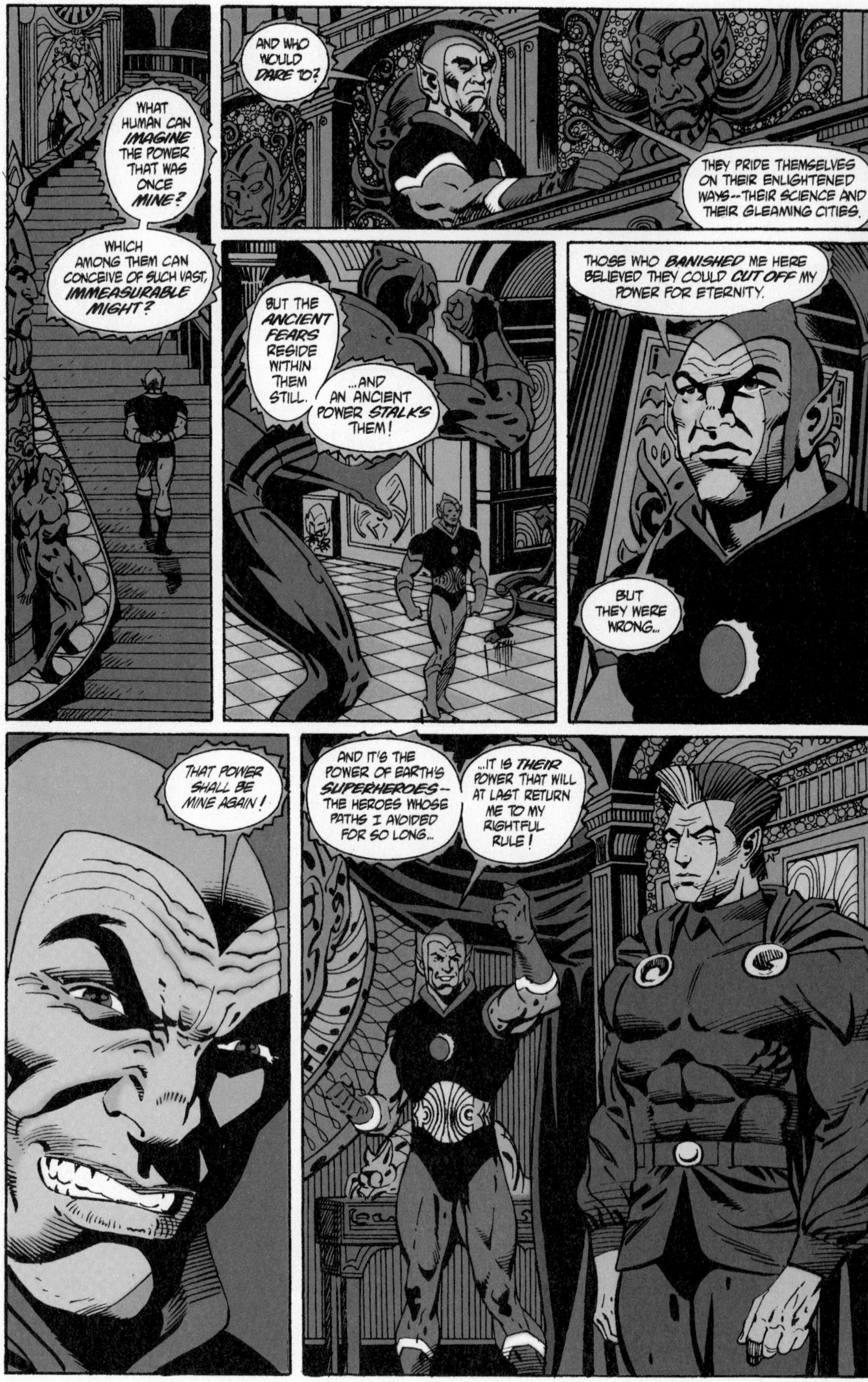
WHAT HUMAN CAN IMAGINE THE POWER THAT WAS ONCE MINE?
WHICH AMONG THEM CAN CONCEIVE OF SUCH VAST, IMMEASURABLE MIGHT?
AND WHO WOULD DARE TO?
THEY PRIDE THEMSELVES ON THEIR ENLIGHTENED WAYS--THEIR SCIENCE AND THEIR GLEAMING CITIES.
BUT THE ANCIENT FEARS RESIDE WITHIN THEM STILL.
...AND AN ANCIENT POWER STALKS THEM!
THOSE WHO BANISHED ME HERE BELIEVED THEY COULD CUT OFF MY POWER FOR ETERNITY.
BUT THEY WERE WRONG...
THAT POWER SHALL BE MINE AGAIN!
AND IT'S THE POWER OF EARTH'S SUPERHEROES--THE HEROES WHOSE PATHS I AVOIDED FOR SO LONG...
...IT IS THEIR POWER THAT WILL AT LAST RETURN ME TO MY RIGHTFUL RULE!

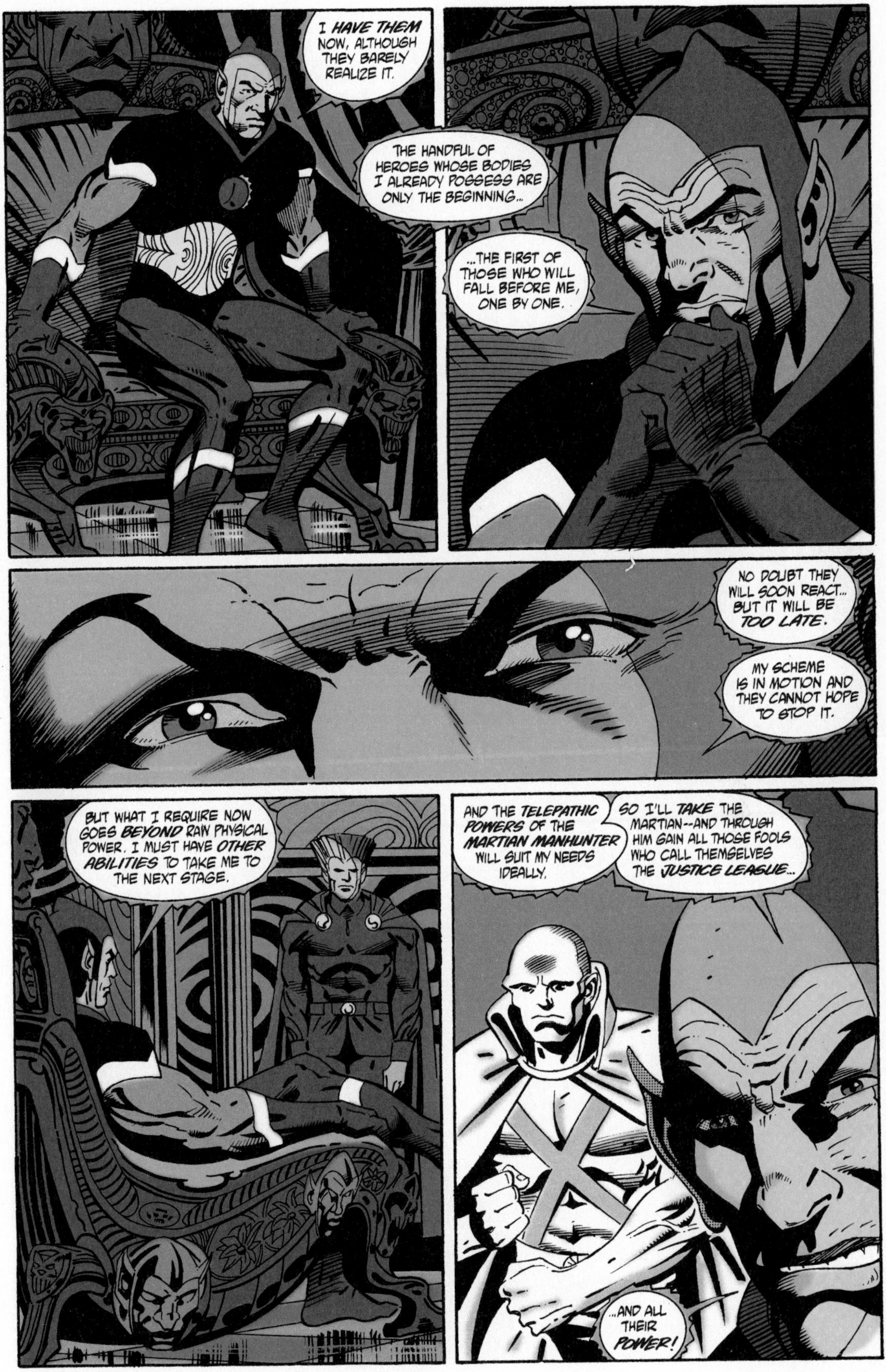
I HAVE THEM NOW, ALTHOUGH THEY BARELY REALIZE IT.
THE HANDFUL OF HEROES WHOSE BODIES I ALREADY POSSESS ARE ONLY THE BEGINNING...
...THE FIRST OF THOSE WHO WILL FALL BEFORE ME, ONE BY ONE.
NO DOUBT THEY WILL SOON REACT... BUT IT WILL BE TOO LATE.
MY SCHEME IS IN MOTION AND THEY CANNOT HOPE TO STOP IT.
BUT WHAT I REQUIRE NOW GOES BEYOND RAW PHYSICAL POWER. I MUST HAVE OTHER ABILITIES TO TAKE ME TO THE NEXT STAGE.
AND THE TELEPATHIC POWERS OF THE MARTIAN MANHUNTER WILL SUIT MY NEEDS IDEALLY.
SO I'LL TAKE THE MARTIAN--AND THROUGH HIM GAIN ALL THOSE FOOLS WHO CALL THEMSELVES THE JUSTICE LEAGUE...
...AND ALL THEIR POWER!

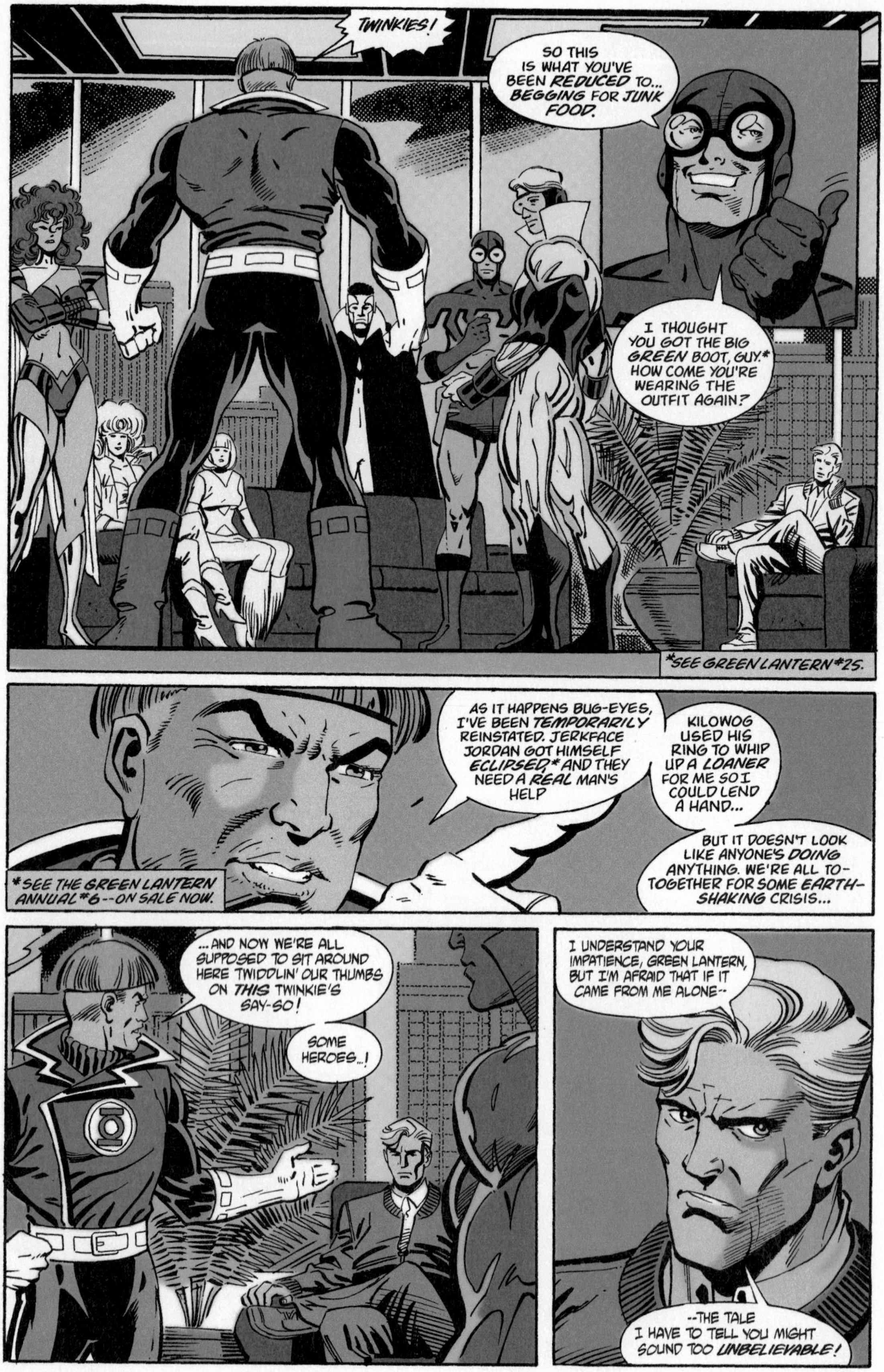
TWINKIES!
SO THIS IS WHAT YOU'VE BEEN REDUCED TO... BEGGING FOR JUNK FOOD.
I THOUGHT YOU GOT THE BIG GREEN BOOT, GUY.* HOW COME YOU'RE WEARING THE OUTFIT AGAIN?
*SEE GREEN LANTERN #25.
AS IT HAPPENS BUG-EYES, I'VE BEEN TEMPORARILY REINSTATED. JERKFACE JORDAN GOT HIMSELF ECLIPSED,* AND THEY NEED A REAL MAN'S HELP
KILOWOG USED HIS RING TO WHIP UP A LOANER FOR ME SO I COULD LEND A HAND...
BUT IT DOESN'T LOOK LIKE ANYONE'S DOING ANYTHING. WE'RE ALL TO-TOGETHER FOR SOME EARTH-SHAKING CRISIS...
*SEE THE GREEN LANTERN ANNUAL #6--ON SALE NOW.
...AND NOW WE'RE ALL SUPPOSED TO SIT AROUND HERE TWIDDLIN' OUR THUMBS ON THIS TWINKIE'S SAY-SO!
SOME HEROES...!
I UNDERSTAND YOUR IMPATIENCE, GREEN LANTERN, BUT I'M AFRAID THAT IF IT CAME FROM ME ALONE--
--THE TALE I HAVE TO TELL YOU MIGHT SOUND TOO UNBELIEVABLE!

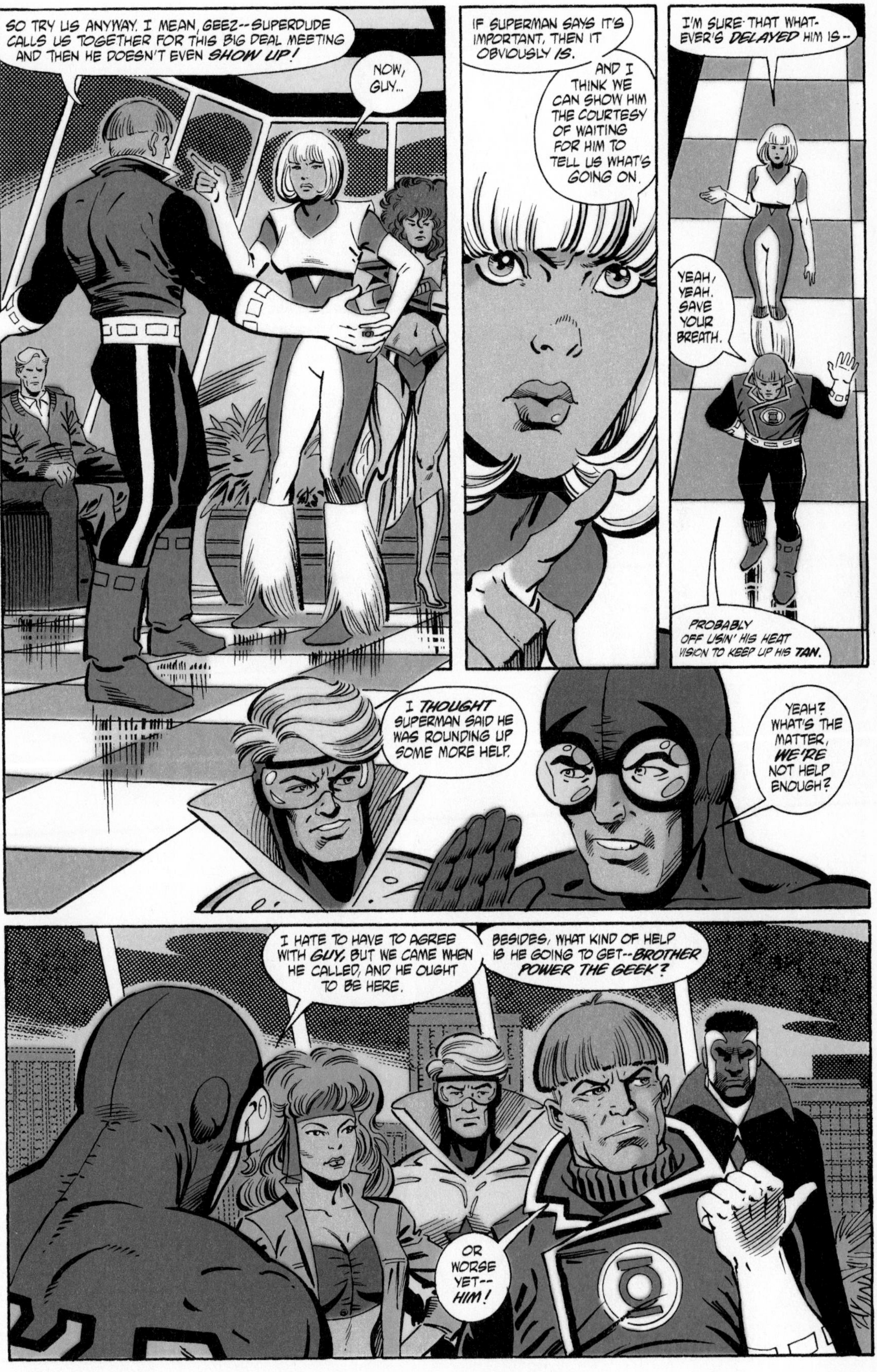
SO TRY US ANYWAY. I MEAN, GEEZ--SUPERDUDE CALLS US TOGETHER FOR THIS BIG DEAL MEETING AND THEN HE DOESN'T EVEN *SHOW UP!*
NOW, GUY...
IF SUPERMAN SAYS IT'S IMPORTANT, THEN IT OBVIOUSLY *IS*.
AND I THINK WE CAN SHOW HIM THE COURTESY OF WAITING FOR HIM TO TELL US WHAT'S GOING ON.
I'M SURE THAT WHAT-EVER'S *DELAYED* HIM IS--
YEAH, YEAH. SAVE YOUR BREATH.
PROBABLY OFF USIN' HIS HEAT VISION TO KEEP UP HIS *TAN*.
I *THOUGHT* SUPERMAN SAID HE WAS ROUNDING UP SOME MORE HELP.
YEAH? WHAT'S THE MATTER, *WE'RE* NOT HELP ENOUGH?
I HATE TO HAVE TO AGREE WITH *GUY*, BUT WE CAME WHEN HE CALLED, AND HE OUGHT TO BE HERE.
BESIDES, WHAT KIND OF HELP IS HE GOING TO GET--*BROTHER POWER THE GEEK?*
OR WORSE YET--*HIM!*

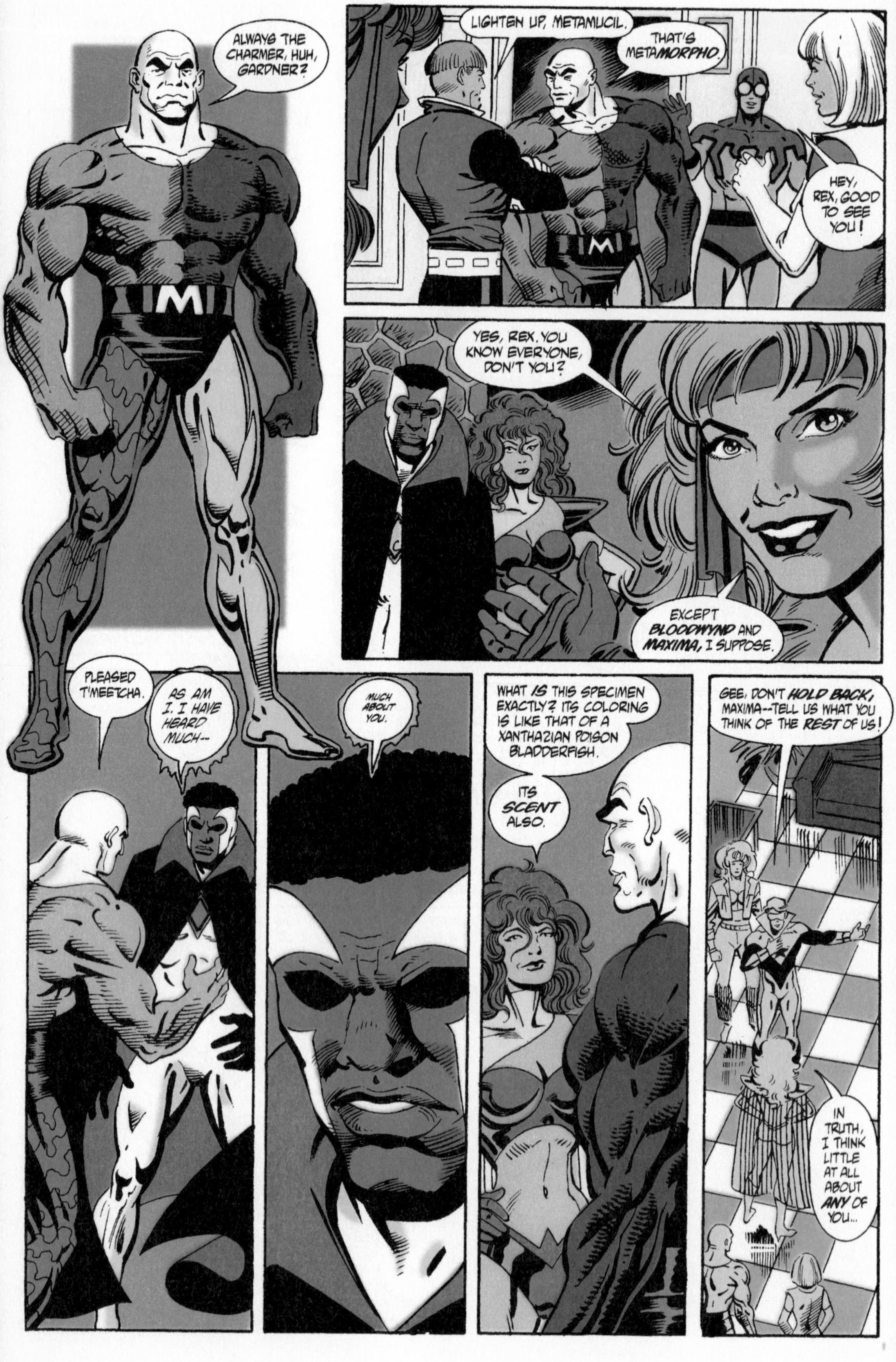
ALWAYS THE CHARMER, HUH, GARDNER?
LIGHTEN UP, METAMUCIL.
THAT'S METAMORPHO.
HEY, REX, GOOD TO SEE YOU!
YES, REX. YOU KNOW EVERYONE, DON'T YOU?
EXCEPT BLOODWYND AND MAXIMA, I SUPPOSE.
PLEASED T'MEETCHA.
AS AM I. I HAVE HEARD MUCH--
MUCH ABOUT YOU.
WHAT IS THIS SPECIMEN EXACTLY? ITS COLORING IS LIKE THAT OF A XANTHAZIAN POISON BLADDERFISH.
ITS SCENT ALSO.
GEE, DON'T HOLD BACK, MAXIMA--TELL US WHAT YOU THINK OF THE REST OF US!
IN TRUTH, I THINK LITTLE AT ALL ABOUT ANY OF YOU...

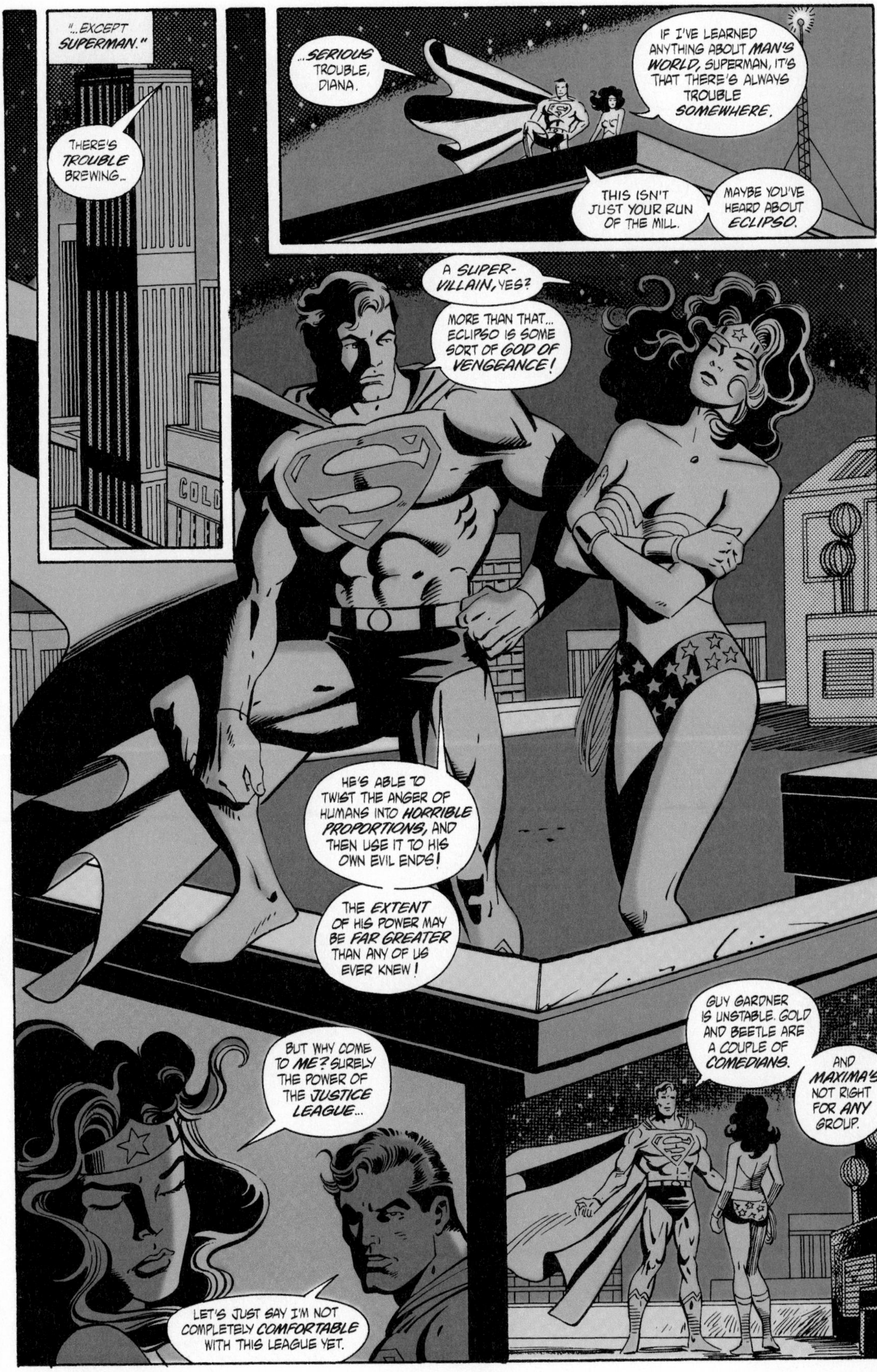

"...EXCEPT SUPERMAN."
THERE'S TROUBLE BREWING...
...SERIOUS TROUBLE, DIANA.
IF I'VE LEARNED ANYTHING ABOUT MAN'S WORLD, SUPERMAN, IT'S THAT THERE'S ALWAYS TROUBLE SOMEWHERE.
THIS ISN'T JUST YOUR RUN OF THE MILL.
MAYBE YOU'VE HEARD ABOUT ECLIPSO.
A SUPER-VILLAIN, YES?
MORE THAN THAT... ECLIPSO IS SOME SORT OF GOD OF VENGEANCE!
HE'S ABLE TO TWIST THE ANGER OF HUMANS INTO HORRIBLE PROPORTIONS, AND THEN USE IT TO HIS OWN EVIL ENDS!
THE EXTENT OF HIS POWER MAY BE FAR GREATER THAN ANY OF US EVER KNEW!
BUT WHY COME TO ME? SURELY THE POWER OF THE JUSTICE LEAGUE...
LET'S JUST SAY I'M NOT COMPLETELY COMFORTABLE WITH THIS LEAGUE YET.
GUY GARDNER IS UNSTABLE. GOLD AND BEETLE ARE A COUPLE OF COMEDIANS.
AND MAXIMA'S NOT RIGHT FOR ANY GROUP.

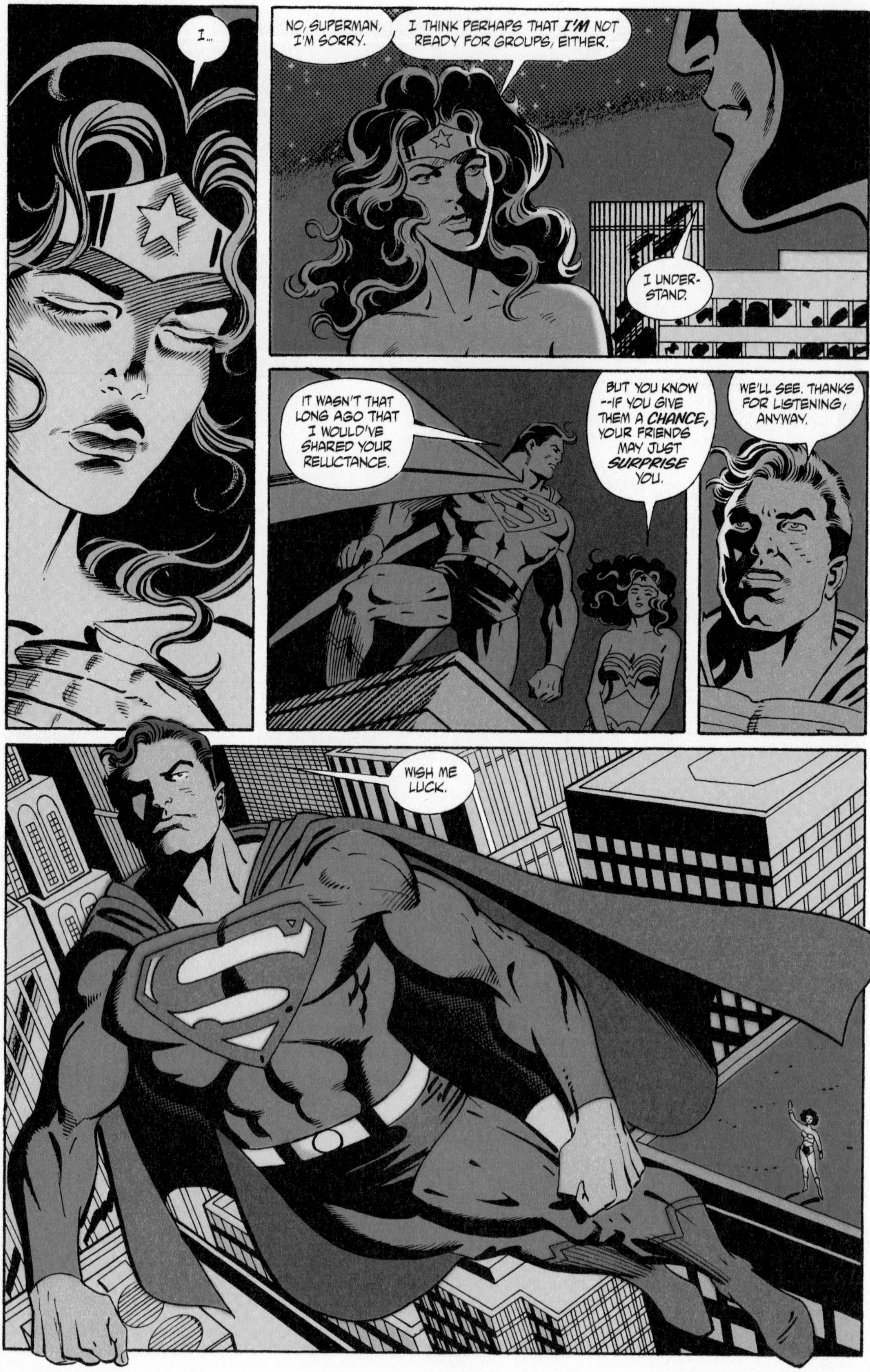
I...
NO, SUPERMAN, I'M SORRY.
I THINK PERHAPS THAT I'M NOT READY FOR GROUPS, EITHER.
I UNDER-STAND.
IT WASN'T THAT LONG AGO THAT I WOULD'VE SHARED YOUR RELUCTANCE.
BUT YOU KNOW --IF YOU GIVE THEM A CHANCE, YOUR FRIENDS MAY JUST SURPRISE YOU.
WE'LL SEE. THANKS FOR LISTENING, ANYWAY.
WISH ME LUCK.

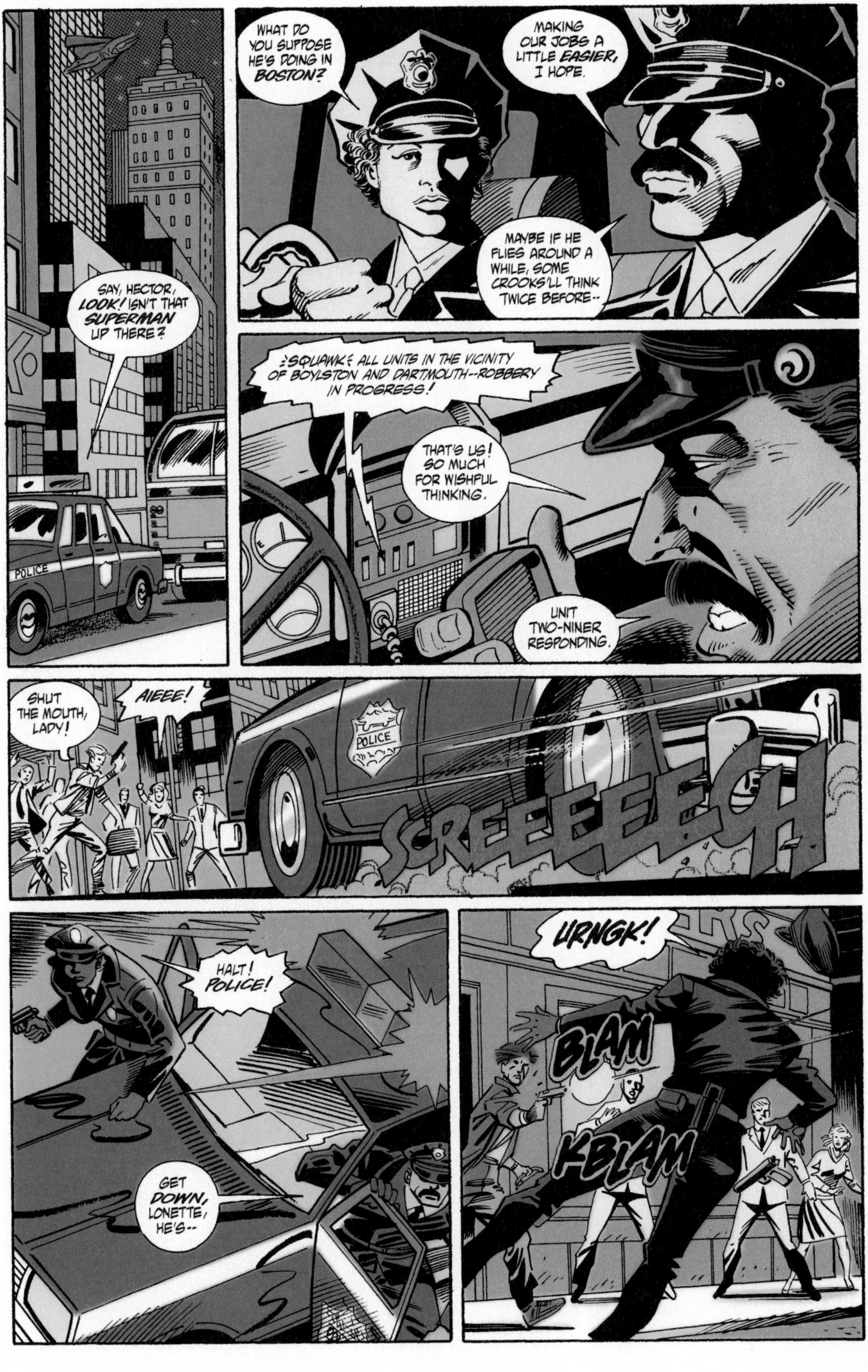
SAY, HECTOR, LOOK! ISN'T THAT SUPERMAN UP THERE?
POLICE
WHAT DO YOU SUPPOSE HE'S DOING IN BOSTON?
MAKING OUR JOBS A LITTLE EASIER, I HOPE.
MAYBE IF HE FLIES AROUND A WHILE, SOME CROOKS'LL THINK TWICE BEFORE--
≤SQUAWK≤ ALL UNITS IN THE VICINITY OF BOYLSTON AND DARTMOUTH--ROBBERY IN PROGRESS!
THAT'S US! SO MUCH FOR WISHFUL THINKING.
UNIT TWO-NINER RESPONDING.
SHUT THE MOUTH, LADY!
AIEEE!
POLICE
SCREEEEECH
HALT! POLICE!
GET DOWN, LONETTE, HE'S--
URNGK!
BLAM
KBLAM

LONETTE!!

ANIMAL! YOU STINKING ANIMAL!

CHK-KASH

OOF!

OUTTA MY FACE, COP!

SHE HAD TWO KIDS, DAMN YOU!

AND I'M GONNA TELL THOSE KIDS THAT HER KILLER GOT THE JUSTICE HE DESERVED!

I'M GONNA TELL THEM AN ANIMAL MURDERED THEIR MOTHER...

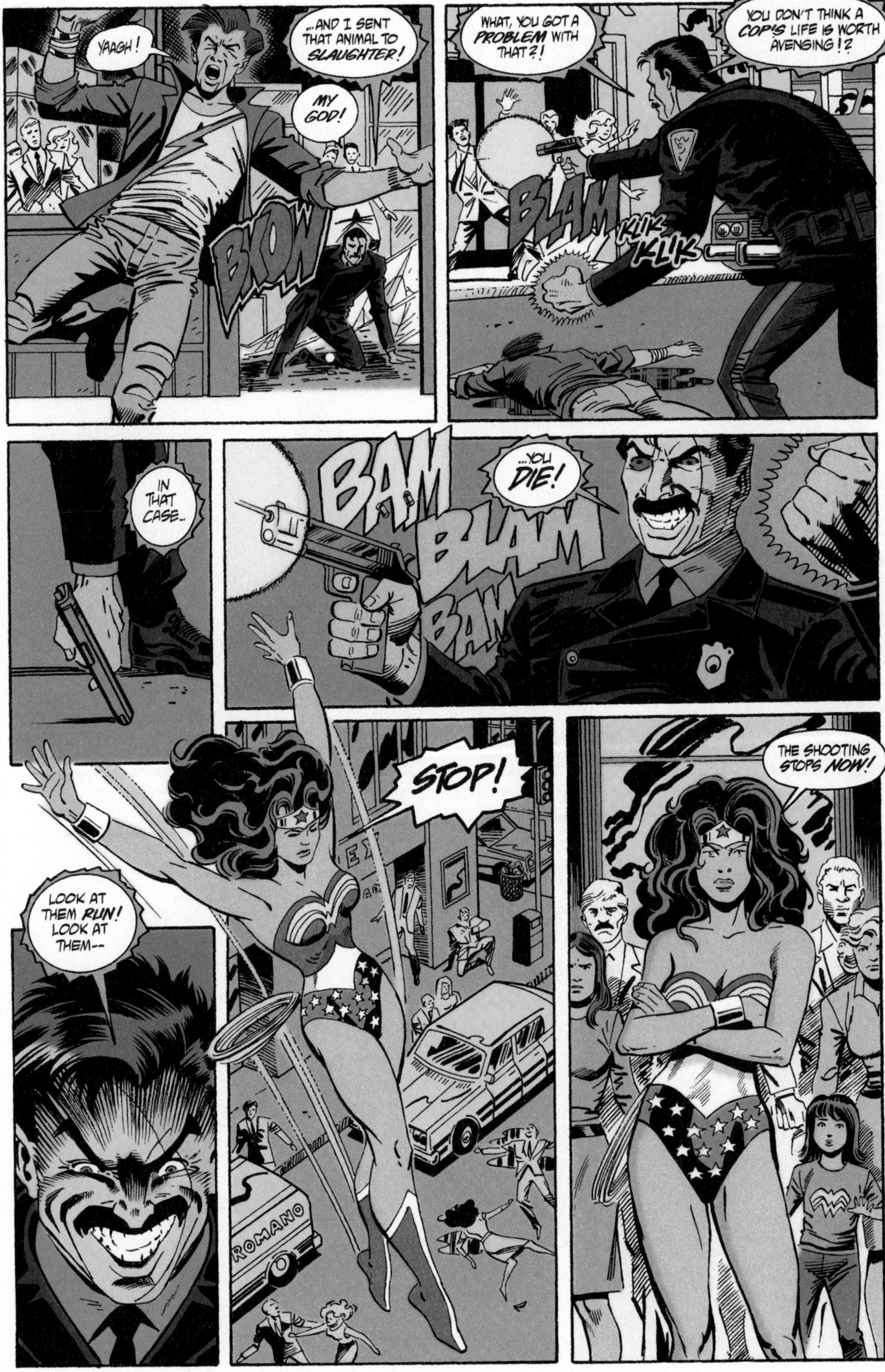

YAAGH!
...AND I SENT THAT ANIMAL TO SLAUGHTER!
MY GOD!
BKOW
WHAT, YOU GOT A PROBLEM WITH THAT?!
YOU DON'T THINK A COP'S LIFE IS WORTH AVENGING!?
BLAM
KLIK KLIK
IN THAT CASE...
BAM
...YOU DIE!
BLAM
BAM
STOP!
THE SHOOTING STOPS NOW!
LOOK AT THEM RUN! LOOK AT THEM--
ROMANO

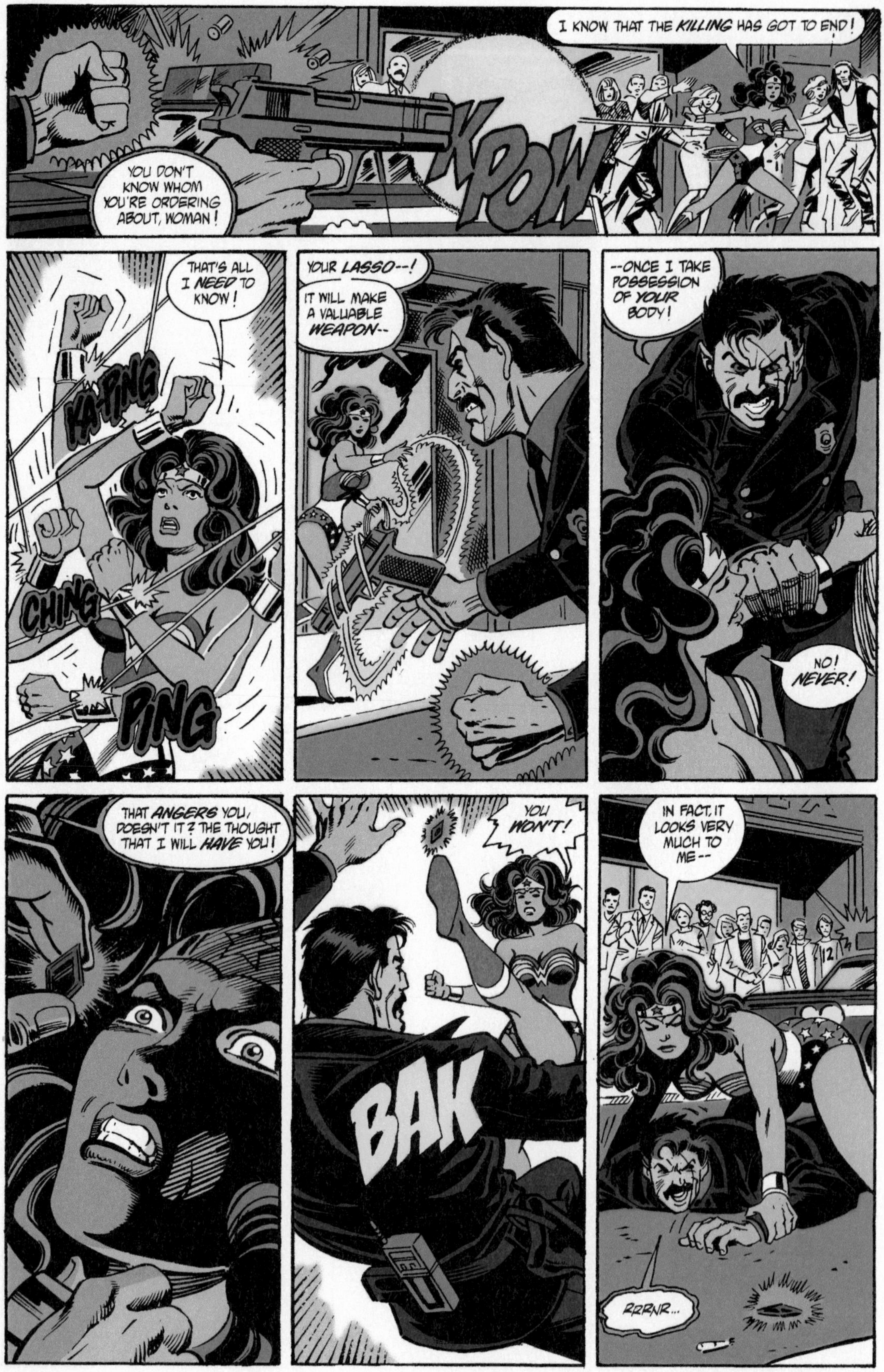
I KNOW THAT THE KILLING HAS GOT TO END!
YOU DON'T KNOW WHOM YOU'RE ORDERING ABOUT, WOMAN!
KPOW
THAT'S ALL I NEED TO KNOW!
KA-PING
CHING
PING
YOUR LASSO--!
IT WILL MAKE A VALUABLE WEAPON--
--ONCE I TAKE POSSESSION OF YOUR BODY!
NO! NEVER!
THAT ANGERS YOU, DOESN'T IT? THE THOUGHT THAT I WILL HAVE YOU!
YOU WON'T!
BAK
IN FACT, IT LOOKS VERY MUCH TO ME--
RRRNR...

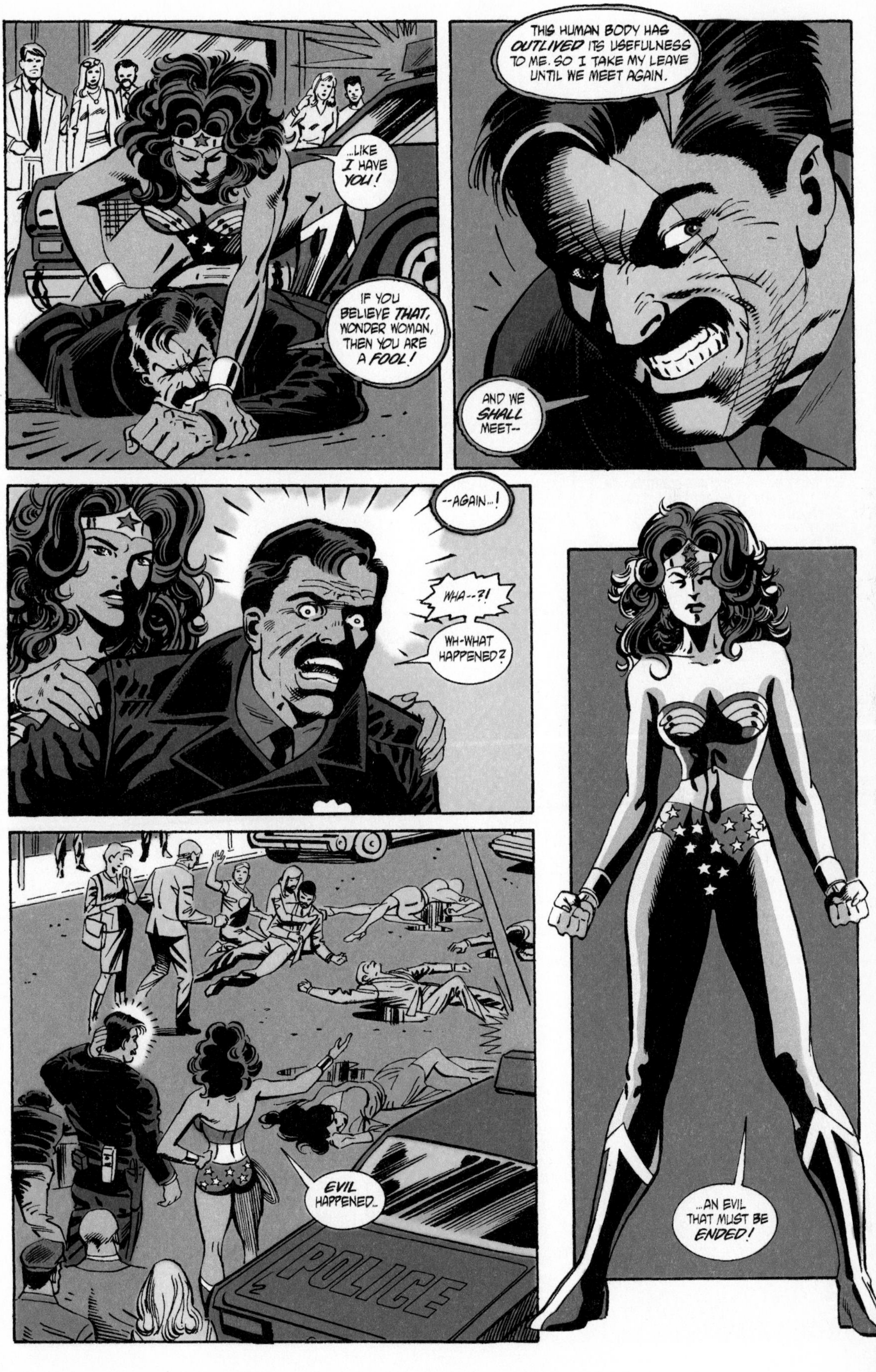
...LIKE I HAVE YOU!
IF YOU BELIEVE THAT, WONDER WOMAN, THEN YOU ARE A FOOL!
THIS HUMAN BODY HAS OUTLIVED ITS USEFULNESS TO ME. SO I TAKE MY LEAVE UNTIL WE MEET AGAIN.
AND WE SHALL MEET--
--AGAIN...!
WHA--?!
WH-WHAT HAPPENED?
EVIL HAPPENED...
POLICE
...AN EVIL THAT MUST BE ENDED!

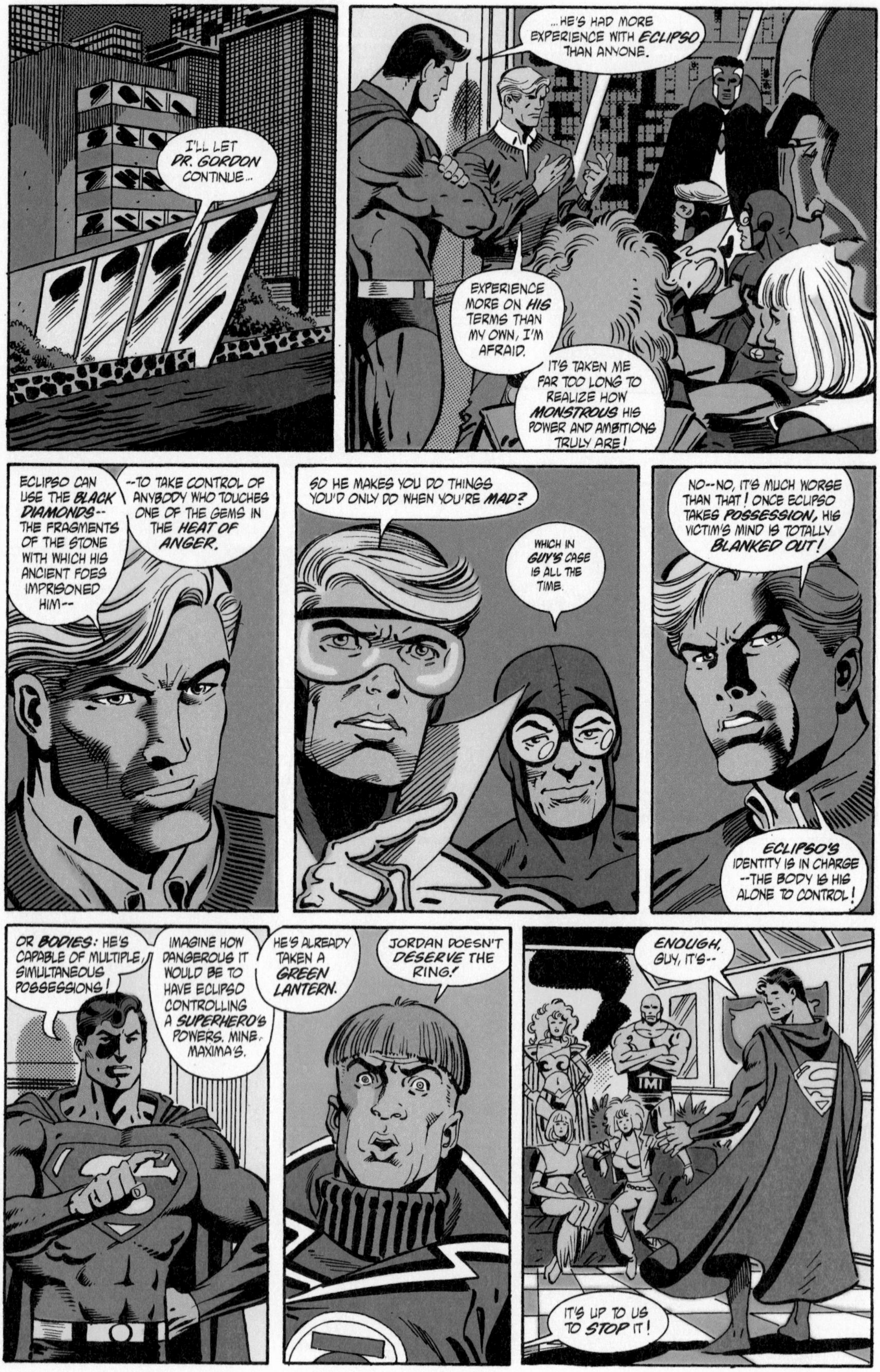
I'LL LET DR. GORDON CONTINUE...
...HE'S HAD MORE EXPERIENCE WITH ECLIPSO THAN ANYONE.
EXPERIENCE MORE ON HIS TERMS THAN MY OWN, I'M AFRAID.
IT'S TAKEN ME FAR TOO LONG TO REALIZE HOW MONSTROUS HIS POWER AND AMBITIONS TRULY ARE!
ECLIPSO CAN USE THE BLACK DIAMONDS-- THE FRAGMENTS OF THE STONE WITH WHICH HIS ANCIENT FOES IMPRISONED HIM--
--TO TAKE CONTROL OF ANYBODY WHO TOUCHES ONE OF THE GEMS IN THE HEAT OF ANGER.
SO HE MAKES YOU DO THINGS YOU'D ONLY DO WHEN YOU'RE MAD?
WHICH IN GUY'S CASE IS ALL THE TIME.
NO--NO, IT'S MUCH WORSE THAN THAT! ONCE ECLIPSO TAKES POSSESSION, HIS VICTIM'S MIND IS TOTALLY BLANKED OUT!
ECLIPSO'S IDENTITY IS IN CHARGE --THE BODY IS HIS ALONE TO CONTROL!
OR BODIES: HE'S CAPABLE OF MULTIPLE, SIMULTANEOUS POSSESSIONS!
IMAGINE HOW DANGEROUS IT WOULD BE TO HAVE ECLIPSO CONTROLLING A SUPERHERO'S POWERS. MINE. MAXIMA'S.
HE'S ALREADY TAKEN A GREEN LANTERN.
JORDAN DOESN'T DESERVE THE RING!
ENOUGH, GUY, IT'S--
IT'S UP TO US TO STOP IT!

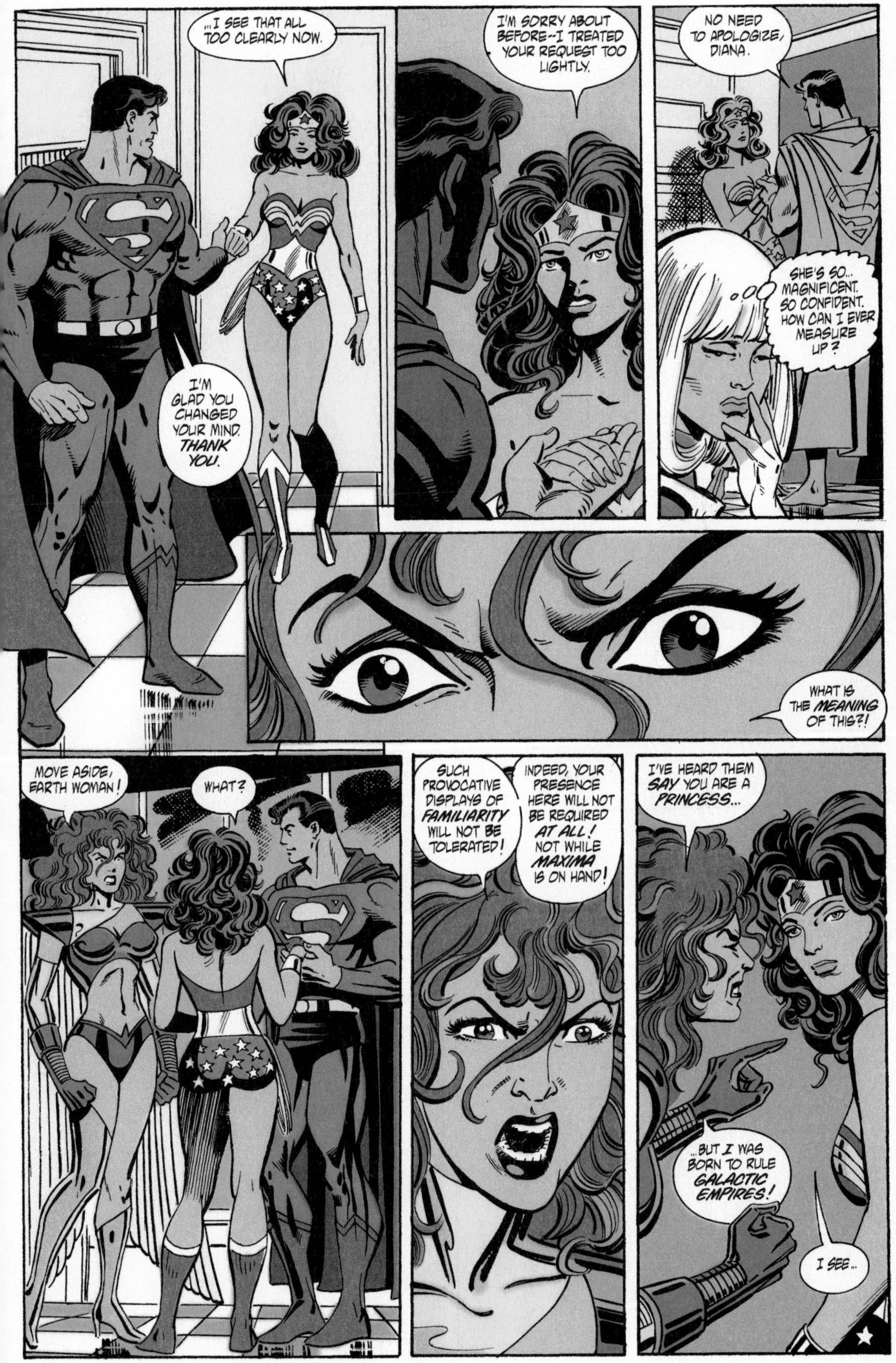
...I SEE THAT ALL TOO CLEARLY NOW.
I'M GLAD YOU CHANGED YOUR MIND. THANK YOU.
I'M SORRY ABOUT BEFORE--I TREATED YOUR REQUEST TOO LIGHTLY.
NO NEED TO APOLOGIZE, DIANA.
SHE'S SO... MAGNIFICENT. SO CONFIDENT. HOW CAN I EVER MEASURE UP?
WHAT IS THE MEANING OF THIS?!
MOVE ASIDE, EARTH WOMAN!
WHAT?
SUCH PROVOCATIVE DISPLAYS OF FAMILIARITY WILL NOT BE TOLERATED!
INDEED, YOUR PRESENCE HERE WILL NOT BE REQUIRED AT ALL! NOT WHILE MAXIMA IS ON HAND!
I'VE HEARD THEM SAY YOU ARE A PRINCESS...
...BUT I WAS BORN TO RULE GALACTIC EMPIRES!
I SEE...

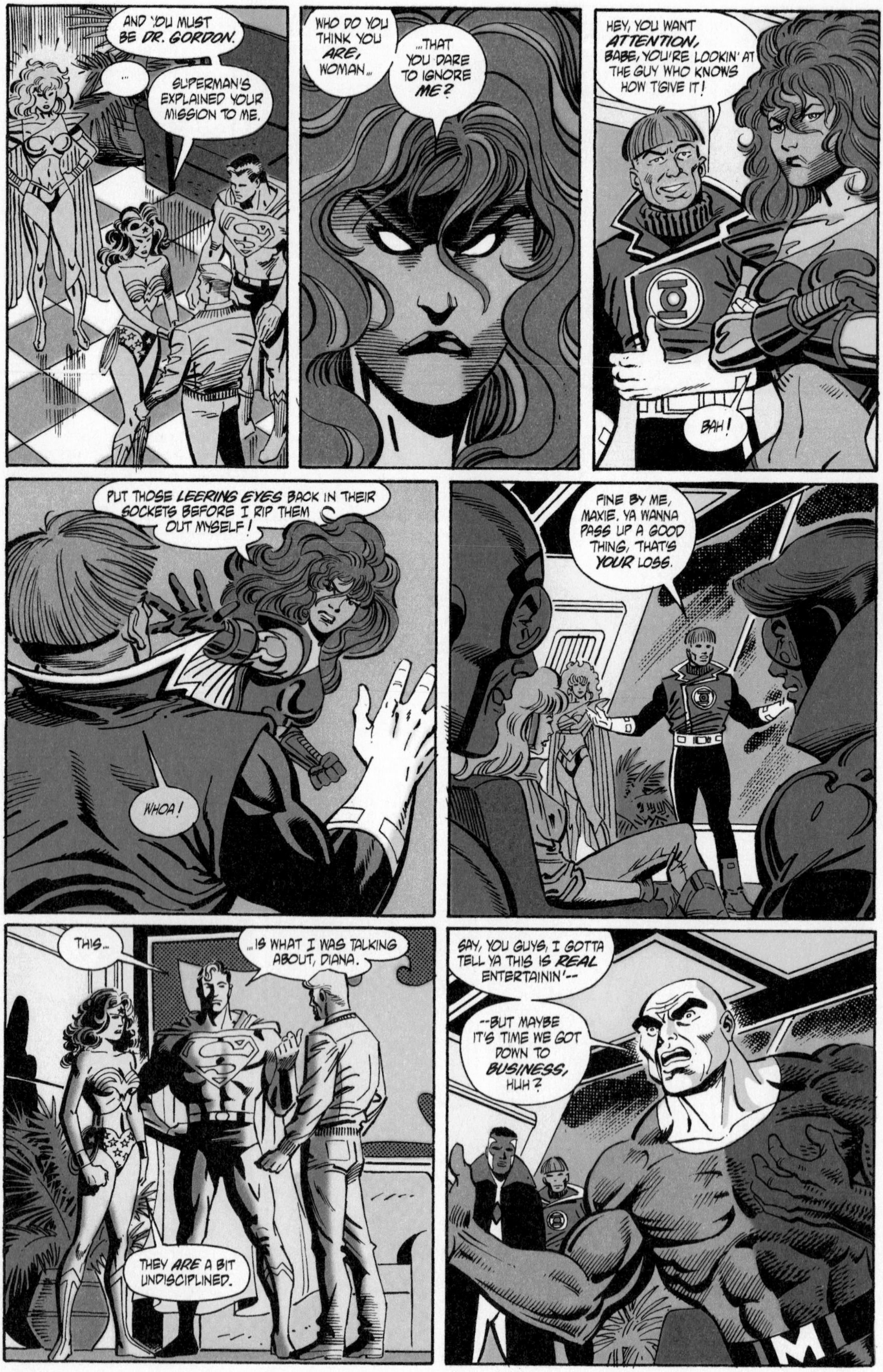
AND YOU MUST BE DR. GORDON.
...
SUPERMAN'S EXPLAINED YOUR MISSION TO ME.
WHO DO YOU THINK YOU ARE, WOMAN...
...THAT YOU DARE TO IGNORE ME?
HEY, YOU WANT ATTENTION, BABE, YOU'RE LOOKIN' AT THE GUY WHO KNOWS HOW T'GIVE IT!
BAH!
PUT THOSE LEERING EYES BACK IN THEIR SOCKETS BEFORE I RIP THEM OUT MYSELF!
WHOA!
FINE BY ME, MAXIE. YA WANNA PASS UP A GOOD THING, THAT'S YOUR LOSS.
THIS...
...IS WHAT I WAS TALKING ABOUT, DIANA.
THEY ARE A BIT UNDISCIPLINED.
SAY, YOU GUYS, I GOTTA TELL YA THIS IS REAL ENTERTAININ'--
--BUT MAYBE IT'S TIME WE GOT DOWN TO BUSINESS, HUH?

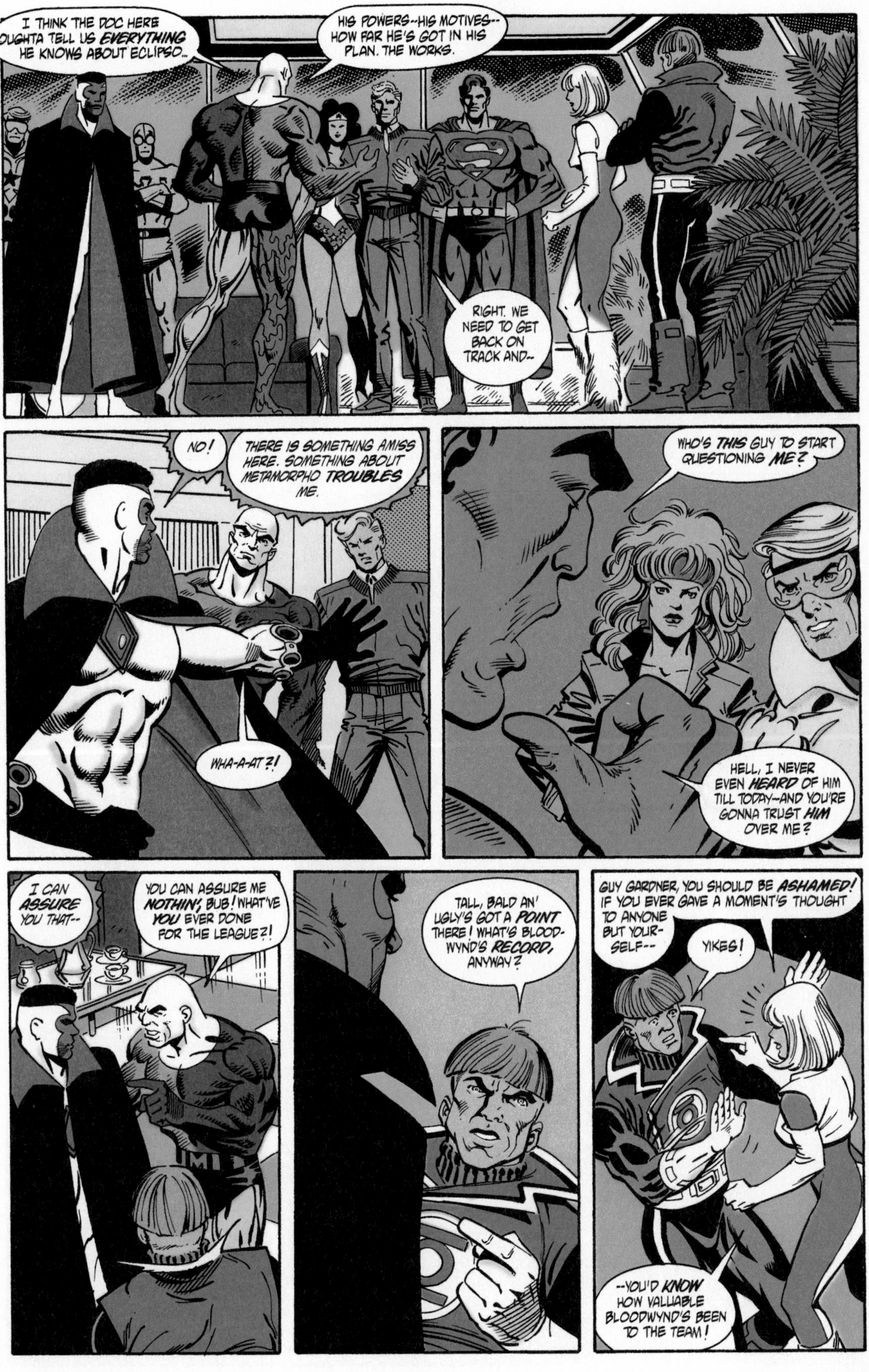
I THINK THE DOC HERE OUGHTA TELL US EVERYTHING HE KNOWS ABOUT ECLIPSO..
HIS POWERS--HIS MOTIVES--HOW FAR HE'S GOT IN HIS PLAN. THE WORKS.
RIGHT. WE NEED TO GET BACK ON TRACK AND--
NO!
THERE IS SOMETHING AMISS HERE. SOMETHING ABOUT METAMORPHO TROUBLES ME.
WHA-A-AT?!
WHO'S THIS GUY TO START QUESTIONING ME?
HELL, I NEVER EVEN HEARD OF HIM TILL TODAY--AND YOU'RE GONNA TRUST HIM OVER ME?
I CAN ASSURE YOU THAT--
YOU CAN ASSURE ME NOTHIN', BUB! WHAT'VE YOU EVER DONE FOR THE LEAGUE?!
TALL, BALD AN' UGLY'S GOT A POINT THERE! WHAT'S BLOOD-WYND'S RECORD, ANYWAY?
GUY GARDNER, YOU SHOULD BE ASHAMED! IF YOU EVER GAVE A MOMENT'S THOUGHT TO ANYONE BUT YOUR-SELF--
YIKES!
--YOU'D KNOW HOW VALUABLE BLOODWYND'S BEEN TO THE TEAM!

SO WHAT'S HE GOING AROUND PICKING *FIGHTS* FOR?

TAKE IT EASY, REX-- WE'RE ALL ON THE *SAME SIDE!* YOU'RE JUST BEING *PARANOID!*

AM NOT!

AM TOO!

I'M ONLY SAYIN' THAT--

CALLING ME A *LIAR?*

WHO MADE *HIM* BOSS ALL OF A SUDD--

NEVER LIKED THE WAY HE--

SO'S YER OLD MAN!

AND ANOTHER THING--

I GUESS *METAMORPHO'S* NOT THE SOUL OF REASON, EITHER.

FIRST HE WANTS EVERY-BODY QUIET, AND NOW HE WON'T--

ENOUGH!

WHILE YOU'RE ALL *BICKERING,* ECLIPSO'S SCHEME IS *RUSHING* FORWARD!

IT'S TIME YOU PEOPLE LEARNED TO STRAIGHTEN UP AND TAKE *ORDERS!*

YEAH, WELL, I DON'T *NEED* THESE KINDA HASSLES...

...I'M *OUTTA HERE!*

I AGREE WITH THE *BLADDERFISH!* FAREWELL!

NOT BAD. WE HAVEN'T EVEN *STARTED* YET--

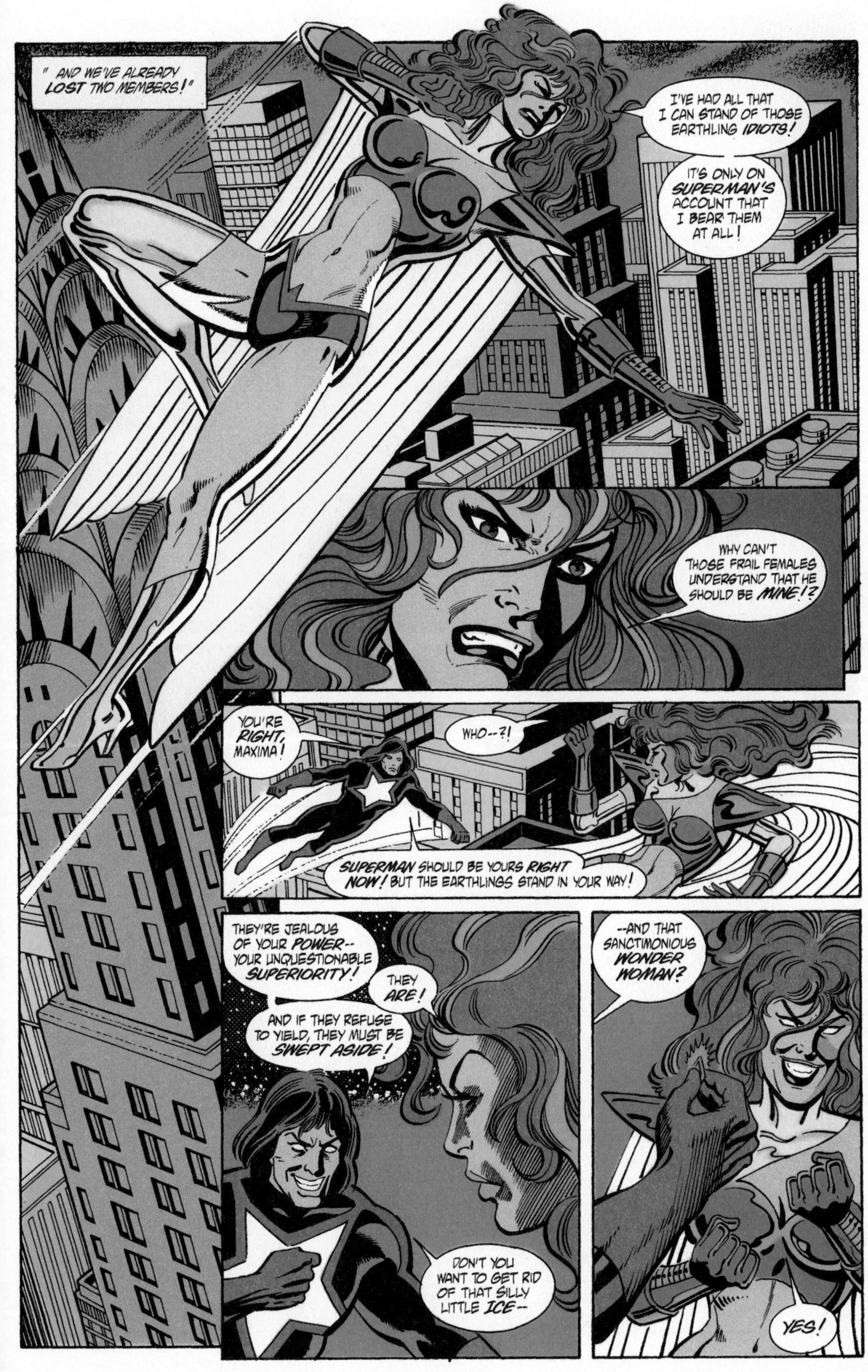
" AND WE'VE ALREADY LOST TWO MEMBERS!"
I'VE HAD ALL THAT I CAN STAND OF THOSE EARTHLING IDIOTS!
IT'S ONLY ON SUPERMAN'S ACCOUNT THAT I BEAR THEM AT ALL!
WHY CAN'T THOSE FRAIL FEMALES UNDERSTAND THAT HE SHOULD BE MINE!?
YOU'RE RIGHT, MAXIMA!
WHO--?!
SUPERMAN SHOULD BE YOURS RIGHT NOW! BUT THE EARTHLINGS STAND IN YOUR WAY!
THEY'RE JEALOUS OF YOUR POWER-- YOUR UNQUESTIONABLE SUPERIORITY!
THEY ARE!
AND IF THEY REFUSE TO YIELD, THEY MUST BE SWEPT ASIDE!
DON'T YOU WANT TO GET RID OF THAT SILLY LITTLE ICE--
--AND THAT SANCTIMONIOUS WONDER WOMAN?
YES!

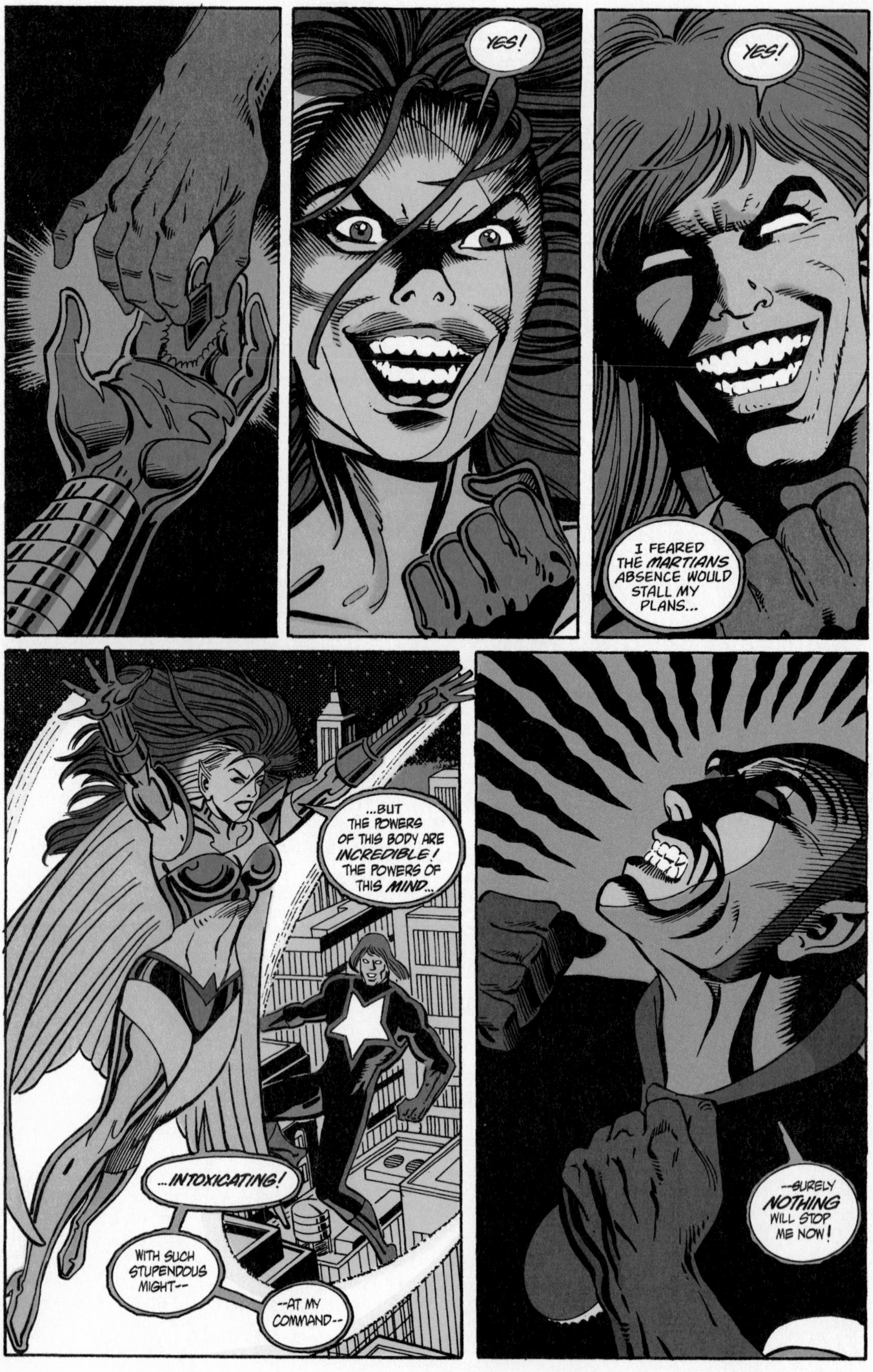
YES!
YES!
I FEARED THE MARTIANS ABSENCE WOULD STALL MY PLANS...
...BUT THE POWERS OF THIS BODY ARE INCREDIBLE! THE POWERS OF THIS MIND...
...INTOXICATING!
WITH SUCH STUPENDOUS MIGHT--
--AT MY COMMAND--
--SURELY NOTHING WILL STOP ME NOW!

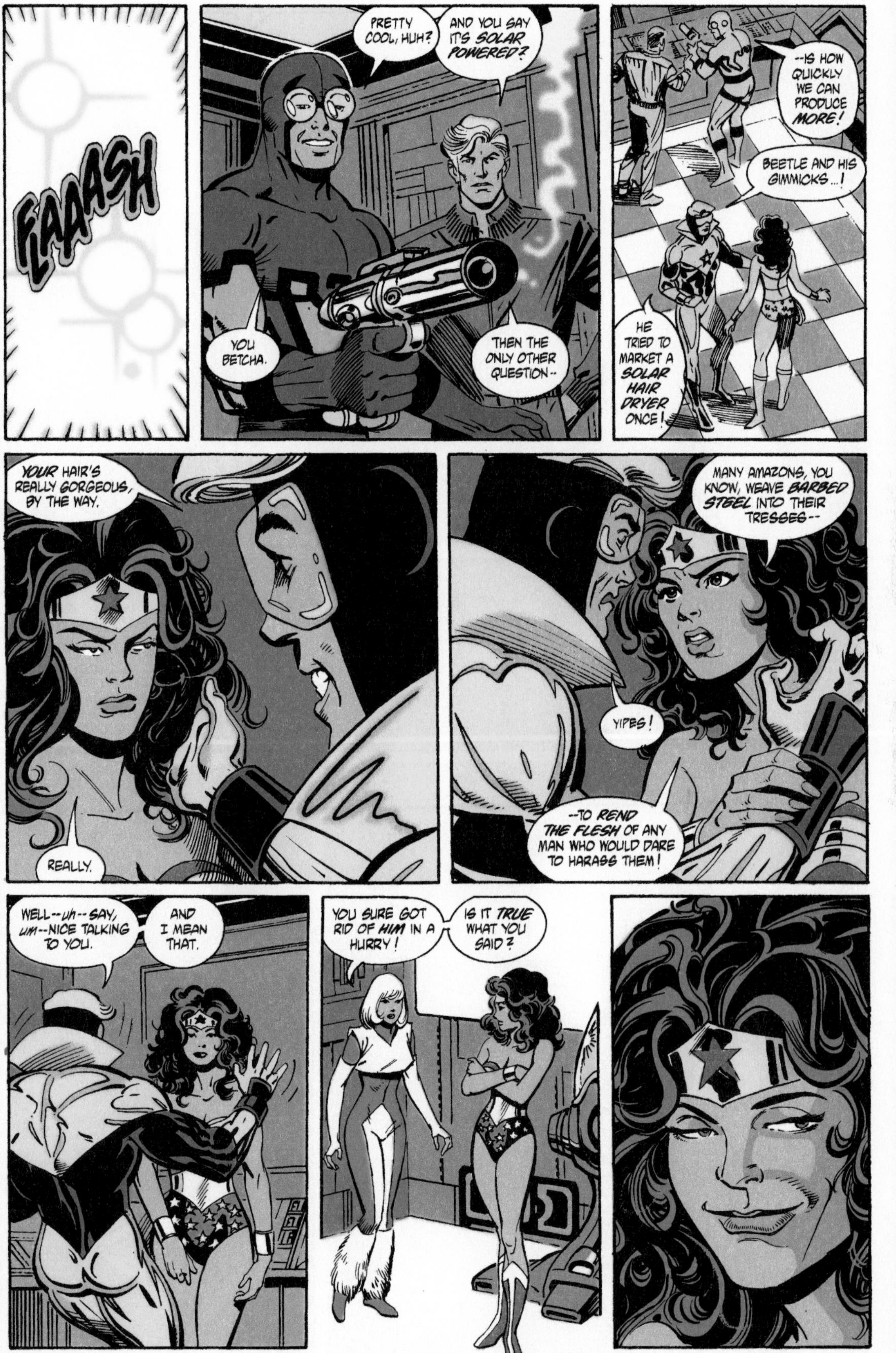
FLAAASH
PRETTY COOL, HUH?
AND YOU SAY IT'S SOLAR POWERED?
YOU BETCHA.
THEN THE ONLY OTHER QUESTION--
--IS HOW QUICKLY WE CAN PRODUCE MORE!
BEETLE AND HIS GIMMICKS...!
HE TRIED TO MARKET A SOLAR HAIR DRYER ONCE!
YOUR HAIR'S REALLY GORGEOUS, BY THE WAY.
REALLY.
MANY AMAZONS, YOU KNOW, WEAVE BARBED STEEL INTO THEIR TRESSES--
YIPES!
--TO REND THE FLESH OF ANY MAN WHO WOULD DARE TO HARASS THEM!
WELL--uh--SAY, um--NICE TALKING TO YOU.
AND I MEAN THAT.
YOU SURE GOT RID OF HIM IN A HURRY!
IS IT TRUE WHAT YOU SAID?

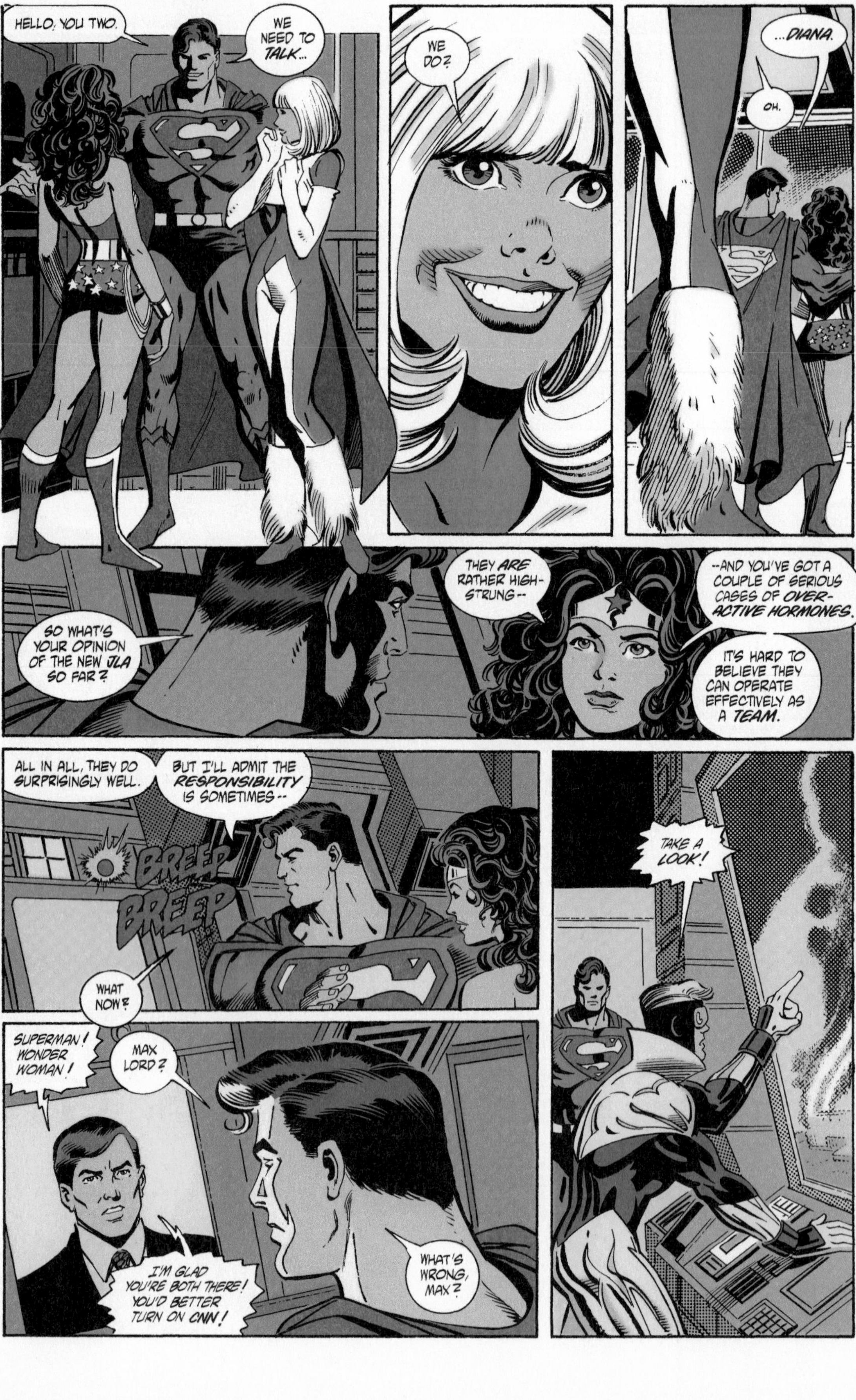

HELLO, YOU TWO.
WE NEED TO TALK...
WE DO?
...DIANA.
OH.
SO WHAT'S YOUR OPINION OF THE NEW JLA SO FAR?
THEY ARE RATHER HIGH-STRUNG--
--AND YOU'VE GOT A COUPLE OF SERIOUS CASES OF OVER-ACTIVE HORMONES.
IT'S HARD TO BELIEVE THEY CAN OPERATE EFFECTIVELY AS A TEAM.
ALL IN ALL, THEY DO SURPRISINGLY WELL.
BUT I'LL ADMIT THE RESPONSIBILITY IS SOMETIMES--
BREEP
BREEP
WHAT NOW?
SUPERMAN! WONDER WOMAN!
MAX LORD?
I'M GLAD YOU'RE BOTH THERE! YOU'D BETTER TURN ON CNN!
WHAT'S WRONG, MAX?
TAKE A LOOK!

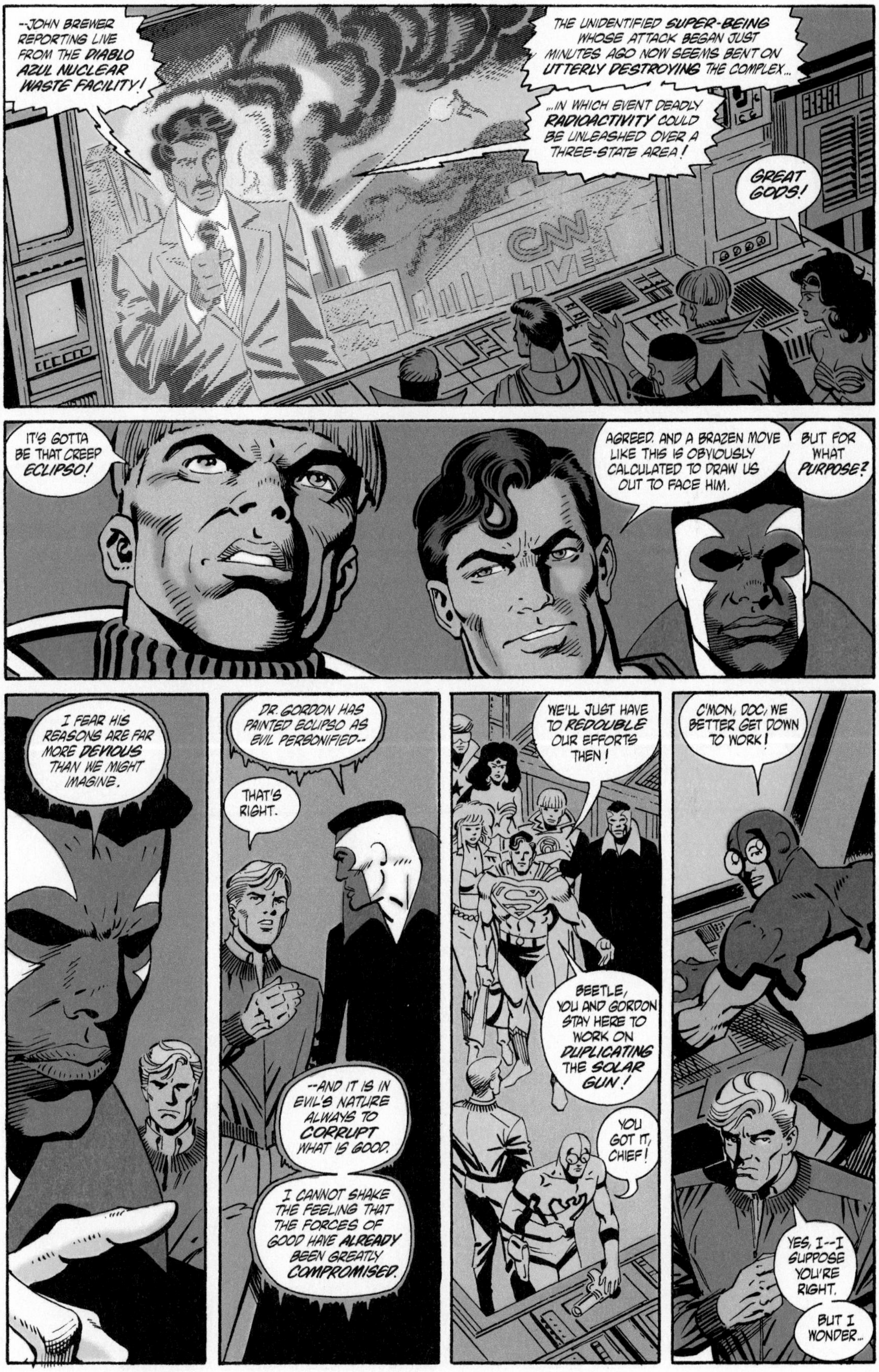
--JOHN BREWER REPORTING LIVE FROM THE DIABLO AZUL NUCLEAR WASTE FACILITY!
THE UNIDENTIFIED SUPER-BEING WHOSE ATTACK BEGAN JUST MINUTES AGO NOW SEEMS BENT ON UTTERLY DESTROYING THE COMPLEX...
...IN WHICH EVENT DEADLY RADIOACTIVITY COULD BE UNLEASHED OVER A THREE-STATE AREA!
CNN LIVE
GREAT GODS!
IT'S GOTTA BE THAT CREEP ECLIPSO!
AGREED. AND A BRAZEN MOVE LIKE THIS IS OBVIOUSLY CALCULATED TO DRAW US OUT TO FACE HIM.
BUT FOR WHAT PURPOSE?
I FEAR HIS REASONS ARE FAR MORE DEVIOUS THAN WE MIGHT IMAGINE.
DR. GORDON HAS PAINTED ECLIPSO AS EVIL PERSONIFIED--
THAT'S RIGHT.
--AND IT IS IN EVIL'S NATURE ALWAYS TO CORRUPT WHAT IS GOOD.
I CANNOT SHAKE THE FEELING THAT THE FORCES OF GOOD HAVE ALREADY BEEN GREATLY COMPROMISED.
WE'LL JUST HAVE TO REDOUBLE OUR EFFORTS THEN!
BEETLE, YOU AND GORDON STAY HERE TO WORK ON DUPLICATING THE SOLAR GUN!
YOU GOT IT, CHIEF!
C'MON, DOC, WE BETTER GET DOWN TO WORK!
YES, I--I SUPPOSE YOU'RE RIGHT.
BUT I WONDER...

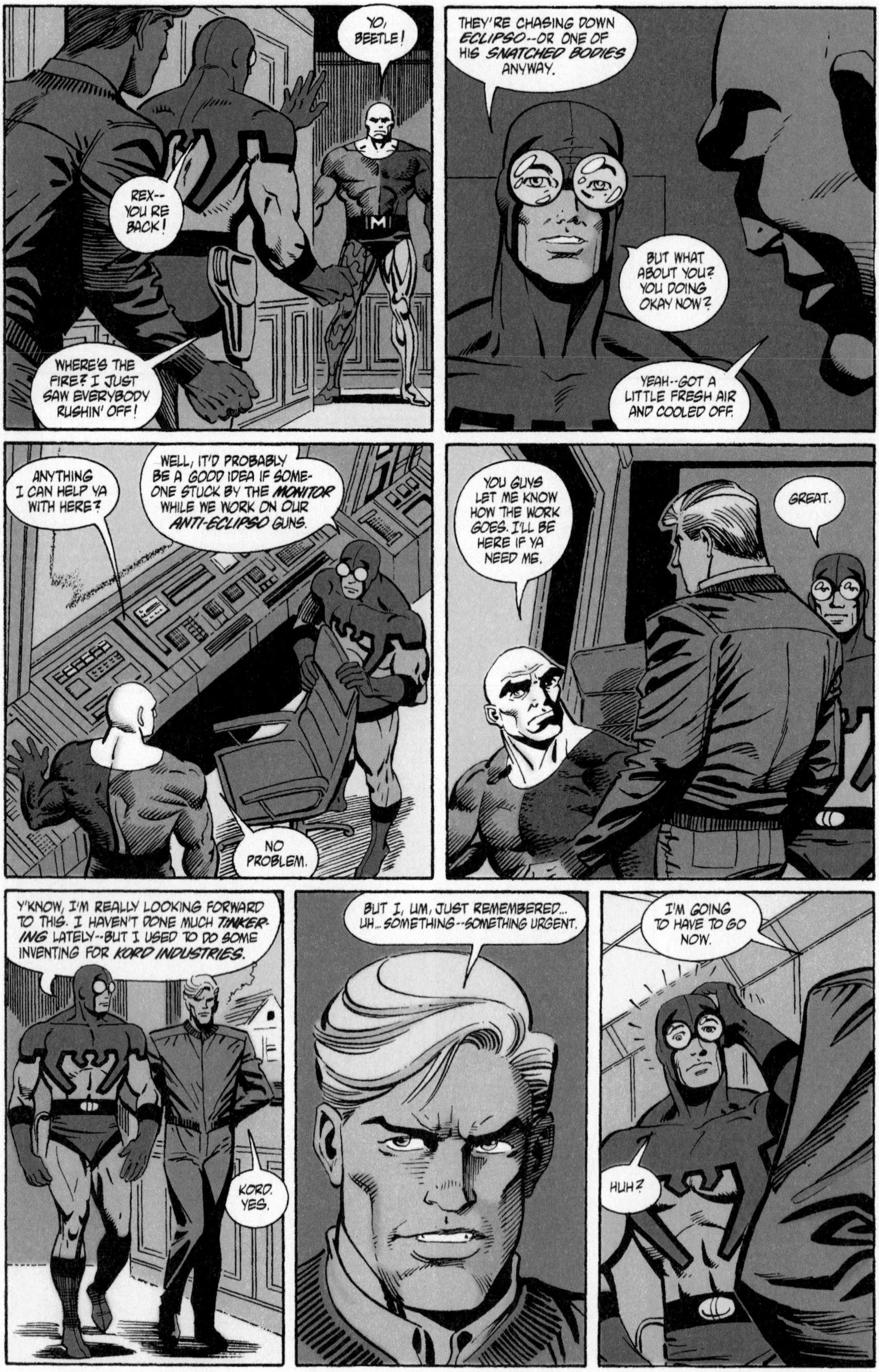
YO, BEETLE!
REX-- YOU'RE BACK!
WHERE'S THE FIRE? I JUST SAW EVERYBODY RUSHIN' OFF!
THEY'RE CHASING DOWN ECLIPSO--OR ONE OF HIS SNATCHED BODIES ANYWAY.
BUT WHAT ABOUT YOU? YOU DOING OKAY NOW?
YEAH--GOT A LITTLE FRESH AIR AND COOLED OFF.
ANYTHING I CAN HELP YA WITH HERE?
WELL, IT'D PROBABLY BE A GOOD IDEA IF SOME-ONE STUCK BY THE MONITOR WHILE WE WORK ON OUR ANTI-ECLIPSO GUNS.
NO PROBLEM.
YOU GUYS LET ME KNOW HOW THE WORK GOES. I'LL BE HERE IF YA NEED ME.
GREAT.
Y'KNOW, I'M REALLY LOOKING FORWARD TO THIS. I HAVEN'T DONE MUCH TINKER-ING LATELY--BUT I USED TO DO SOME INVENTING FOR KORD INDUSTRIES.
KORD. YES.
BUT I, UM, JUST REMEMBERED... UH... SOMETHING--SOMETHING URGENT.
I'M GOING TO HAVE TO GO NOW.
HUH?

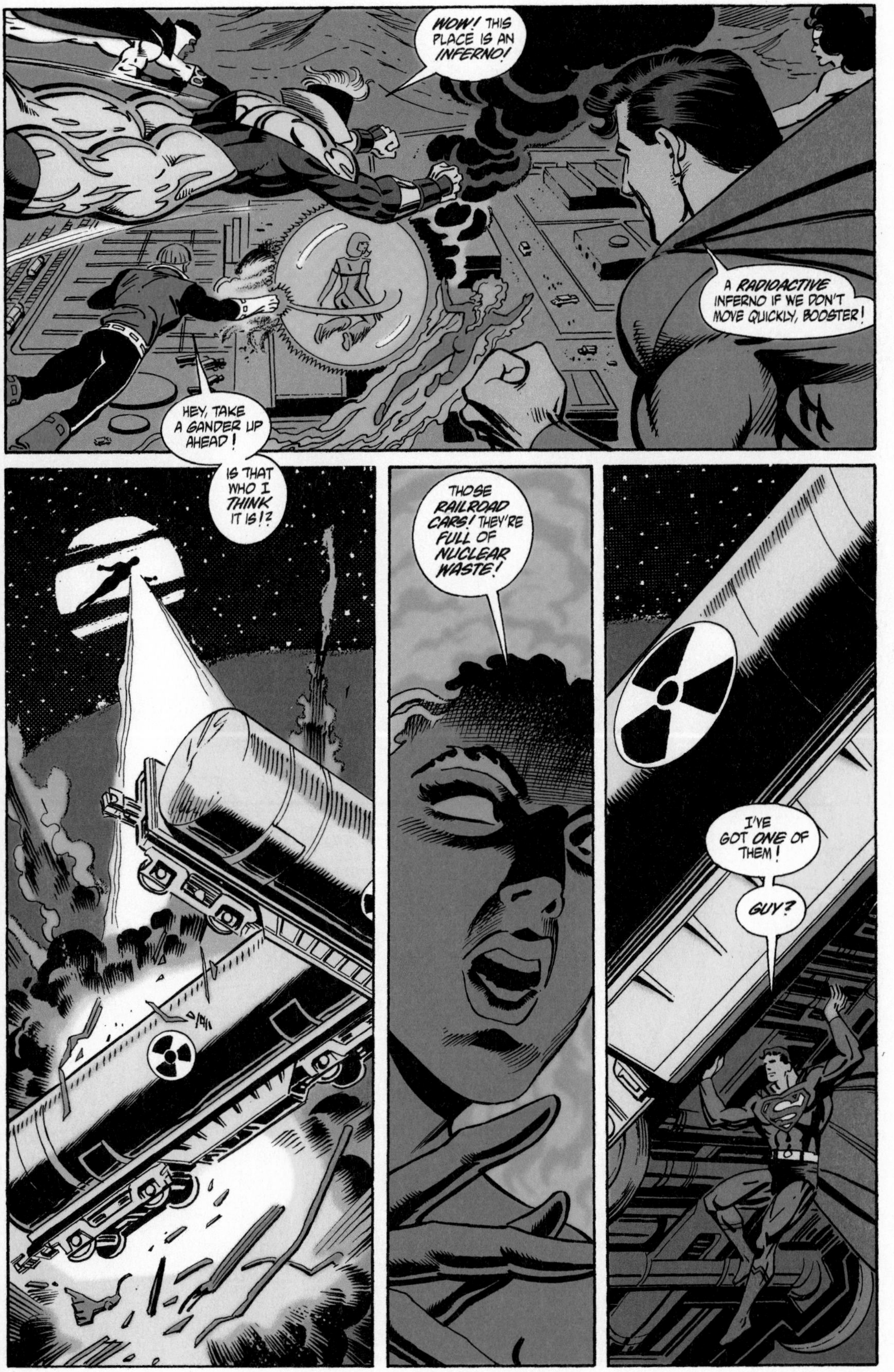
WOW! THIS PLACE IS AN INFERNO!
A RADIOACTIVE INFERNO IF WE DON'T MOVE QUICKLY, BOOSTER!
HEY, TAKE A GANDER UP AHEAD!
IS THAT WHO I THINK IT IS!?
THOSE RAILROAD CARS! THEY'RE FULL OF NUCLEAR WASTE!
I'VE GOT ONE OF THEM!
GUY?

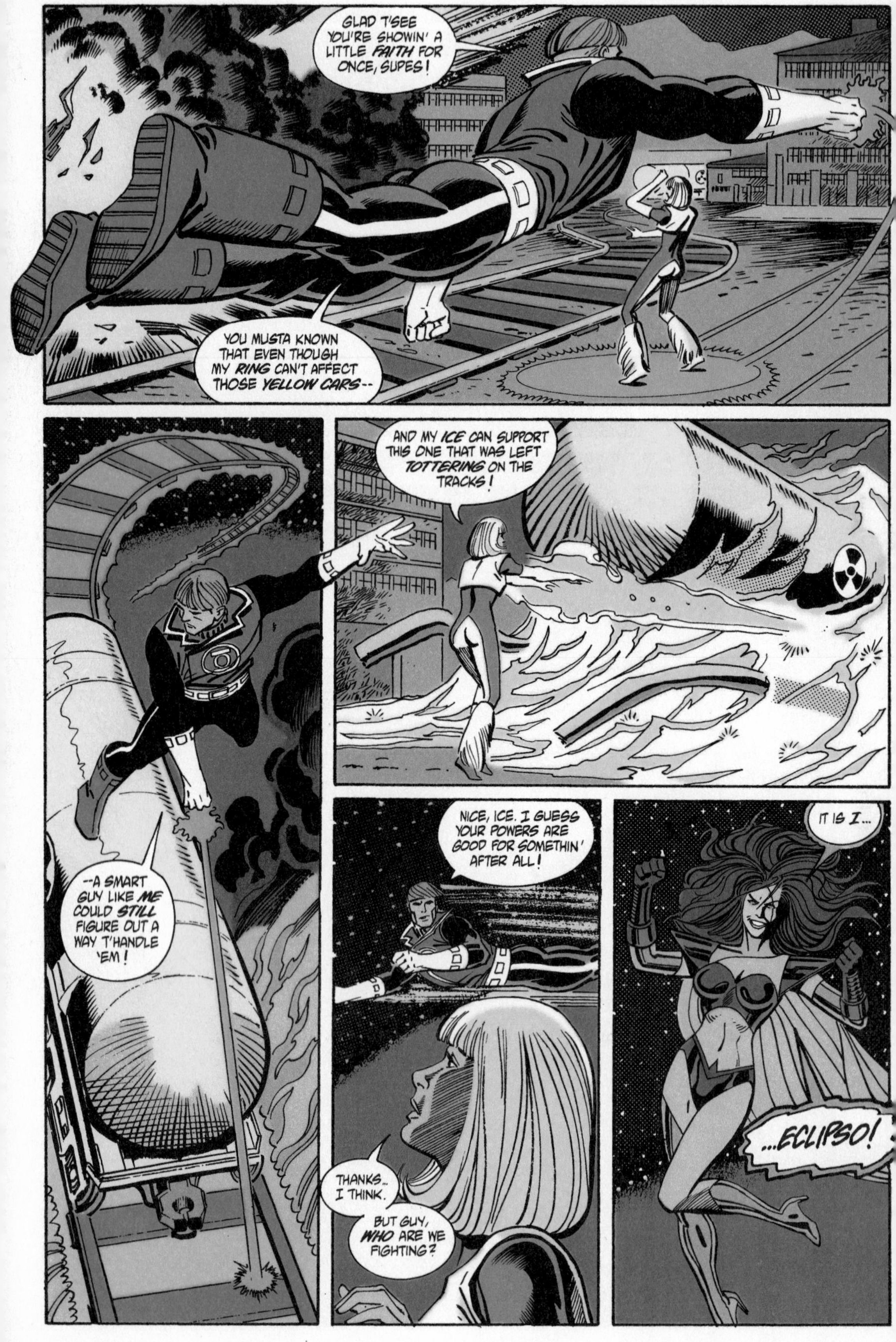
GLAD T'SEE YOU'RE SHOWIN' A LITTLE FAITH FOR ONCE, SUPES!
YOU MUSTA KNOWN THAT EVEN THOUGH MY RING CAN'T AFFECT THOSE YELLOW CARS--
--A SMART GUY LIKE ME COULD STILL FIGURE OUT A WAY T'HANDLE 'EM!
AND MY ICE CAN SUPPORT THIS ONE THAT WAS LEFT TOTTERING ON THE TRACKS!
NICE, ICE. I GUESS YOUR POWERS ARE GOOD FOR SOMETHIN' AFTER ALL!
THANKS... I THINK.
BUT GUY, WHO ARE WE FIGHTING?
IT IS I...
...ECLIPSO!

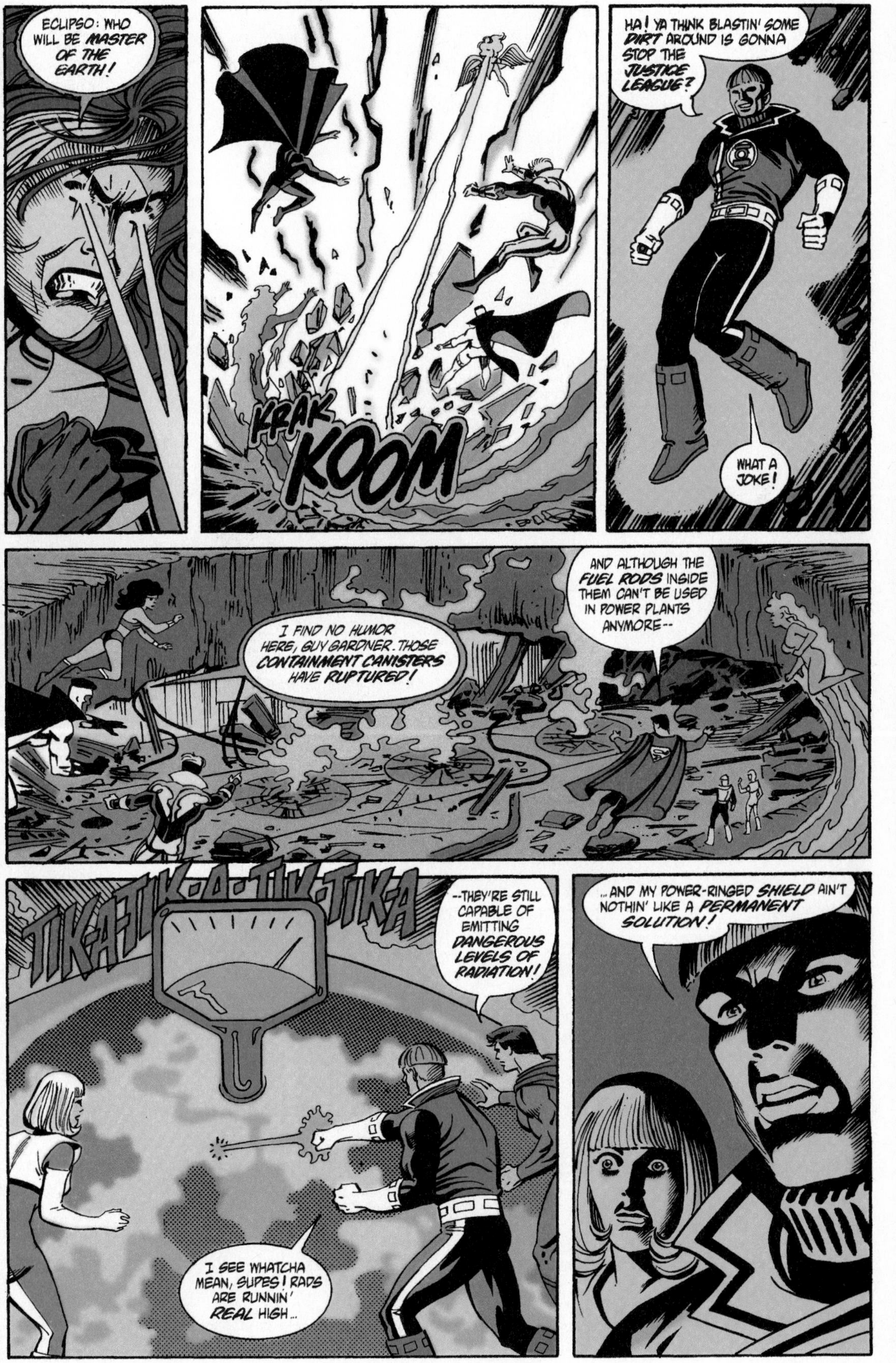
ECLIPSO: WHO WILL BE MASTER OF THE EARTH!
KRAK
KOOM
HA! YA THINK BLASTIN' SOME DIRT AROUND IS GONNA STOP THE JUSTICE LEAGUE?
WHAT A JOKE!
I FIND NO HUMOR HERE, GUY GARDNER. THOSE CONTAINMENT CANISTERS HAVE RUPTURED!
AND ALTHOUGH THE FUEL RODS INSIDE THEM CAN'T BE USED IN POWER PLANTS ANYMORE--
TIK-A-TIK-A-TIK-TIKA
--THEY'RE STILL CAPABLE OF EMITTING DANGEROUS LEVELS OF RADIATION!
I SEE WHATCHA MEAN, SUPES! RADS ARE RUNNIN' REAL HIGH...
...AND MY POWER-RINGED SHIELD AIN'T NOTHIN' LIKE A PERMANENT SOLUTION!

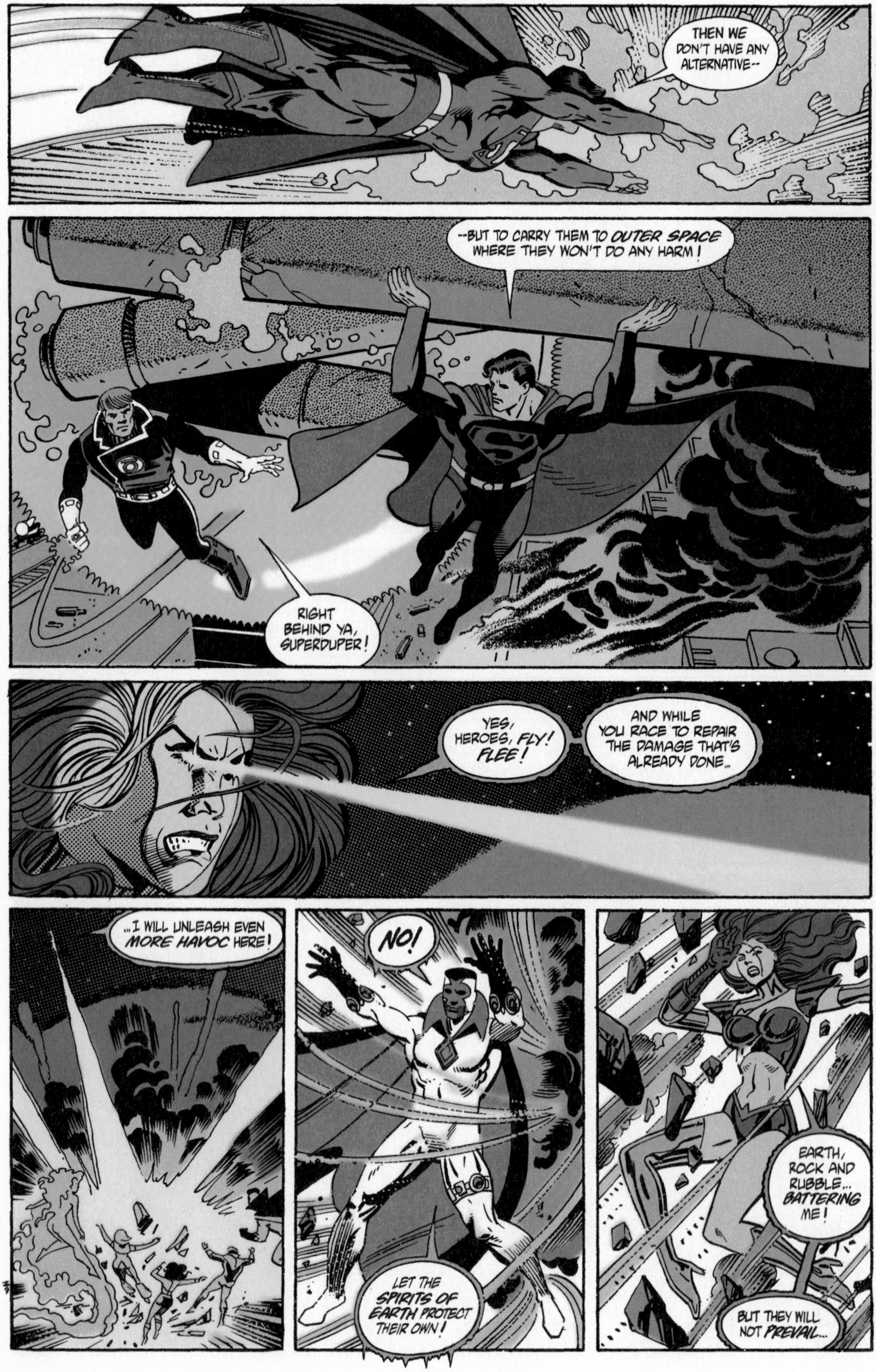
THEN WE DON'T HAVE ANY ALTERNATIVE--
--BUT TO CARRY THEM TO OUTER SPACE WHERE THEY WON'T DO ANY HARM!
RIGHT BEHIND YA, SUPERDUPER!
YES, HEROES, FLY! FLEE!
AND WHILE YOU RACE TO REPAIR THE DAMAGE THAT'S ALREADY DONE...
...I WILL UNLEASH EVEN MORE HAVOC HERE!
NO!
LET THE SPIRITS OF EARTH PROTECT THEIR OWN!
EARTH, ROCK AND RUBBLE... BATTERING ME!
BUT THEY WILL NOT PREVAIL...

"...FOR ECLIPSO FIGHTS ON *MANY FRONTS!*"

DON'T KNOW *WHAT* GOT INTO BRUCE GORDON--

--BUT EVEN WORKING *ALONE,* I CAN COBBLE TOGETHER SOME BASIC *SOLAR GUNS* IN NO TIME!

IT MIGHT EVEN REMIND SOME PEOPLE JUST WHAT I HAVE TO OFFER TO THIS--

HUH?

EMERGENCY LIGHTS COMING ON. BUT IT SOUNDS LIKE SOMEONE'S...

IS ANYBODY THERE?

REX, IS THAT YOU?

YOWWW!

MANAGED TO GET OUT OF THE WAY OF THAT BLAST IN TIME, BUT--

uh-oh.

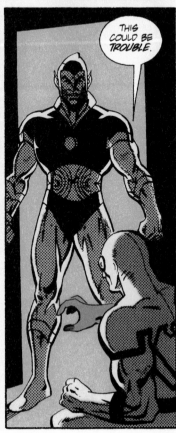

THIS COULD BE TROUBLE.

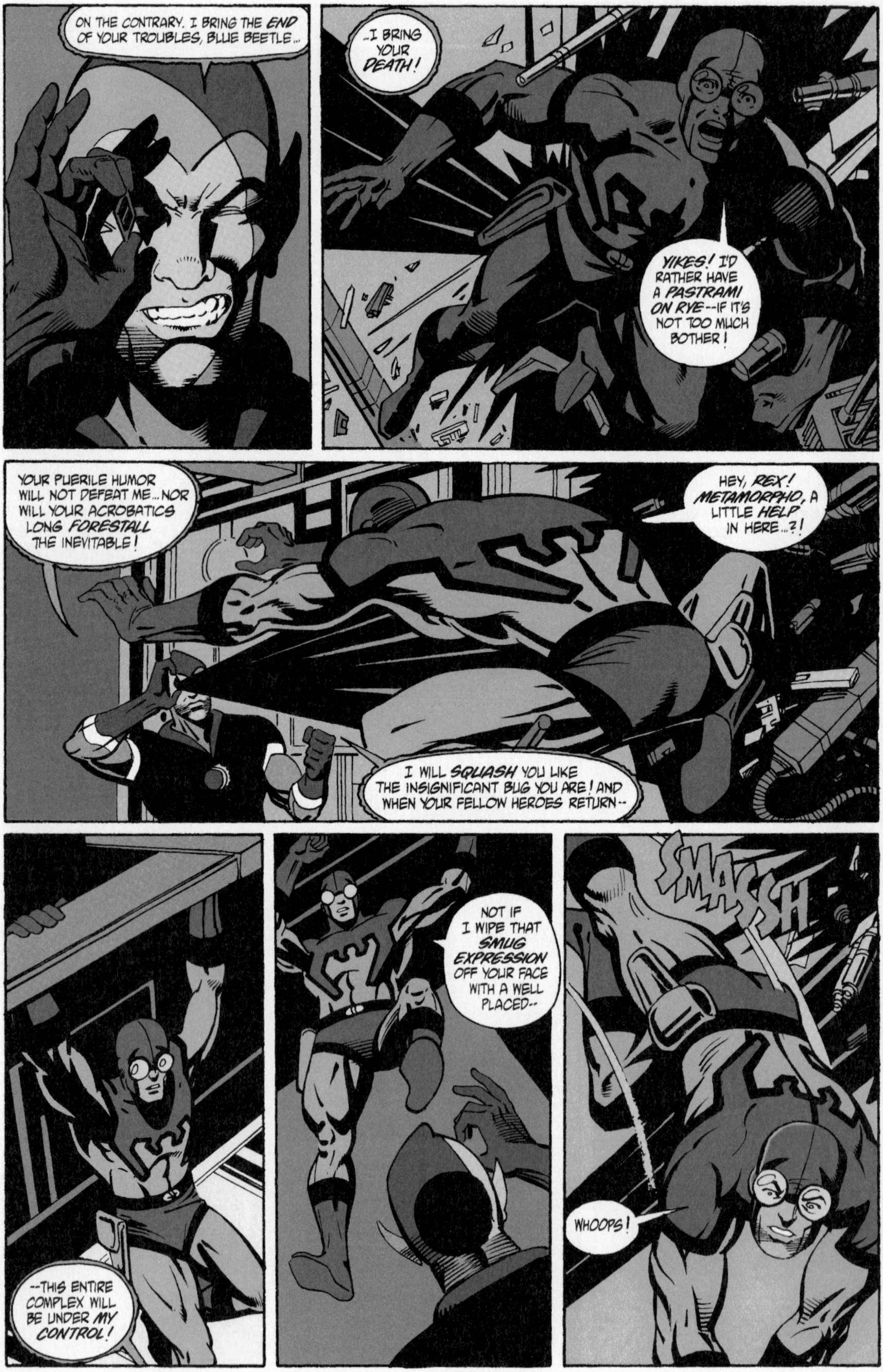
ON THE CONTRARY. I BRING THE END OF YOUR TROUBLES, BLUE BEETLE...
...I BRING YOUR DEATH!
YIKES! I'D RATHER HAVE A PASTRAMI ON RYE--IF IT'S NOT TOO MUCH BOTHER!
YOUR PUERILE HUMOR WILL NOT DEFEAT ME...NOR WILL YOUR ACROBATICS LONG FORESTALL THE INEVITABLE!
HEY, REX! METAMORPHO, A LITTLE HELP IN HERE...?!
I WILL SQUASH YOU LIKE THE INSIGNIFICANT BUG YOU ARE! AND WHEN YOUR FELLOW HEROES RETURN--
--THIS ENTIRE COMPLEX WILL BE UNDER MY CONTROL!
NOT IF I WIPE THAT SMUG EXPRESSION OFF YOUR FACE WITH A WELL PLACED--
SMASSH
WHOOPS!

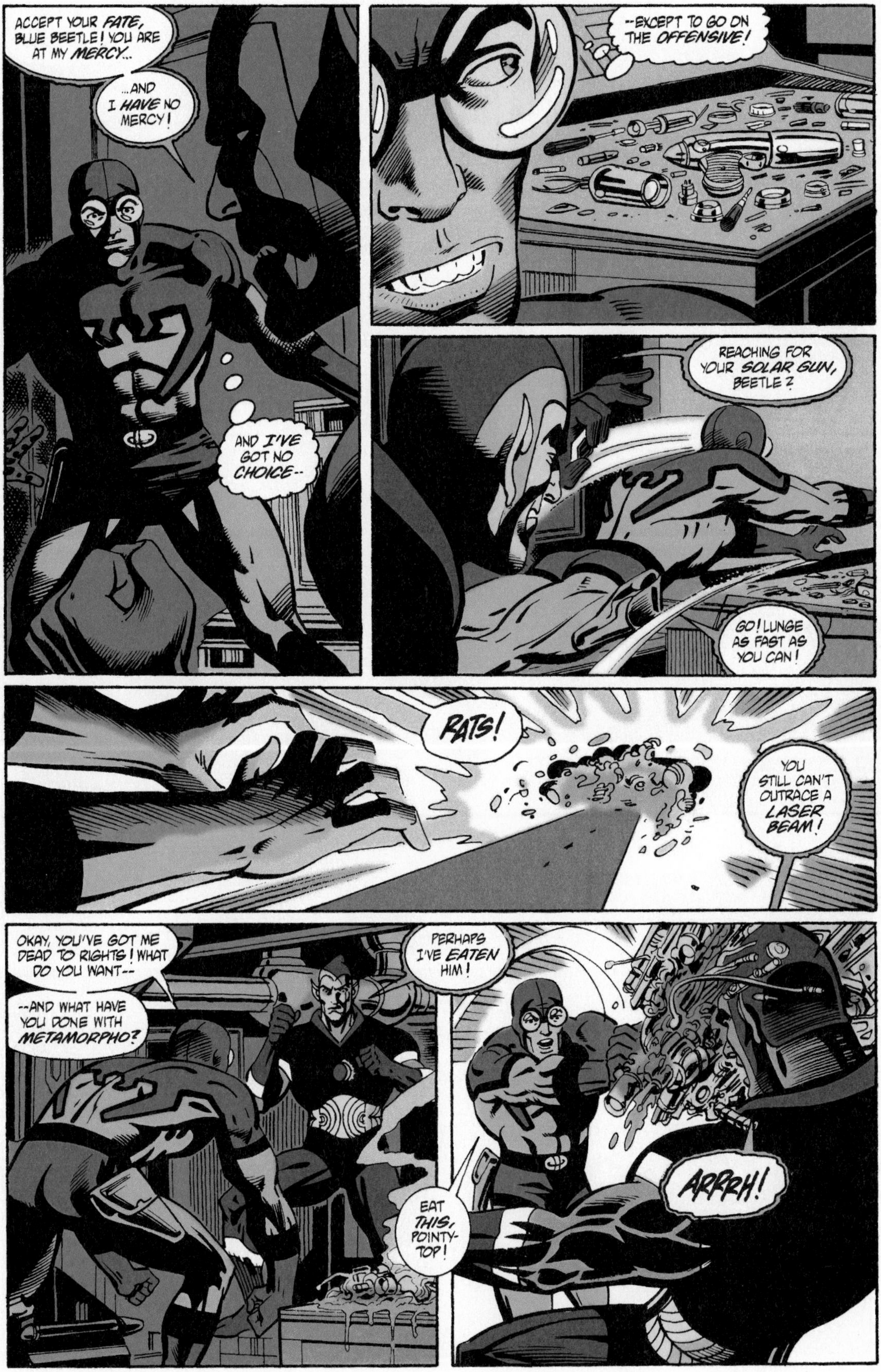

ACCEPT YOUR FATE, BLUE BEETLE! YOU ARE AT MY MERCY...
...AND I HAVE NO MERCY!
AND I'VE GOT NO CHOICE--
--EXCEPT TO GO ON THE OFFENSIVE!
REACHING FOR YOUR SOLAR GUN, BEETLE?
GO! LUNGE AS FAST AS YOU CAN!
RATS!
YOU STILL CAN'T OUTRACE A LASER BEAM!
OKAY, YOU'VE GOT ME DEAD TO RIGHTS! WHAT DO YOU WANT--
--AND WHAT HAVE YOU DONE WITH METAMORPHO?
PERHAPS I'VE EATEN HIM!
EAT THIS, POINTY-TOP!
ARRRH!

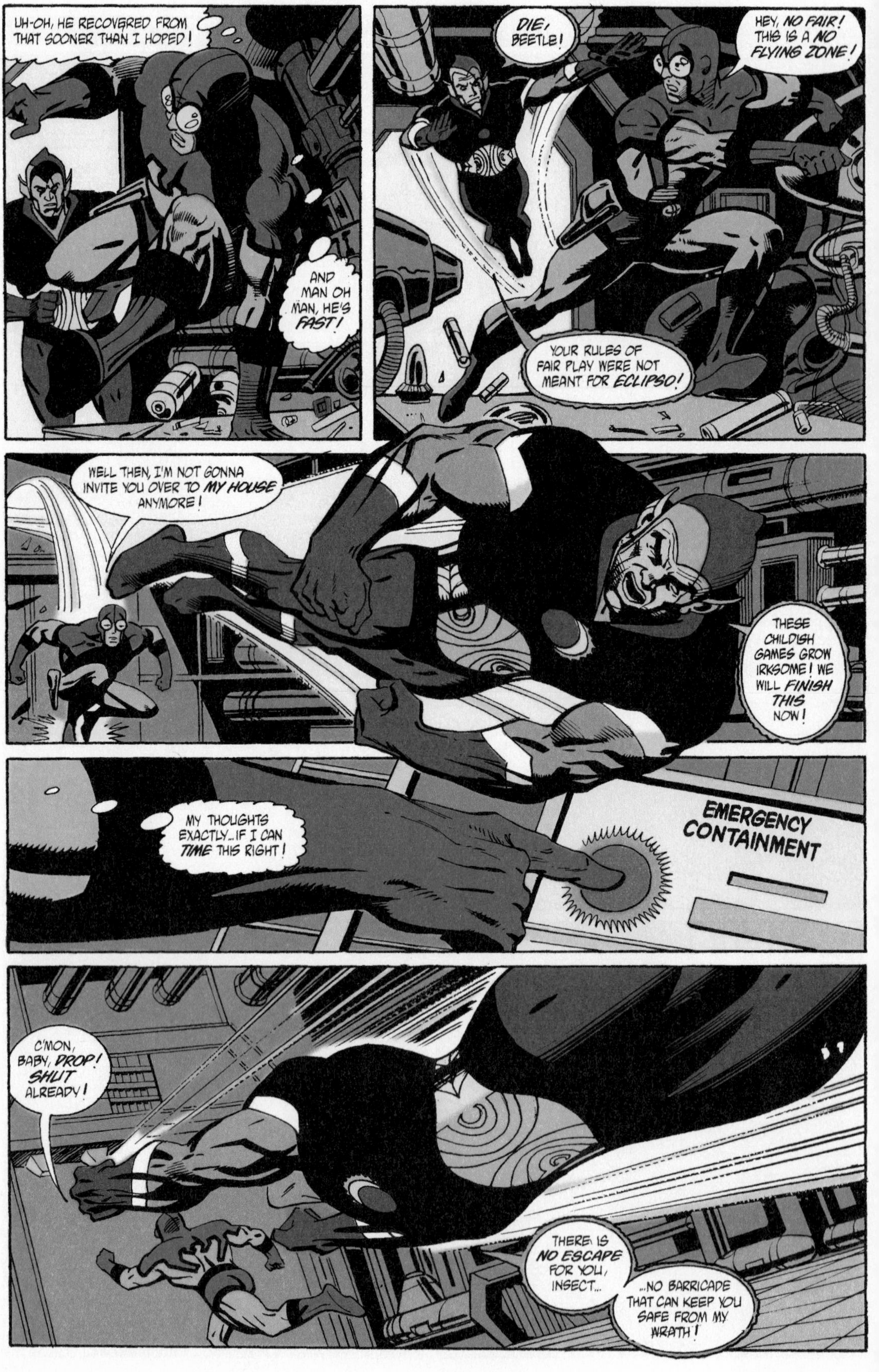
UH-OH, HE RECOVERED FROM THAT SOONER THAN I HOPED!
AND MAN OH MAN, HE'S FAST!
DIE, BEETLE!
HEY, NO FAIR! THIS IS A NO FLYING ZONE!
YOUR RULES OF FAIR PLAY WERE NOT MEANT FOR ECLIPSO!
WELL THEN, I'M NOT GONNA INVITE YOU OVER TO MY HOUSE ANYMORE!
THESE CHILDISH GAMES GROW IRKSOME! WE WILL FINISH THIS NOW!
MY THOUGHTS EXACTLY... IF I CAN TIME THIS RIGHT!
EMERGENCY CONTAINMENT
C'MON, BABY, DROP! SHUT ALREADY!
THERE IS NO ESCAPE FOR YOU, INSECT...
...NO BARRICADE THAT CAN KEEP YOU SAFE FROM MY WRATH!

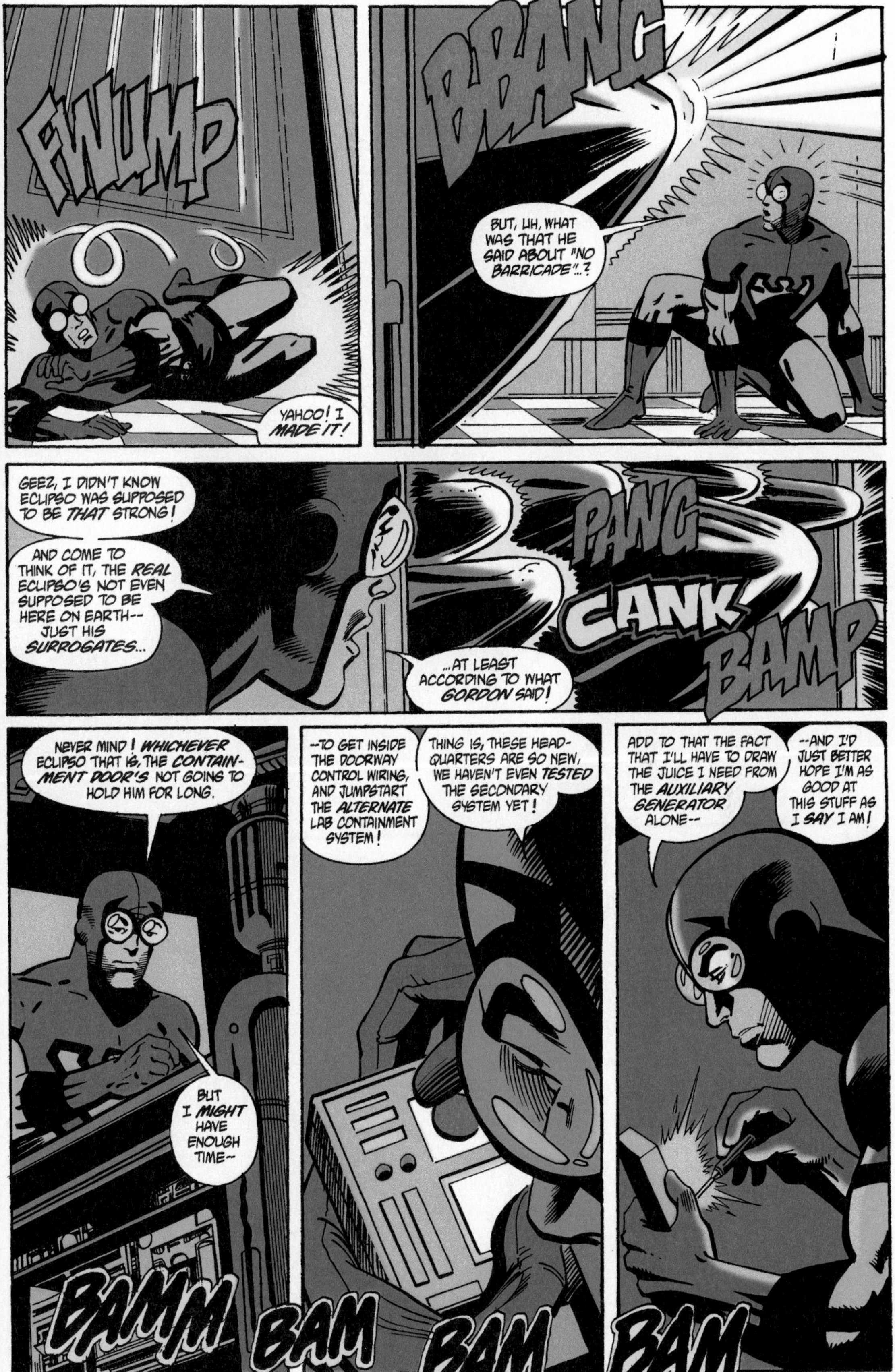
FWUMP
YAHOO! I MADE IT!
BBRANG
BUT, UH, WHAT WAS THAT HE SAID ABOUT "NO BARRICADE"...?
GEEZ, I DIDN'T KNOW ECLIPSO WAS SUPPOSED TO BE THAT STRONG!
AND COME TO THINK OF IT, THE REAL ECLIPSO'S NOT EVEN SUPPOSED TO BE HERE ON EARTH-- JUST HIS SURROGATES...
PANG
CANK
BAMP
...AT LEAST ACCORDING TO WHAT GORDON SAID!
NEVER MIND! WHICHEVER ECLIPSO THAT IS, THE CONTAIN-MENT DOOR'S NOT GOING TO HOLD HIM FOR LONG.
BUT I MIGHT HAVE ENOUGH TIME--
--TO GET INSIDE THE DOORWAY CONTROL WIRING, AND JUMPSTART THE ALTERNATE LAB CONTAINMENT SYSTEM!
THING IS, THESE HEAD-QUARTERS ARE SO NEW, WE HAVEN'T EVEN TESTED THE SECONDARY SYSTEM YET!
ADD TO THAT THE FACT THAT I'LL HAVE TO DRAW THE JUICE I NEED FROM THE AUXILIARY GENERATOR ALONE--
--AND I'D JUST BETTER HOPE I'M AS GOOD AT THIS STUFF AS I SAY I AM!
BAMM BAM BAM BAM

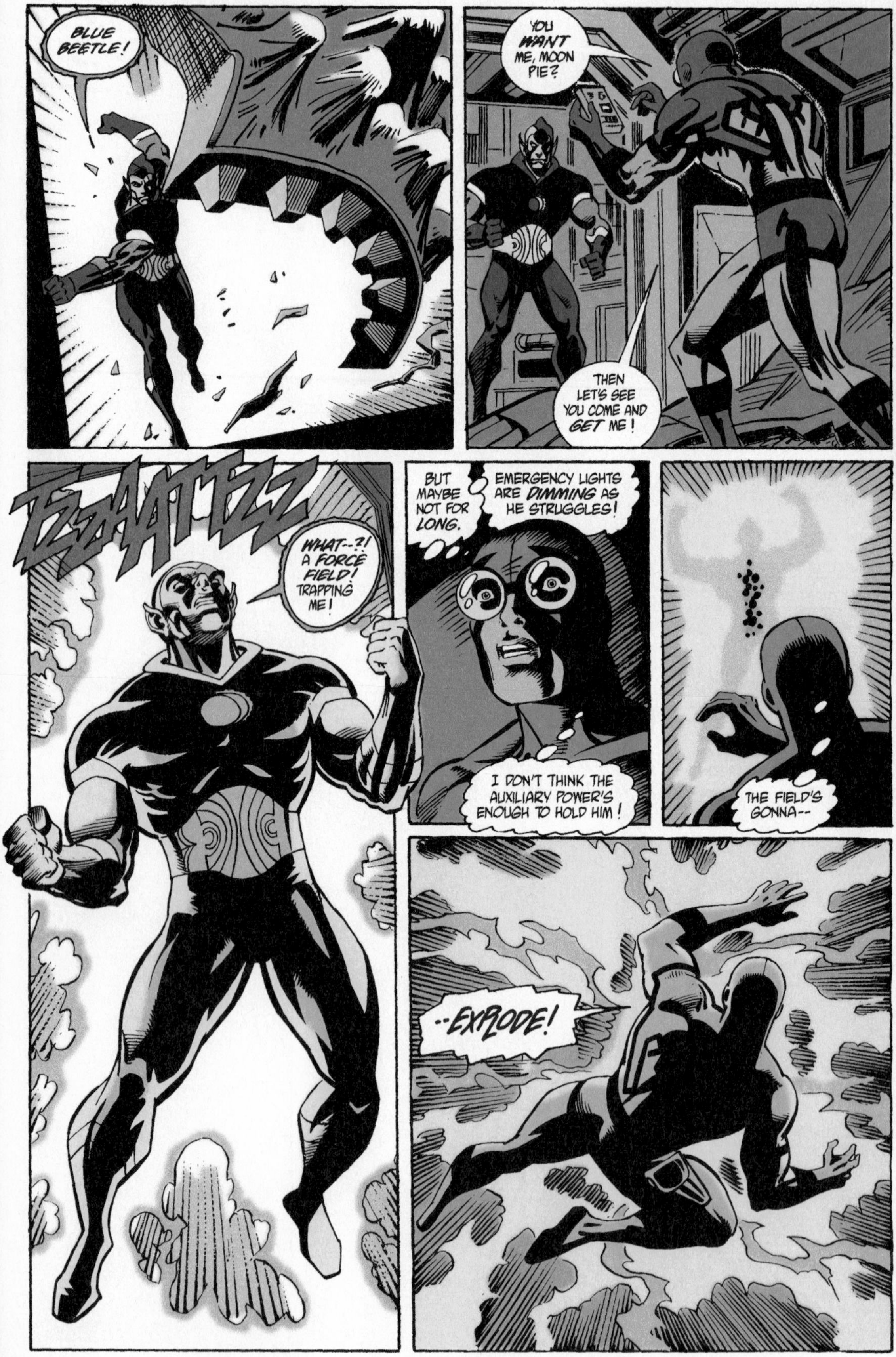
BLUE BEETLE!
YOU WANT ME, MOON PIE?
THEN LET'S SEE YOU COME AND GET ME!
TZZAATTZZ
WHAT--?! A FORCE FIELD! TRAPPING ME!
BUT MAYBE NOT FOR LONG.
EMERGENCY LIGHTS ARE DIMMING AS HE STRUGGLES!
I DON'T THINK THE AUXILIARY POWER'S ENOUGH TO HOLD HIM!
THE FIELD'S GONNA--
--EXPLODE!

:WHEW!: THAT BLOWED UP REAL GOOD!

AND IT LOOKS LIKE IT TOOK ECLIPSO ALONG WITH IT!

HE'S GONE!

OR ELSE HE'S JUST LURKING AROUND THE NEXT CORNER!

BEST BET'S TO GET INTO MY BUG AND--

UHNNH...

WHO...?

HEY, OLD BUDDY, YOU OKAY?

P-PINNED... IN THE WRECKAGE...

REX!

YOU MUST'VE BEEN COMING TO THE RESCUE AND GOT CAUGHT IN THE BLAST!

YEAH... THINK YOU COULD GIVE ME A HAND? OR MAYBE...

...YOUR LIFE, BLUE BEETLE!

HUH?! I THOUGHT YOU WERE PINNED!

YOU ALSO BELIEVED I WAS METAMORPHO!

OH NO!

AND THAT WAS A DEADLY MISTAKE!

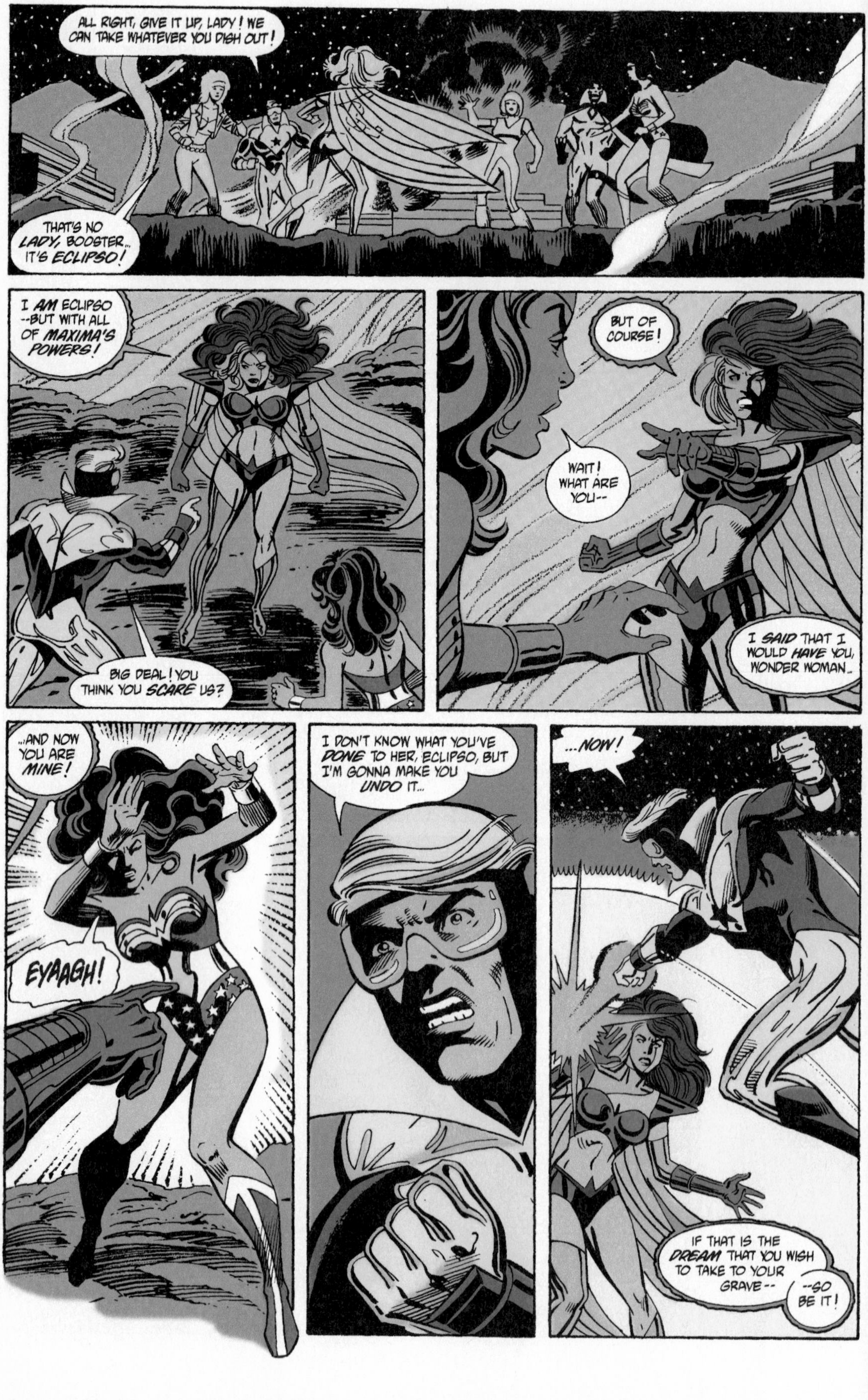
ALL RIGHT, GIVE IT UP, LADY! WE CAN TAKE WHATEVER YOU DISH OUT!
THAT'S NO LADY, BOOSTER... IT'S ECLIPSO!
I AM ECLIPSO --BUT WITH ALL OF MAXIMA'S POWERS!
BIG DEAL! YOU THINK YOU SCARE US?
BUT OF COURSE!
WAIT! WHAT ARE YOU--
I SAID THAT I WOULD HAVE YOU, WONDER WOMAN...
...AND NOW YOU ARE MINE!
EYAAGH!
I DON'T KNOW WHAT YOU'VE DONE TO HER, ECLIPSO, BUT I'M GONNA MAKE YOU UNDO IT...
...NOW!
IF THAT IS THE DREAM THAT YOU WISH TO TAKE TO YOUR GRAVE--
--SO BE IT!

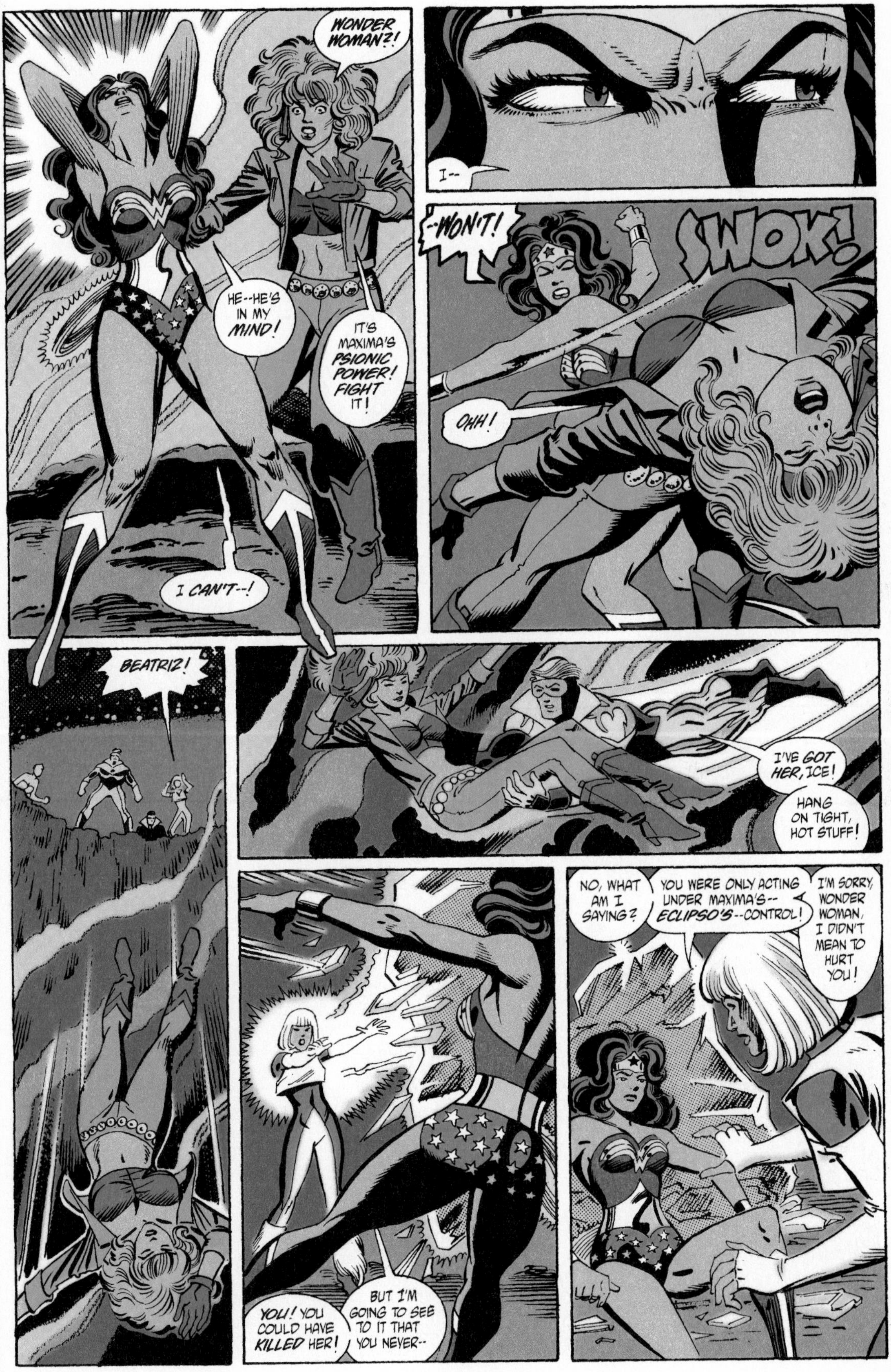
WONDER WOMAN?!
HE--HE'S IN MY MIND!
IT'S MAXIMA'S PSIONIC POWER! FIGHT IT!
I CAN'T--!
I--
--WON'T!
SWOK!
OHH!
BEATRIZ!
I'VE GOT HER, ICE!
HANG ON TIGHT, HOT STUFF!
YOU! YOU COULD HAVE KILLED HER!
BUT I'M GOING TO SEE TO IT THAT YOU NEVER--
NO, WHAT AM I SAYING?
YOU WERE ONLY ACTING UNDER MAXIMA'S-- ECLIPSO'S--CONTROL!
I'M SORRY, WONDER WOMAN, I DIDN'T MEAN TO HURT YOU!

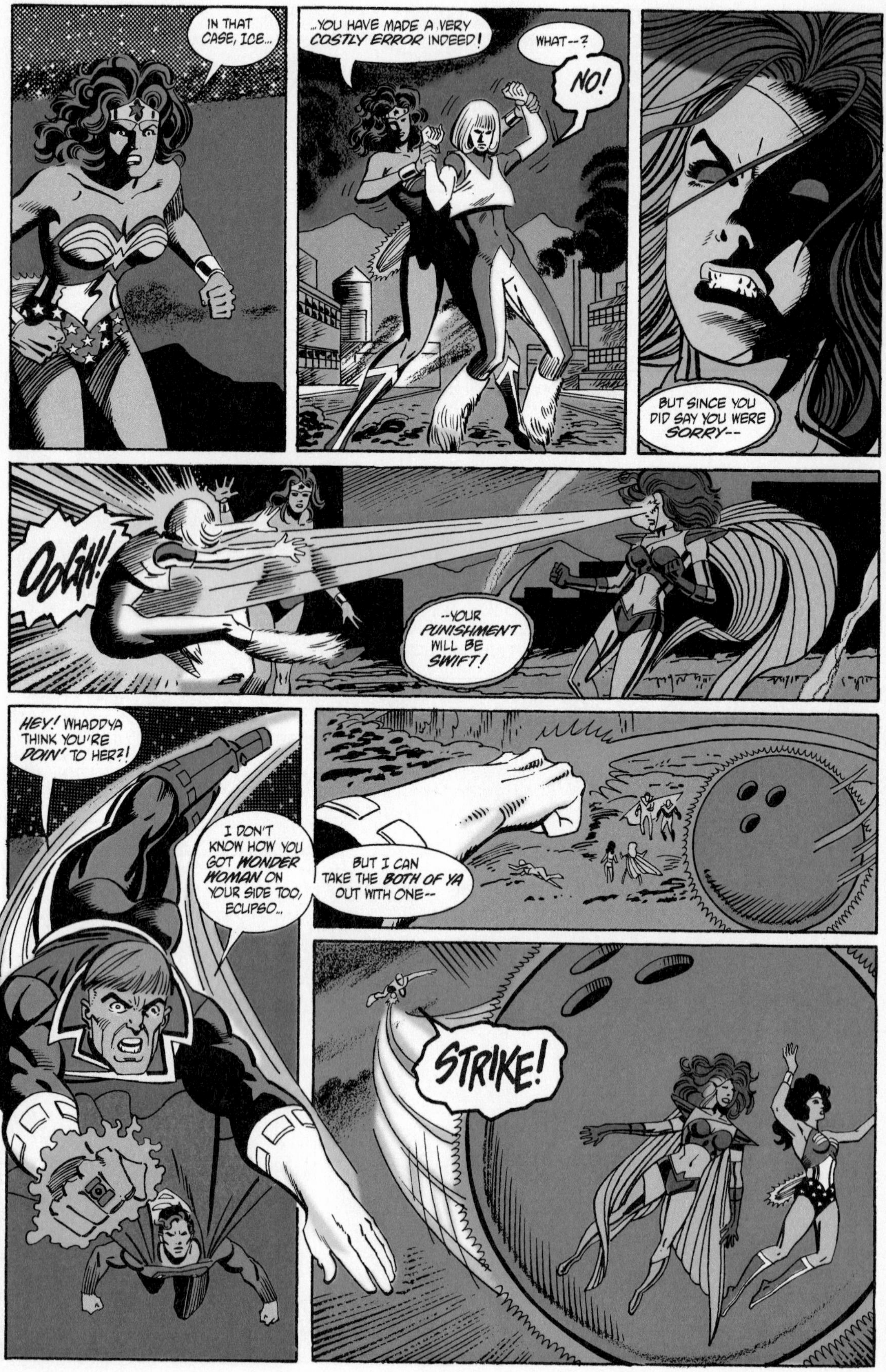
IN THAT CASE, ICE...
...YOU HAVE MADE A VERY COSTLY ERROR INDEED!
WHAT--?
NO!
BUT SINCE YOU DID SAY YOU WERE SORRY--
OOGH!
--YOUR PUNISHMENT WILL BE SWIFT!
HEY! WHADDYA THINK YOU'RE DOIN' TO HER?!
I DON'T KNOW HOW YOU GOT WONDER WOMAN ON YOUR SIDE TOO, ECLIPSO...
BUT I CAN TAKE THE BOTH OF YA OUT WITH ONE--
STRIKE!

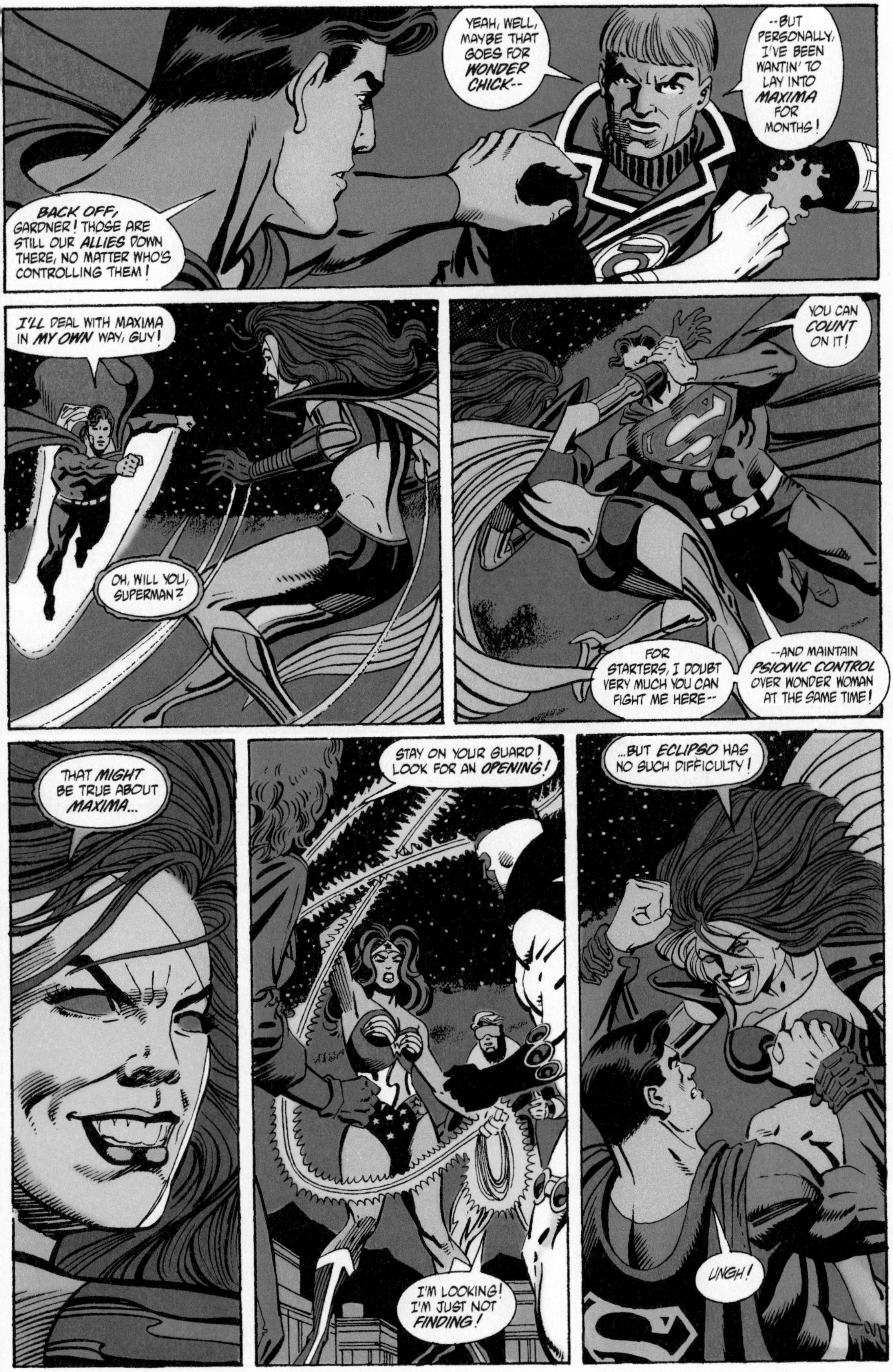
BACK OFF, GARDNER! THOSE ARE STILL OUR ALLIES DOWN THERE, NO MATTER WHO'S CONTROLLING THEM!
YEAH, WELL, MAYBE THAT GOES FOR WONDER CHICK--
--BUT PERSONALLY, I'VE BEEN WANTIN' TO LAY INTO MAXIMA FOR MONTHS!
I'LL DEAL WITH MAXIMA IN MY OWN WAY, GUY!
OH, WILL YOU, SUPERMAN?
YOU CAN COUNT ON IT!
FOR STARTERS, I DOUBT VERY MUCH YOU CAN FIGHT ME HERE--
--AND MAINTAIN PSIONIC CONTROL OVER WONDER WOMAN AT THE SAME TIME!
THAT MIGHT BE TRUE ABOUT MAXIMA...
STAY ON YOUR GUARD! LOOK FOR AN OPENING!
I'M LOOKING! I'M JUST NOT FINDING!
...BUT ECLIPSO HAS NO SUCH DIFFICULTY!
UNGH!

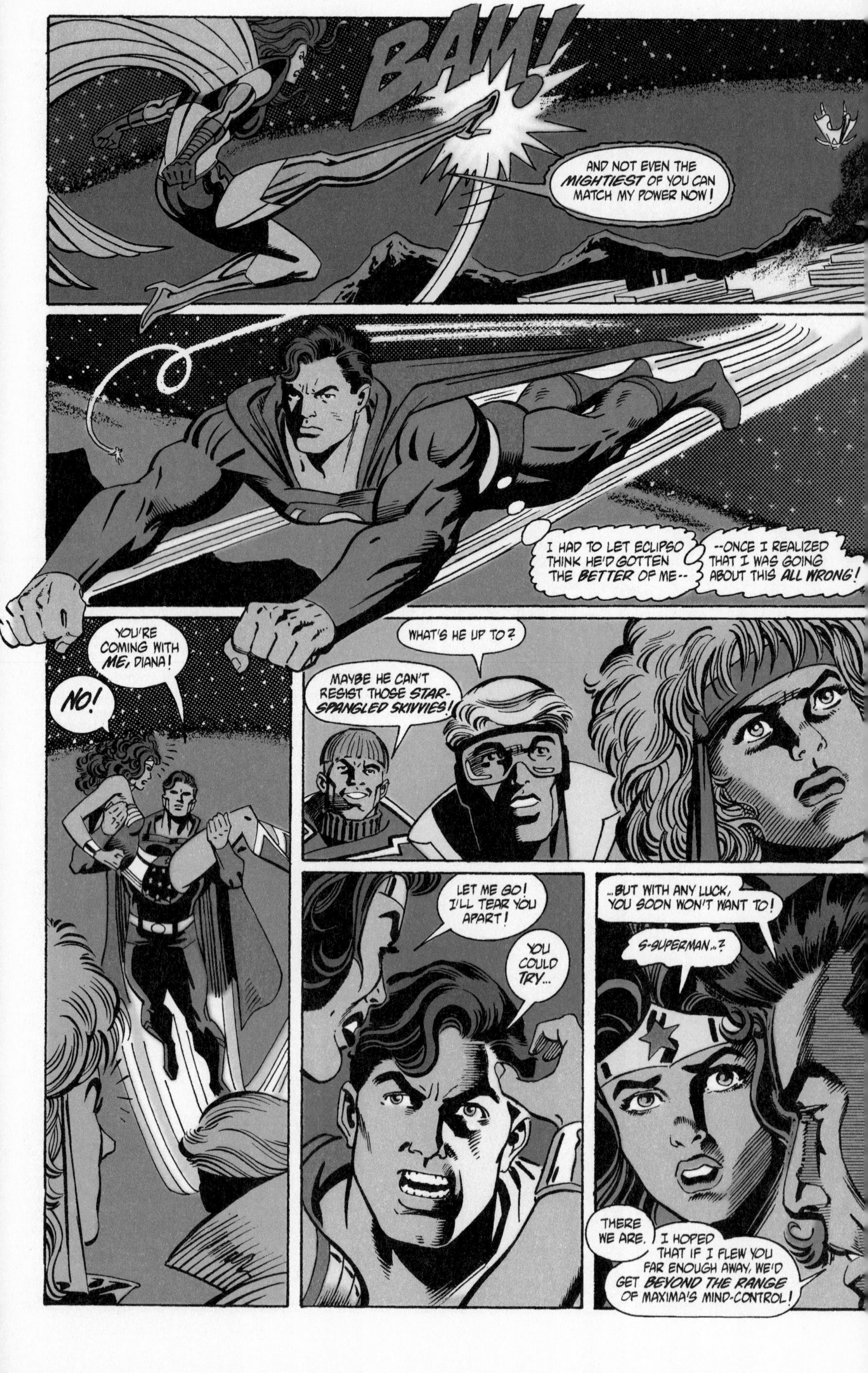
BAM!
AND NOT EVEN THE MIGHTIEST OF YOU CAN MATCH MY POWER NOW!
I HAD TO LET ECLIPSO THINK HE'D GOTTEN THE BETTER OF ME--
--ONCE I REALIZED THAT I WAS GOING ABOUT THIS ALL WRONG!
YOU'RE COMING WITH ME, DIANA!
NO!
WHAT'S HE UP TO?
MAYBE HE CAN'T RESIST THOSE STAR-SPANGLED SKIVVIES!
LET ME GO! I'LL TEAR YOU APART!
YOU COULD TRY...
...BUT WITH ANY LUCK, YOU SOON WON'T WANT TO!
S-SUPERMAN...?
THERE WE ARE.
I HOPED THAT IF I FLEW YOU FAR ENOUGH AWAY, WE'D GET BEYOND THE RANGE OF MAXIMA'S MIND-CONTROL!

IT WAS IN NOT TAKING CONTROL OF THE MOST *POWERFUL* HERO OF ALL...

I SEE MY *MISTAKE* NOW.

SUPERMAN!

HEY, ECLIPSO...

...WATCH WHO YOU'RE CALLIN' *MOST* POWERFUL!

NOOO!

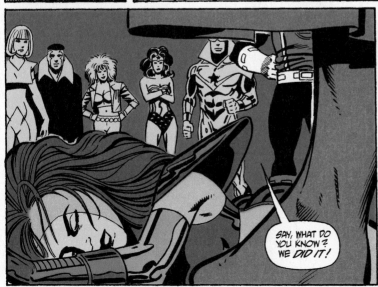

SAY, WHAT DO YOU KNOW? WE *DID* IT!

LET'S HAUL HER BACK TO *HEADQUARTERS* AND SEE IF BEETLE'S GUN CAN REALLY KNOCK ECLIPSO OUT OF HER!

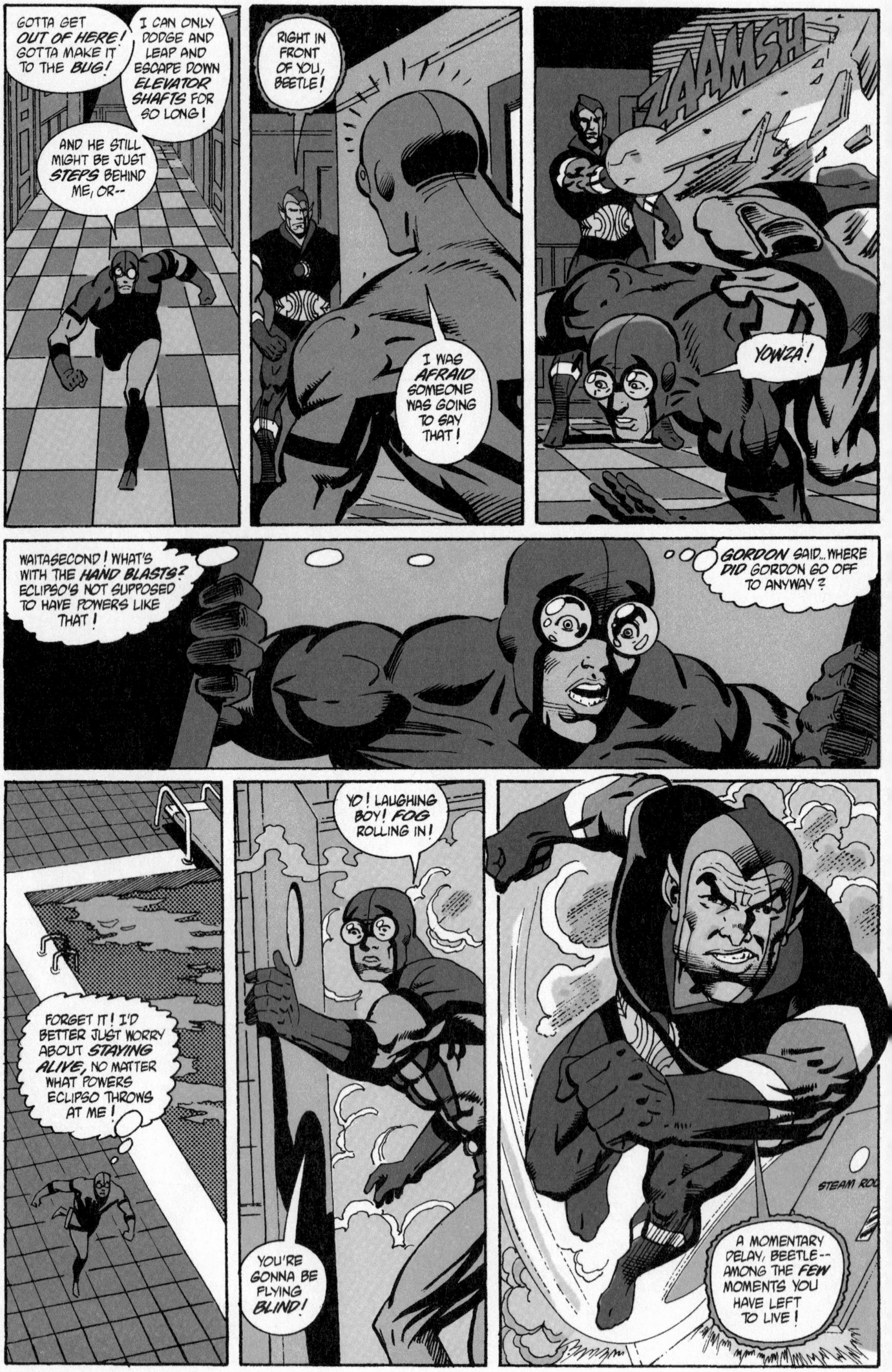
GOTTA GET OUT OF HERE! GOTTA MAKE IT TO THE BUG!
I CAN ONLY DODGE AND LEAP AND ESCAPE DOWN ELEVATOR SHAFTS FOR SO LONG!
AND HE STILL MIGHT BE JUST STEPS BEHIND ME, OR--
RIGHT IN FRONT OF YOU, BEETLE!
I WAS AFRAID SOMEONE WAS GOING TO SAY THAT!
ZAAMSH
YOWZA!
WAITASECOND! WHAT'S WITH THE HAND BLASTS? ECLIPSO'S NOT SUPPOSED TO HAVE POWERS LIKE THAT!
GORDON SAID... WHERE DID GORDON GO OFF TO ANYWAY?
FORGET IT! I'D BETTER JUST WORRY ABOUT STAYING ALIVE, NO MATTER WHAT POWERS ECLIPSO THROWS AT ME!
YO! LAUGHING BOY! FOG ROLLING IN!
YOU'RE GONNA BE FLYING BLIND!
STEAM ROO
A MOMENTARY DELAY, BEETLE-- AMONG THE FEW MOMENTS YOU HAVE LEFT TO LIVE!

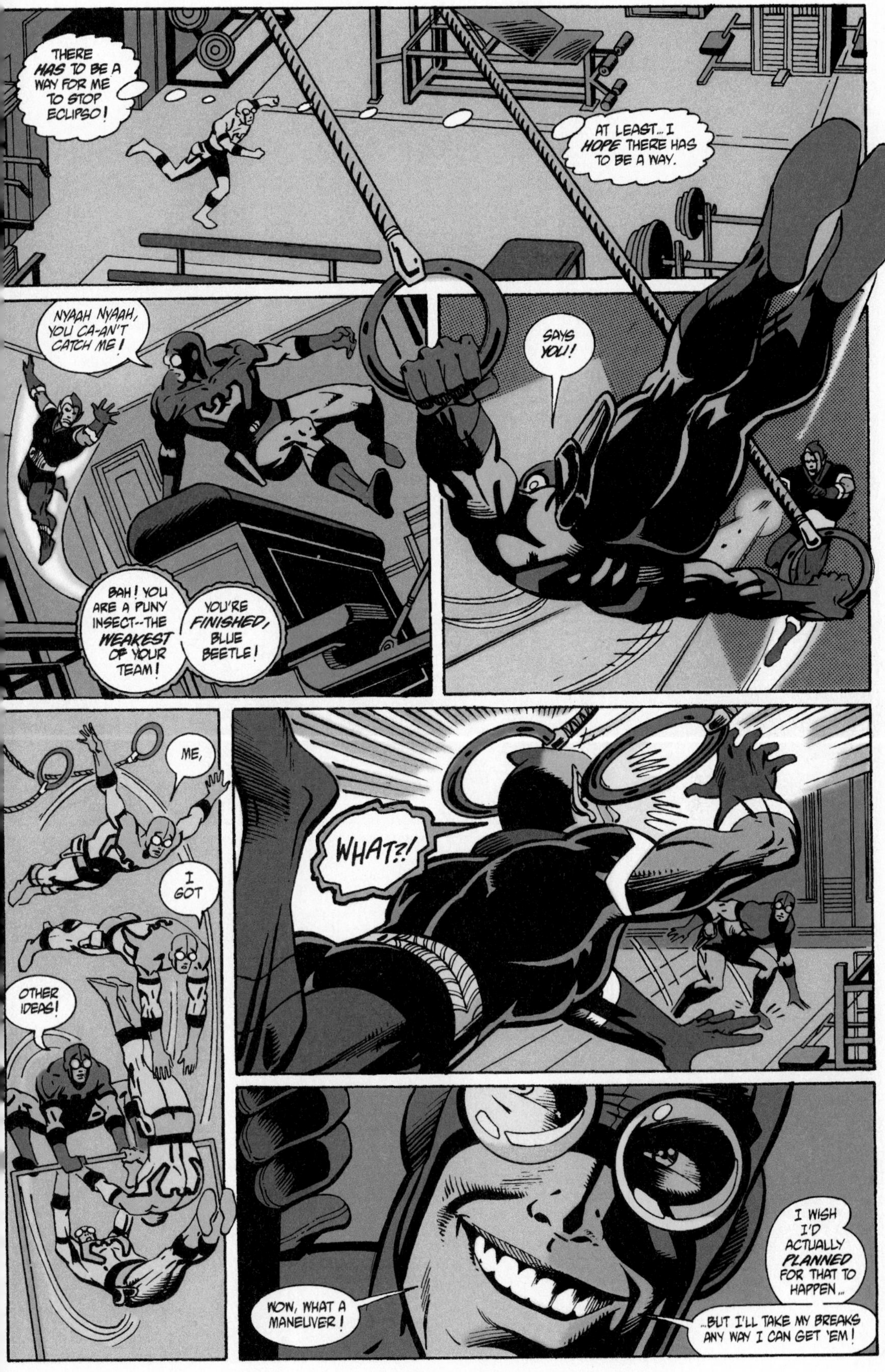
THERE HAS TO BE A WAY FOR ME TO STOP ECLIPSO!
AT LEAST... I HOPE THERE HAS TO BE A WAY.
NYAAH NYAAH, YOU CA-AN'T CATCH ME!
BAH! YOU ARE A PUNY INSECT--THE WEAKEST OF YOUR TEAM!
YOU'RE FINISHED, BLUE BEETLE!
SAYS YOU!
ME,
I GOT
OTHER IDEAS!
WHAT?!
WOW, WHAT A MANEUVER!
I WISH I'D ACTUALLY PLANNED FOR THAT TO HAPPEN...
...BUT I'LL TAKE MY BREAKS ANY WAY I CAN GET 'EM!

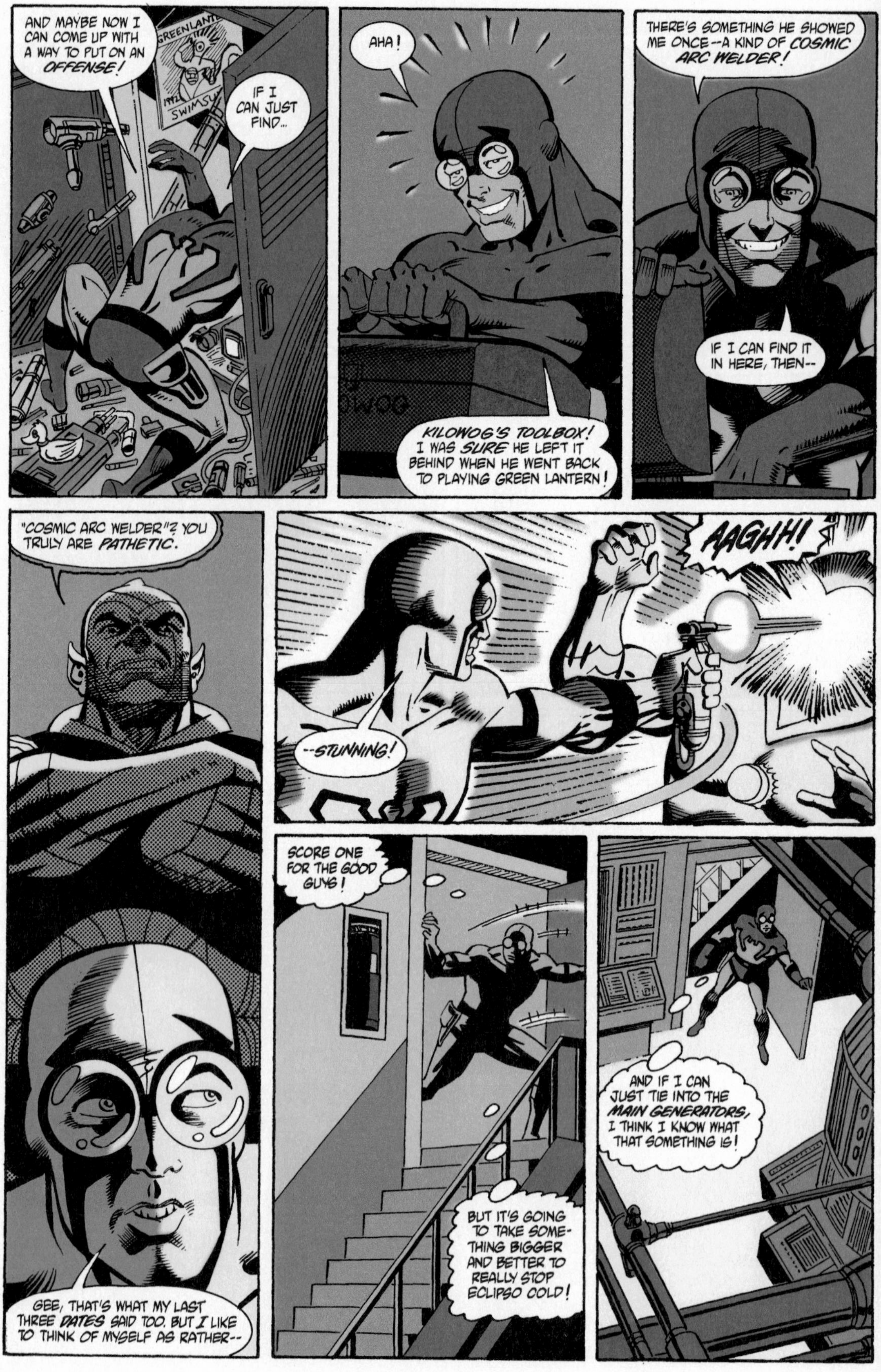
AND MAYBE NOW I CAN COME UP WITH A WAY TO PUT ON AN OFFENSE!
IF I CAN JUST FIND...
AHA!
KILOWOG'S TOOLBOX! I WAS SURE HE LEFT IT BEHIND WHEN HE WENT BACK TO PLAYING GREEN LANTERN!
THERE'S SOMETHING HE SHOWED ME ONCE--A KIND OF COSMIC ARC WELDER!
IF I CAN FIND IT IN HERE, THEN--
"COSMIC ARC WELDER"? YOU TRULY ARE PATHETIC.
GEE, THAT'S WHAT MY LAST THREE DATES SAID TOO. BUT I LIKE TO THINK OF MYSELF AS RATHER--
--STUNNING!
AAGHH!
SCORE ONE FOR THE GOOD GUYS!
BUT IT'S GOING TO TAKE SOMETHING BIGGER AND BETTER TO REALLY STOP ECLIPSO COLD!
AND IF I CAN JUST TIE INTO THE MAIN GENERATORS, I THINK I KNOW WHAT THAT SOMETHING IS!

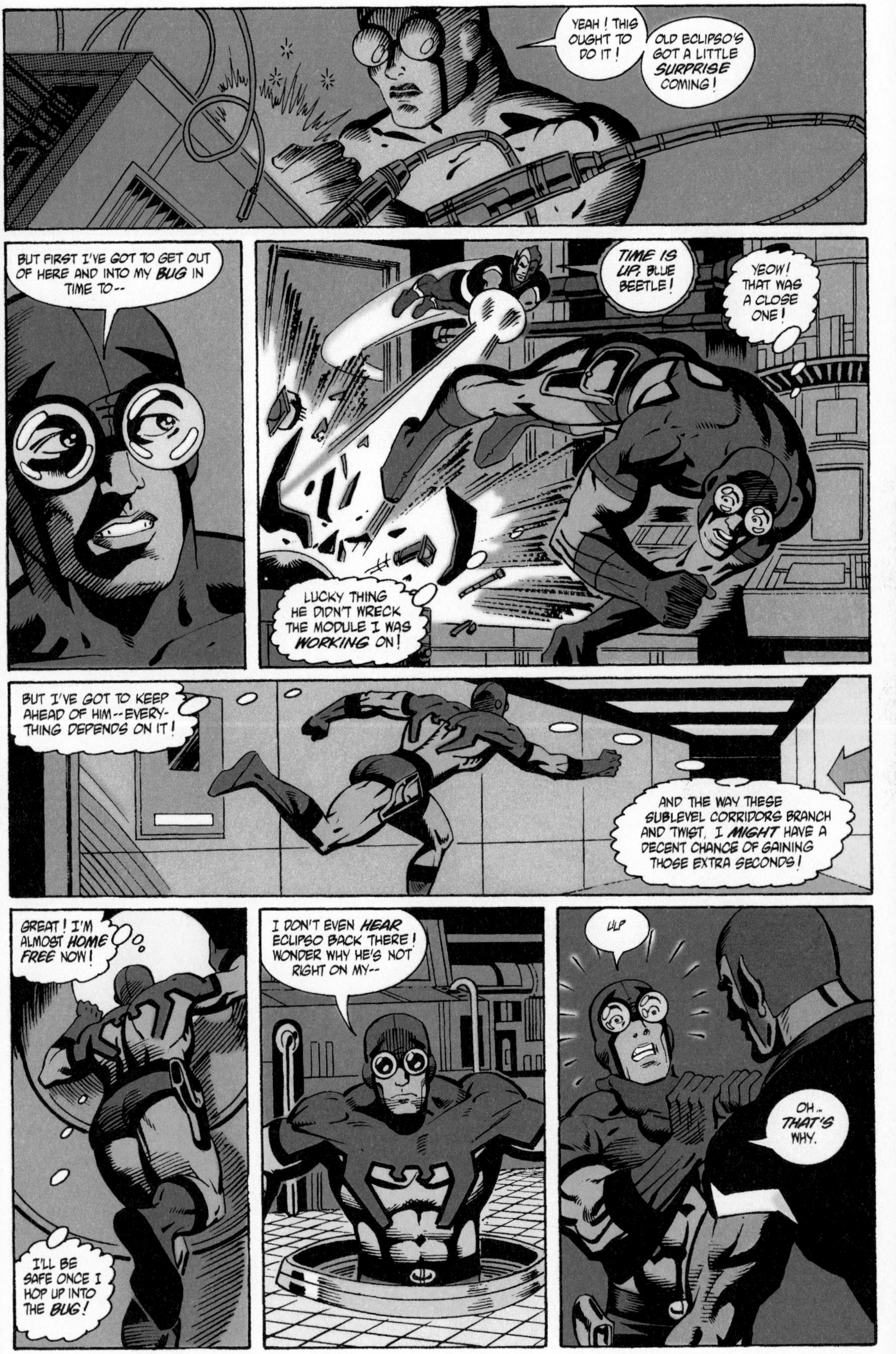
YEAH! THIS OUGHT TO DO IT!
OLD ECLIPSO'S GOT A LITTLE SURPRISE COMING!
BUT FIRST I'VE GOT TO GET OUT OF HERE AND INTO MY BUG IN TIME TO--
TIME IS UP, BLUE BEETLE!
YEOW! THAT WAS A CLOSE ONE!
LUCKY THING HE DIDN'T WRECK THE MODULE I WAS WORKING ON!
BUT I'VE GOT TO KEEP AHEAD OF HIM--EVERY-THING DEPENDS ON IT!
AND THE WAY THESE SUBLEVEL CORRIDORS BRANCH AND TWIST, I MIGHT HAVE A DECENT CHANCE OF GAINING THOSE EXTRA SECONDS!
GREAT! I'M ALMOST HOME FREE NOW!
I'LL BE SAFE ONCE I HOP UP INTO THE BUG!
I DON'T EVEN HEAR ECLIPSO BACK THERE! WONDER WHY HE'S NOT RIGHT ON MY--
ULP
OH.. THAT'S WHY.

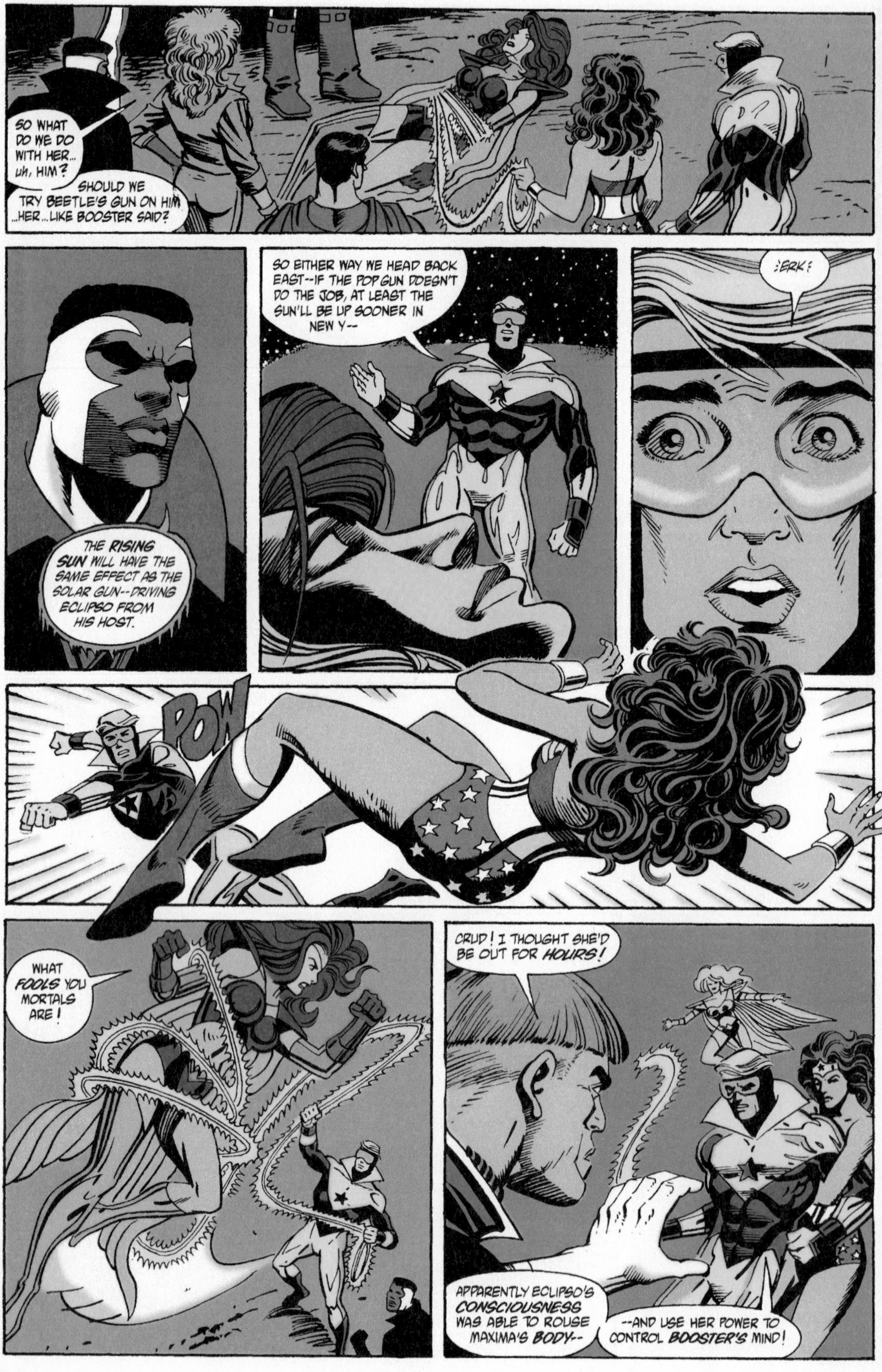
SO WHAT DO WE DO WITH HER... uh, HIM?
SHOULD WE TRY BEETLE'S GUN ON HIM ...HER... LIKE BOOSTER SAID?
THE RISING SUN WILL HAVE THE SAME EFFECT AS THE SOLAR GUN--DRIVING ECLIPSO FROM HIS HOST.
SO EITHER WAY WE HEAD BACK EAST--IF THE POPGUN DOESN'T DO THE JOB, AT LEAST THE SUN'LL BE UP SOONER IN NEW Y--
¡ERK!
POW
WHAT FOOLS YOU MORTALS ARE!
CRUD! I THOUGHT SHE'D BE OUT FOR HOURS!
APPARENTLY ECLIPSO'S CONSCIOUSNESS WAS ABLE TO ROUSE MAXIMA'S BODY--
--AND USE HER POWER TO CONTROL BOOSTER'S MIND!

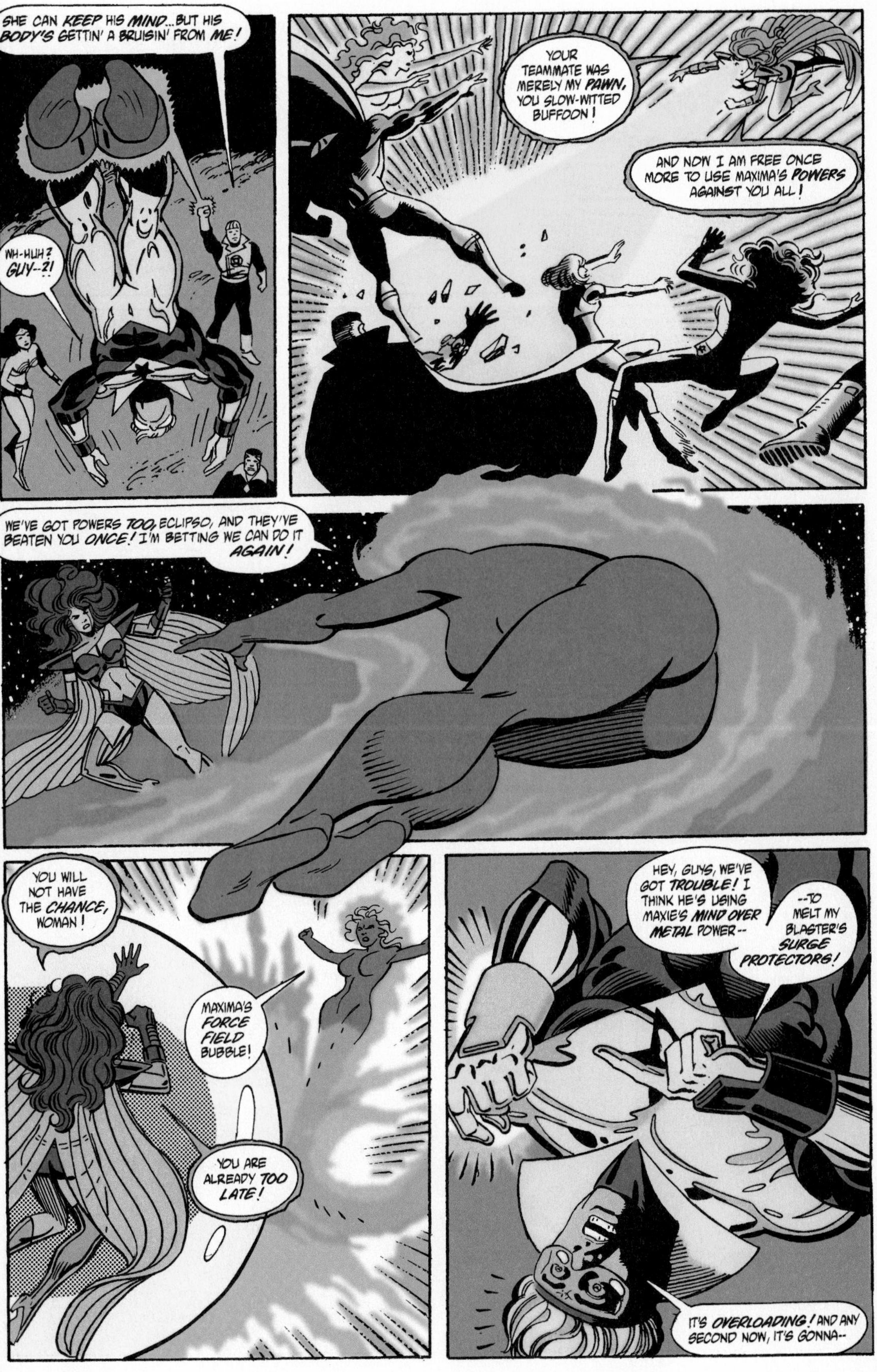

SHE CAN KEEP HIS MIND... BUT HIS BODY'S GETTIN' A BRUISIN' FROM ME!
WH-HUH? GUY--?!
YOUR TEAMMATE WAS MERELY MY PAWN, YOU SLOW-WITTED BUFFOON!
AND NOW I AM FREE ONCE MORE TO USE MAXIMA'S POWERS AGAINST YOU ALL!
WE'VE GOT POWERS TOO, ECLIPSO, AND THEY'VE BEATEN YOU ONCE! I'M BETTING WE CAN DO IT AGAIN!
YOU WILL NOT HAVE THE CHANCE, WOMAN!
MAXIMA'S FORCE FIELD BUBBLE!
YOU ARE ALREADY TOO LATE!
HEY, GUYS, WE'VE GOT TROUBLE! I THINK HE'S USING MAXIE'S MIND OVER METAL POWER--
--TO MELT MY BLASTER'S SURGE PROTECTORS!
IT'S OVERLOADING! AND ANY SECOND NOW, IT'S GONNA--

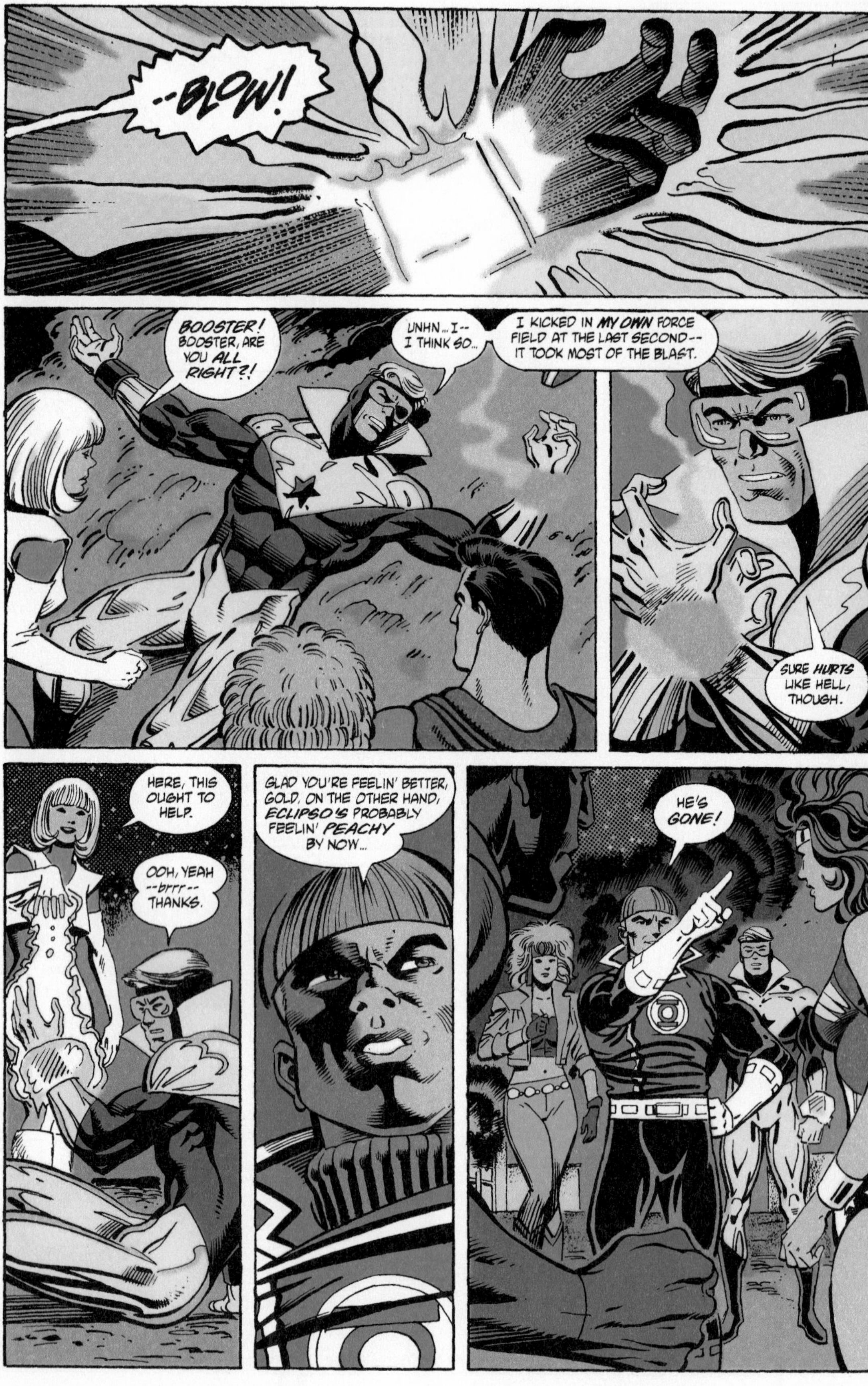
--BLOW!
BOOSTER! BOOSTER, ARE YOU ALL RIGHT?!
UNHN... I-- I THINK SO...
I KICKED IN MY OWN FORCE FIELD AT THE LAST SECOND-- IT TOOK MOST OF THE BLAST.
SURE HURTS LIKE HELL, THOUGH.
HERE, THIS OUGHT TO HELP.
OOH, YEAH --brrr-- THANKS.
GLAD YOU'RE FEELIN' BETTER, GOLD. ON THE OTHER HAND, ECLIPSO'S PROBABLY FEELIN' PEACHY BY NOW...
HE'S GONE!

I'M A GONER!

ECLIPSO'S GOT A GRIP LIKE IRON, AND ALL I'VE GOT IS--

ONE LAST CHANCE!

WHAT?!

IT *WORKED!* HE LOST HIS FOOTING WHEN THE BUG LURCHED FORWARD!

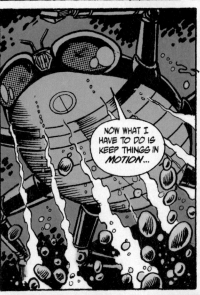

NOW WHAT I HAVE TO DO IS KEEP THINGS IN *MOTION...*

CRAASSH

...AND HOPE THE *U.N.* TOOK OUT LOTS OF *INSURANCE* WHEN THEY PROMISED TO PAY FOR THE UPKEEP ON THIS PLACE!

IF YOUR GOAL IS TO MAKE A *SHAMBLES* OF THESE HEADQUARTERS--

--I COMMEND YOUR SUCCESS!

BUT IN TRUTH, YOU HAVE ONLY DELAYED THE *INEVITABLE!*

BAMM!

I FIGURE EVERY SECOND I'M STILL BREATHING--

BASH!

--IS ANOTHER SECOND CLOSER TO PUTTING YOU IN THE HOT SEAT!

ALL IN HOW YOU LOOK AT IT, CRATER-BREATH!

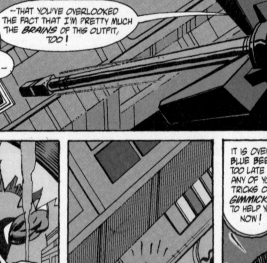

I MEAN, YOU'RE PROBABLY SO IMPRESSED WITH MY SPEED, STRENGTH, AGILITY AND DEATH-DEFYING ACROBATICS--

--THAT YOU'VE OVERLOOKED THE FACT THAT I'M PRETTY MUCH THE BRAINS OF THIS OUTFIT, TOO!

PROOF THAT EARTH'S HEROES ARE IN A SORRY STATE INDEED!

I WILL BROOK NO MORE OF THIS!

UH-OH, BETTER HURRY UP!

CHUK

IT IS OVER, BLUE BEETLE! TOO LATE FOR ANY OF YOUR TRICKS OR GIMMICKRY TO HELP YOU NOW!

MAYBE...

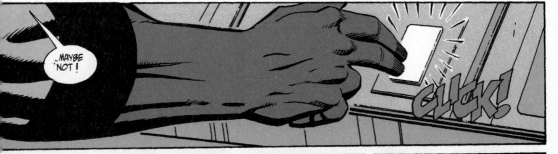

...MAYBE 'NOT!

CLICK!

SHUNK!

SHUNK!

SHUNK!

WHAT HAVE YOU--?

OH...SO YOU'VE MANAGED TO RESTORE THIS BUILDING'S MAIN POWER.

NOT TO MENTION ALL THE LIGHTS!

IS *THAT* YOUR PLAN? DIDN'T GORDON TELL YOU THAT MERE ELECTRIC LIGHTS MEAN *NOTHING* TO ME?

AH, BUT THOSE AREN'T JUST *ANY* LIGHTS, CLIPSTER!

WHAT DO YOU MEAN?! EXPLAIN YOURSELF!

SEE, I TAPPED INTO THE *SOLAR COLLECTORS* THAT POWER MY *BUG*--

--AND NOW THEY'RE HOOKED UP TO THE HEADQUARTERS' MAIN POWER SYSTEM!

WHICH MEANS...

WHICH MEANS THAT THIS ENTIRE COMPLEX WILL SOON BE BATHED IN *SOLAR-POWERED ENERGY.*

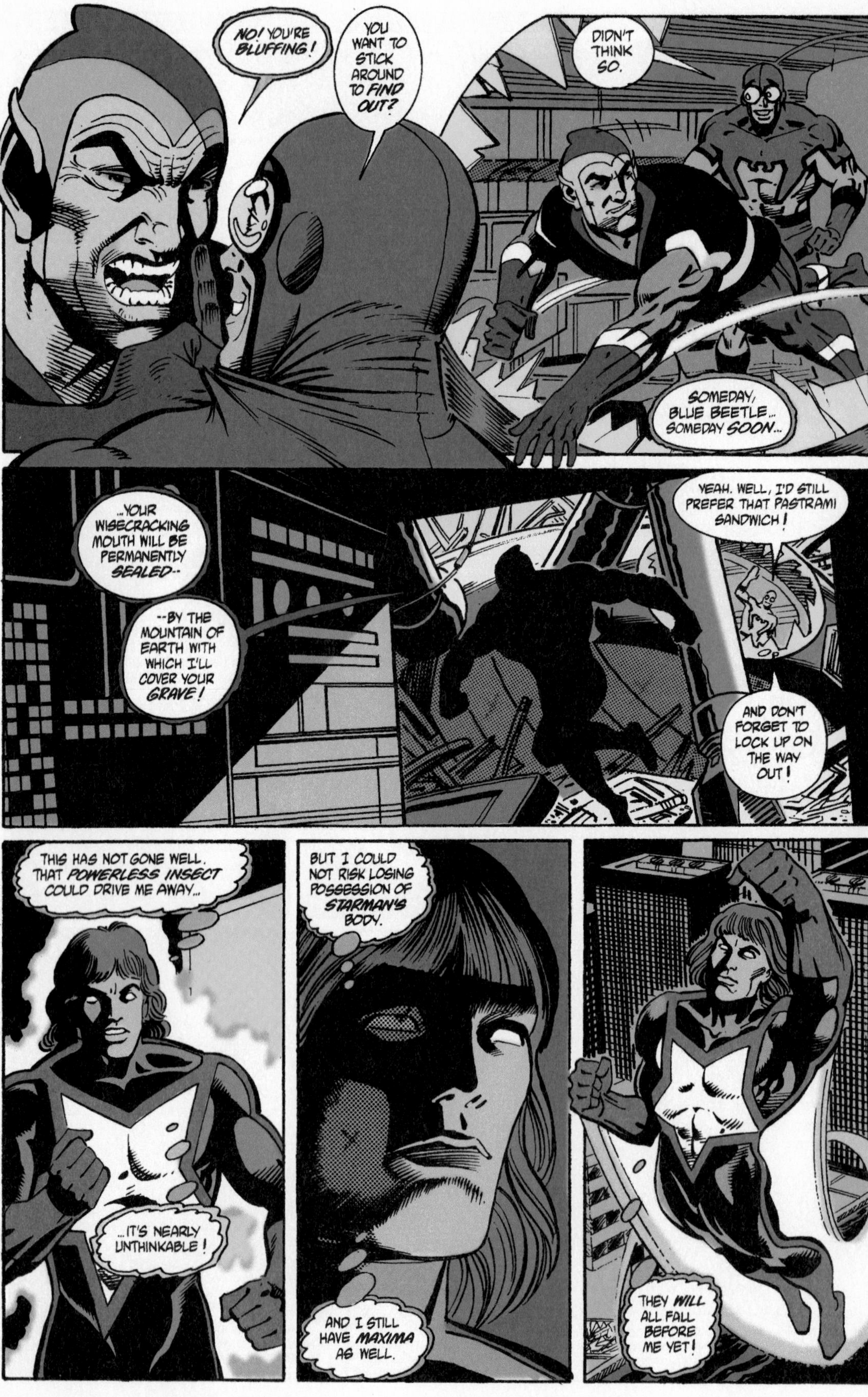
NO! YOU'RE BLUFFING!
YOU WANT TO STICK AROUND TO FIND OUT?
DIDN'T THINK SO.
SOMEDAY, BLUE BEETLE... SOMEDAY SOON...
...YOUR WISECRACKING MOUTH WILL BE PERMANENTLY SEALED--
--BY THE MOUNTAIN OF EARTH WITH WHICH I'LL COVER YOUR GRAVE!
YEAH. WELL, I'D STILL PREFER THAT PASTRAMI SANDWICH!
AND DON'T FORGET TO LOCK UP ON THE WAY OUT!
THIS HAS NOT GONE WELL. THAT POWERLESS INSECT COULD DRIVE ME AWAY...
...IT'S NEARLY UNTHINKABLE!
BUT I COULD NOT RISK LOSING POSSESSION OF STARMAN'S BODY.
AND I STILL HAVE MAXIMA AS WELL.
THEY WILL ALL FALL BEFORE ME YET!

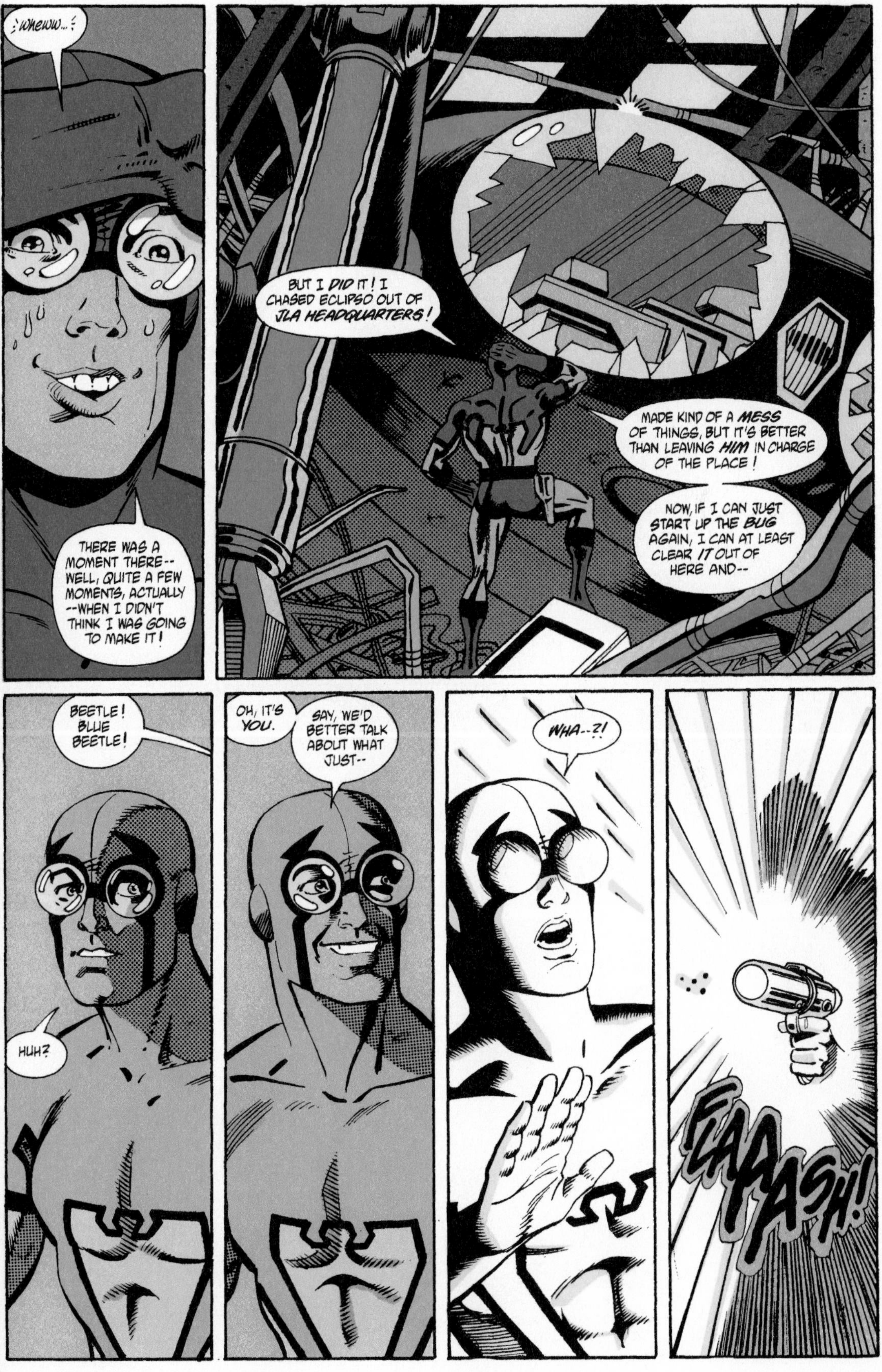

WHEWW...
THERE WAS A MOMENT THERE-- WELL, QUITE A FEW MOMENTS, ACTUALLY --WHEN I DIDN'T THINK I WAS GOING TO MAKE IT!
BUT I DID IT! I CHASED ECLIPSO OUT OF JLA HEADQUARTERS!
MADE KIND OF A MESS OF THINGS, BUT IT'S BETTER THAN LEAVING HIM IN CHARGE OF THE PLACE!
NOW, IF I CAN JUST START UP THE BUG AGAIN, I CAN AT LEAST CLEAR IT OUT OF HERE AND--
BEETLE! BLUE BEETLE!
HUH?
OH, IT'S YOU.
SAY, WE'D BETTER TALK ABOUT WHAT JUST--
WHA--?!
FLAAASH!

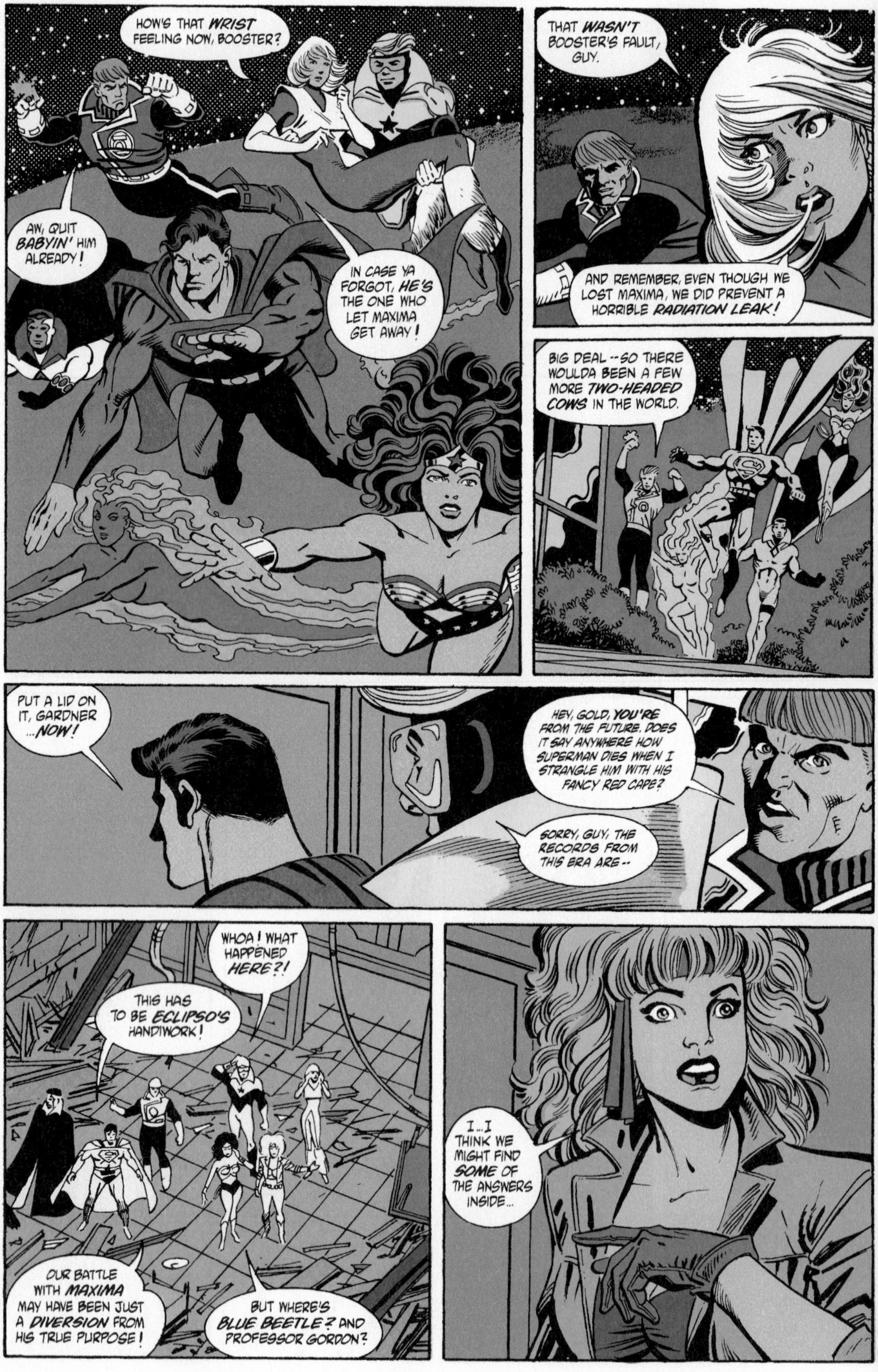
HOW'S THAT WRIST FEELING NOW, BOOSTER?
AW, QUIT BABYIN' HIM ALREADY!
IN CASE YA FORGOT, HE'S THE ONE WHO LET MAXIMA GET AWAY!
THAT WASN'T BOOSTER'S FAULT, GUY.
AND REMEMBER, EVEN THOUGH WE LOST MAXIMA, WE DID PREVENT A HORRIBLE RADIATION LEAK!
BIG DEAL -- SO THERE WOULDA BEEN A FEW MORE TWO-HEADED COWS IN THE WORLD.
PUT A LID ON IT, GARDNER ...NOW!
HEY, GOLD, YOU'RE FROM THE FUTURE. DOES IT SAY ANYWHERE HOW SUPERMAN DIES WHEN I STRANGLE HIM WITH HIS FANCY RED CAPE?
SORRY, GUY, THE RECORDS FROM THIS ERA ARE --
WHOA! WHAT HAPPENED HERE?!
THIS HAS TO BE ECLIPSO'S HANDIWORK!
OUR BATTLE WITH MAXIMA MAY HAVE BEEN JUST A DIVERSION FROM HIS TRUE PURPOSE!
BUT WHERE'S BLUE BEETLE? AND PROFESSOR GORDON?
I...I THINK WE MIGHT FIND SOME OF THE ANSWERS INSIDE...

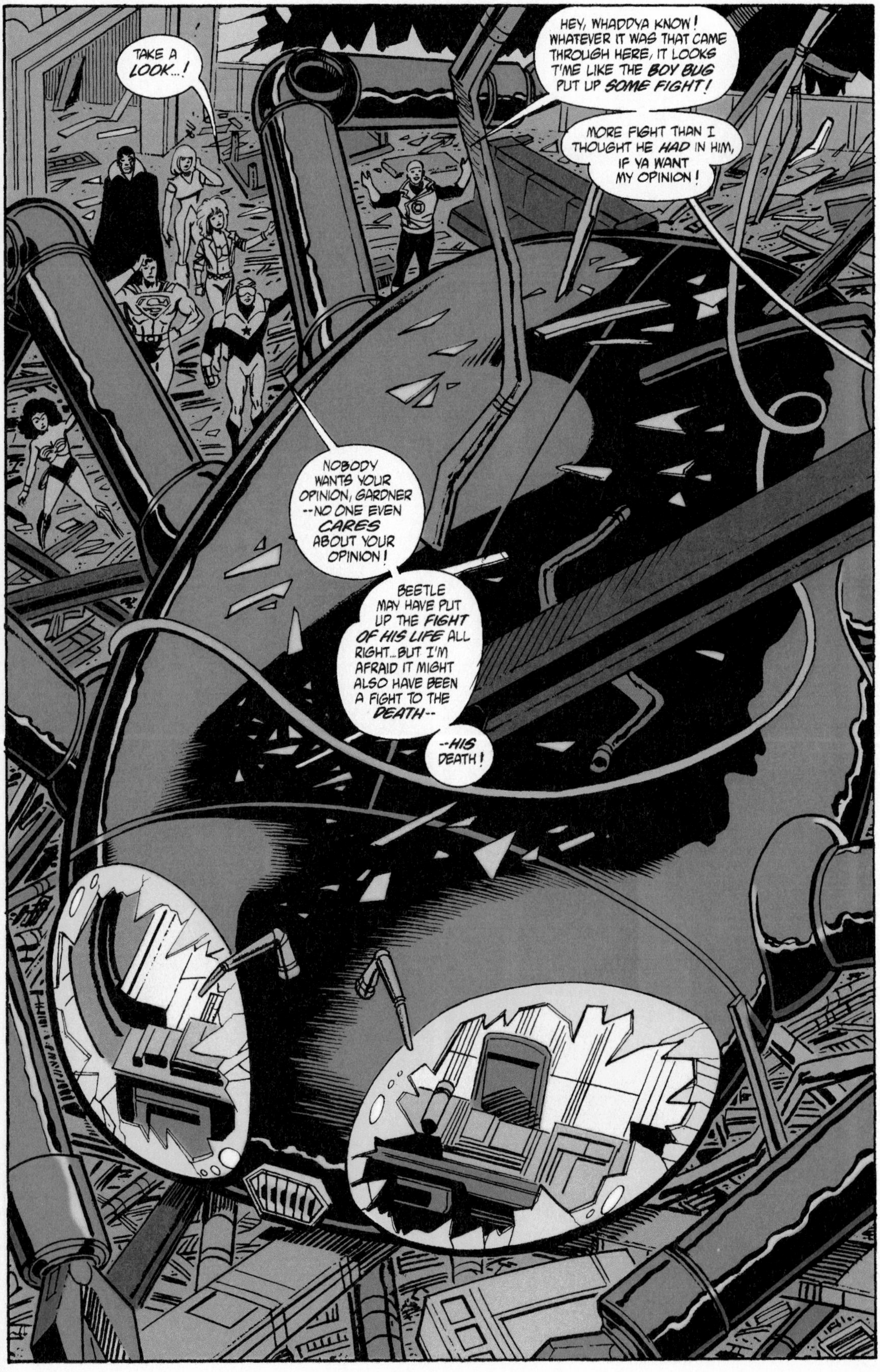
TAKE A LOOK...!
HEY, WHADDYA KNOW! WHATEVER IT WAS THAT CAME THROUGH HERE, IT LOOKS T'ME LIKE THE BOY BUG PUT UP SOME FIGHT!
MORE FIGHT THAN I THOUGHT HE HAD IN HIM, IF YA WANT MY OPINION!
NOBODY WANTS YOUR OPINION, GARDNER --NO ONE EVEN CARES ABOUT YOUR OPINION!
BEETLE MAY HAVE PUT UP THE FIGHT OF HIS LIFE ALL RIGHT...BUT I'M AFRAID IT MIGHT ALSO HAVE BEEN A FIGHT TO THE DEATH--
--HIS DEATH!

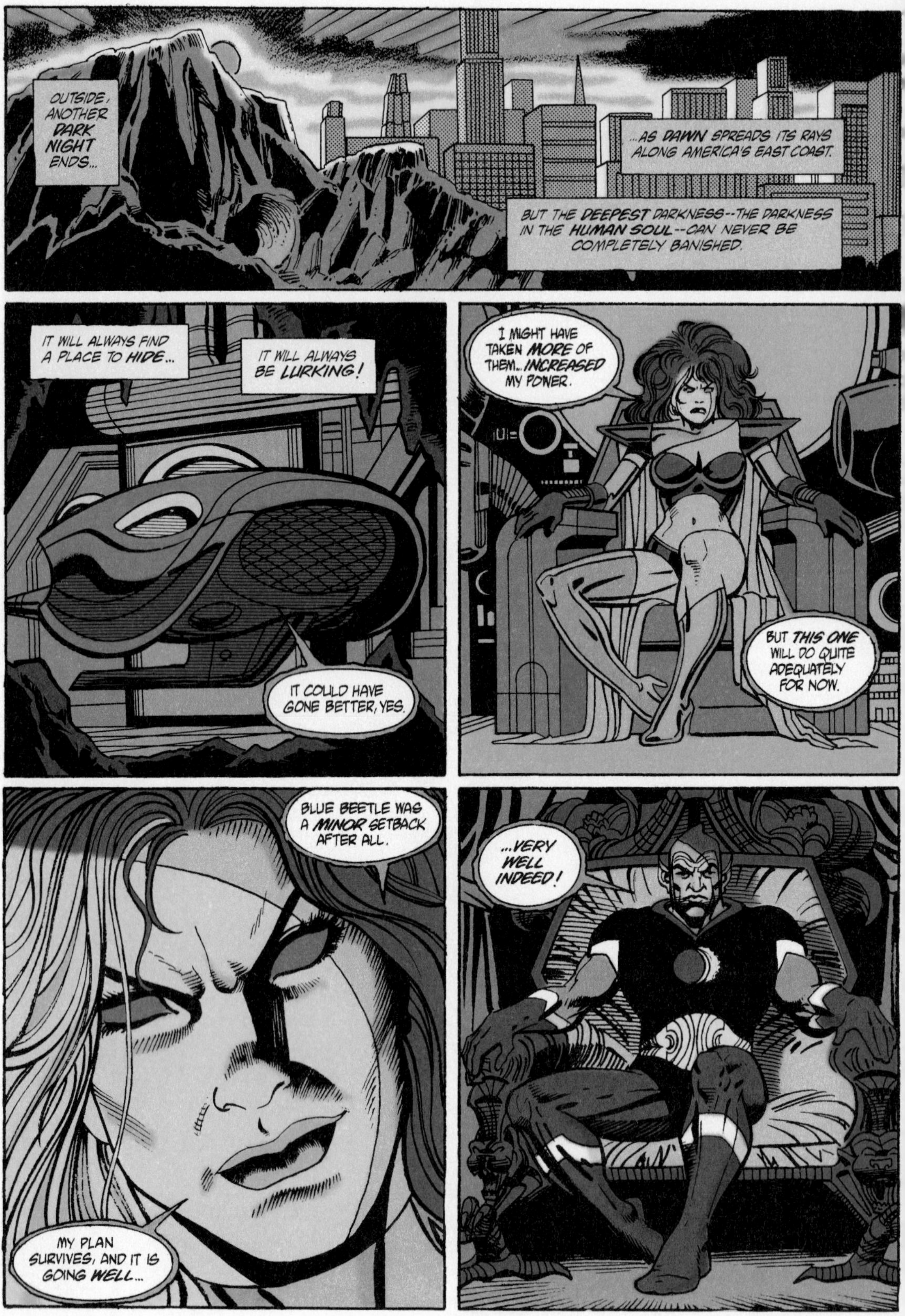
OUTSIDE, ANOTHER DARK NIGHT ENDS...
...AS DAWN SPREADS ITS RAYS ALONG AMERICA'S EAST COAST.
BUT THE DEEPEST DARKNESS--THE DARKNESS IN THE HUMAN SOUL--CAN NEVER BE COMPLETELY BANISHED.
IT WILL ALWAYS FIND A PLACE TO HIDE...
IT WILL ALWAYS BE LURKING!
IT COULD HAVE GONE BETTER, YES.
I MIGHT HAVE TAKEN MORE OF THEM... INCREASED MY POWER.
BUT THIS ONE WILL DO QUITE ADEQUATELY FOR NOW.
BLUE BEETLE WAS A MINOR SETBACK AFTER ALL.
MY PLAN SURVIVES, AND IT IS GOING WELL...
...VERY WELL INDEED!

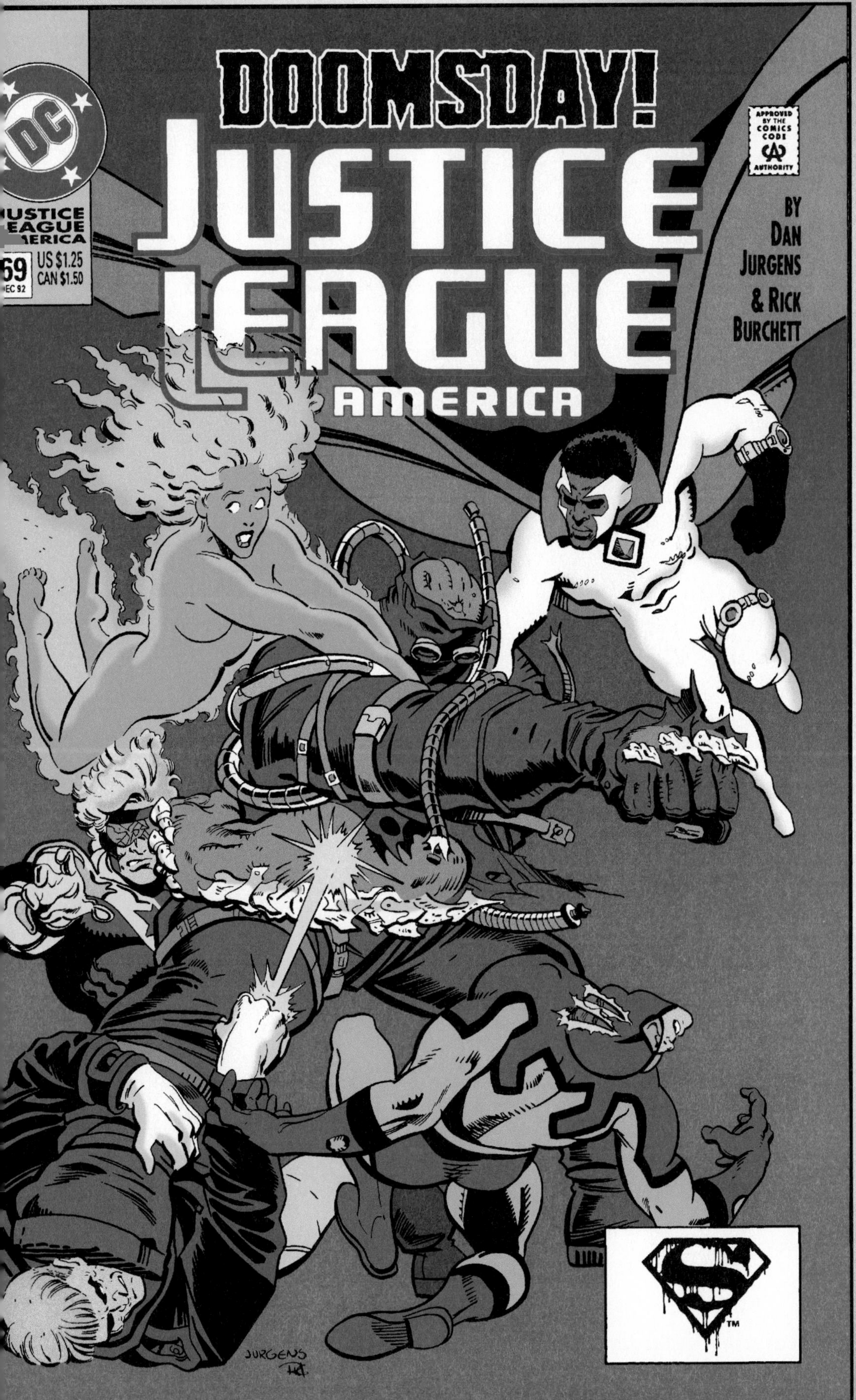
DOOMSDAY!
JUSTICE LEAGUE AMERICA
DC
JUSTICE LEAGUE AMERICA
69 DEC 92
US $1.25
CAN $1.50
APPROVED BY THE COMICS CODE AUTHORITY
BY DAN JURGENS & RICK BURCHETT
JURGENS
TM

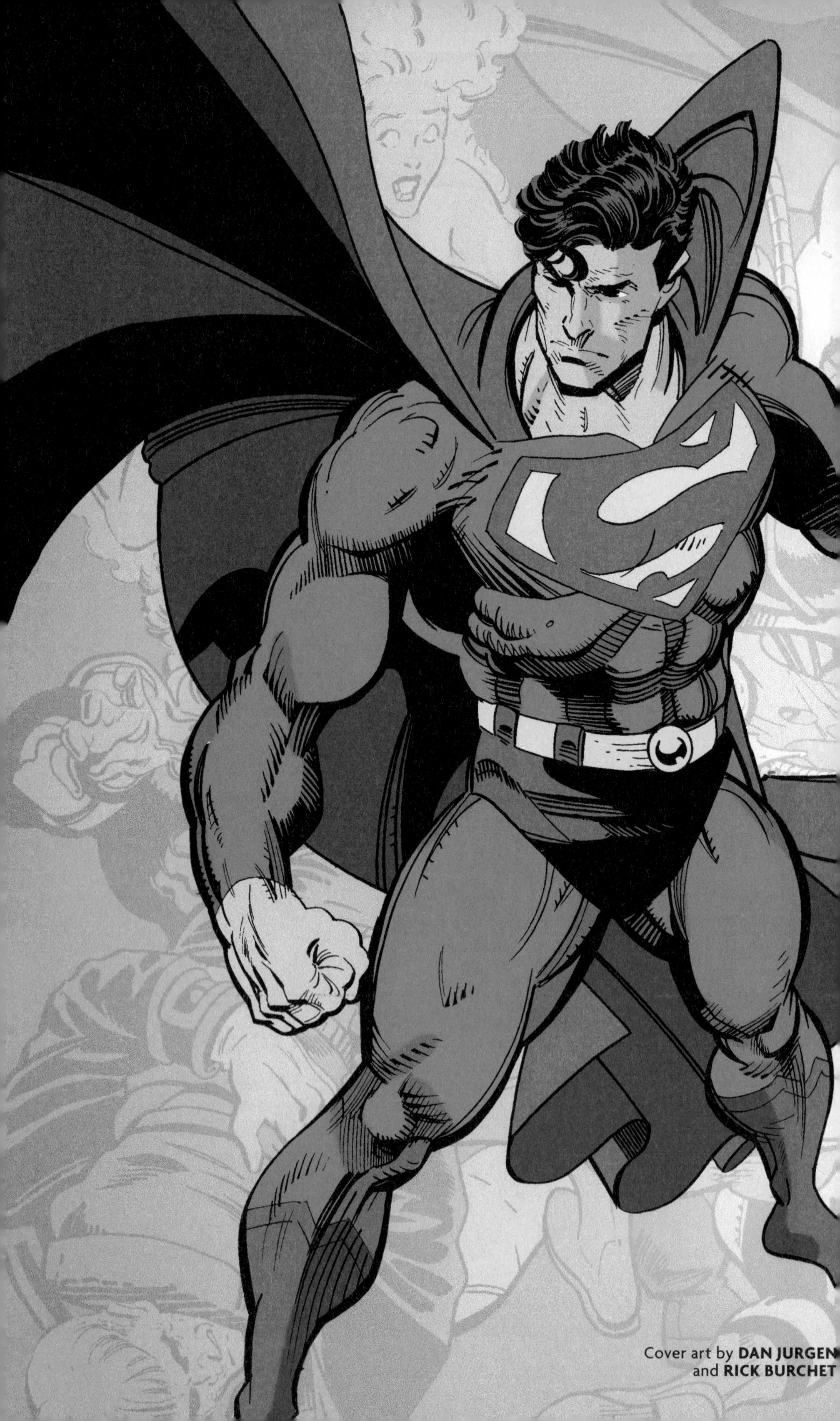

Cover art by **DAN JURGEN**
and **RICK BURCHET**

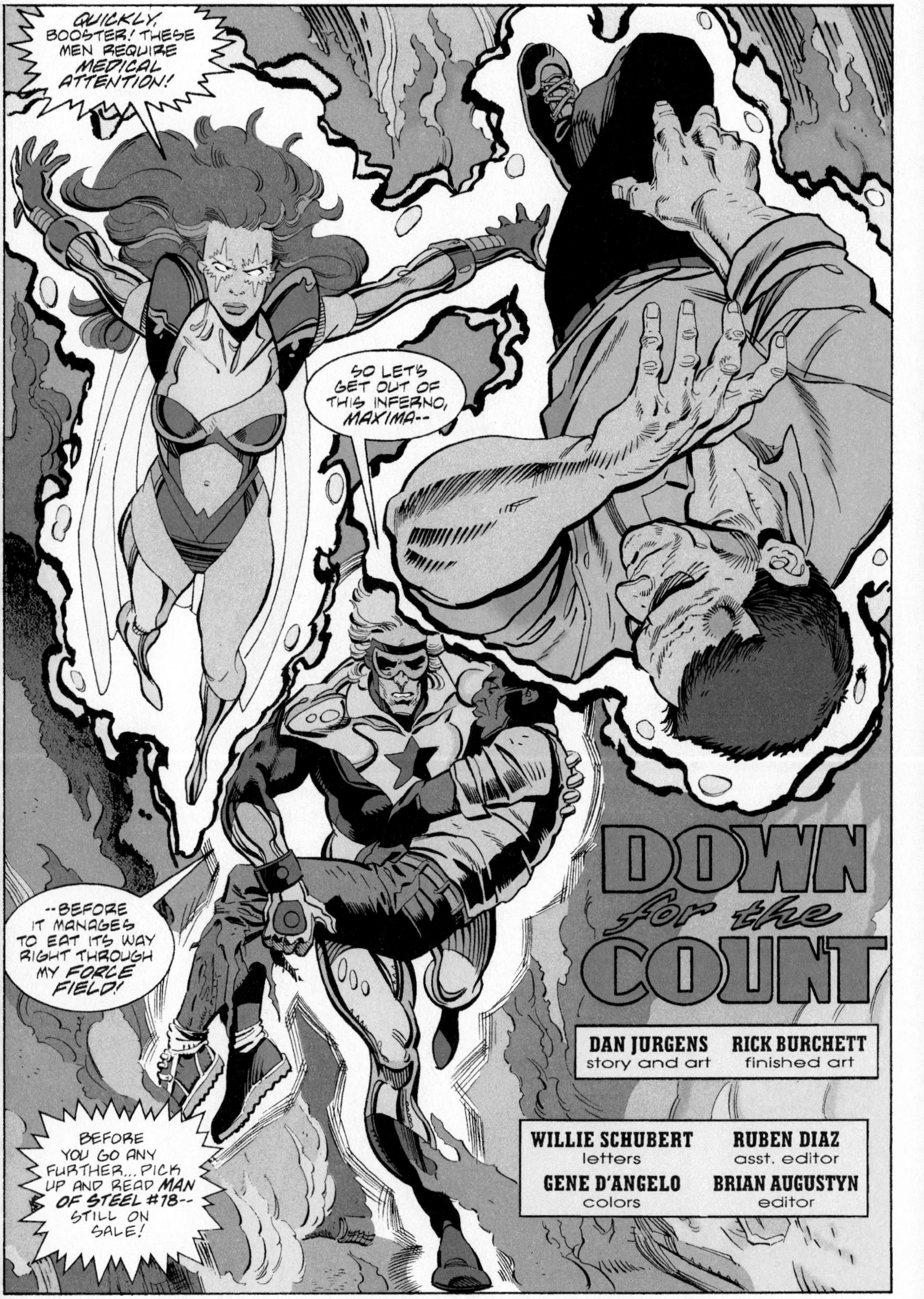
QUICKLY, BOOSTER! THESE MEN REQUIRE MEDICAL ATTENTION!
SO LET'S GET OUT OF THIS INFERNO, MAXIMA--
--BEFORE IT MANAGES TO EAT ITS WAY RIGHT THROUGH MY FORCE FIELD!
BEFORE YOU GO ANY FURTHER...PICK UP AND READ MAN OF STEEL #18-- STILL ON SALE!
DOWN for the COUNT
DAN JURGENS story and art
RICK BURCHETT finished art
WILLIE SCHUBERT letters
RUBEN DIAZ asst. editor
GENE D'ANGELO colors
BRIAN AUGUSTYN editor

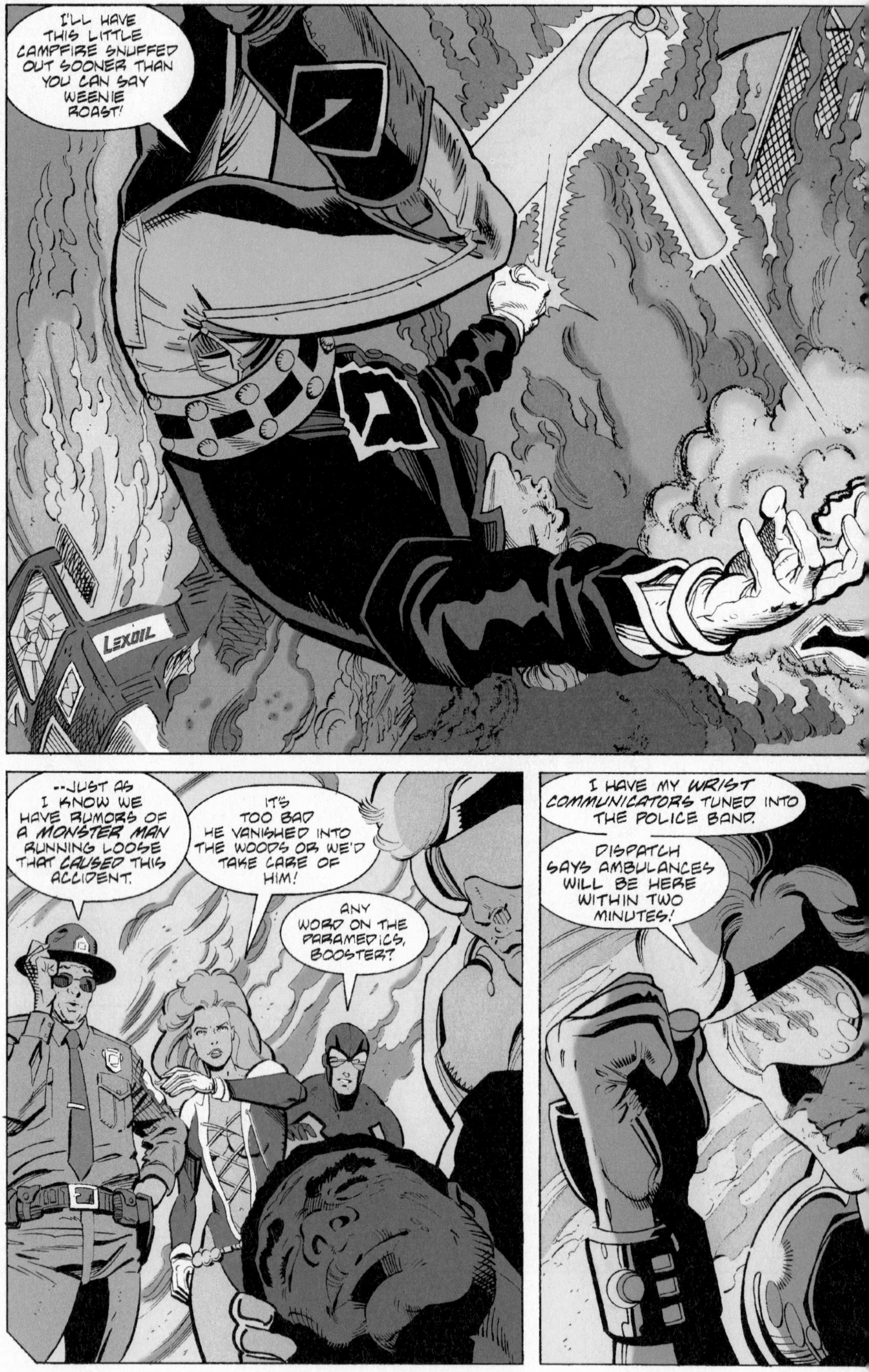
I'LL HAVE THIS LITTLE CAMPFIRE SNUFFED OUT SOONER THAN YOU CAN SAY WEENIE ROAST!
LEXOIL
--JUST AS I KNOW WE HAVE RUMORS OF A *MONSTER MAN* RUNNING LOOSE THAT *CAUSED* THIS ACCIDENT.
IT'S TOO BAD HE VANISHED INTO THE WOODS OR WE'D TAKE CARE OF HIM!
ANY WORD ON THE PARAMEDICS, BOOSTER?
I HAVE MY *WRIST COMMUNICATORS* TUNED INTO THE POLICE BAND.
DISPATCH SAYS AMBULANCES WILL BE HERE WITHIN TWO MINUTES!

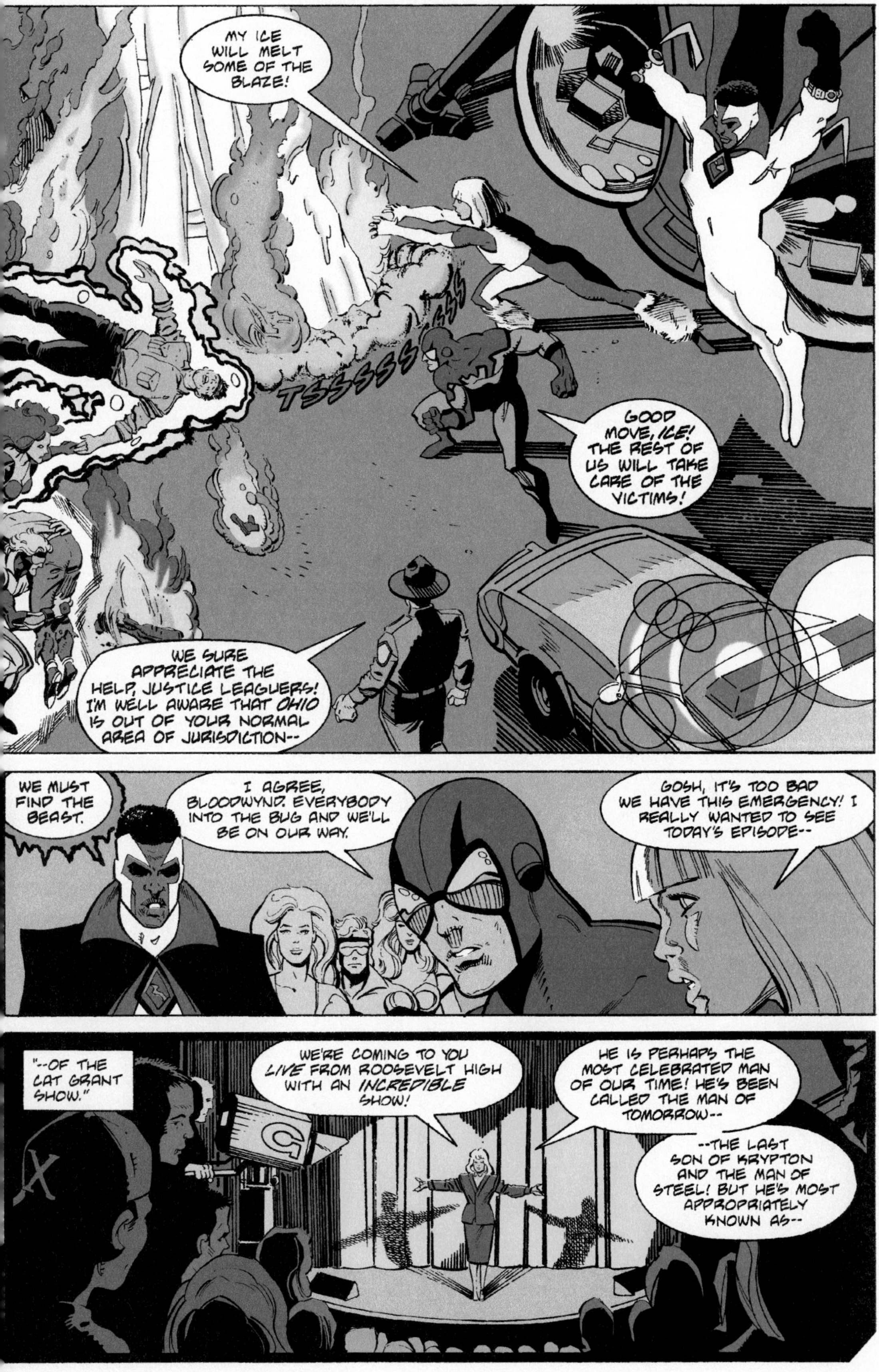
MY ICE WILL MELT SOME OF THE BLAZE!
TSSSSSSSSS
GOOD MOVE, ICE! THE REST OF US WILL TAKE CARE OF THE VICTIMS!
WE SURE APPRECIATE THE HELP, JUSTICE LEAGUERS! I'M WELL AWARE THAT OHIO IS OUT OF YOUR NORMAL AREA OF JURISDICTION--
WE MUST FIND THE BEAST.
I AGREE, BLOODWYND. EVERYBODY INTO THE BUG AND WE'LL BE ON OUR WAY.
GOSH, IT'S TOO BAD WE HAVE THIS EMERGENCY! I REALLY WANTED TO SEE TODAY'S EPISODE--
"--OF THE CAT GRANT SHOW."
WE'RE COMING TO YOU LIVE FROM ROOSEVELT HIGH WITH AN INCREDIBLE SHOW!
HE IS PERHAPS THE MOST CELEBRATED MAN OF OUR TIME! HE'S BEEN CALLED THE MAN OF TOMORROW--
--THE LAST SON OF KRYPTON AND THE MAN OF STEEL! BUT HE'S MOST APPROPRIATELY KNOWN AS--

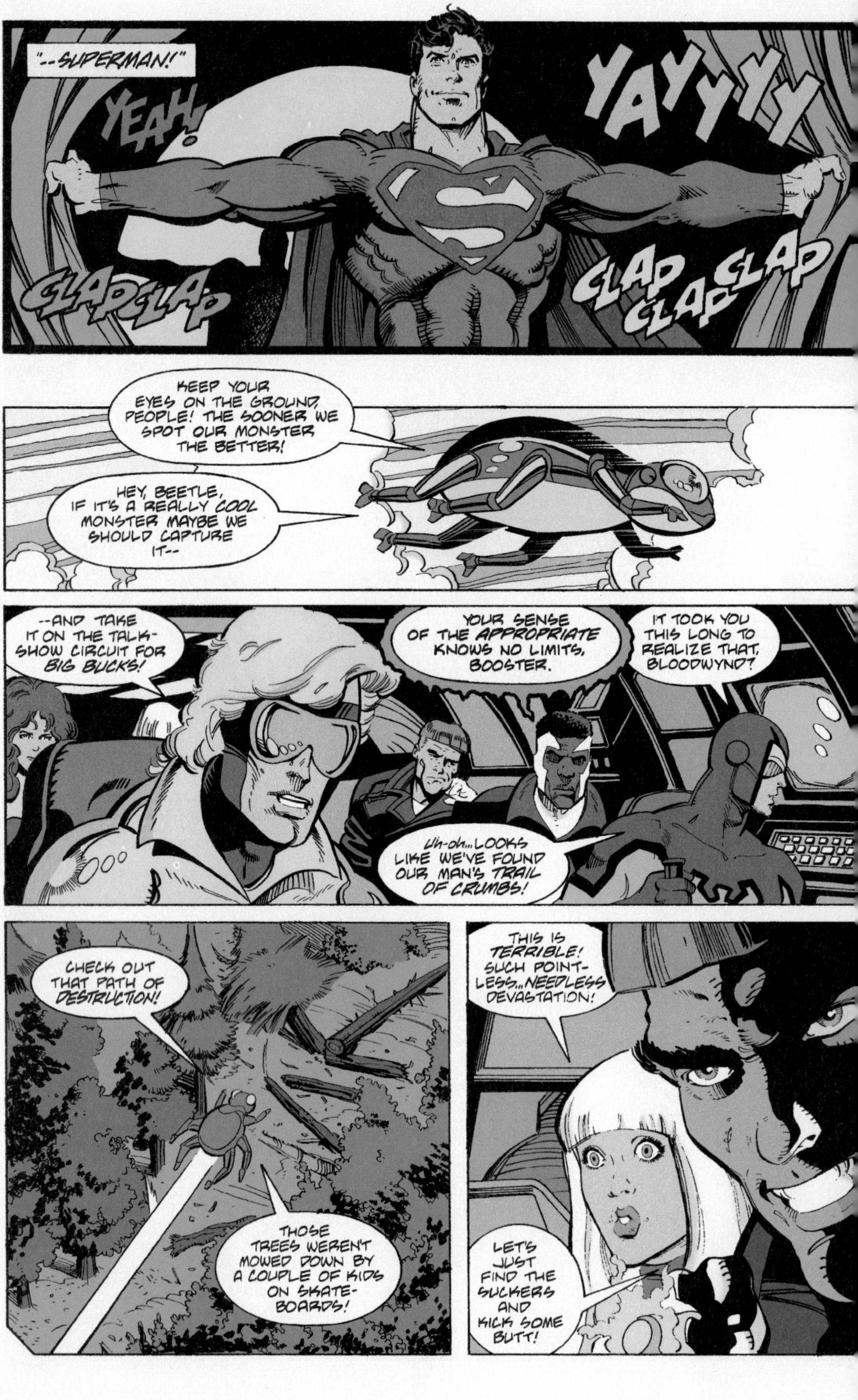
"--SUPERMAN!"
YEAH!
YAYYYY
CLAP CLAP
CLAP CLAP CLAP
KEEP YOUR EYES ON THE GROUND, PEOPLE! THE SOONER WE SPOT OUR MONSTER THE BETTER!
HEY, BEETLE, IF IT'S A REALLY COOL MONSTER MAYBE WE SHOULD CAPTURE IT--
--AND TAKE IT ON THE TALK-SHOW CIRCUIT FOR BIG BUCKS!
YOUR SENSE OF THE APPROPRIATE KNOWS NO LIMITS, BOOSTER.
IT TOOK YOU THIS LONG TO REALIZE THAT, BLOODWYND?
Uh-oh... LOOKS LIKE WE'VE FOUND OUR MAN'S TRAIL OF CRUMBS!
CHECK OUT THAT PATH OF DESTRUCTION!
THOSE TREES WEREN'T MOWED DOWN BY A COUPLE OF KIDS ON SKATE-BOARDS!
THIS IS TERRIBLE! SUCH POINT-LESS... NEEDLESS DEVASTATION!
LET'S JUST FIND THE SUCKERS AND KICK SOME BUTT!

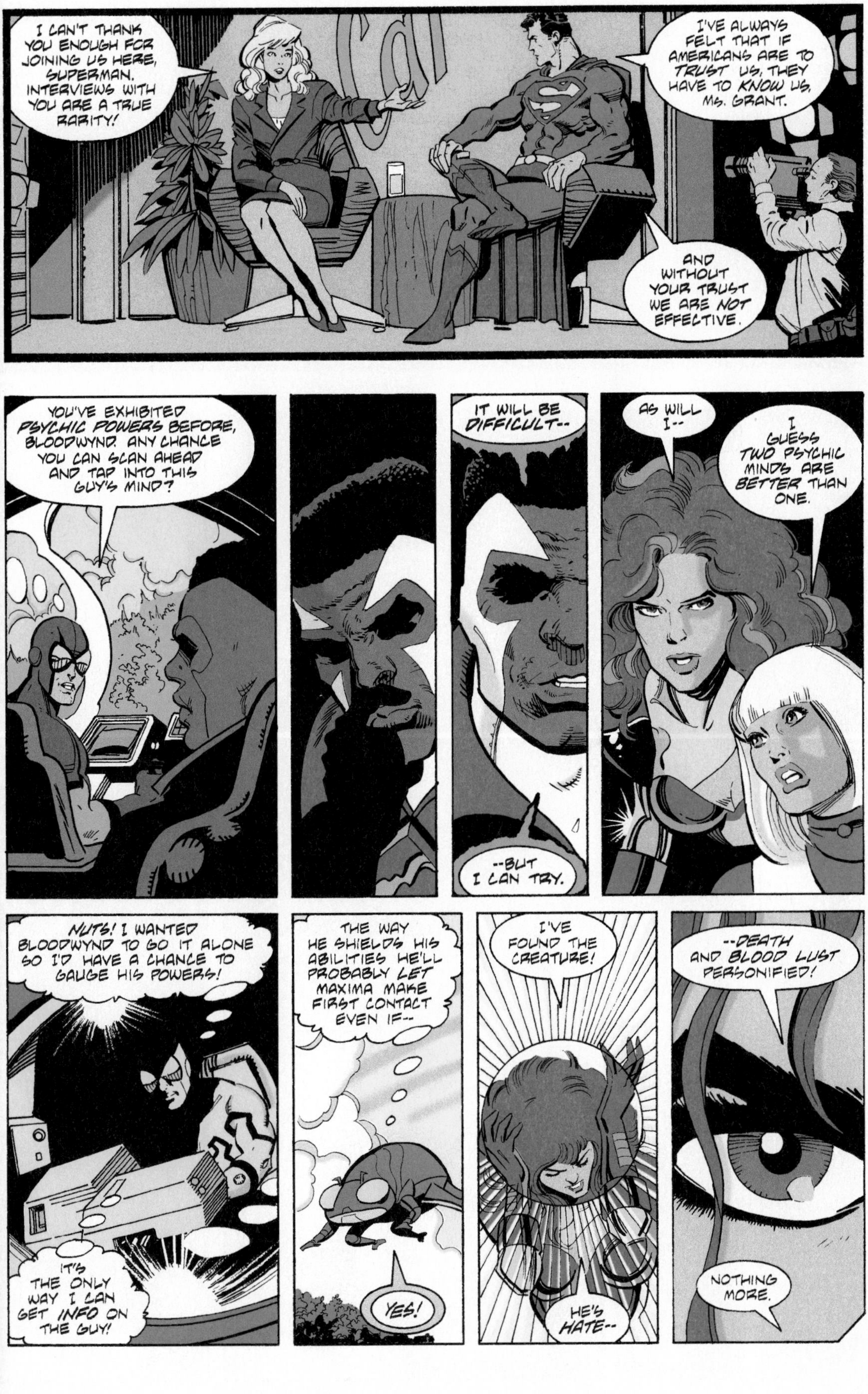
I CAN'T THANK YOU ENOUGH FOR JOINING US HERE, SUPERMAN. INTERVIEWS WITH YOU ARE A TRUE RARITY!
I'VE ALWAYS FELT THAT IF AMERICANS ARE TO TRUST US, THEY HAVE TO KNOW US, MS. GRANT.
AND WITHOUT YOUR TRUST WE ARE NOT EFFECTIVE.
YOU'VE EXHIBITED PSYCHIC POWERS BEFORE, BLOODWYND. ANY CHANCE YOU CAN SCAN AHEAD AND TAP INTO THIS GUY'S MIND?
IT WILL BE DIFFICULT--
--BUT I CAN TRY.
AS WILL I--
I GUESS TWO PSYCHIC MINDS ARE BETTER THAN ONE.
NUTS! I WANTED BLOODWYND TO GO IT ALONE SO I'D HAVE A CHANCE TO GAUGE HIS POWERS!
IT'S THE ONLY WAY I CAN GET INFO ON THE GUY!
THE WAY HE SHIELDS HIS ABILITIES HE'LL PROBABLY LET MAXIMA MAKE FIRST CONTACT EVEN IF--
YES!
I'VE FOUND THE CREATURE!
HE'S HATE--
--DEATH AND BLOOD LUST PERSONIFIED!
NOTHING MORE.

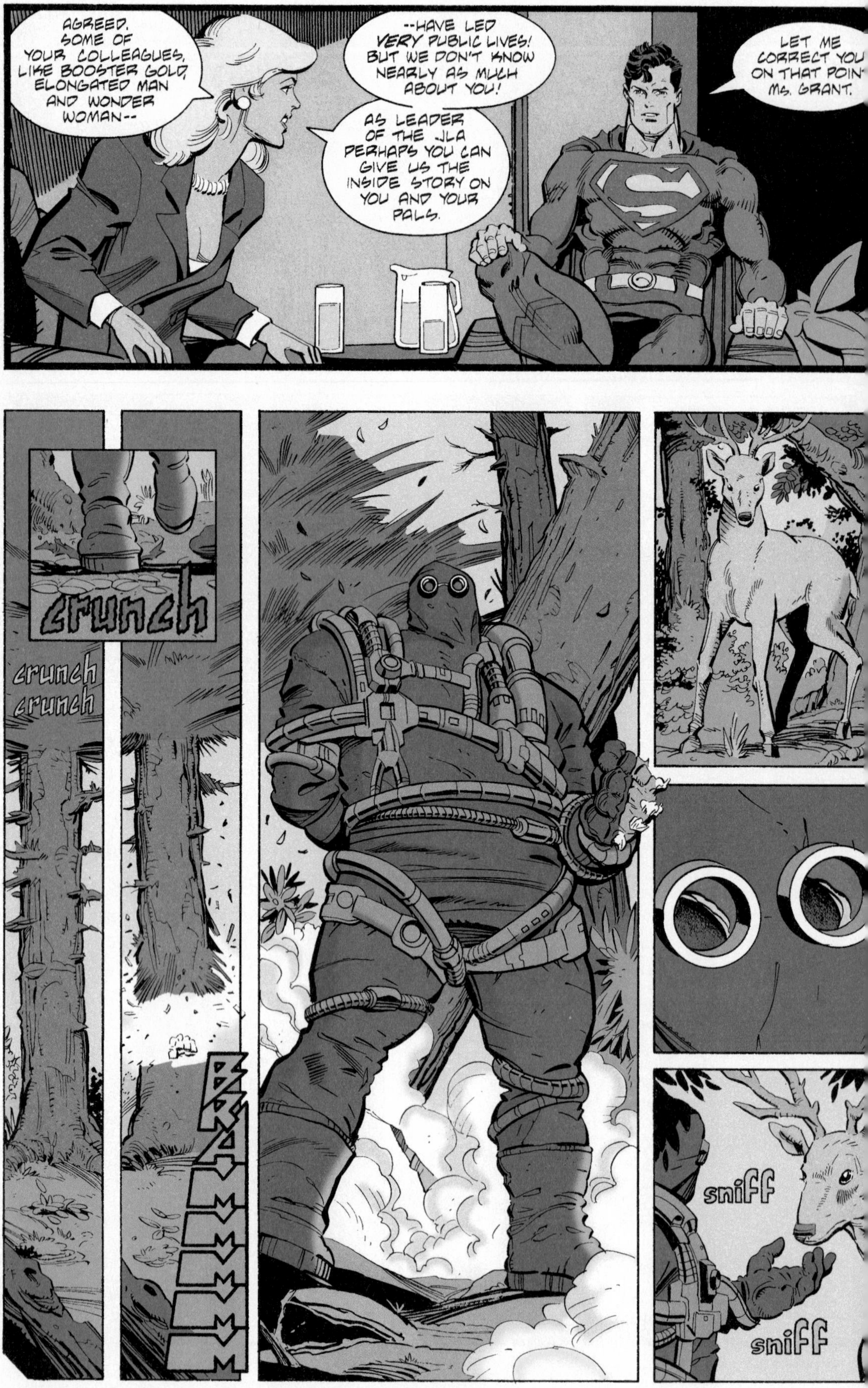
AGREED. SOME OF YOUR COLLEAGUES, LIKE BOOSTER GOLD, ELONGATED MAN AND WONDER WOMAN--
--HAVE LED VERY PUBLIC LIVES! BUT WE DON'T KNOW NEARLY AS MUCH ABOUT YOU!
AS LEADER OF THE JLA PERHAPS YOU CAN GIVE US THE INSIDE STORY ON YOU AND YOUR PALS.
LET ME CORRECT YOU ON THAT POINT MS. GRANT.
crunch
crunch
crunch
sniff
sniff

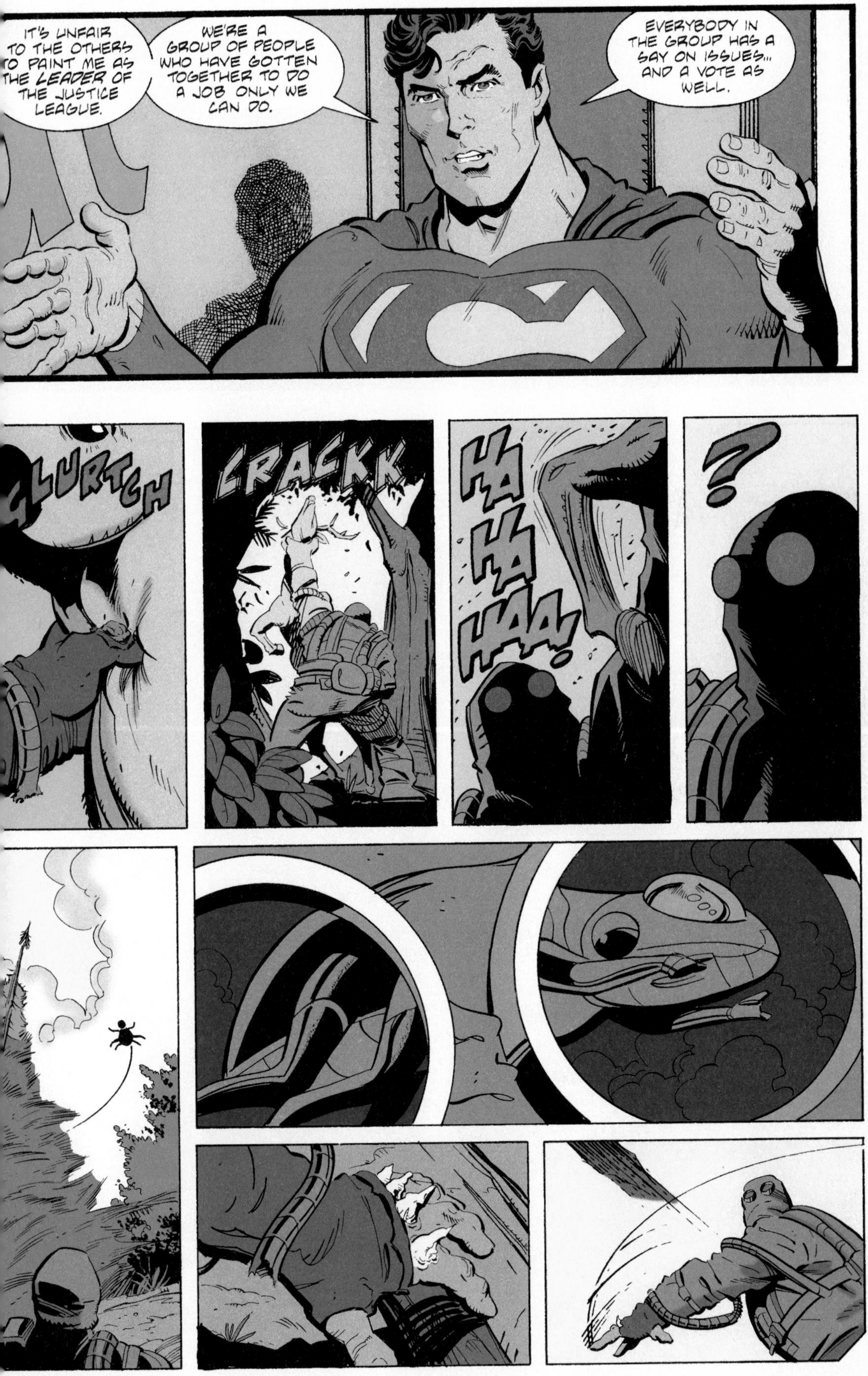
IT'S UNFAIR TO THE OTHERS TO PAINT ME AS THE *LEADER* OF THE JUSTICE LEAGUE.
WE'RE A GROUP OF PEOPLE WHO HAVE GOTTEN TOGETHER TO DO A JOB ONLY WE CAN DO.
EVERYBODY IN THE GROUP HAS A SAY ON ISSUES... AND A VOTE AS WELL.
GLURTCH
CRACKK
HA HA HAA!
?

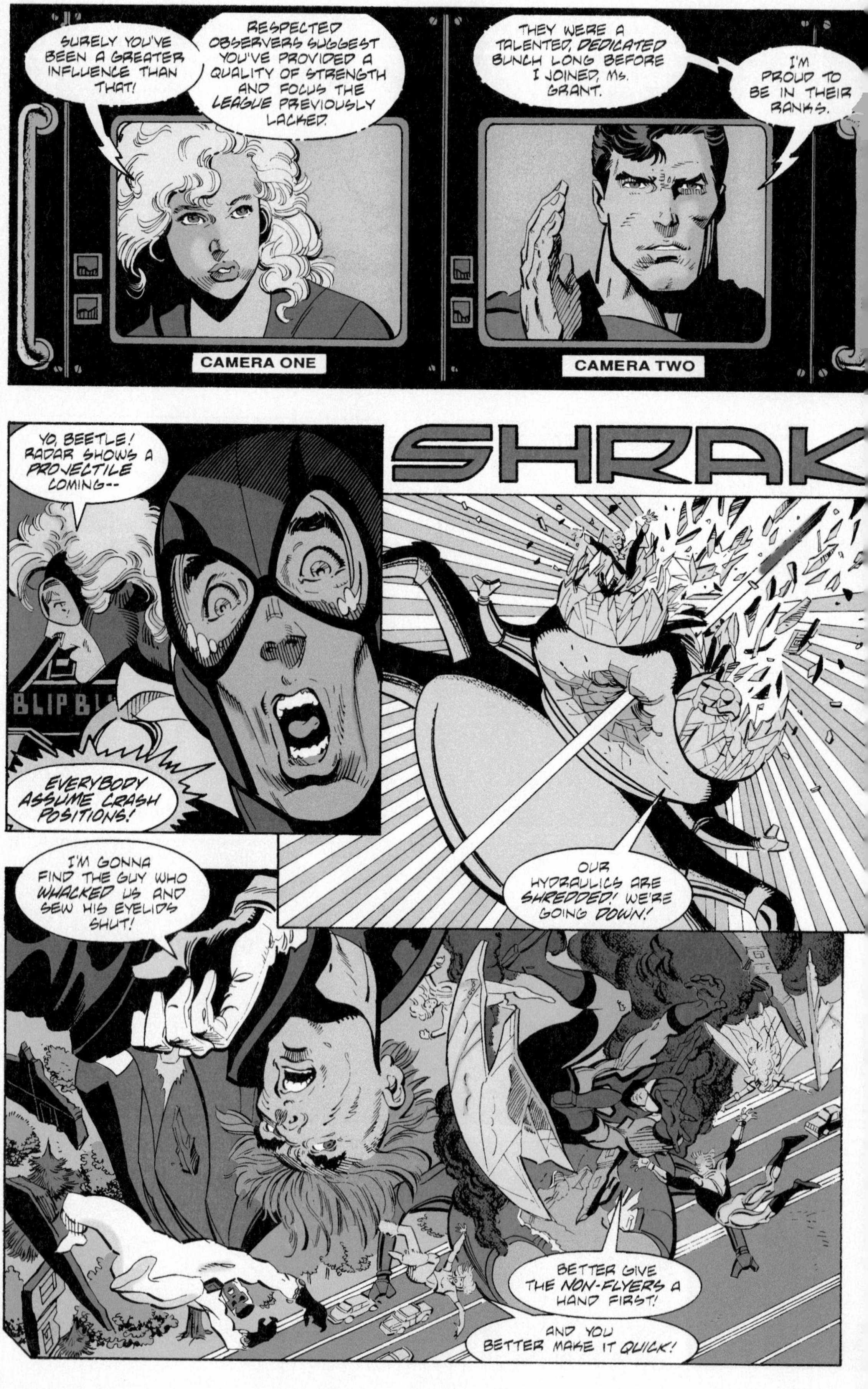
SURELY YOU'VE BEEN A GREATER INFLUENCE THAN THAT!
RESPECTED OBSERVERS SUGGEST YOU'VE PROVIDED A QUALITY OF STRENGTH AND FOCUS THE LEAGUE PREVIOUSLY LACKED.
CAMERA ONE
THEY WERE A TALENTED, DEDICATED BUNCH LONG BEFORE I JOINED, Ms. GRANT.
I'M PROUD TO BE IN THEIR RANKS.
CAMERA TWO
YO, BEETLE! RADAR SHOWS A PROJECTILE COMING--
BLIP BL
EVERYBODY ASSUME CRASH POSITIONS!
SHRAK
OUR HYDRAULICS ARE SHREDDED! WE'RE GOING DOWN!
I'M GONNA FIND THE GUY WHO WHACKED US AND SEW HIS EYELIDS SHUT!
BETTER GIVE THE NON-FLYERS A HAND FIRST!
AND YOU BETTER MAKE IT QUICK!

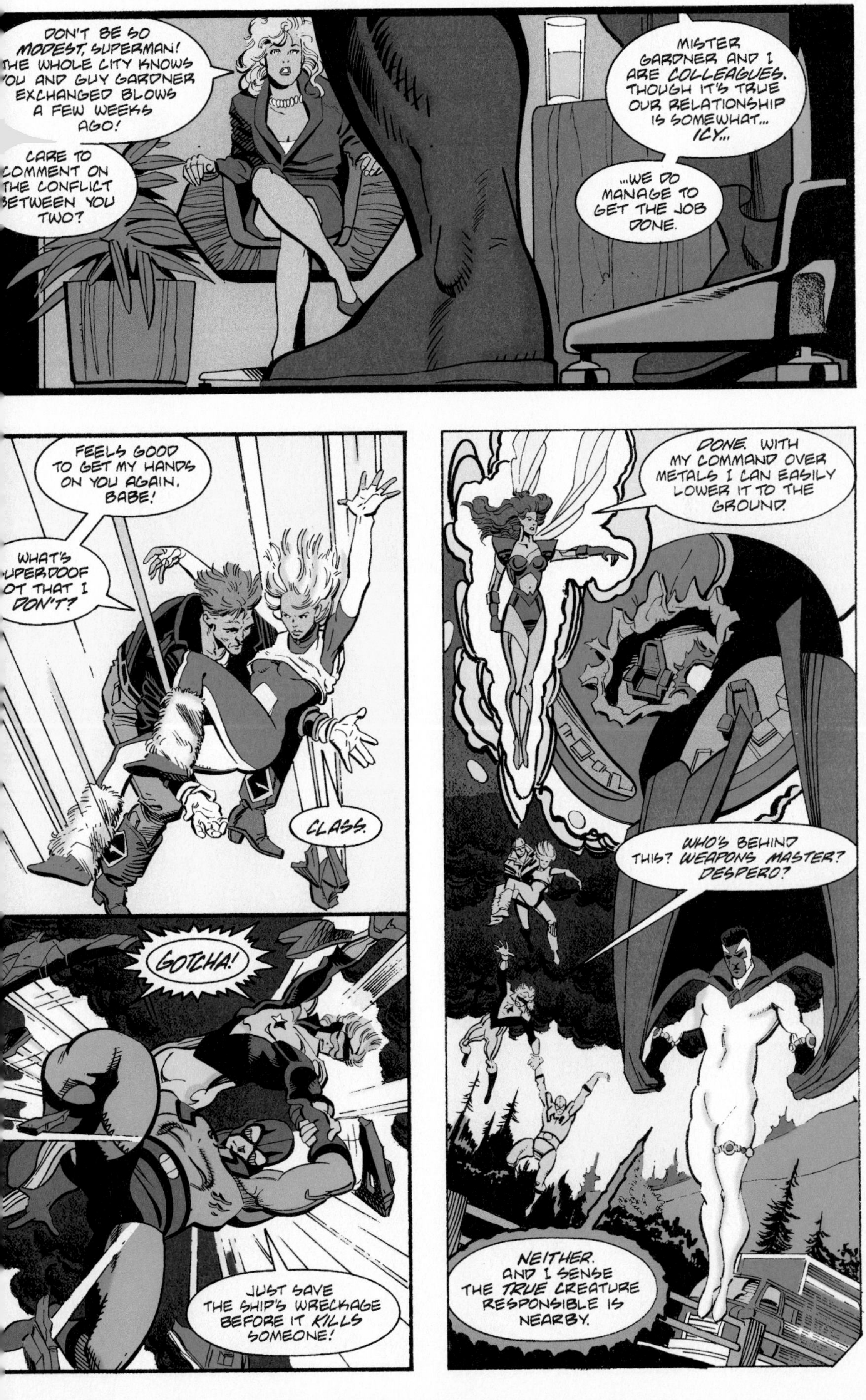
DON'T BE SO MODEST, SUPERMAN! THE WHOLE CITY KNOWS YOU AND GUY GARDNER EXCHANGED BLOWS A FEW WEEKS AGO!
CARE TO COMMENT ON THE CONFLICT BETWEEN YOU TWO?
MISTER GARDNER AND I ARE COLLEAGUES. THOUGH IT'S TRUE OUR RELATIONSHIP IS SOMEWHAT... ICY...
...WE DO MANAGE TO GET THE JOB DONE.
FEELS GOOD TO GET MY HANDS ON YOU AGAIN, BABE!
WHAT'S UPERDOOF OT THAT I DON'T?
CLASS.
GOTCHA!
JUST SAVE THE SHIP'S WRECKAGE BEFORE IT KILLS SOMEONE!
DONE. WITH MY COMMAND OVER METALS I CAN EASILY LOWER IT TO THE GROUND.
WHO'S BEHIND THIS? WEAPONS MASTER? DESPERO?
NEITHER. AND I SENSE THE TRUE CREATURE RESPONSIBLE IS NEARBY.

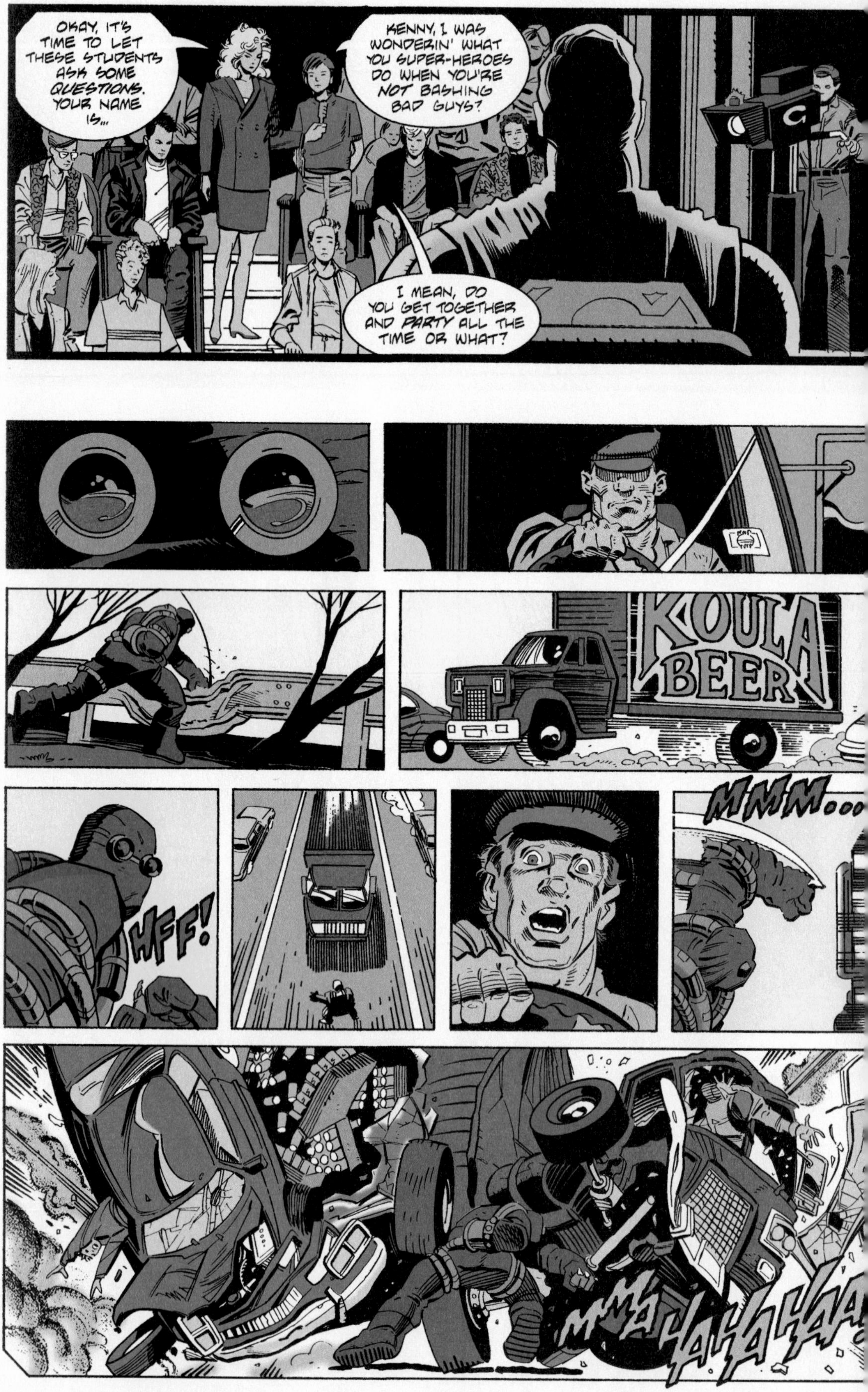
OKAY, IT'S TIME TO LET THESE STUDENTS ASK SOME QUESTIONS. YOUR NAME IS...
KENNY. I WAS WONDERIN' WHAT YOU SUPER-HEROES DO WHEN YOU'RE NOT BASHING BAD GUYS?
I MEAN, DO YOU GET TOGETHER AND PARTY ALL THE TIME OR WHAT?
KOULA BEER
HFF!
MMM...
MMMAHAHAHAHA

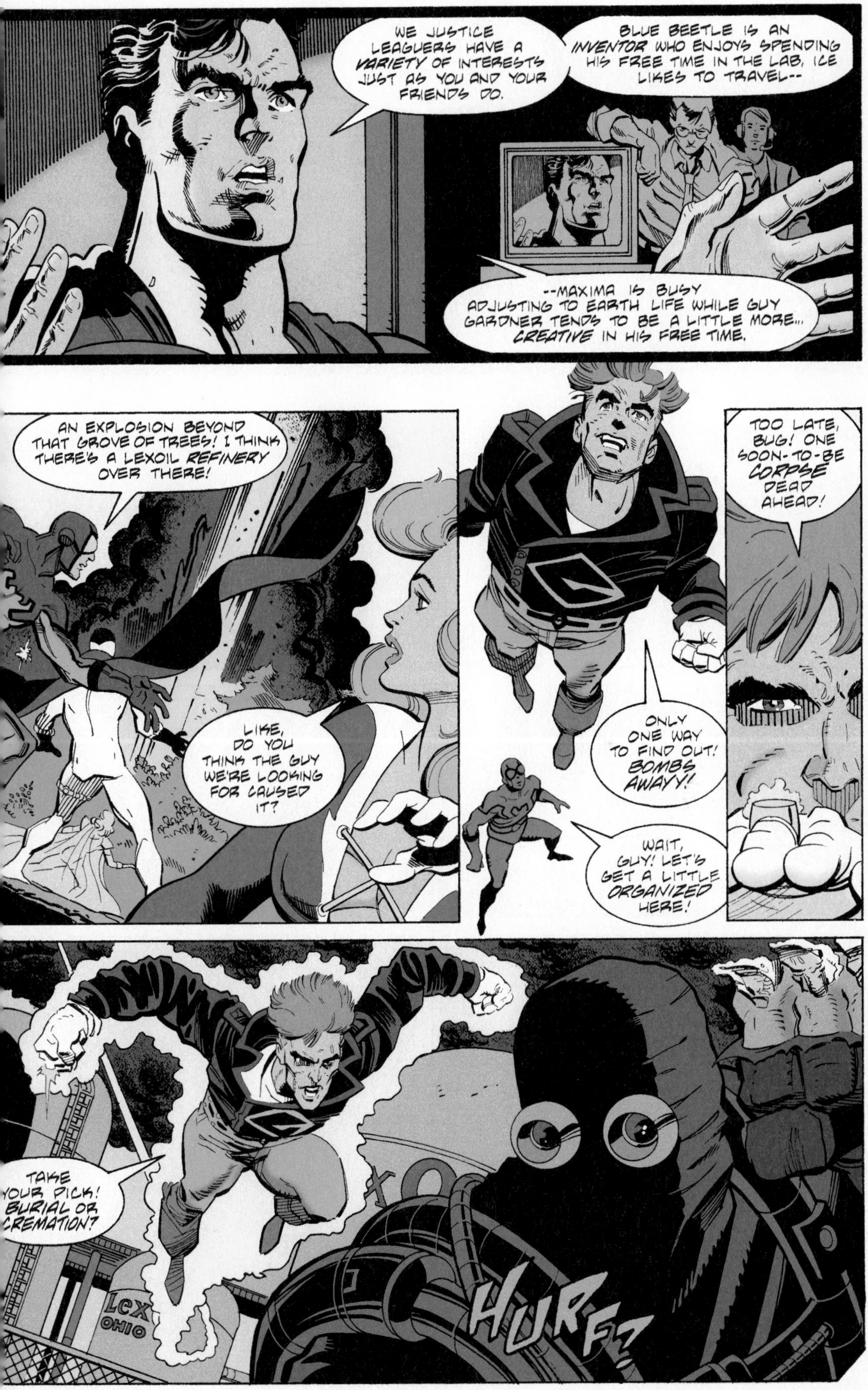
WE JUSTICE LEAGUERS HAVE A VARIETY OF INTERESTS JUST AS YOU AND YOUR FRIENDS DO.
BLUE BEETLE IS AN INVENTOR WHO ENJOYS SPENDING HIS FREE TIME IN THE LAB, ICE LIKES TO TRAVEL--
--MAXIMA IS BUSY ADJUSTING TO EARTH LIFE WHILE GUY GARDNER TENDS TO BE A LITTLE MORE... CREATIVE IN HIS FREE TIME.
AN EXPLOSION BEYOND THAT GROVE OF TREES! I THINK THERE'S A LEXOIL REFINERY OVER THERE!
LIKE, DO YOU THINK THE GUY WE'RE LOOKING FOR CAUSED IT?
TOO LATE, BUG! ONE SOON-TO-BE CORPSE DEAD AHEAD!
ONLY ONE WAY TO FIND OUT! BOMBS AWAY!
WAIT, GUY! LET'S GET A LITTLE ORGANIZED HERE!
TAKE YOUR PICK! BURIAL OR CREMATION?
LEX OHIO
HURF?

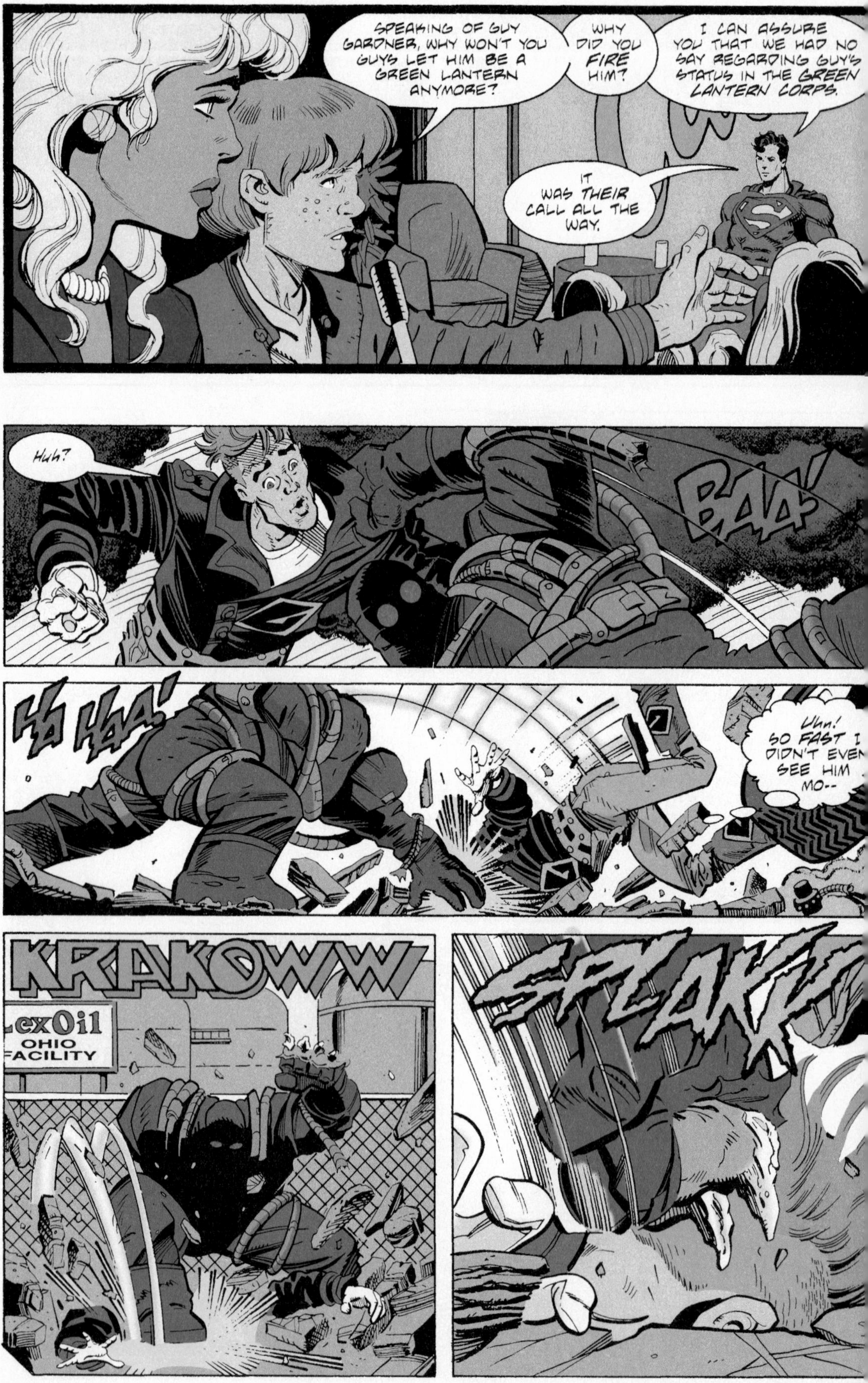
SPEAKING OF GUY GARDNER, WHY WON'T YOU GUYS LET HIM BE A GREEN LANTERN ANYMORE?
WHY DID YOU FIRE HIM?
I CAN ASSURE YOU THAT WE HAD NO SAY REGARDING GUY'S STATUS IN THE GREEN LANTERN CORPS.
IT WAS THEIR CALL ALL THE WAY.
Huh?
BAM!
HO HAA!
Uhn! SO FAST I DIDN'T EVEN SEE HIM MO--
KRAKOWW!
LexOil
OHIO FACILITY

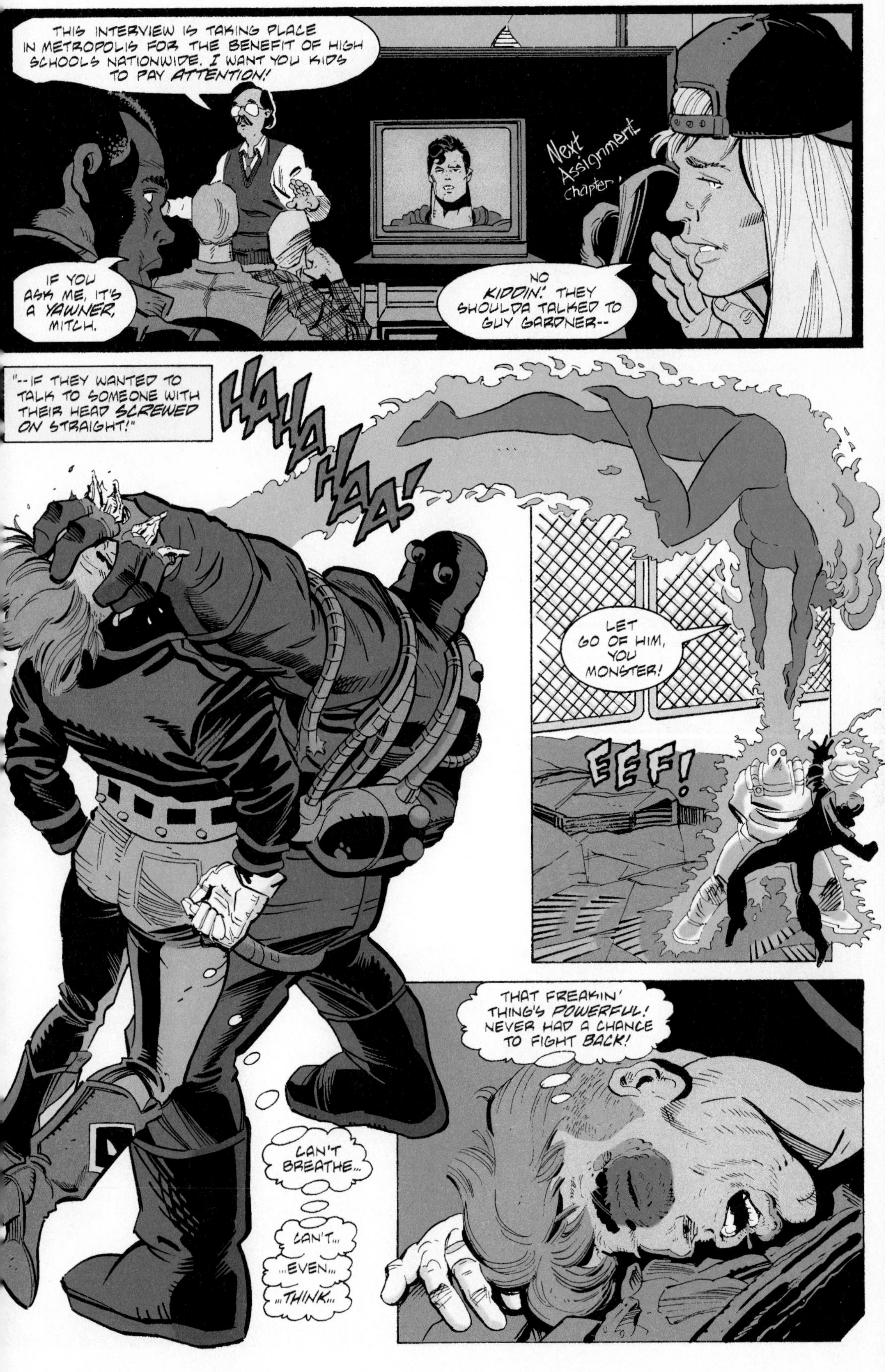
THIS INTERVIEW IS TAKING PLACE IN METROPOLIS FOR THE BENEFIT OF HIGH SCHOOLS NATIONWIDE. I WANT YOU KIDS TO PAY ATTENTION!
Next Assignment: chapter
IF YOU ASK ME, IT'S A YAWNER, MITCH.
NO KIDDIN'! THEY SHOULDA TALKED TO GUY GARDNER--
"--IF THEY WANTED TO TALK TO SOMEONE WITH THEIR HEAD SCREWED ON STRAIGHT!"
HAHAHAHAA!
LET GO OF HIM, YOU MONSTER!
EEF!
THAT FREAKIN' THING'S POWERFUL! NEVER HAD A CHANCE TO FIGHT BACK!
CAN'T BREATHE...
CAN'T...
...EVEN...
...THINK...

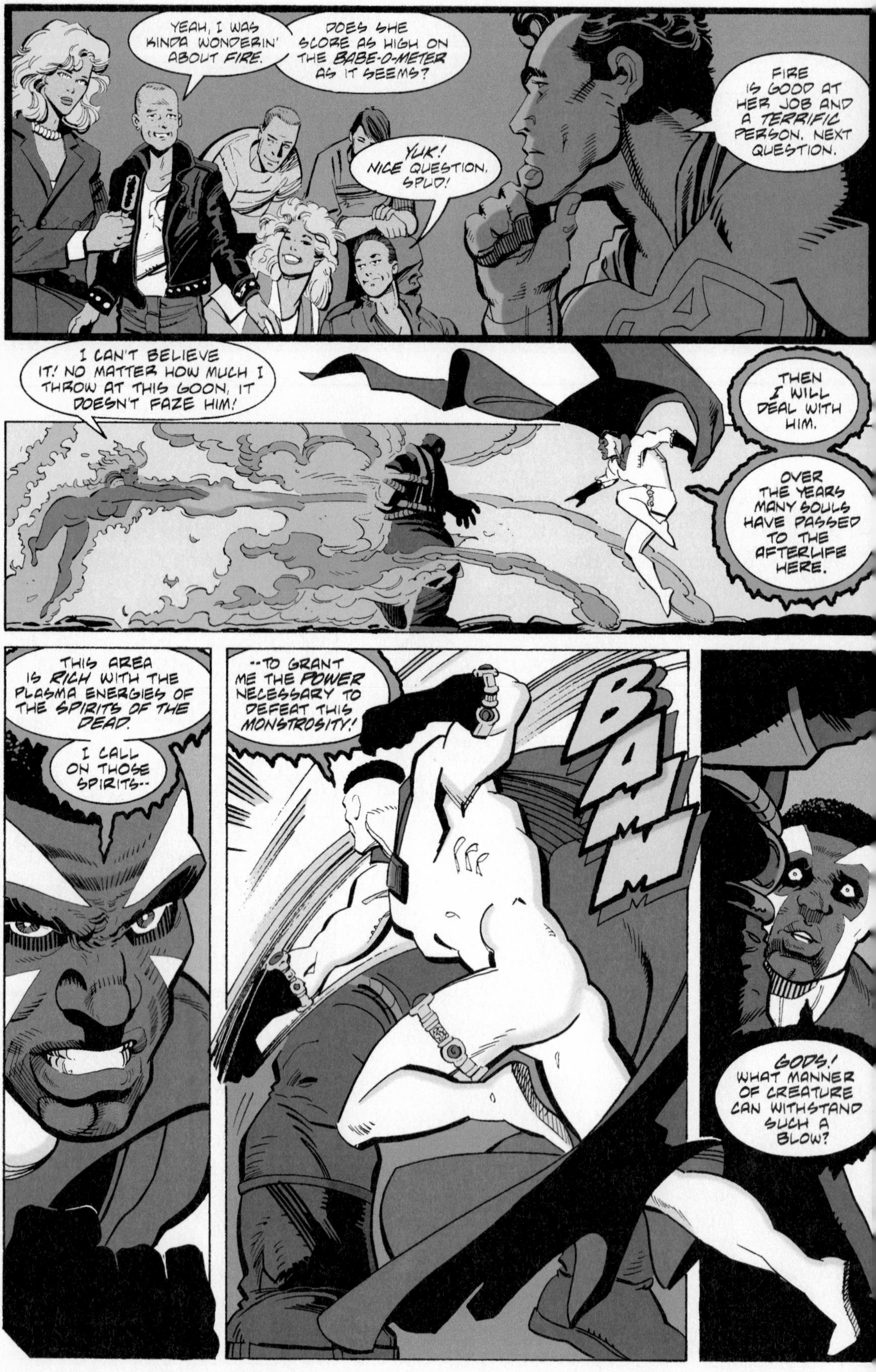
YEAH, I WAS KINDA WONDERIN' ABOUT FIRE.
DOES SHE SCORE AS HIGH ON THE BABE-O-METER AS IT SEEMS?
YUK! NICE QUESTION, SPUD!
FIRE IS GOOD AT HER JOB AND A TERRIFIC PERSON. NEXT QUESTION.
I CAN'T BELIEVE IT! NO MATTER HOW MUCH I THROW AT THIS GOON, IT DOESN'T FAZE HIM!
THEN I WILL DEAL WITH HIM.
OVER THE YEARS MANY SOULS HAVE PASSED TO THE AFTERLIFE HERE.
THIS AREA IS RICH WITH THE PLASMA ENERGIES OF THE SPIRITS OF THE DEAD.
I CALL ON THOSE SPIRITS--
--TO GRANT ME THE POWER NECESSARY TO DEFEAT THIS MONSTROSITY!
BAM!
GODS! WHAT MANNER OF CREATURE CAN WITHSTAND SUCH A BLOW?

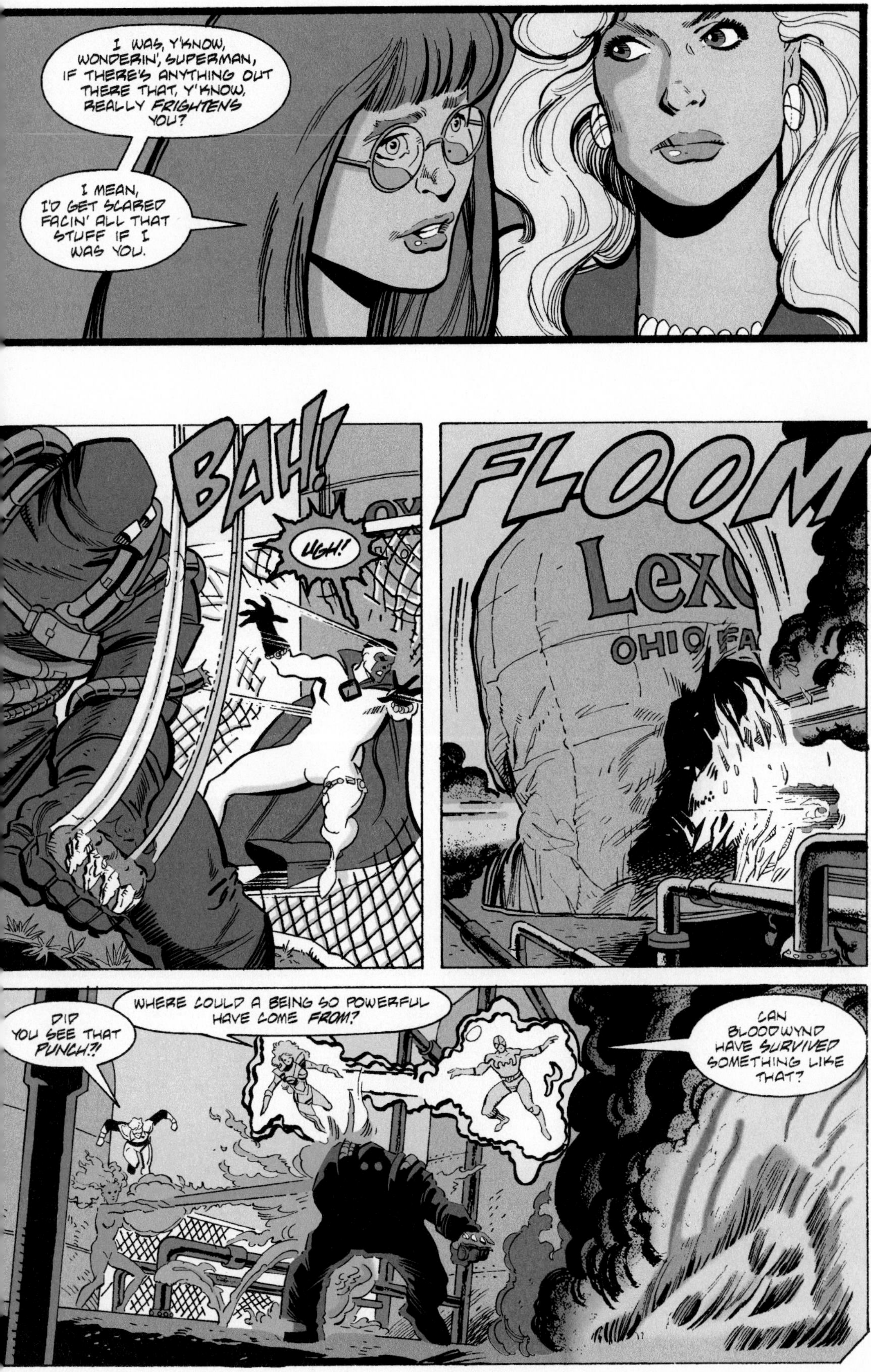
I WAS, Y'KNOW, WONDERIN', SUPERMAN, IF THERE'S ANYTHING OUT THERE THAT, Y'KNOW, REALLY FRIGHTENS YOU?
I MEAN, I'D GET SCARED FACIN' ALL THAT STUFF IF I WAS YOU.
BAH!
UGH!
FLOOM
LexC
OHIO FA
DID YOU SEE THAT PUNCH?!
WHERE COULD A BEING SO POWERFUL HAVE COME FROM?
CAN BLOODWYND HAVE SURVIVED SOMETHING LIKE THAT?

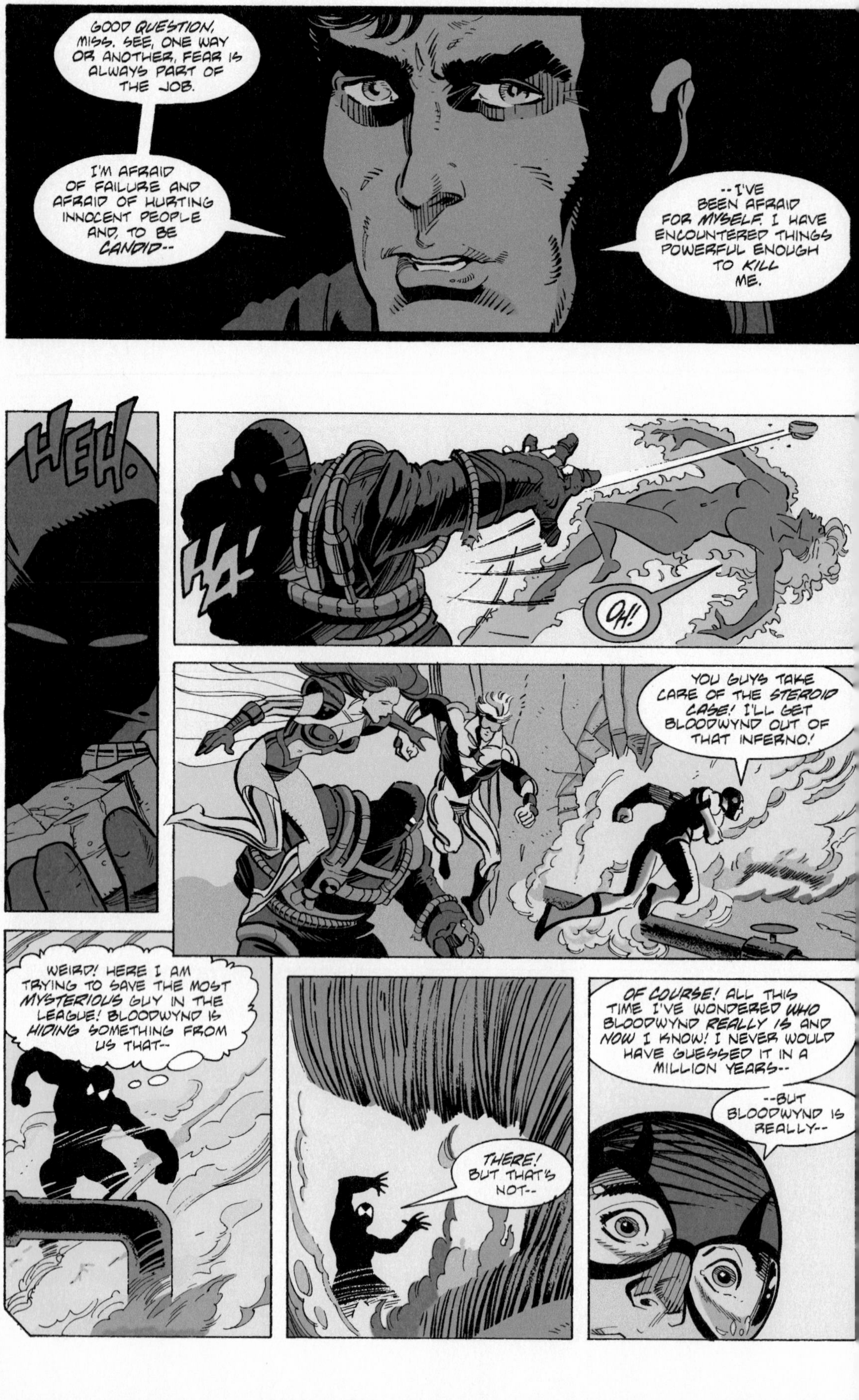

GOOD QUESTION, MISS. SEE, ONE WAY OR ANOTHER, FEAR IS ALWAYS PART OF THE JOB.
I'M AFRAID OF FAILURE AND AFRAID OF HURTING INNOCENT PEOPLE AND, TO BE CANDID--
--I'VE BEEN AFRAID FOR MYSELF. I HAVE ENCOUNTERED THINGS POWERFUL ENOUGH TO KILL ME.
HEH.
HA!
OH!
YOU GUYS TAKE CARE OF THE STEROID CASE! I'LL GET BLOODWYND OUT OF THAT INFERNO!
WEIRD! HERE I AM TRYING TO SAVE THE MOST MYSTERIOUS GUY IN THE LEAGUE! BLOODWYND IS HIDING SOMETHING FROM US THAT--
THERE! BUT THAT'S NOT--
OF COURSE! ALL THIS TIME I'VE WONDERED WHO BLOODWYND REALLY IS AND NOW I KNOW! I NEVER WOULD HAVE GUESSED IT IN A MILLION YEARS--
--BUT BLOODWYND IS REALLY--

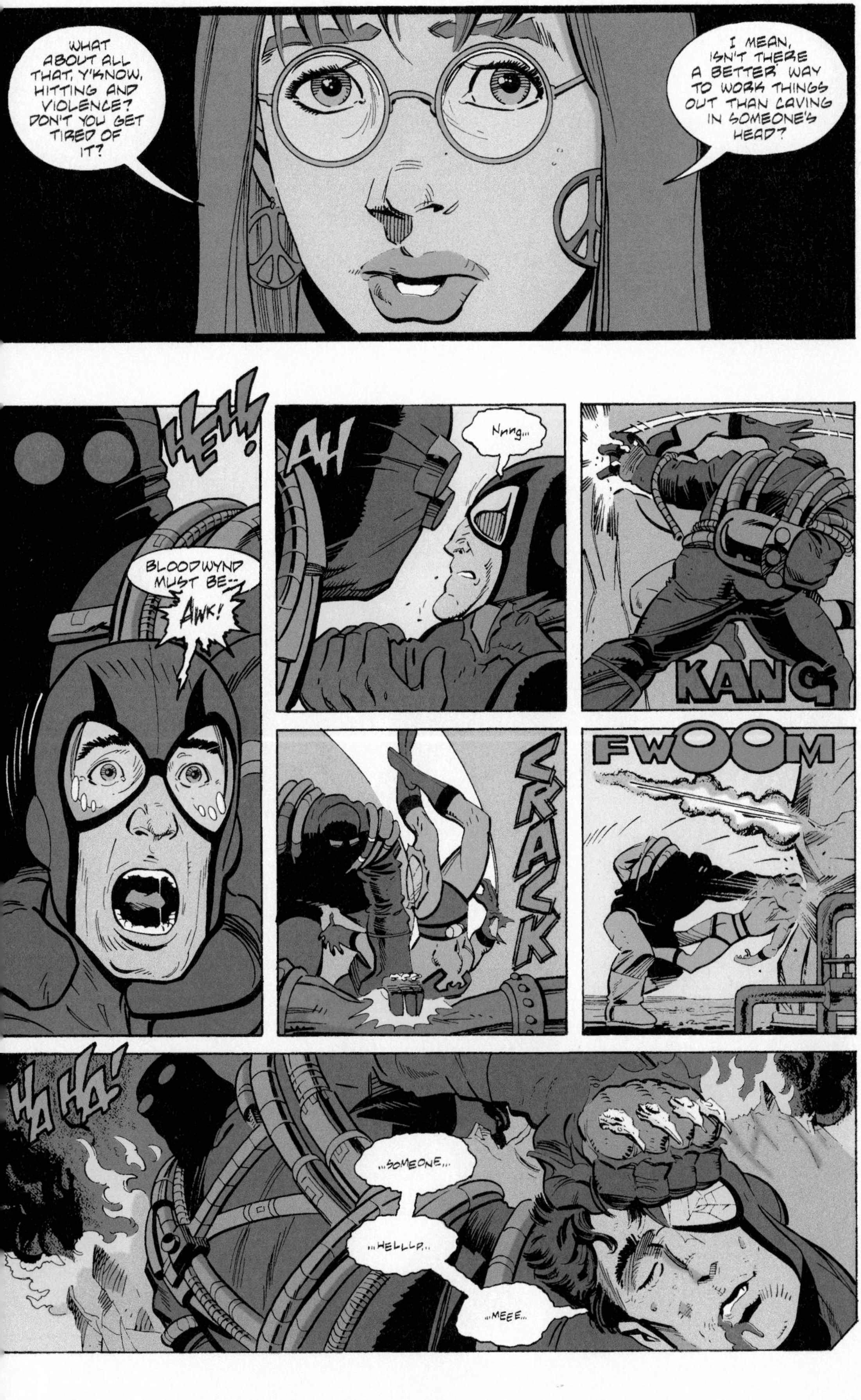
WHAT ABOUT ALL THAT, Y'KNOW, HITTING AND VIOLENCE? DON'T YOU GET TIRED OF IT?
I MEAN, ISN'T THERE A BETTER WAY TO WORK THINGS OUT THAN CAVING IN SOMEONE'S HEAD?
HEH!
BLOODWYND MUST BE--
AWK!
AH
Nnng...
KANG
CRACK
FWOOM
HA HA!
...SOMEONE...
...HELLLP...
...MEEE...

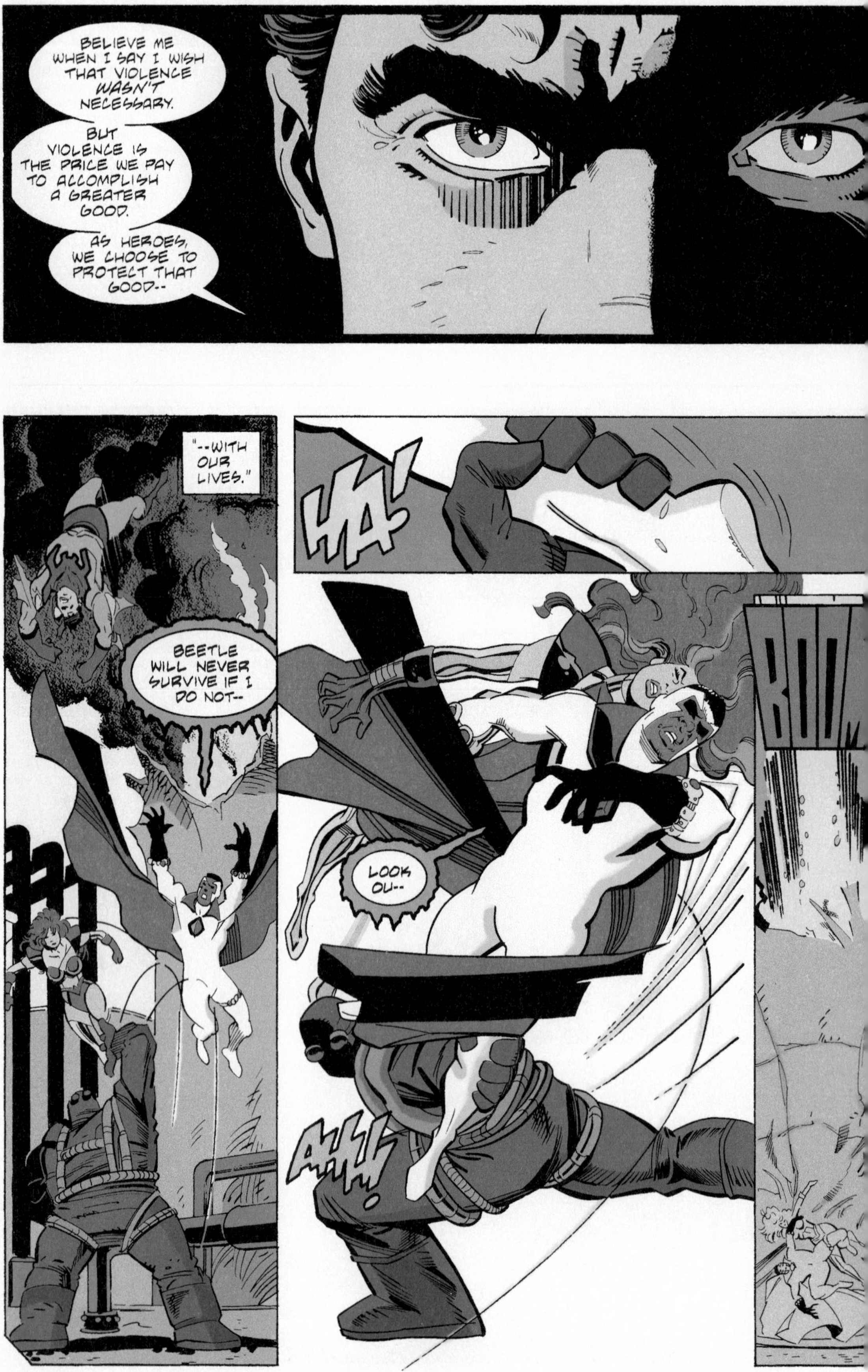
BELIEVE ME WHEN I SAY I WISH THAT VIOLENCE *WASN'T* NECESSARY.
BUT VIOLENCE IS THE PRICE WE PAY TO ACCOMPLISH A GREATER GOOD.
AS HEROES, WE CHOOSE TO PROTECT THAT GOOD--
"--WITH OUR LIVES."
BEETLE WILL NEVER SURVIVE IF I DO NOT--
HA!
LOOK OU--
AHH!
BOO

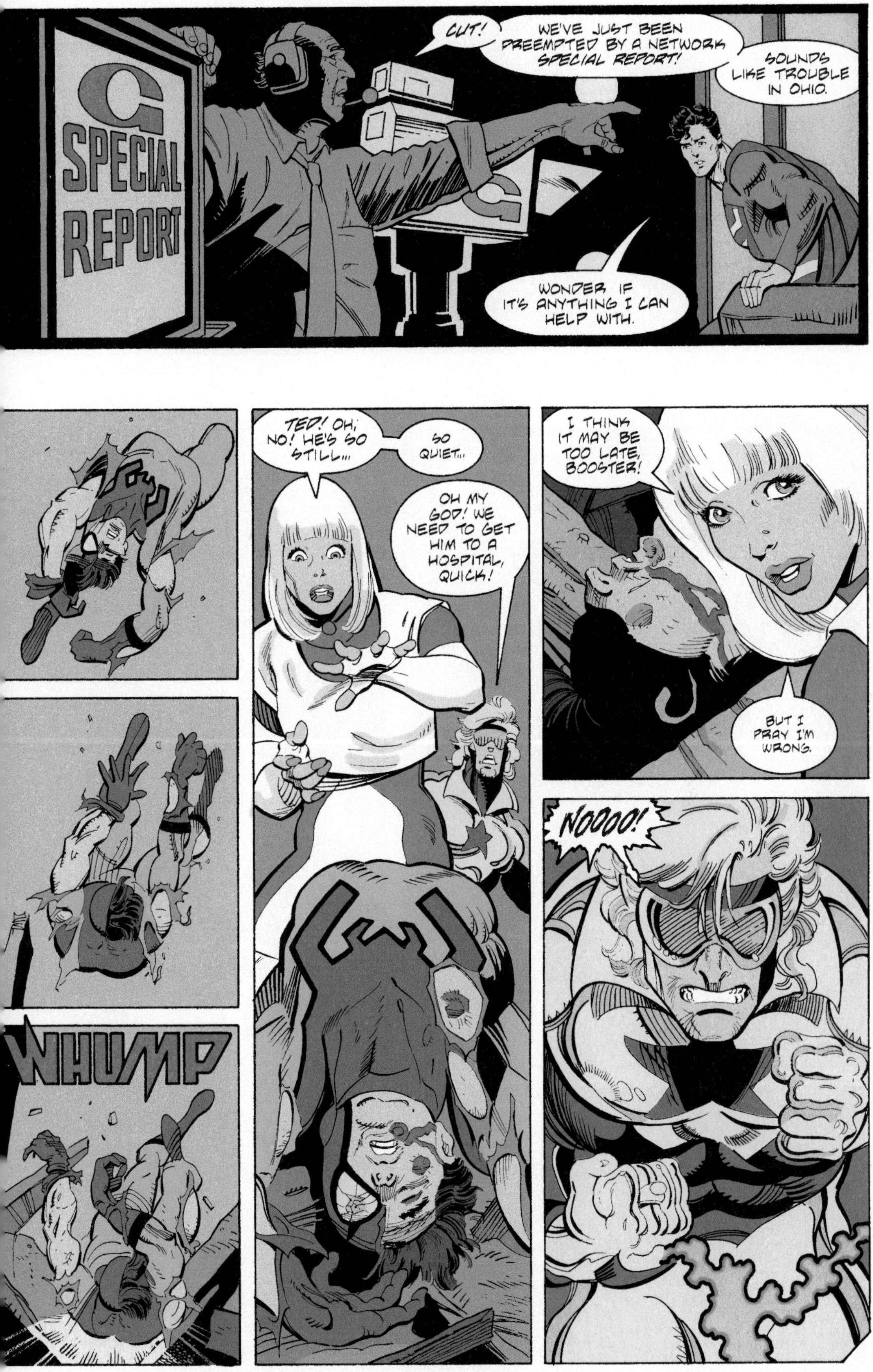
SPECIAL REPORT
CUT!
WE'VE JUST BEEN PREEMPTED BY A NETWORK SPECIAL REPORT!
SOUNDS LIKE TROUBLE IN OHIO.
WONDER IF IT'S ANYTHING I CAN HELP WITH.
WHUMP
TED! OH, NO! HE'S SO STILL...
SO QUIET...
OH MY GOD! WE NEED TO GET HIM TO A HOSPITAL, QUICK!
I THINK IT MAY BE TOO LATE, BOOSTER!
BUT I PRAY I'M WRONG.
NOOOO!

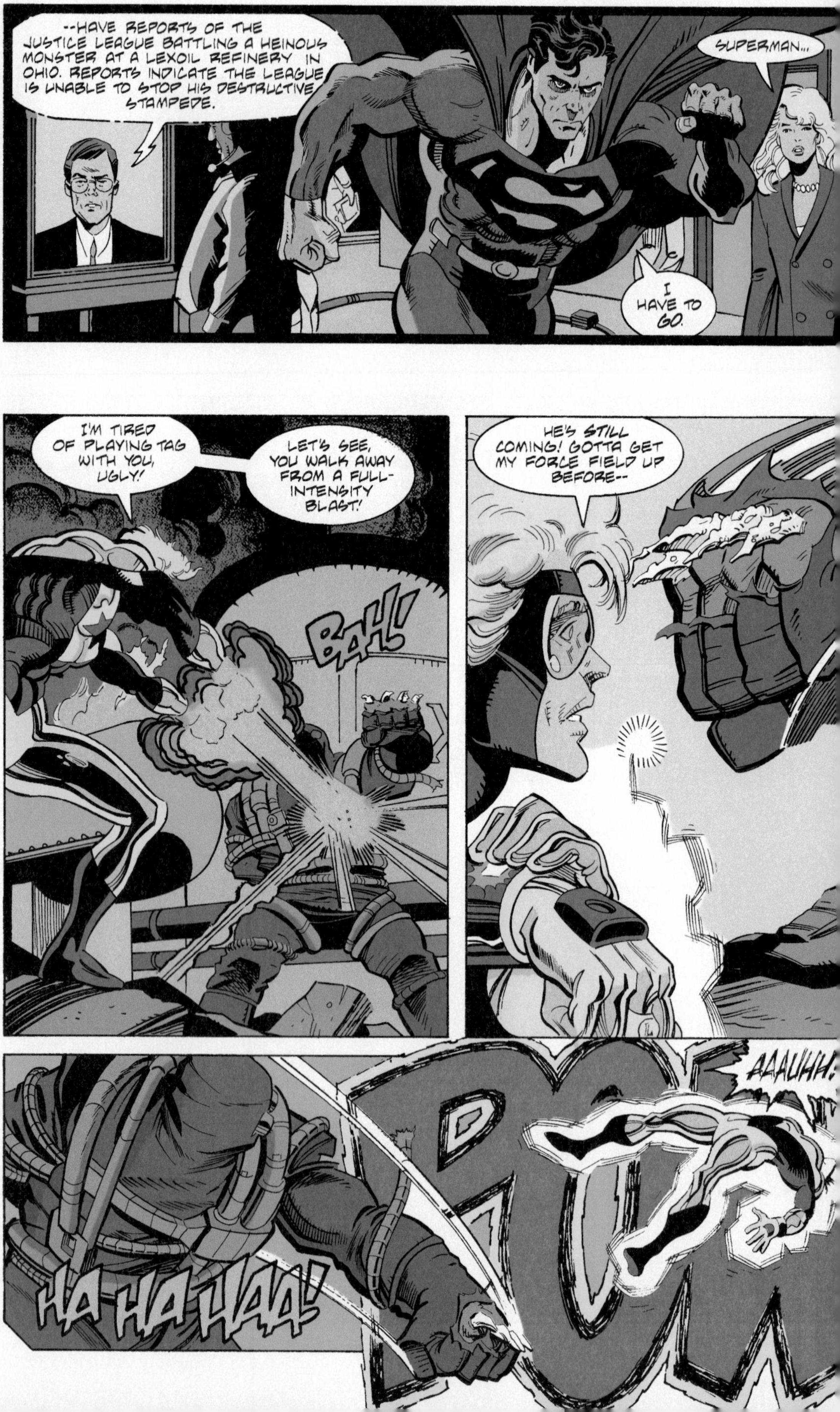
--HAVE REPORTS OF THE JUSTICE LEAGUE BATTLING A HEINOUS MONSTER AT A LEXOIL REFINERY IN OHIO. REPORTS INDICATE THE LEAGUE IS UNABLE TO STOP HIS DESTRUCTIVE STAMPEDE.
SUPERMAN...
I HAVE TO GO.
I'M TIRED OF PLAYING TAG WITH YOU, UGLY!
LET'S SEE, YOU WALK AWAY FROM A FULL-INTENSITY BLAST!
BAH!
HE'S STILL COMING! GOTTA GET MY FORCE FIELD UP BEFORE--
AAAUHH!
HA HA HAA!
POW

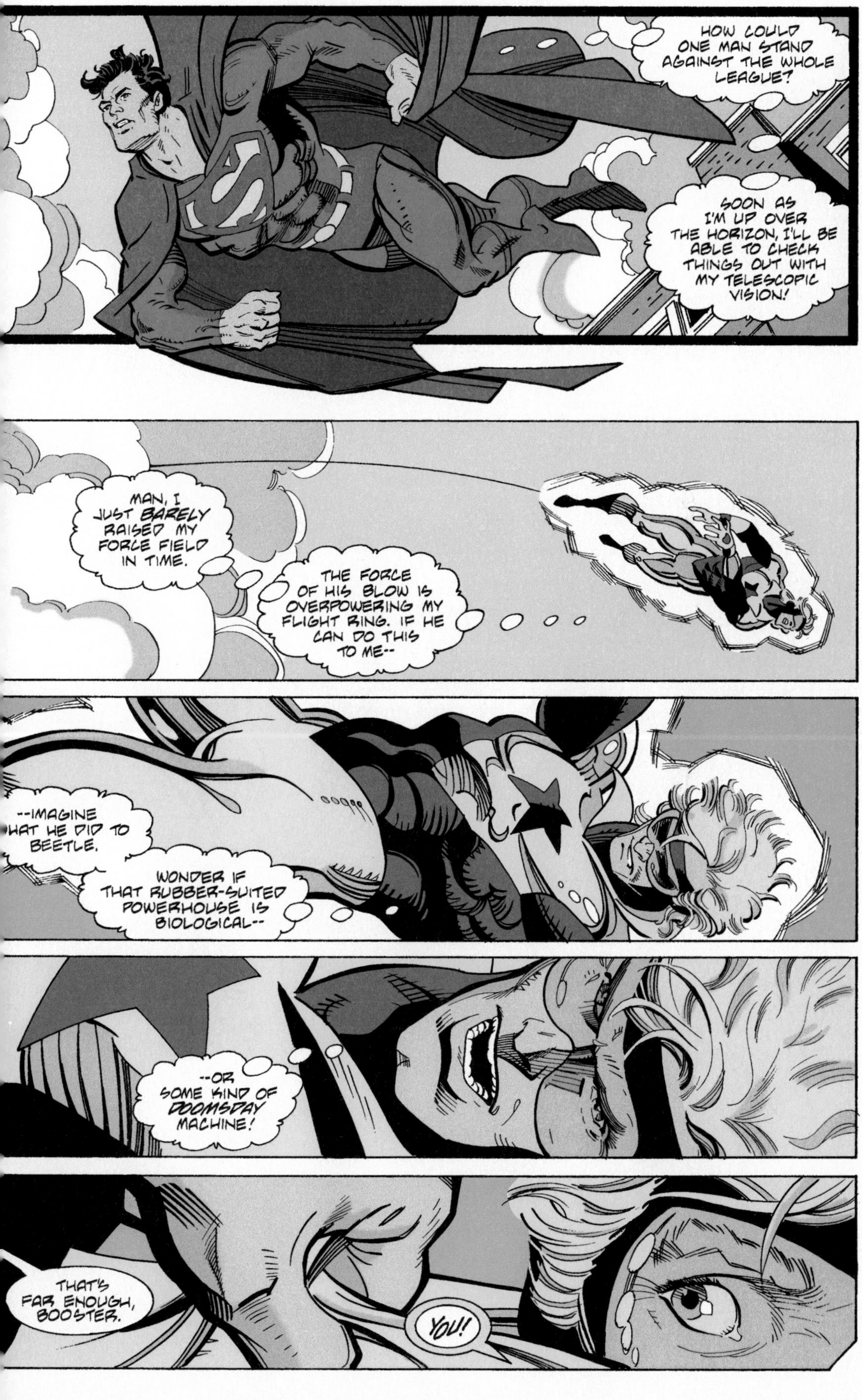

HOW COULD ONE MAN STAND AGAINST THE WHOLE LEAGUE?
SOON AS I'M UP OVER THE HORIZON, I'LL BE ABLE TO CHECK THINGS OUT WITH MY TELESCOPIC VISION!
MAN, I JUST BARELY RAISED MY FORCE FIELD IN TIME.
THE FORCE OF HIS BLOW IS OVERPOWERING MY FLIGHT RING. IF HE CAN DO THIS TO ME--
--IMAGINE WHAT HE DID TO BEETLE.
WONDER IF THAT RUBBER-SUITED POWERHOUSE IS BIOLOGICAL--
--OR SOME KIND OF DOOMSDAY MACHINE!
THAT'S FAR ENOUGH, BOOSTER.
YOU!

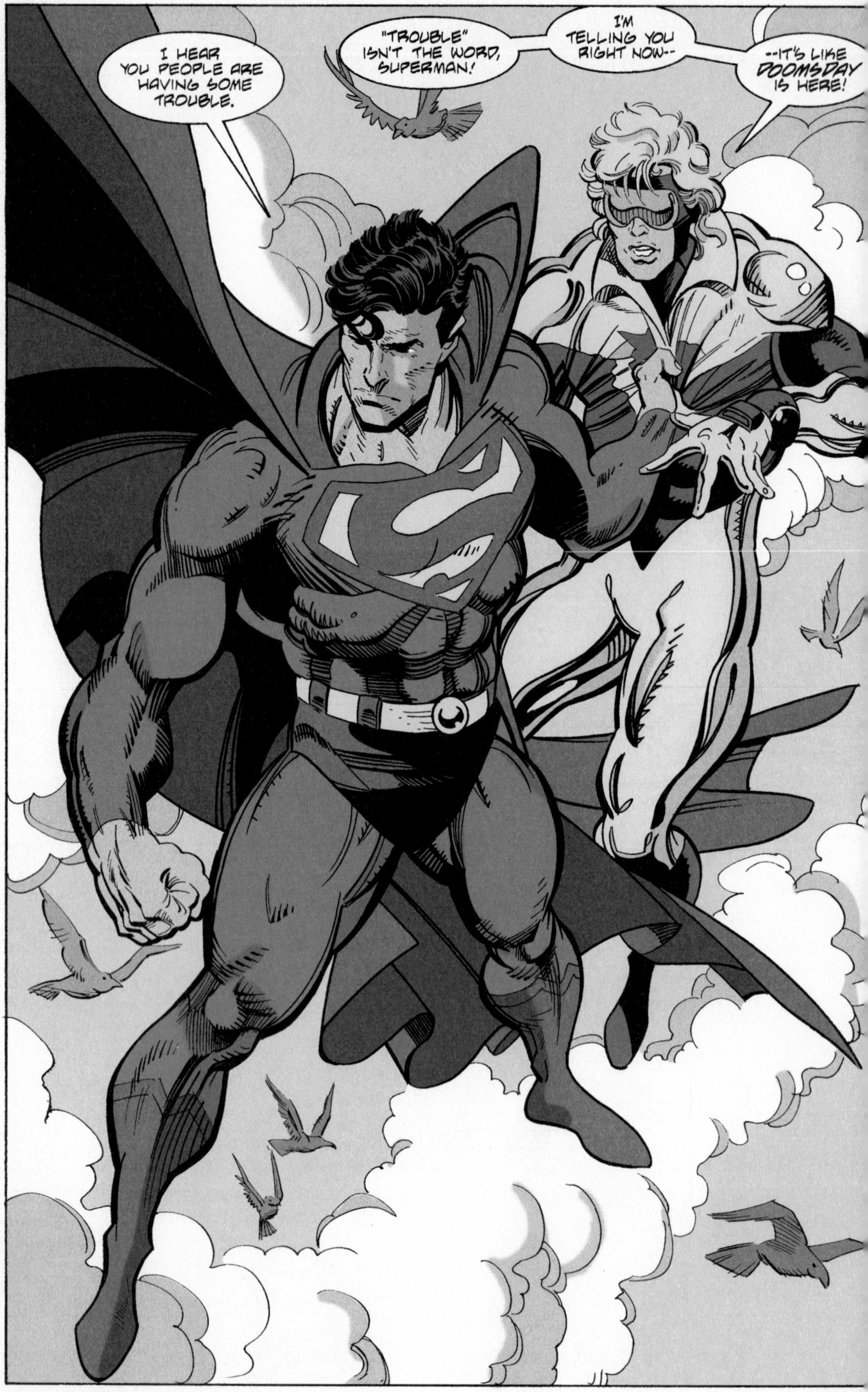
I HEAR YOU PEOPLE ARE HAVING SOME TROUBLE.
"TROUBLE" ISN'T THE WORD, SUPERMAN!
I'M TELLING YOU RIGHT NOW--
--IT'S LIKE DOOMSDAY IS HERE!

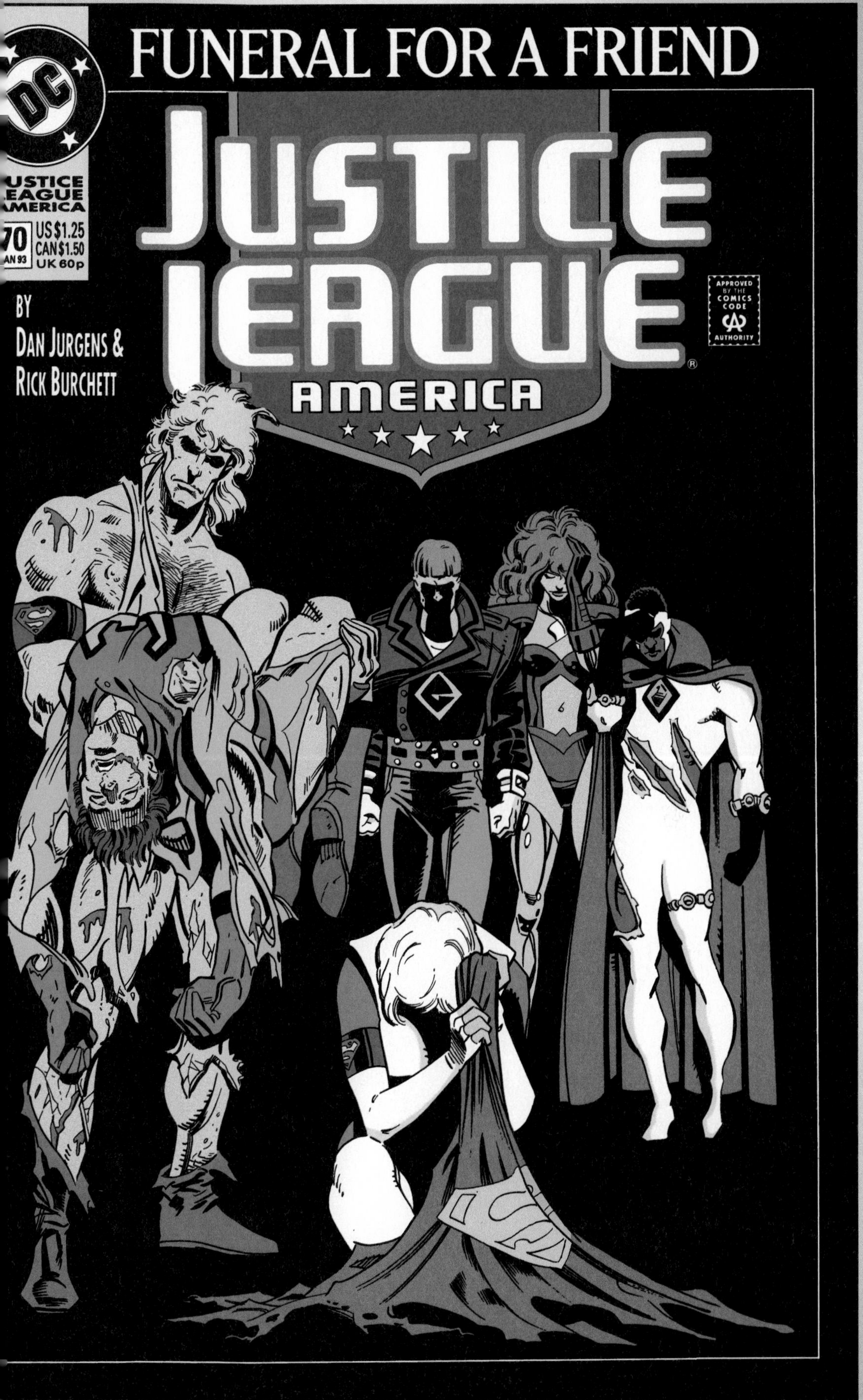
FUNERAL FOR A FRIEND
DC
JUSTICE LEAGUE AMERICA
70
JAN 93
US $1.25
CAN $1.50
UK 60p
JUSTICE LEAGUE AMERICA
APPROVED BY THE COMICS CODE AUTHORITY
BY
DAN JURGENS &
RICK BURCHETT

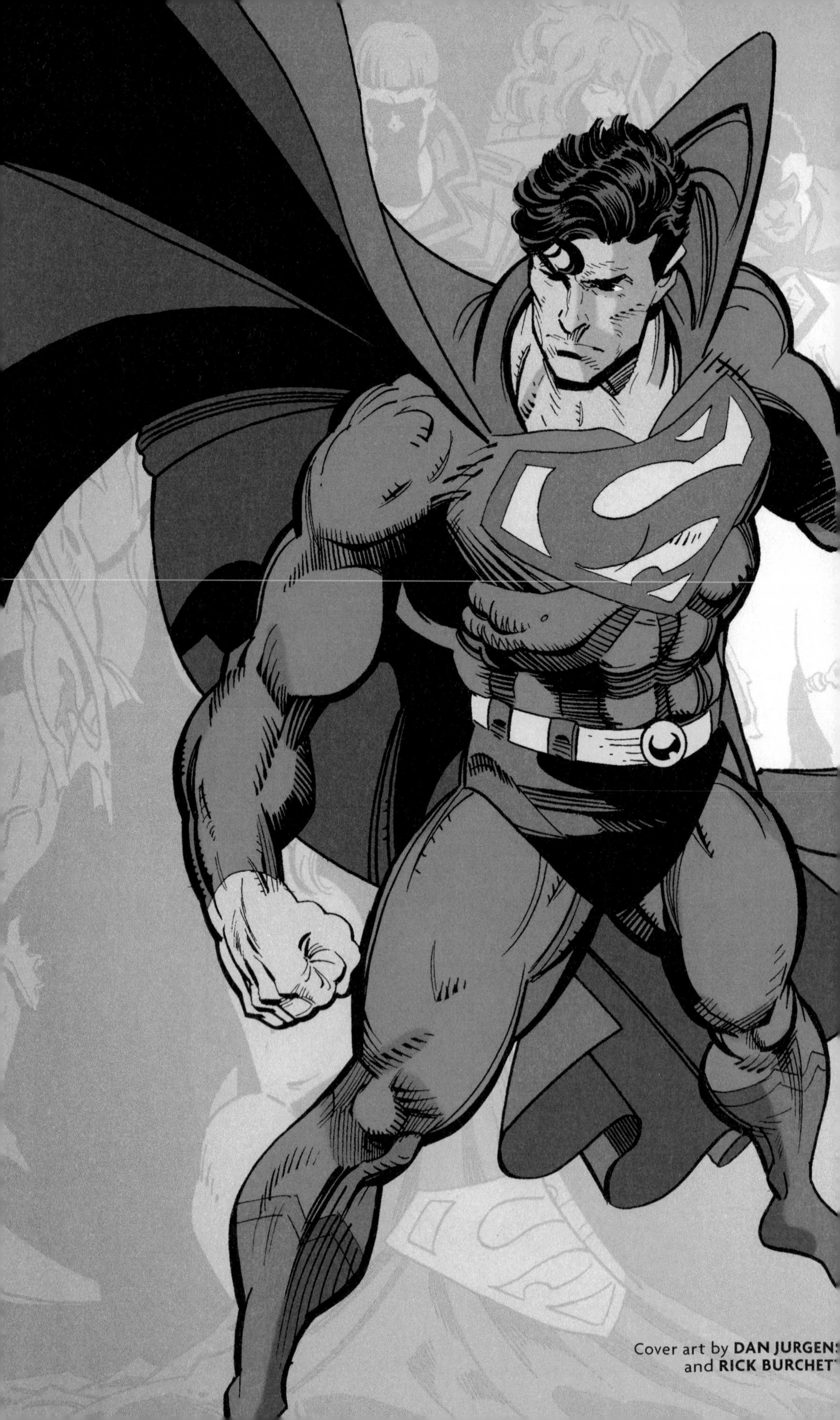

Cover art by **DAN JURGENS**
and **RICK BURCHETT**

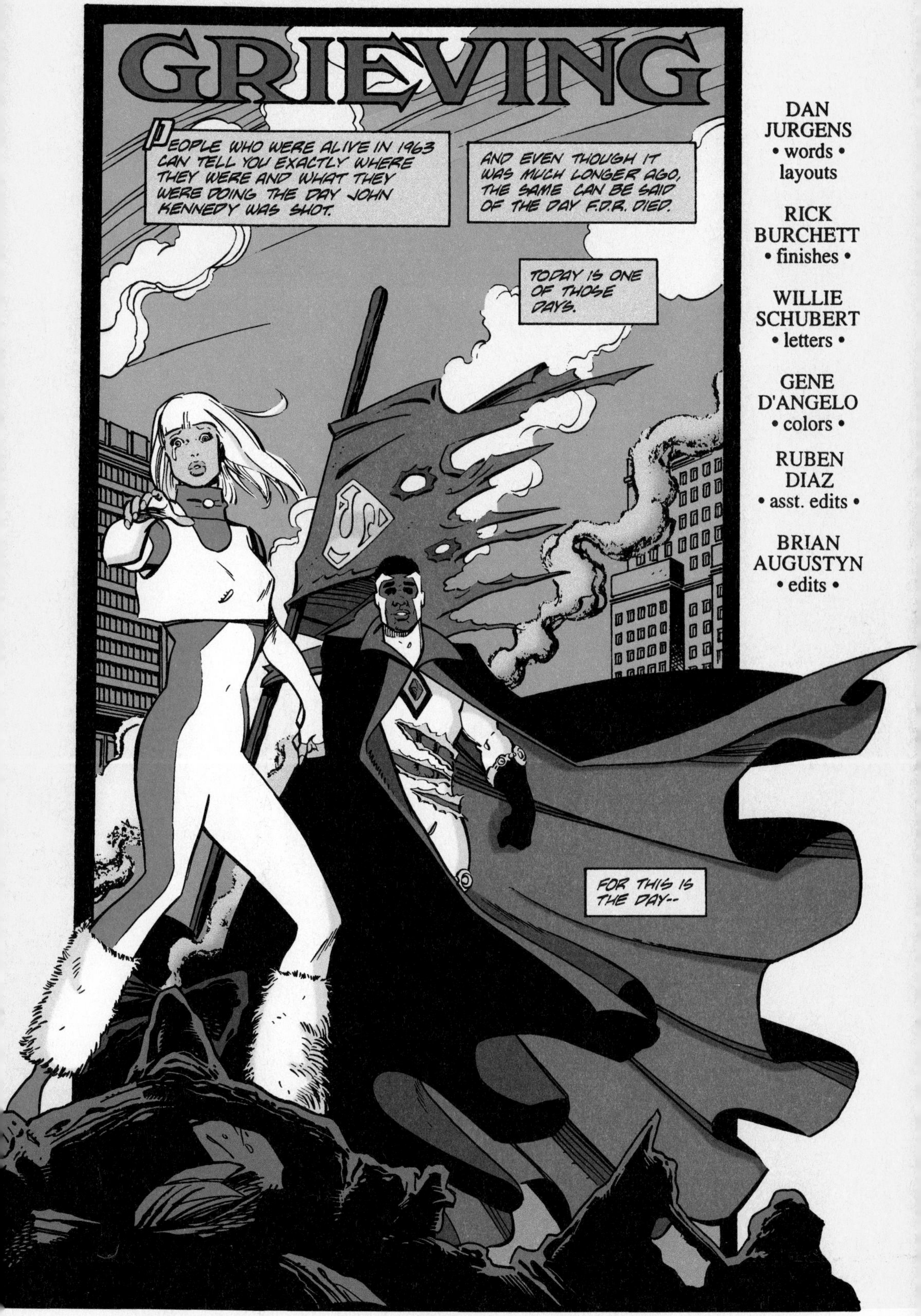
GRIEVING
PEOPLE WHO WERE ALIVE IN 1963 CAN TELL YOU EXACTLY WHERE THEY WERE AND WHAT THEY WERE DOING THE DAY JOHN KENNEDY WAS SHOT.
AND EVEN THOUGH IT WAS MUCH LONGER AGO, THE SAME CAN BE SAID OF THE DAY F.D.R. DIED.
TODAY IS ONE OF THOSE DAYS.
FOR THIS IS THE DAY--

DAN JURGENS
• words •
layouts

RICK BURCHETT
• finishes •

WILLIE SCHUBERT
• letters •

GENE D'ANGELO
• colors •

RUBEN DIAZ
• asst. edits •

BRIAN AUGUSTYN
• edits •

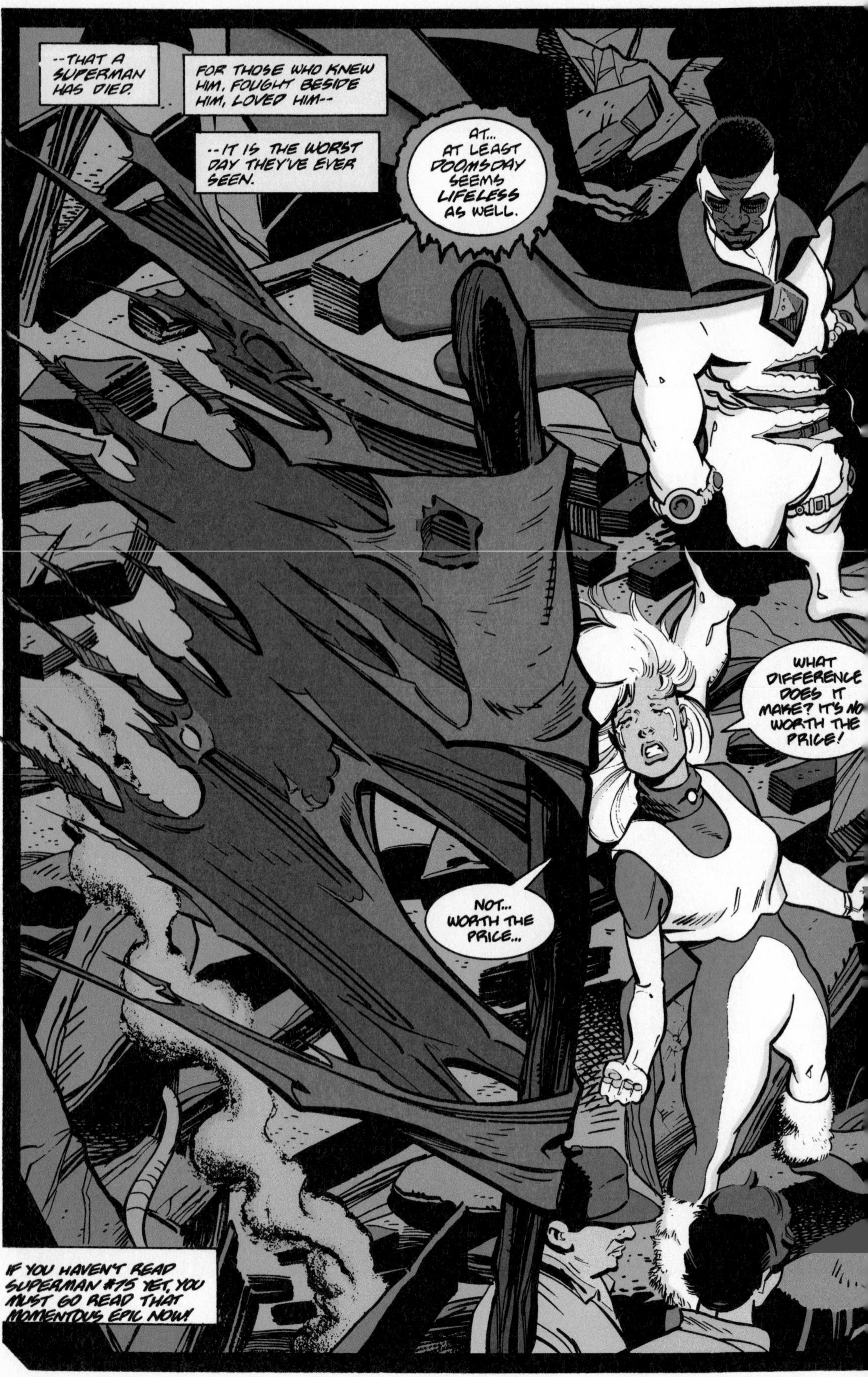

--THAT A SUPERMAN HAS DIED.
FOR THOSE WHO KNEW HIM, FOUGHT BESIDE HIM, LOVED HIM--
--IT IS THE WORST DAY THEY'VE EVER SEEN.
AT... AT LEAST DOOMSDAY SEEMS LIFELESS AS WELL.
WHAT DIFFERENCE DOES IT MAKE? IT'S NO WORTH THE PRICE!
NOT... WORTH THE PRICE...
IF YOU HAVEN'T READ SUPERMAN #75 YET, YOU MUST GO READ THAT MOMENTOUS EPIC NOW!

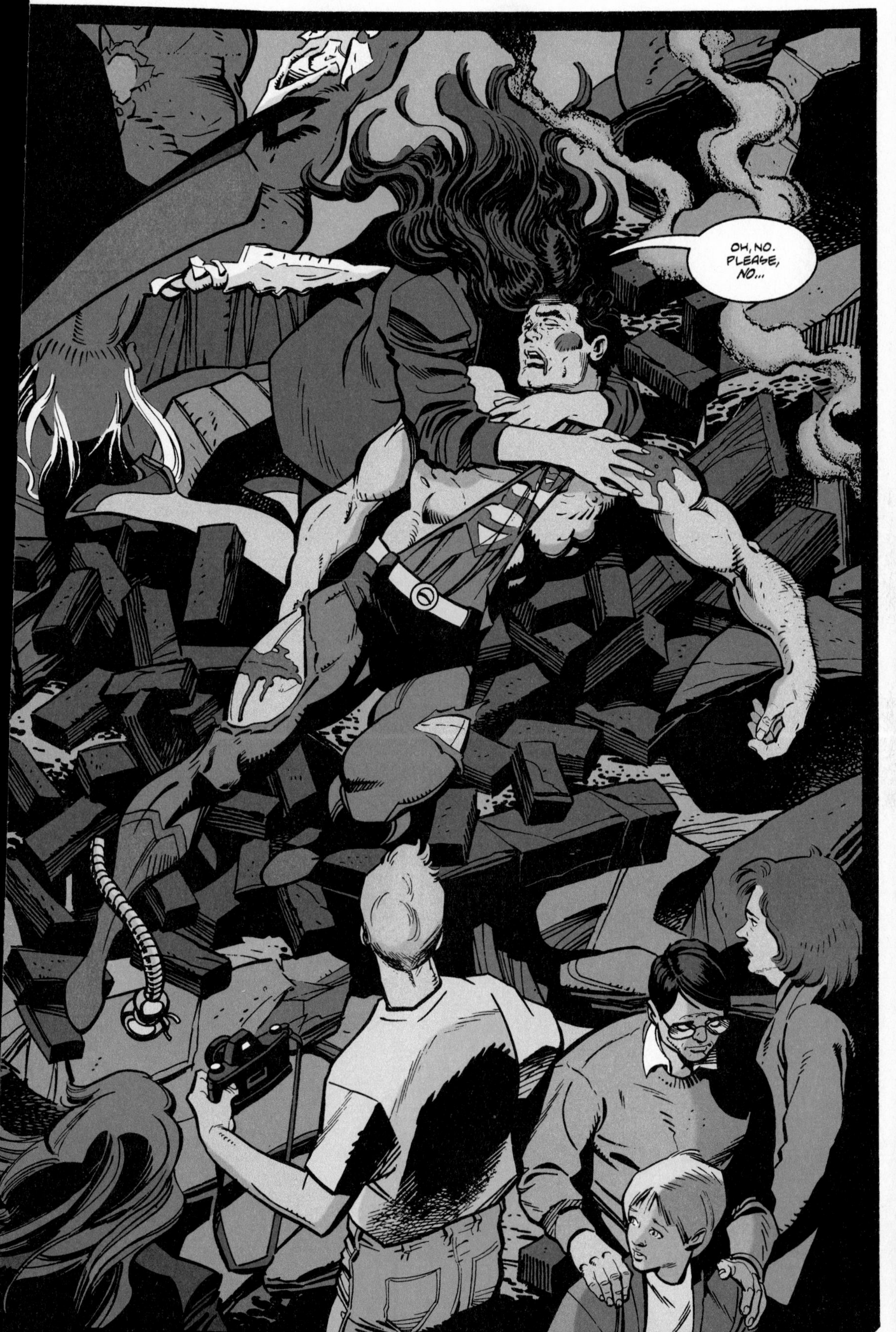
OH, NO. PLEASE, NO...

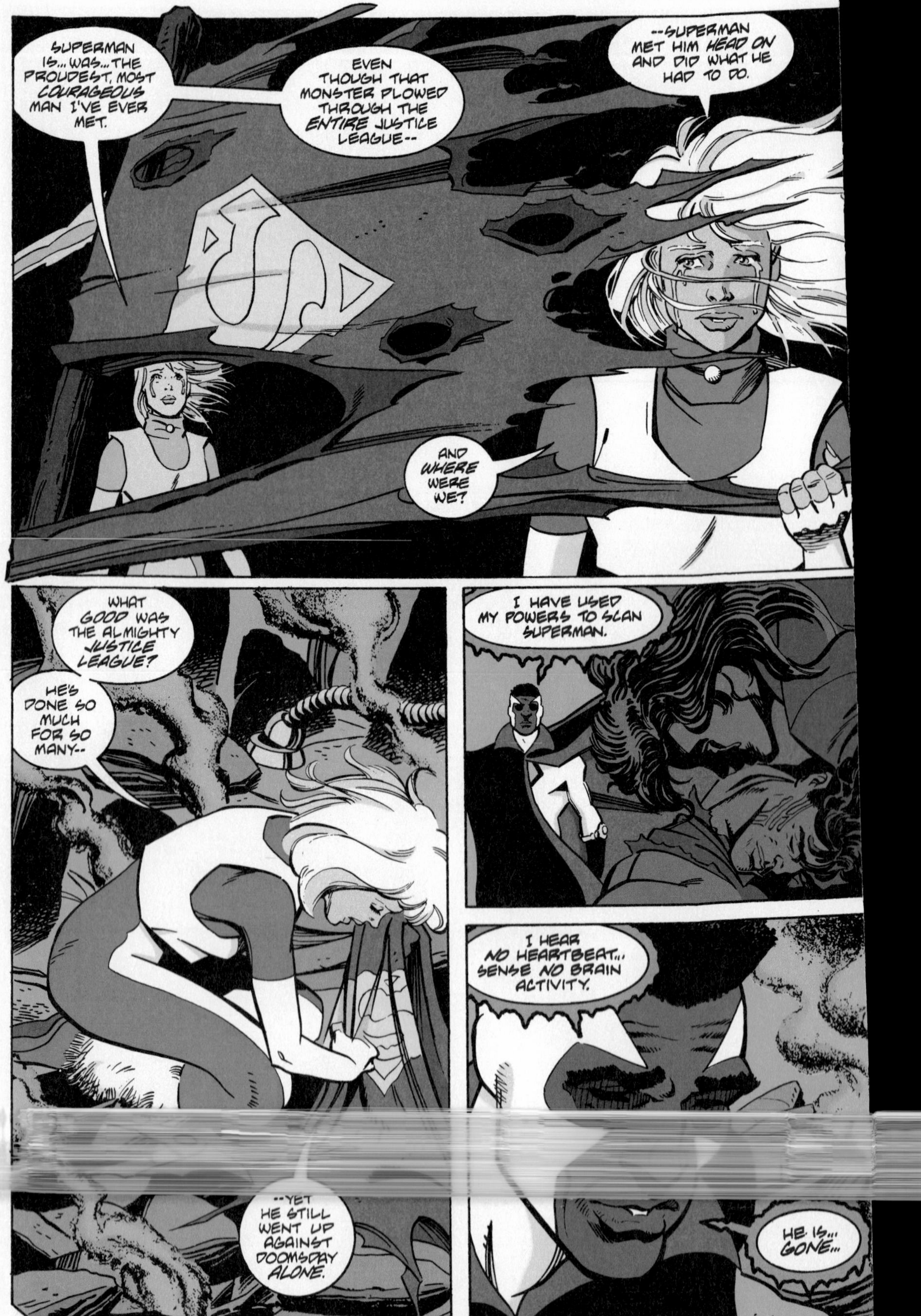
SUPERMAN IS... WAS... THE PROUDEST, MOST COURAGEOUS MAN I'VE EVER MET.
EVEN THOUGH THAT MONSTER PLOWED THROUGH THE ENTIRE JUSTICE LEAGUE--
--SUPERMAN MET HIM HEAD ON AND DID WHAT HE HAD TO DO.
AND WHERE WERE WE?
WHAT GOOD WAS THE ALMIGHTY JUSTICE LEAGUE?
HE'S DONE SO MUCH FOR SO MANY--
--YET HE STILL WENT UP AGAINST DOOMSDAY ALONE.
I HAVE USED MY POWERS TO SCAN SUPERMAN.
I HEAR NO HEARTBEAT... SENSE NO BRAIN ACTIVITY.
HE IS... GONE...

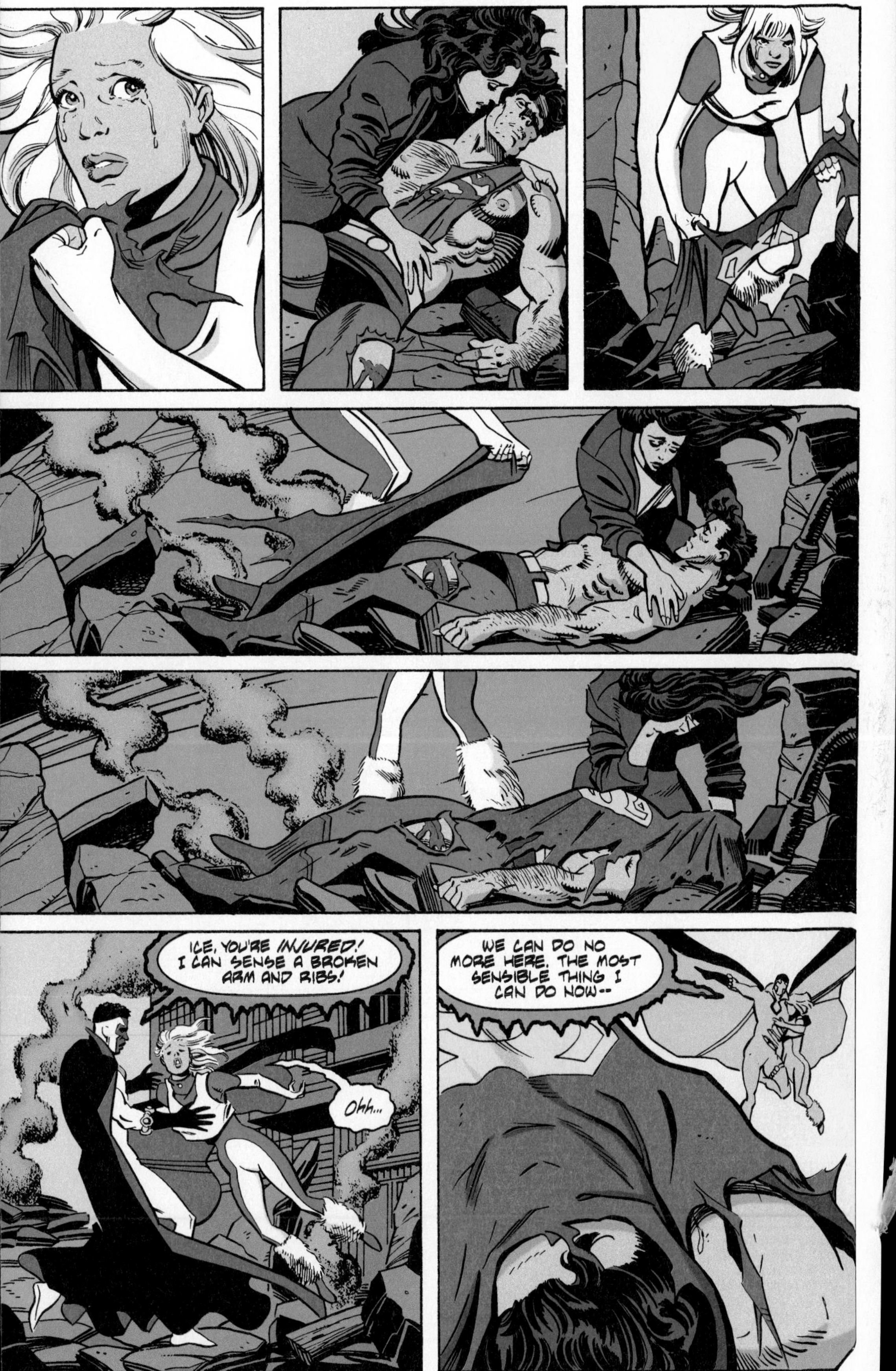
ICE, YOU'RE INJURED! I CAN SENSE A BROKEN ARM AND RIBS!
Ohh...
WE CAN DO NO MORE HERE. THE MOST SENSIBLE THING I CAN DO NOW--

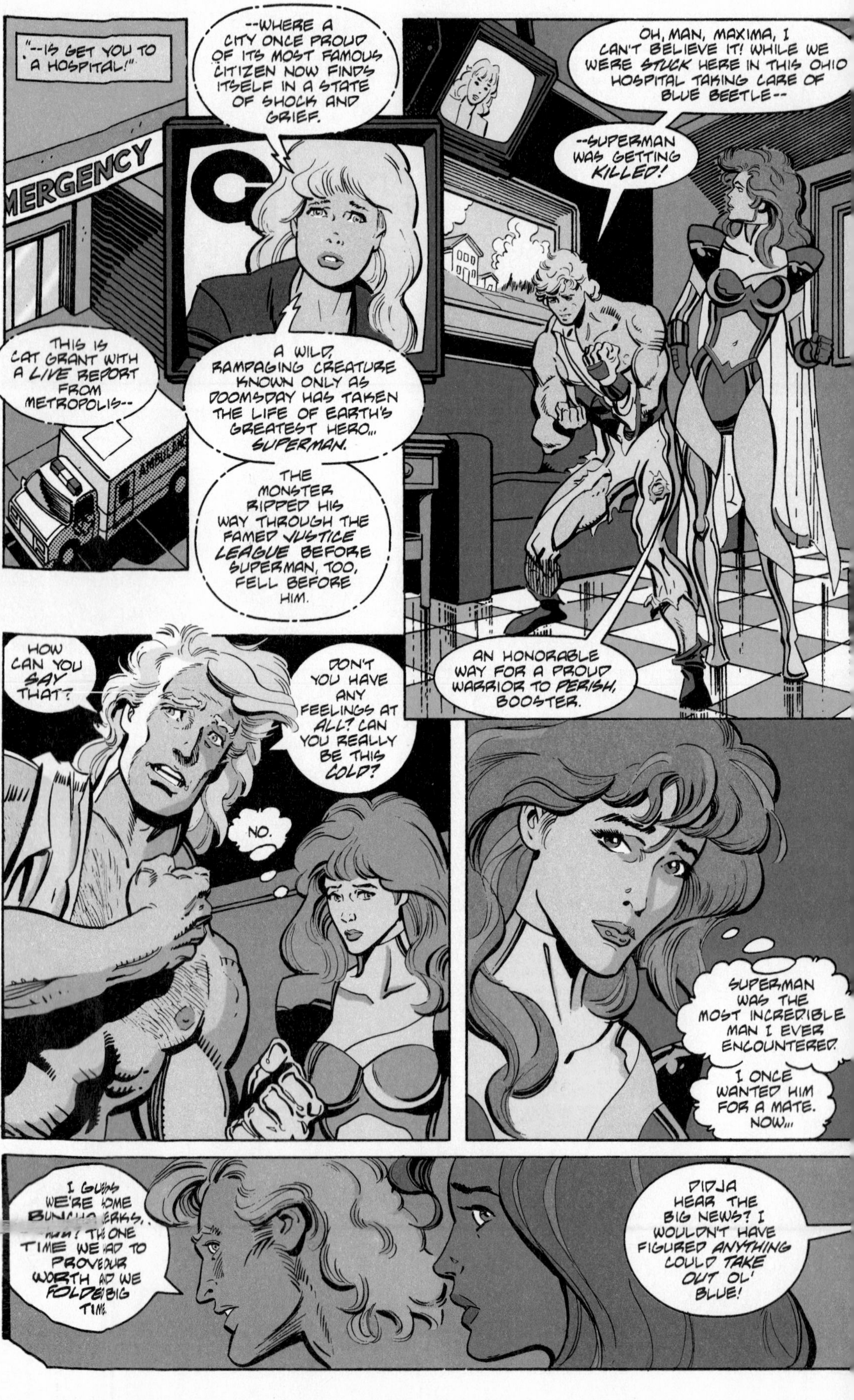
"--IS GET YOU TO A HOSPITAL!"
--WHERE A CITY ONCE PROUD OF ITS MOST FAMOUS CITIZEN NOW FINDS ITSELF IN A STATE OF SHOCK AND GRIEF.
EMERGENCY
THIS IS CAT GRANT WITH A *LIVE* REPORT FROM METROPOLIS--
A WILD, RAMPAGING CREATURE KNOWN ONLY AS DOOMSDAY HAS TAKEN THE LIFE OF EARTH'S GREATEST HERO... *SUPERMAN.*
THE MONSTER RIPPED HIS WAY THROUGH THE FAMED *JUSTICE LEAGUE* BEFORE SUPERMAN, TOO, FELL BEFORE HIM.
OH, MAN, MAXIMA, I CAN'T BELIEVE IT! WHILE WE WERE *STUCK* HERE IN THIS OHIO HOSPITAL TAKING CARE OF BLUE BEETLE--
--SUPERMAN WAS GETTING *KILLED!*
AN HONORABLE WAY FOR A PROUD WARRIOR TO *PERISH,* BOOSTER.
HOW CAN YOU *SAY* THAT?
DON'T YOU HAVE ANY FEELINGS AT *ALL?* CAN YOU REALLY BE THIS *COLD?*
NO.
SUPERMAN WAS THE MOST INCREDIBLE MAN I EVER ENCOUNTERED.
I ONCE WANTED HIM FOR A MATE. NOW...
I GUESS WE'RE SOME
THE ONE TIME WE HAD TO PROVE OUR WORTH AND WE *FOLDED* BIG TIME.
DIDJA HEAR THE BIG NEWS? I WOULDN'T HAVE FIGURED *ANYTHING* COULD *TAKE OUT* OL' BLUE!

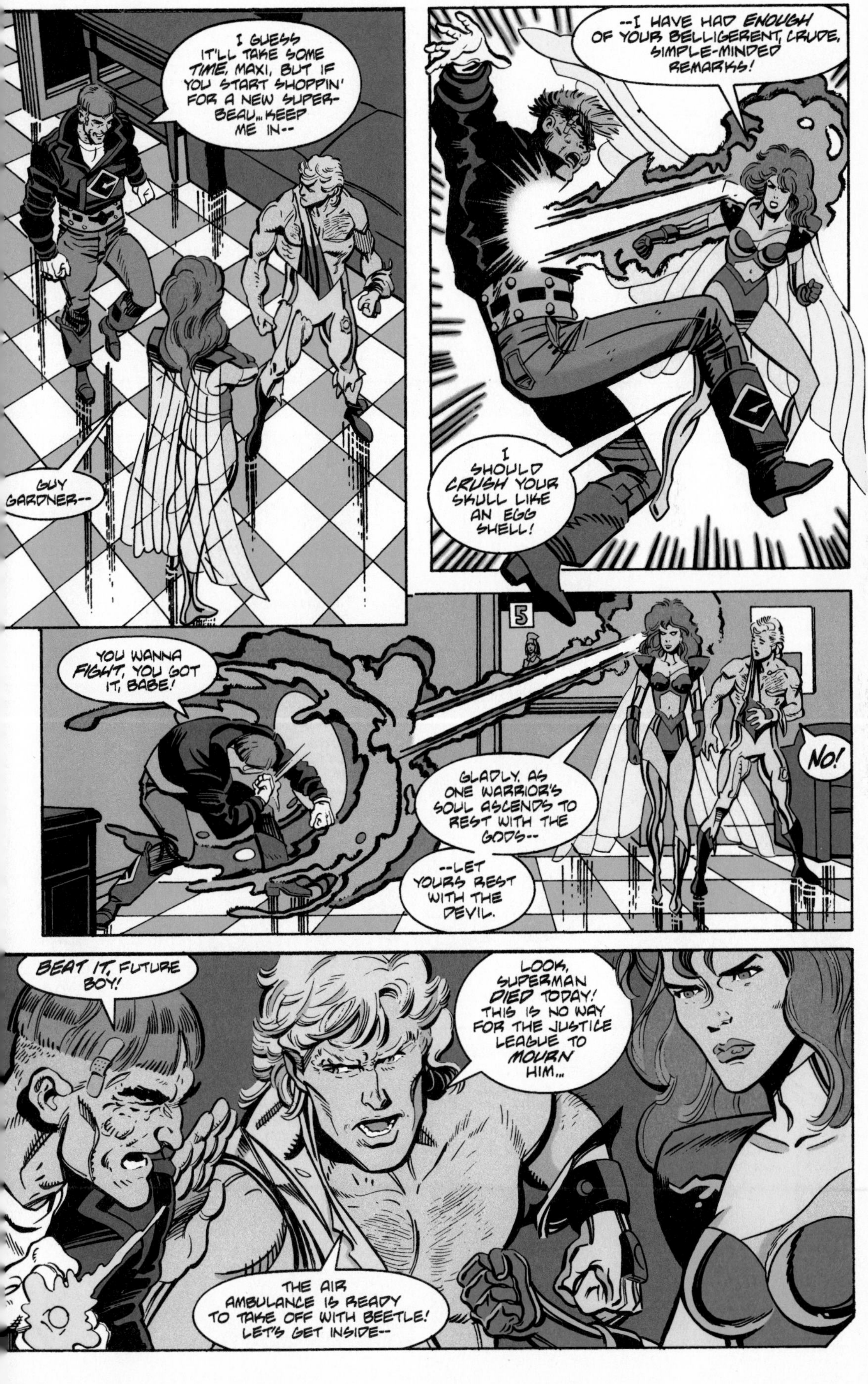
I GUESS IT'LL TAKE SOME TIME, MAXI, BUT IF YOU START SHOPPIN' FOR A NEW SUPER-BEAU... KEEP ME IN--
GUY GARDNER--
--I HAVE HAD ENOUGH OF YOUR BELLIGERENT, CRUDE, SIMPLE-MINDED REMARKS!
I SHOULD CRUSH YOUR SKULL LIKE AN EGG SHELL!
YOU WANNA FIGHT, YOU GOT IT, BABE!
GLADLY. AS ONE WARRIOR'S SOUL ASCENDS TO REST WITH THE GODS--
--LET YOURS REST WITH THE DEVIL.
NO!
BEAT IT, FUTURE BOY!
LOOK, SUPERMAN DIED TODAY! THIS IS NO WAY FOR THE JUSTICE LEAGUE TO MOURN HIM...
THE AIR AMBULANCE IS READY TO TAKE OFF WITH BEETLE! LET'S GET INSIDE--

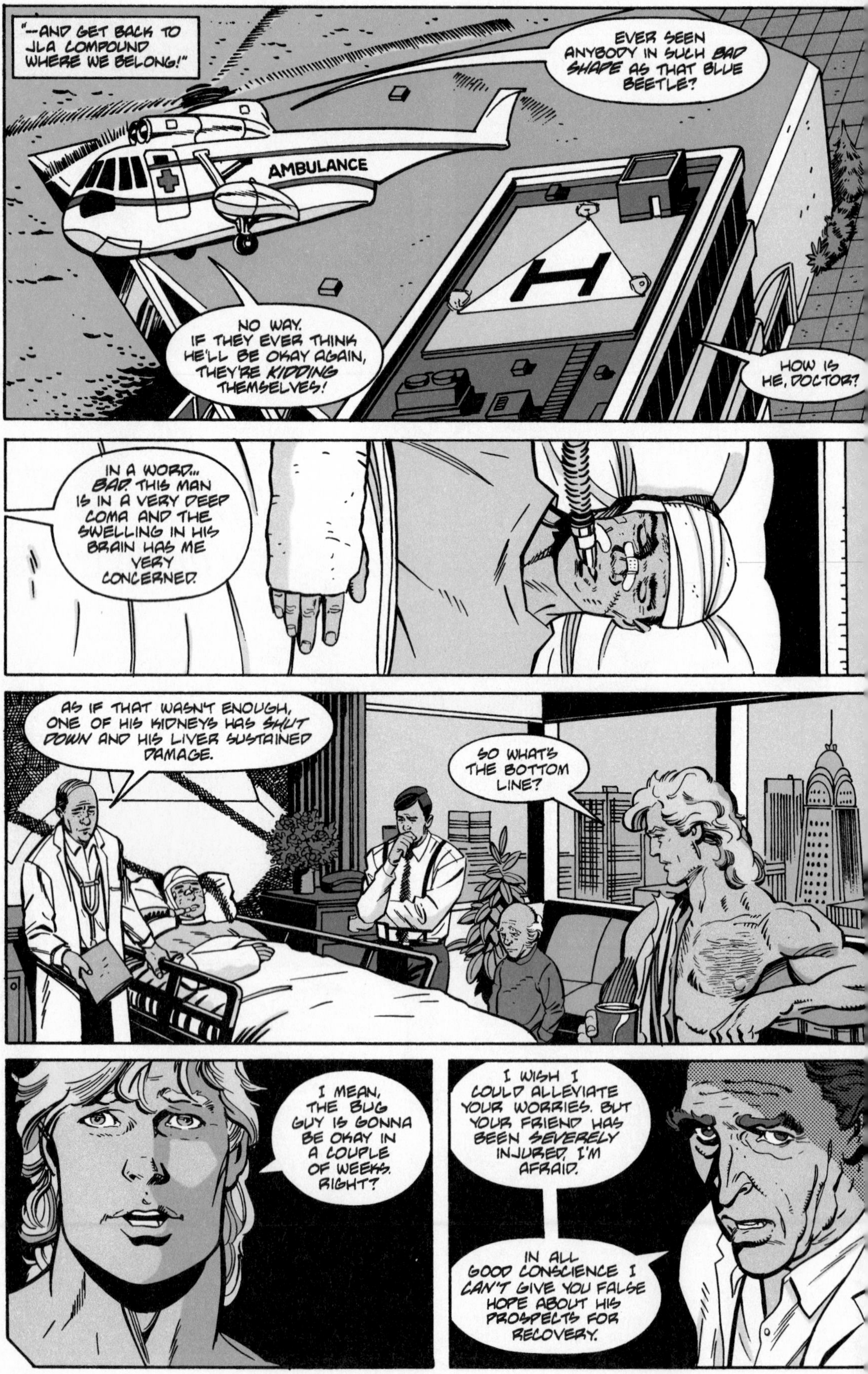
"--AND GET BACK TO JLA COMPOUND WHERE WE BELONG!"
EVER SEEN ANYBODY IN SUCH BAD SHAPE AS THAT BLUE BEETLE?
AMBULANCE
NO WAY. IF THEY EVER THINK HE'LL BE OKAY AGAIN, THEY'RE KIDDING THEMSELVES!
HOW IS HE, DOCTOR?
IN A WORD... BAD. THIS MAN IS IN A VERY DEEP COMA AND THE SWELLING IN HIS BRAIN HAS ME VERY CONCERNED.
AS IF THAT WASN'T ENOUGH, ONE OF HIS KIDNEYS HAS SHUT DOWN AND HIS LIVER SUSTAINED DAMAGE.
SO WHAT'S THE BOTTOM LINE?
I MEAN, THE BUG GUY IS GONNA BE OKAY IN A COUPLE OF WEEKS. RIGHT?
I WISH I COULD ALLEVIATE YOUR WORRIES. BUT YOUR FRIEND HAS BEEN SEVERELY INJURED, I'M AFRAID.
IN ALL GOOD CONSCIENCE I CAN'T GIVE YOU FALSE HOPE ABOUT HIS PROSPECTS FOR RECOVERY.

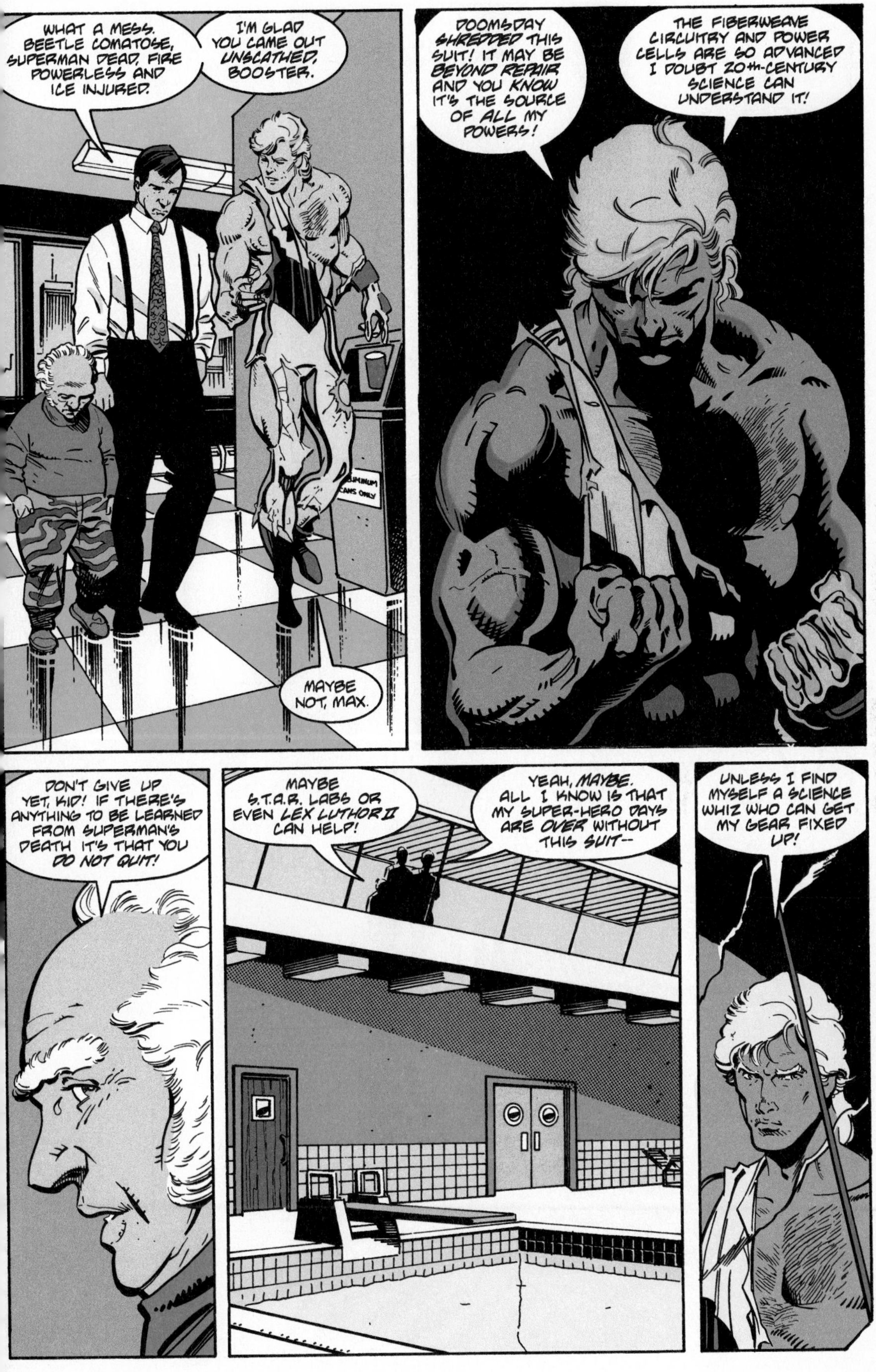
WHAT A MESS. BEETLE COMATOSE, SUPERMAN DEAD, FIRE POWERLESS AND ICE INJURED.
I'M GLAD YOU CAME OUT UNSCATHED, BOOSTER.
MAYBE NOT, MAX.
DOOMSDAY SHREDDED THIS SUIT! IT MAY BE BEYOND REPAIR AND YOU KNOW IT'S THE SOURCE OF ALL MY POWERS!
THE FIBERWEAVE CIRCUITRY AND POWER CELLS ARE SO ADVANCED I DOUBT 20th-CENTURY SCIENCE CAN UNDERSTAND IT!
DON'T GIVE UP YET, KID! IF THERE'S ANYTHING TO BE LEARNED FROM SUPERMAN'S DEATH IT'S THAT YOU DO NOT QUIT!
MAYBE S.T.A.R. LABS OR EVEN LEX LUTHOR II CAN HELP!
YEAH, MAYBE. ALL I KNOW IS THAT MY SUPER-HERO DAYS ARE OVER WITHOUT THIS SUIT--
UNLESS I FIND MYSELF A SCIENCE WHIZ WHO CAN GET MY GEAR FIXED UP!

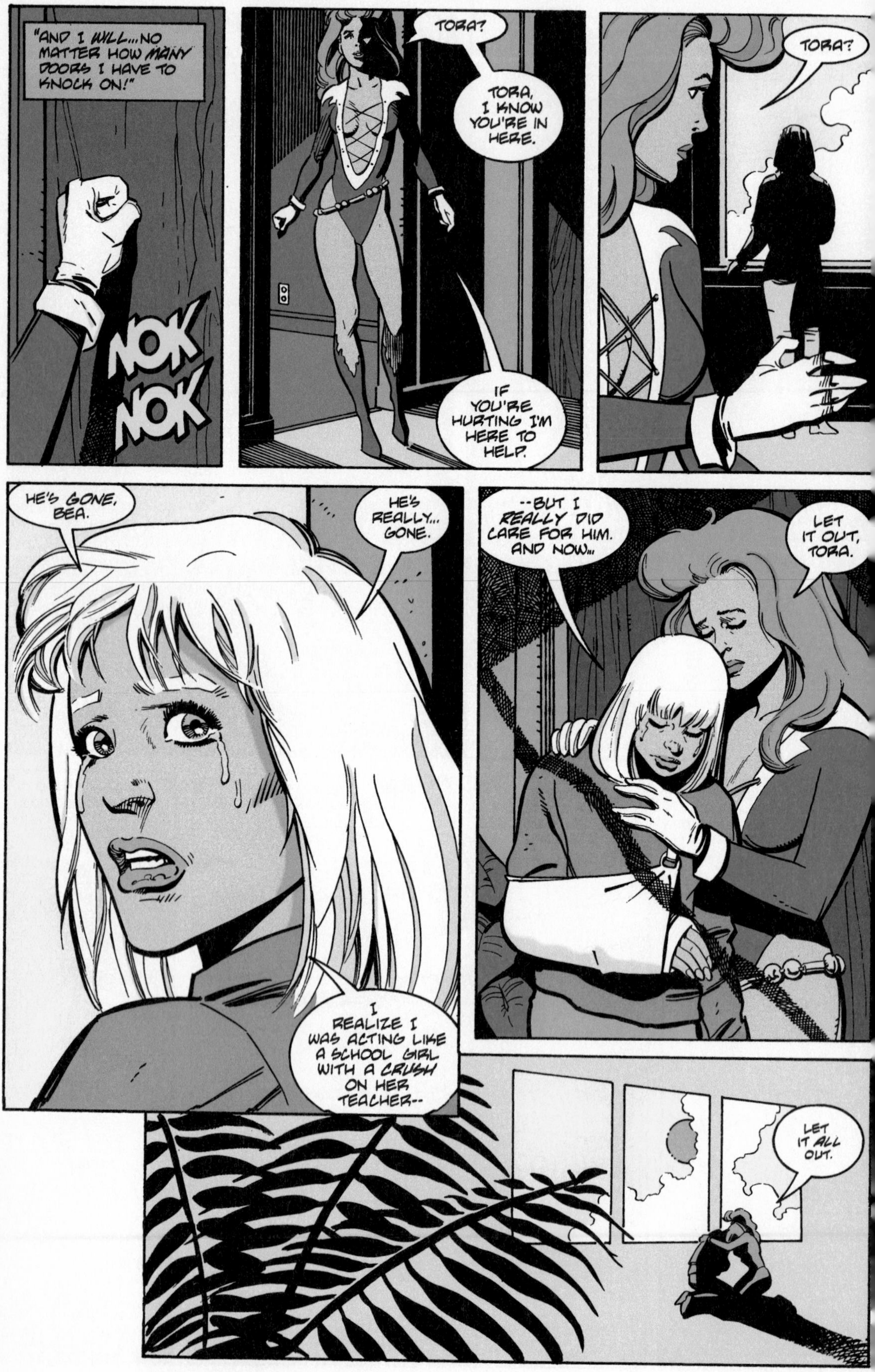
"AND I WILL...NO MATTER HOW MANY DOORS I HAVE TO KNOCK ON!"
NOK NOK
TORA?
TORA, I KNOW YOU'RE IN HERE.
IF YOU'RE HURTING I'M HERE TO HELP.
TORA?
HE'S GONE, BEA.
HE'S REALLY... GONE.
I REALIZE I WAS ACTING LIKE A SCHOOL GIRL WITH A CRUSH ON HER TEACHER--
--BUT I REALLY DID CARE FOR HIM. AND NOW...
LET IT OUT, TORA.
LET IT ALL OUT.

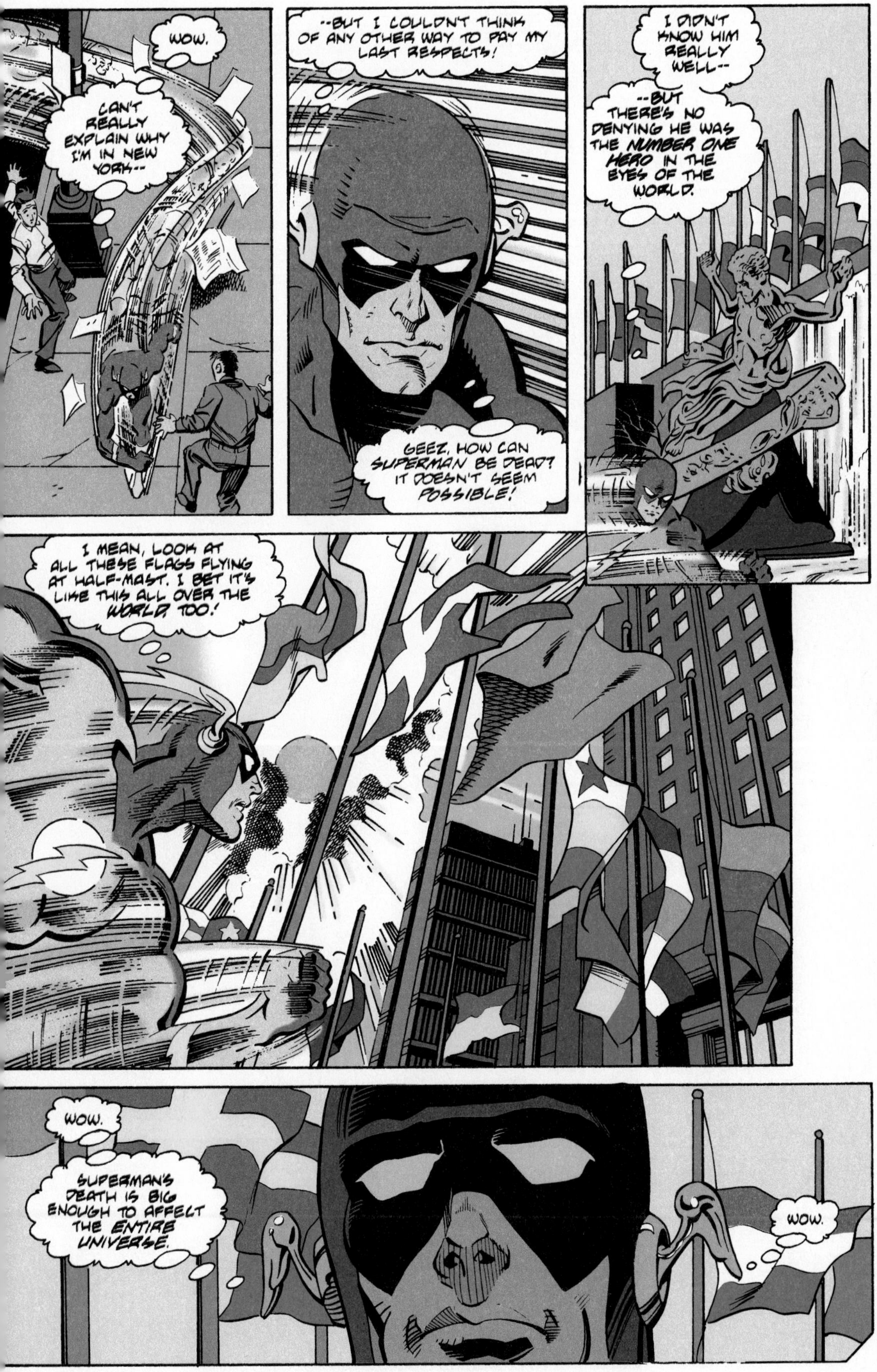
WOW.
CAN'T REALLY EXPLAIN WHY I'M IN NEW YORK--
--BUT I COULDN'T THINK OF ANY OTHER WAY TO PAY MY LAST RESPECTS!
GEEZ, HOW CAN SUPERMAN BE DEAD? IT DOESN'T SEEM POSSIBLE!
I DIDN'T KNOW HIM REALLY WELL--
--BUT THERE'S NO DENYING HE WAS THE NUMBER ONE HERO IN THE EYES OF THE WORLD.
I MEAN, LOOK AT ALL THESE FLAGS FLYING AT HALF-MAST. I BET IT'S LIKE THIS ALL OVER THE WORLD, TOO!
WOW.
SUPERMAN'S DEATH IS BIG ENOUGH TO AFFECT THE ENTIRE UNIVERSE.
WOW.

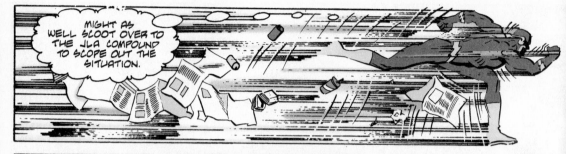

MIGHT AS WELL SCOOT OVER TO THE JLA COMPOUND TO SCOPE OUT THE SITUATION.

IF THERE'S ANY KIND OF MEMORIAL SERVICE I DEFINITELY WANT TO BE A PART OF IT.

FIRST UNCLE BARRY AND NOW SUPERMAN.

WHAT'S THE WORLD COMING TO?

YO, BOOSTEROO! YOU LOSE A FIGHT WITH A TIGER OR SOMETHING?

A TIGER NAMED DOOMSDAY, FLASH.

WHAT'S THIS? YOU ALWAYS CARRY ALONG YOUR OWN TRASH?

SORRY. SOMETIMES MY SPEED CREATES SUCH A VORTEX--

--THAT I TEND TO PICK THINGS UP AS I GO.

TELL ME WHAT HAPPENED, MAN. WAS DOOMSDAY REALLY THAT TOUGH?

IT WAS... A WAR.

STRAIGHT-UP, FLAT-OUT, TAKE-NO-PRISONERS WAR.

JEEZ.

NO LIE. AND I'M LEFT FEELING LIKE A TOTAL WASH-OUT!

WE'RE THE JUSTICE LEAGUE, WALLY! WE'RE SUPPOSED TO BEAT THREATS LIKE DOOMSDAY!

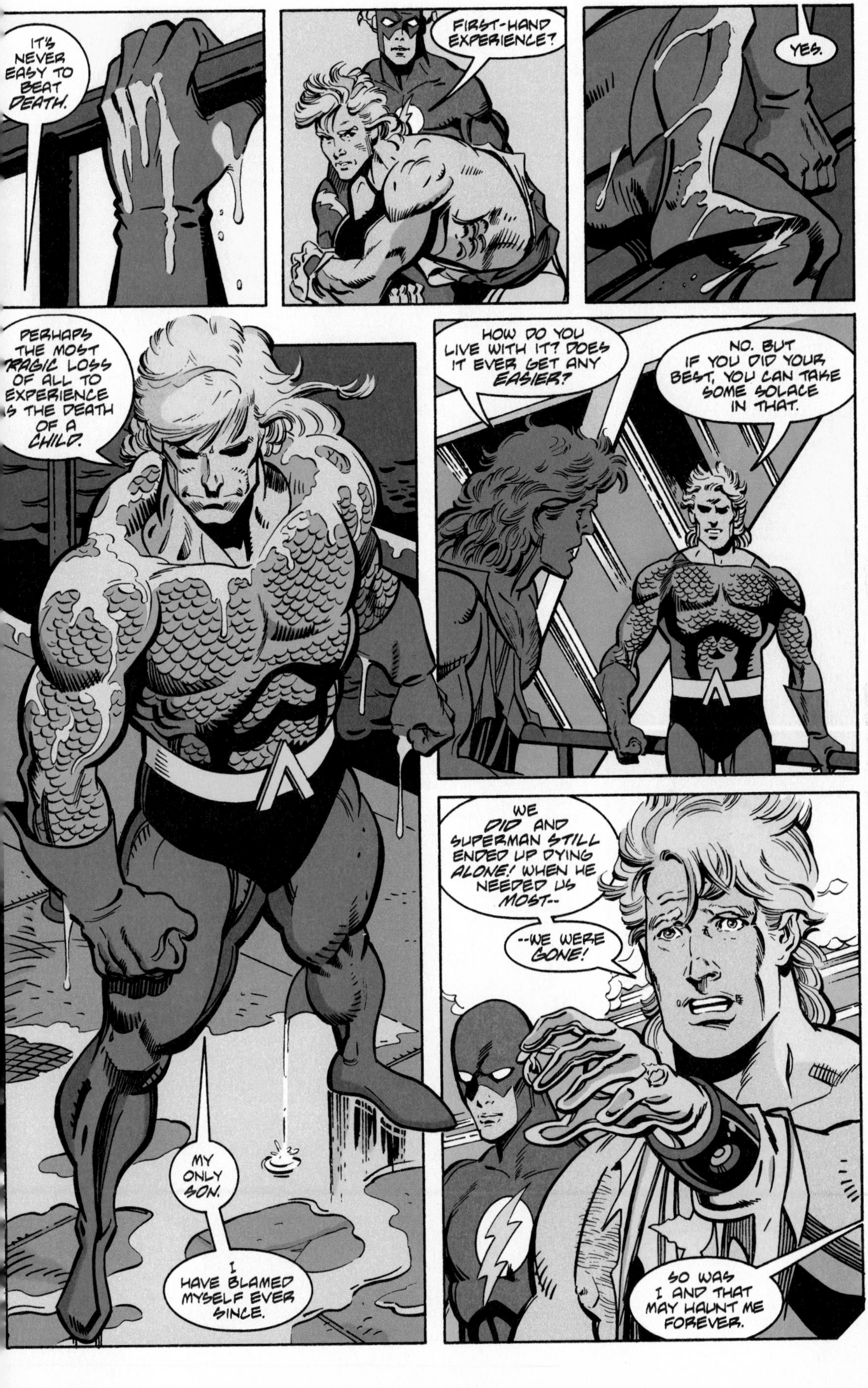
IT'S NEVER EASY TO BEAT DEATH.
FIRST-HAND EXPERIENCE?
YES.
PERHAPS THE MOST RAGIC LOSS OF ALL TO EXPERIENCE S THE DEATH OF A CHILD.
MY ONLY SON.
I HAVE BLAMED MYSELF EVER SINCE.
HOW DO YOU LIVE WITH IT? DOES IT EVER GET ANY EASIER?
NO. BUT IF YOU DID YOUR BEST, YOU CAN TAKE SOME SOLACE IN THAT.
WE DID AND SUPERMAN STILL ENDED UP DYING ALONE! WHEN HE NEEDED US MOST--
--WE WERE GONE!
SO WAS I AND THAT MAY HAUNT ME FOREVER.

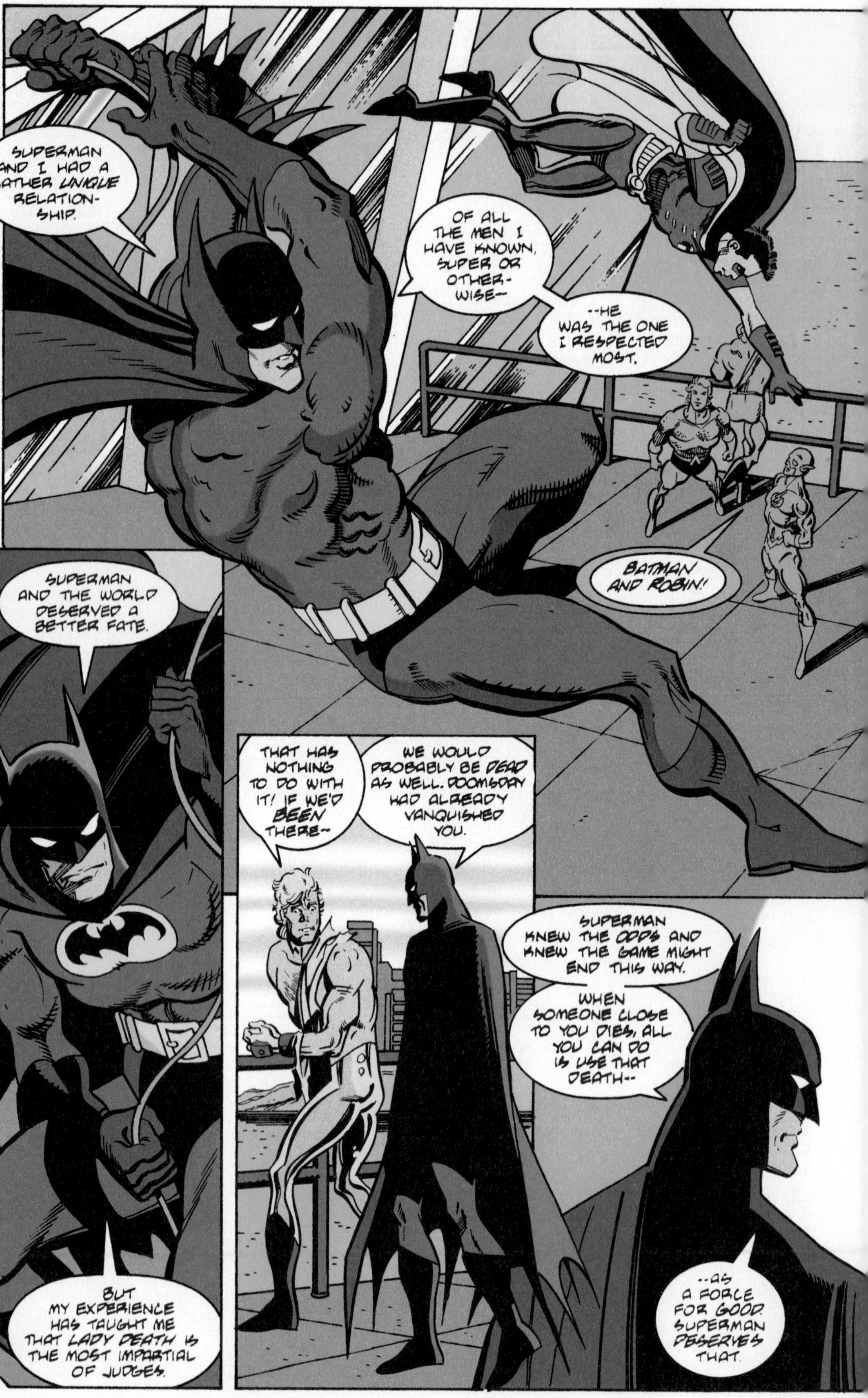
SUPERMAN AND I HAD A RATHER UNIQUE RELATION-SHIP.
OF ALL THE MEN I HAVE KNOWN, SUPER OR OTHER-WISE--
--HE WAS THE ONE I RESPECTED MOST.
BATMAN AND ROBIN!
SUPERMAN AND THE WORLD DESERVED A BETTER FATE.
BUT MY EXPERIENCE HAS TAUGHT ME THAT LADY DEATH IS THE MOST IMPARTIAL OF JUDGES.
THAT HAS NOTHING TO DO WITH IT! IF WE'D BEEN THERE--
WE WOULD PROBABLY BE DEAD AS WELL. DOOMSDAY HAD ALREADY VANQUISHED YOU.
SUPERMAN KNEW THE ODDS AND KNEW THE GAME MIGHT END THIS WAY.
WHEN SOMEONE CLOSE TO YOU DIES, ALL YOU CAN DO IS USE THAT DEATH--
--AS A FORCE FOR GOOD. SUPERMAN DESERVES THAT.

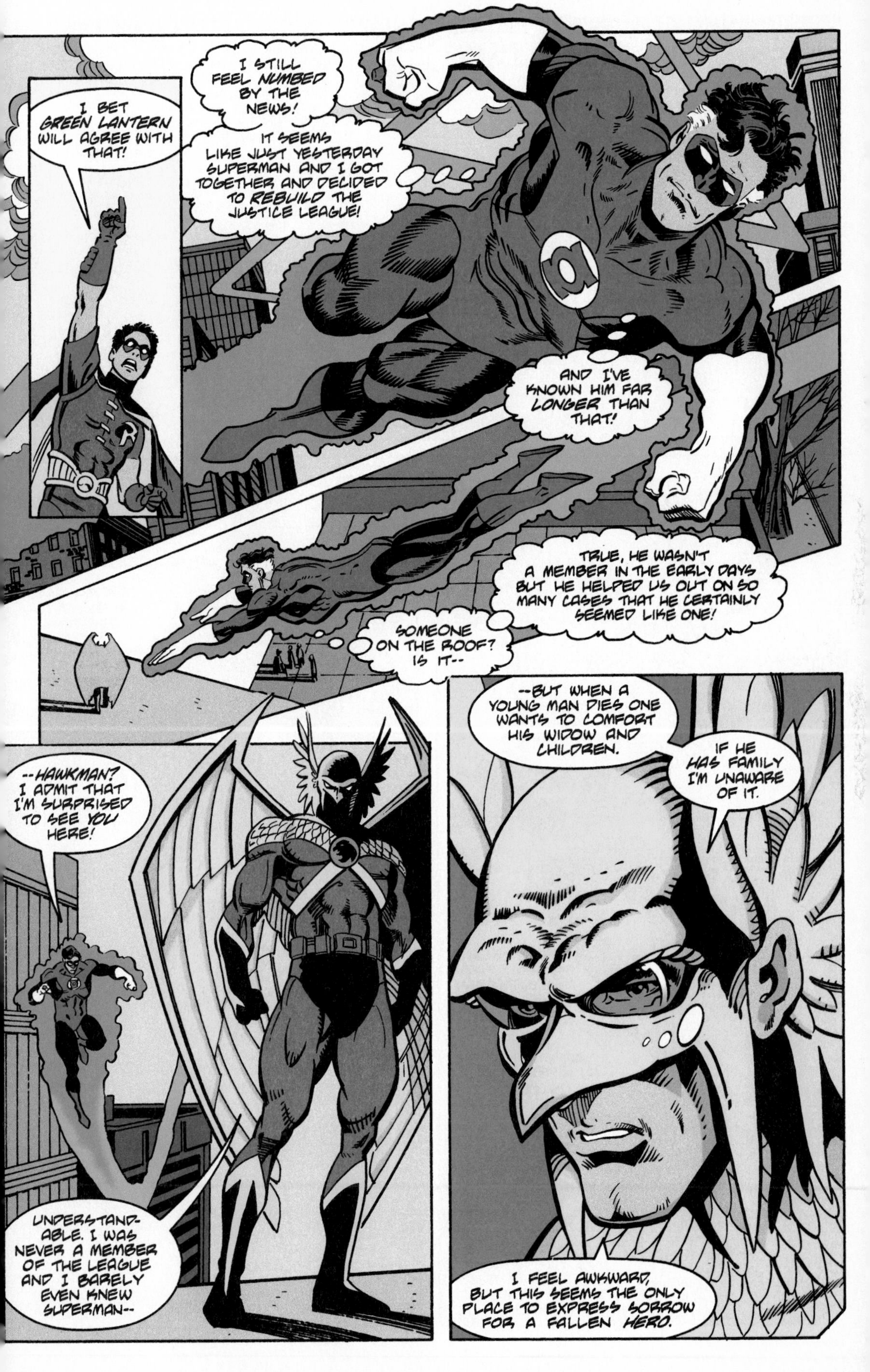
I BET GREEN LANTERN WILL AGREE WITH THAT!
I STILL FEEL NUMBED BY THE NEWS!
IT SEEMS LIKE JUST YESTERDAY SUPERMAN AND I GOT TOGETHER AND DECIDED TO REBUILD THE JUSTICE LEAGUE!
AND I'VE KNOWN HIM FAR LONGER THAN THAT!
TRUE, HE WASN'T A MEMBER IN THE EARLY DAYS BUT HE HELPED US OUT ON SO MANY CASES THAT HE CERTAINLY SEEMED LIKE ONE!
SOMEONE ON THE ROOF? IS IT--
--HAWKMAN? I ADMIT THAT I'M SURPRISED TO SEE YOU HERE!
UNDERSTAND-ABLE. I WAS NEVER A MEMBER OF THE LEAGUE AND I BARELY EVEN KNEW SUPERMAN--
--BUT WHEN A YOUNG MAN DIES ONE WANTS TO COMFORT HIS WIDOW AND CHILDREN.
IF HE HAS FAMILY I'M UNAWARE OF IT.
I FEEL AWKWARD, BUT THIS SEEMS THE ONLY PLACE TO EXPRESS SORROW FOR A FALLEN HERO.

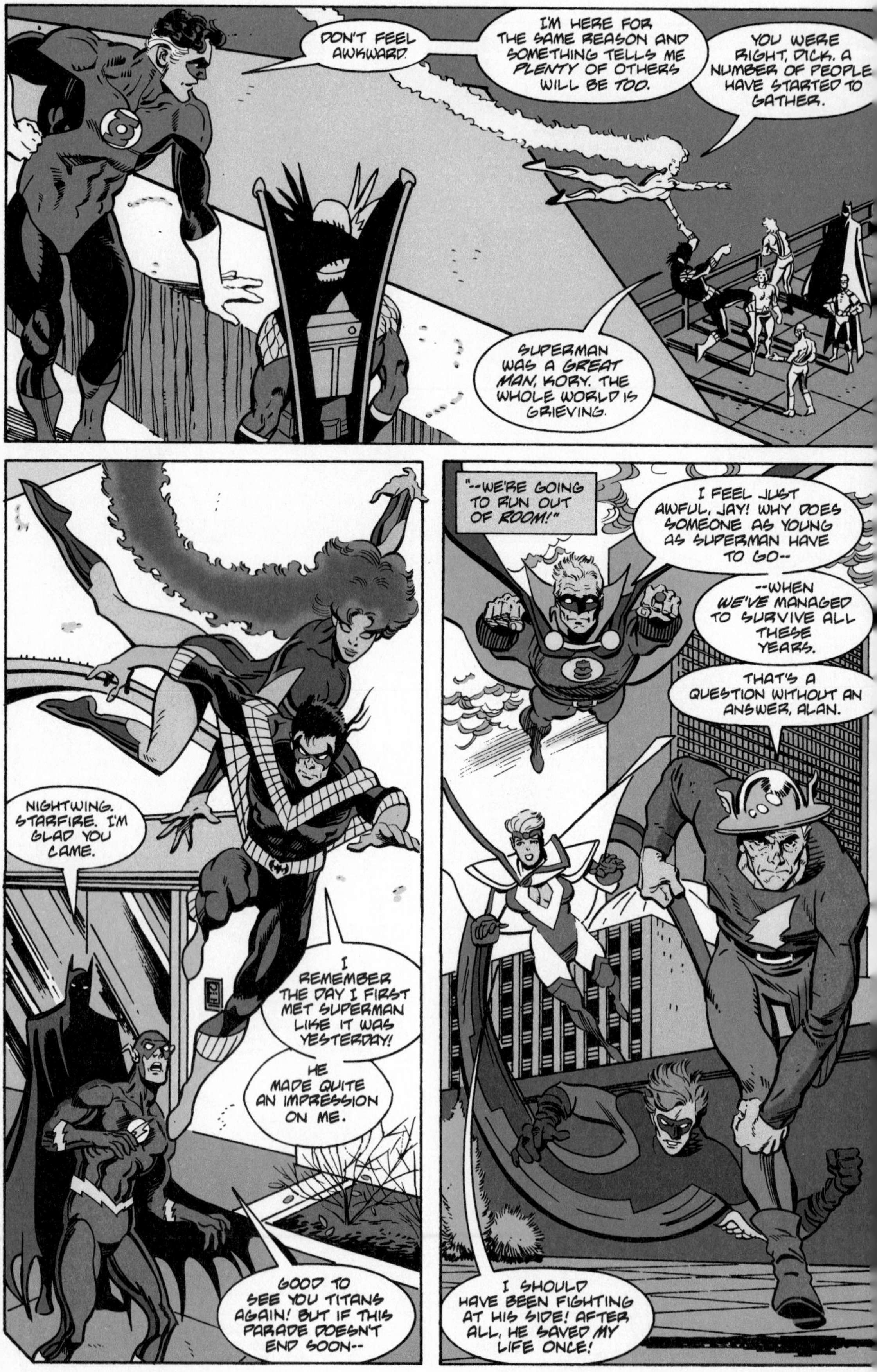
DON'T FEEL AWKWARD.
I'M HERE FOR THE SAME REASON AND SOMETHING TELLS ME PLENTY OF OTHERS WILL BE TOO.
YOU WERE RIGHT, DICK. A NUMBER OF PEOPLE HAVE STARTED TO GATHER.
SUPERMAN WAS A GREAT MAN, KORY. THE WHOLE WORLD IS GRIEVING.
NIGHTWING. STARFIRE. I'M GLAD YOU CAME.
I REMEMBER THE DAY I FIRST MET SUPERMAN LIKE IT WAS YESTERDAY!
HE MADE QUITE AN IMPRESSION ON ME.
GOOD TO SEE YOU TITANS AGAIN! BUT IF THIS PARADE DOESN'T END SOON--
"--WE'RE GOING TO RUN OUT OF ROOM!"
I FEEL JUST AWFUL, JAY! WHY DOES SOMEONE AS YOUNG AS SUPERMAN HAVE TO GO--
--WHEN WE'VE MANAGED TO SURVIVE ALL THESE YEARS.
THAT'S A QUESTION WITHOUT AN ANSWER, ALAN.
I SHOULD HAVE BEEN FIGHTING AT HIS SIDE! AFTER ALL, HE SAVED MY LIFE ONCE!

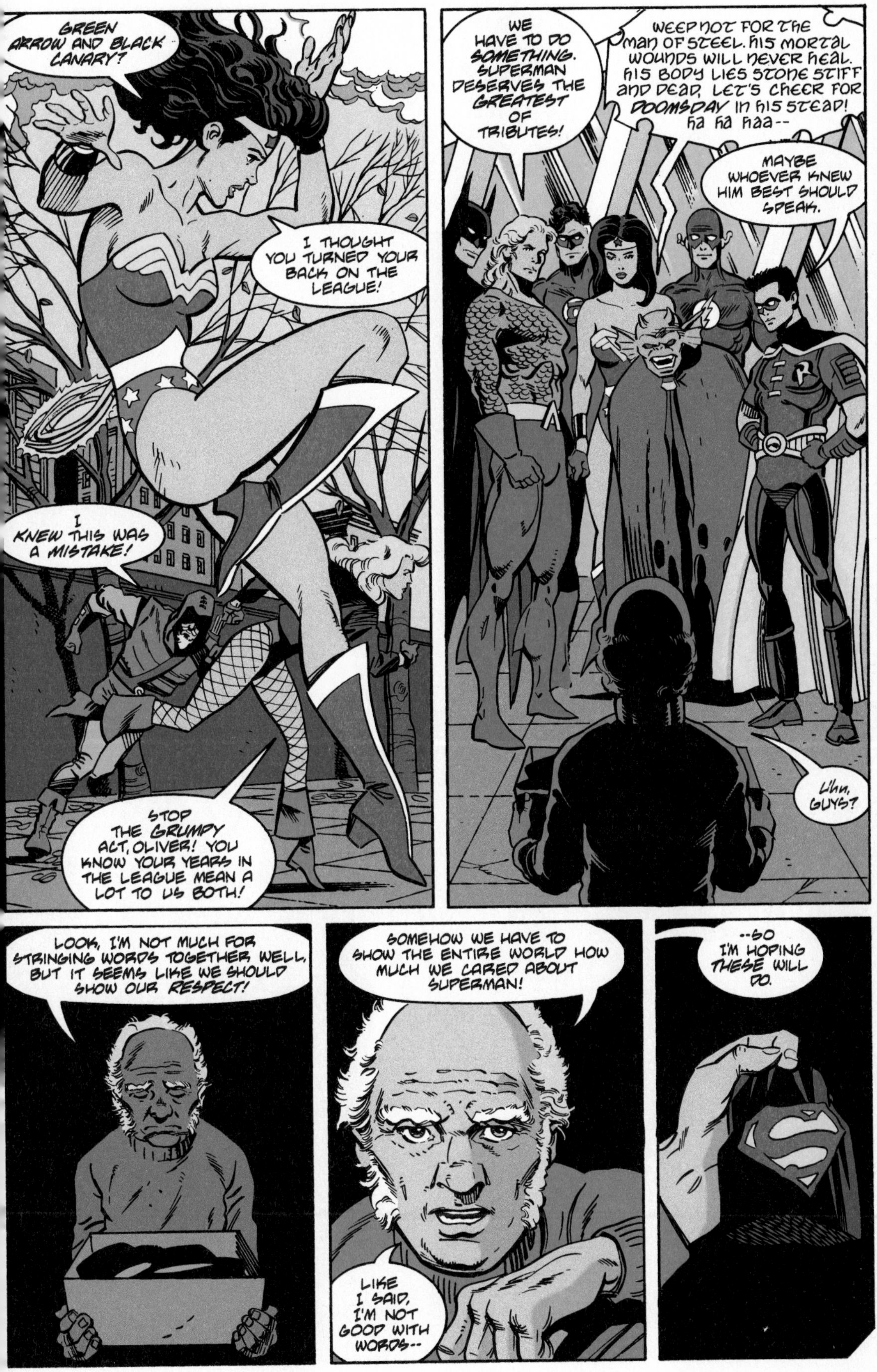
GREEN ARROW AND BLACK CANARY?
I THOUGHT YOU TURNED YOUR BACK ON THE LEAGUE!
I KNEW THIS WAS A MISTAKE!
STOP THE GRUMPY ACT, OLIVER! YOU KNOW YOUR YEARS IN THE LEAGUE MEAN A LOT TO US BOTH!
WE HAVE TO DO SOMETHING. SUPERMAN DESERVES THE GREATEST OF TRIBUTES!
WEEP NOT FOR THE MAN OF STEEL. HIS MORTAL WOUNDS WILL NEVER HEAL. HIS BODY LIES STONE STIFF AND DEAD, LET'S CHEER FOR DOOMSDAY IN HIS STEAD! HA HA HAA--
MAYBE WHOEVER KNEW HIM BEST SHOULD SPEAK.
UHN, GUYS?
LOOK, I'M NOT MUCH FOR STRINGING WORDS TOGETHER WELL, BUT IT SEEMS LIKE WE SHOULD SHOW OUR RESPECT!
SOMEHOW WE HAVE TO SHOW THE ENTIRE WORLD HOW MUCH WE CARED ABOUT SUPERMAN!
LIKE I SAID, I'M NOT GOOD WITH WORDS--
--SO I'M HOPING THESE WILL DO.

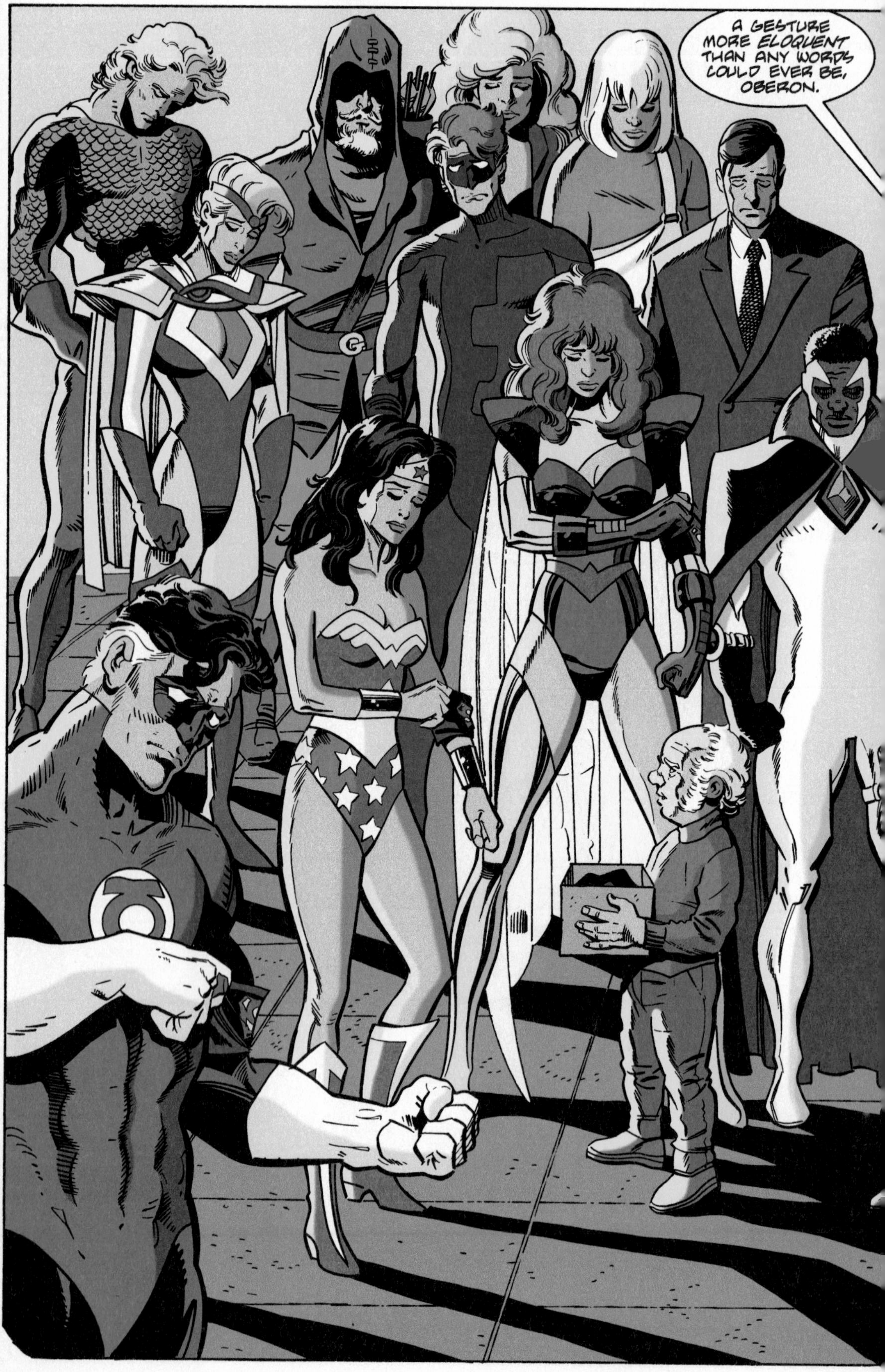
A GESTURE MORE ELOQUENT THAN ANY WORDS COULD EVER BE, OBERON.

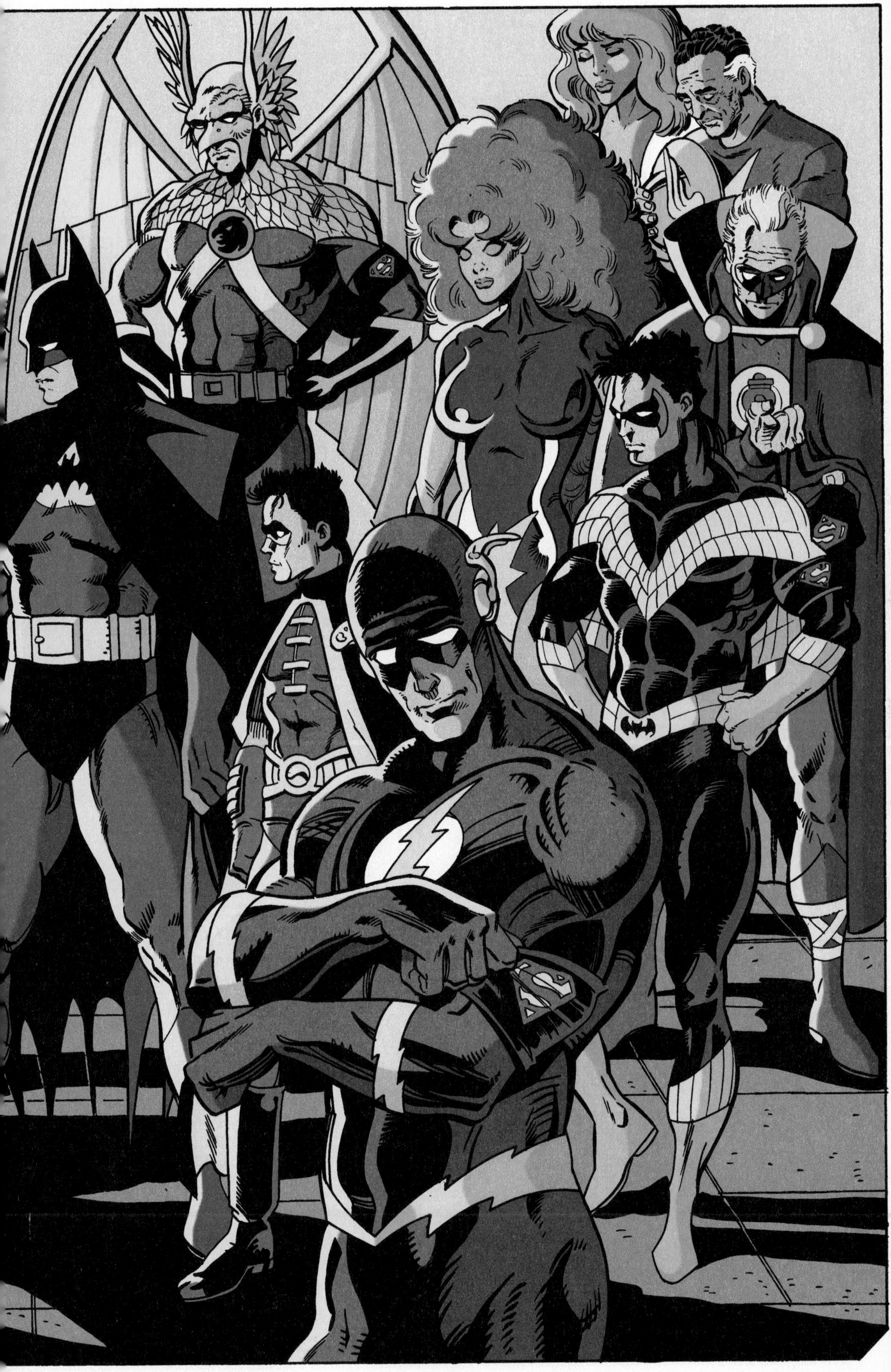

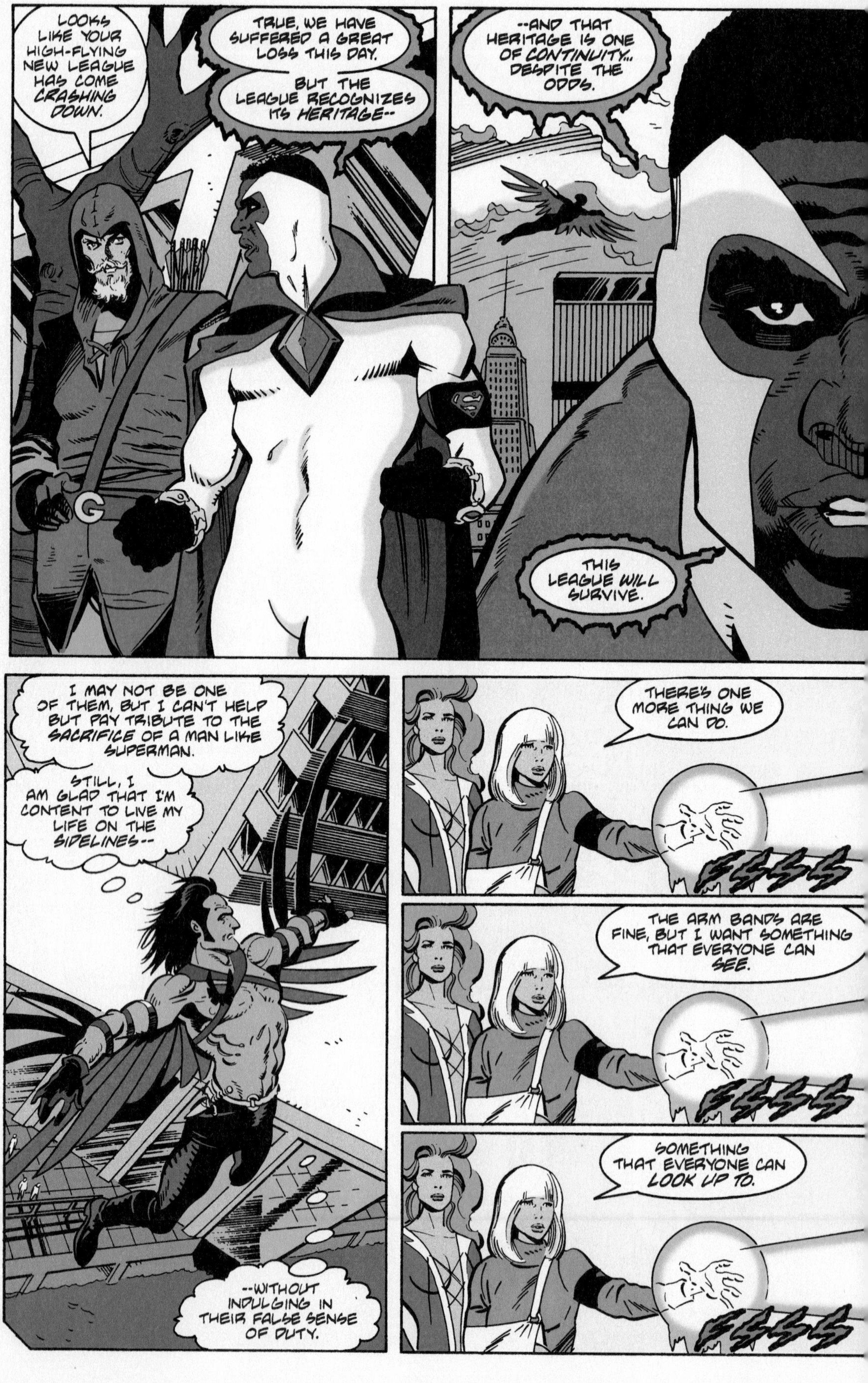
LOOKS LIKE YOUR HIGH-FLYING NEW LEAGUE HAS COME CRASHING DOWN.
TRUE, WE HAVE SUFFERED A GREAT LOSS THIS DAY.
BUT THE LEAGUE RECOGNIZES ITS HERITAGE--
--AND THAT HERITAGE IS ONE OF CONTINUITY... DESPITE THE ODDS.
THIS LEAGUE WILL SURVIVE.
I MAY NOT BE ONE OF THEM, BUT I CAN'T HELP BUT PAY TRIBUTE TO THE SACRIFICE OF A MAN LIKE SUPERMAN.
STILL, I AM GLAD THAT I'M CONTENT TO LIVE MY LIFE ON THE SIDELINES--
--WITHOUT INDULGING IN THEIR FALSE SENSE OF DUTY.
THERE'S ONE MORE THING WE CAN DO.
FSSSS
THE ARM BANDS ARE FINE, BUT I WANT SOMETHING THAT EVERYONE CAN SEE.
FSSSS
SOMETHING THAT EVERYONE CAN LOOK UP TO.
FSSSS

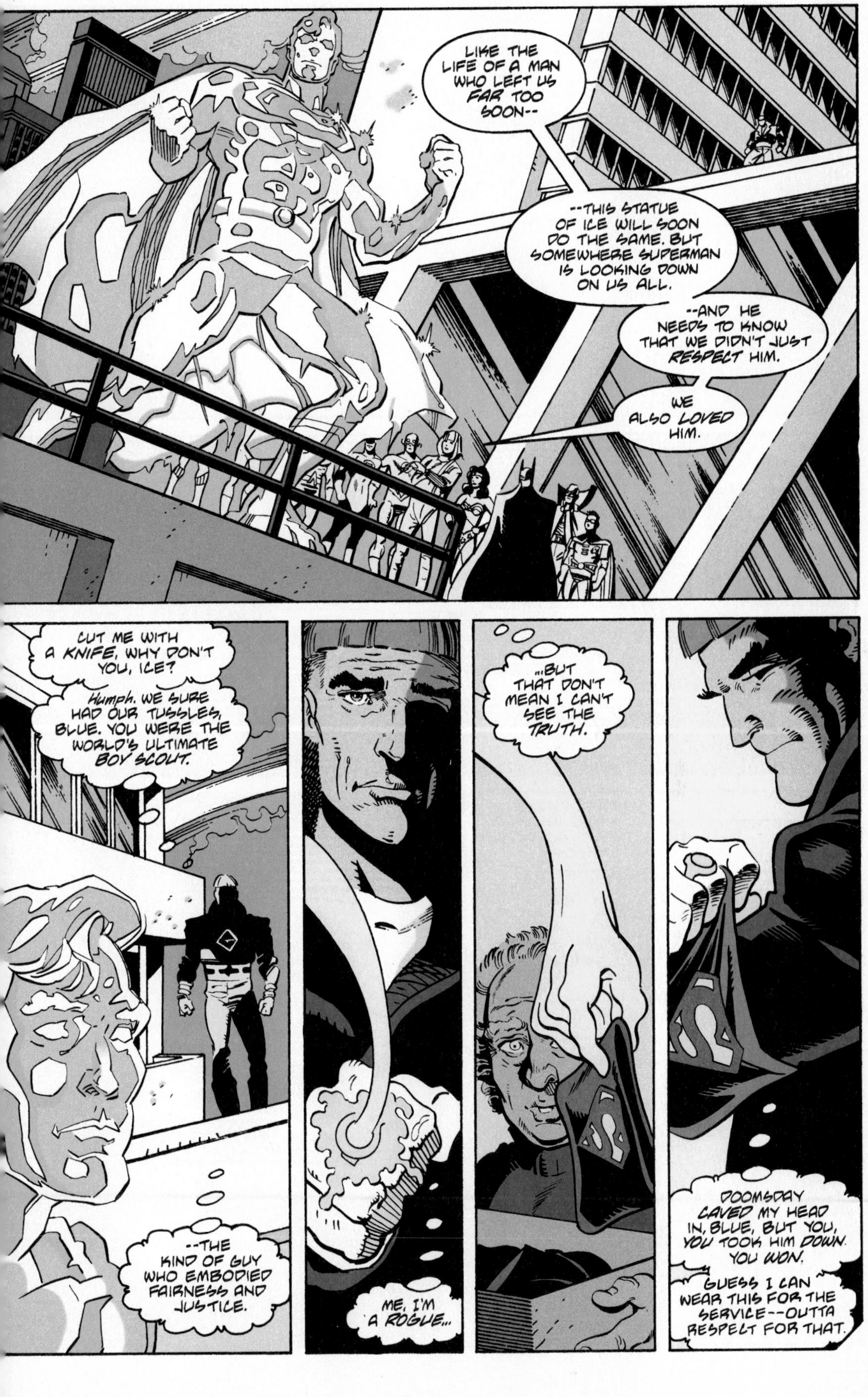
LIKE THE LIFE OF A MAN WHO LEFT US FAR TOO SOON--
--THIS STATUE OF ICE WILL SOON DO THE SAME. BUT SOMEWHERE SUPERMAN IS LOOKING DOWN ON US ALL.
--AND HE NEEDS TO KNOW THAT WE DIDN'T JUST RESPECT HIM.
WE ALSO LOVED HIM.
CUT ME WITH A KNIFE, WHY DON'T YOU, ICE?
Humph. WE SURE HAD OUR TUSSLES, BLUE. YOU WERE THE WORLD'S ULTIMATE BOY SCOUT.
--THE KIND OF GUY WHO EMBODIED FAIRNESS AND JUSTICE.
ME, I'M A ROGUE...
...BUT THAT DON'T MEAN I CAN'T SEE THE TRUTH.
DOOMSDAY CAVED MY HEAD IN, BLUE, BUT YOU, YOU TOOK HIM DOWN. YOU WON.
GUESS I CAN WEAR THIS FOR THE SERVICE--OUTTA RESPECT FOR THAT.

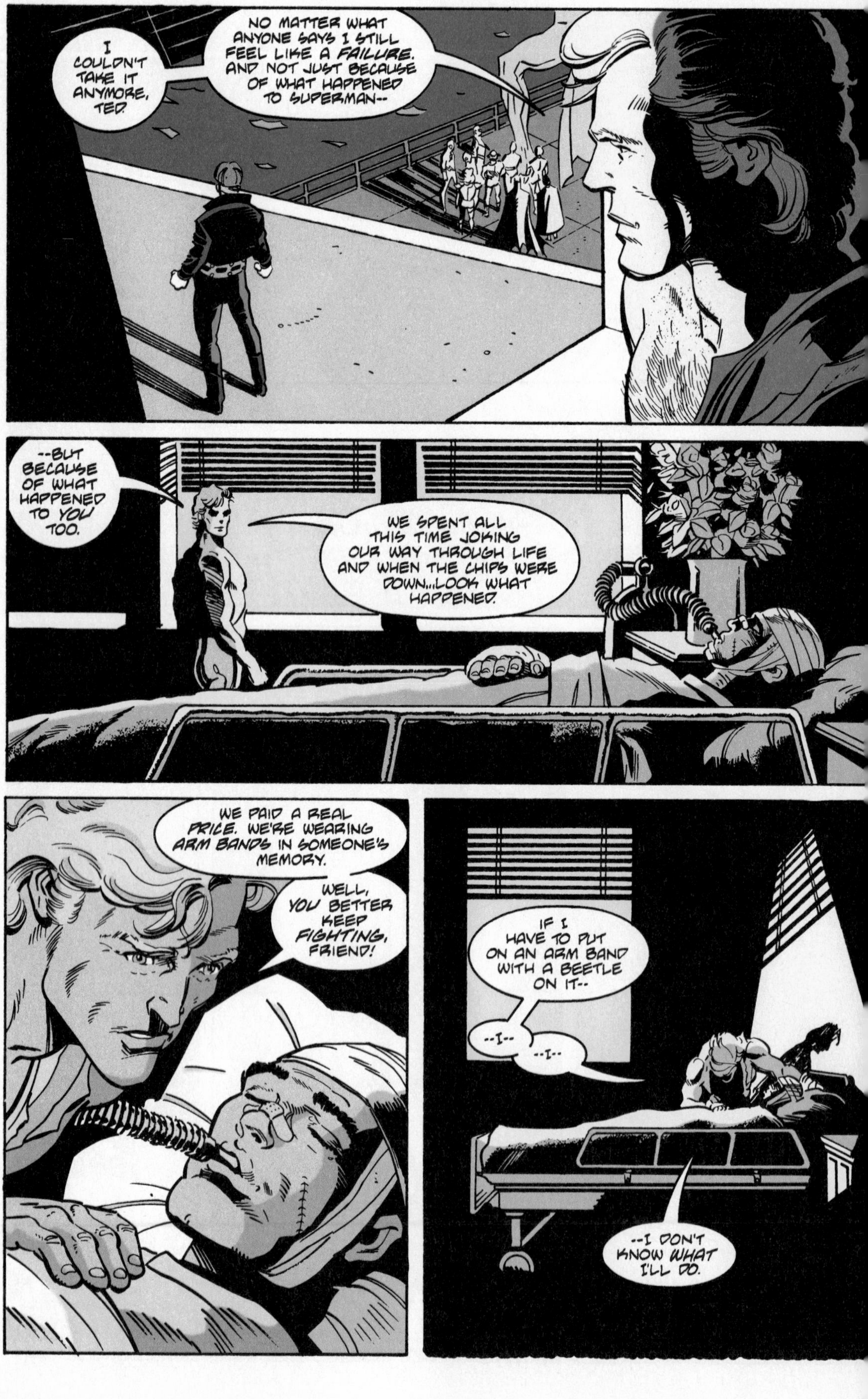
I COULDN'T TAKE IT ANYMORE, TED.
NO MATTER WHAT ANYONE SAYS I STILL FEEL LIKE A FAILURE. AND NOT JUST BECAUSE OF WHAT HAPPENED TO SUPERMAN--
--BUT BECAUSE OF WHAT HAPPENED TO YOU TOO.
WE SPENT ALL THIS TIME JOKING OUR WAY THROUGH LIFE AND WHEN THE CHIPS WERE DOWN...LOOK WHAT HAPPENED.
WE PAID A REAL PRICE. WE'RE WEARING ARM BANDS IN SOMEONE'S MEMORY.
WELL, YOU BETTER KEEP FIGHTING, FRIEND!
IF I HAVE TO PUT ON AN ARM BAND WITH A BEETLE ON IT--
--I--
--I--
--I DON'T KNOW WHAT I'LL DO.

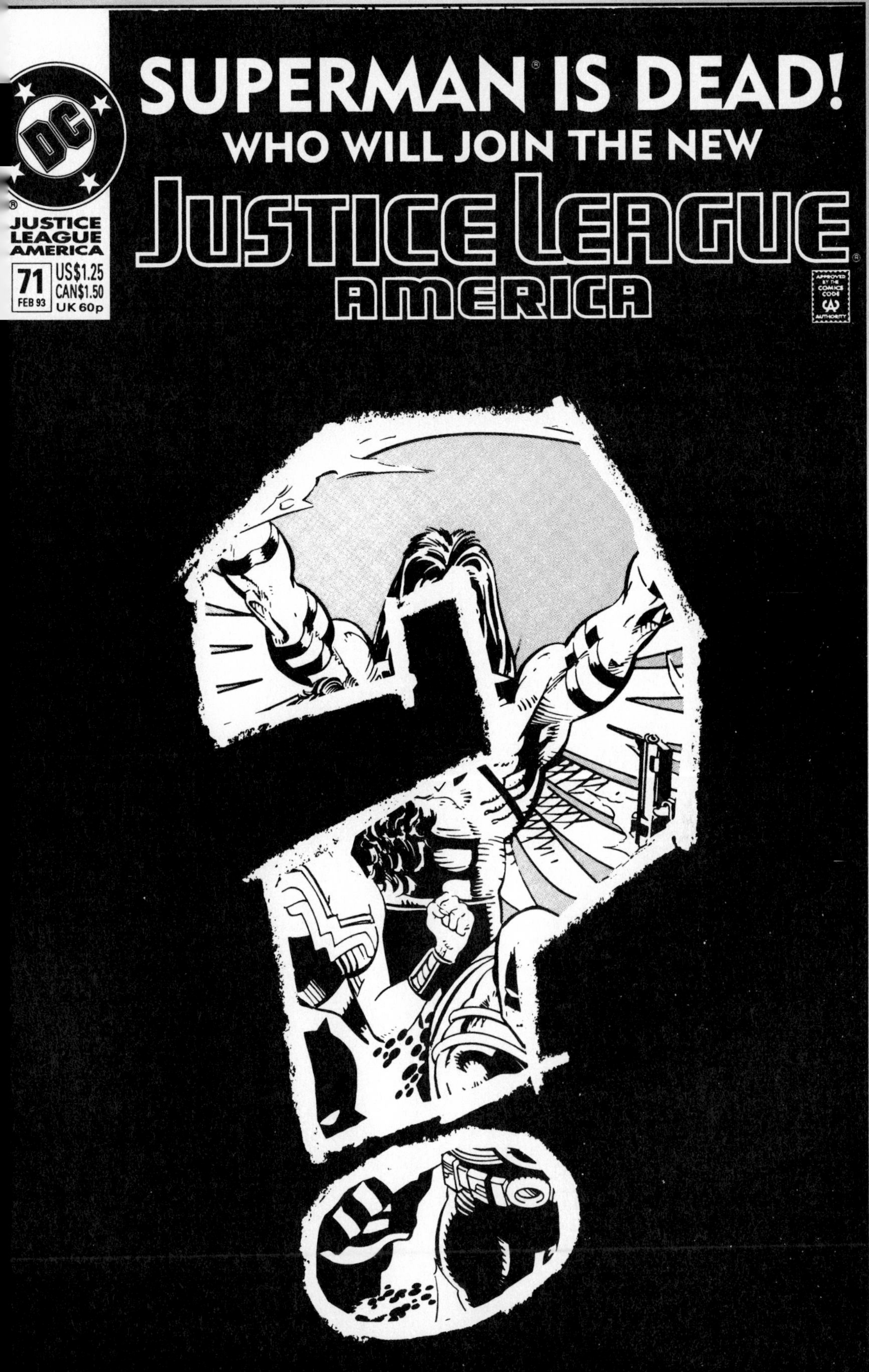

DC
JUSTICE LEAGUE AMERICA
71
FEB 93
US$1.25
CAN$1.50
UK 60p
SUPERMAN IS DEAD!
WHO WILL JOIN THE NEW
JUSTICE LEAGUE AMERICA
APPROVED BY THE COMICS CODE AUTHORITY

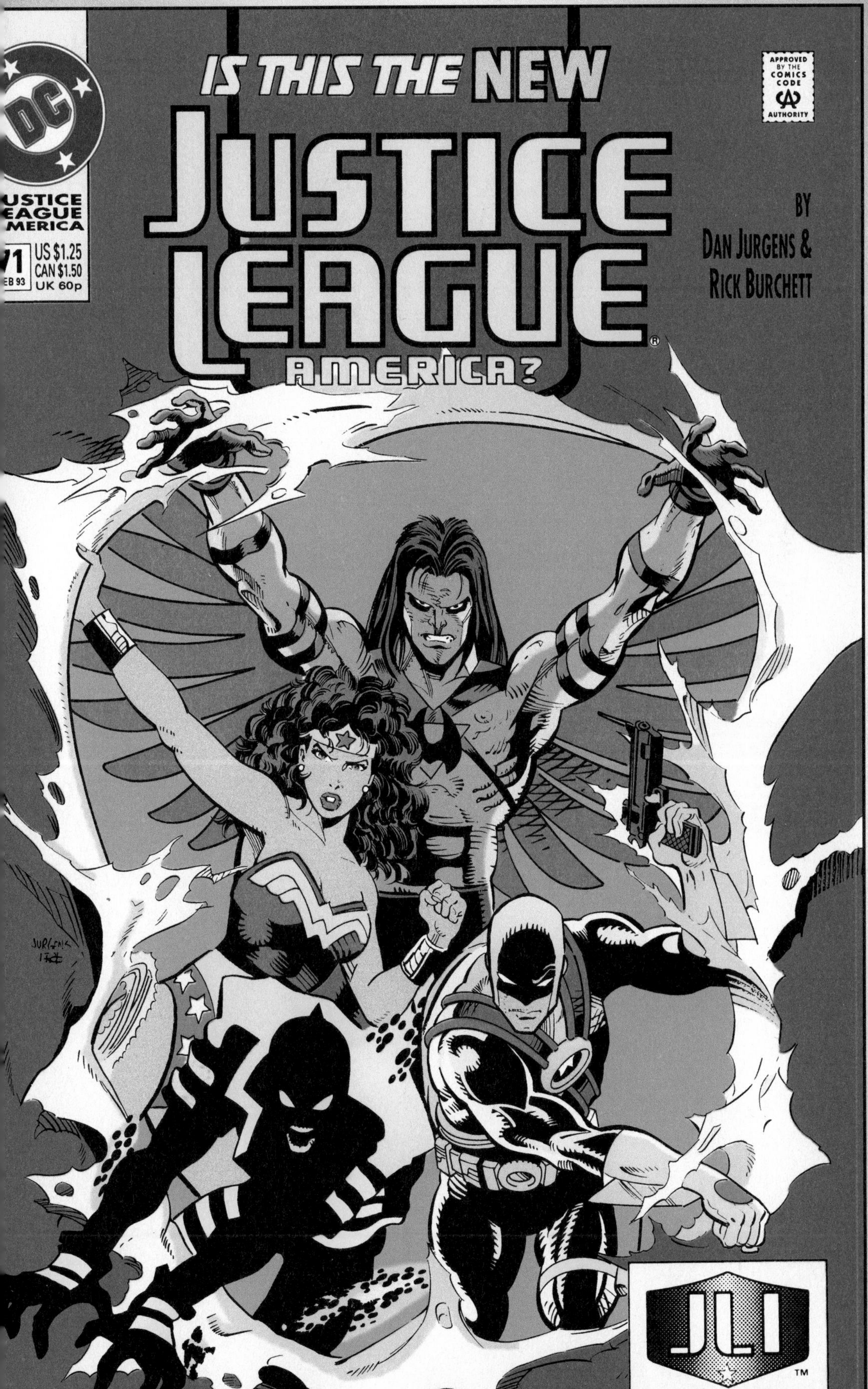
IS THIS THE NEW
JUSTICE LEAGUE AMERICA?
BY
DAN JURGENS &
RICK BURCHETT
JUSTICE LEAGUE AMERICA
71 FEB 93
US $1.25
CAN $1.50
UK 60p
APPROVED BY THE COMICS CODE AUTHORITY
JLI
JURGENS

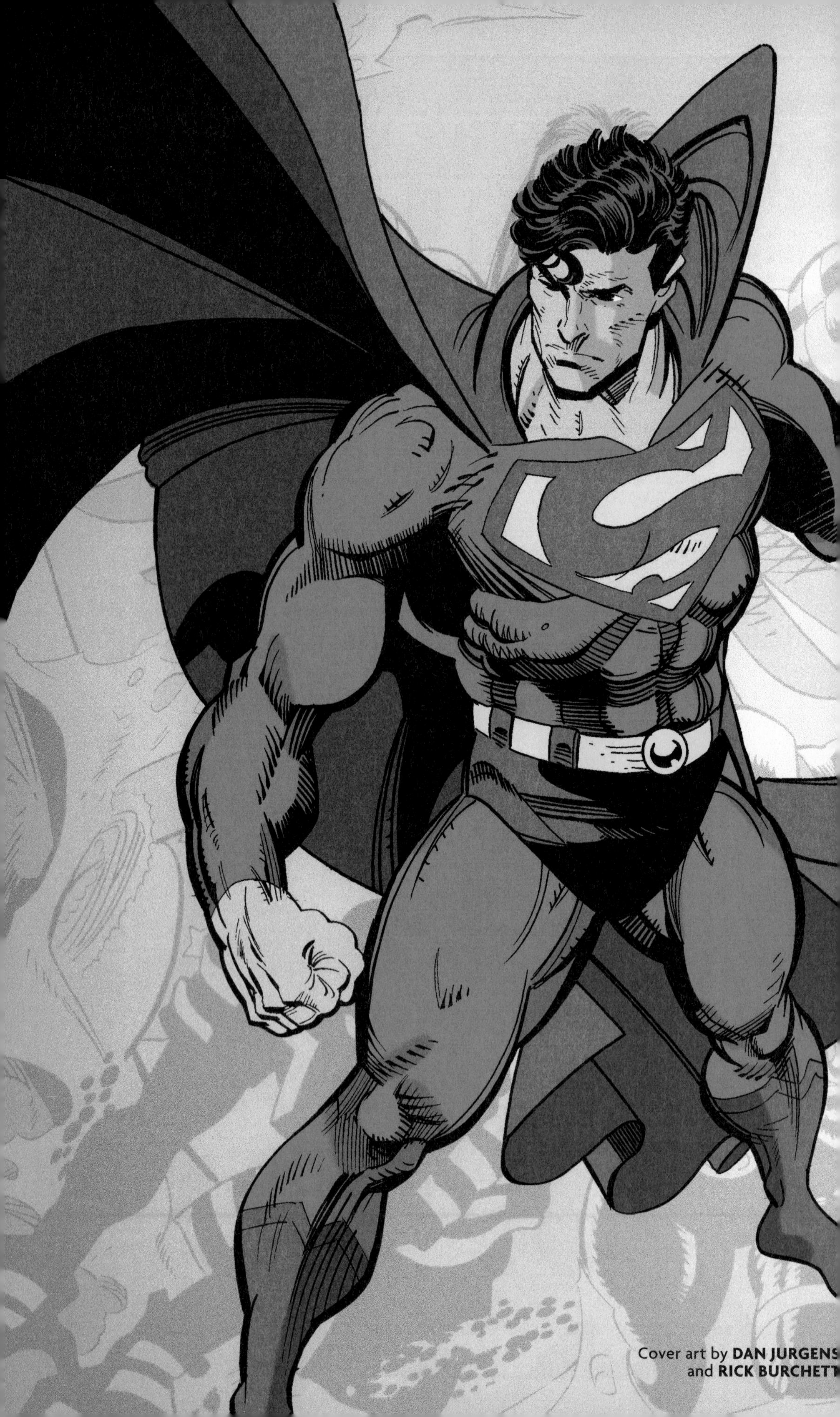

Cover art by **DAN JURGENS**
and **RICK BURCHETT**

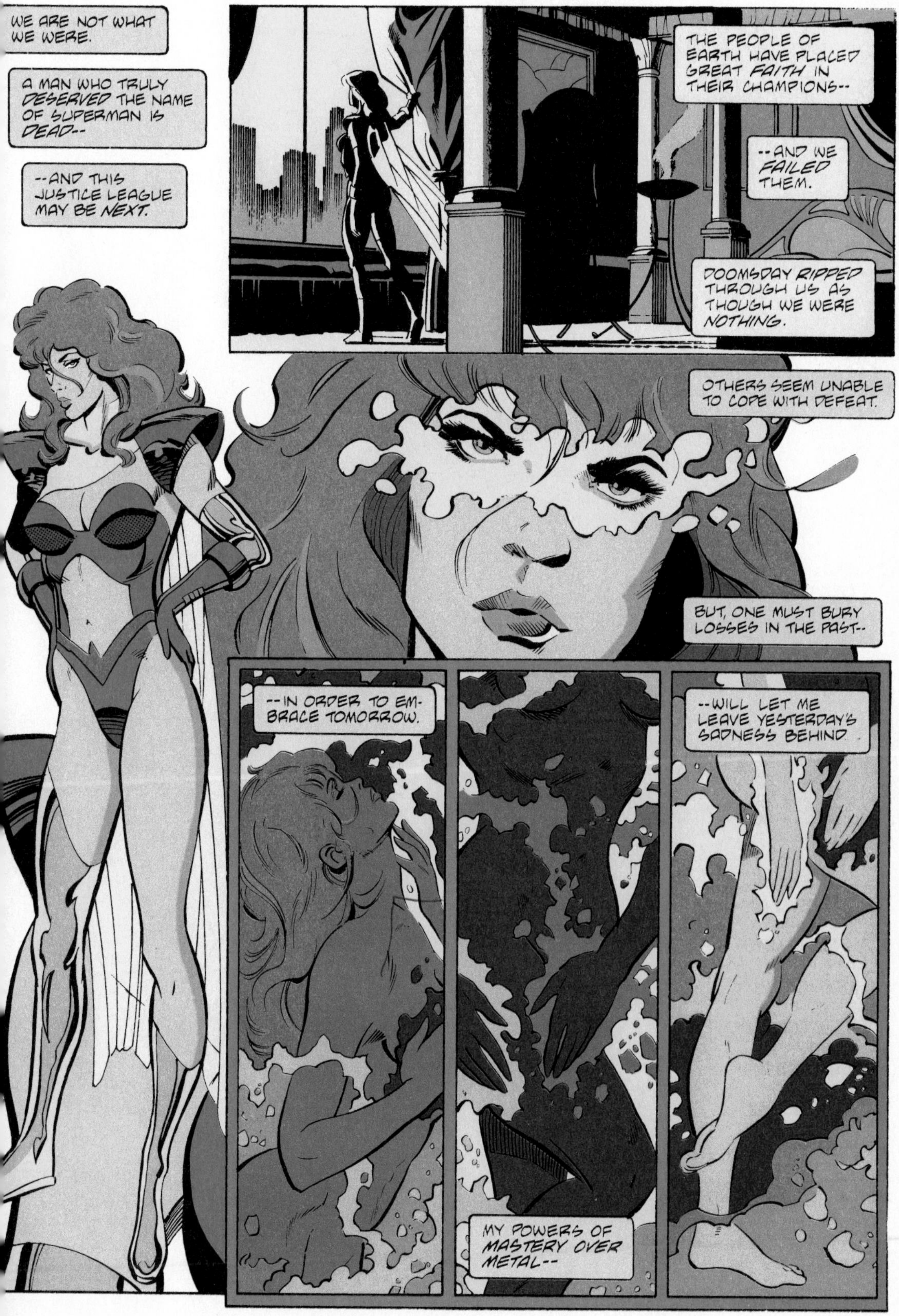
WE ARE NOT WHAT WE WERE.
A MAN WHO TRULY DESERVED THE NAME OF SUPERMAN IS DEAD--
--AND THIS JUSTICE LEAGUE MAY BE NEXT.
THE PEOPLE OF EARTH HAVE PLACED GREAT FAITH IN THEIR CHAMPIONS--
--AND WE FAILED THEM.
DOOMSDAY RIPPED THROUGH US AS THOUGH WE WERE NOTHING.
OTHERS SEEM UNABLE TO COPE WITH DEFEAT.
BUT, ONE MUST BURY LOSSES IN THE PAST--
--IN ORDER TO EMBRACE TOMORROW.
MY POWERS OF MASTERY OVER METAL--
--WILL LET ME LEAVE YESTERDAY'S SADNESS BEHIND

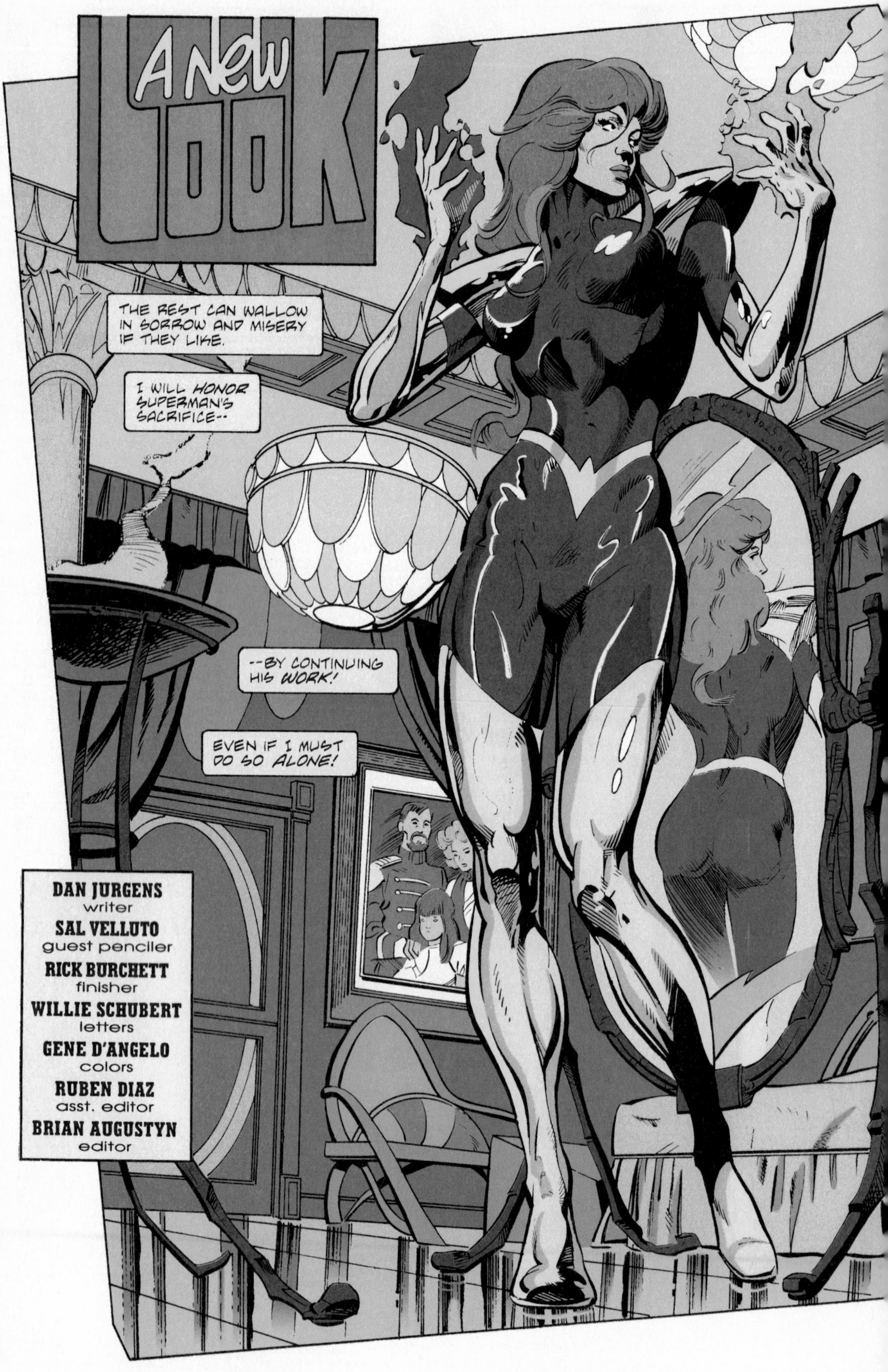
A NEW LOOK
THE REST CAN WALLOW IN SORROW AND MISERY IF THEY LIKE.
I WILL HONOR SUPERMAN'S SACRIFICE--
--BY CONTINUING HIS WORK!
EVEN IF I MUST DO SO ALONE!
DAN JURGENS writer
SAL VELLUTO guest penciler
RICK BURCHETT finisher
WILLIE SCHUBERT letters
GENE D'ANGELO colors
RUBEN DIAZ asst. editor
BRIAN AUGUSTYN editor

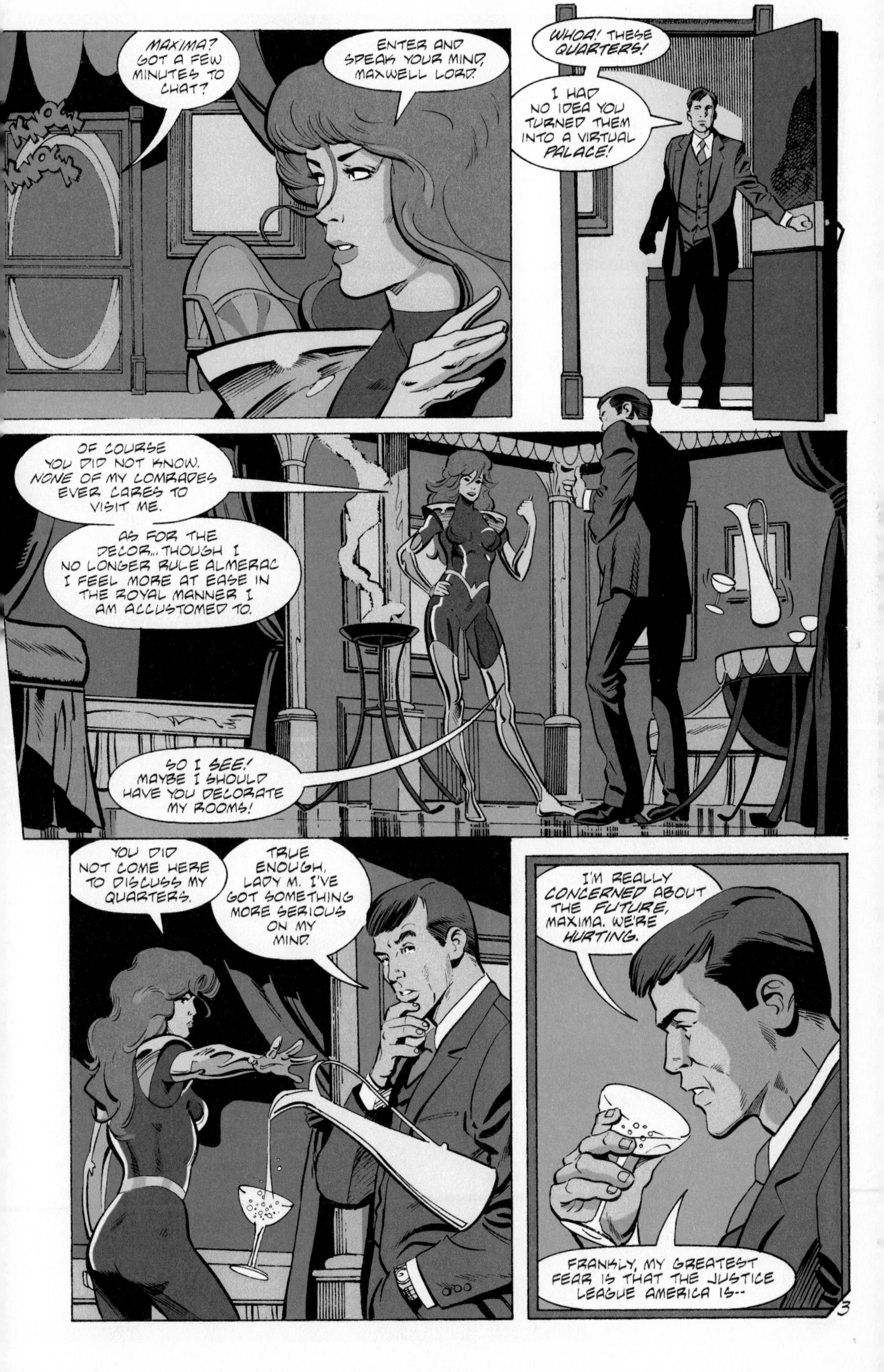
KNOCK KNOCK
MAXIMA? GOT A FEW MINUTES TO CHAT?
ENTER AND SPEAK YOUR MIND, MAXWELL LORD.
WHOA! THESE QUARTERS!
I HAD NO IDEA YOU TURNED THEM INTO A VIRTUAL PALACE!
OF COURSE YOU DID NOT KNOW. NONE OF MY COMRADES EVER CARES TO VISIT ME.
AS FOR THE DECOR... THOUGH I NO LONGER RULE ALMERAC I FEEL MORE AT EASE IN THE ROYAL MANNER I AM ACCUSTOMED TO.
SO I SEE! MAYBE I SHOULD HAVE YOU DECORATE MY ROOMS!
YOU DID NOT COME HERE TO DISCUSS MY QUARTERS.
TRUE ENOUGH, LADY M. I'VE GOT SOMETHING MORE SERIOUS ON MY MIND.
I'M REALLY CONCERNED ABOUT THE FUTURE, MAXIMA. WE'RE HURTING.
FRANKLY, MY GREATEST FEAR IS THAT THE JUSTICE LEAGUE AMERICA IS--

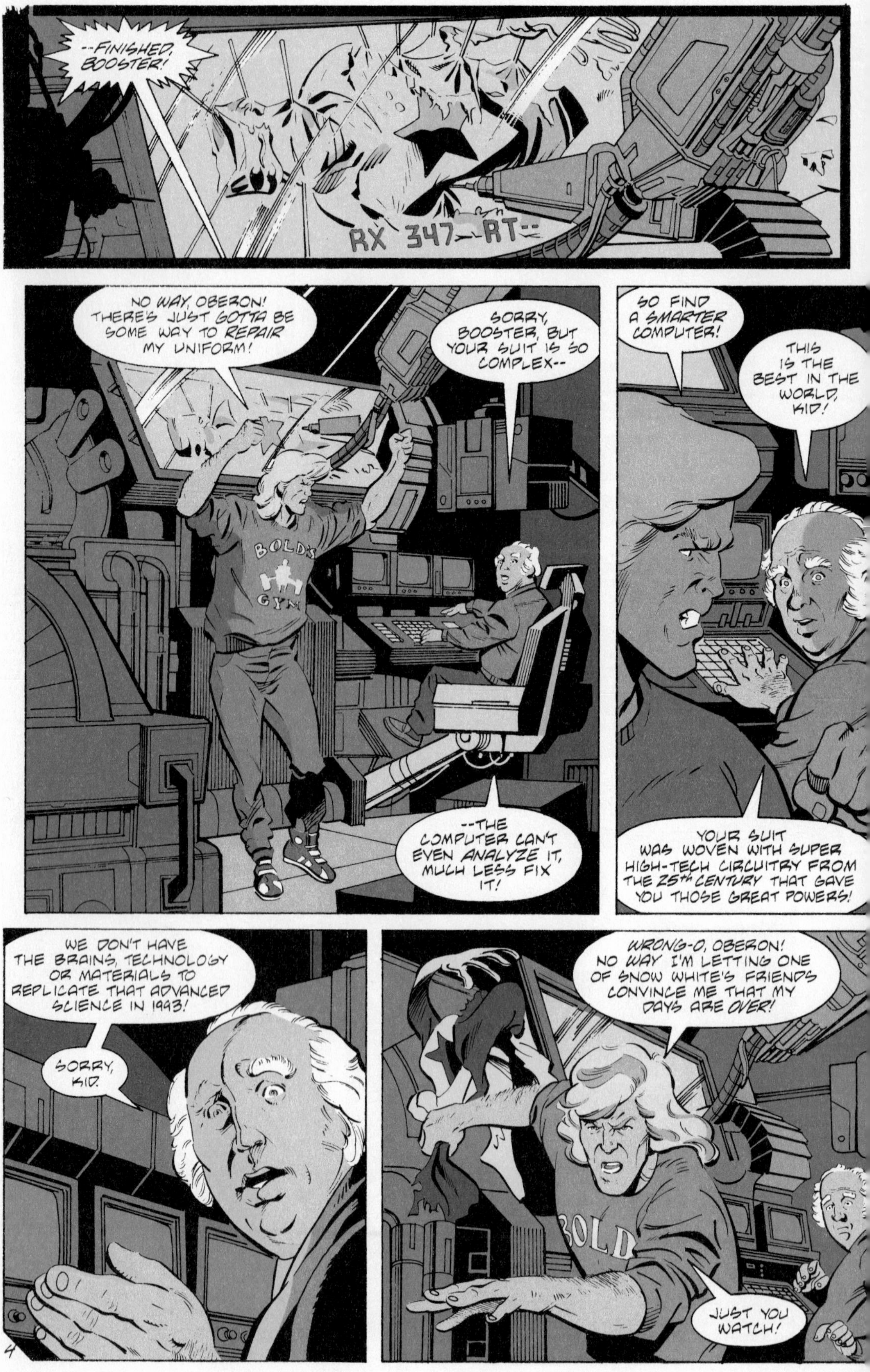
--FINISHED, BOOSTER!
RX 347--RT--
NO WAY, OBERON! THERE'S JUST GOTTA BE SOME WAY TO REPAIR MY UNIFORM!
SORRY, BOOSTER, BUT YOUR SUIT IS SO COMPLEX--
--THE COMPUTER CAN'T EVEN ANALYZE IT, MUCH LESS FIX IT!
BOLD'S GYM
SO FIND A SMARTER COMPUTER!
THIS IS THE BEST IN THE WORLD, KID!
YOUR SUIT WAS WOVEN WITH SUPER HIGH-TECH CIRCUITRY FROM THE 25TH CENTURY THAT GAVE YOU THOSE GREAT POWERS!
WE DON'T HAVE THE BRAINS, TECHNOLOGY OR MATERIALS TO REPLICATE THAT ADVANCED SCIENCE IN 1993!
SORRY, KID.
WRONG-O, OBERON! NO WAY I'M LETTING ONE OF SNOW WHITE'S FRIENDS CONVINCE ME THAT MY DAYS ARE OVER!
JUST YOU WATCH!

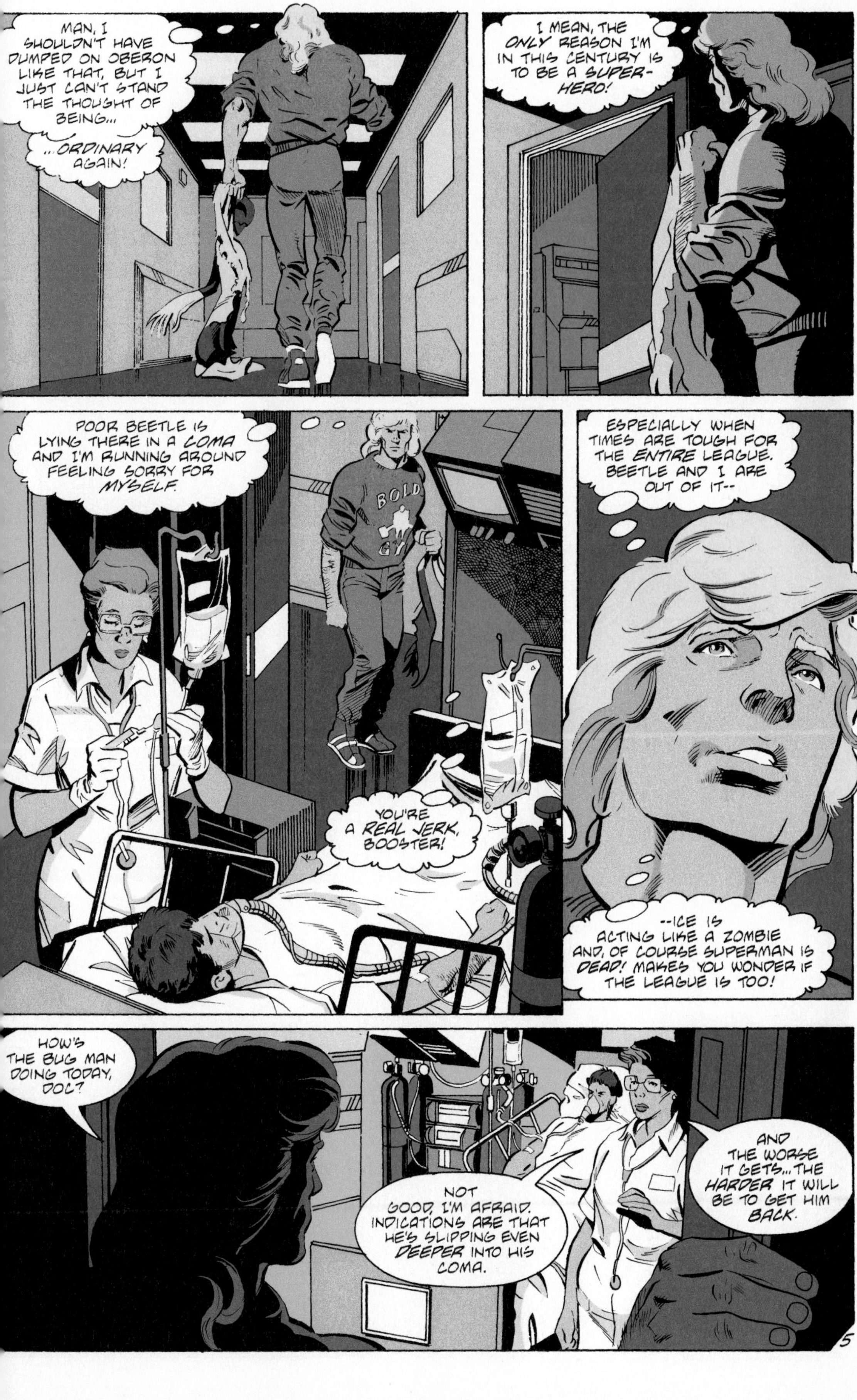
MAN, I SHOULDN'T HAVE DUMPED ON OBERON LIKE THAT, BUT I JUST CAN'T STAND THE THOUGHT OF BEING...
...ORDINARY AGAIN!
I MEAN, THE ONLY REASON I'M IN THIS CENTURY IS TO BE A SUPER-HERO!
POOR BEETLE IS LYING THERE IN A COMA AND I'M RUNNING AROUND FEELING SORRY FOR MYSELF.
BOLD GYM
YOU'RE A REAL JERK, BOOSTER!
ESPECIALLY WHEN TIMES ARE TOUGH FOR THE ENTIRE LEAGUE. BEETLE AND I ARE OUT OF IT--
--ICE IS ACTING LIKE A ZOMBIE AND, OF COURSE SUPERMAN IS DEAD! MAKES YOU WONDER IF THE LEAGUE IS TOO!
HOW'S THE BUG MAN DOING TODAY, DOC?
NOT GOOD, I'M AFRAID. INDICATIONS ARE THAT HE'S SLIPPING EVEN DEEPER INTO HIS COMA.
AND THE WORSE IT GETS... THE HARDER IT WILL BE TO GET HIM BACK.

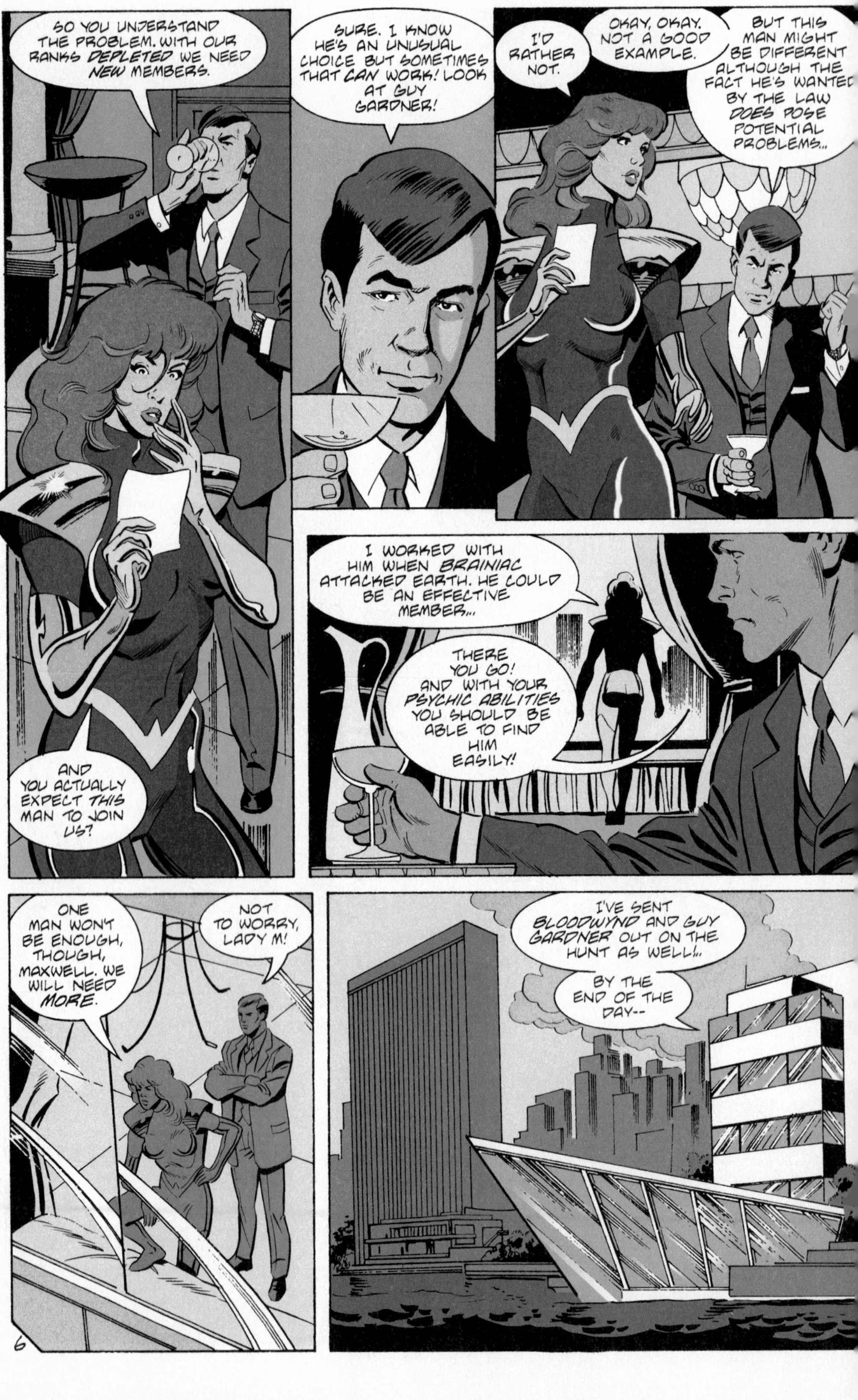
SO YOU UNDERSTAND THE PROBLEM. WITH OUR RANKS *DEPLETED* WE NEED *NEW* MEMBERS.
AND YOU ACTUALLY EXPECT *THIS* MAN TO JOIN US?
SURE. I KNOW HE'S AN UNUSUAL CHOICE BUT SOMETIMES THAT *CAN* WORK! LOOK AT GUY GARDNER!
I'D RATHER NOT.
OKAY, OKAY. NOT A GOOD EXAMPLE.
BUT THIS MAN MIGHT BE DIFFERENT ALTHOUGH THE FACT HE'S WANTED BY THE LAW *DOES* POSE POTENTIAL PROBLEMS...
I WORKED WITH HIM WHEN *BRAINIAC* ATTACKED EARTH. HE COULD BE AN EFFECTIVE MEMBER...
THERE YOU GO! AND WITH YOUR *PSYCHIC ABILITIES* YOU SHOULD BE ABLE TO FIND HIM EASILY!
ONE MAN WON'T BE ENOUGH, THOUGH, MAXWELL. WE WILL NEED *MORE*.
NOT TO WORRY, LADY M!
I'VE SENT *BLOODWYND* AND *GUY GARDNER* OUT ON THE HUNT AS WELL!...
BY THE END OF THE DAY--

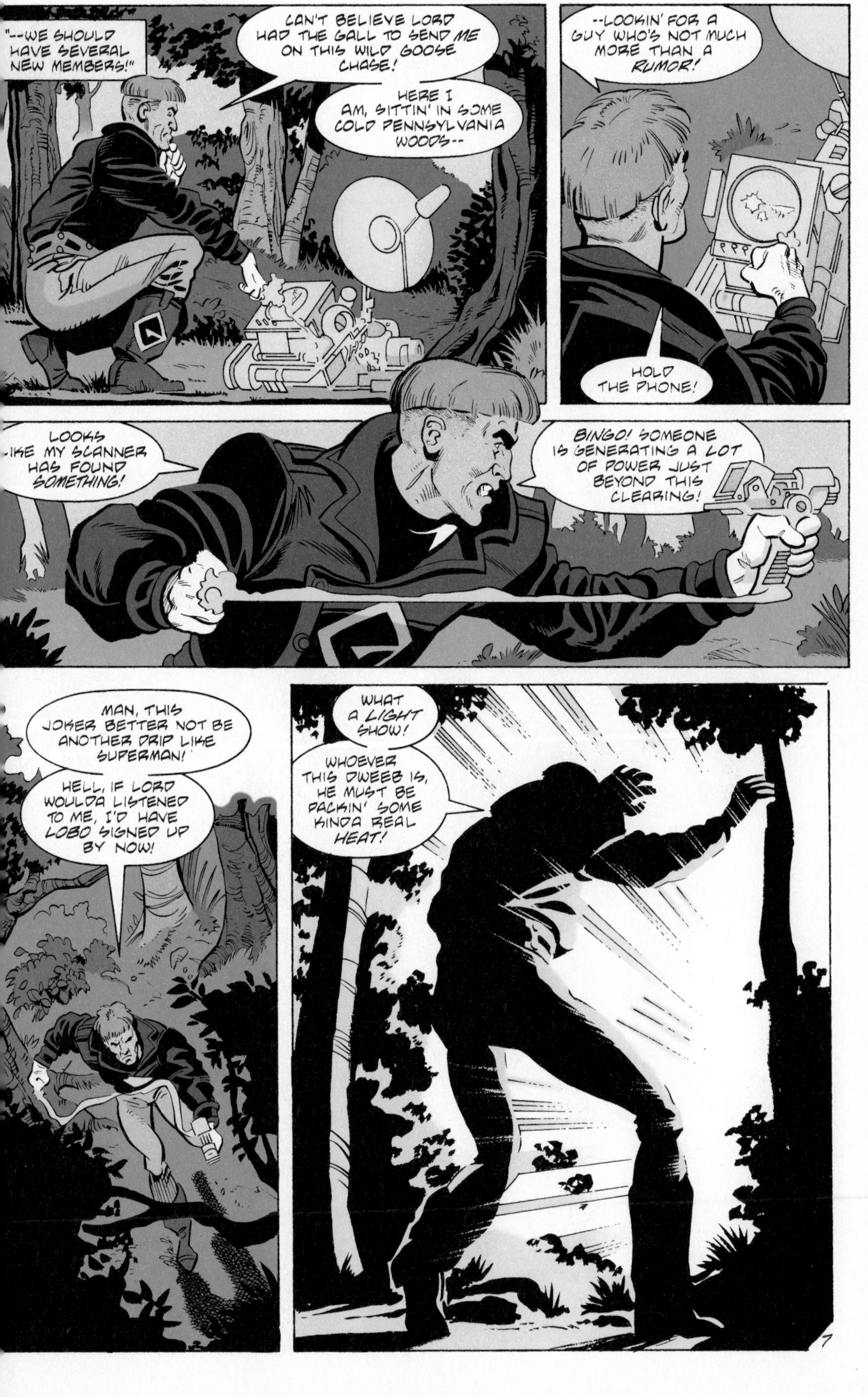
"--WE SHOULD HAVE SEVERAL NEW MEMBERS!"
CAN'T BELIEVE LORD HAD THE GALL TO SEND ME ON THIS WILD GOOSE CHASE!
HERE I AM, SITTIN' IN SOME COLD PENNSYLVANIA WOODS--
--LOOKIN' FOR A GUY WHO'S NOT MUCH MORE THAN A RUMOR!
HOLD THE PHONE!
LOOKS LIKE MY SCANNER HAS FOUND SOMETHING!
BINGO! SOMEONE IS GENERATING A LOT OF POWER JUST BEYOND THIS CLEARING!
MAN, THIS JOKER BETTER NOT BE ANOTHER DRIP LIKE SUPERMAN!
HELL, IF LORD WOULDA LISTENED TO ME, I'D HAVE LOBO SIGNED UP BY NOW!
WHAT A LIGHT SHOW!
WHOEVER THIS DWEEB IS, HE MUST BE PACKIN' SOME KINDA REAL HEAT!

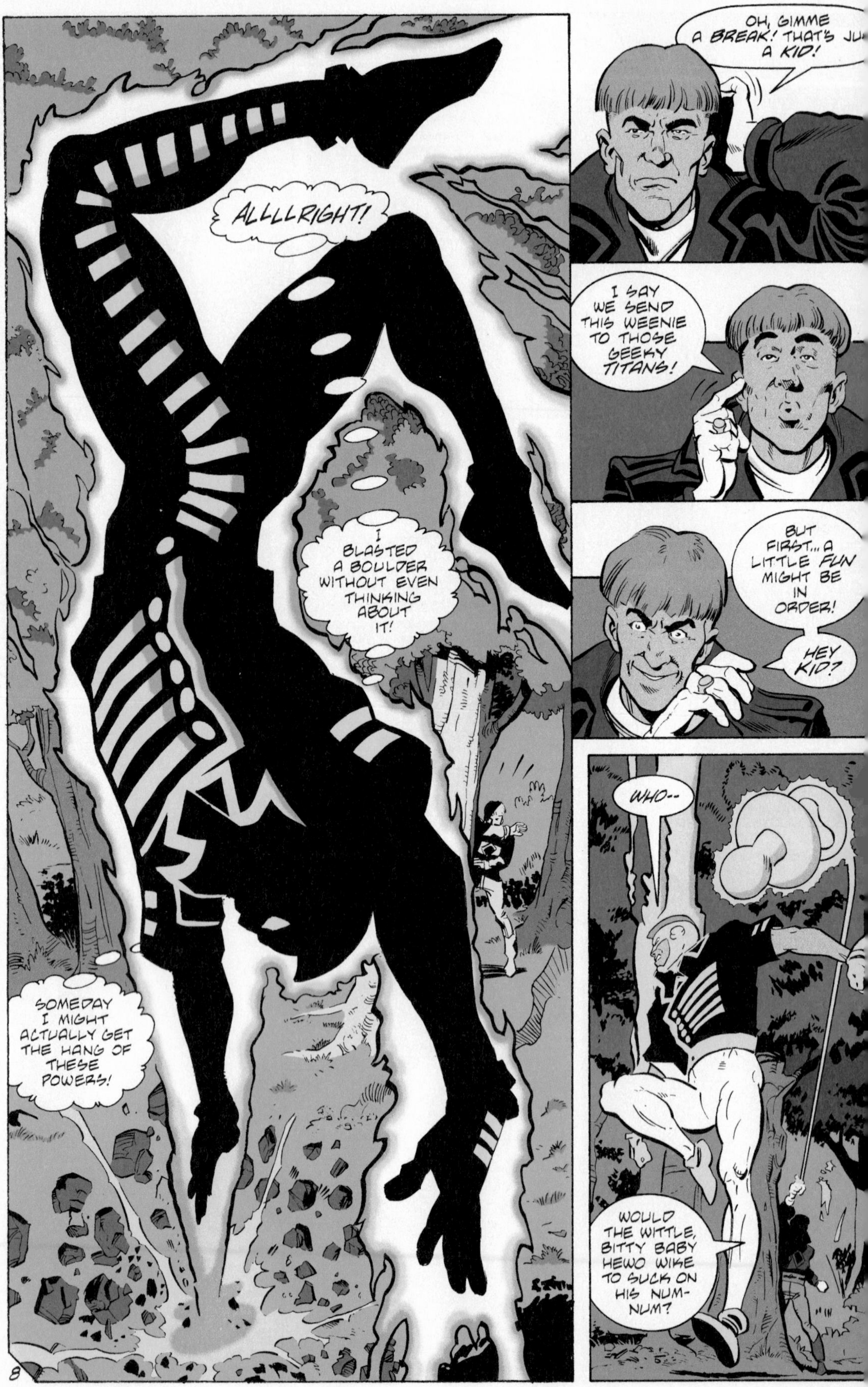
ALLLLRIGHT!
I BLASTED A BOULDER WITHOUT EVEN THINKING ABOUT IT!
SOMEDAY I MIGHT ACTUALLY GET THE HANG OF THESE POWERS!
OH, GIMME A BREAK! THAT'S JU A KID!
I SAY WE SEND THIS WEENIE TO THOSE GEEKY TITANS!
BUT FIRST... A LITTLE FUN MIGHT BE IN ORDER!
HEY KID?
WHO--
WOULD THE WITTLE, BITTY BABY HEWO WIKE TO SUCK ON HIS NUM-NUM?

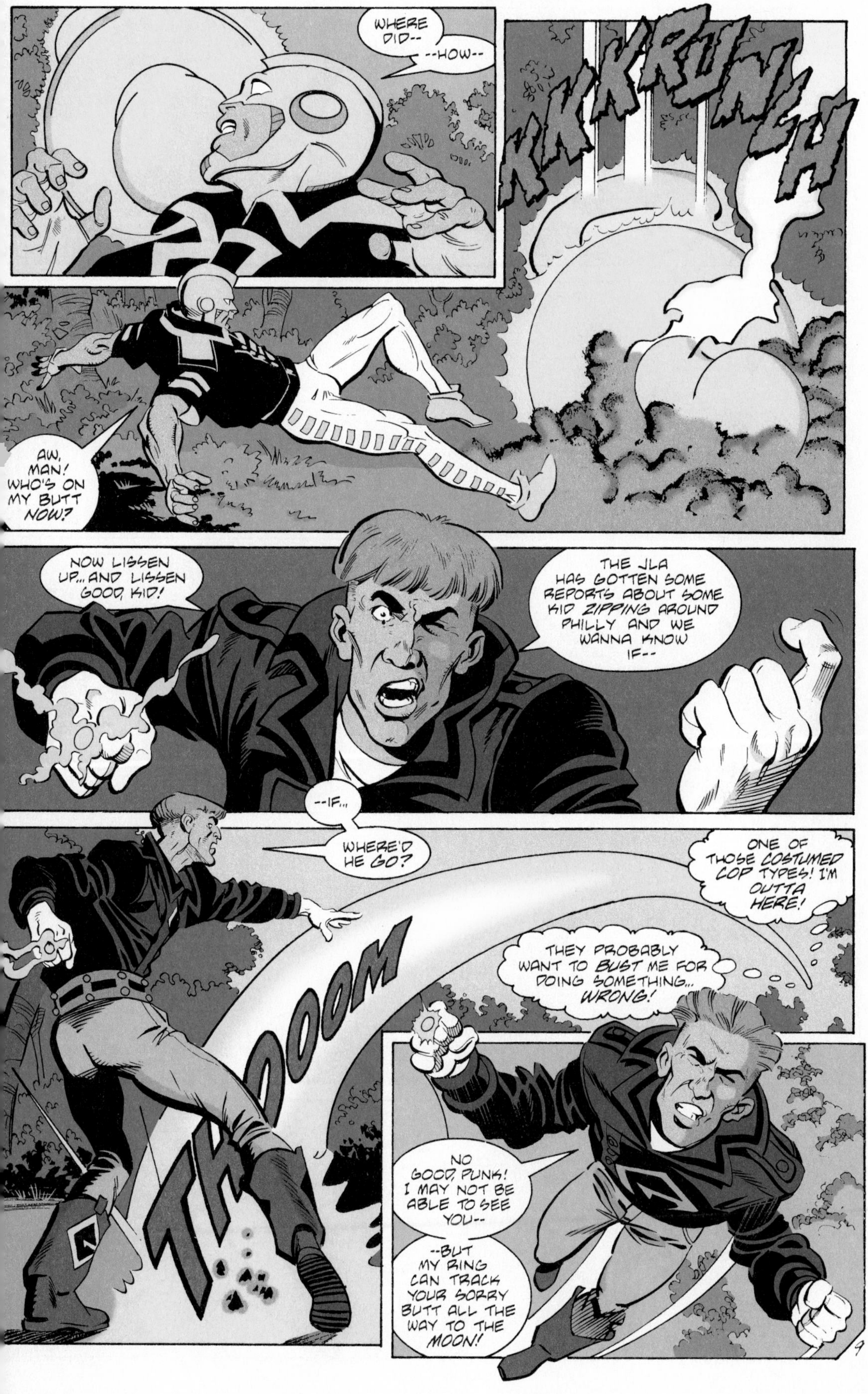
WHERE DID--
--HOW--
KKKRUNCH
AW, MAN! WHO'S ON MY BUTT NOW?
NOW LISSEN UP... AND LISSEN GOOD, KID!
THE JLA HAS GOTTEN SOME REPORTS ABOUT SOME KID ZIPPING AROUND PHILLY AND WE WANNA KNOW IF--
--IF...
WHERE'D HE GO?
ONE OF THOSE COSTUMED COP TYPES! I'M OUTTA HERE!
THEY PROBABLY WANT TO BUST ME FOR DOING SOMETHING... WRONG!
THRDOOOM
NO GOOD, PUNK! I MAY NOT BE ABLE TO SEE YOU--
--BUT MY RING CAN TRACK YOUR SORRY BUTT ALL THE WAY TO THE MOON!

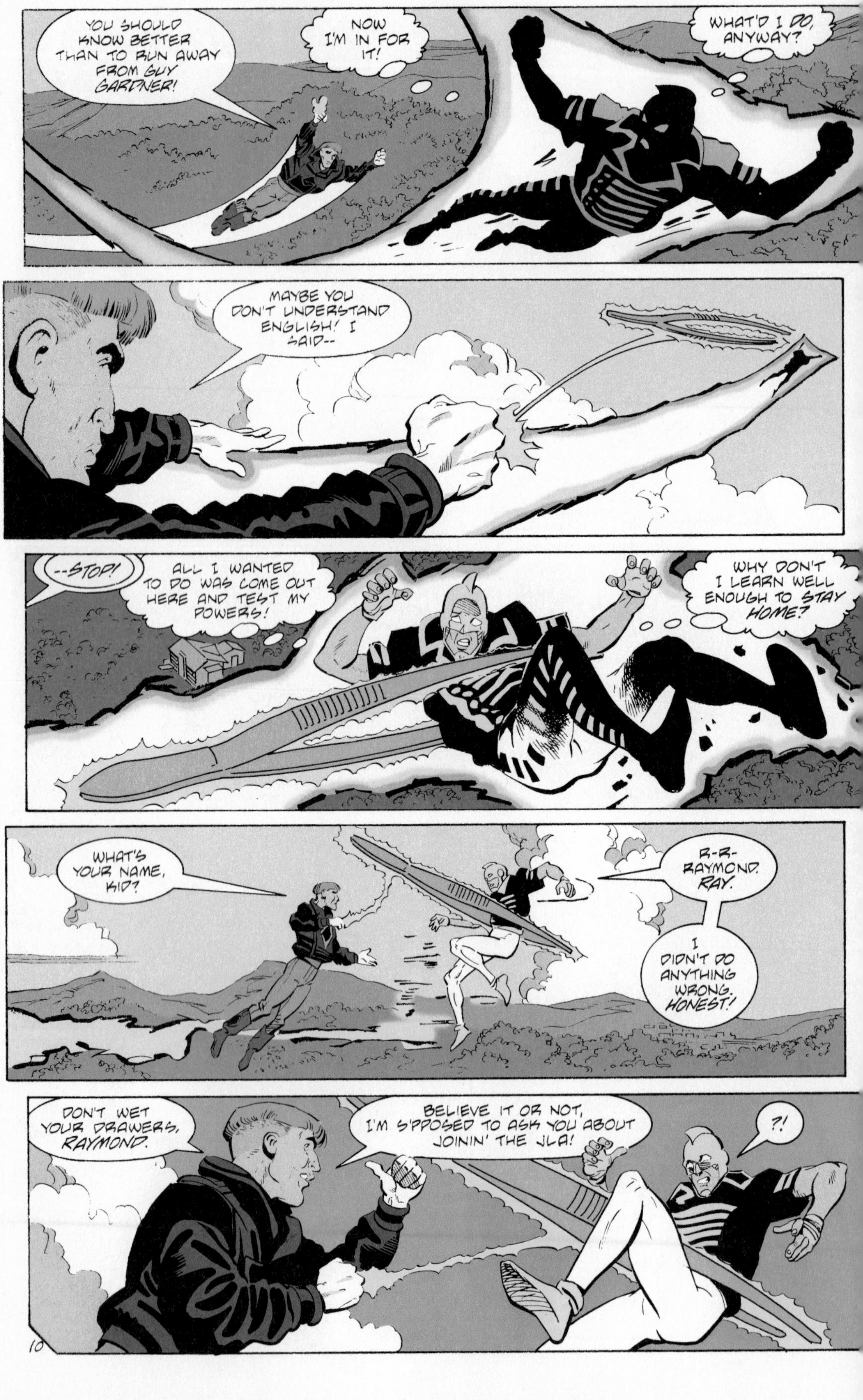
YOU SHOULD KNOW BETTER THAN TO RUN AWAY FROM GUY GARDNER!
NOW I'M IN FOR IT!
WHAT'D I DO, ANYWAY?
MAYBE YOU DON'T UNDERSTAND ENGLISH! I SAID--
--STOP!
ALL I WANTED TO DO WAS COME OUT HERE AND TEST MY POWERS!
WHY DON'T I LEARN WELL ENOUGH TO STAY HOME?
WHAT'S YOUR NAME, KID?
R-R-RAYMOND. RAY.
I DIDN'T DO ANYTHING WRONG. HONEST!
DON'T WET YOUR DRAWERS, RAYMOND.
BELIEVE IT OR NOT, I'M S'PPOSED TO ASK YOU ABOUT JOININ' THE JLA!
?!

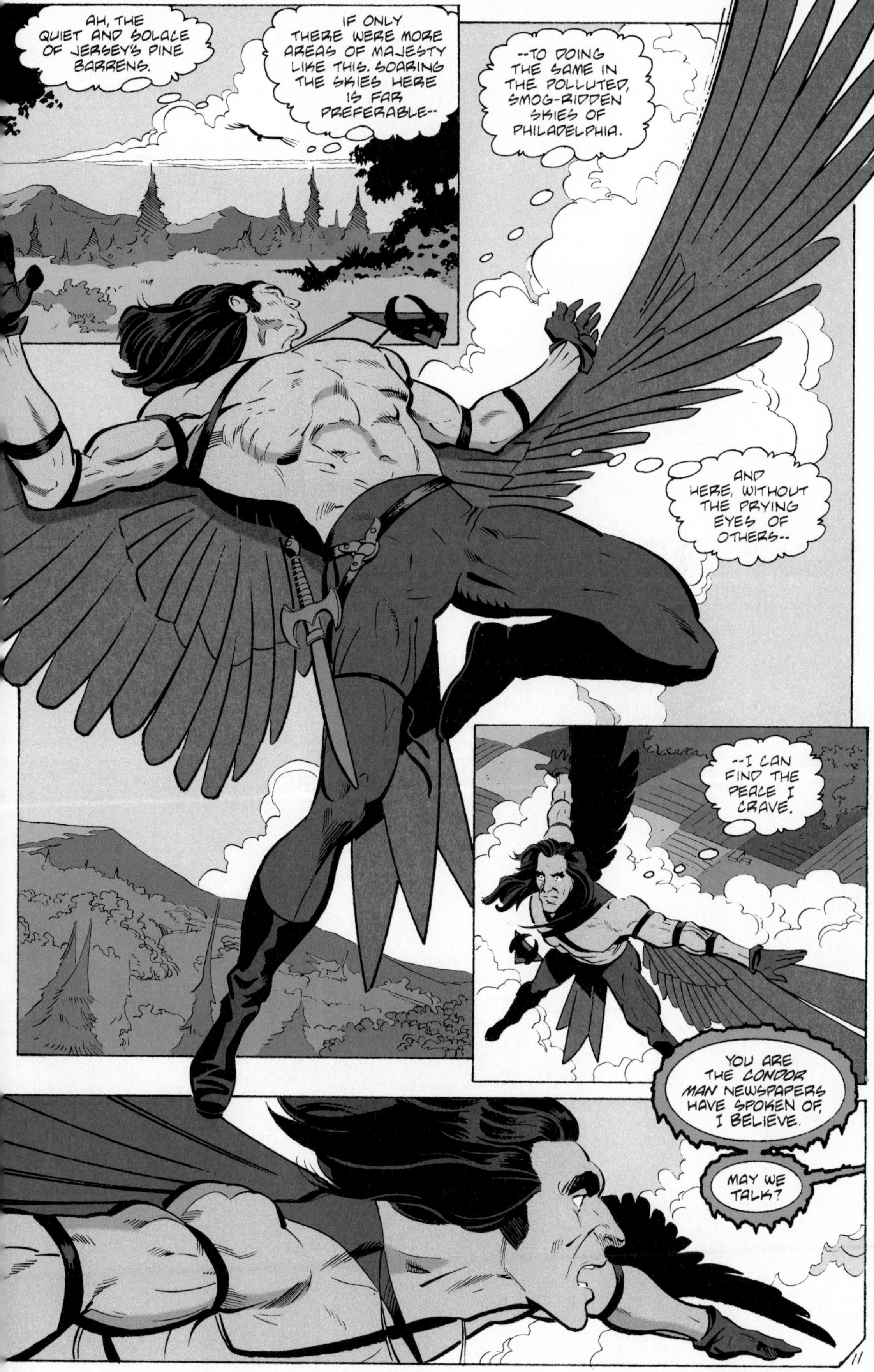
AH, THE QUIET AND SOLACE OF JERSEY'S PINE BARRENS.
IF ONLY THERE WERE MORE AREAS OF MAJESTY LIKE THIS. SOARING THE SKIES HERE IS FAR PREFERABLE--
--TO DOING THE SAME IN THE POLLUTED, SMOG-RIDDEN SKIES OF PHILADELPHIA.
AND HERE, WITHOUT THE PRYING EYES OF OTHERS--
--I CAN FIND THE PEACE I CRAVE.
YOU ARE THE *CONDOR MAN* NEWSPAPERS HAVE SPOKEN OF, I BELIEVE.
MAY WE TALK?

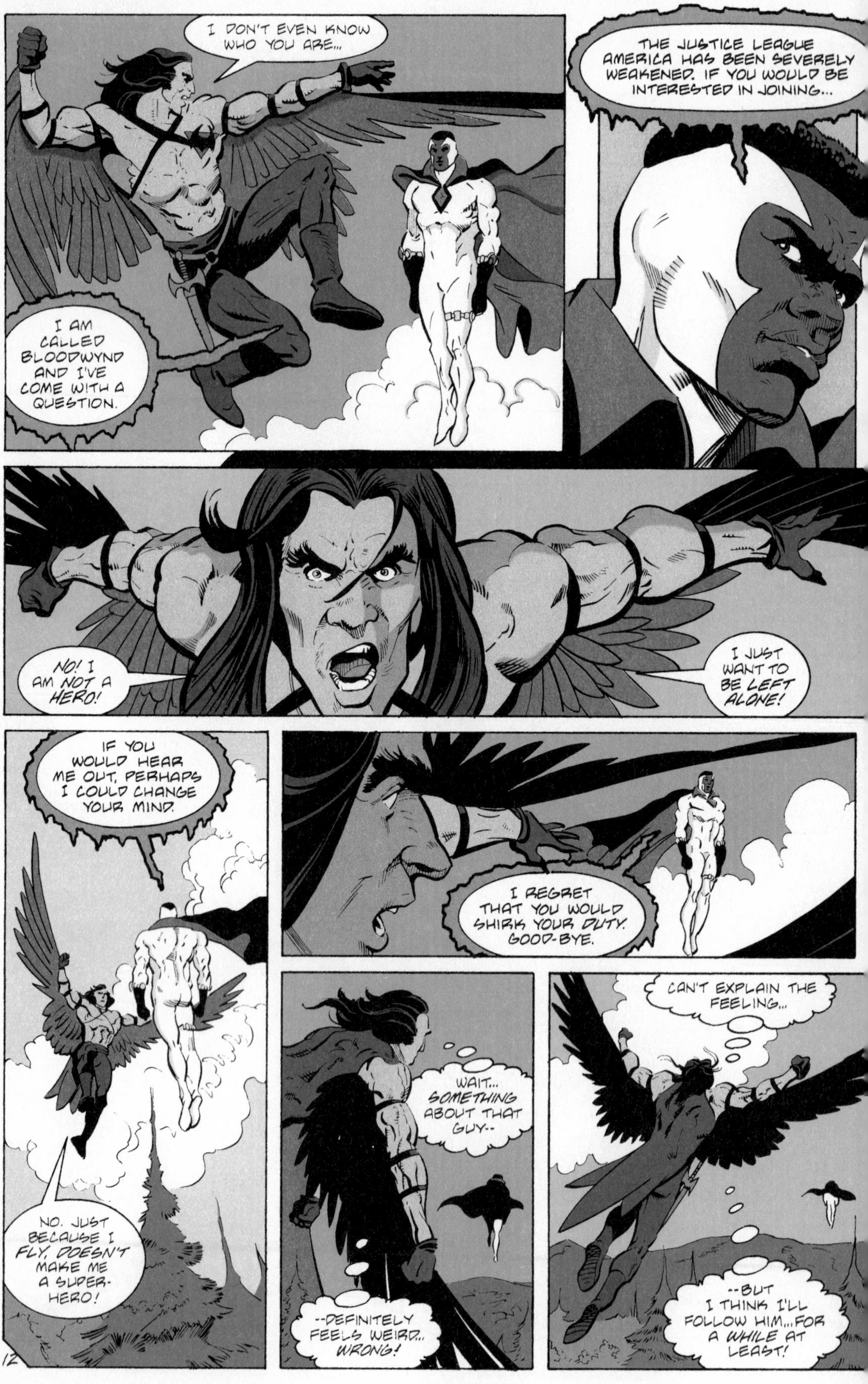
I DON'T EVEN KNOW WHO YOU ARE...
I AM CALLED BLOODWYND AND I'VE COME WITH A QUESTION.
THE JUSTICE LEAGUE AMERICA HAS BEEN SEVERELY WEAKENED. IF YOU WOULD BE INTERESTED IN JOINING...
NO! I AM NOT A HERO!
I JUST WANT TO BE LEFT ALONE!
IF YOU WOULD HEAR ME OUT, PERHAPS I COULD CHANGE YOUR MIND.
NO. JUST BECAUSE I FLY, DOESN'T MAKE ME A SUPER-HERO!
I REGRET THAT YOU WOULD SHIRK YOUR DUTY. GOOD-BYE.
WAIT... SOMETHING ABOUT THAT GUY--
--DEFINITELY FEELS WEIRD... WRONG!
CAN'T EXPLAIN THE FEELING...
--BUT I THINK I'LL FOLLOW HIM...FOR A WHILE AT LEAST!

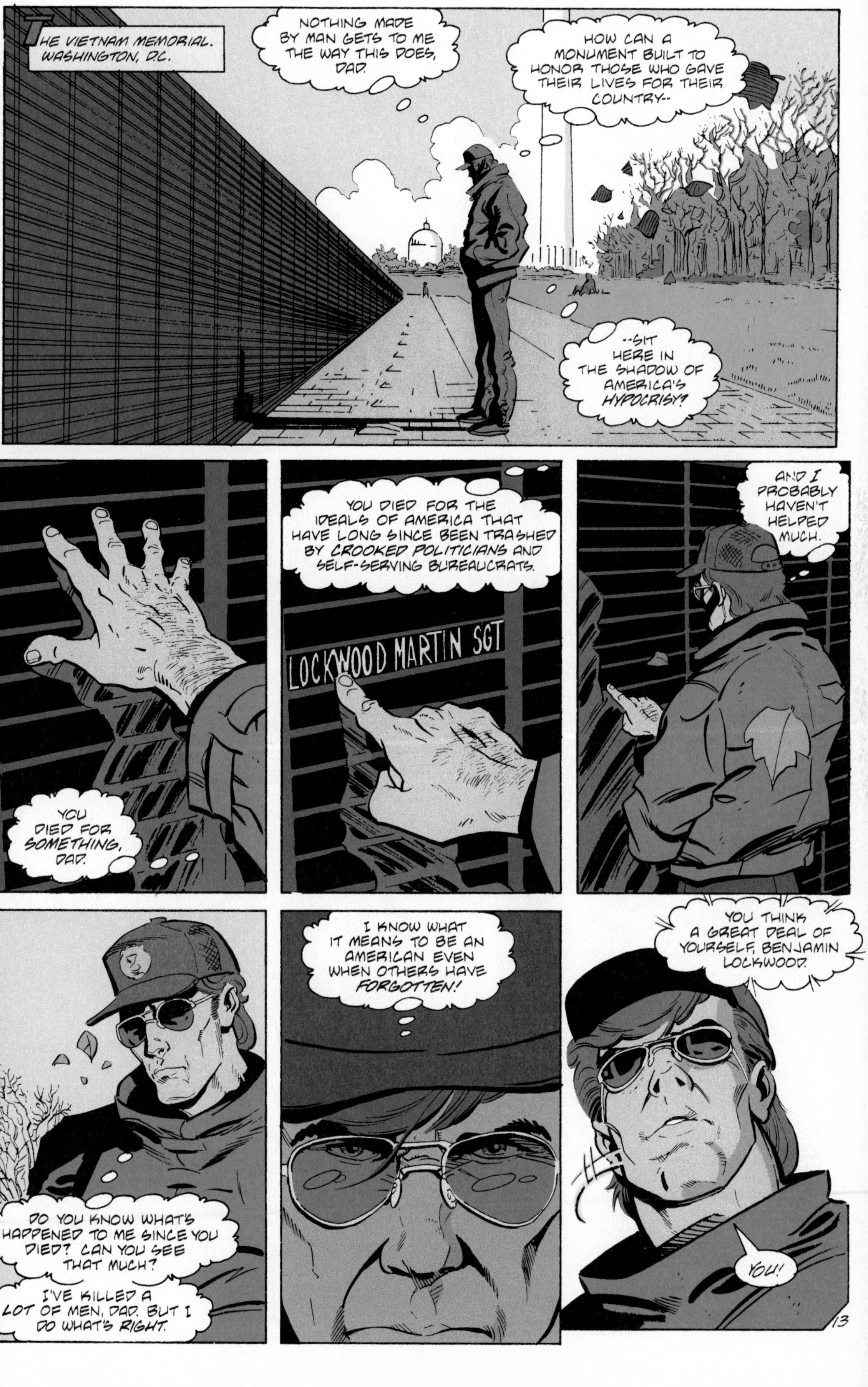
THE VIETNAM MEMORIAL. WASHINGTON, D.C.
NOTHING MADE BY MAN GETS TO ME THE WAY THIS DOES, DAD.
HOW CAN A MONUMENT BUILT TO HONOR THOSE WHO GAVE THEIR LIVES FOR THEIR COUNTRY--
--SIT HERE IN THE SHADOW OF AMERICA'S *HYPOCRISY?*
YOU DIED FOR *SOMETHING,* DAD.
YOU DIED FOR THE IDEALS OF AMERICA THAT HAVE LONG SINCE BEEN TRASHED BY *CROOKED POLITICIANS* AND SELF-SERVING BUREAUCRATS.
LOCKWOOD MARTIN SGT
AND *I* PROBABLY HAVEN'T HELPED MUCH.
DO YOU KNOW WHAT'S HAPPENED TO ME SINCE YOU DIED? CAN YOU SEE THAT MUCH?
I'VE KILLED A LOT OF MEN, DAD. BUT I DO WHAT'S *RIGHT.*
I KNOW WHAT IT MEANS TO BE AN AMERICAN EVEN WHEN OTHERS HAVE *FORGOTTEN!*
YOU THINK A GREAT DEAL OF YOURSELF, BENJAMIN LOCKWOOD.
YOU!

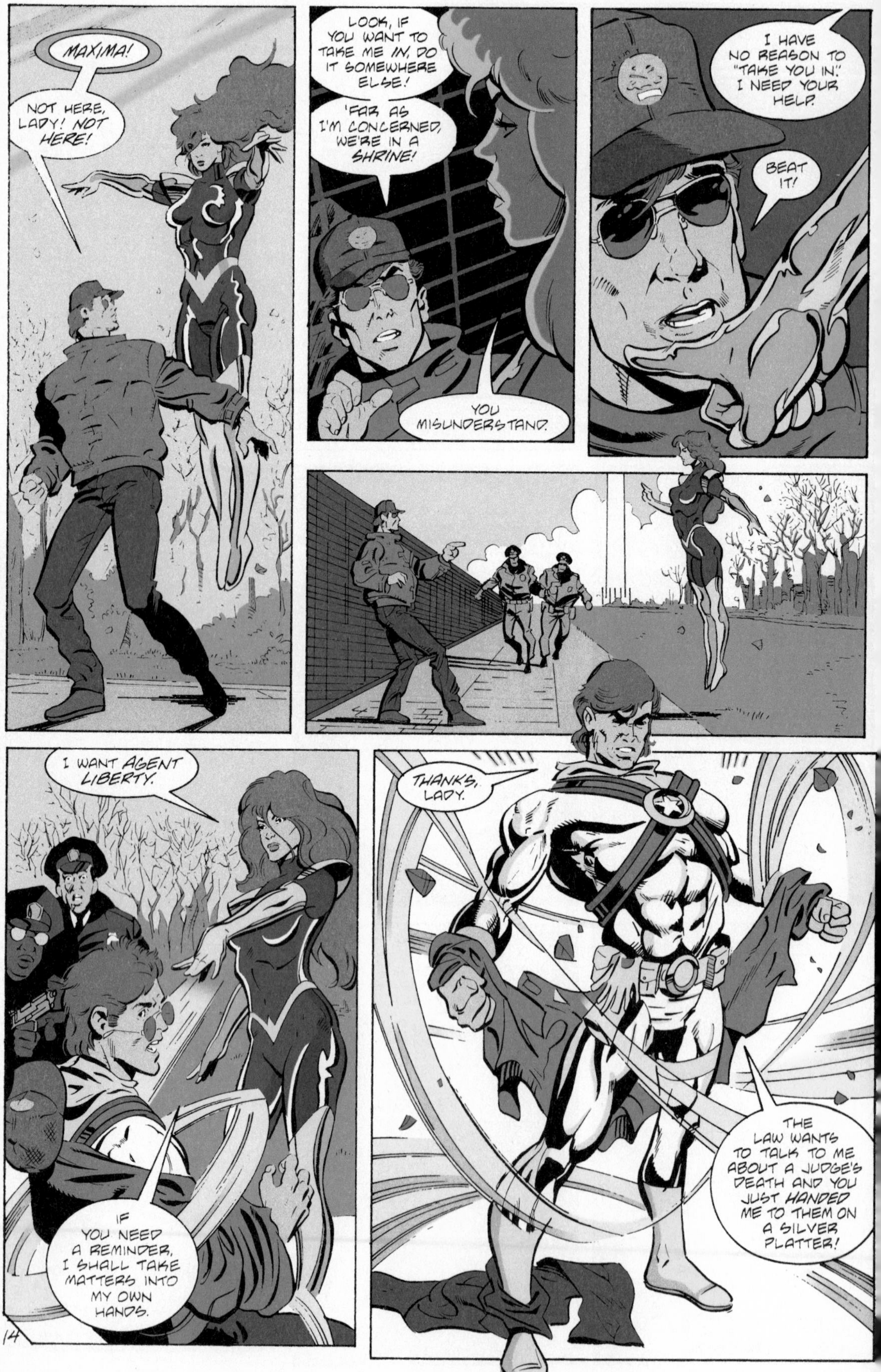
MAXIMA!
NOT HERE, LADY! NOT HERE!
LOOK, IF YOU WANT TO TAKE ME IN, DO IT SOMEWHERE ELSE!
'FAR AS I'M CONCERNED, WE'RE IN A SHRINE!
YOU MISUNDERSTAND.
I HAVE NO REASON TO "TAKE YOU IN." I NEED YOUR HELP.
BEAT IT!
I WANT AGENT LIBERTY.
IF YOU NEED A REMINDER, I SHALL TAKE MATTERS INTO MY OWN HANDS.
THANKS, LADY.
THE LAW WANTS TO TALK TO ME ABOUT A JUDGE'S DEATH AND YOU JUST HANDED ME TO THEM ON A SILVER PLATTER!

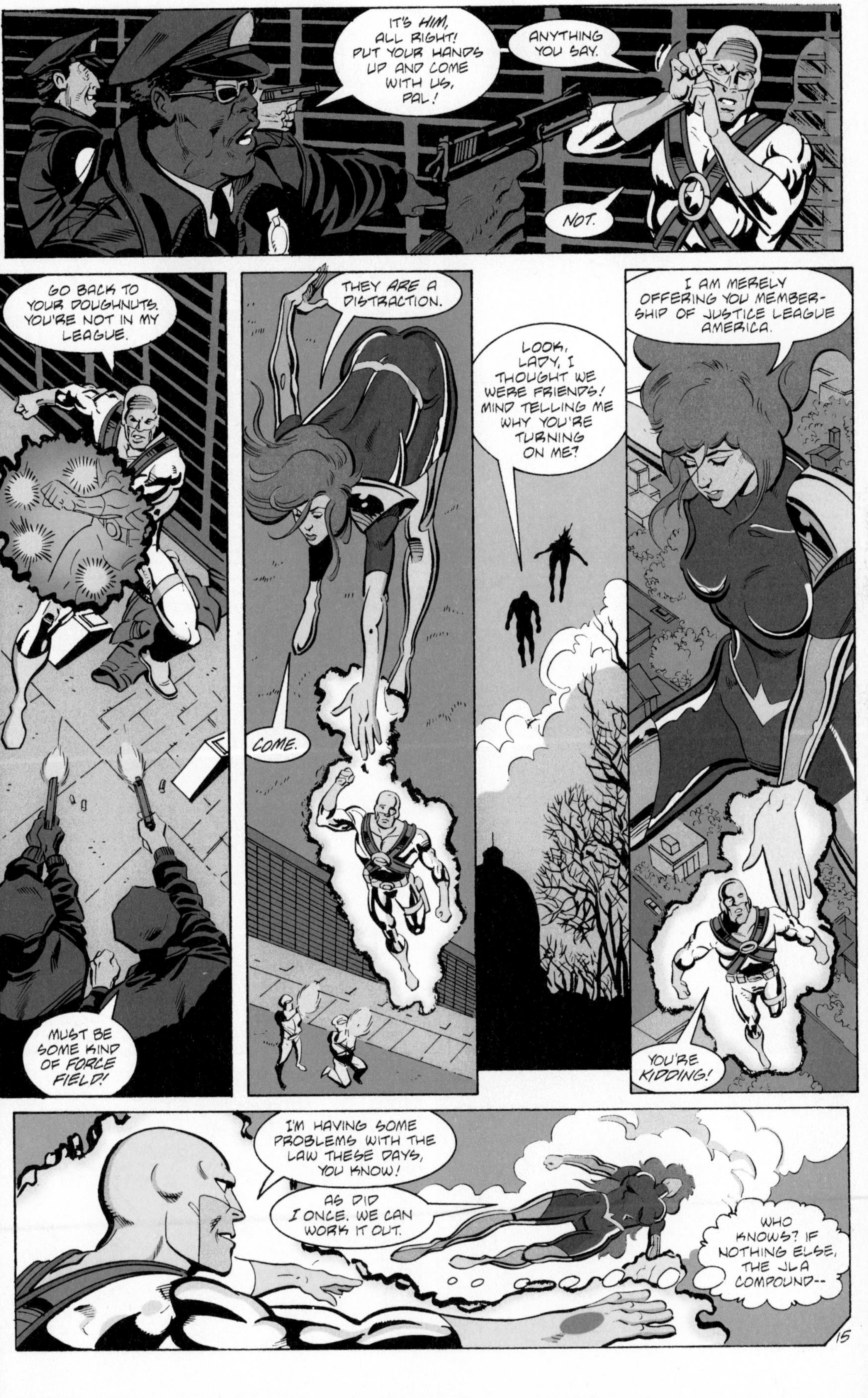
IT'S HIM, ALL RIGHT! PUT YOUR HANDS UP AND COME WITH US, PAL!
ANYTHING YOU SAY.
NOT.
GO BACK TO YOUR DOUGHNUTS. YOU'RE NOT IN MY LEAGUE.
MUST BE SOME KIND OF FORCE FIELD!
THEY ARE A DISTRACTION.
COME.
LOOK, LADY, I THOUGHT WE WERE FRIENDS! MIND TELLING ME WHY YOU'RE TURNING ON ME?
I AM MERELY OFFERING YOU MEMBERSHIP OF JUSTICE LEAGUE AMERICA.
YOU'RE KIDDING!
I'M HAVING SOME PROBLEMS WITH THE LAW THESE DAYS, YOU KNOW!
AS DID I ONCE. WE CAN WORK IT OUT.
WHO KNOWS? IF NOTHING ELSE, THE JLA COMPOUND--

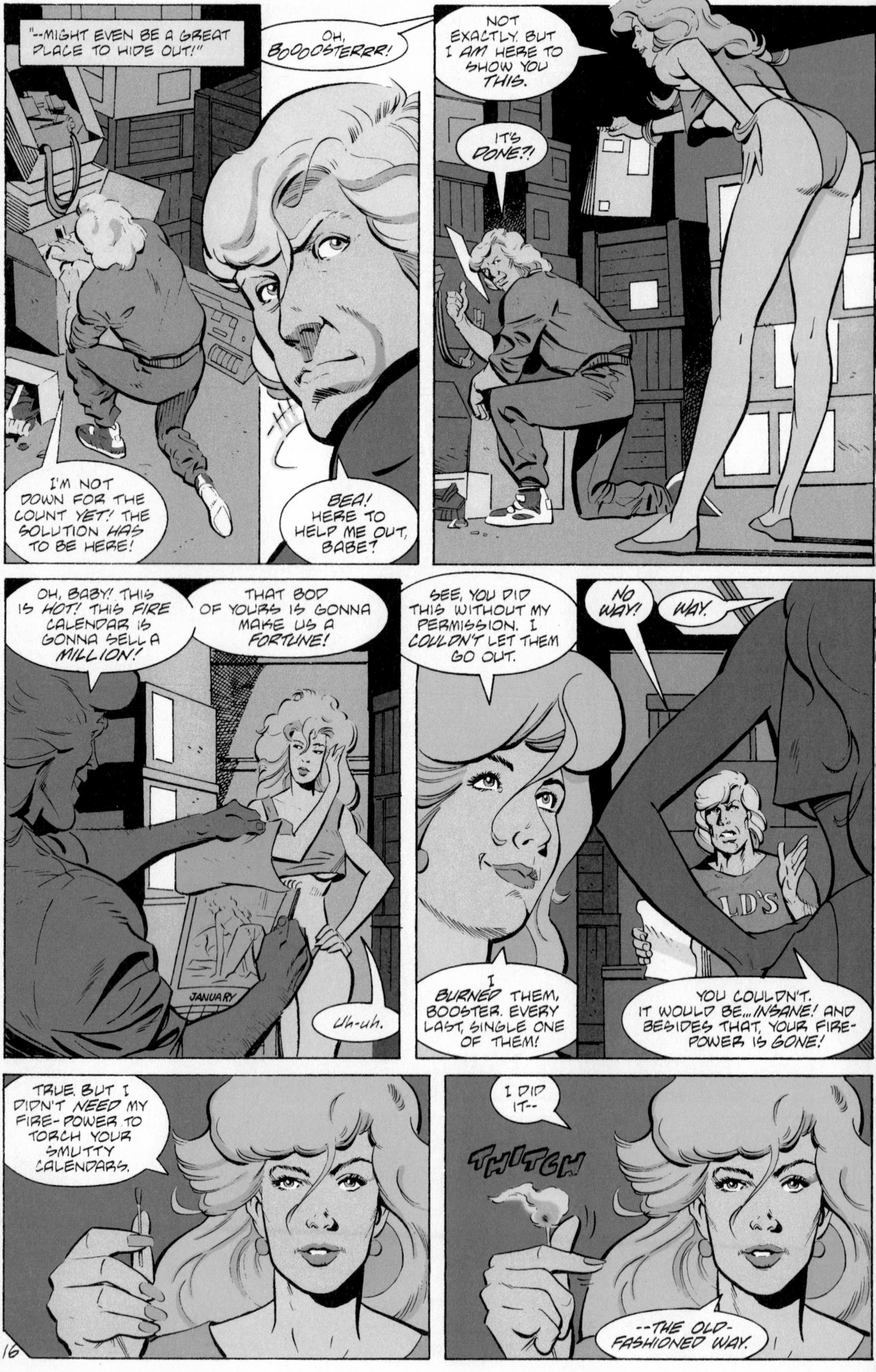

"--MIGHT EVEN BE A GREAT PLACE TO HIDE OUT!"
I'M NOT DOWN FOR THE COUNT YET! THE SOLUTION HAS TO BE HERE!
OH, BOOOOSTERRR!
BEA! HERE TO HELP ME OUT, BABE?
NOT EXACTLY. BUT I AM HERE TO SHOW YOU THIS.
IT'S DONE?!
OH, BABY! THIS IS HOT! THIS FIRE CALENDAR IS GONNA SELL A MILLION!
THAT BOD OF YOURS IS GONNA MAKE US A FORTUNE!
JANUARY
Uh-uh.
SEE, YOU DID THIS WITHOUT MY PERMISSION. I COULDN'T LET THEM GO OUT.
I BURNED THEM, BOOSTER. EVERY LAST, SINGLE ONE OF THEM!
NO WAY!
WAY.
LD'S
YOU COULDN'T. IT WOULD BE...INSANE! AND BESIDES THAT, YOUR FIRE-POWER IS GONE!
TRUE. BUT I DIDN'T NEED MY FIRE-POWER TO TORCH YOUR SMUTTY CALENDARS.
I DID IT--
THITCH
--THE OLD-FASHIONED WAY.

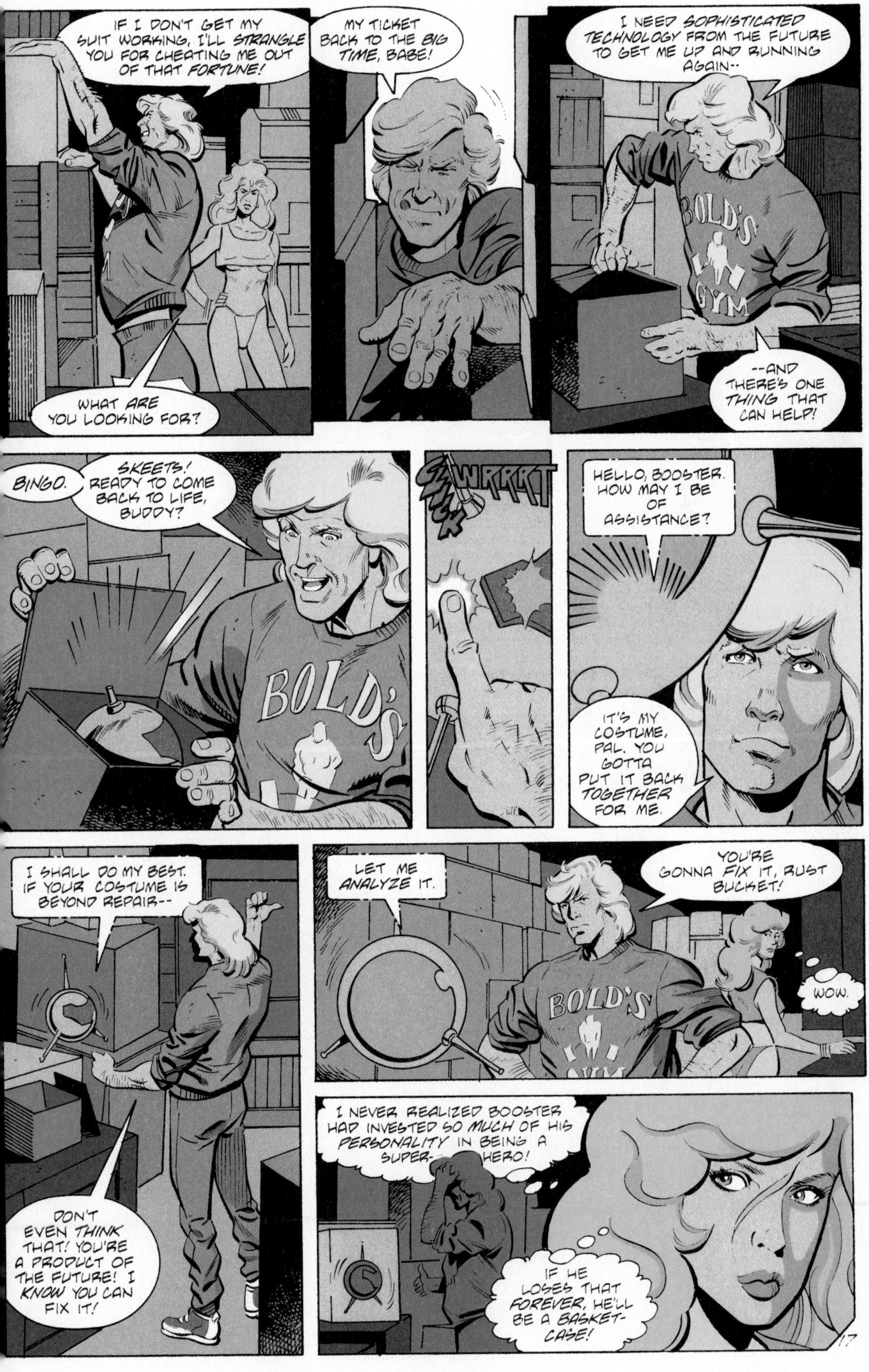

IF I DON'T GET MY SUIT WORKING, I'LL STRANGLE YOU FOR CHEATING ME OUT OF THAT FORTUNE!
WHAT ARE YOU LOOKING FOR?
MY TICKET BACK TO THE BIG TIME, BABE!
I NEED SOPHISTICATED TECHNOLOGY FROM THE FUTURE TO GET ME UP AND RUNNING AGAIN--
BOLD'S GYM
--AND THERE'S ONE THING THAT CAN HELP!
BINGO.
SKEETS! READY TO COME BACK TO LIFE, BUDDY?
BOLD'S
SWICK
WRRRT
HELLO, BOOSTER. HOW MAY I BE OF ASSISTANCE?
IT'S MY COSTUME, PAL. YOU GOTTA PUT IT BACK TOGETHER FOR ME.
I SHALL DO MY BEST. IF YOUR COSTUME IS BEYOND REPAIR--
DON'T EVEN THINK THAT! YOU'RE A PRODUCT OF THE FUTURE! I KNOW YOU CAN FIX IT!
LET ME ANALYZE IT.
YOU'RE GONNA FIX IT, RUST BUCKET!
BOLD'S
WOW.
I NEVER REALIZED BOOSTER HAD INVESTED SO MUCH OF HIS PERSONALITY IN BEING A SUPER-HERO!
IF HE LOSES THAT FOREVER, HE'LL BE A BASKET-CASE!

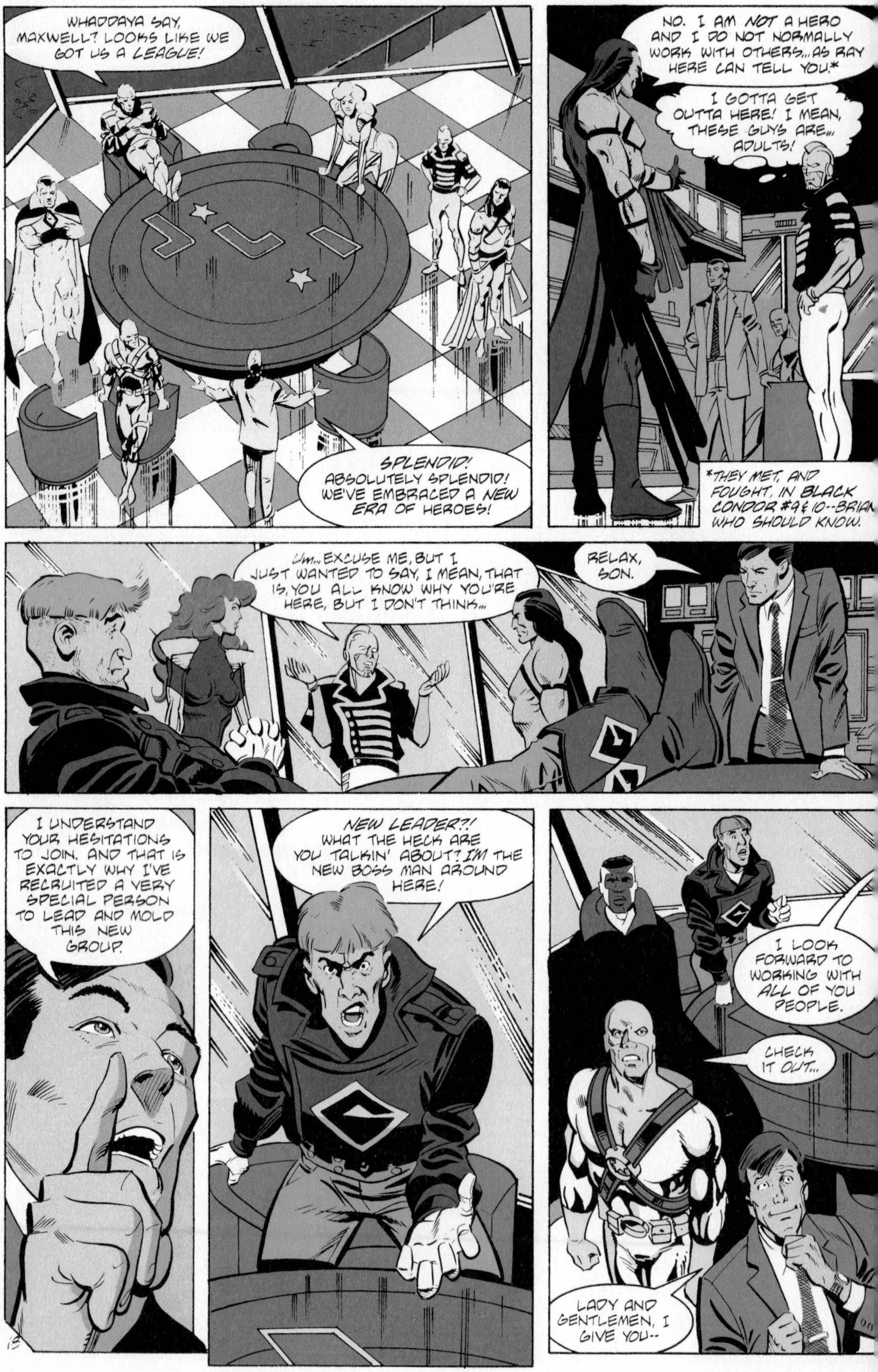

WHADDAYA SAY, MAXWELL? LOOKS LIKE WE GOT US A LEAGUE!
SPLENDID! ABSOLUTELY SPLENDID! WE'VE EMBRACED A NEW ERA OF HEROES!
NO. I AM NOT A HERO AND I DO NOT NORMALLY WORK WITH OTHERS...AS RAY HERE CAN TELL YOU.*
I GOTTA GET OUTTA HERE! I MEAN, THESE GUYS ARE... ADULTS!
*THEY MET, AND FOUGHT, IN BLACK CONDOR #9 & 10--BRIAN WHO SHOULD KNOW.
UM... EXCUSE ME, BUT I JUST WANTED TO SAY, I MEAN, THAT IS, YOU ALL KNOW WHY YOU'RE HERE, BUT I DON'T THINK...
RELAX, SON.
I UNDERSTAND YOUR HESITATIONS TO JOIN. AND THAT IS EXACTLY WHY I'VE RECRUITED A VERY SPECIAL PERSON TO LEAD AND MOLD THIS NEW GROUP.
NEW LEADER?! WHAT THE HECK ARE YOU TALKIN' ABOUT? I'M THE NEW BOSS MAN AROUND HERE!
I LOOK FORWARD TO WORKING WITH ALL OF YOU PEOPLE.
CHECK IT OUT...
LADY AND GENTLEMEN, I GIVE YOU--

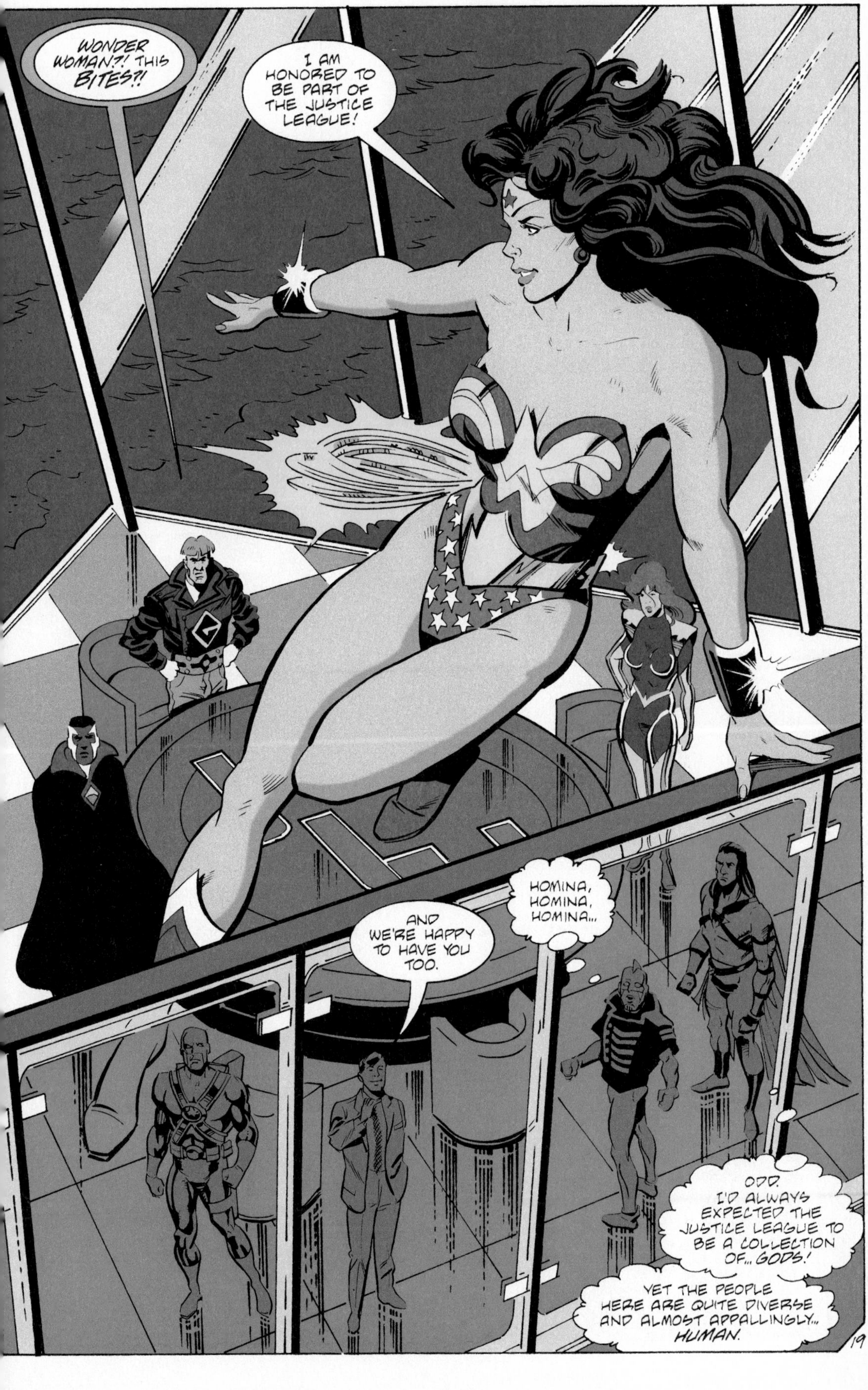
WONDER WOMAN?! THIS BITES?!
I AM HONORED TO BE PART OF THE JUSTICE LEAGUE!
HOMINA, HOMINA, HOMINA...
AND WE'RE HAPPY TO HAVE YOU TOO.
ODD. I'D ALWAYS EXPECTED THE JUSTICE LEAGUE TO BE A COLLECTION OF... GODS!
YET THE PEOPLE HERE ARE QUITE DIVERSE AND ALMOST APPALLINGLY... HUMAN.

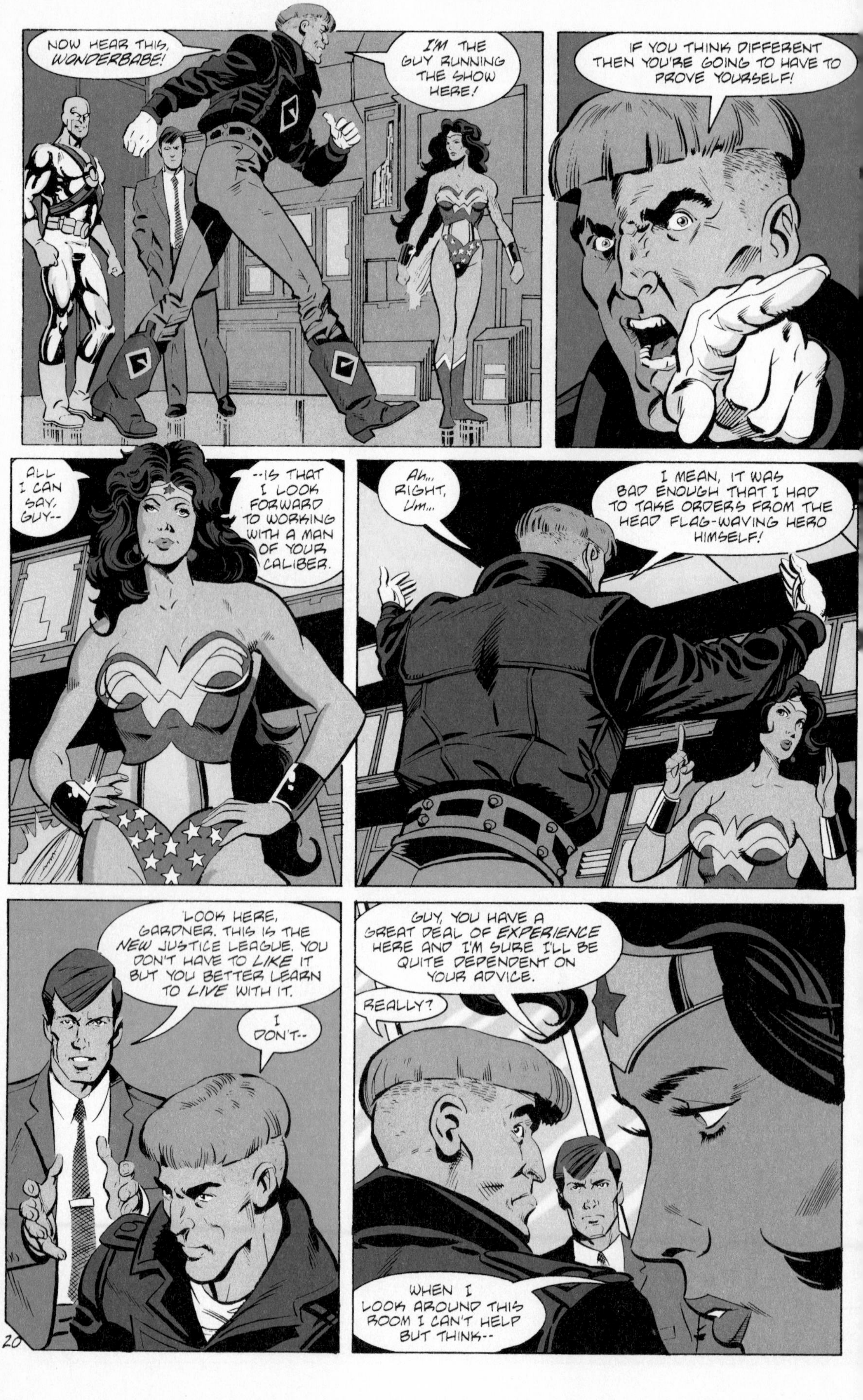
NOW HEAR THIS, WONDERBABE!
I'M THE GUY RUNNING THE SHOW HERE!
IF YOU THINK DIFFERENT THEN YOU'RE GOING TO HAVE TO PROVE YOURSELF!
ALL I CAN SAY, GUY--
--IS THAT I LOOK FORWARD TO WORKING WITH A MAN OF YOUR CALIBER.
Ah... RIGHT, Um...
I MEAN, IT WAS BAD ENOUGH THAT I HAD TO TAKE ORDERS FROM THE HEAD FLAG-WAVING HERO HIMSELF!
LOOK HERE, GARDNER. THIS IS THE NEW JUSTICE LEAGUE. YOU DON'T HAVE TO LIKE IT BUT YOU BETTER LEARN TO LIVE WITH IT.
I DON'T--
GUY, YOU HAVE A GREAT DEAL OF EXPERIENCE HERE AND I'M SURE I'LL BE QUITE DEPENDENT ON YOUR ADVICE.
REALLY?
WHEN I LOOK AROUND THIS ROOM I CAN'T HELP BUT THINK--

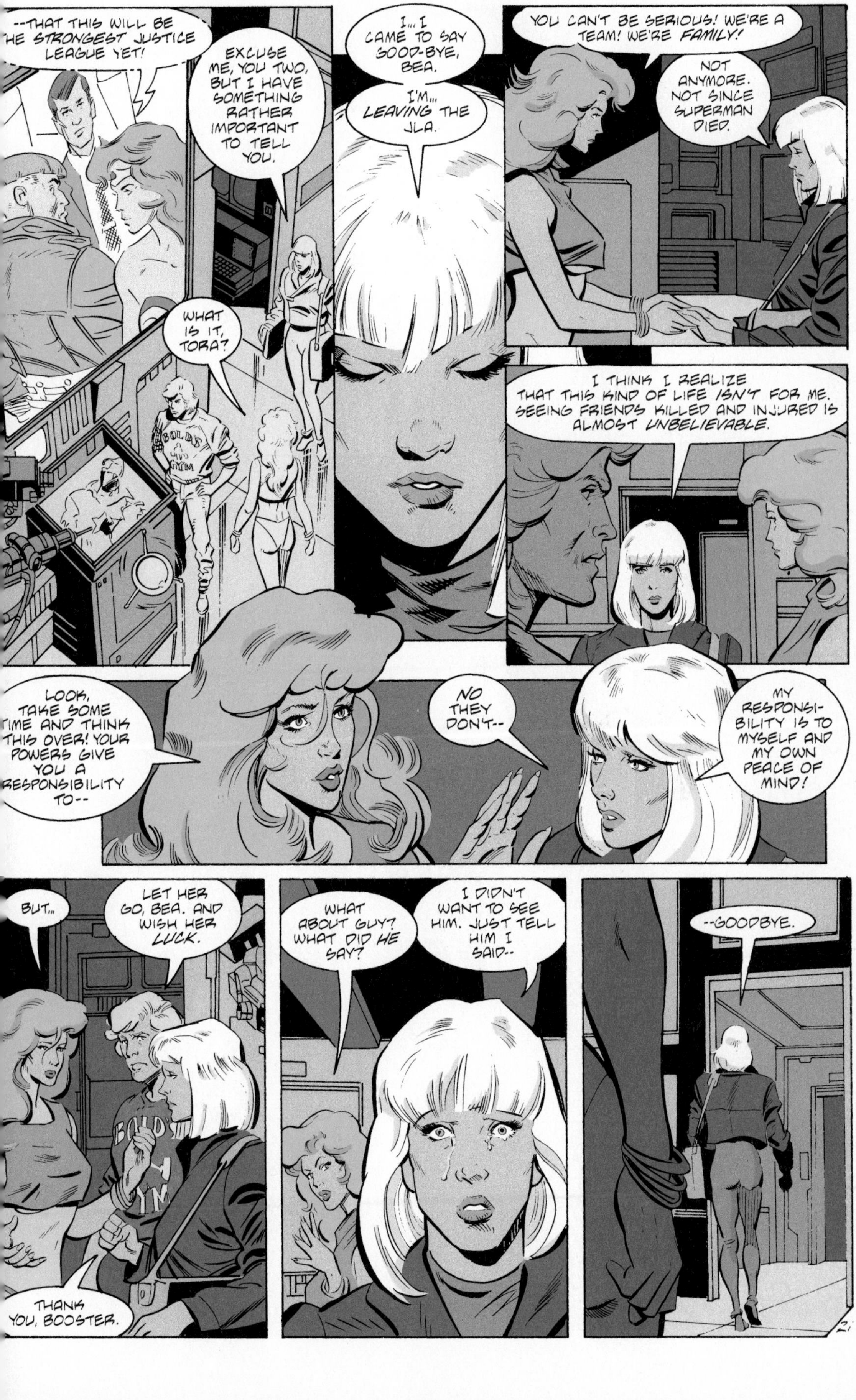
--THAT THIS WILL BE THE STRONGEST JUSTICE LEAGUE YET!
EXCUSE ME, YOU TWO, BUT I HAVE SOMETHING RATHER IMPORTANT TO TELL YOU.
WHAT IS IT, TORA?
I... I CAME TO SAY GOOD-BYE, BEA.
I'M... LEAVING THE JLA.
YOU CAN'T BE SERIOUS! WE'RE A TEAM! WE'RE FAMILY!
NOT ANYMORE. NOT SINCE SUPERMAN DIED.
I THINK I REALIZE THAT THIS KIND OF LIFE ISN'T FOR ME. SEEING FRIENDS KILLED AND INJURED IS ALMOST UNBELIEVABLE.
LOOK, TAKE SOME TIME AND THINK THIS OVER! YOUR POWERS GIVE YOU A RESPONSIBILITY TO--
NO THEY DON'T--
MY RESPONSI-BILITY IS TO MYSELF AND MY OWN PEACE OF MIND!
BUT...
LET HER GO, BEA. AND WISH HER LUCK.
THANK YOU, BOOSTER.
WHAT ABOUT GUY? WHAT DID HE SAY?
I DIDN'T WANT TO SEE HIM. JUST TELL HIM I SAID--
--GOODBYE.
BOLD'S GYM

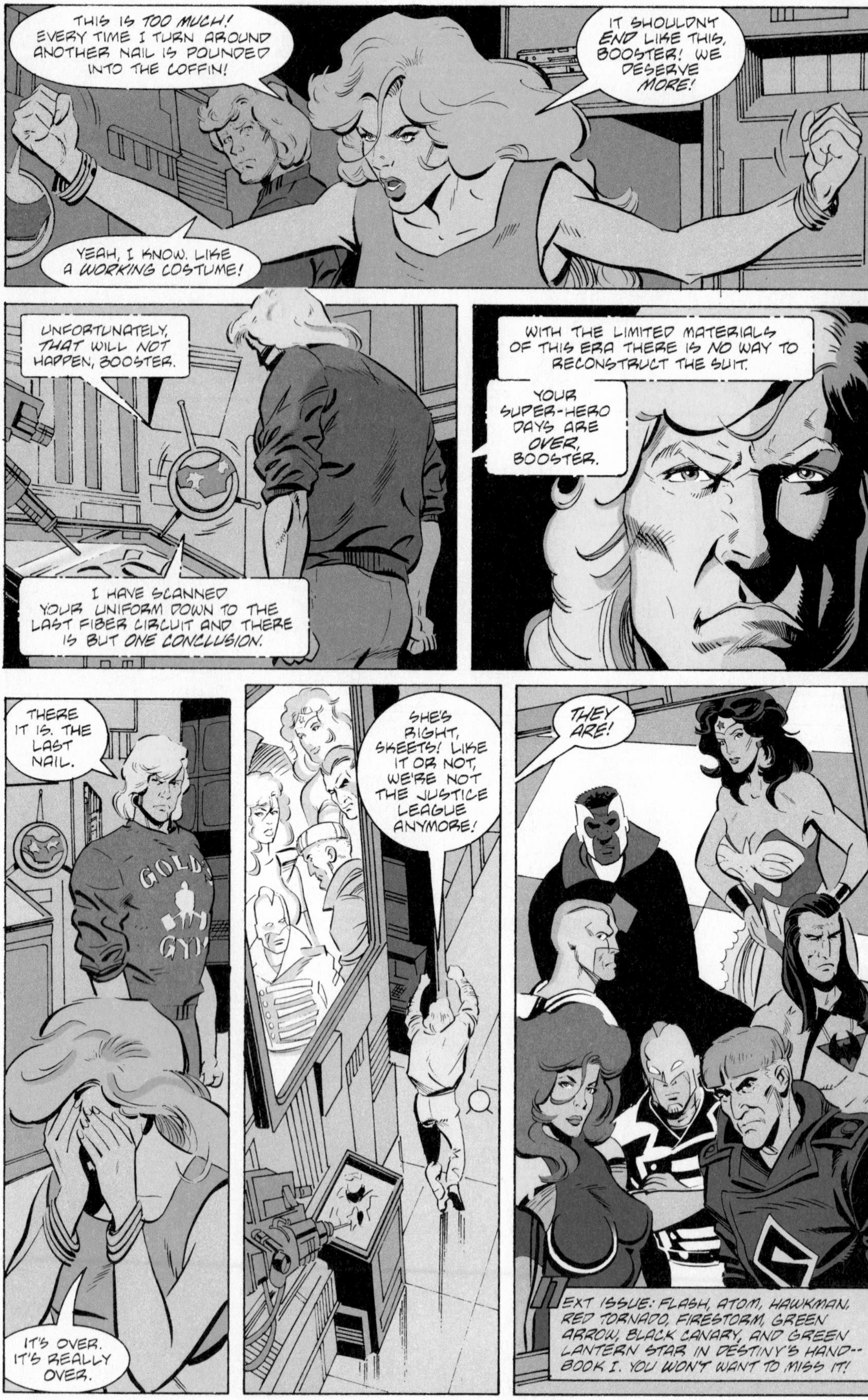

THIS IS TOO MUCH! EVERY TIME I TURN AROUND ANOTHER NAIL IS POUNDED INTO THE COFFIN!
IT SHOULDN'T END LIKE THIS, BOOSTER! WE DESERVE MORE!
YEAH, I KNOW. LIKE A WORKING COSTUME!
UNFORTUNATELY, THAT WILL NOT HAPPEN, BOOSTER.
I HAVE SCANNED YOUR UNIFORM DOWN TO THE LAST FIBER CIRCUIT AND THERE IS BUT ONE CONCLUSION.
WITH THE LIMITED MATERIALS OF THIS ERA THERE IS NO WAY TO RECONSTRUCT THE SUIT.
YOUR SUPER-HERO DAYS ARE OVER, BOOSTER.
THERE IT IS. THE LAST NAIL.
GOLD'S GYM
IT'S OVER. IT'S REALLY OVER.
SHE'S RIGHT, SKEETS! LIKE IT OR NOT, WE'RE NOT THE JUSTICE LEAGUE ANYMORE!
THEY ARE!
NEXT ISSUE: FLASH, ATOM, HAWKMAN, RED TORNADO, FIRESTORM, GREEN ARROW, BLACK CANARY, AND GREEN LANTERN STAR IN DESTINY'S HAND--BOOK I. YOU WON'T WANT TO MISS IT!

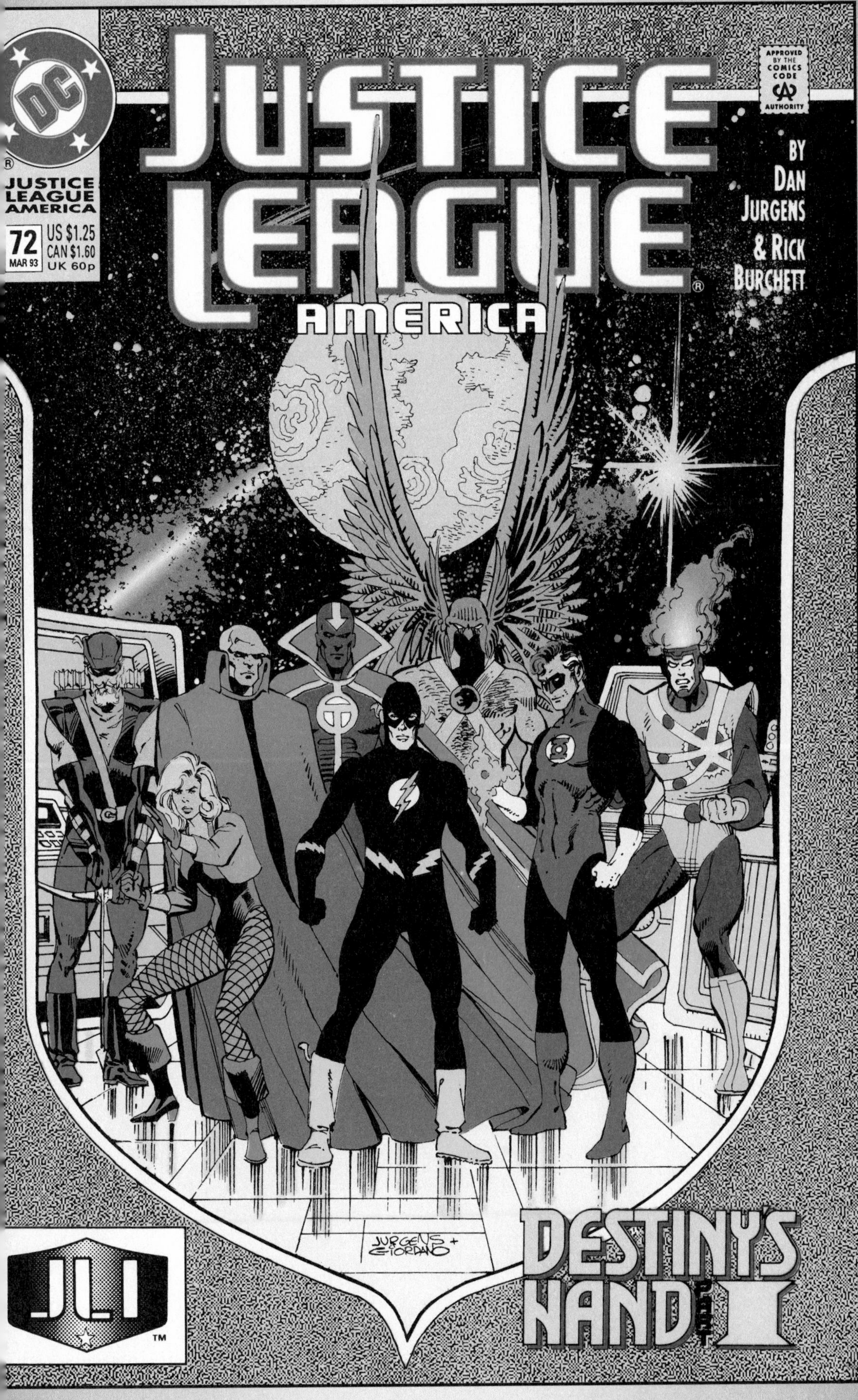

JUSTICE LEAGUE AMERICA
JUSTICE LEAGUE AMERICA
72
MAR 93
US $1.25
CAN $1.60
UK 60p
APPROVED BY THE COMICS CODE AUTHORITY
BY DAN JURGENS & RICK BURCHETT
JURGENS + GIORDANO
JLI
DESTINY'S HAND PART I

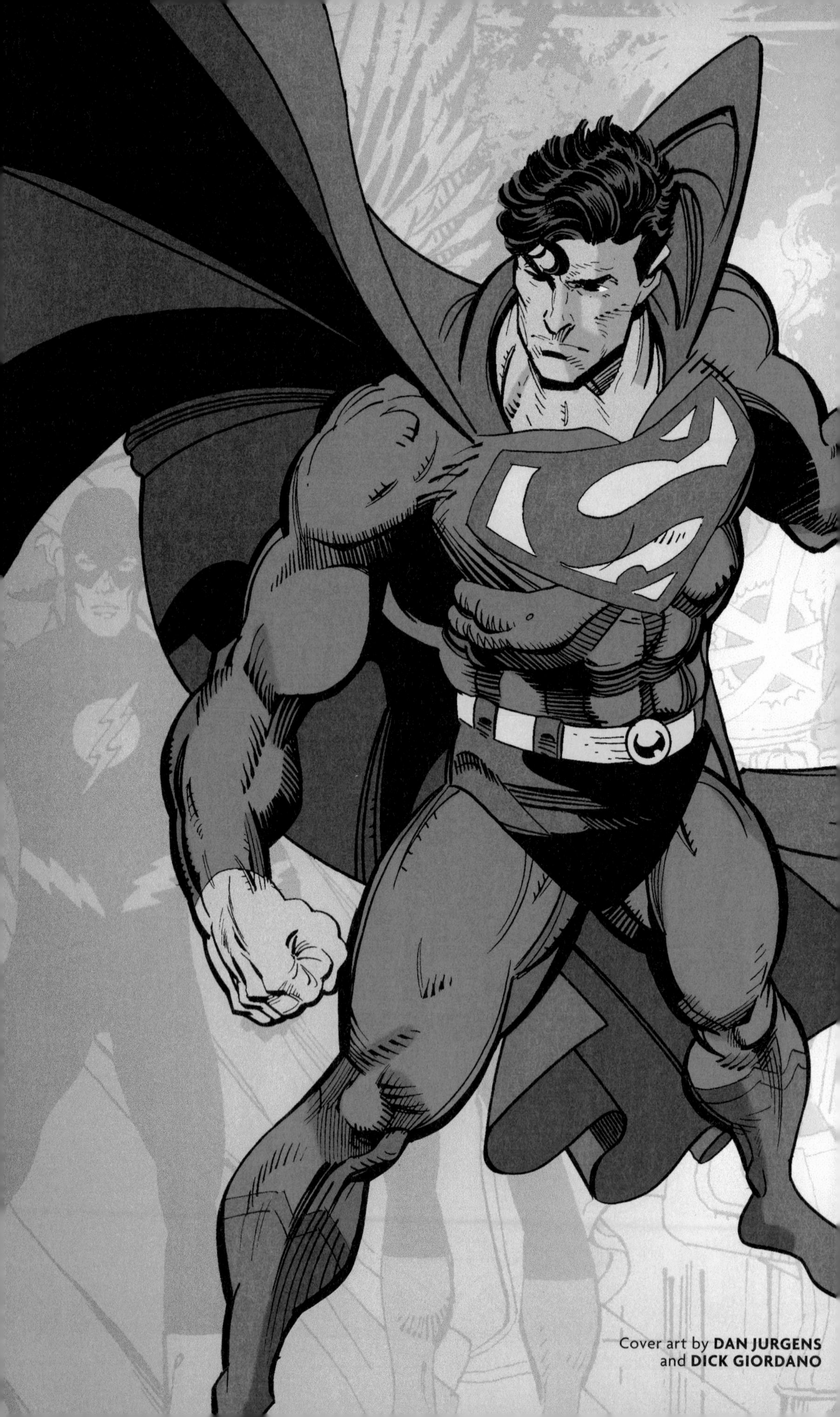

Cover art by **DAN JURGENS**
and **DICK GIORDANO**

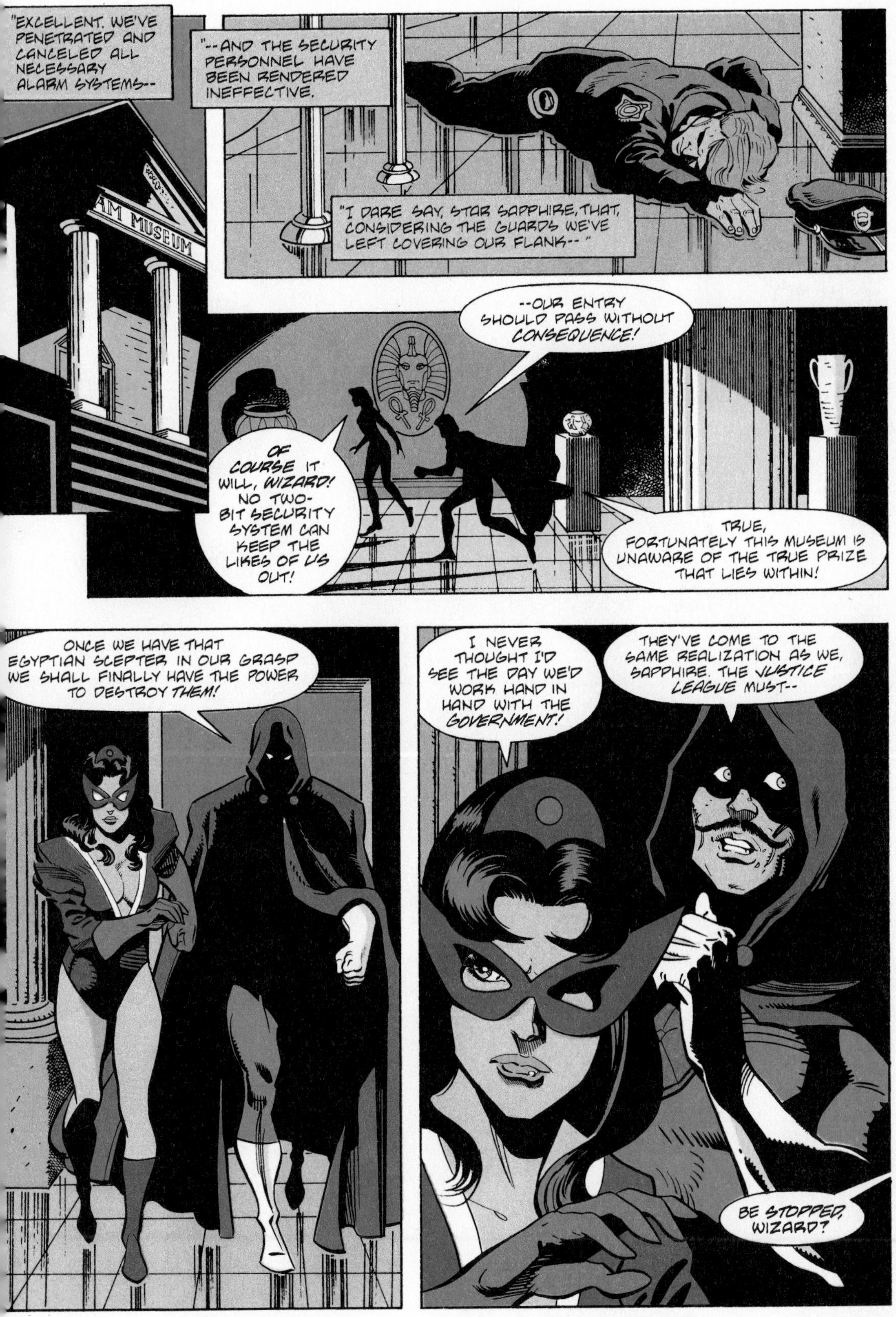
"EXCELLENT. WE'VE PENETRATED AND CANCELED ALL NECESSARY ALARM SYSTEMS--
"--AND THE SECURITY PERSONNEL HAVE BEEN RENDERED INEFFECTIVE.
AM MUSEUM
"I DARE SAY, STAR SAPPHIRE, THAT, CONSIDERING THE GUARDS WE'VE LEFT COVERING OUR FLANK-- "
--OUR ENTRY SHOULD PASS WITHOUT CONSEQUENCE!
OF COURSE IT WILL, WIZARD! NO TWO-BIT SECURITY SYSTEM CAN KEEP THE LIKES OF US OUT!
TRUE, FORTUNATELY THIS MUSEUM IS UNAWARE OF THE TRUE PRIZE THAT LIES WITHIN!
ONCE WE HAVE THAT EGYPTIAN SCEPTER IN OUR GRASP WE SHALL FINALLY HAVE THE POWER TO DESTROY THEM!
I NEVER THOUGHT I'D SEE THE DAY WE'D WORK HAND IN HAND WITH THE GOVERNMENT!
THEY'VE COME TO THE SAME REALIZATION AS WE, SAPPHIRE. THE JUSTICE LEAGUE MUST--
BE STOPPED, WIZARD?

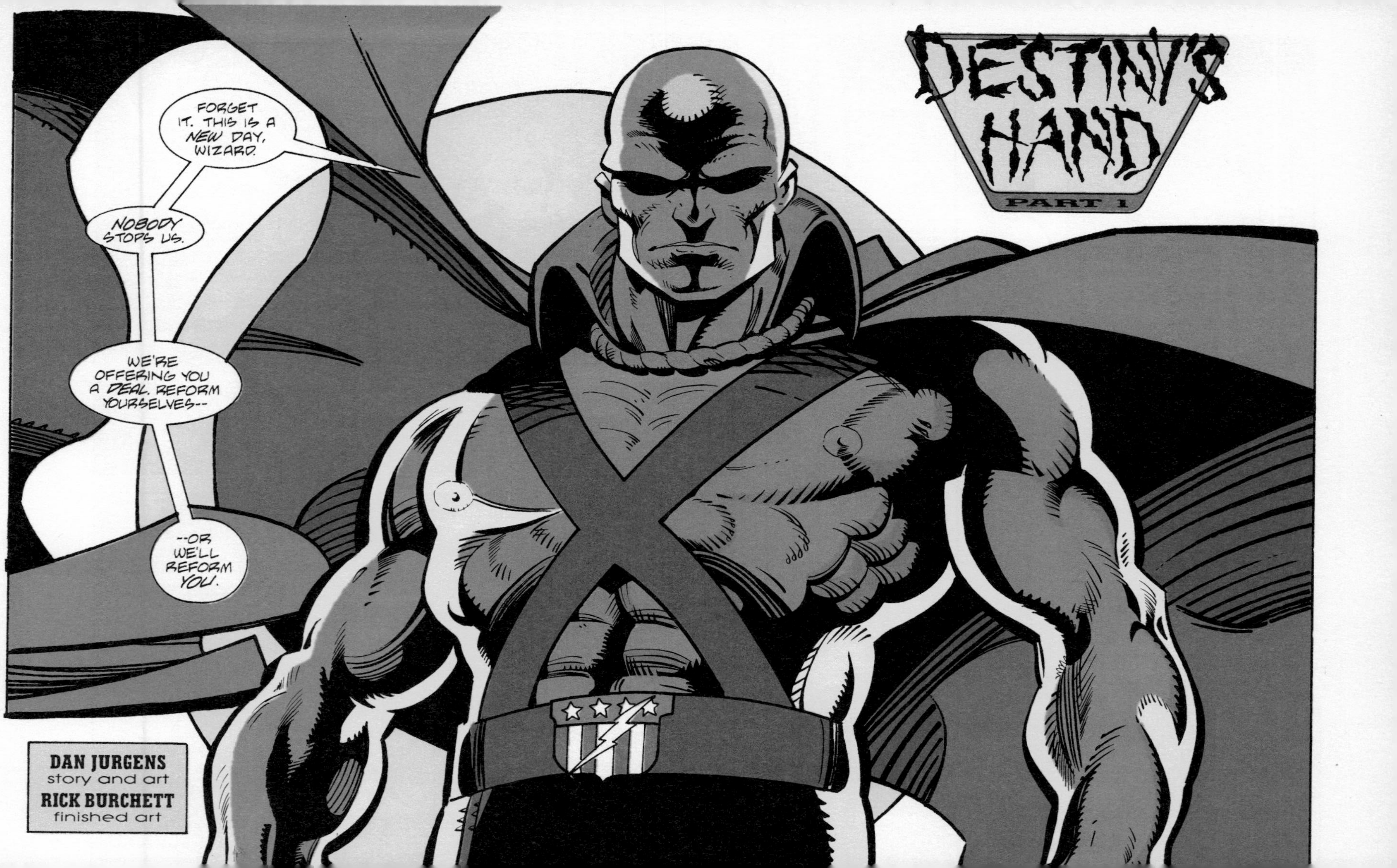
DESTINY'S HAND
PART 1
FORGET IT. THIS IS A NEW DAY, WIZARD.
NOBODY STOPS US.
WE'RE OFFERING YOU A DEAL. REFORM YOURSELVES--
--OR WE'LL REFORM YOU.
DAN JURGENS story and art
RICK BURCHETT finished art

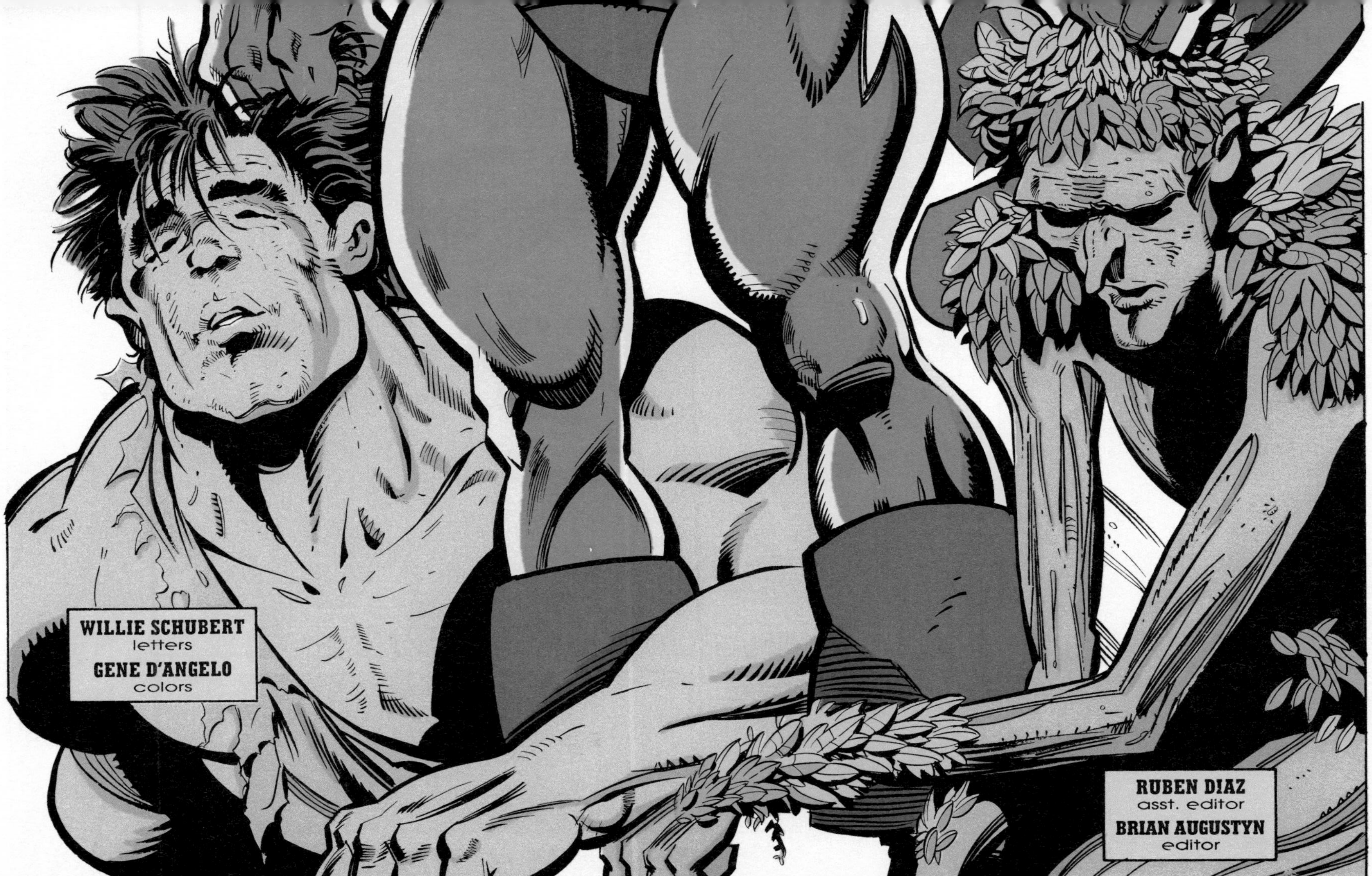
WILLIE SCHUBERT
letters
GENE D'ANGELO
colors
RUBEN DIAZ
asst. editor
BRIAN AUGUSTYN
editor

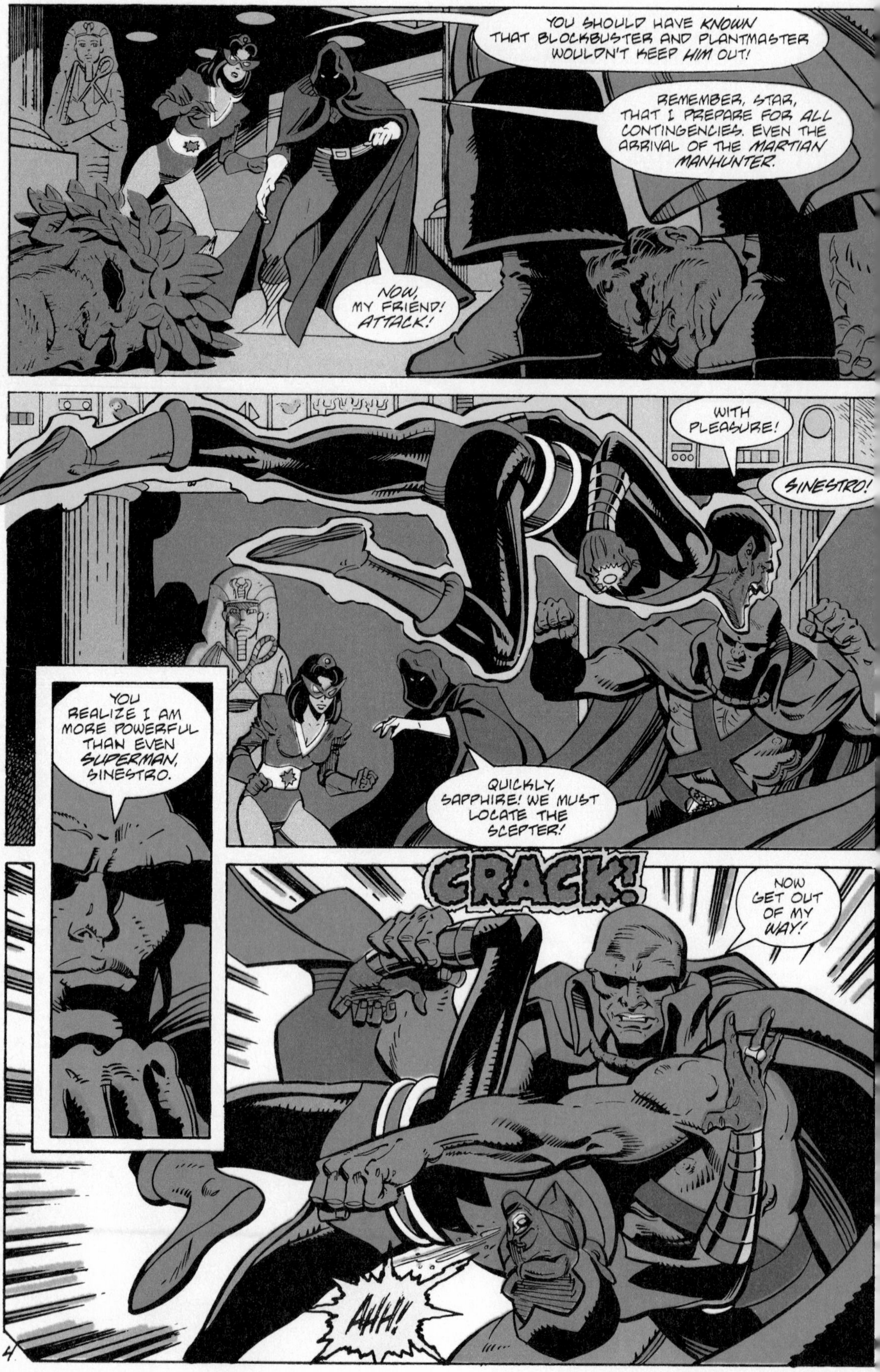
YOU SHOULD HAVE KNOWN THAT BLOCKBUSTER AND PLANTMASTER WOULDN'T KEEP HIM OUT!
REMEMBER, STAR, THAT I PREPARE FOR ALL CONTINGENCIES. EVEN THE ARRIVAL OF THE MARTIAN MANHUNTER.
NOW, MY FRIEND! ATTACK!
WITH PLEASURE!
SINESTRO!
QUICKLY, SAPPHIRE! WE MUST LOCATE THE SCEPTER!
YOU REALIZE I AM MORE POWERFUL THAN EVEN SUPERMAN, SINESTRO.
CRACK!
NOW GET OUT OF MY WAY!
AHH!

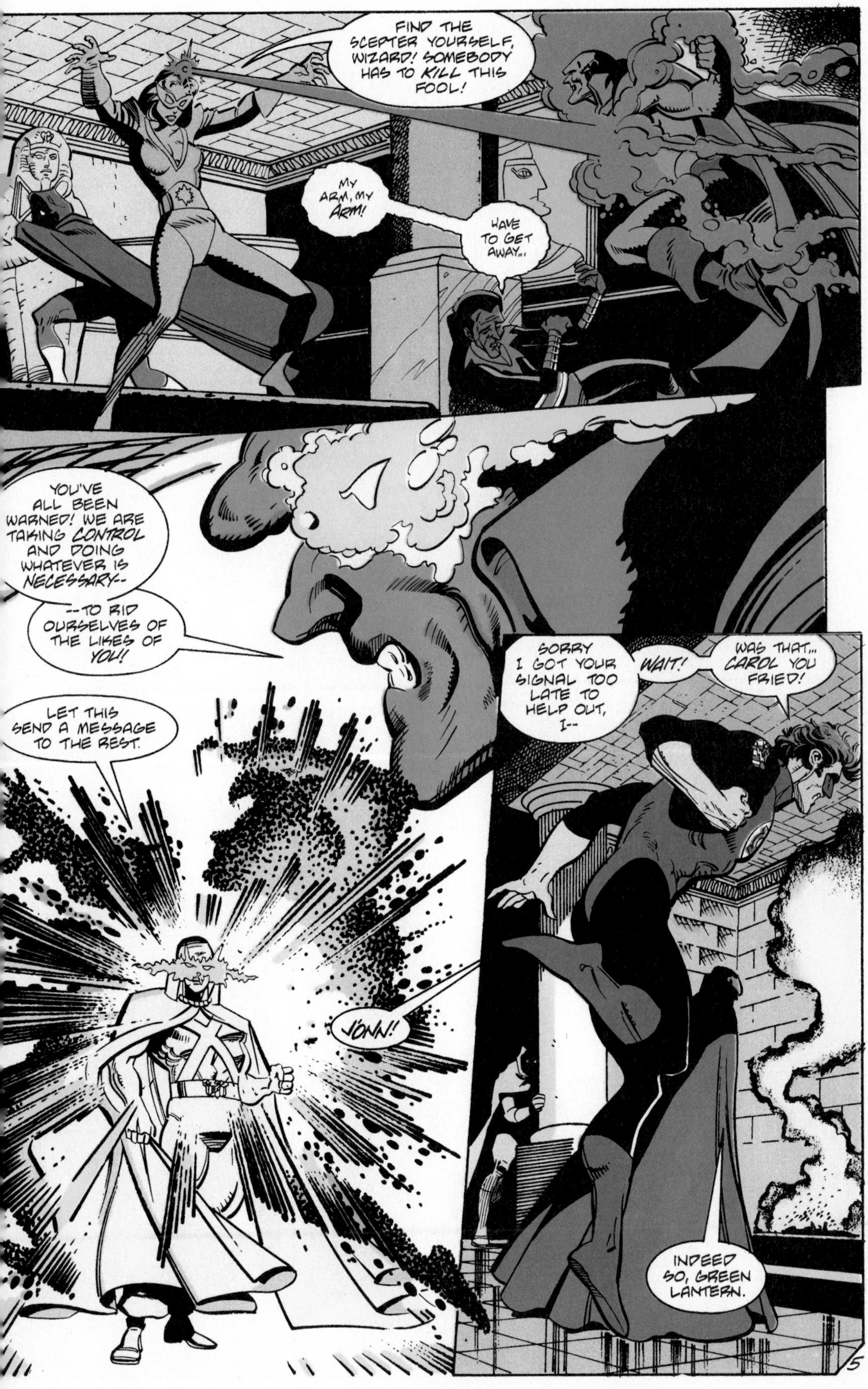
FIND THE SCEPTER YOURSELF, WIZARD! SOMEBODY HAS TO KILL THIS FOOL!
MY ARM, MY ARM!
HAVE TO GET AWAY...
YOU'VE ALL BEEN WARNED! WE ARE TAKING CONTROL AND DOING WHATEVER IS NECESSARY--
--TO RID OURSELVES OF THE LIKES OF YOU!
LET THIS SEND A MESSAGE TO THE REST.
J'ONN!
SORRY I GOT YOUR SIGNAL TOO LATE TO HELP OUT, I--
WAIT!
WAS THAT... CAROL YOU FRIED!
INDEED SO, GREEN LANTERN.

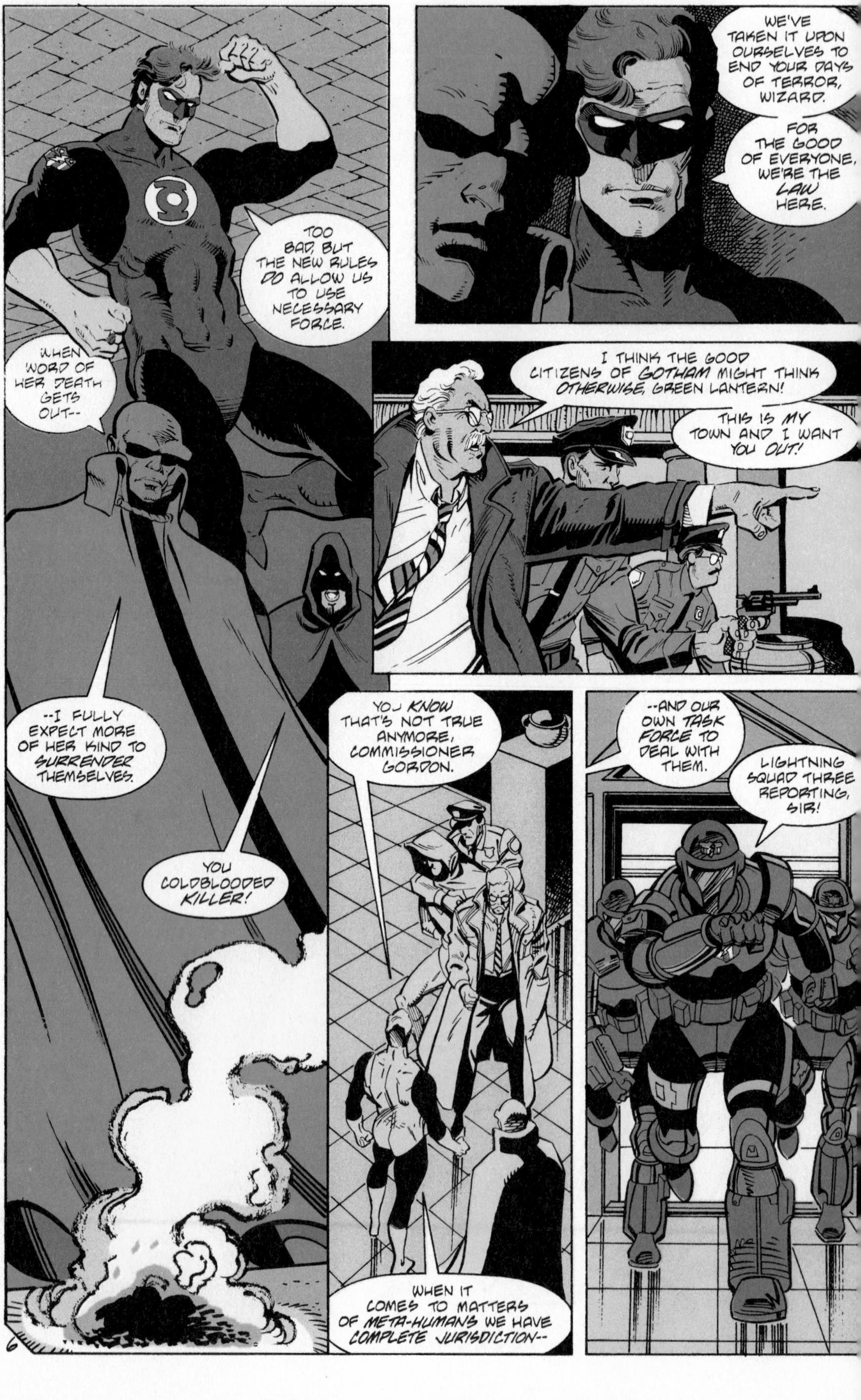
TOO BAD, BUT THE NEW RULES DO ALLOW US TO USE NECESSARY FORCE.
WE'VE TAKEN IT UPON OURSELVES TO END YOUR DAYS OF TERROR, WIZARD.
FOR THE GOOD OF EVERYONE, WE'RE THE LAW HERE.
WHEN WORD OF HER DEATH GETS OUT--
I THINK THE GOOD CITIZENS OF GOTHAM MIGHT THINK OTHERWISE, GREEN LANTERN!
THIS IS MY TOWN AND I WANT YOU OUT!
--I FULLY EXPECT MORE OF HER KIND TO SURRENDER THEMSELVES.
YOU COLDBLOODED KILLER!
YOU KNOW THAT'S NOT TRUE ANYMORE, COMMISSIONER GORDON.
WHEN IT COMES TO MATTERS OF META-HUMANS WE HAVE COMPLETE JURISDICTION--
--AND OUR OWN TASK FORCE TO DEAL WITH THEM.
LIGHTNING SQUAD THREE REPORTING, SIR!

SECURE THE AREA AND GET THOSE CREEPS OUT OF HERE.
JUST ONE MINUTE, LANTERN. IT'S MY JOB TO ARREST THEM!
IT IS OUR JOB TO TAKE AND REFORM THEM.
IS THIS WHAT YOU WANT, GORDON? NINE OR TEN SUPER-POWERED, SELF-APPOINTED GODS RUNNING THE PLANET?
SURE, THEY'LL START WITH US--BUT MARK MY WORDS--
--YOU ARE NEXT!
WHERE ARE YOU TAKING THESE PEOPLE?
THE JLA INCARCERATION COMPLEX IN NEVADA, COMMISSIONER.
BLEEDING FASCISTS! IF SOMETHING ISN'T DONE TO STOP THEM SOON--
--THEY'LL TAKE OVER THE WHOLE BLASTED PLANET!
ONCE THEY GO THROUGH THE INTENSE PSI-SCRUBBING PROCESS THEY'LL NO LONGER PREY ON SOCIETY!
TOO BAD SINESTRO GOT AWAY. I'D REALLY LIKE TO GET MY MITTS ON HIM!
ALERT ALL MEMBERS AND LIGHTNING TROOPS TO LAUNCH A FULL-SCALE SEARCH. WITH LUCK--
7

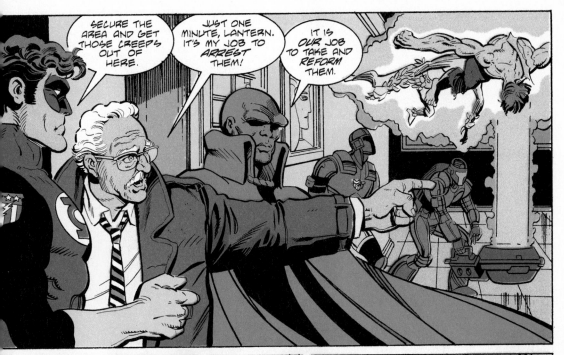

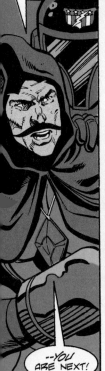

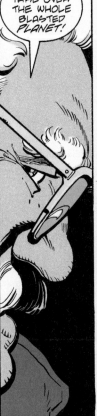

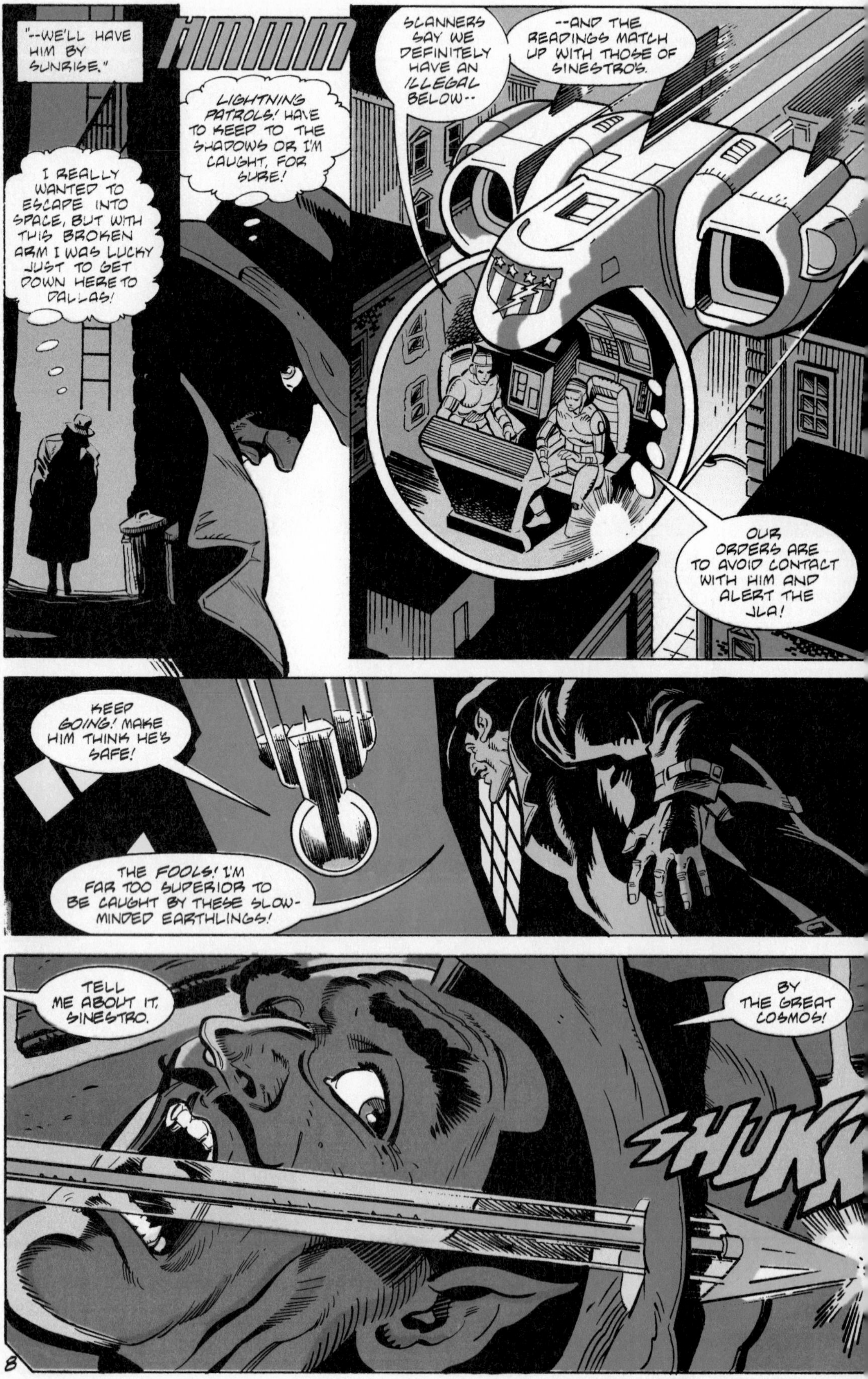
"--WE'LL HAVE HIM BY SUNRISE."
HMMMM
I REALLY WANTED TO ESCAPE INTO SPACE, BUT WITH THIS BROKEN ARM I WAS LUCKY JUST TO GET DOWN HERE TO DALLAS!
LIGHTNING PATROLS! HAVE TO KEEP TO THE SHADOWS OR I'M CAUGHT, FOR SURE!
SCANNERS SAY WE DEFINITELY HAVE AN ILLEGAL BELOW--
--AND THE READINGS MATCH UP WITH THOSE OF SINESTRO'S.
OUR ORDERS ARE TO AVOID CONTACT WITH HIM AND ALERT THE JLA!
KEEP GOING! MAKE HIM THINK HE'S SAFE!
THE FOOLS! I'M FAR TOO SUPERIOR TO BE CAUGHT BY THESE SLOW-MINDED EARTHLINGS!
TELL ME ABOUT IT, SINESTRO.
BY THE GREAT COSMOS!

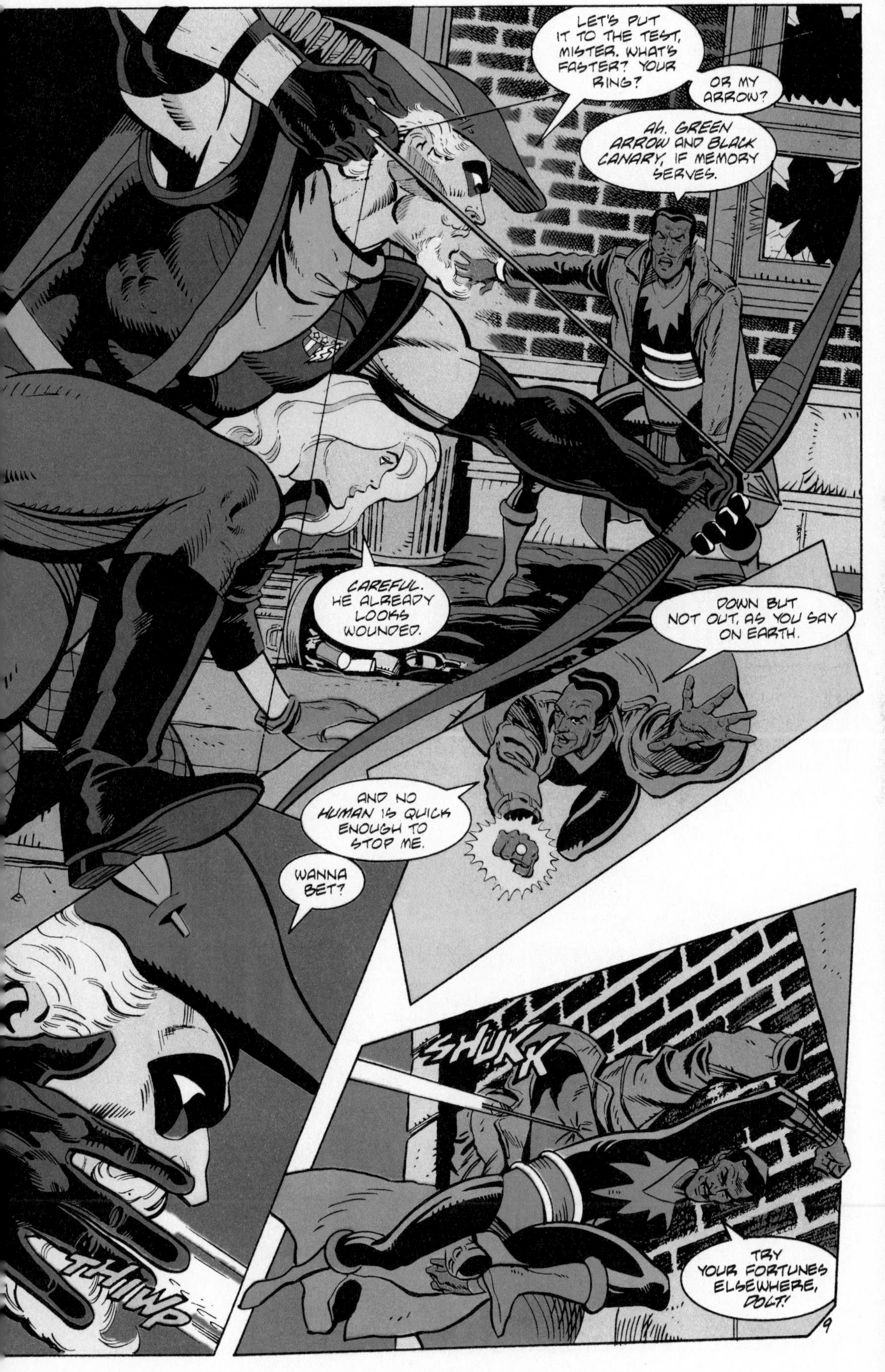
LET'S PUT IT TO THE TEST, MISTER. WHAT'S FASTER? YOUR RING?
OR MY ARROW?
AH. GREEN ARROW AND BLACK CANARY, IF MEMORY SERVES.
CAREFUL. HE ALREADY LOOKS WOUNDED.
DOWN BUT NOT OUT, AS YOU SAY ON EARTH.
AND NO HUMAN IS QUICK ENOUGH TO STOP ME.
WANNA BET?
THWIP
SHUKK
TRY YOUR FORTUNES ELSEWHERE, DOLT!

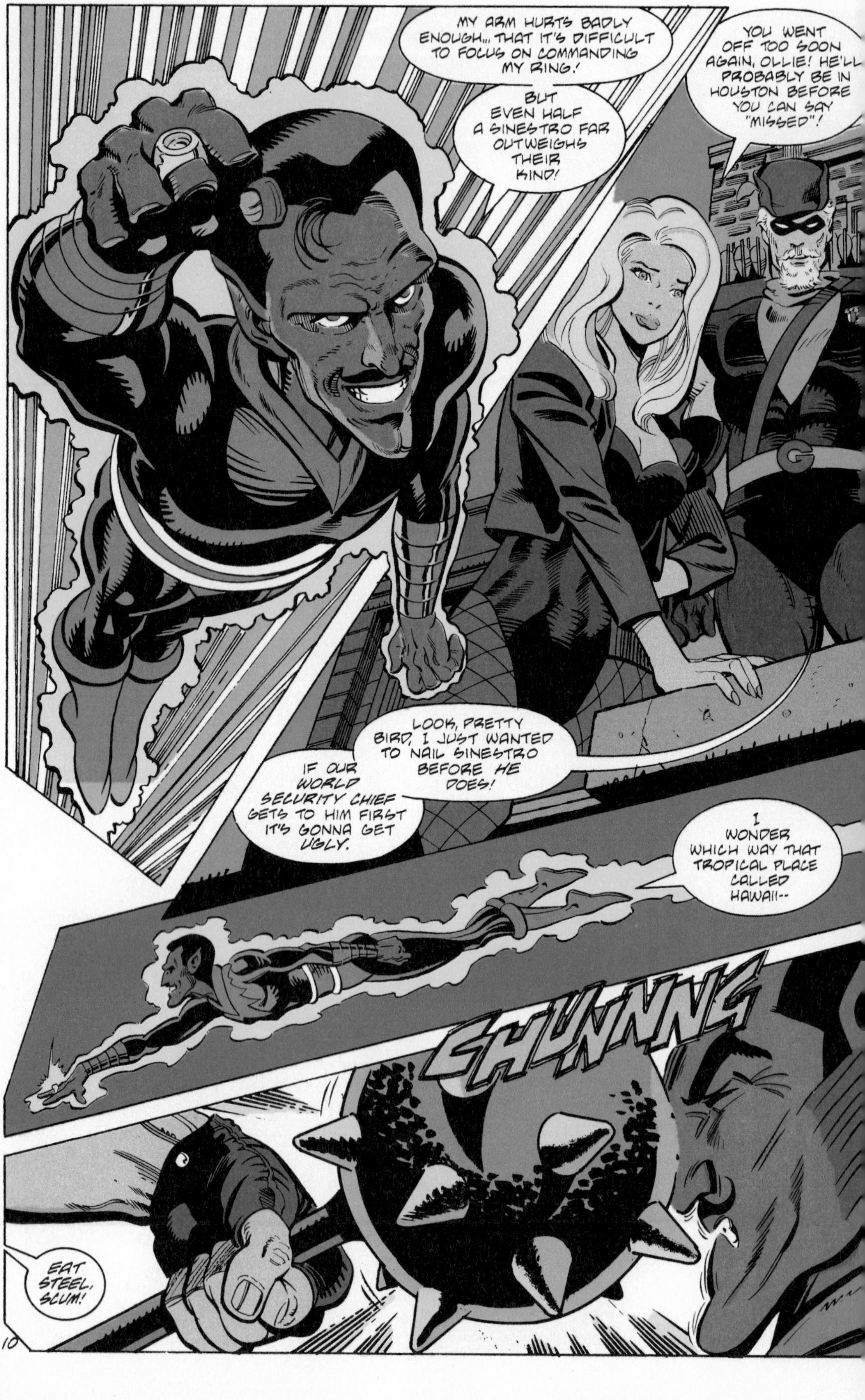
MY ARM HURTS BADLY ENOUGH... THAT IT'S DIFFICULT TO FOCUS ON COMMANDING MY RING!
BUT EVEN HALF A SINESTRO FAR OUTWEIGHS THEIR KIND!
YOU WENT OFF TOO SOON AGAIN, OLLIE! HE'LL PROBABLY BE IN HOUSTON BEFORE YOU CAN SAY "MISSED"!
LOOK, PRETTY BIRD, I JUST WANTED TO NAIL SINESTRO BEFORE HE DOES!
IF OUR WORLD SECURITY CHIEF GETS TO HIM FIRST IT'S GONNA GET UGLY.
I WONDER WHICH WAY THAT TROPICAL PLACE CALLED HAWAII--
CHUNNNG
EAT STEEL, SCUM!

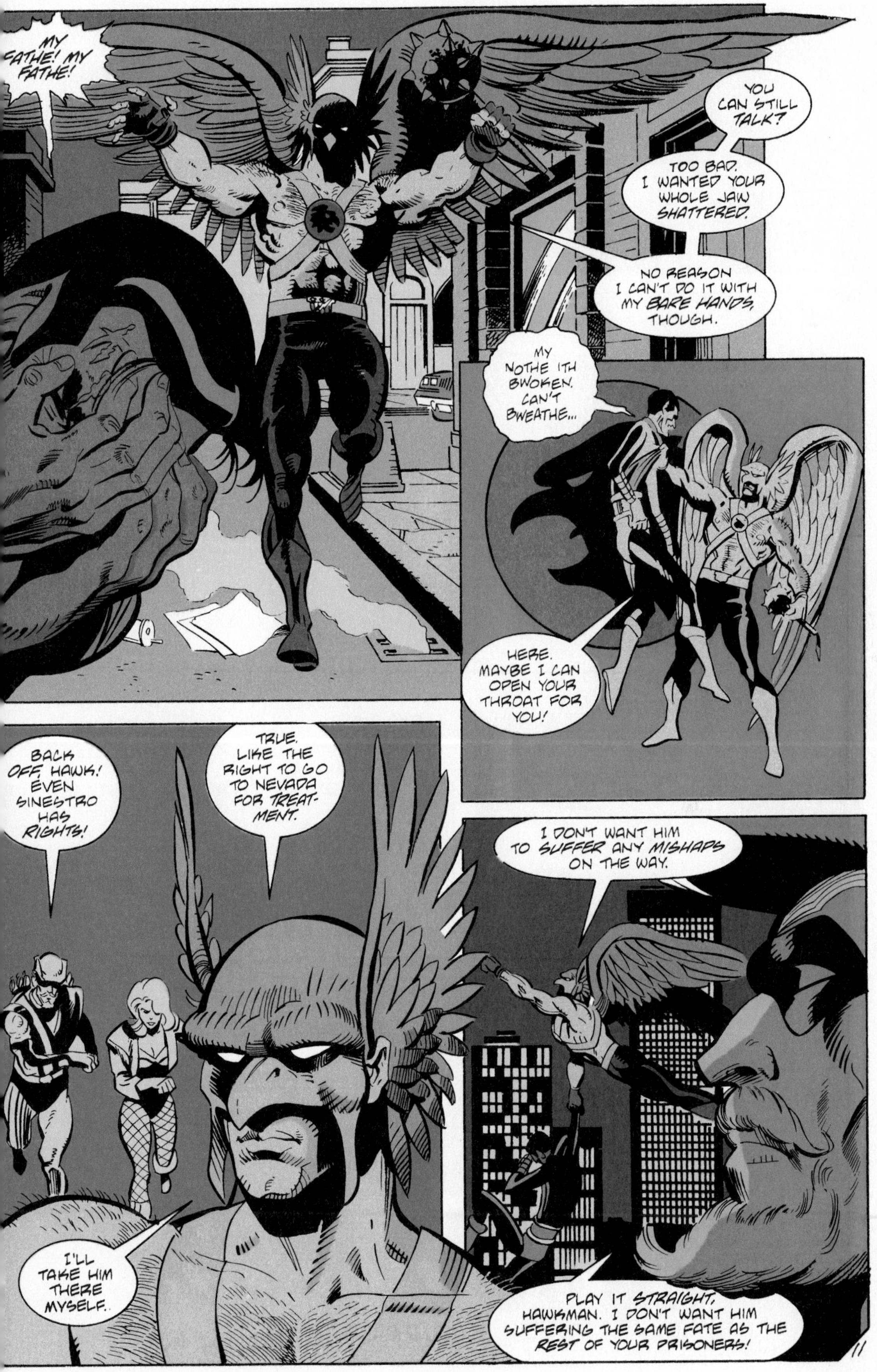
MY FATHE! MY FATHE!
YOU CAN STILL TALK?
TOO BAD. I WANTED YOUR WHOLE JAW SHATTERED.
NO REASON I CAN'T DO IT WITH MY BARE HANDS, THOUGH.
MY NOTHE ITH BWOKEN. CAN'T BWEATHE...
HERE. MAYBE I CAN OPEN YOUR THROAT FOR YOU!
BACK OFF, HAWK! EVEN SINESTRO HAS RIGHTS!
TRUE. LIKE THE RIGHT TO GO TO NEVADA FOR TREAT-MENT.
I'LL TAKE HIM THERE MYSELF.
I DON'T WANT HIM TO SUFFER ANY MISHAPS ON THE WAY.
PLAY IT STRAIGHT, HAWKMAN. I DON'T WANT HIM SUFFERING THE SAME FATE AS THE REST OF YOUR PRISONERS!

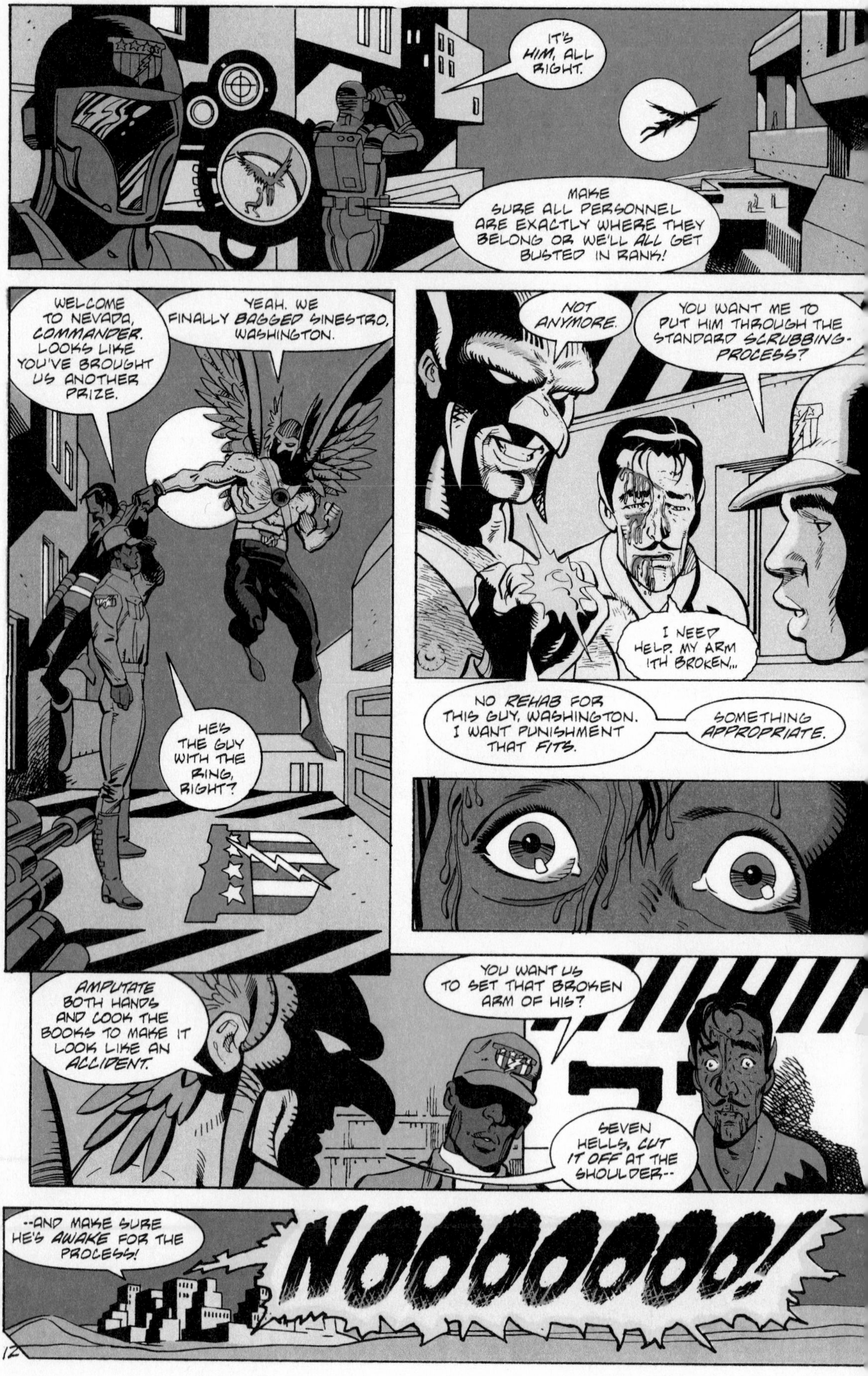
IT'S HIM, ALL RIGHT.
MAKE SURE ALL PERSONNEL ARE EXACTLY WHERE THEY BELONG OR WE'LL ALL GET BUSTED IN RANK!
WELCOME TO NEVADA, COMMANDER. LOOKS LIKE YOU'VE BROUGHT US ANOTHER PRIZE.
YEAH. WE FINALLY BAGGED SINESTRO, WASHINGTON.
HE'S THE GUY WITH THE RING, RIGHT?
NOT ANYMORE.
YOU WANT ME TO PUT HIM THROUGH THE STANDARD SCRUBBING-PROCESS?
I NEED HELP. MY ARM ITH BROKEN...
NO REHAB FOR THIS GUY, WASHINGTON. I WANT PUNISHMENT THAT FITS.
SOMETHING APPROPRIATE.
AMPUTATE BOTH HANDS AND COOK THE BOOKS TO MAKE IT LOOK LIKE AN ACCIDENT.
YOU WANT US TO SET THAT BROKEN ARM OF HIS?
SEVEN HELLS, CUT IT OFF AT THE SHOULDER--
--AND MAKE SURE HE'S AWAKE FOR THE PROCESS!
NOOOOOOO!

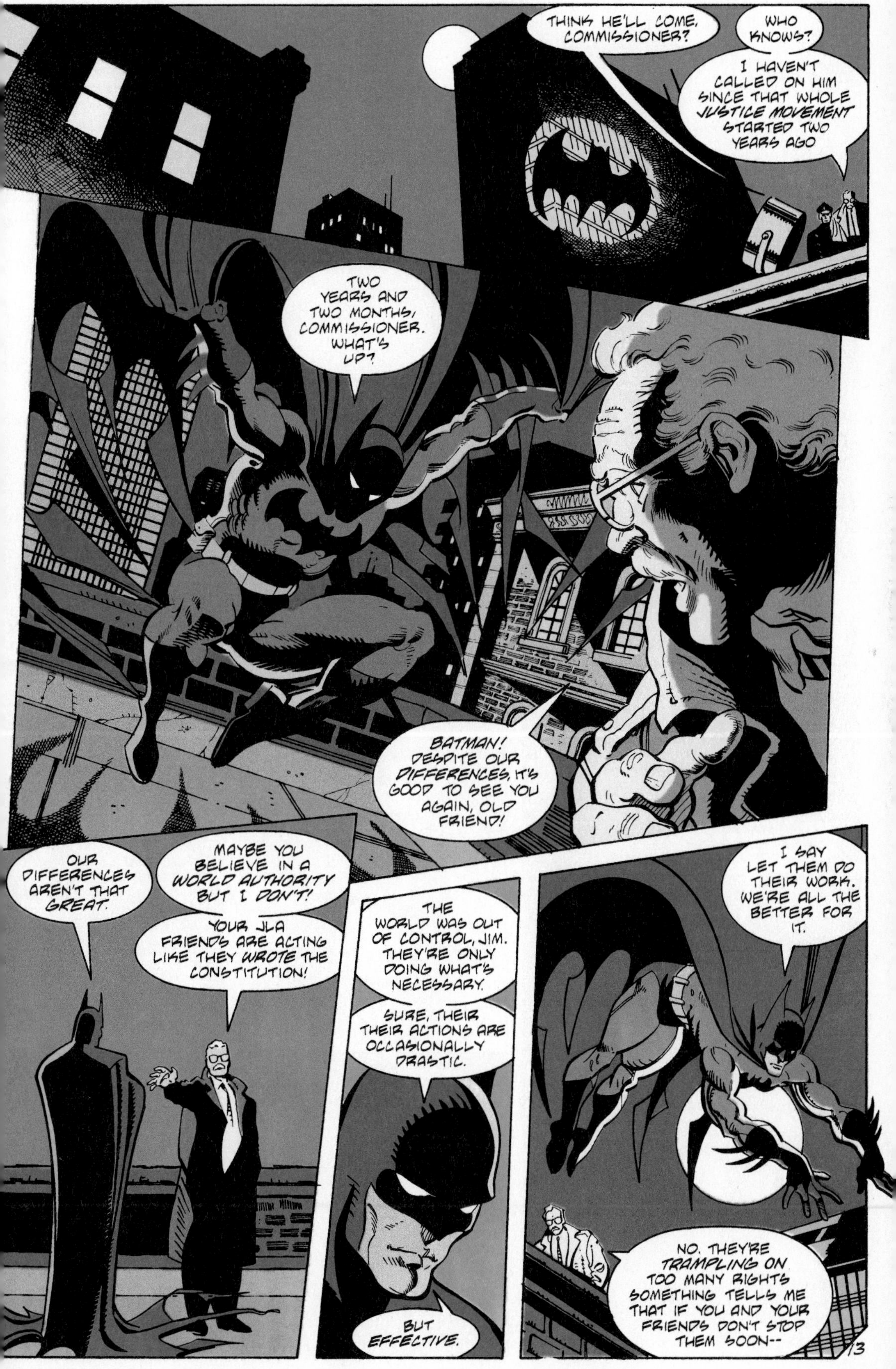
THINK HE'LL COME, COMMISSIONER?
WHO KNOWS?
I HAVEN'T CALLED ON HIM SINCE THAT WHOLE JUSTICE MOVEMENT STARTED TWO YEARS AGO
TWO YEARS AND TWO MONTHS, COMMISSIONER. WHAT'S UP?
BATMAN! DESPITE OUR DIFFERENCES, IT'S GOOD TO SEE YOU AGAIN, OLD FRIEND!
OUR DIFFERENCES AREN'T THAT GREAT.
MAYBE YOU BELIEVE IN A WORLD AUTHORITY BUT I DON'T!
YOUR JLA FRIENDS ARE ACTING LIKE THEY WROTE THE CONSTITUTION!
THE WORLD WAS OUT OF CONTROL, JIM. THEY'RE ONLY DOING WHAT'S NECESSARY.
SURE, THEIR THEIR ACTIONS ARE OCCASIONALLY DRASTIC.
BUT EFFECTIVE.
I SAY LET THEM DO THEIR WORK. WE'RE ALL THE BETTER FOR IT.
NO. THEY'RE TRAMPLING ON TOO MANY RIGHTS SOMETHING TELLS ME THAT IF YOU AND YOUR FRIENDS DON'T STOP THEM SOON--

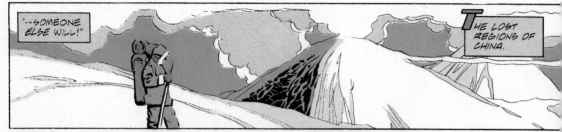

"--SOMEONE ELSE WILL!"

THE LOST REGIONS OF CHINA.

<EVERYTHING IS IN PROPER ALIGNMENT. LET THE COUNTDOWN CONTINUE.>

<ARM ALL MISSILES AND OPEN THE SILOS.>

<MISSILES ARMED AND SILOS OPEN.>

<ARE YOU CERTAIN OF THE WISDOM OF THIS ACTION, COMRADE. IF WE SHOULD FAIL...>

<WE SHALL NOT. IT IS ALWAYS WISE TO CONTROL YOUR OWN DESTINY RATHER THAN SUBJUGATE IT TO THE WILL OF UNWORTHY RULERS!>

<IGNITION!>

<WE HAVE IGNITION! LAUNCH PROCEDURE INITIATED!>

<LET THEIR DREAMS OF WORLD DOMINATION DIE IN A BALL OF NUCLEAR DEATH!>

BRRRT

<GUN FIRE?!>

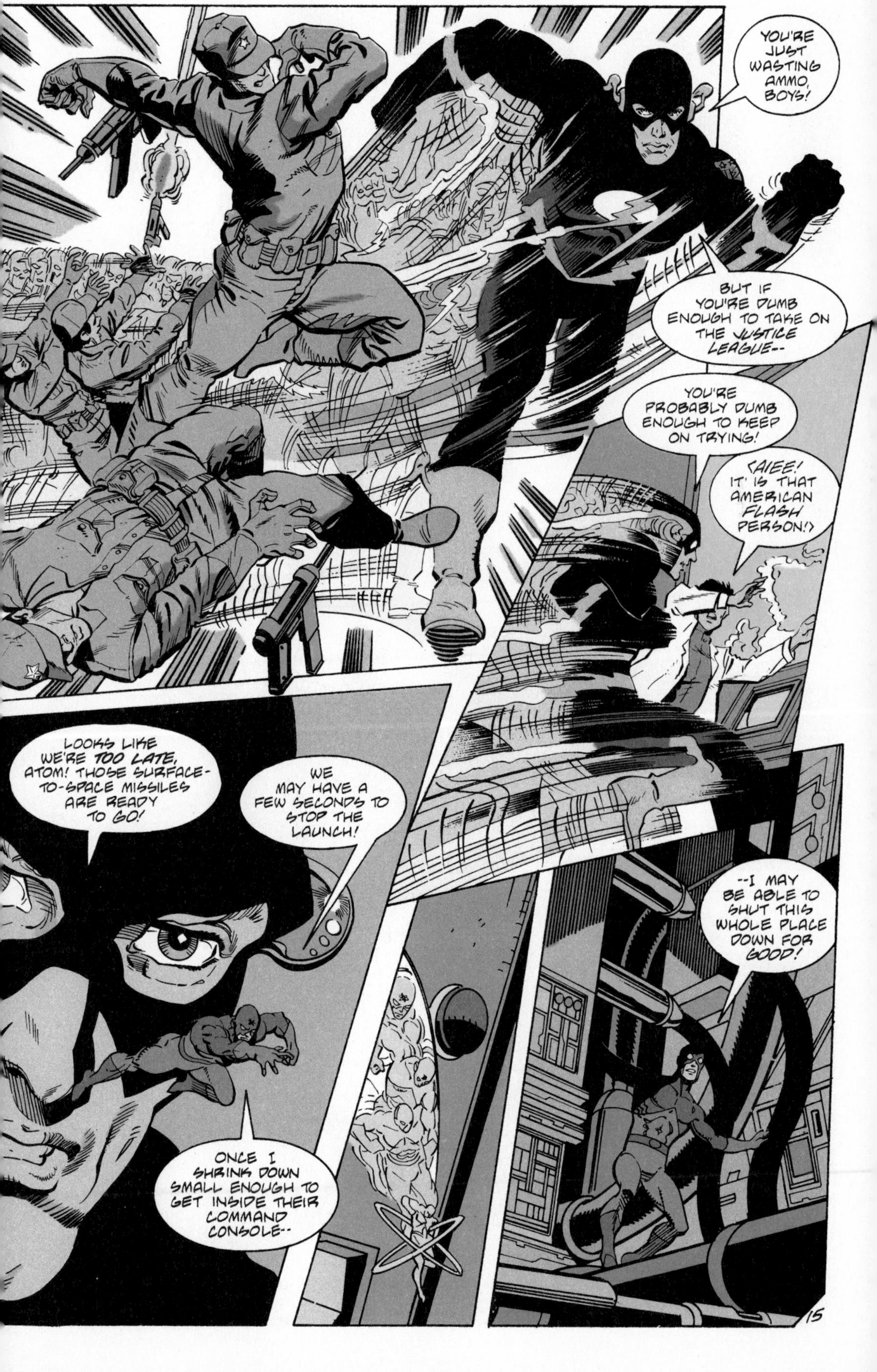

YOU'RE JUST WASTING AMMO, BOYS!
BUT IF YOU'RE DUMB ENOUGH TO TAKE ON THE JUSTICE LEAGUE--
YOU'RE PROBABLY DUMB ENOUGH TO KEEP ON TRYING!
<AIEE! IT IS THAT AMERICAN FLASH PERSON!>
LOOKS LIKE WE'RE TOO LATE, ATOM! THOSE SURFACE-TO-SPACE MISSILES ARE READY TO GO!
WE MAY HAVE A FEW SECONDS TO STOP THE LAUNCH!
ONCE I SHRINK DOWN SMALL ENOUGH TO GET INSIDE THEIR COMMAND CONSOLE--
--I MAY BE ABLE TO SHUT THIS WHOLE PLACE DOWN FOR GOOD!

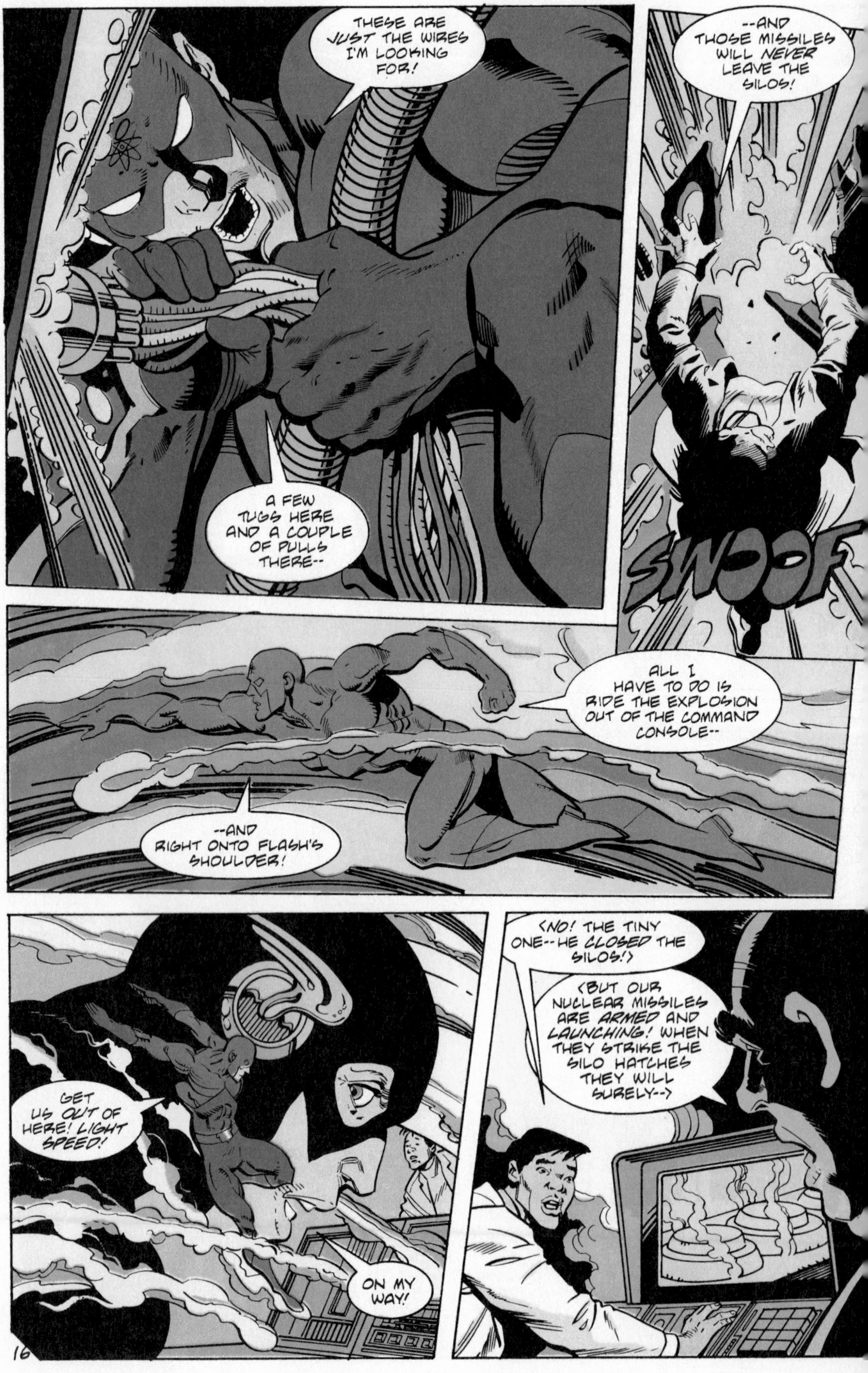
THESE ARE JUST THE WIRES I'M LOOKING FOR!
A FEW TUGS HERE AND A COUPLE OF PULLS THERE--
--AND THOSE MISSILES WILL NEVER LEAVE THE SILOS!
SWOOF
ALL I HAVE TO DO IS RIDE THE EXPLOSION OUT OF THE COMMAND CONSOLE--
--AND RIGHT ONTO FLASH'S SHOULDER!
GET US OUT OF HERE! LIGHT SPEED!
ON MY WAY!
<NO! THE TINY ONE--HE CLOSED THE SILOS!>
<BUT OUR NUCLEAR MISSILES ARE ARMED AND LAUNCHING! WHEN THEY STRIKE THE SILO HATCHES THEY WILL SURELY-->

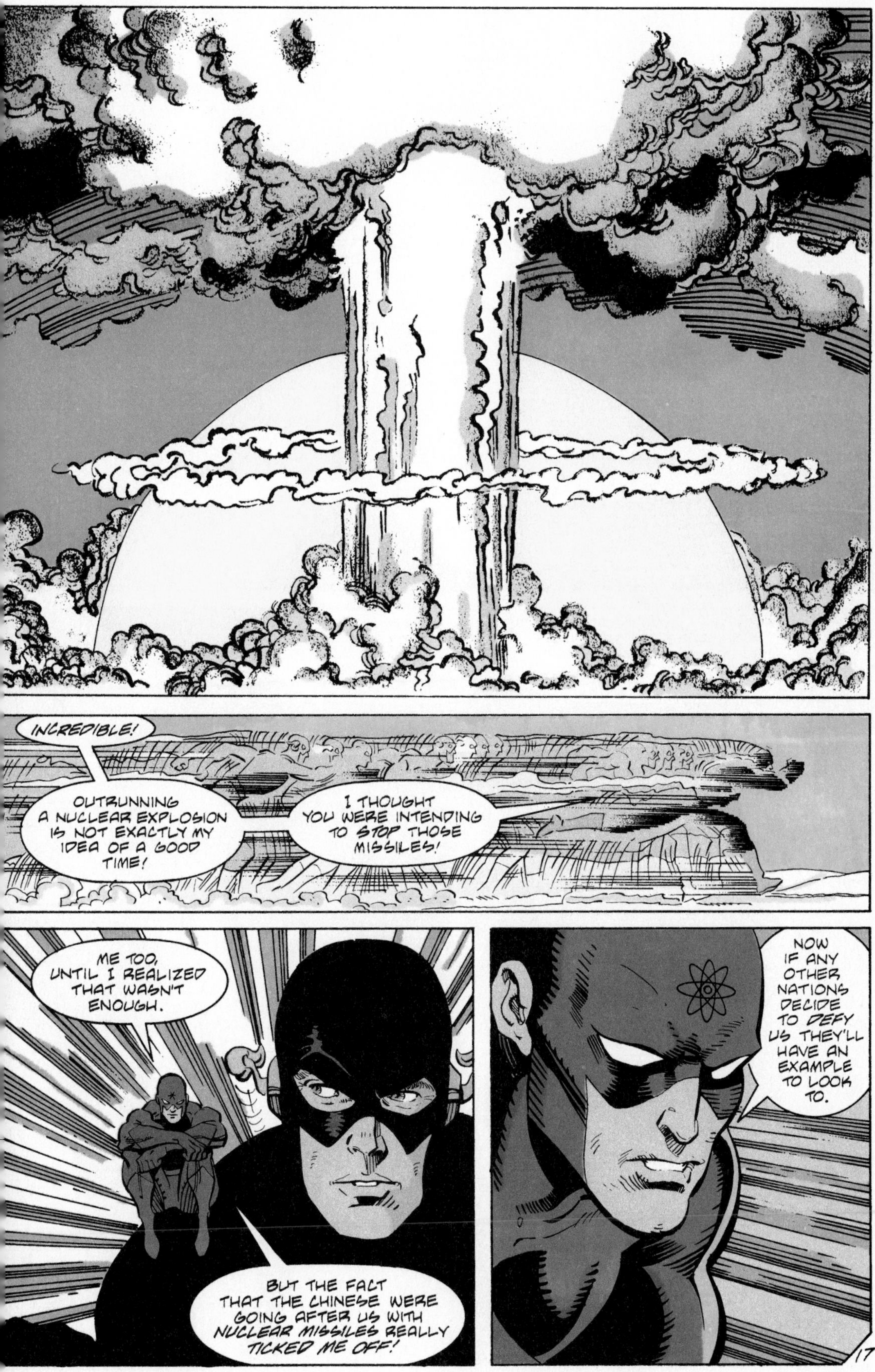

INCREDIBLE!
OUTRUNNING A NUCLEAR EXPLOSION IS NOT EXACTLY MY IDEA OF A GOOD TIME!
I THOUGHT YOU WERE INTENDING TO STOP THOSE MISSILES!
ME TOO, UNTIL I REALIZED THAT WASN'T ENOUGH.
BUT THE FACT THAT THE CHINESE WERE GOING AFTER US WITH NUCLEAR MISSILES REALLY TICKED ME OFF!
NOW IF ANY OTHER NATIONS DECIDE TO DEFY US THEY'LL HAVE AN EXAMPLE TO LOOK TO.

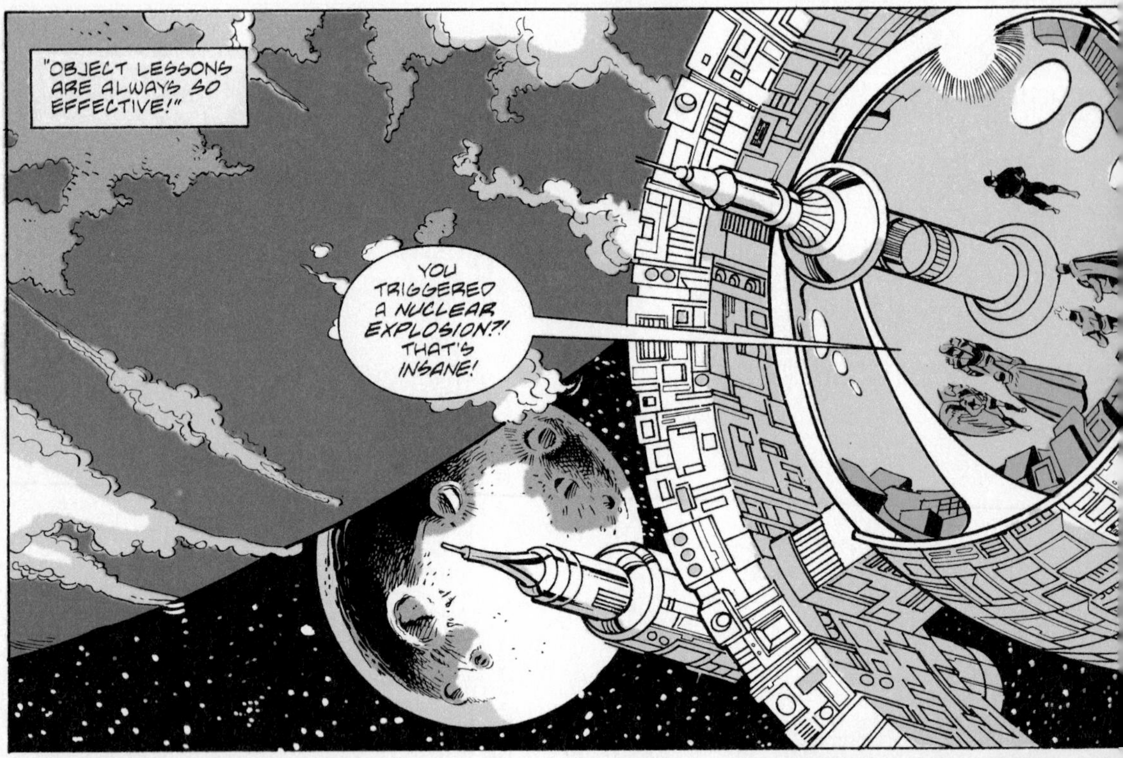
"OBJECT LESSONS ARE ALWAYS SO EFFECTIVE!"
YOU TRIGGERED A NUCLEAR EXPLOSION?! THAT'S INSANE!

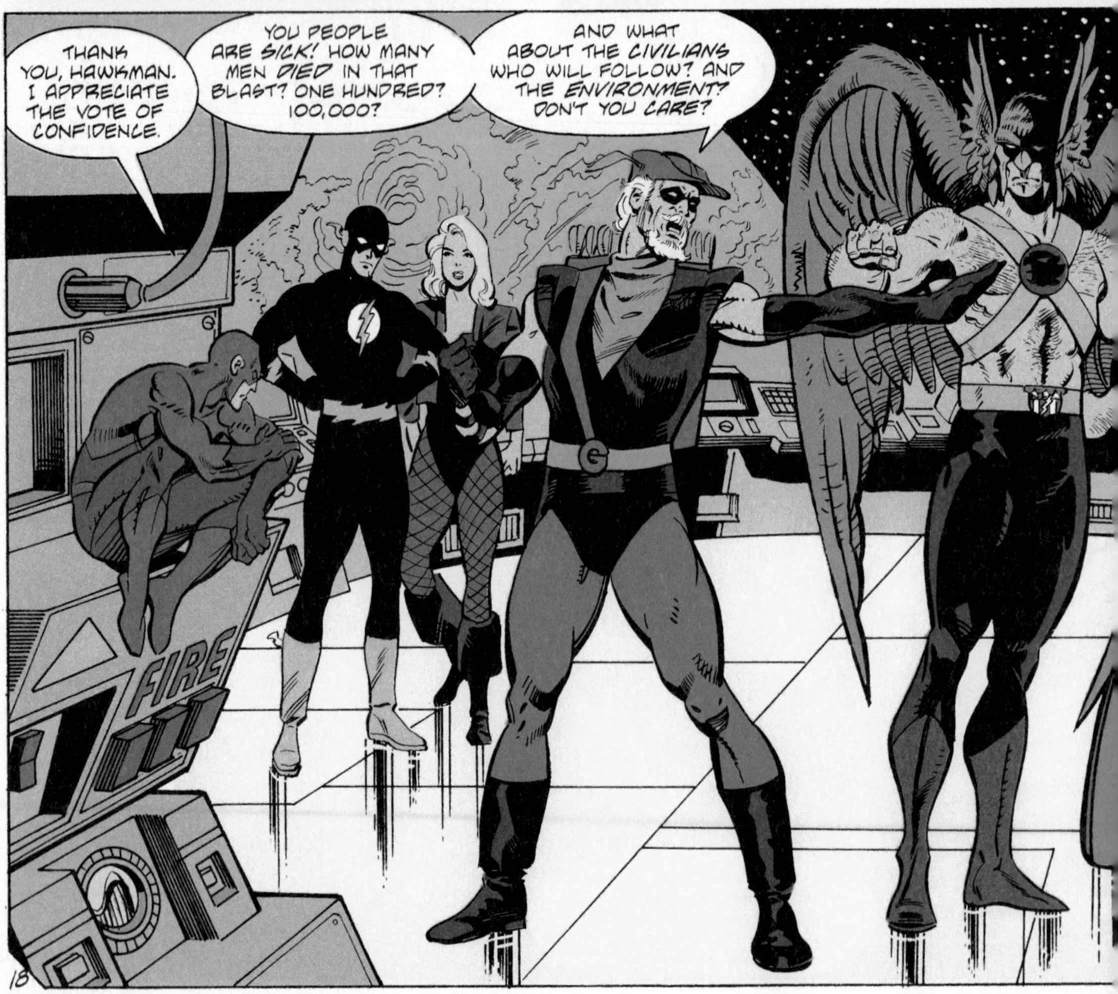
THANK YOU, HAWKMAN. I APPRECIATE THE VOTE OF CONFIDENCE.
YOU PEOPLE ARE SICK! HOW MANY MEN DIED IN THAT BLAST? ONE HUNDRED? 100,000?
AND WHAT ABOUT THE CIVILIANS WHO WILL FOLLOW? AND THE ENVIRONMENT? DON'T YOU CARE?
FIRE

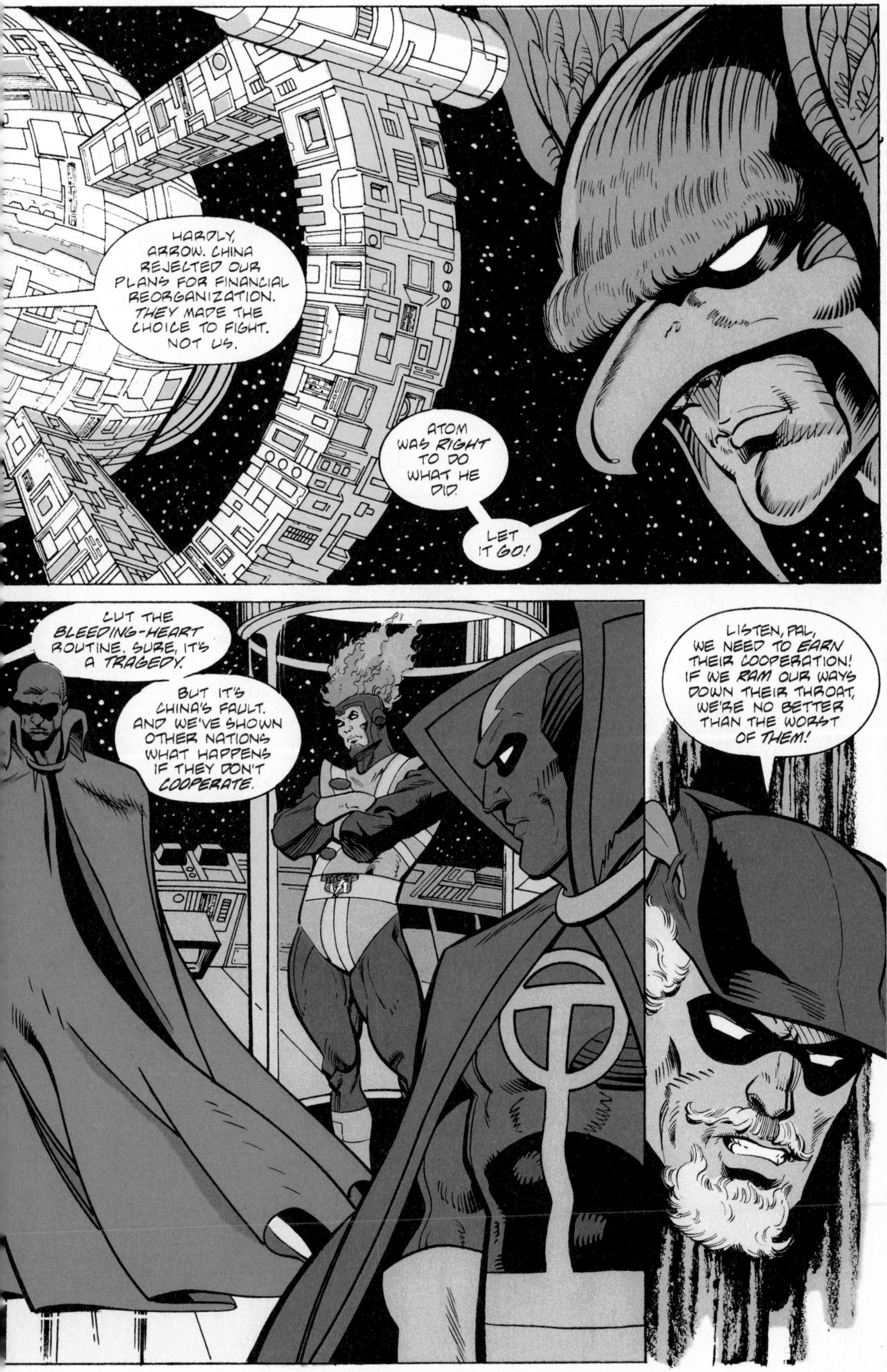
HARDLY, ARROW. CHINA REJECTED OUR PLANS FOR FINANCIAL REORGANIZATION. THEY MADE THE CHOICE TO FIGHT. NOT US.
ATOM WAS RIGHT TO DO WHAT HE DID.
LET IT GO!
CUT THE BLEEDING-HEART ROUTINE. SURE, IT'S A TRAGEDY.
BUT IT'S CHINA'S FAULT. AND WE'VE SHOWN OTHER NATIONS WHAT HAPPENS IF THEY DON'T COOPERATE.
LISTEN, PAL, WE NEED TO EARN THEIR COOPERATION! IF WE RAM OUR WAYS DOWN THEIR THROAT, WE'RE NO BETTER THAN THE WORST OF THEM!

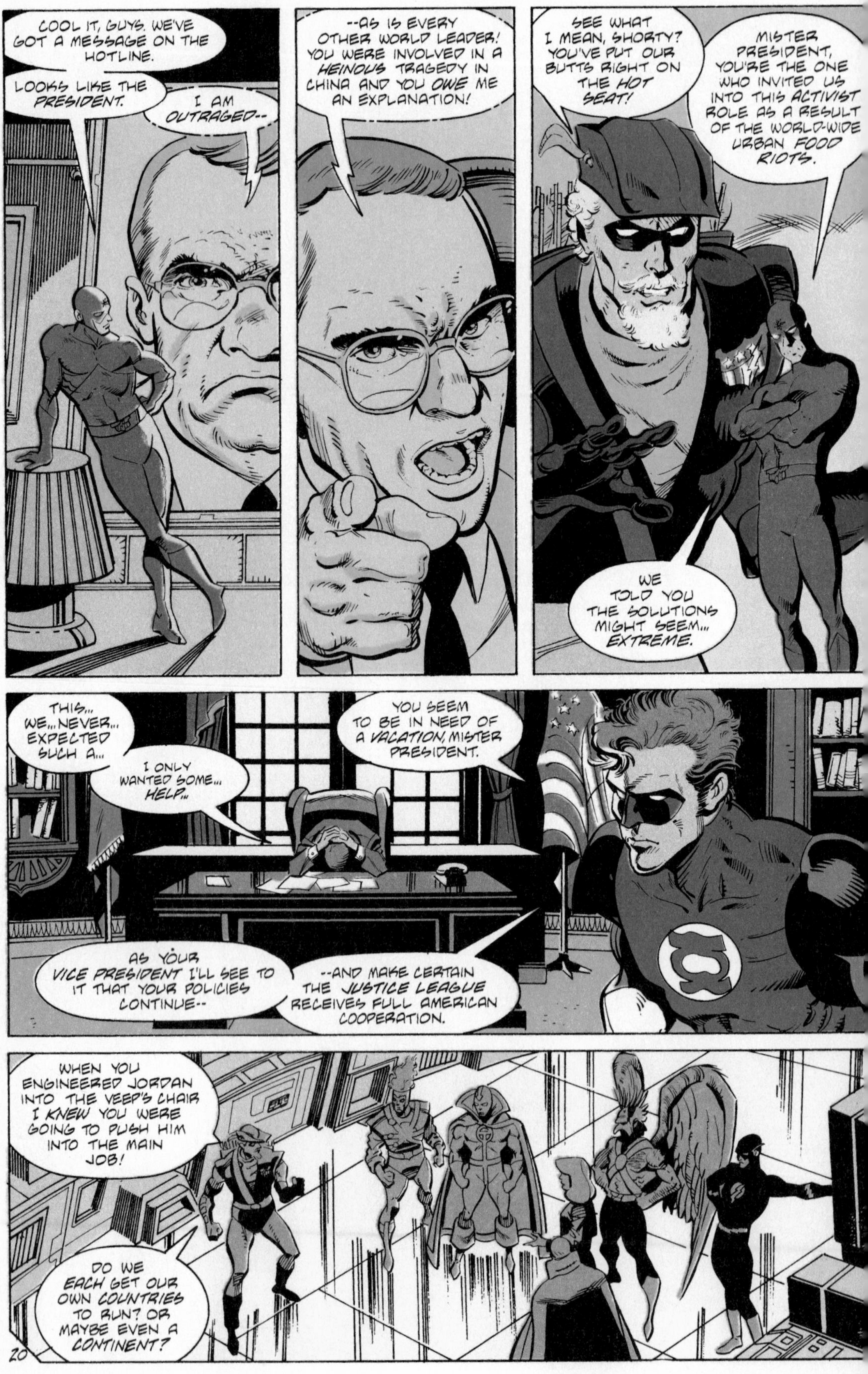
COOL IT, GUYS. WE'VE GOT A MESSAGE ON THE HOTLINE.
LOOKS LIKE THE PRESIDENT.
I AM OUTRAGED--
--AS IS EVERY OTHER WORLD LEADER! YOU WERE INVOLVED IN A HEINOUS TRAGEDY IN CHINA AND YOU OWE ME AN EXPLANATION!
SEE WHAT I MEAN, SHORTY? YOU'VE PUT OUR BUTTS RIGHT ON THE HOT SEAT!
MISTER PRESIDENT, YOU'RE THE ONE WHO INVITED US INTO THIS ACTIVIST ROLE AS A RESULT OF THE WORLD-WIDE URBAN FOOD RIOTS.
WE TOLD YOU THE SOLUTIONS MIGHT SEEM... EXTREME.
THIS... WE... NEVER... EXPECTED SUCH A...
I ONLY WANTED SOME... HELP...
YOU SEEM TO BE IN NEED OF A VACATION, MISTER PRESIDENT.
AS YOUR VICE PRESIDENT I'LL SEE TO IT THAT YOUR POLICIES CONTINUE--
--AND MAKE CERTAIN THE JUSTICE LEAGUE RECEIVES FULL AMERICAN COOPERATION.
WHEN YOU ENGINEERED JORDAN INTO THE VEEP'S CHAIR I KNEW YOU WERE GOING TO PUSH HIM INTO THE MAIN JOB!
DO WE EACH GET OUR OWN COUNTRIES TO RUN? OR MAYBE EVEN A CONTINENT?

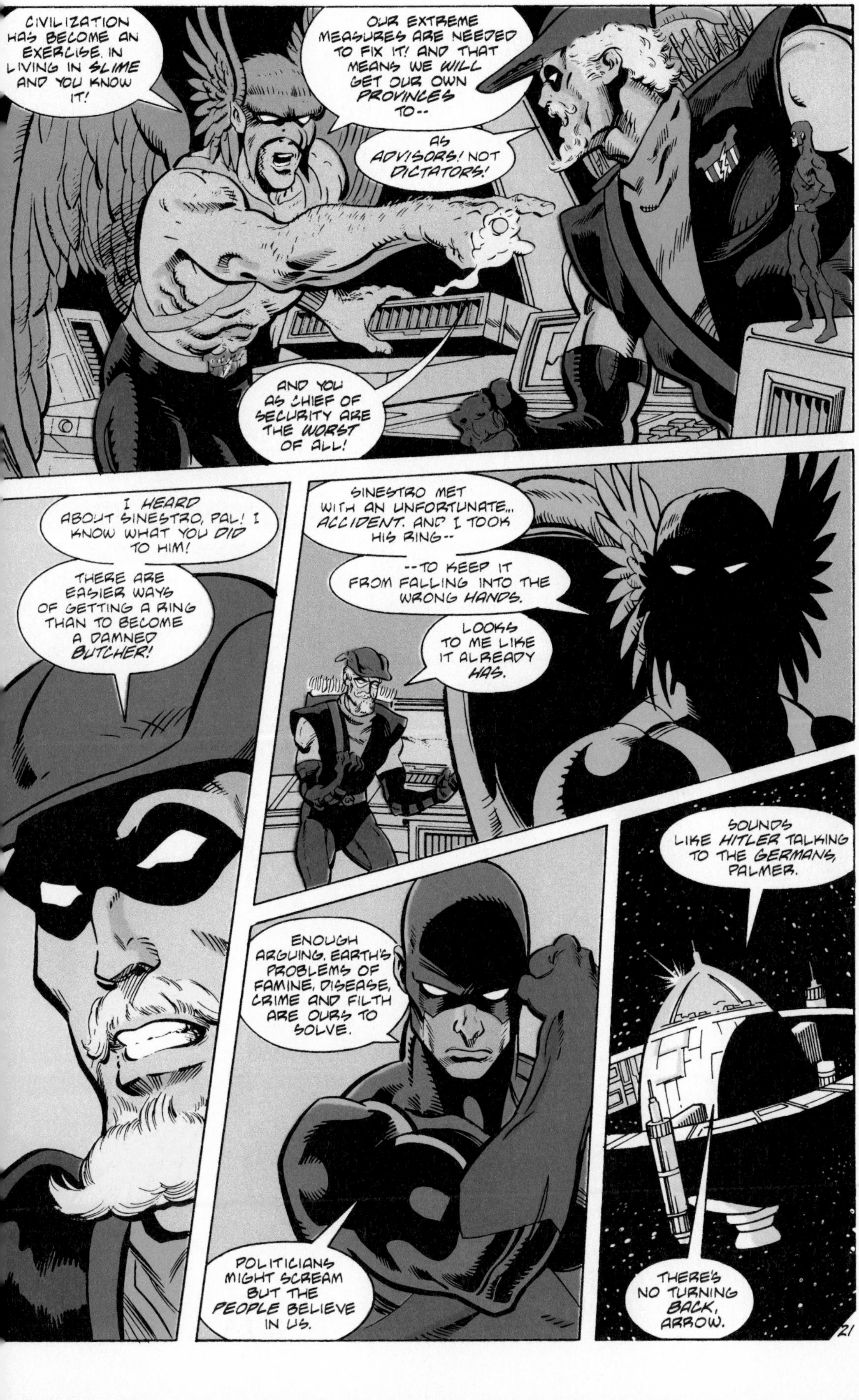
CIVILIZATION HAS BECOME AN EXERCISE IN LIVING IN SLIME AND YOU KNOW IT!
OUR EXTREME MEASURES ARE NEEDED TO FIX IT! AND THAT MEANS WE WILL GET OUR OWN PROVINCES TO--
AS ADVISORS! NOT DICTATORS!
AND YOU AS CHIEF OF SECURITY ARE THE WORST OF ALL!
I HEARD ABOUT SINESTRO, PAL! I KNOW WHAT YOU DID TO HIM!
THERE ARE EASIER WAYS OF GETTING A RING THAN TO BECOME A DAMNED BUTCHER!
SINESTRO MET WITH AN UNFORTUNATE... ACCIDENT. AND I TOOK HIS RING--
--TO KEEP IT FROM FALLING INTO THE WRONG HANDS.
LOOKS TO ME LIKE IT ALREADY HAS.
ENOUGH ARGUING. EARTH'S PROBLEMS OF FAMINE, DISEASE, CRIME AND FILTH ARE OURS TO SOLVE.
POLITICIANS MIGHT SCREAM BUT THE PEOPLE BELIEVE IN US.
SOUNDS LIKE HITLER TALKING TO THE GERMANS, PALMER.
THERE'S NO TURNING BACK, ARROW.

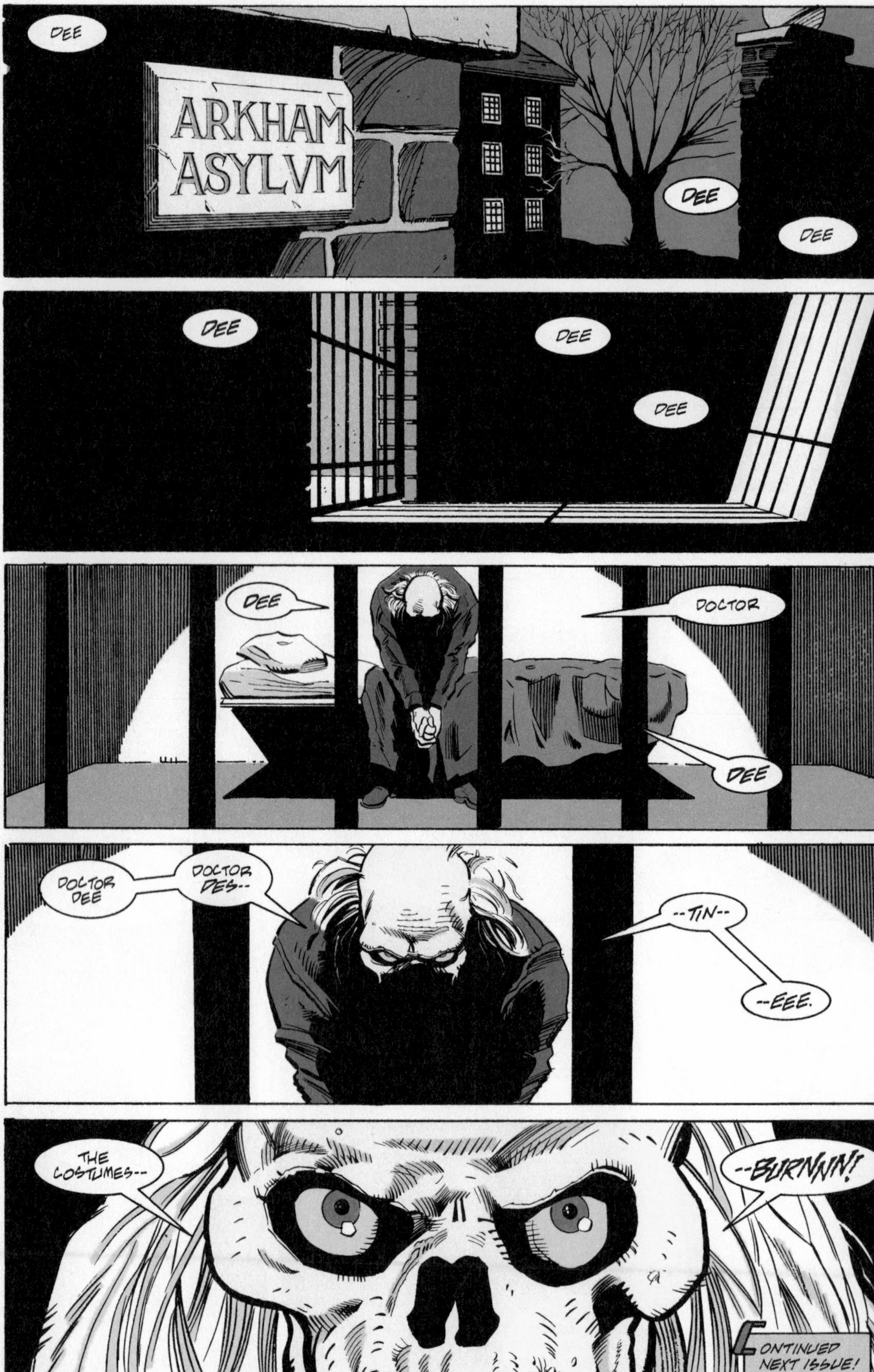

DEE
ARKHAM ASYLVM
DEE
DEE
DEE
DEE
DEE
DEE
DOCTOR
DEE
DOCTOR DEE
DOCTOR DES--
--TIN--
--EEE.
THE COSTUMES--
--BURNNN!
CONTINUED NEXT ISSUE!

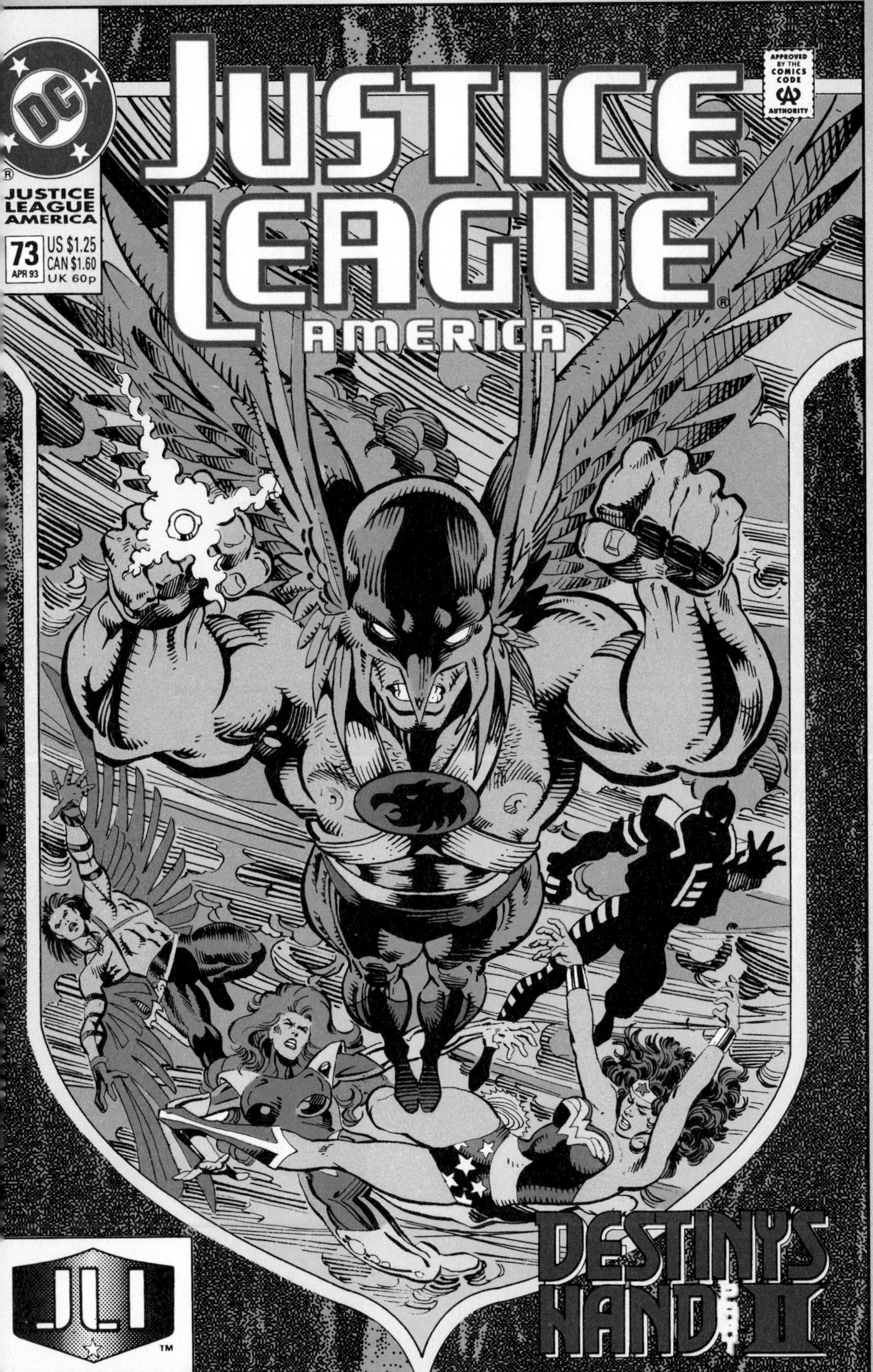

DC
JUSTICE LEAGUE AMERICA
73
APR 93
US $1.25
CAN $1.60
UK 60p
APPROVED BY THE COMICS CODE AUTHORITY
JUSTICE LEAGUE AMERICA
JLI
DESTINY'S HAND PART II

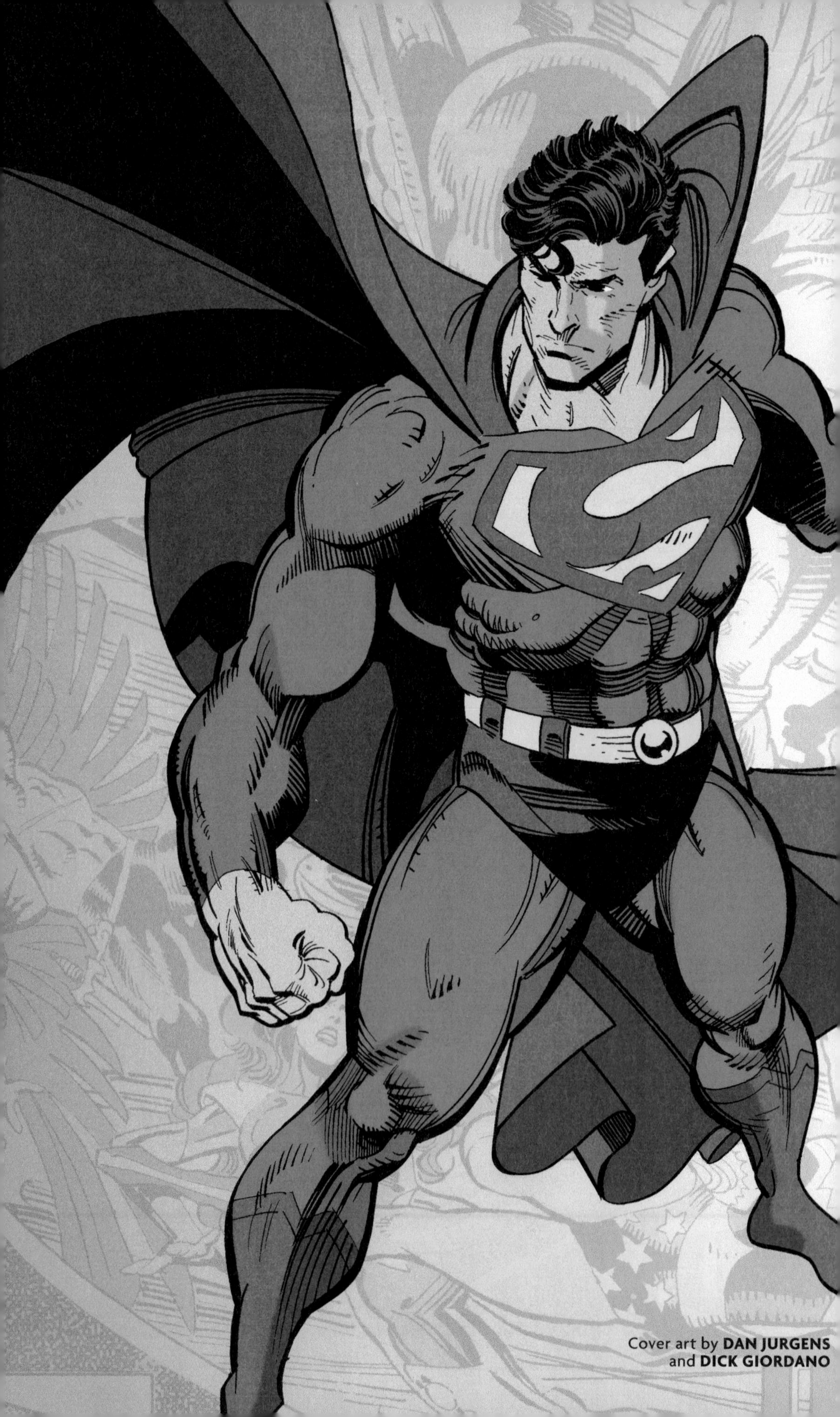

Cover art by **DAN JURGENS**
and **DICK GIORDANO**

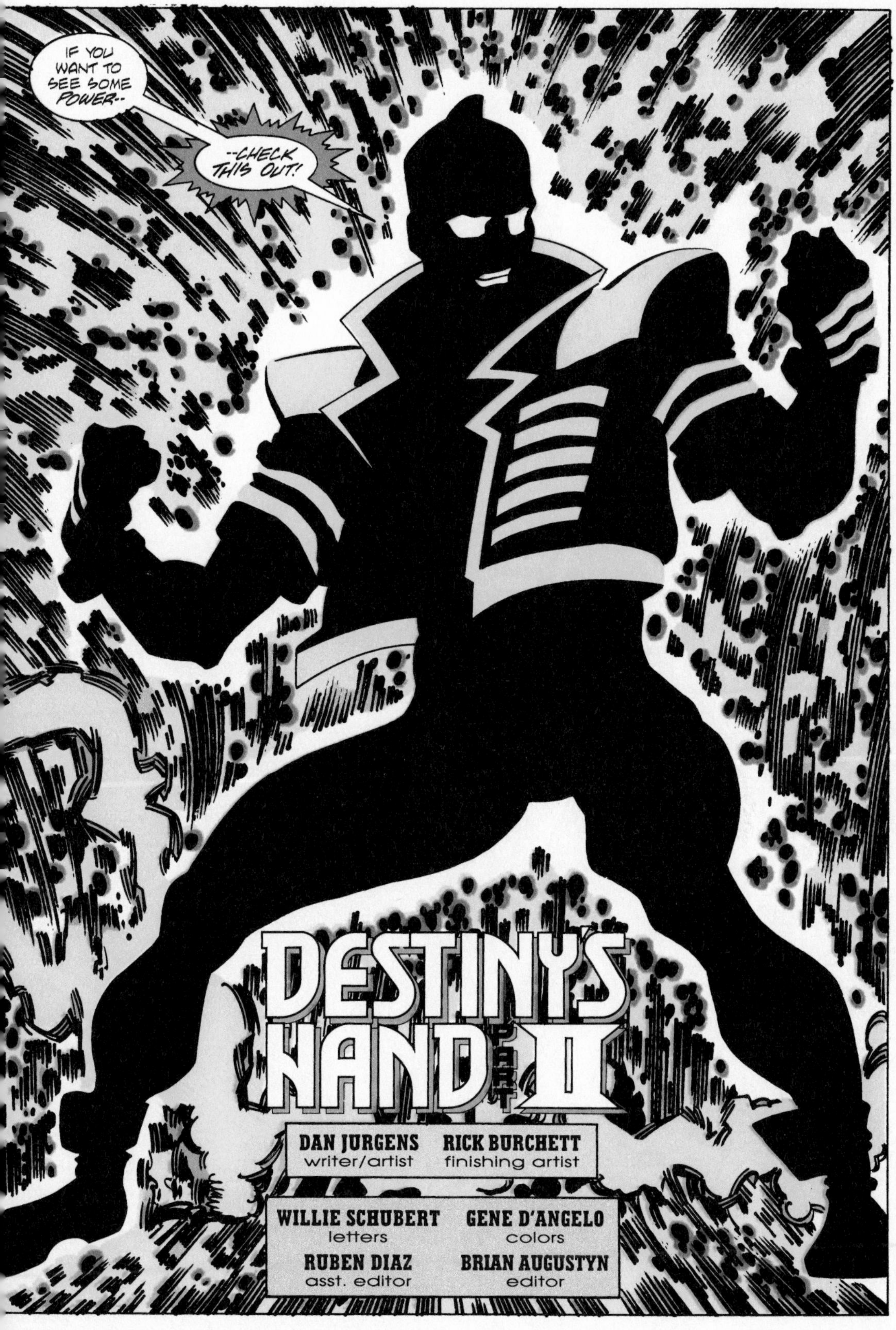
IF YOU WANT TO SEE SOME POWER--
--CHECK THIS OUT!
DESTINY'S HAND PART II
DAN JURGENS writer/artist
RICK BURCHETT finishing artist
WILLIE SCHUBERT letters
GENE D'ANGELO colors
RUBEN DIAZ asst. editor
BRIAN AUGUSTYN editor

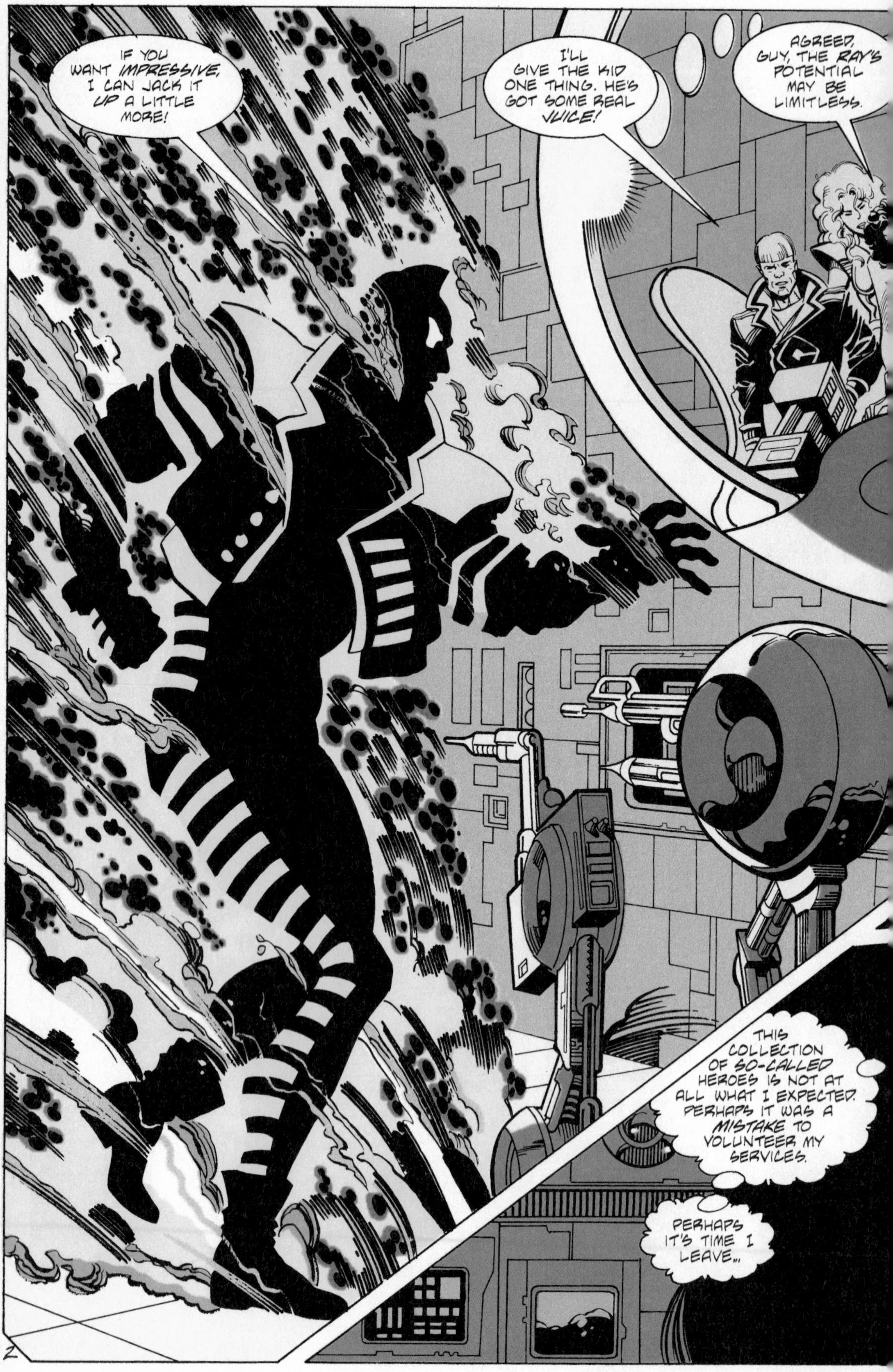
IF YOU WANT IMPRESSIVE, I CAN JACK IT UP A LITTLE MORE!
I'LL GIVE THE KID ONE THING. HE'S GOT SOME REAL JUICE!
AGREED, GUY, THE RAY'S POTENTIAL MAY BE LIMITLESS.
THIS COLLECTION OF SO-CALLED HEROES IS NOT AT ALL WHAT I EXPECTED. PERHAPS IT WAS A MISTAKE TO VOLUNTEER MY SERVICES.
PERHAPS IT'S TIME I LEAVE...

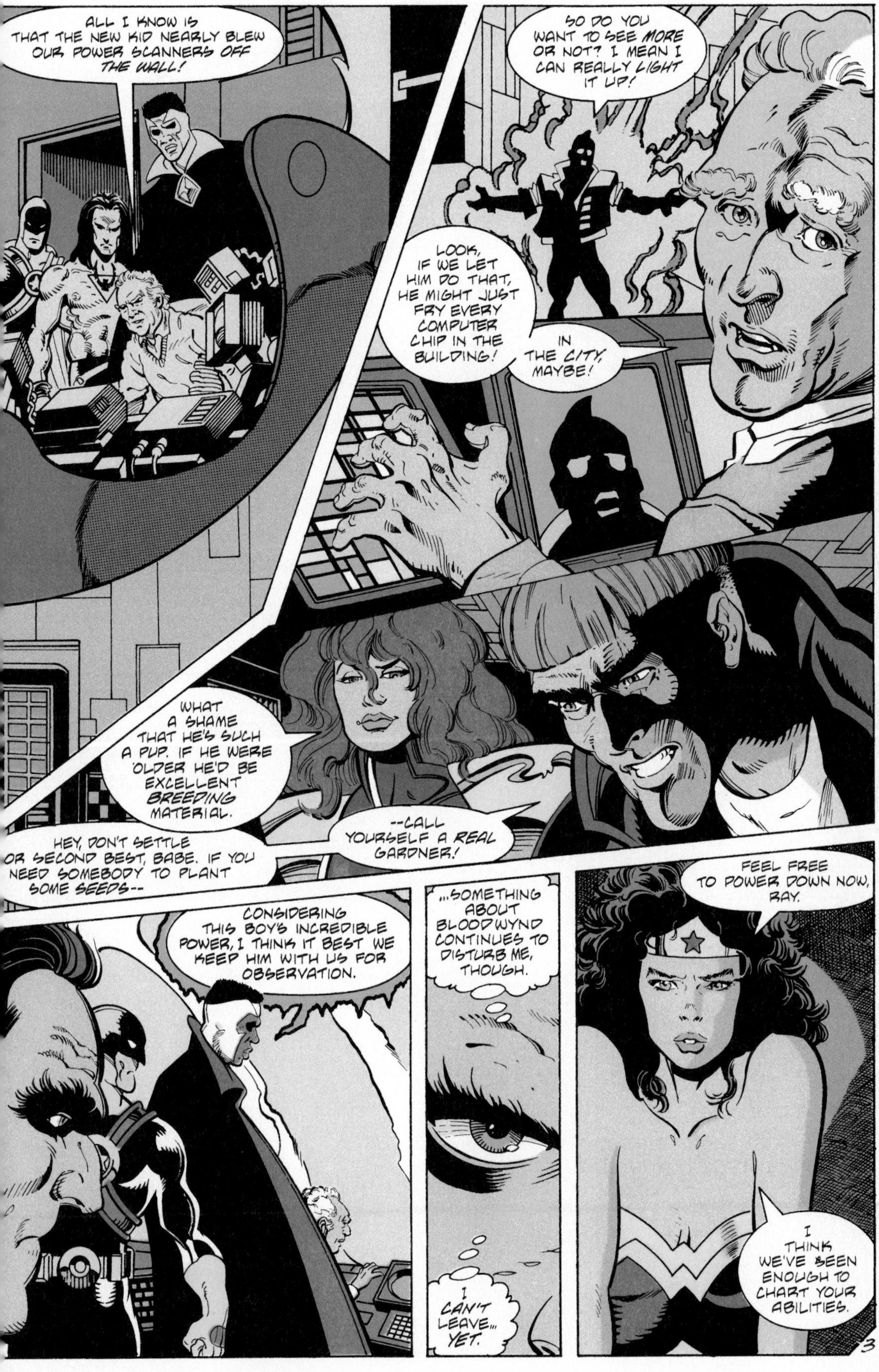
ALL I KNOW IS THAT THE NEW KID NEARLY BLEW OUR POWER SCANNERS OFF THE WALL!
SO DO YOU WANT TO SEE MORE OR NOT? I MEAN I CAN REALLY LIGHT IT UP!
LOOK, IF WE LET HIM DO THAT, HE MIGHT JUST FRY EVERY COMPUTER CHIP IN THE BUILDING!
IN THE CITY, MAYBE!
WHAT A SHAME THAT HE'S SUCH A PUP. IF HE WERE OLDER HE'D BE EXCELLENT BREEDING MATERIAL.
HEY, DON'T SETTLE OR SECOND BEST, BABE. IF YOU NEED SOMEBODY TO PLANT SOME SEEDS--
--CALL YOURSELF A REAL GARDNER!
CONSIDERING THIS BOY'S INCREDIBLE POWER, I THINK IT BEST WE KEEP HIM WITH US FOR OBSERVATION.
...SOMETHING ABOUT BLOODWYND CONTINUES TO DISTURB ME, THOUGH.
I CAN'T LEAVE... YET.
FEEL FREE TO POWER DOWN NOW, RAY.
I THINK WE'VE SEEN ENOUGH TO CHART YOUR ABILITIES.

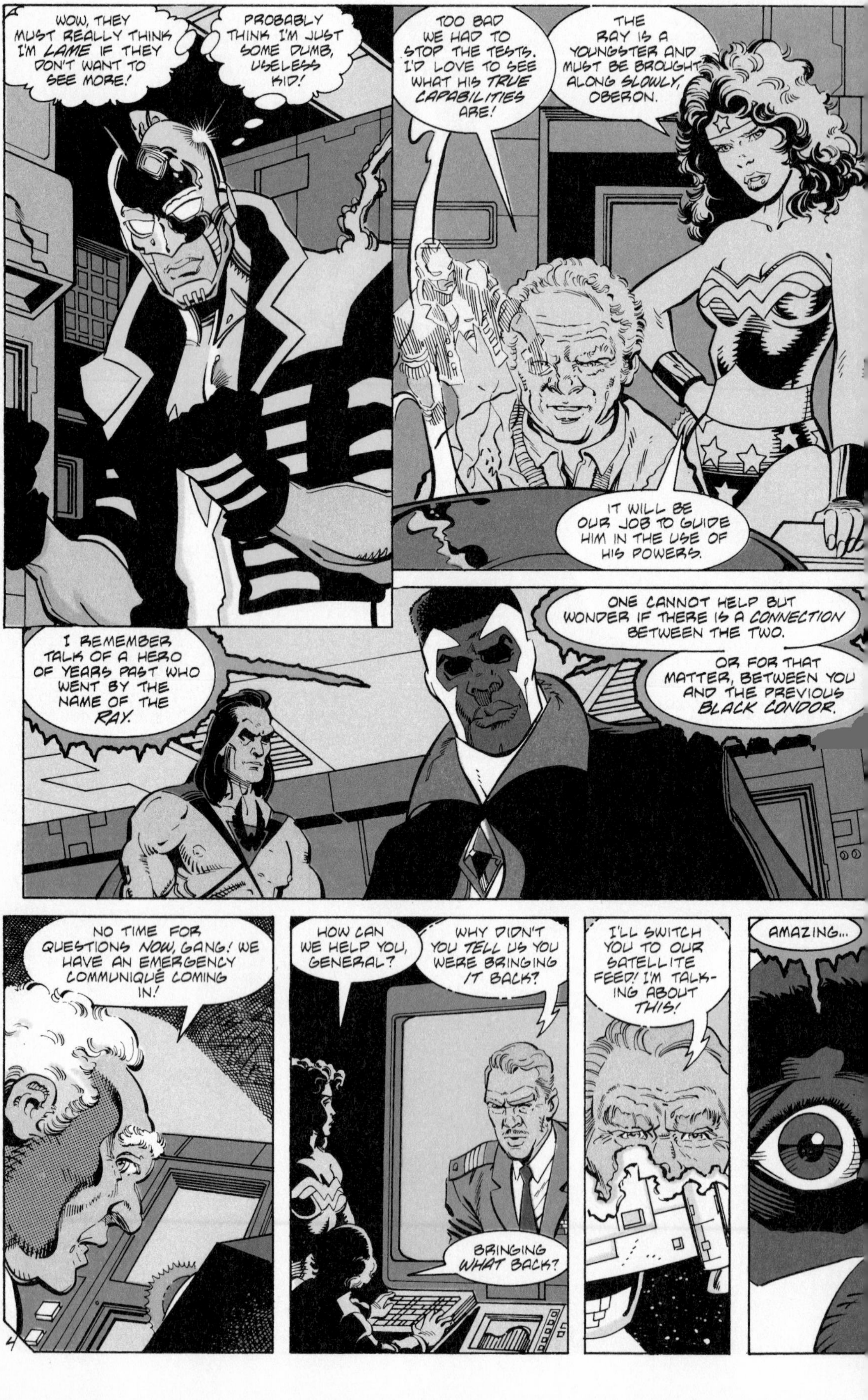
WOW, THEY MUST REALLY THINK I'M LAME IF THEY DON'T WANT TO SEE MORE!
PROBABLY THINK I'M JUST SOME DUMB, USELESS KID!
TOO BAD WE HAD TO STOP THE TESTS. I'D LOVE TO SEE WHAT HIS TRUE CAPABILITIES ARE!
THE RAY IS A YOUNGSTER AND MUST BE BROUGHT ALONG SLOWLY, OBERON.
IT WILL BE OUR JOB TO GUIDE HIM IN THE USE OF HIS POWERS.
I REMEMBER TALK OF A HERO OF YEARS PAST WHO WENT BY THE NAME OF THE RAY.
ONE CANNOT HELP BUT WONDER IF THERE IS A CONNECTION BETWEEN THE TWO.
OR FOR THAT MATTER, BETWEEN YOU AND THE PREVIOUS BLACK CONDOR.
NO TIME FOR QUESTIONS NOW, GANG! WE HAVE AN EMERGENCY COMMUNIQUÉ COMING IN!
HOW CAN WE HELP YOU, GENERAL?
WHY DIDN'T YOU TELL US YOU WERE BRINGING IT BACK?
BRINGING WHAT BACK?
I'LL SWITCH YOU TO OUR SATELLITE FEED! I'M TALKING ABOUT THIS!
AMAZING...
4

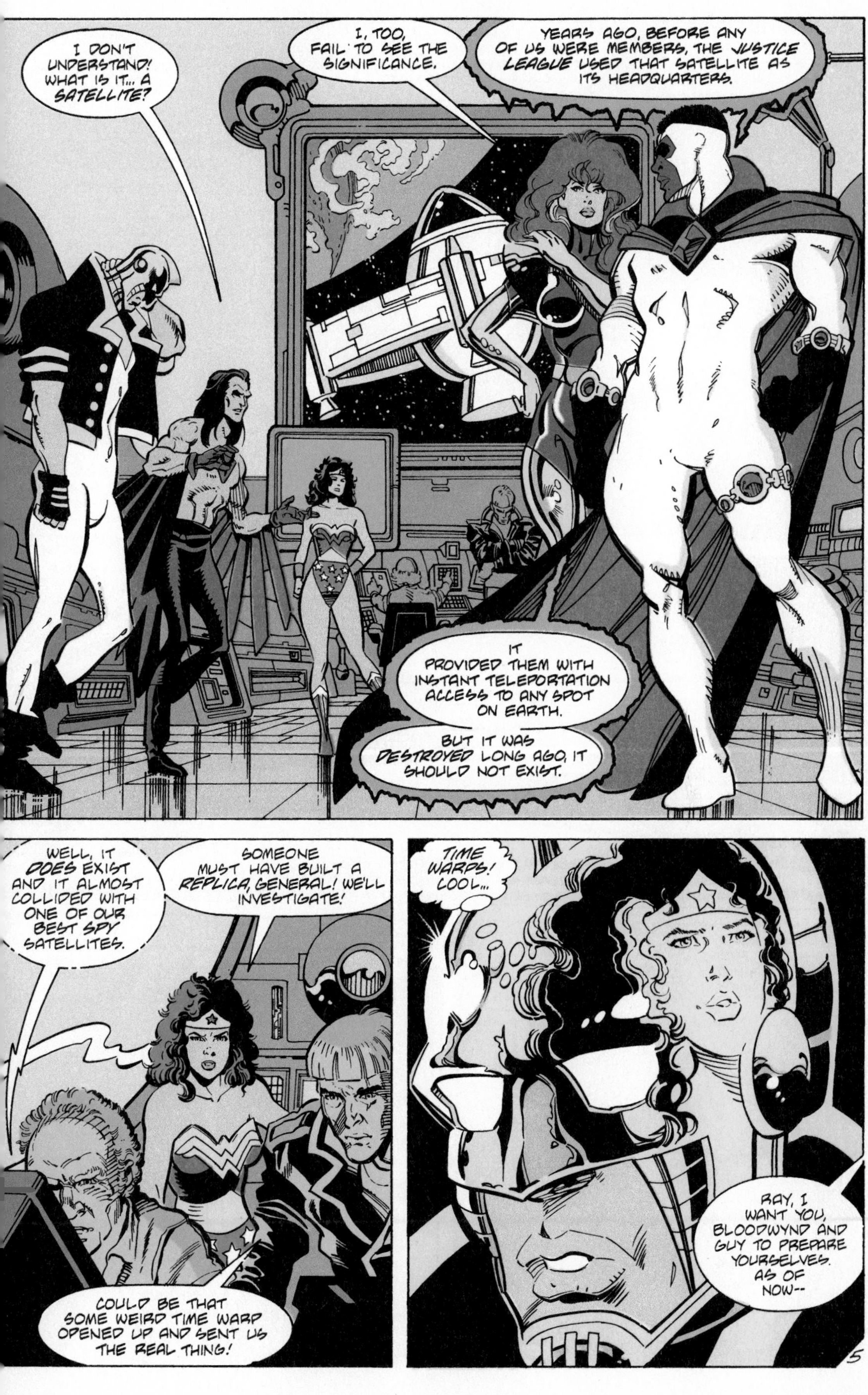
I DON'T UNDERSTAND! WHAT IS IT... A SATELLITE?
I, TOO, FAIL TO SEE THE SIGNIFICANCE.
YEARS AGO, BEFORE ANY OF US WERE MEMBERS, THE JUSTICE LEAGUE USED THAT SATELLITE AS ITS HEADQUARTERS.
IT PROVIDED THEM WITH INSTANT TELEPORTATION ACCESS TO ANY SPOT ON EARTH.
BUT IT WAS DESTROYED LONG AGO. IT SHOULD NOT EXIST.
WELL, IT DOES EXIST AND IT ALMOST COLLIDED WITH ONE OF OUR BEST SPY SATELLITES.
SOMEONE MUST HAVE BUILT A REPLICA, GENERAL! WE'LL INVESTIGATE!
COULD BE THAT SOME WEIRD TIME WARP OPENED UP AND SENT US THE REAL THING!
TIME WARPS! COOL...
RAY, I WANT YOU, BLOODWYND AND GUY TO PREPARE YOURSELVES. AS OF NOW--

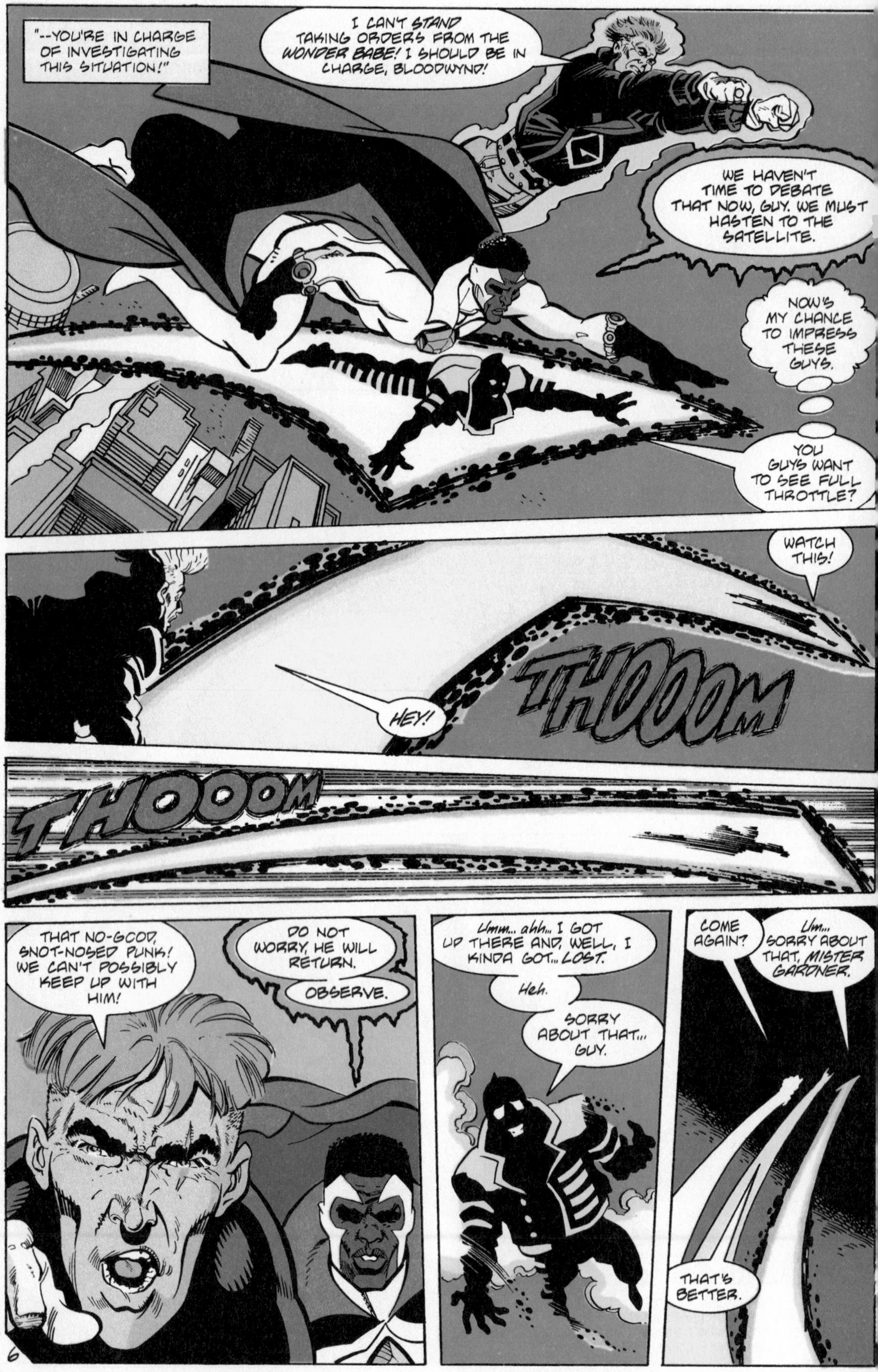
"--YOU'RE IN CHARGE OF INVESTIGATING THIS SITUATION!"
I CAN'T STAND TAKING ORDERS FROM THE WONDER BABE! I SHOULD BE IN CHARGE, BLOODWYND!
WE HAVEN'T TIME TO DEBATE THAT NOW, GUY. WE MUST HASTEN TO THE SATELLITE.
NOW'S MY CHANCE TO IMPRESS THESE GUYS.
YOU GUYS WANT TO SEE FULL THROTTLE?
WATCH THIS!
HEY!
THOOOM
THOOOM
THAT NO-GOOD, SNOT-NOSED PUNK! WE CAN'T POSSIBLY KEEP UP WITH HIM!
DO NOT WORRY, HE WILL RETURN.
OBSERVE.
Umm... ahh... I GOT UP THERE AND, WELL, I KINDA GOT... LOST.
Heh.
SORRY ABOUT THAT... GUY.
COME AGAIN?
Um... SORRY ABOUT THAT, MISTER GARDNER.
THAT'S BETTER.

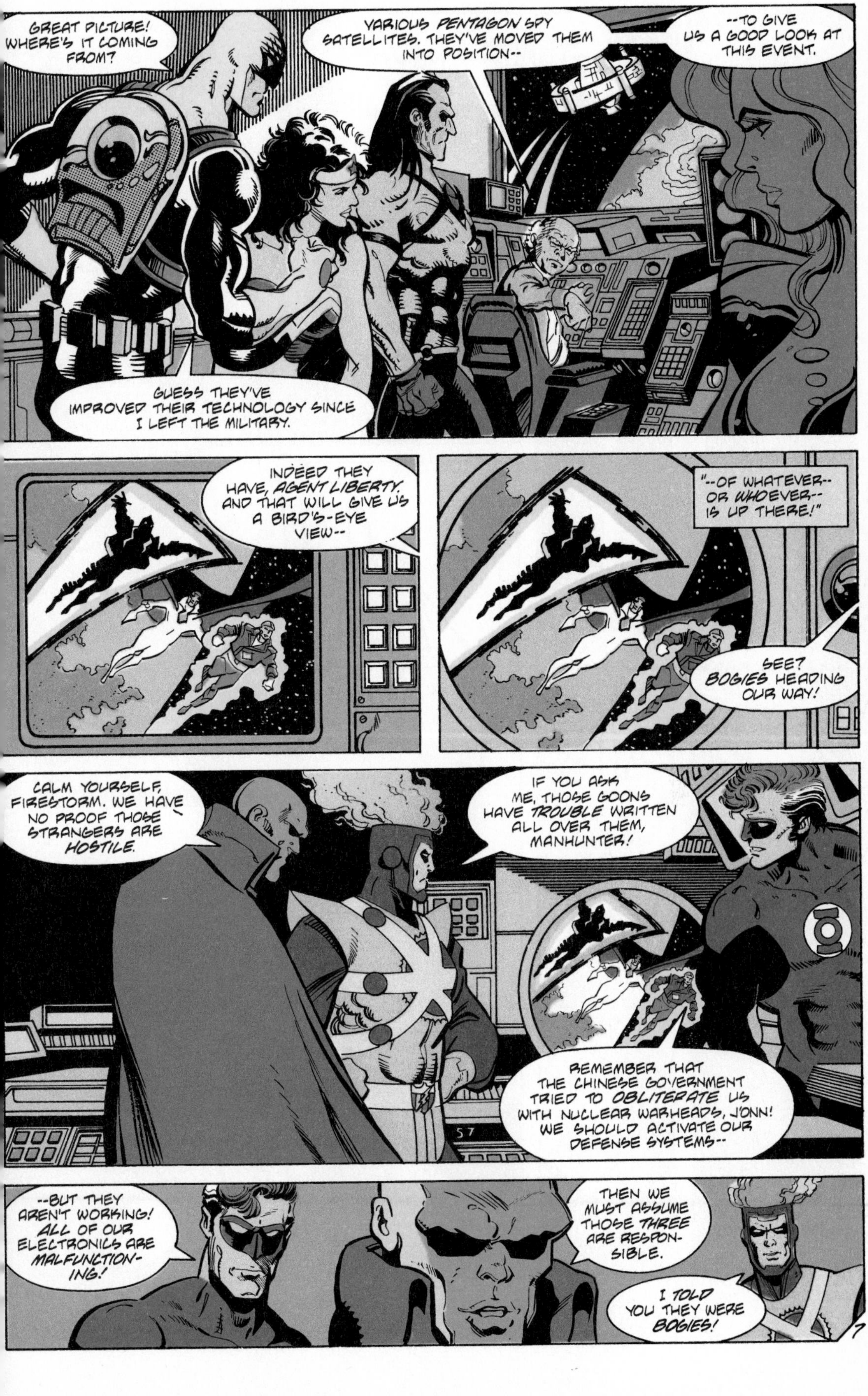
GREAT PICTURE! WHERE'S IT COMING FROM?
VARIOUS PENTAGON SPY SATELLITES. THEY'VE MOVED THEM INTO POSITION--
--TO GIVE US A GOOD LOOK AT THIS EVENT.
GUESS THEY'VE IMPROVED THEIR TECHNOLOGY SINCE I LEFT THE MILITARY.
INDEED THEY HAVE, AGENT LIBERTY. AND THAT WILL GIVE US A BIRD'S-EYE VIEW--
"--OF WHATEVER-- OR WHOEVER-- IS UP THERE!"
SEE? BOGIES HEADING OUR WAY!
CALM YOURSELF, FIRESTORM. WE HAVE NO PROOF THOSE STRANGERS ARE HOSTILE.
IF YOU ASK ME, THOSE GOONS HAVE TROUBLE WRITTEN ALL OVER THEM, MANHUNTER!
REMEMBER THAT THE CHINESE GOVERNMENT TRIED TO OBLITERATE US WITH NUCLEAR WARHEADS, J'ONN! WE SHOULD ACTIVATE OUR DEFENSE SYSTEMS--
57
--BUT THEY AREN'T WORKING! ALL OF OUR ELECTRONICS ARE MALFUNCTION-ING!
THEN WE MUST ASSUME THOSE THREE ARE RESPON-SIBLE.
I TOLD YOU THEY WERE BOGIES!

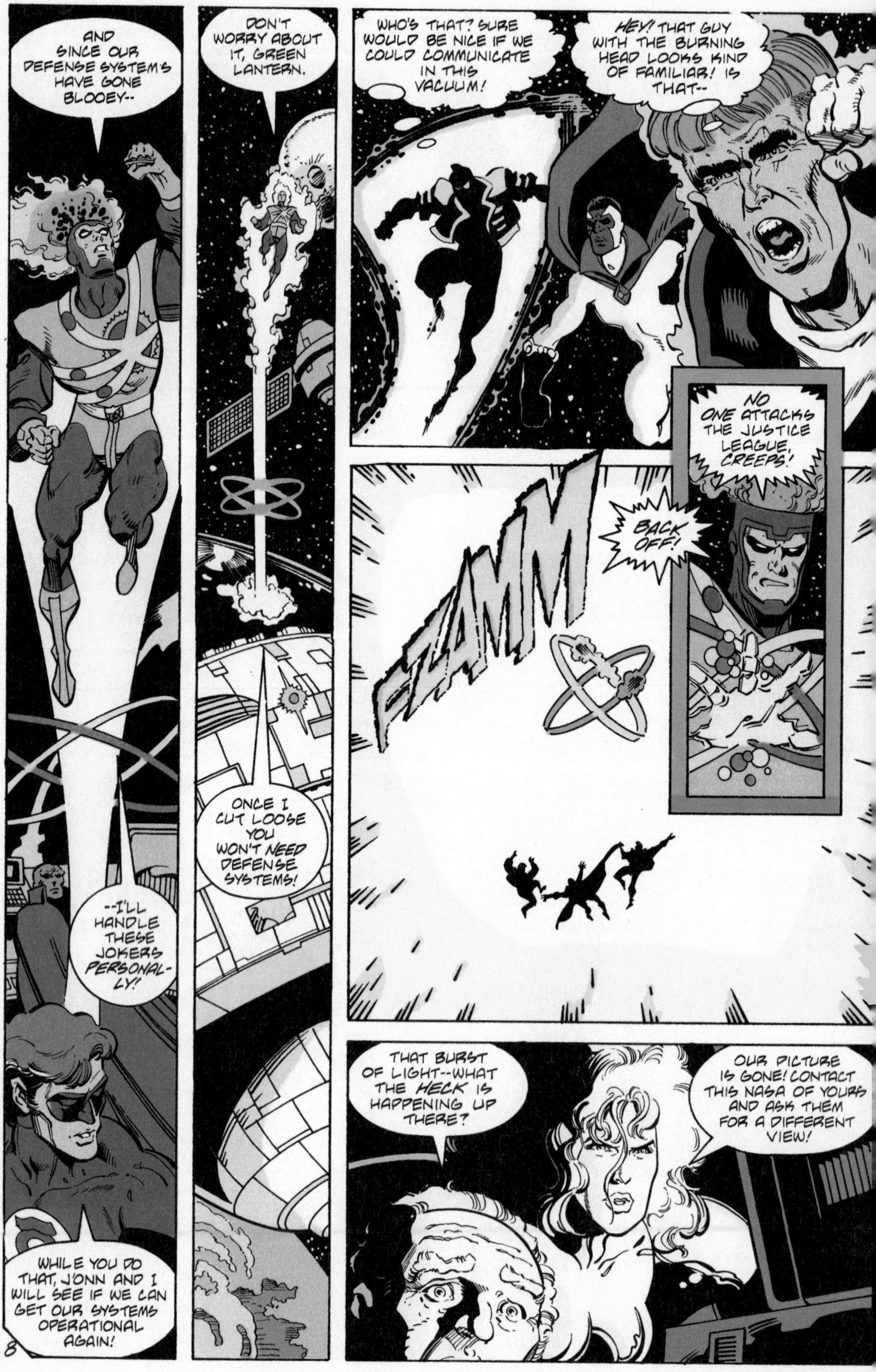
AND SINCE OUR DEFENSE SYSTEM'S HAVE GONE BLOOEY--
--I'LL HANDLE THESE JOKERS PERSONAL-LY!
WHILE YOU DO THAT, J'ONN AND I WILL SEE IF WE CAN GET OUR SYSTEMS OPERATIONAL AGAIN!
DON'T WORRY ABOUT IT, GREEN LANTERN.
ONCE I CUT LOOSE YOU WON'T NEED DEFENSE SYSTEMS!
WHO'S THAT? SURE WOULD BE NICE IF WE COULD COMMUNICATE IN THIS VACUUM!
HEY! THAT GUY WITH THE BURNING HEAD LOOKS KIND OF FAMILIAR! IS THAT--
NO ONE ATTACKS THE JUSTICE LEAGUE, CREEPS!
BACK OFF!
FZAMM
THAT BURST OF LIGHT--WHAT THE HECK IS HAPPENING UP THERE?
OUR PICTURE IS GONE! CONTACT THIS NASA OF YOURS AND ASK THEM FOR A DIFFERENT VIEW!

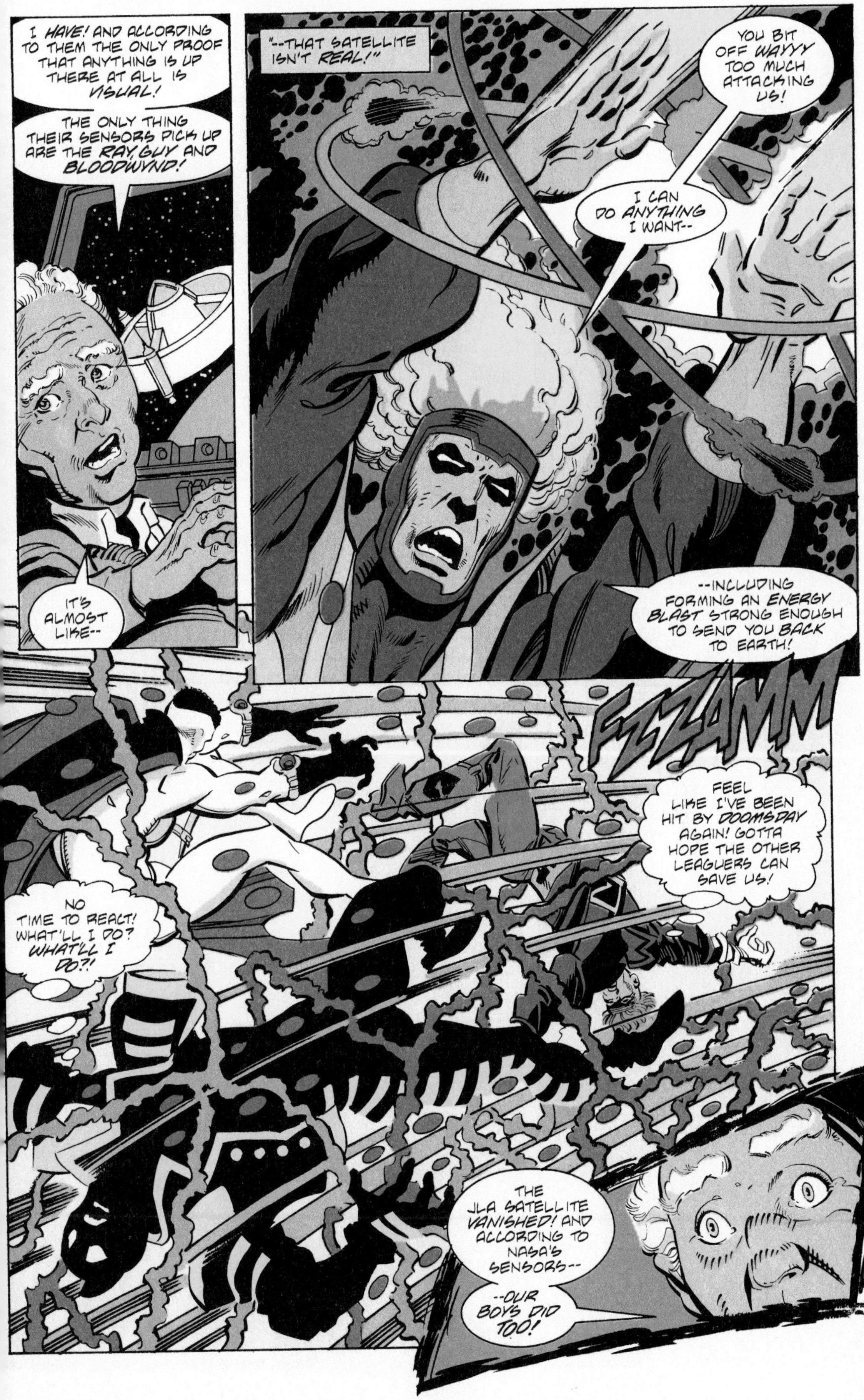
I HAVE! AND ACCORDING TO THEM THE ONLY PROOF THAT ANYTHING IS UP THERE AT ALL IS VISUAL!
THE ONLY THING THEIR SENSORS PICK UP ARE THE RAY, GUY AND BLOODWYND!
IT'S ALMOST LIKE--
"--THAT SATELLITE ISN'T REAL!"
YOU BIT OFF WAYYY TOO MUCH ATTACKING US!
I CAN DO ANYTHING I WANT--
--INCLUDING FORMING AN ENERGY BLAST STRONG ENOUGH TO SEND YOU BACK TO EARTH!
FZZAMM
FEEL LIKE I'VE BEEN HIT BY DOOMSDAY AGAIN! GOTTA HOPE THE OTHER LEAGUERS CAN SAVE US!
NO TIME TO REACT! WHAT'LL I DO? WHAT'LL I DO?!
THE JLA SATELLITE VANISHED! AND ACCORDING TO NASA'S SENSORS--
--OUR BOYS DID TOO!

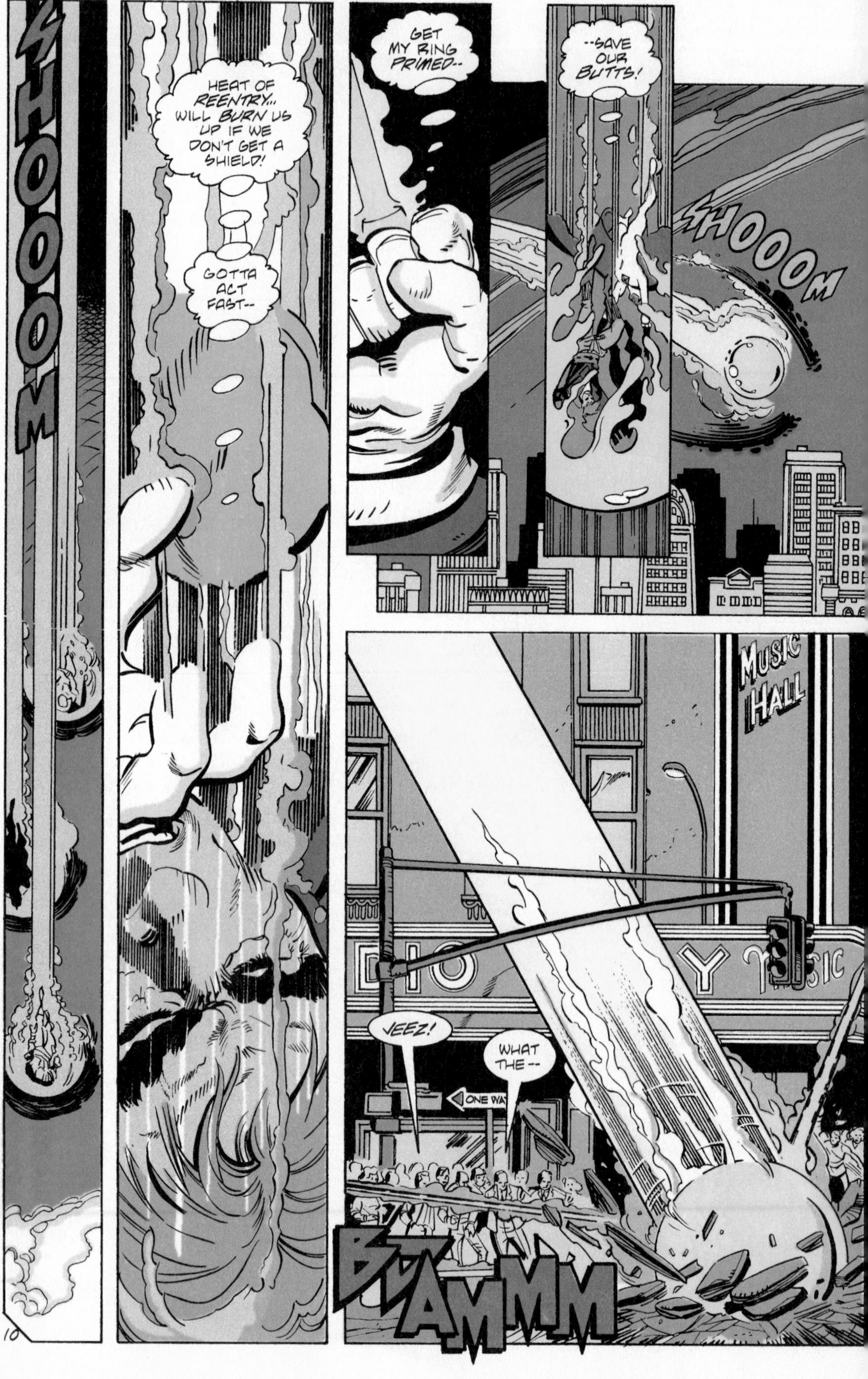
SHOOOM
HEAT OF REENTRY... WILL BURN US UP IF WE DON'T GET A SHIELD!
GOTTA ACT FAST--
GET MY RING PRIMED--
--SAVE OUR BUTTS!
SHOOOM
MUSIC HALL
JEEZ!
WHAT THE --
BLAMMM

THIS SUCKS!

WHOEVER IS UP THERE IN THAT SCREWY SATELLITE--

--IS GONNA *PAY BIG TIME* FOR DOIN' THIS TO US!

I AGREE. IT WOULD CERTAINLY SEEM THAT A *FULL POWERED* ASSAULT IS CALLED FOR.

DAMN STRAIGHT!

I'M WITH YOU GUYS!

I MEAN, WE *GOTTA* HAVE MORE GOING FOR US, RIGHT?

HOLD.

THAT SIGN FLASHING BELOW...

A *MASSIVE NUCLEAR ATTACK* LAUNCHED AGAINST *CHINA?!*

SOMETHING HAS OBVIOUSLY GONE QUITE WRONG DURING THE BRIEF TIME WE WERE IN SPACE.

CHINA DEVA... BY NUCLEAR AT TACK

11

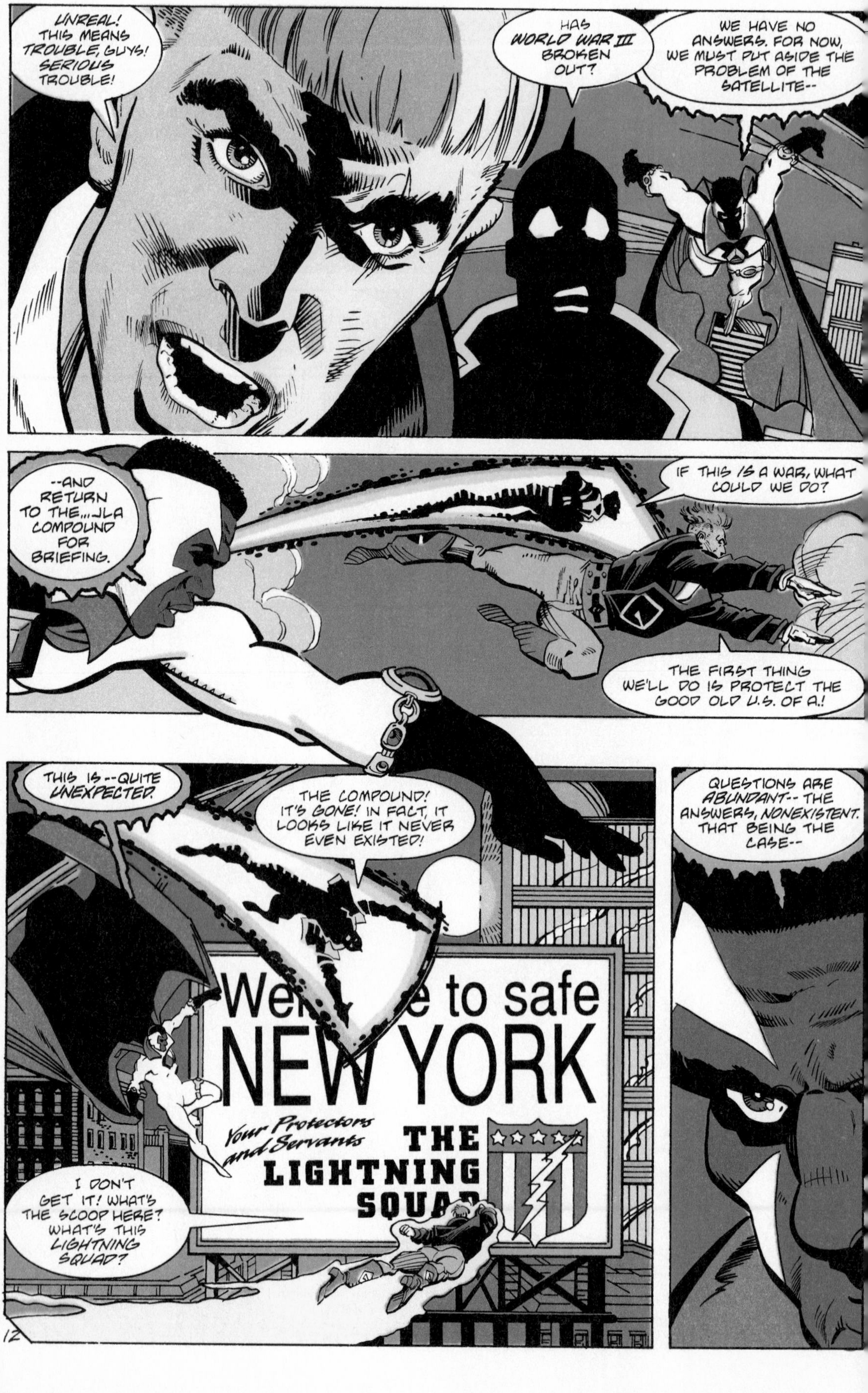
UNREAL! THIS MEANS TROUBLE, GUYS! SERIOUS TROUBLE!
HAS WORLD WAR III BROKEN OUT?
WE HAVE NO ANSWERS. FOR NOW, WE MUST PUT ASIDE THE PROBLEM OF THE SATELLITE--
--AND RETURN TO THE...JLA COMPOUND FOR BRIEFING.
IF THIS IS A WAR, WHAT COULD WE DO?
THE FIRST THING WE'LL DO IS PROTECT THE GOOD OLD U.S. OF A.!
THIS IS --QUITE UNEXPECTED.
THE COMPOUND! IT'S GONE! IN FACT, IT LOOKS LIKE IT NEVER EVEN EXISTED!
We e to safe
NEW YORK
Your Protectors and Servants
THE LIGHTNING SQUA
I DON'T GET IT! WHAT'S THE SCOOP HERE? WHAT'S THIS LIGHTNING SQUAD?
QUESTIONS ARE ABUNDANT-- THE ANSWERS, NONEXISTENT. THAT BEING THE CASE--

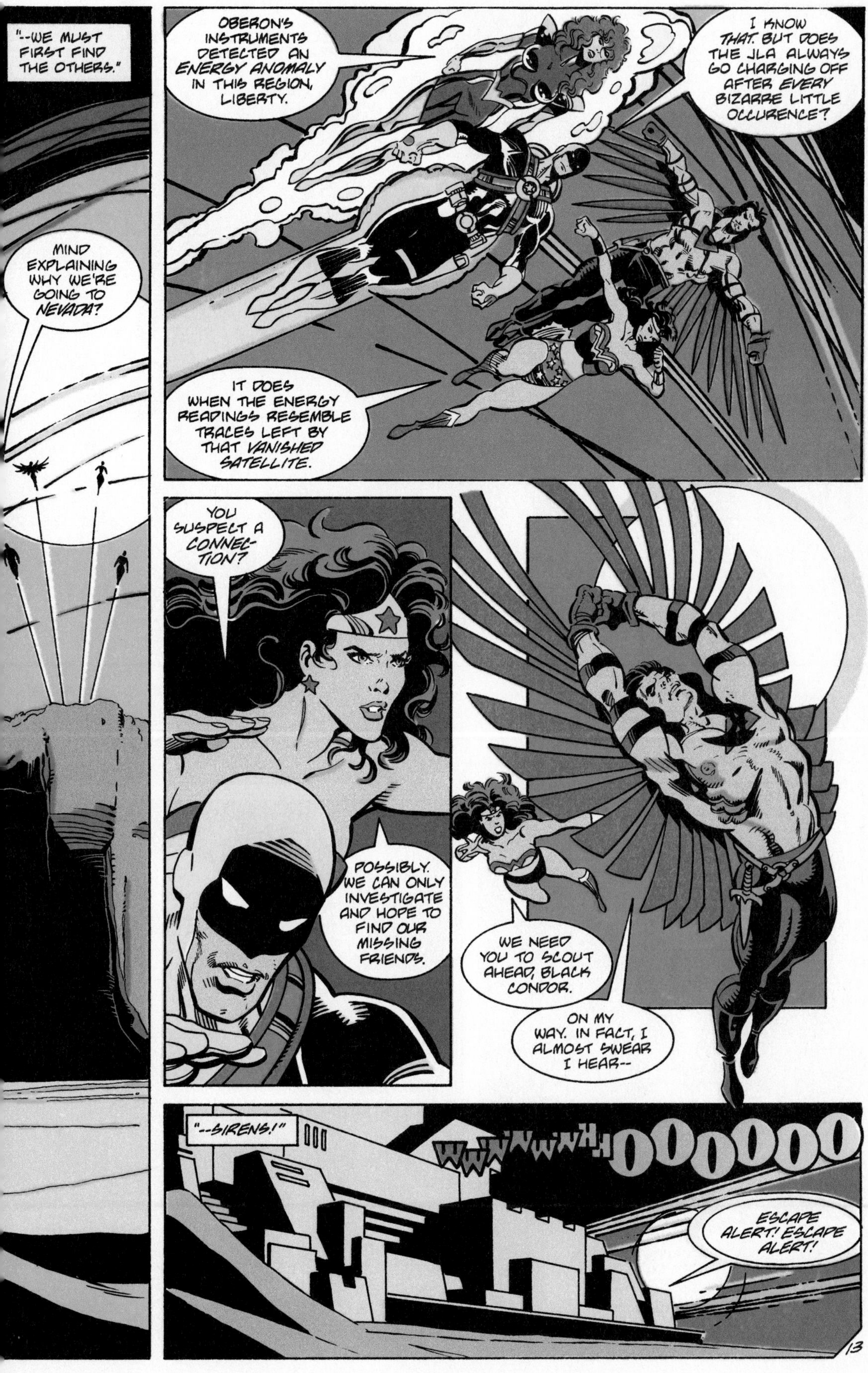
"--WE MUST FIRST FIND THE OTHERS."
OBERON'S INSTRUMENTS DETECTED AN ENERGY ANOMALY IN THIS REGION, LIBERTY.
I KNOW THAT. BUT DOES THE JLA ALWAYS GO CHARGING OFF AFTER EVERY BIZARRE LITTLE OCCURENCE?
MIND EXPLAINING WHY WE'RE GOING TO NEVADA?
IT DOES WHEN THE ENERGY READINGS RESEMBLE TRACES LEFT BY THAT VANISHED SATELLITE.
YOU SUSPECT A CONNECTION?
POSSIBLY. WE CAN ONLY INVESTIGATE AND HOPE TO FIND OUR MISSING FRIENDS.
WE NEED YOU TO SCOUT AHEAD, BLACK CONDOR.
ON MY WAY. IN FACT, I ALMOST SWEAR I HEAR--
"--SIRENS!"
WWWHHHNNNOOOOOOO
ESCAPE ALERT! ESCAPE ALERT!
13

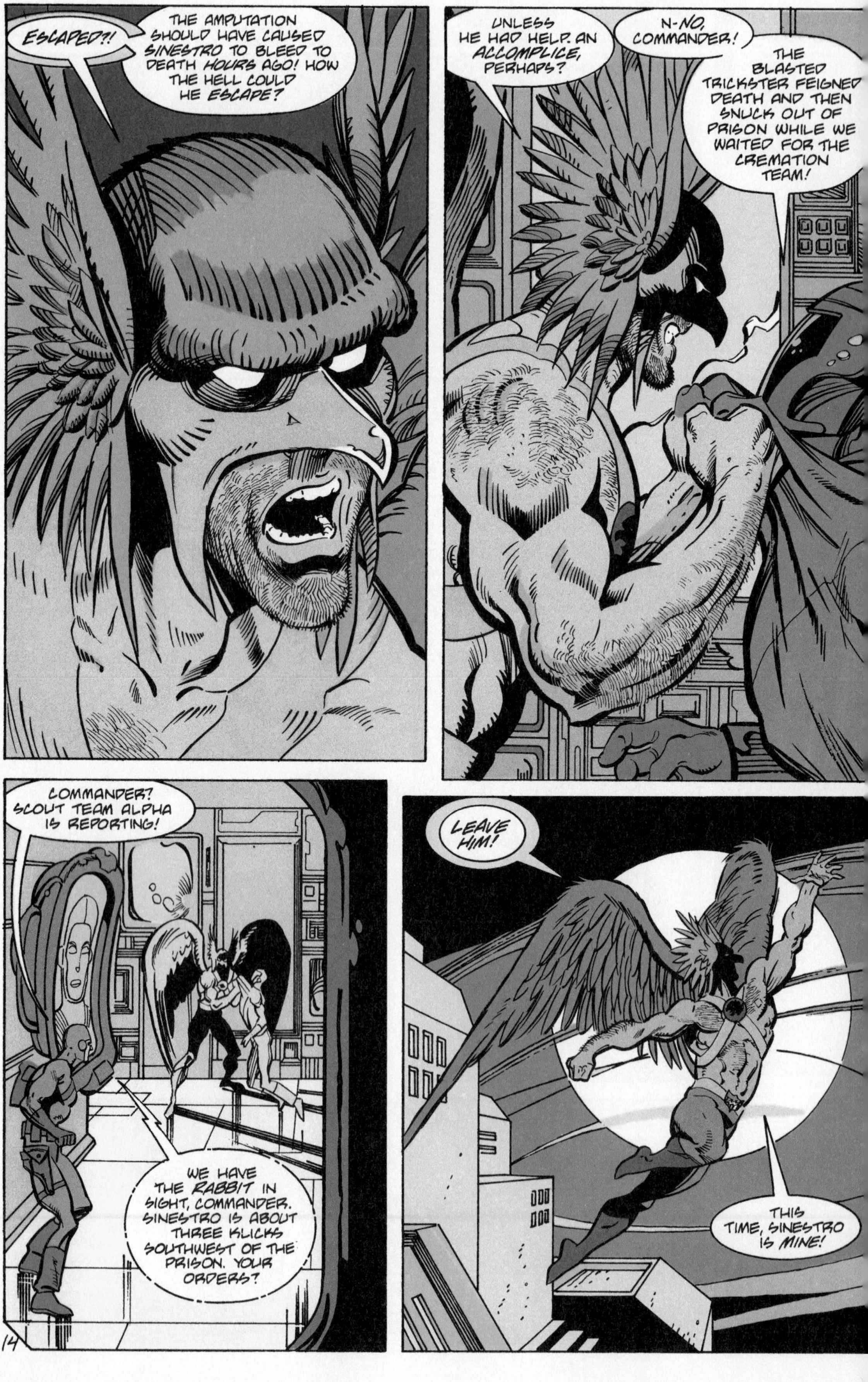
ESCAPED?!
THE AMPUTATION SHOULD HAVE CAUSED SINESTRO TO BLEED TO DEATH HOURS AGO! HOW THE HELL COULD HE ESCAPE?
UNLESS HE HAD HELP. AN ACCOMPLICE, PERHAPS?
N-NO, COMMANDER!
THE BLASTED TRICKSTER FEIGNED DEATH AND THEN SNUCK OUT OF PRISON WHILE WE WAITED FOR THE CREMATION TEAM!
COMMANDER? SCOUT TEAM ALPHA IS REPORTING!
WE HAVE THE RABBIT IN SIGHT, COMMANDER. SINESTRO IS ABOUT THREE KLICKS SOUTHWEST OF THE PRISON. YOUR ORDERS?
LEAVE HIM!
THIS TIME, SINESTRO IS MINE!

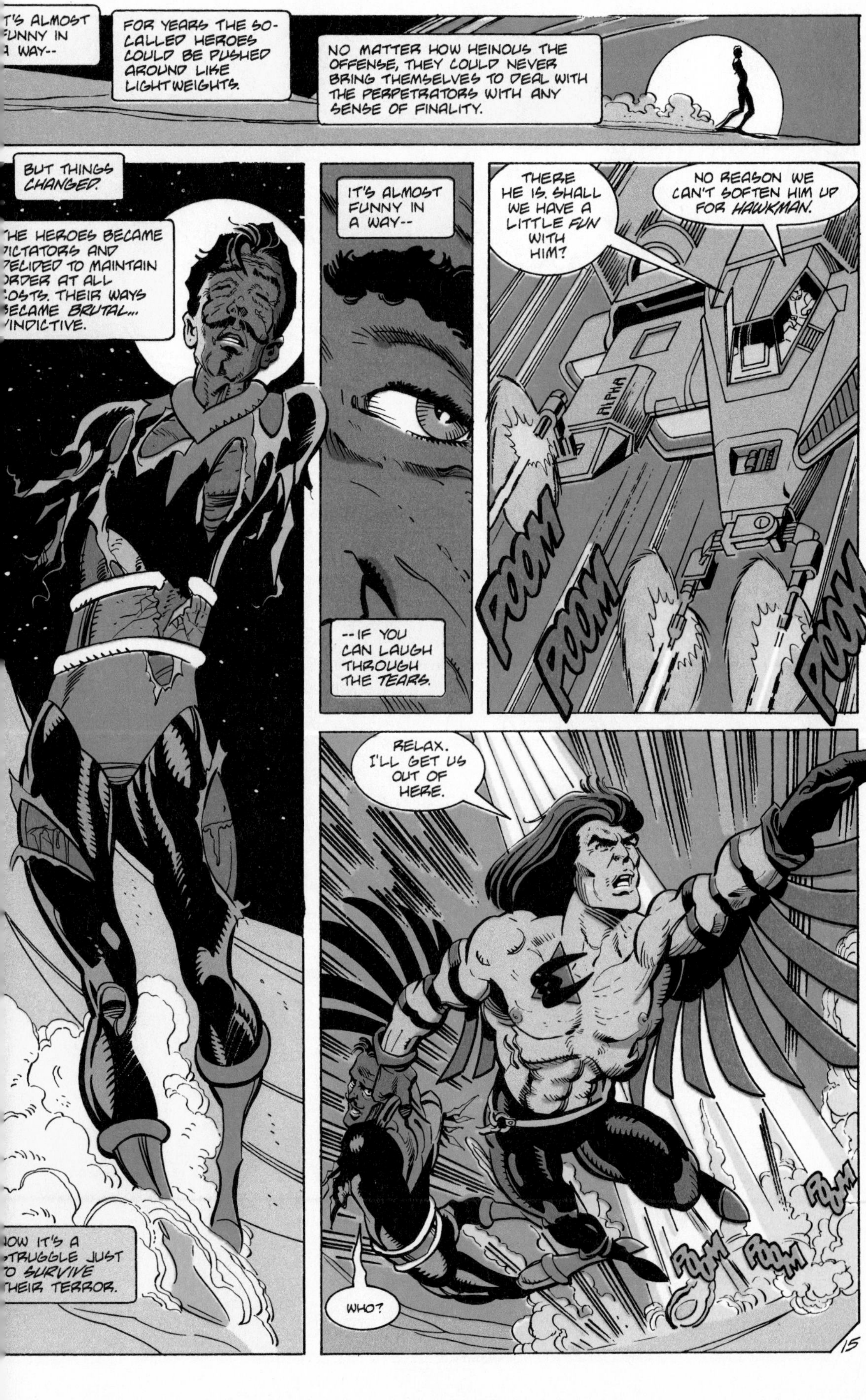

IT'S ALMOST FUNNY IN A WAY--
FOR YEARS THE SO-CALLED HEROES COULD BE PUSHED AROUND LIKE LIGHTWEIGHTS.
NO MATTER HOW HEINOUS THE OFFENSE, THEY COULD NEVER BRING THEMSELVES TO DEAL WITH THE PERPETRATORS WITH ANY SENSE OF FINALITY.
BUT THINGS CHANGED.
THE HEROES BECAME DICTATORS AND DECIDED TO MAINTAIN ORDER AT ALL COSTS. THEIR WAYS BECAME BRUTAL... VINDICTIVE.
NOW IT'S A STRUGGLE JUST TO SURVIVE THEIR TERROR.
IT'S ALMOST FUNNY IN A WAY--
--IF YOU CAN LAUGH THROUGH THE TEARS.
THERE HE IS. SHALL WE HAVE A LITTLE FUN WITH HIM?
NO REASON WE CAN'T SOFTEN HIM UP FOR HAWKMAN.
ALPHA
POOM
POOM
POOM
RELAX. I'LL GET US OUT OF HERE.
WHO?
POOM
POOM
POOM

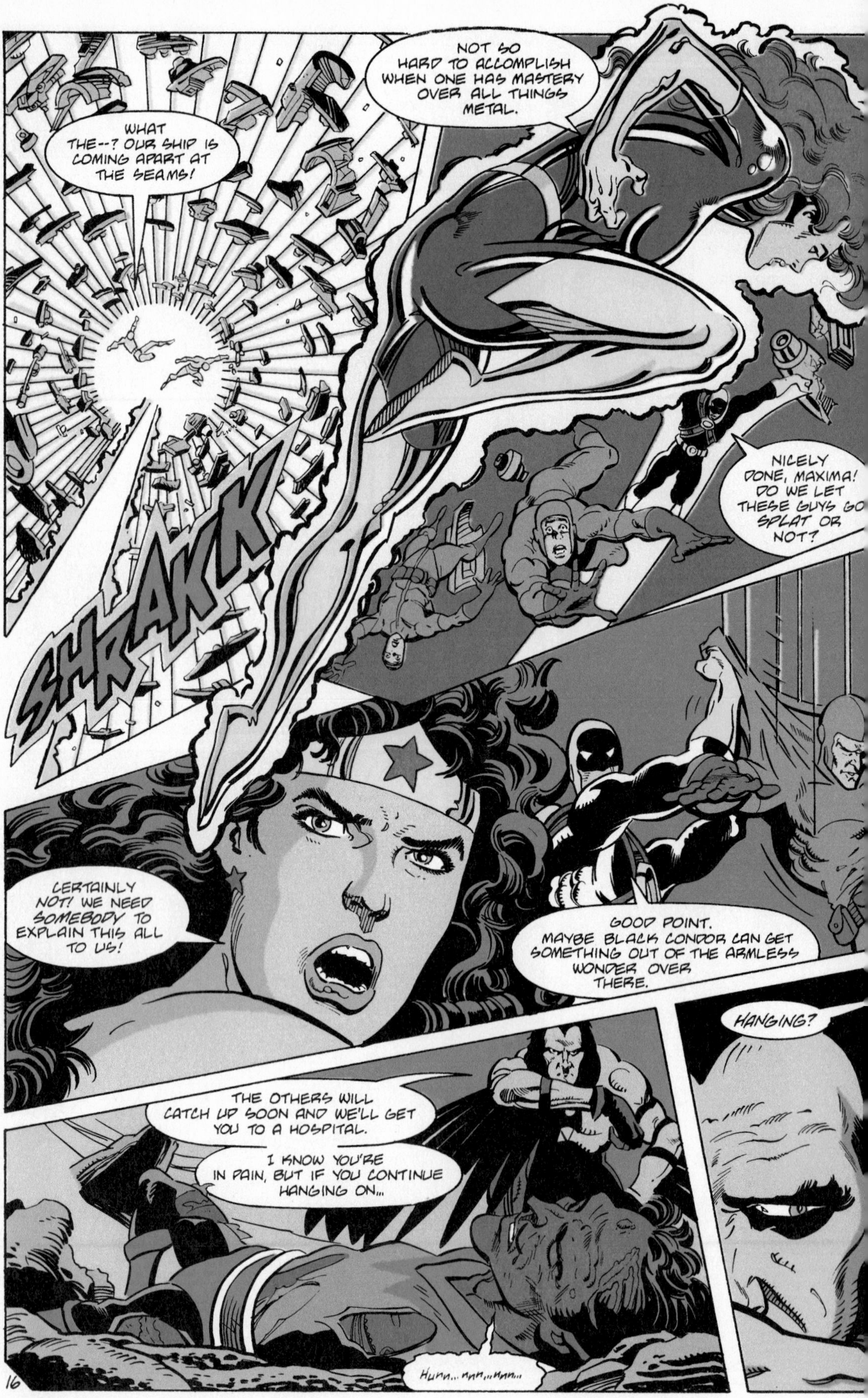
WHAT THE--? OUR SHIP IS COMING APART AT THE SEAMS!
NOT SO HARD TO ACCOMPLISH WHEN ONE HAS MASTERY OVER ALL THINGS METAL.
SHRAKK
NICELY DONE, MAXIMA! DO WE LET THESE GUYS GO SPLAT OR NOT?
CERTAINLY NOT! WE NEED SOMEBODY TO EXPLAIN THIS ALL TO US!
GOOD POINT. MAYBE BLACK CONDOR CAN GET SOMETHING OUT OF THE ARMLESS WONDER OVER THERE.
THE OTHERS WILL CATCH UP SOON AND WE'LL GET YOU TO A HOSPITAL.
I KNOW YOU'RE IN PAIN, BUT IF YOU CONTINUE HANGING ON...
HANGING?
Hunn... nnn... hnn...

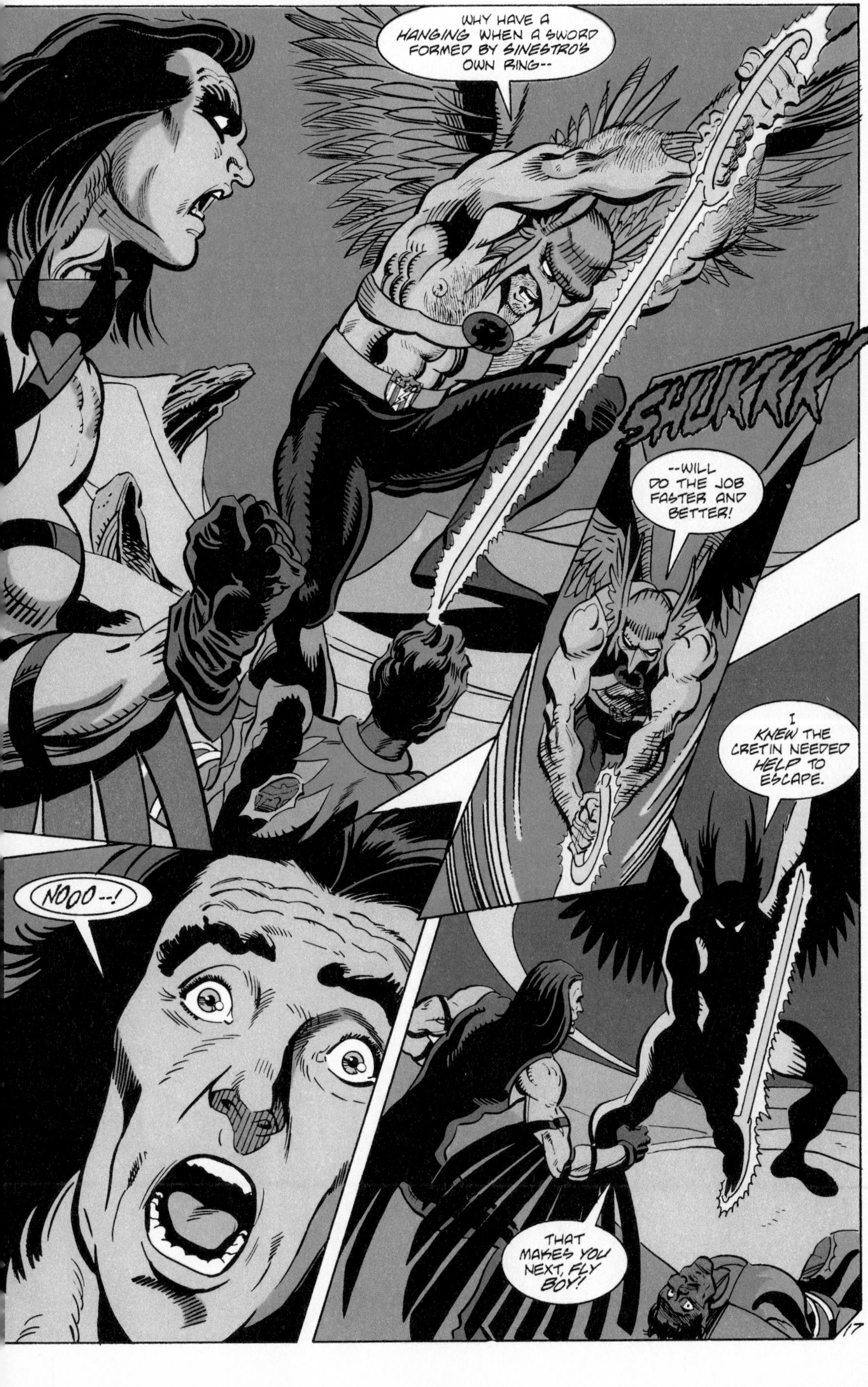
WHY HAVE A HANGING WHEN A SWORD FORMED BY SINESTRO'S OWN RING--
SHUKKK
--WILL DO THE JOB FASTER AND BETTER!
I KNEW THE CRETIN NEEDED HELP TO ESCAPE.
NOOO--!
THAT MAKES YOU NEXT, FLY BOY!

OUR JUSTICE LEAGUE COMPOUND IS *MISSING*. THIS MUCH IS CLEAR...

PERHAPS WE HAVE GONE BACK IN TIME *BEFORE* IT EXISTED. PERHAPS WE ARE ON ANOTHER EARTH. ONE COULD EVEN SPECULATE--

--THAT OUR *ENTIRE* WORLD HAS BEEN SOMEHOW ALTERED.

Welcome to safe NEW YORK
THE LIGHTNING SQUAD

I SAY WE START *DIGGING* TO GET TO THE BOTTOM OF ALL THIS!

SOUNDS GOOD, BUT HOW? I HAVE ENOUGH TROUBLE TRYING TO CHANGE A *FUSE!*

WAIT. I SENSE THE PRESENCE OF *ANOTHER.* WE ARE NOT ALONE!

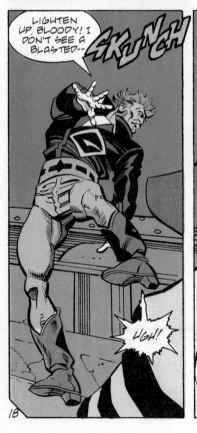

LIGHTEN UP, BLOODY! I DON'T SEE A BLASTED--

SKUNCH

STAKT

UGH!

SHOW YOURSELF. NOW.

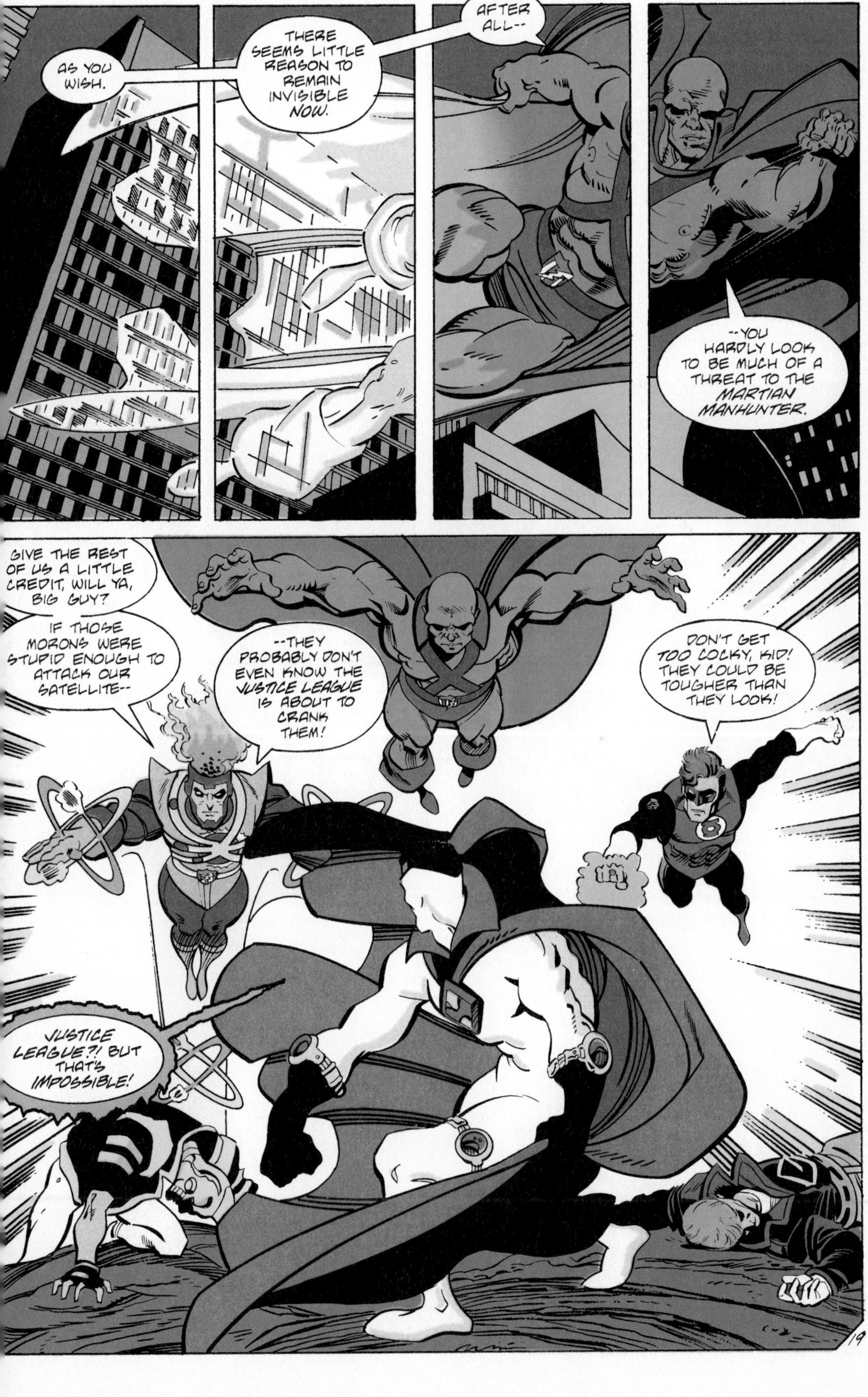

AS YOU WISH.
THERE SEEMS LITTLE REASON TO REMAIN INVISIBLE NOW.
AFTER ALL--
--YOU HARDLY LOOK TO BE MUCH OF A THREAT TO THE MARTIAN MANHUNTER.
GIVE THE REST OF US A LITTLE CREDIT, WILL YA, BIG GUY?
IF THOSE MORONS WERE STUPID ENOUGH TO ATTACK OUR SATELLITE--
--THEY PROBABLY DON'T EVEN KNOW THE JUSTICE LEAGUE IS ABOUT TO CRANK THEM!
DON'T GET TOO COCKY, KID! THEY COULD BE TOUGHER THAN THEY LOOK!
JUSTICE LEAGUE?! BUT THAT'S IMPOSSIBLE!

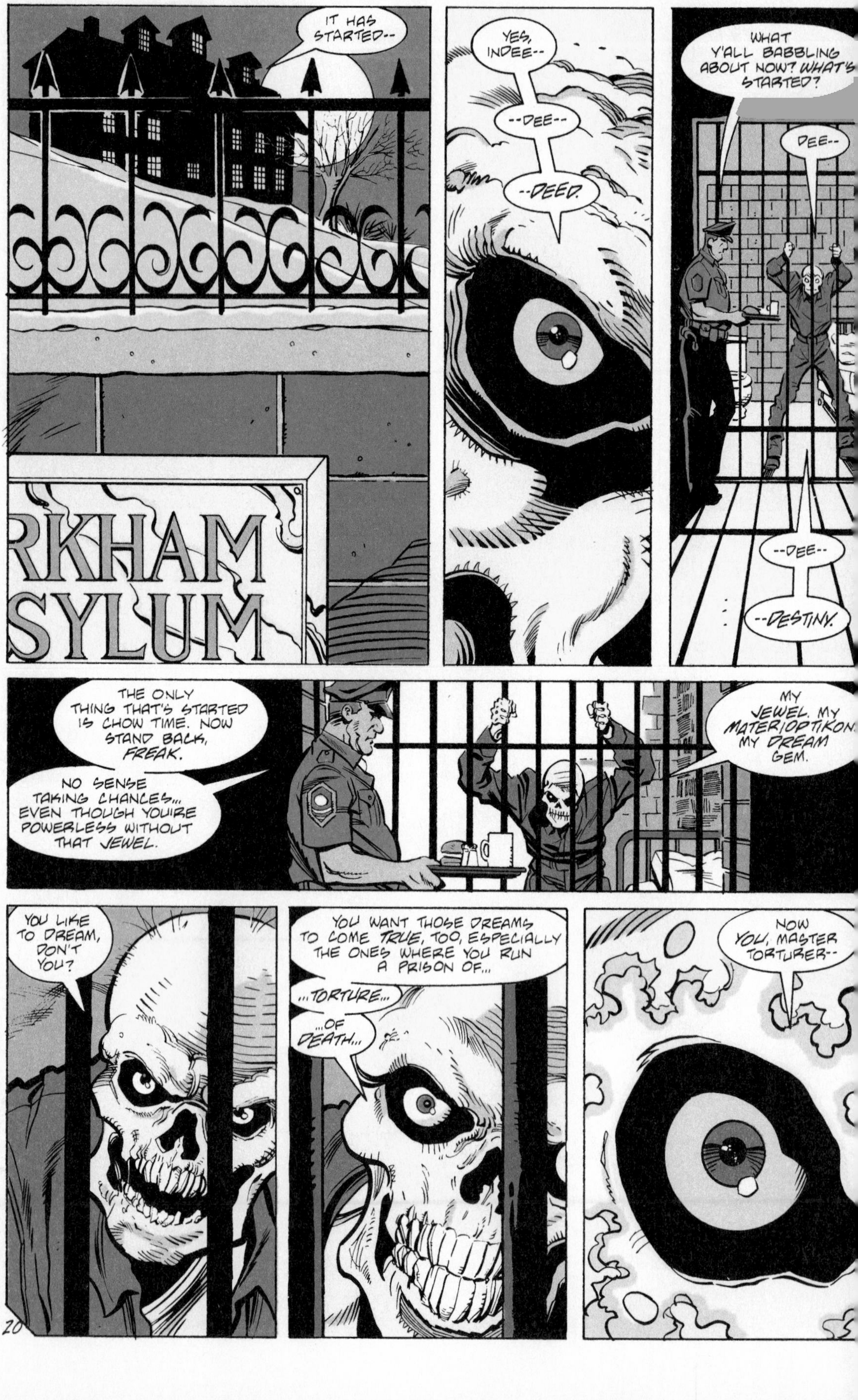

IT HAS STARTED--
RKHAM SYLUM
YES, INDEE--
--DEE--
--DEED.
WHAT Y'ALL BABBLING ABOUT NOW? WHAT'S STARTED?
DEE--
--DEE--
--DESTINY.
THE ONLY THING THAT'S STARTED IS CHOW TIME. NOW STAND BACK, FREAK.
NO SENSE TAKING CHANCES... EVEN THOUGH YOU'RE POWERLESS WITHOUT THAT JEWEL.
MY JEWEL. MY MATERIOPTIKON. MY DREAM GEM.
YOU LIKE TO DREAM, DON'T YOU?
YOU WANT THOSE DREAMS TO COME TRUE, TOO, ESPECIALLY THE ONES WHERE YOU RUN A PRISON OF...
...TORTURE...
...OF DEATH...
NOW YOU, MASTER TORTURER--

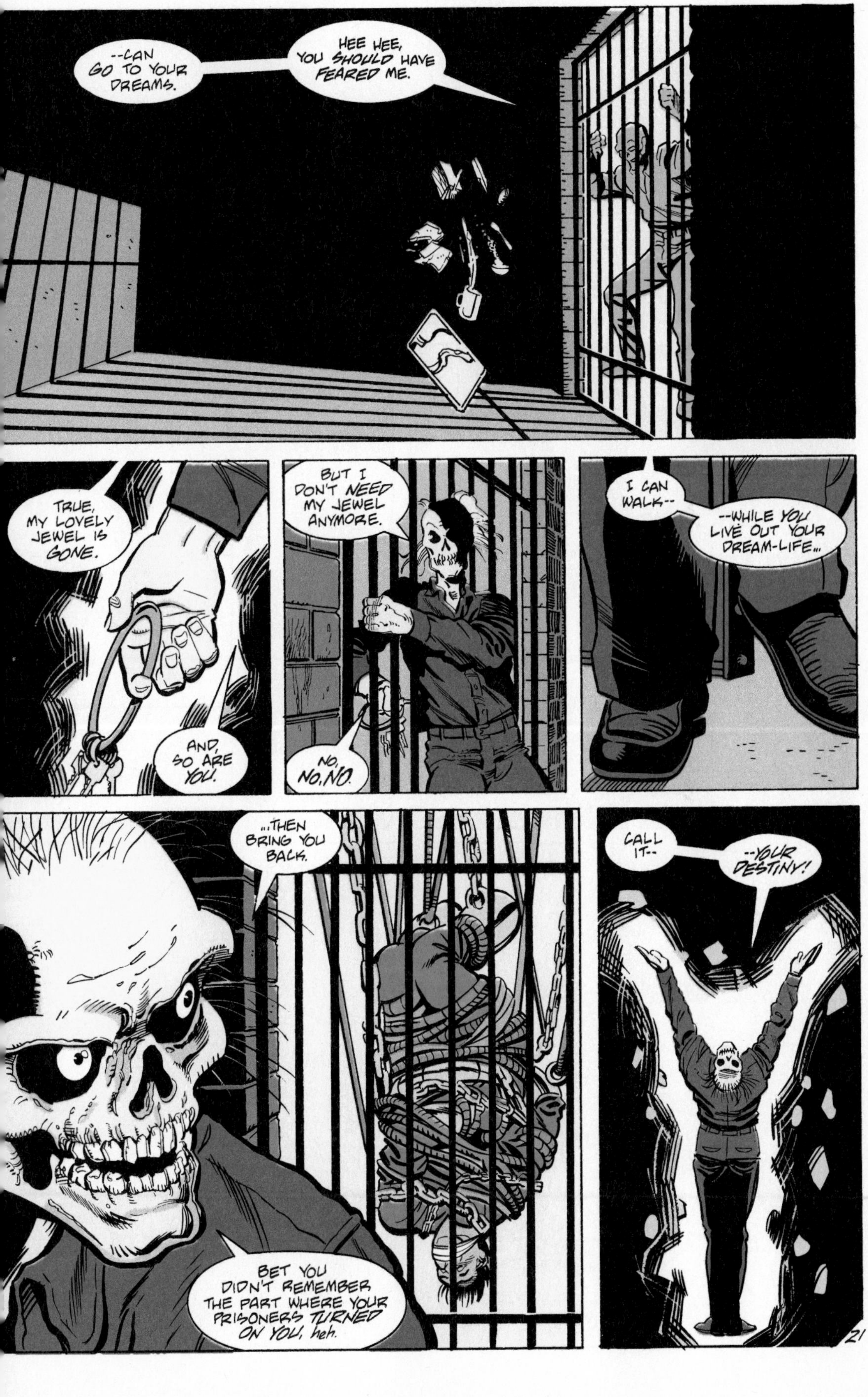
--CAN GO TO YOUR DREAMS.
HEE HEE, YOU SHOULD HAVE FEARED ME.
TRUE, MY LOVELY JEWEL IS GONE.
AND, SO ARE YOU.
BUT I DON'T NEED MY JEWEL ANYMORE.
NO, NO, NO.
I CAN WALK--
--WHILE YOU LIVE OUT YOUR DREAM-LIFE...
...THEN BRING YOU BACK.
BET YOU DIDN'T REMEMBER THE PART WHERE YOUR PRISONERS TURNED ON YOU, heh.
CALL IT--
--YOUR DESTINY!

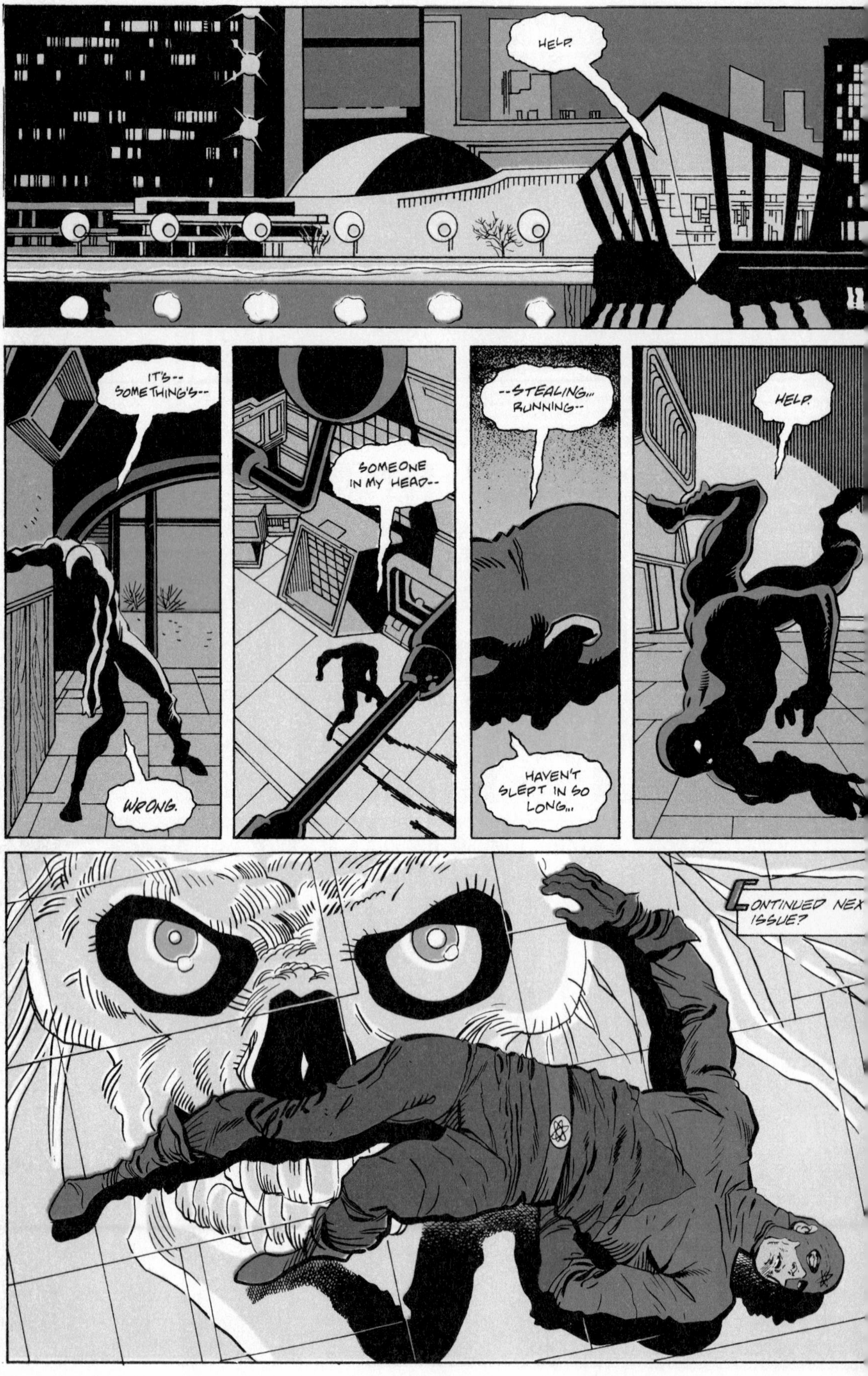
HELP.
IT'S--
SOMETHING'S--
WRONG.
SOMEONE
IN MY HEAD--
--STEALING...
RUNNING--
HAVEN'T
SLEPT IN SO
LONG...
HELP.
CONTINUED NEX
ISSUE?

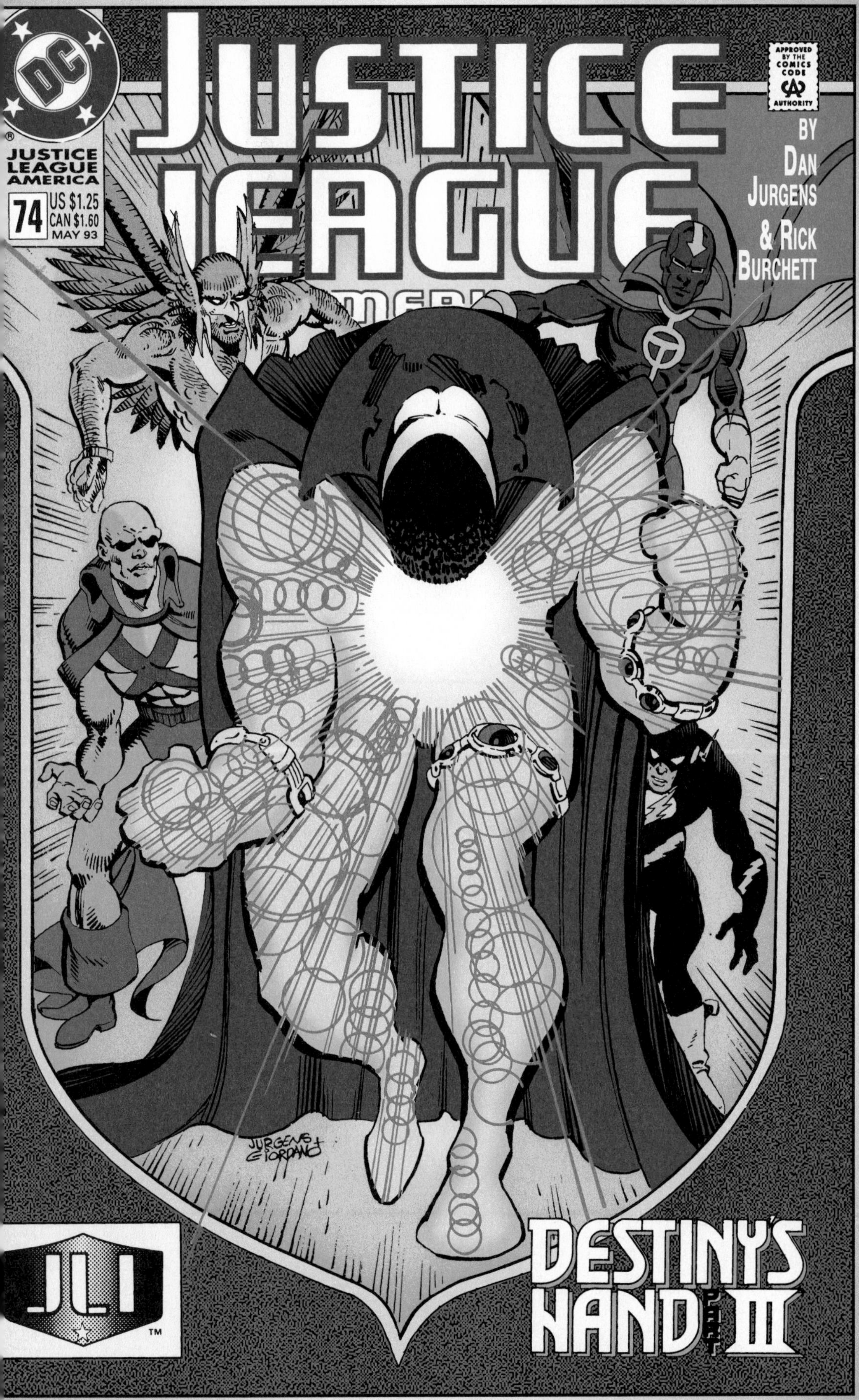

JUSTICE LEAGUE
JUSTICE LEAGUE AMERICA
74 US $1.25 CAN $1.60 MAY 93
APPROVED BY THE COMICS CODE AUTHORITY
BY DAN JURGENS & RICK BURCHETT
JURGENS + GIORDANO
JLI
DESTINY'S HAND PART III

Cover art by **DAN JURGENS**
and **DICK GIORDANO**

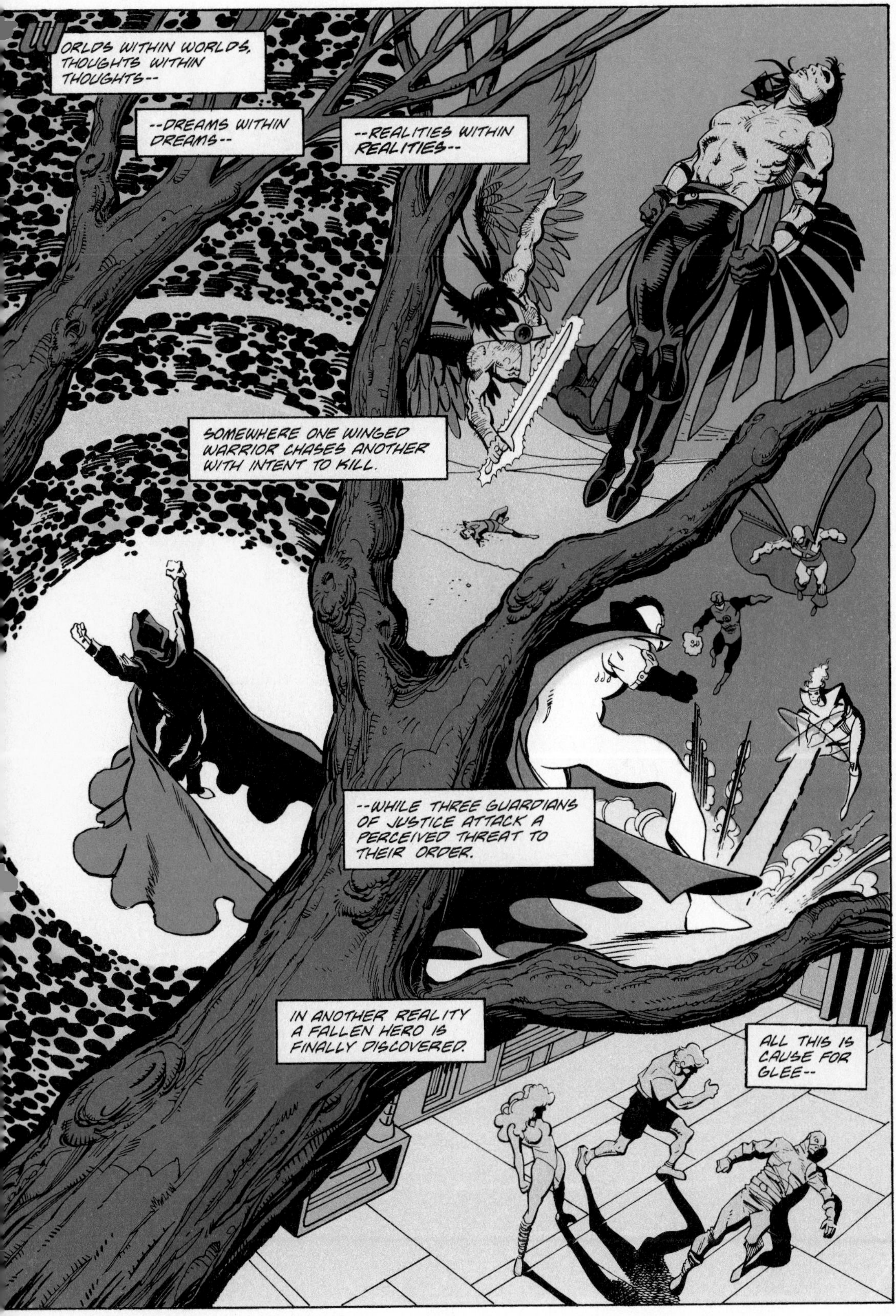
WORLDS WITHIN WORLDS, THOUGHTS WITHIN THOUGHTS--
--DREAMS WITHIN DREAMS--
--REALITIES WITHIN REALITIES--
SOMEWHERE ONE WINGED WARRIOR CHASES ANOTHER WITH INTENT TO KILL.
--WHILE THREE GUARDIANS OF JUSTICE ATTACK A PERCEIVED THREAT TO THEIR ORDER.
IN ANOTHER REALITY A FALLEN HERO IS FINALLY DISCOVERED.
ALL THIS IS CAUSE FOR GLEE--

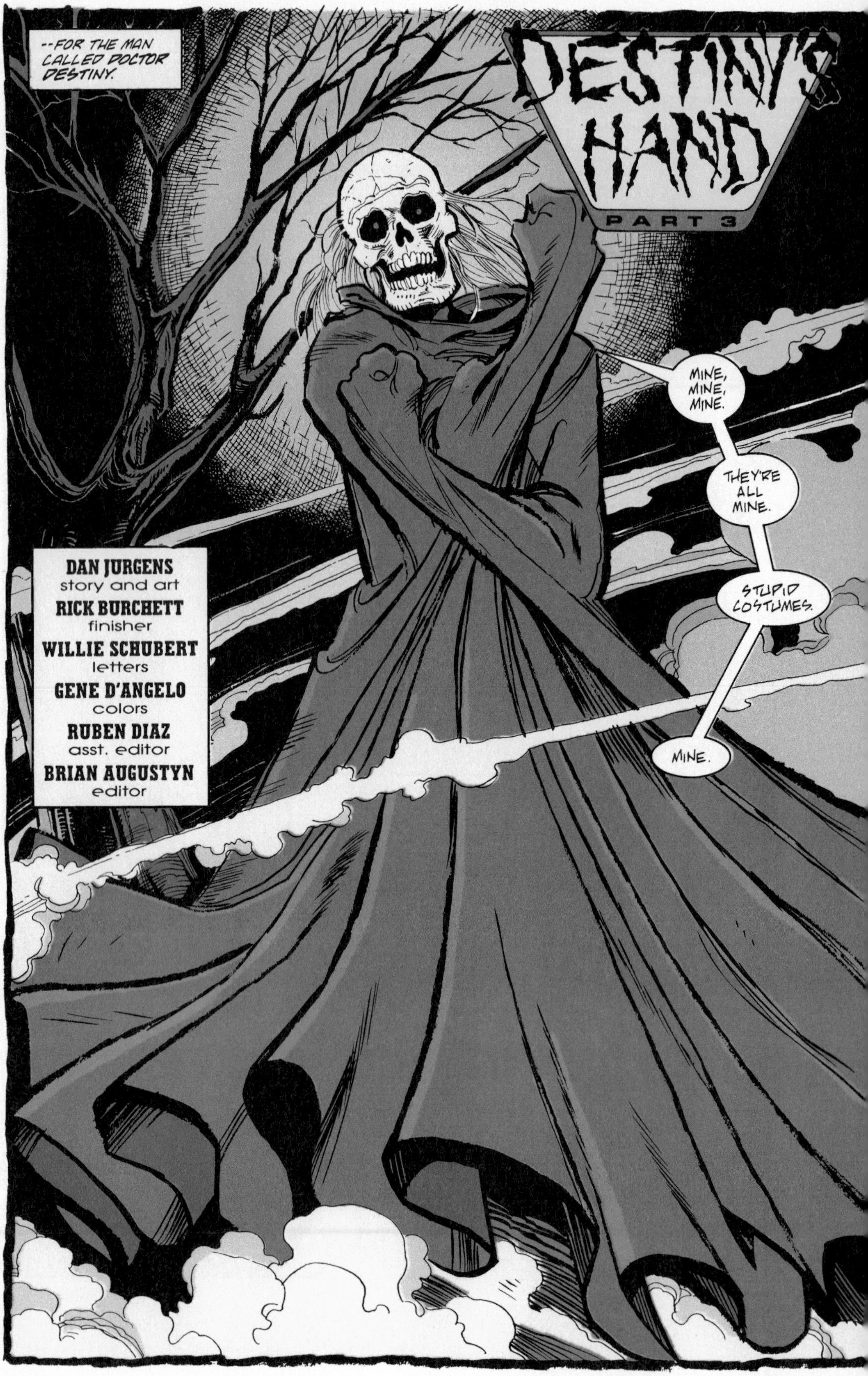
--FOR THE MAN CALLED DOCTOR DESTINY.
DESTINY'S HAND
PART 3
MINE, MINE, MINE.
THEY'RE ALL MINE.
STUPID COSTUMES.
MINE.
DAN JURGENS story and art
RICK BURCHETT finisher
WILLIE SCHUBERT letters
GENE D'ANGELO colors
RUBEN DIAZ asst. editor
BRIAN AUGUSTYN editor

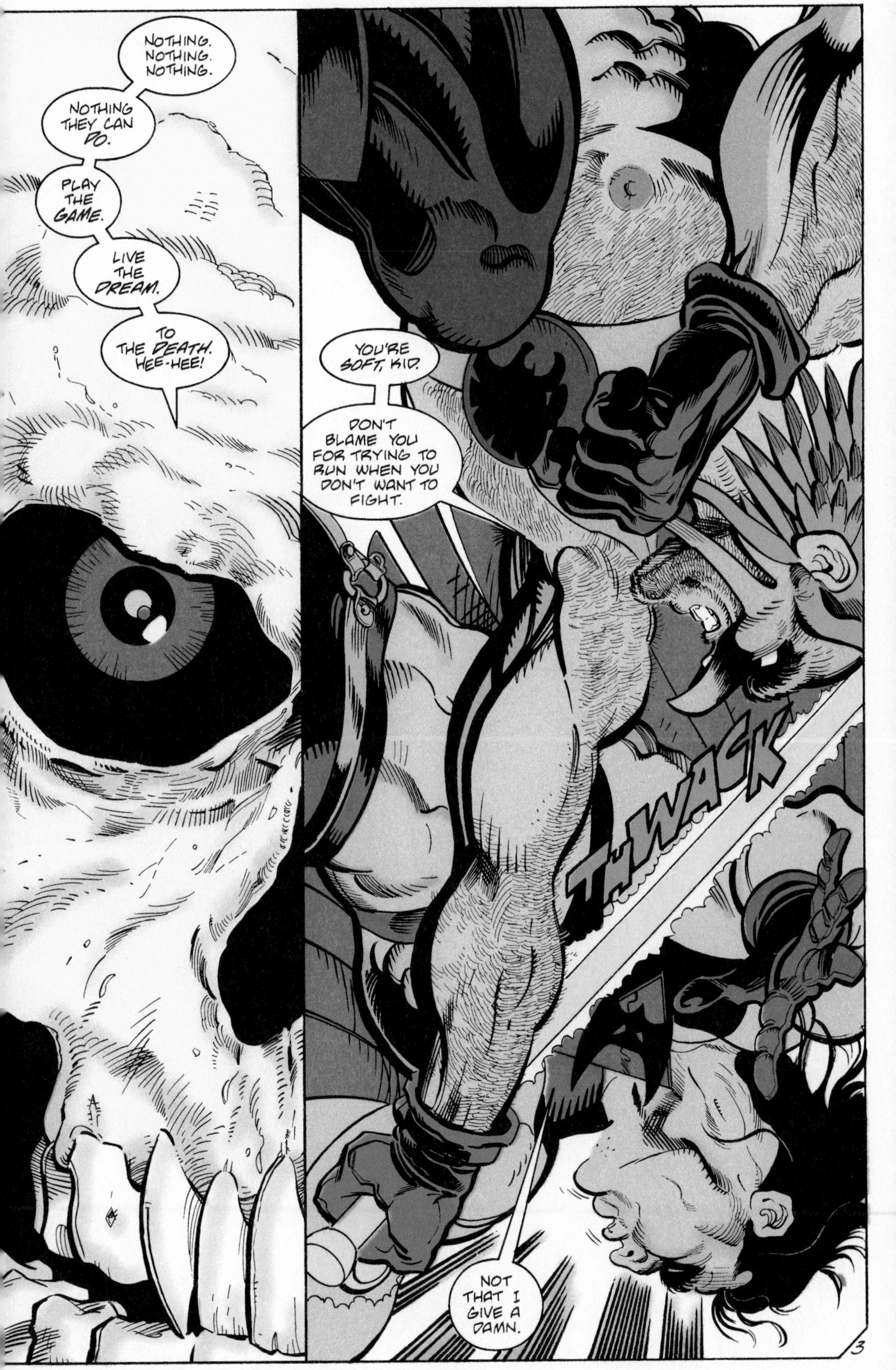
NOTHING. NOTHING. NOTHING.
NOTHING THEY CAN DO.
PLAY THE GAME.
LIVE THE DREAM.
TO THE DEATH. HEE-HEE!
YOU'RE SOFT, KID.
DON'T BLAME YOU FOR TRYING TO RUN WHEN YOU DON'T WANT TO FIGHT.
THWACK
NOT THAT I GIVE A DAMN.

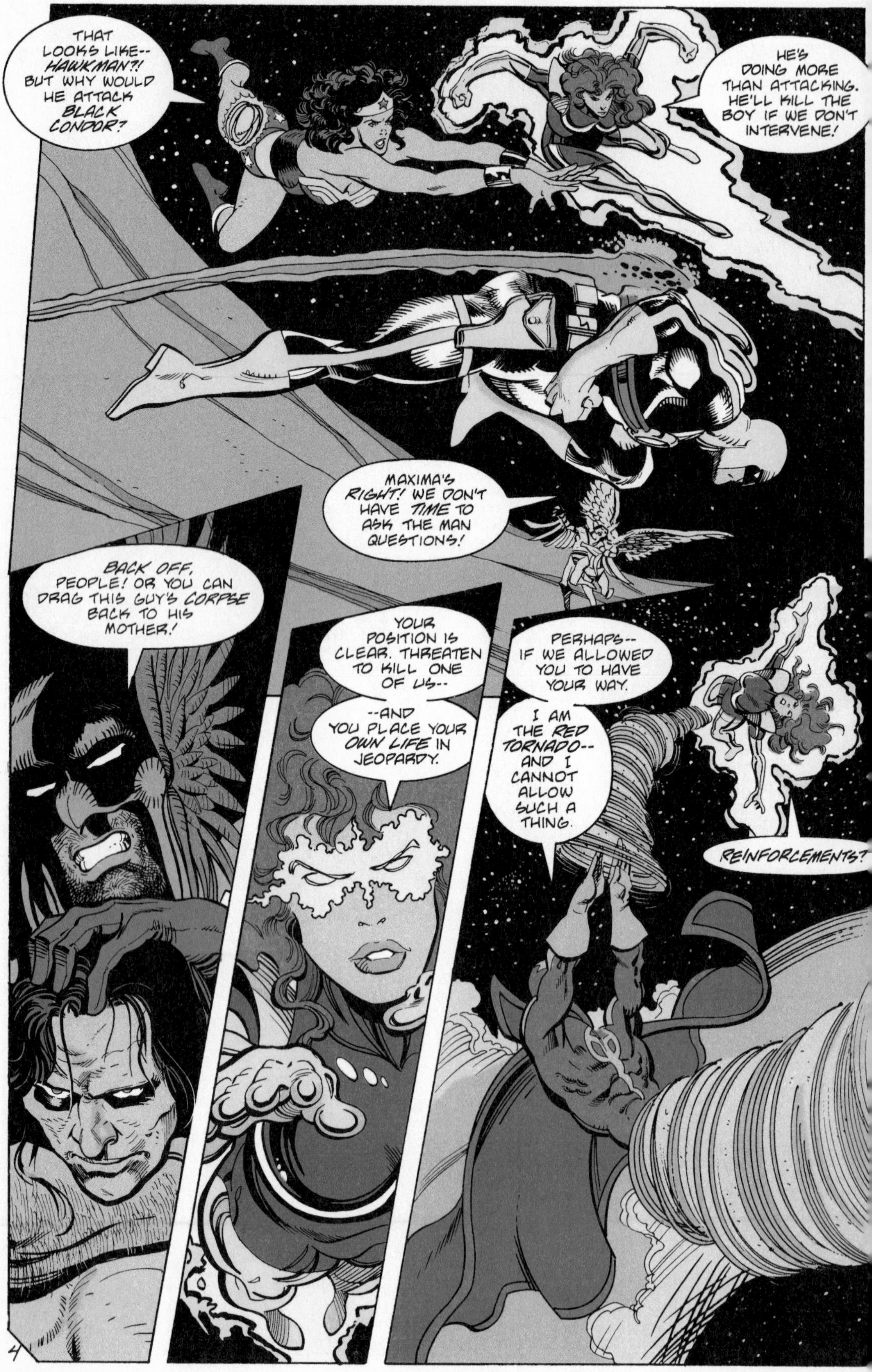
THAT LOOKS LIKE-- HAWKMAN?! BUT WHY WOULD HE ATTACK BLACK CONDOR?
HE'S DOING MORE THAN ATTACKING. HE'LL KILL THE BOY IF WE DON'T INTERVENE!
MAXIMA'S RIGHT! WE DON'T HAVE TIME TO ASK THE MAN QUESTIONS!
BACK OFF, PEOPLE! OR YOU CAN DRAG THIS GUY'S CORPSE BACK TO HIS MOTHER!
YOUR POSITION IS CLEAR. THREATEN TO KILL ONE OF US--
--AND YOU PLACE YOUR OWN LIFE IN JEOPARDY.
PERHAPS-- IF WE ALLOWED YOU TO HAVE YOUR WAY.
I AM THE RED TORNADO-- AND I CANNOT ALLOW SUCH A THING.
REINFORCEMENTS?

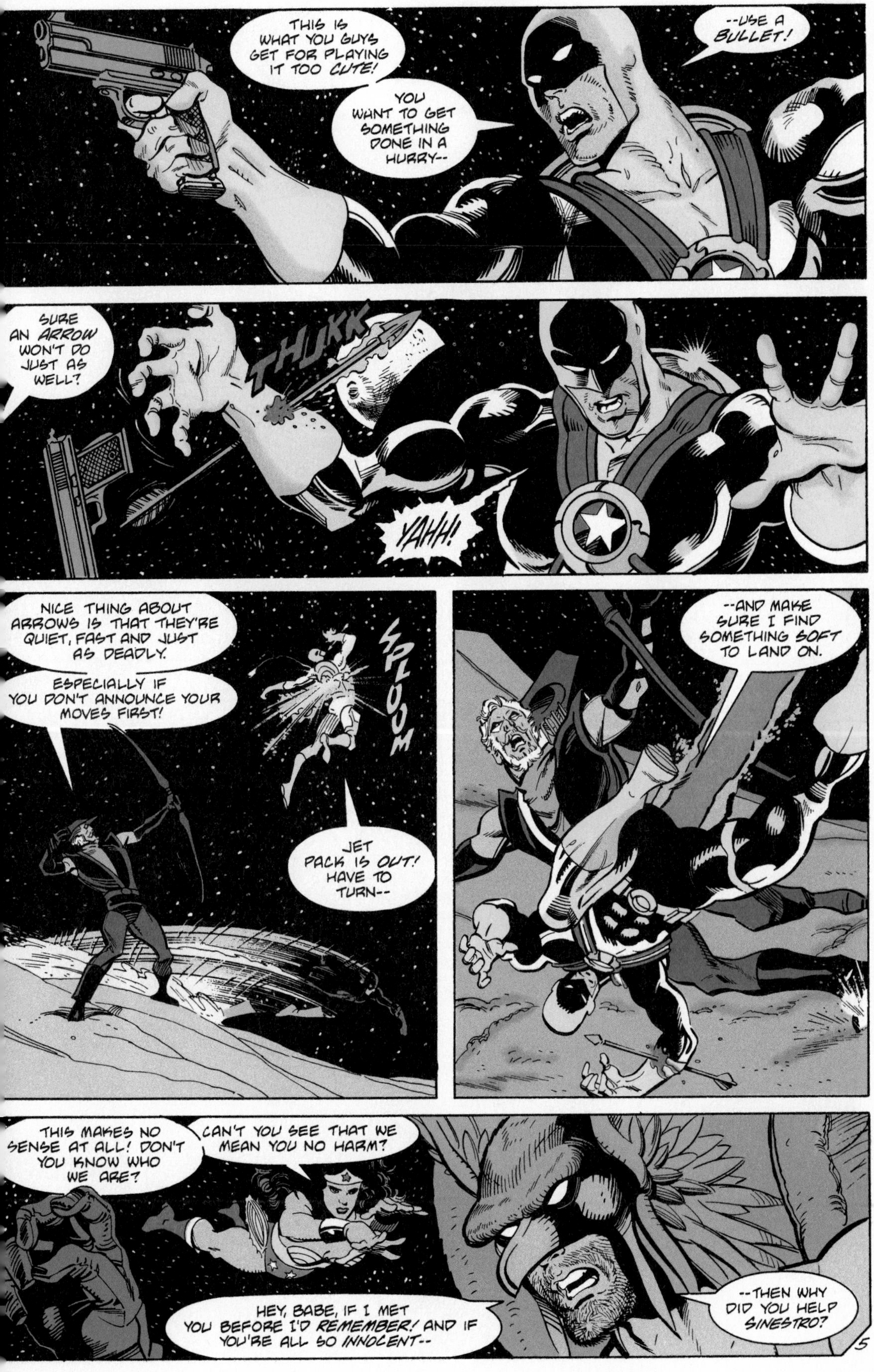
THIS IS WHAT YOU GUYS GET FOR PLAYING IT TOO CUTE!
YOU WANT TO GET SOMETHING DONE IN A HURRY--
--USE A BULLET!
SURE AN ARROW WON'T DO JUST AS WELL?
THUKK
YAHH!
NICE THING ABOUT ARROWS IS THAT THEY'RE QUIET, FAST AND JUST AS DEADLY.
ESPECIALLY IF YOU DON'T ANNOUNCE YOUR MOVES FIRST!
SPLOOOM
JET PACK IS OUT! HAVE TO TURN--
--AND MAKE SURE I FIND SOMETHING SOFT TO LAND ON.
THIS MAKES NO SENSE AT ALL! DON'T YOU KNOW WHO WE ARE?
CAN'T YOU SEE THAT WE MEAN YOU NO HARM?
HEY, BABE, IF I MET YOU BEFORE I'D REMEMBER! AND IF YOU'RE ALL SO INNOCENT--
--THEN WHY DID YOU HELP SINESTRO?

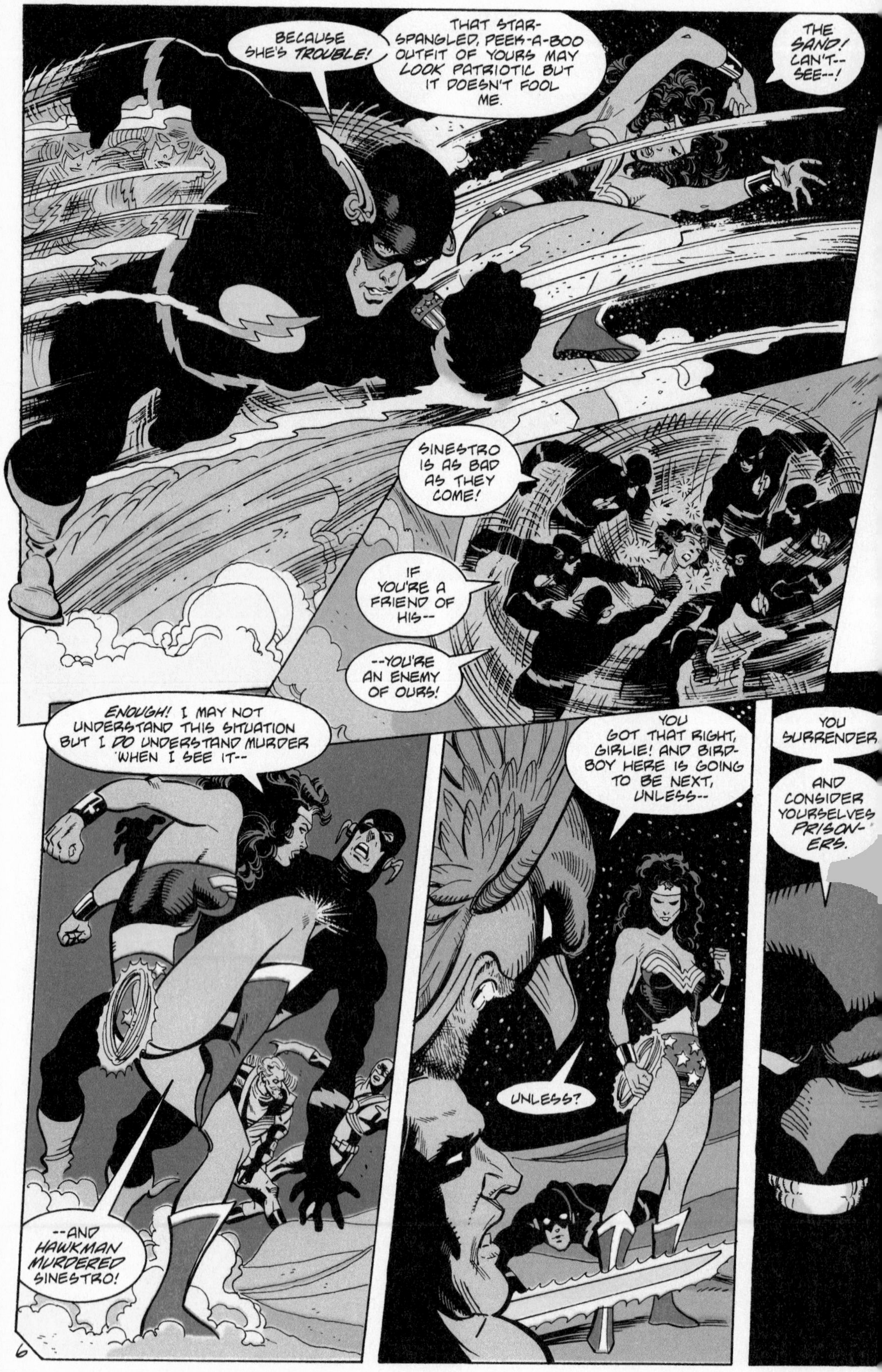
BECAUSE SHE'S TROUBLE!
THAT STAR-SPANGLED, PEEK-A-BOO OUTFIT OF YOURS MAY LOOK PATRIOTIC BUT IT DOESN'T FOOL ME.
THE SAND! CAN'T-- SEE--!
SINESTRO IS AS BAD AS THEY COME!
IF YOU'RE A FRIEND OF HIS--
--YOU'RE AN ENEMY OF OURS!
ENOUGH! I MAY NOT UNDERSTAND THIS SITUATION BUT I DO UNDERSTAND MURDER WHEN I SEE IT--
--AND HAWKMAN MURDERED SINESTRO!
YOU GOT THAT RIGHT, GIRLIE! AND BIRD-BOY HERE IS GOING TO BE NEXT, UNLESS--
UNLESS?
YOU SURRENDER
AND CONSIDER YOURSELVES PRISONERS.

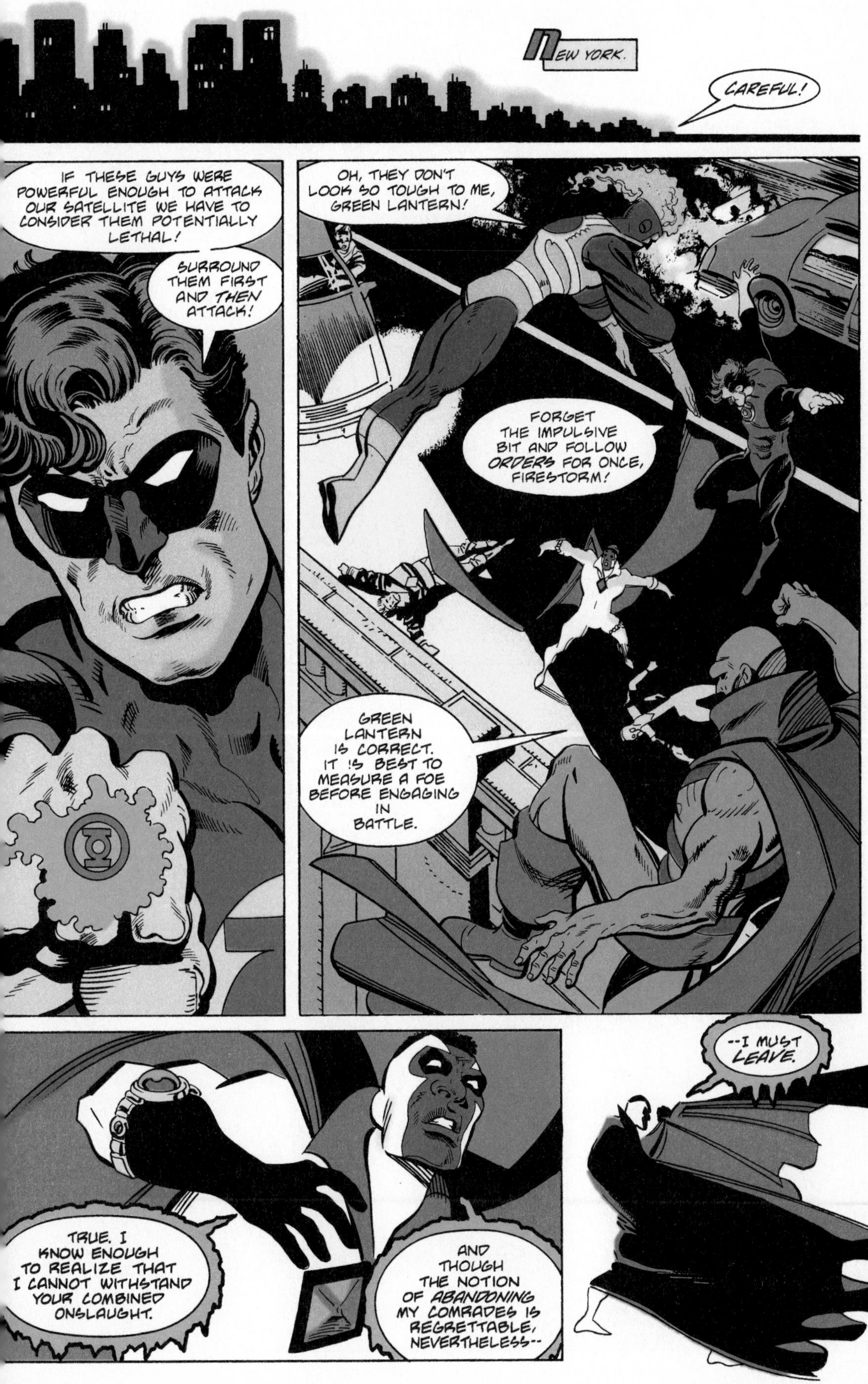
NEW YORK.
CAREFUL!
IF THESE GUYS WERE POWERFUL ENOUGH TO ATTACK OUR SATELLITE WE HAVE TO CONSIDER THEM POTENTIALLY LETHAL!
SURROUND THEM FIRST AND THEN ATTACK!
OH, THEY DON'T LOOK SO TOUGH TO ME, GREEN LANTERN!
FORGET THE IMPULSIVE BIT AND FOLLOW ORDERS FOR ONCE, FIRESTORM!
GREEN LANTERN IS CORRECT. IT IS BEST TO MEASURE A FOE BEFORE ENGAGING IN BATTLE.
TRUE. I KNOW ENOUGH TO REALIZE THAT I CANNOT WITHSTAND YOUR COMBINED ONSLAUGHT.
AND THOUGH THE NOTION OF ABANDONING MY COMRADES IS REGRETTABLE, NEVERTHELESS--
--I MUST LEAVE.

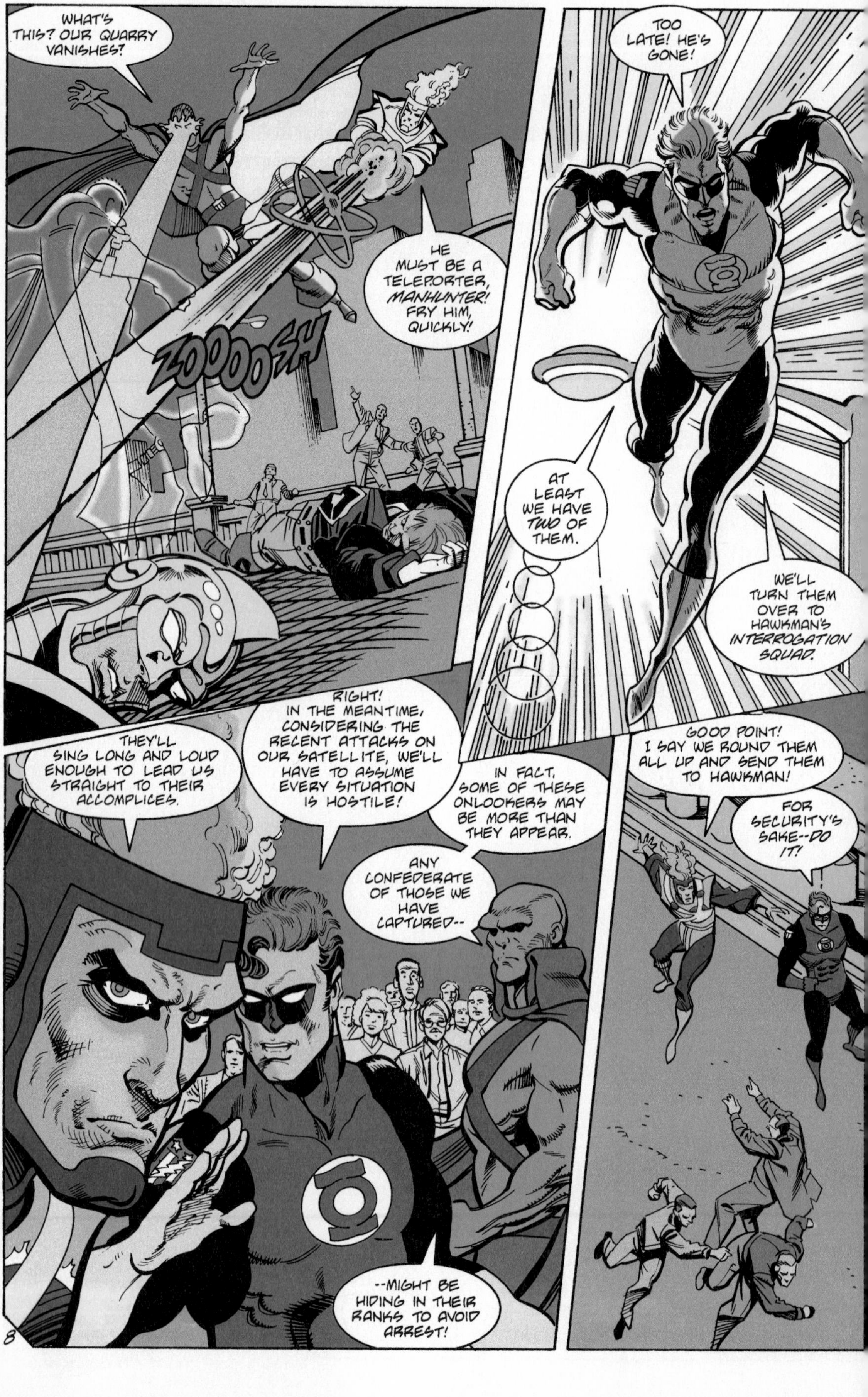
WHAT'S THIS? OUR QUARRY VANISHES?
HE MUST BE A TELEPORTER, *MANHUNTER!* FRY HIM, QUICKLY!
ZOOOOOSH
TOO LATE! HE'S GONE!
AT LEAST WE HAVE *TWO* OF THEM.
WE'LL TURN THEM OVER TO HAWKMAN'S *INTERROGATION SQUAD.*
THEY'LL SING LONG AND LOUD ENOUGH TO LEAD US STRAIGHT TO THEIR ACCOMPLICES.
RIGHT! IN THE MEANTIME, CONSIDERING THE RECENT ATTACKS ON OUR SATELLITE, WE'LL HAVE TO ASSUME EVERY SITUATION IS HOSTILE!
IN FACT, SOME OF THESE ONLOOKERS MAY BE MORE THAN THEY APPEAR.
ANY CONFEDERATE OF THOSE WE HAVE CAPTURED--
--MIGHT BE HIDING IN THEIR RANKS TO AVOID ARREST!
GOOD POINT! I SAY WE ROUND THEM ALL UP AND SEND THEM TO HAWKMAN!
FOR SECURITY'S SAKE--*DO IT!*

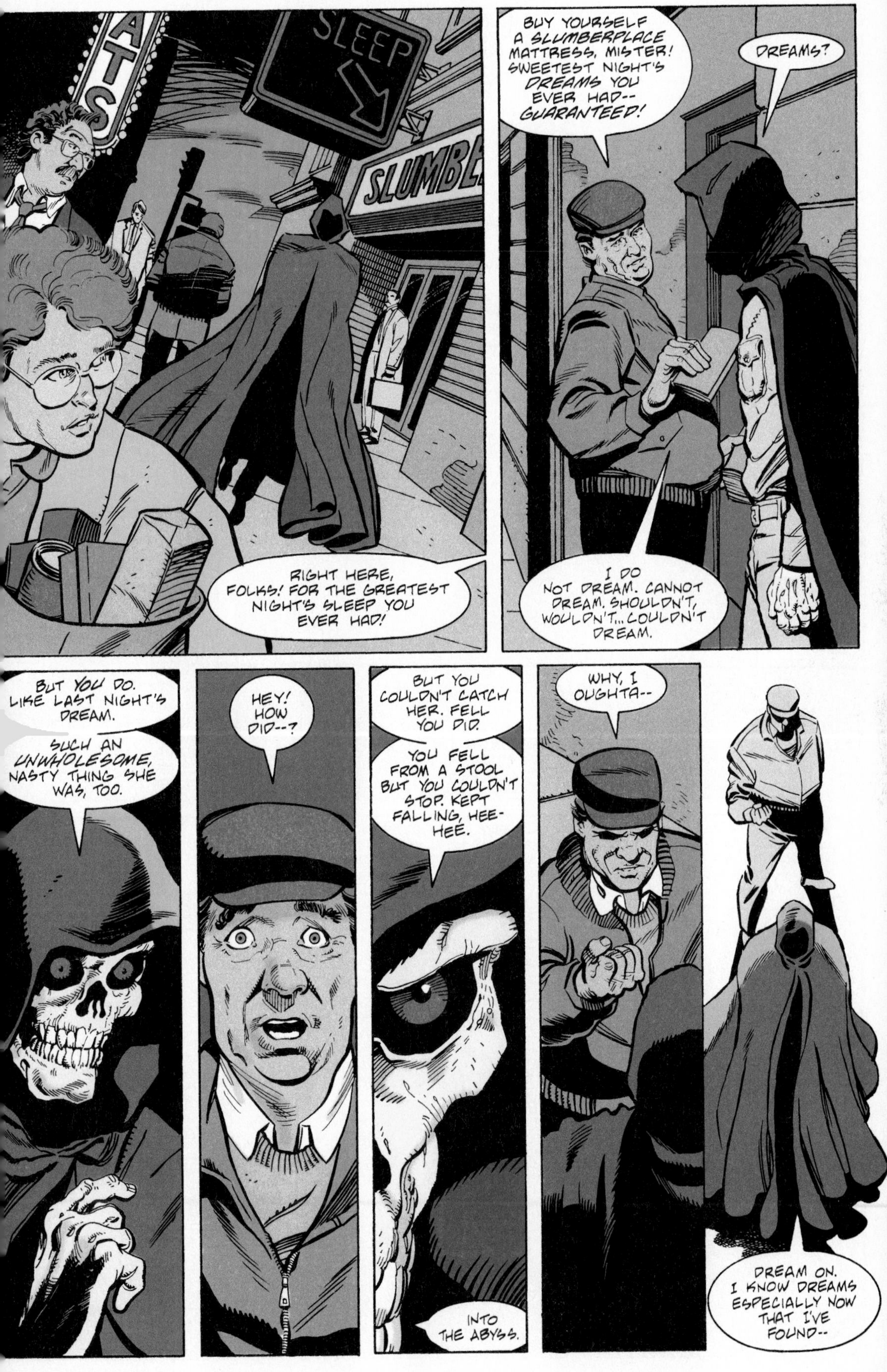
RIGHT HERE, FOLKS! FOR THE GREATEST NIGHT'S SLEEP YOU EVER HAD!
BUY YOURSELF A SLUMBERPLACE MATTRESS, MISTER! SWEETEST NIGHT'S DREAMS YOU EVER HAD-- GUARANTEED!
DREAMS?
I DO NOT DREAM. CANNOT DREAM. SHOULDN'T, WOULDN'T... COULDN'T DREAM.
BUT YOU DO. LIKE LAST NIGHT'S DREAM.
SUCH AN UNWHOLESOME, NASTY THING SHE WAS, TOO.
HEY! HOW DID--?
BUT YOU COULDN'T CATCH HER. FELL YOU DID.
YOU FELL FROM A STOOL BUT YOU COULDN'T STOP. KEPT FALLING, HEE-HEE.
INTO THE ABYSS.
WHY, I OUGHTA--
DREAM ON. I KNOW DREAMS ESPECIALLY NOW THAT I'VE FOUND--

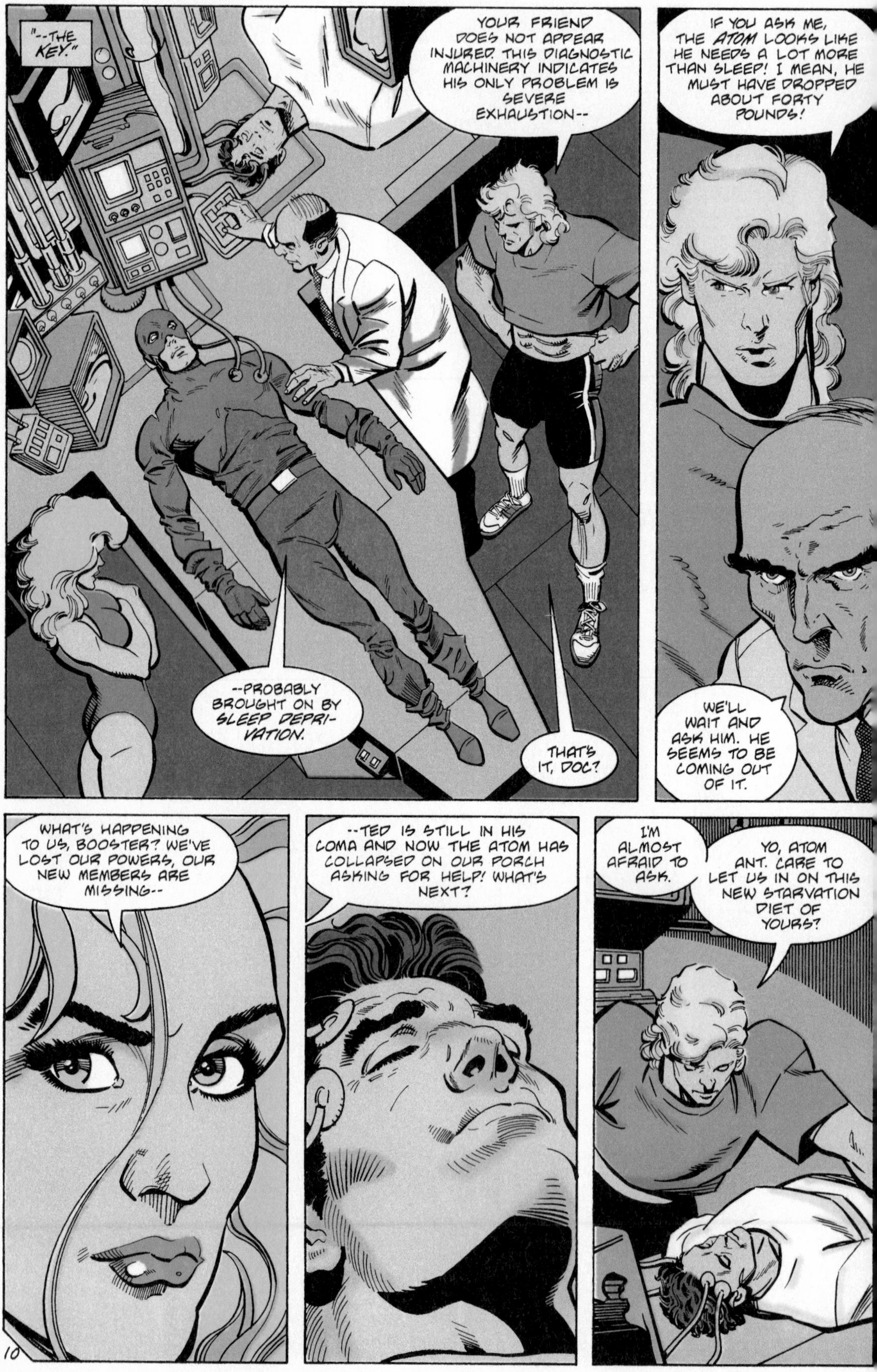
"--THE KEY."
YOUR FRIEND DOES NOT APPEAR INJURED. THIS DIAGNOSTIC MACHINERY INDICATES HIS ONLY PROBLEM IS SEVERE EXHAUSTION--
--PROBABLY BROUGHT ON BY SLEEP DEPRIVATION.
THAT'S IT, DOC?
IF YOU ASK ME, THE ATOM LOOKS LIKE HE NEEDS A LOT MORE THAN SLEEP! I MEAN, HE MUST HAVE DROPPED ABOUT FORTY POUNDS!
WE'LL WAIT AND ASK HIM. HE SEEMS TO BE COMING OUT OF IT.
WHAT'S HAPPENING TO US, BOOSTER? WE'VE LOST OUR POWERS, OUR NEW MEMBERS ARE MISSING--
--TED IS STILL IN HIS COMA AND NOW THE ATOM HAS COLLAPSED ON OUR PORCH ASKING FOR HELP! WHAT'S NEXT?
I'M ALMOST AFRAID TO ASK.
YO, ATOM ANT. CARE TO LET US IN ON THIS NEW STARVATION DIET OF YOURS?

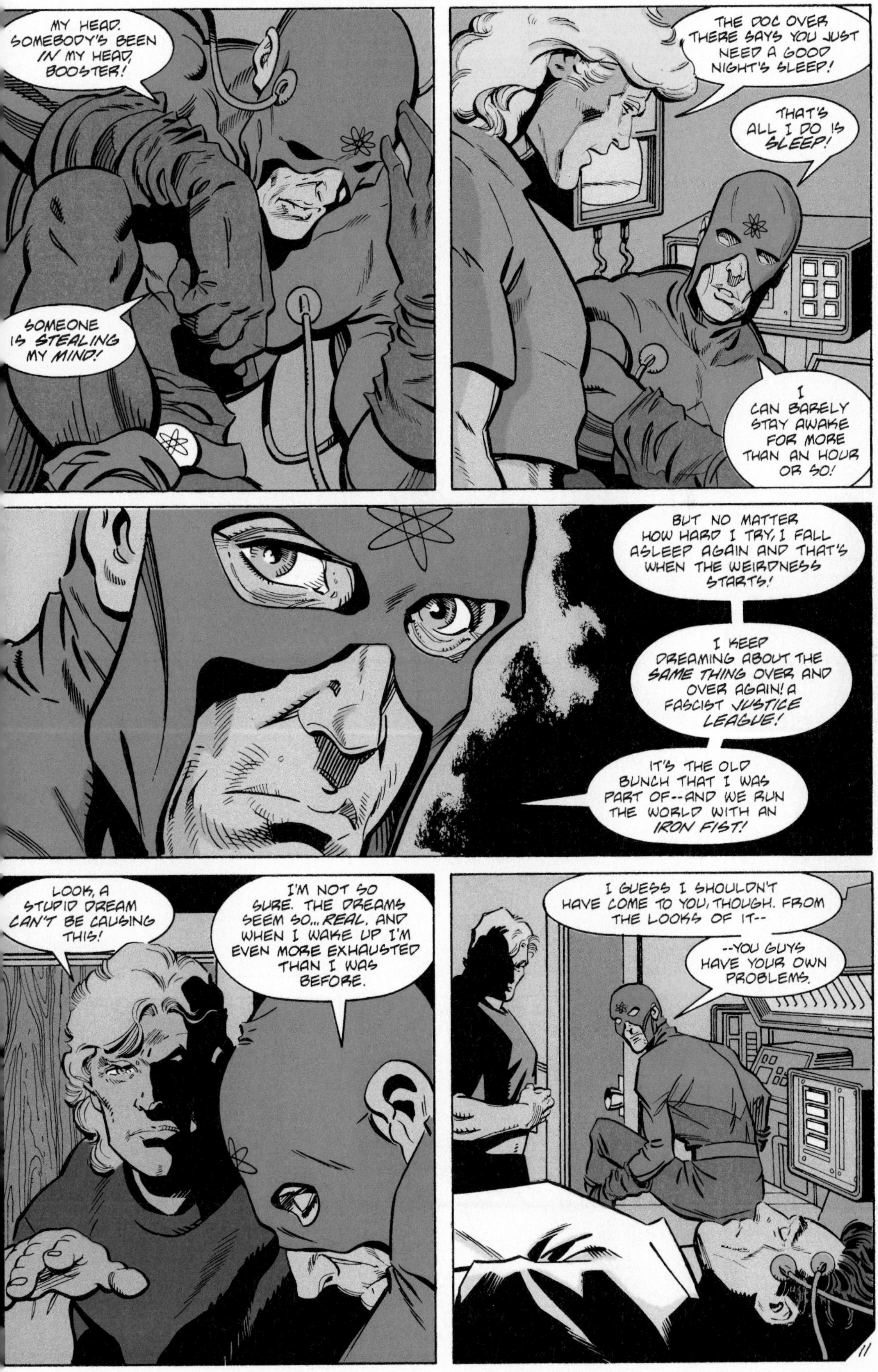
MY HEAD. SOMEBODY'S BEEN IN MY HEAD, BOOSTER!
SOMEONE IS STEALING MY MIND!
THE DOC OVER THERE SAYS YOU JUST NEED A GOOD NIGHT'S SLEEP!
THAT'S ALL I DO IS SLEEP!
I CAN BARELY STAY AWAKE FOR MORE THAN AN HOUR OR SO!
BUT NO MATTER HOW HARD I TRY, I FALL ASLEEP AGAIN AND THAT'S WHEN THE WEIRDNESS STARTS!
I KEEP DREAMING ABOUT THE SAME THING OVER AND OVER AGAIN! A FASCIST JUSTICE LEAGUE!
IT'S THE OLD BUNCH THAT I WAS PART OF--AND WE RUN THE WORLD WITH AN IRON FIST!
LOOK, A STUPID DREAM CAN'T BE CAUSING THIS!
I'M NOT SO SURE. THE DREAMS SEEM SO... REAL. AND WHEN I WAKE UP I'M EVEN MORE EXHAUSTED THAN I WAS BEFORE.
I GUESS I SHOULDN'T HAVE COME TO YOU, THOUGH. FROM THE LOOKS OF IT--
--YOU GUYS HAVE YOUR OWN PROBLEMS.
11

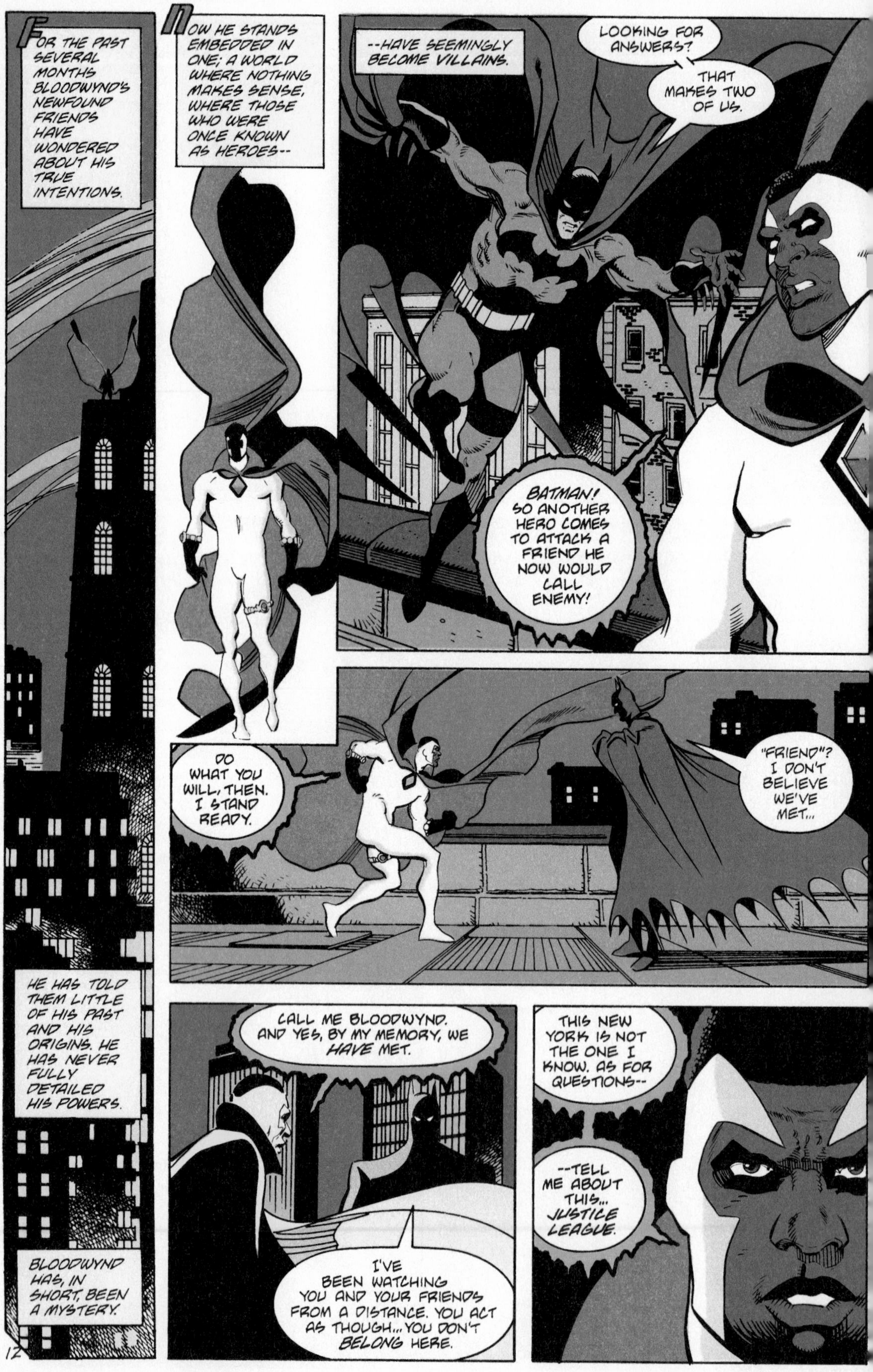
FOR THE PAST SEVERAL MONTHS BLOODWYND'S NEWFOUND FRIENDS HAVE WONDERED ABOUT HIS TRUE INTENTIONS.
NOW HE STANDS EMBEDDED IN ONE; A WORLD WHERE NOTHING MAKES SENSE, WHERE THOSE WHO WERE ONCE KNOWN AS HEROES--
--HAVE SEEMINGLY BECOME VILLAINS.
LOOKING FOR ANSWERS?
THAT MAKES TWO OF US.
BATMAN! SO ANOTHER HERO COMES TO ATTACK A FRIEND HE NOW WOULD CALL ENEMY!
"FRIEND"? I DON'T BELIEVE WE'VE MET...
DO WHAT YOU WILL, THEN. I STAND READY.
HE HAS TOLD THEM LITTLE OF HIS PAST AND HIS ORIGINS. HE HAS NEVER FULLY DETAILED HIS POWERS.
BLOODWYND HAS, IN SHORT, BEEN A MYSTERY.
CALL ME BLOODWYND. AND YES, BY MY MEMORY, WE HAVE MET.
I'VE BEEN WATCHING YOU AND YOUR FRIENDS FROM A DISTANCE. YOU ACT AS THOUGH... YOU DON'T BELONG HERE.
THIS NEW YORK IS NOT THE ONE I KNOW. AS FOR QUESTIONS--
--TELL ME ABOUT THIS... JUSTICE LEAGUE.

THIS WORLD HAD BECOME A WRETCHED PLACE, BLOODWYND. WARS, FAMINE AND STARVATION. RAMPANT UNEMPLOYMENT, ECONOMIC CHAOS, RIOTS-- THE WORKS.

AMERICA WASN'T EXEMPT. SHE WAS ON THE VERGE OF COLLAPSE AND THE GOVERNMENT WAS AT A LOSS TO STOP THE SLIDE.

THE PRESIDENT ASKED THE JUSTICE LEAGUE OF AMERICA TO IGNORE CRIME-FIGHTING AND TAKE A ROLE IN HELPING OUT.

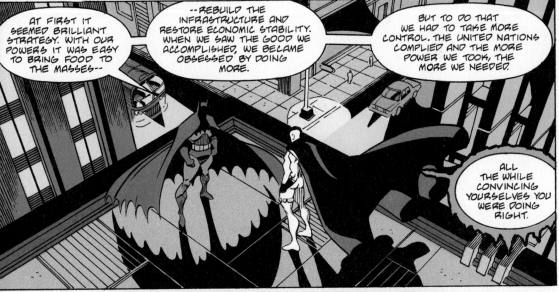

AT FIRST IT SEEMED BRILLIANT STRATEGY. WITH OUR POWERS IT WAS EASY TO BRING FOOD TO THE MASSES--

--REBUILD THE INFRASTRUCTURE AND RESTORE ECONOMIC STABILITY. WHEN WE SAW THE GOOD WE ACCOMPLISHED, WE BECAME OBSESSED BY DOING MORE.

BUT TO DO THAT WE HAD TO TAKE MORE CONTROL. THE UNITED NATIONS COMPLIED AND THE MORE POWER WE TOOK, THE MORE WE NEEDED.

ALL THE WHILE CONVINCING YOURSELVES YOU WERE DOING RIGHT.

AT FIRST WE WERE. BUT IT WASN'T LONG BEFORE WE BECAME A GOVERNMENT.

WE GAVE THE POLITICIANS ORDERS AND THEY JUMPED. WE WERE A *DE FACTO* GOVERNMENT THAT ANSWERED TO NO ONE.

13

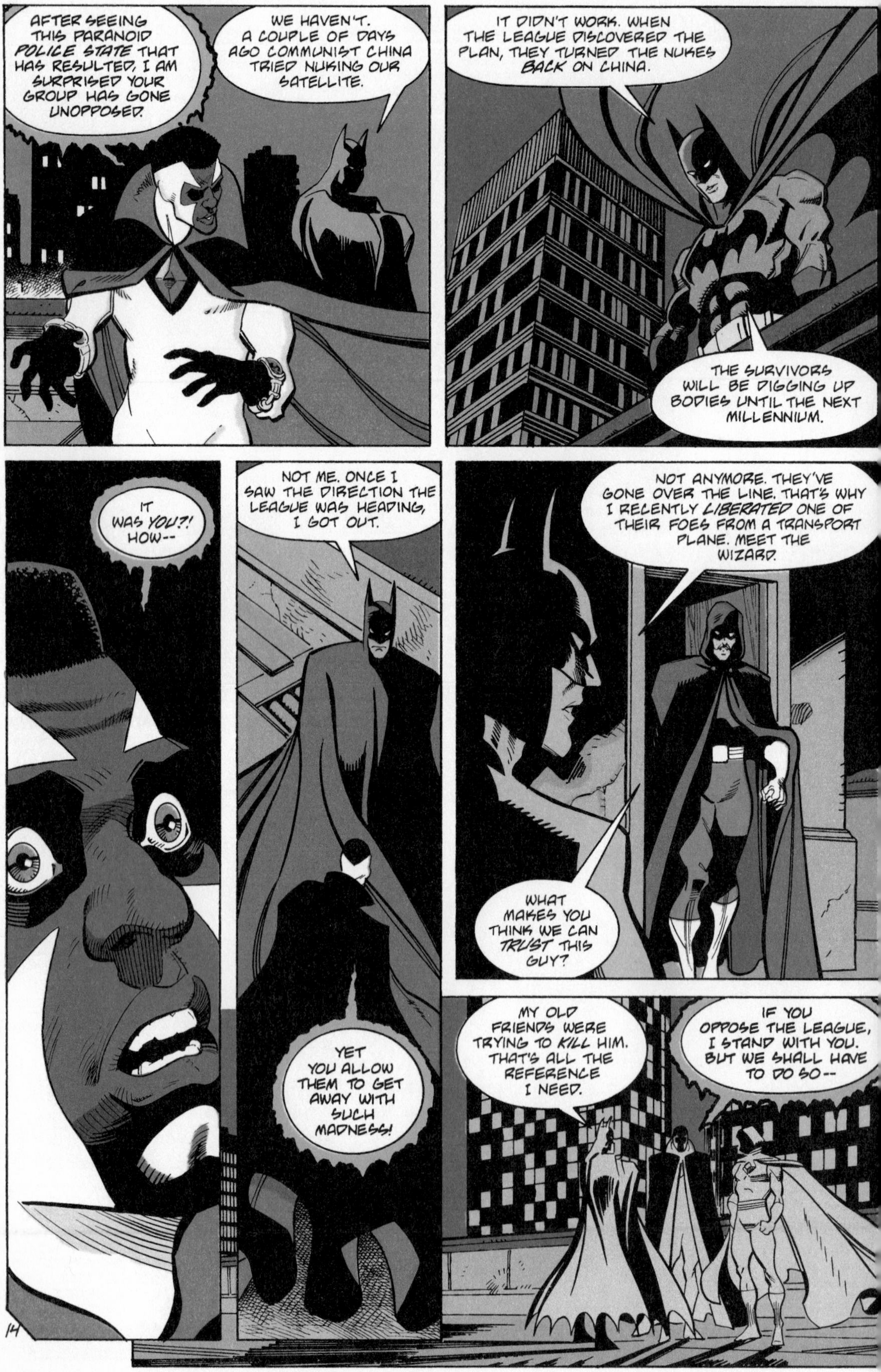

AFTER SEEING THIS PARANOID POLICE STATE THAT HAS RESULTED, I AM SURPRISED YOUR GROUP HAS GONE UNOPPOSED.
WE HAVEN'T. A COUPLE OF DAYS AGO COMMUNIST CHINA TRIED NUKING OUR SATELLITE.
IT DIDN'T WORK. WHEN THE LEAGUE DISCOVERED THE PLAN, THEY TURNED THE NUKES BACK ON CHINA.
THE SURVIVORS WILL BE DIGGING UP BODIES UNTIL THE NEXT MILLENNIUM.
IT WAS YOU?! HOW--
NOT ME. ONCE I SAW THE DIRECTION THE LEAGUE WAS HEADING, I GOT OUT.
YET YOU ALLOW THEM TO GET AWAY WITH SUCH MADNESS!
NOT ANYMORE. THEY'VE GONE OVER THE LINE. THAT'S WHY I RECENTLY LIBERATED ONE OF THEIR FOES FROM A TRANSPORT PLANE. MEET THE WIZARD.
WHAT MAKES YOU THINK WE CAN TRUST THIS GUY?
MY OLD FRIENDS WERE TRYING TO KILL HIM. THAT'S ALL THE REFERENCE I NEED.
IF YOU OPPOSE THE LEAGUE, I STAND WITH YOU. BUT WE SHALL HAVE TO DO SO--

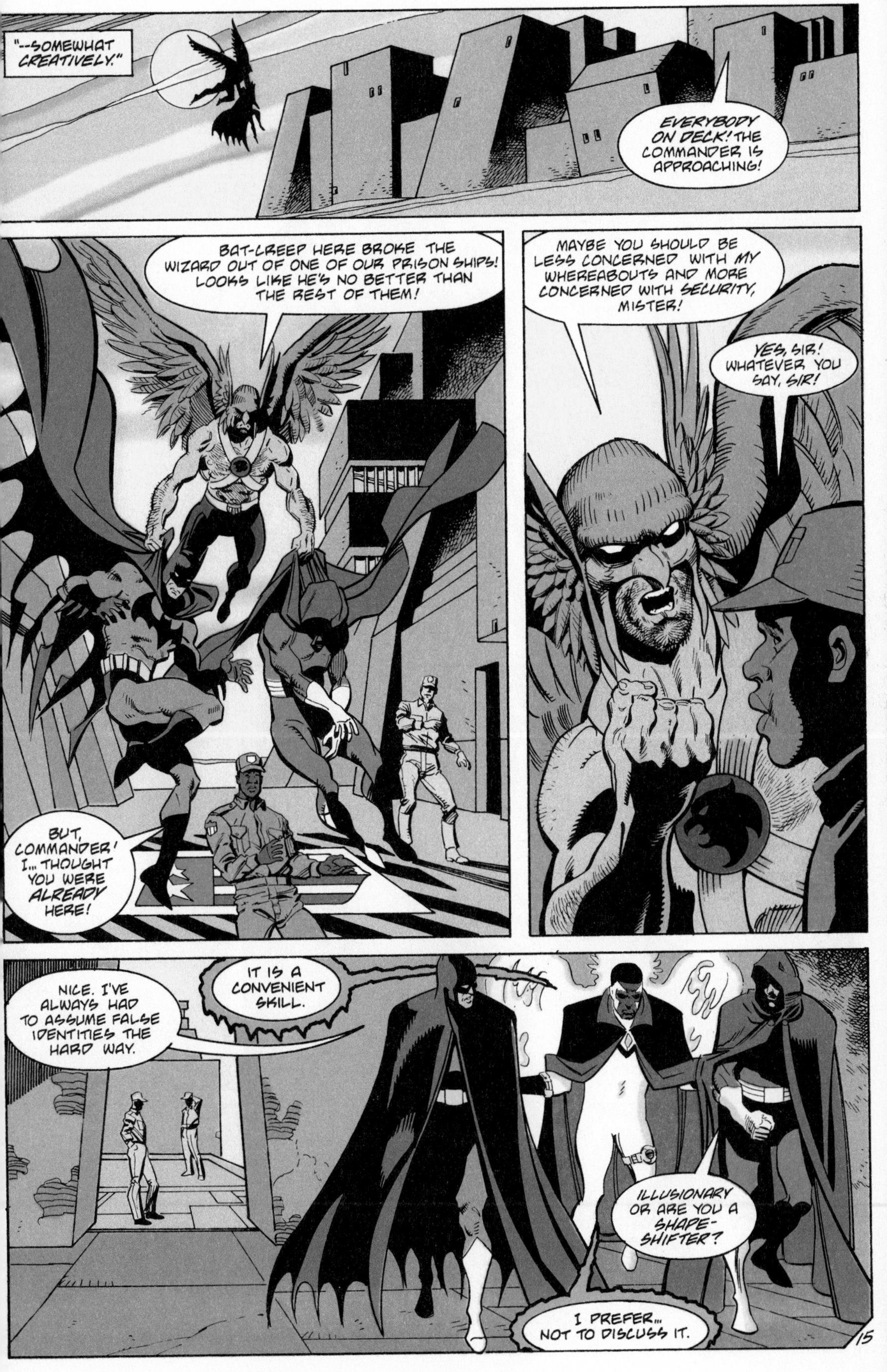
"--SOMEWHAT CREATIVELY."
EVERYBODY ON DECK! THE COMMANDER IS APPROACHING!
BAT-CREEP HERE BROKE THE WIZARD OUT OF ONE OF OUR PRISON SHIPS! LOOKS LIKE HE'S NO BETTER THAN THE REST OF THEM!
BUT, COMMANDER! I... THOUGHT YOU WERE ALREADY HERE!
MAYBE YOU SHOULD BE LESS CONCERNED WITH MY WHEREABOUTS AND MORE CONCERNED WITH SECURITY, MISTER!
YES, SIR! WHATEVER YOU SAY, SIR!
NICE. I'VE ALWAYS HAD TO ASSUME FALSE IDENTITIES THE HARD WAY.
IT IS A CONVENIENT SKILL.
ILLUSIONARY OR ARE YOU A SHAPE-SHIFTER?
I PREFER... NOT TO DISCUSS IT.

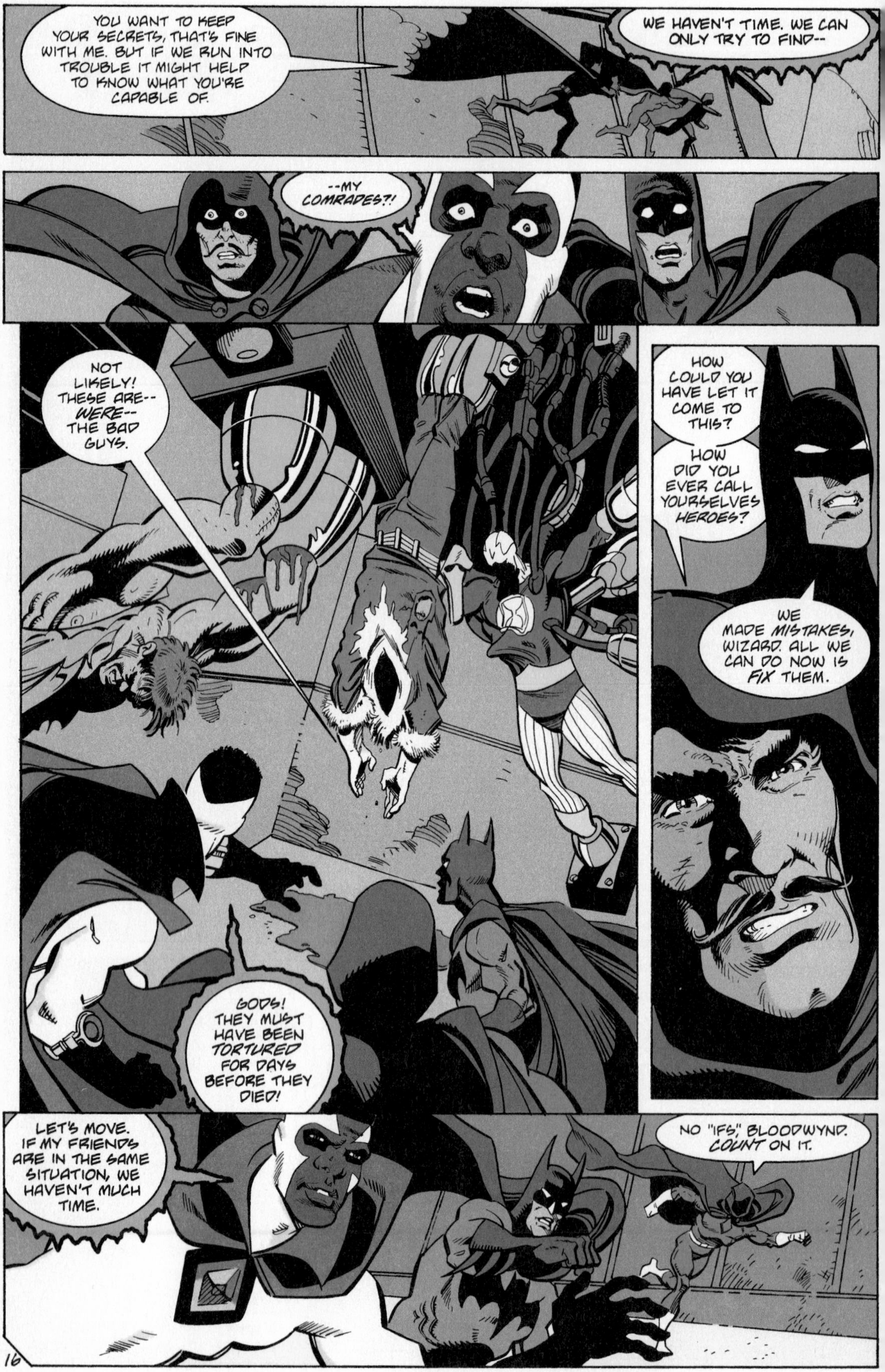
YOU WANT TO KEEP YOUR SECRETS, THAT'S FINE WITH ME. BUT IF WE RUN INTO TROUBLE IT MIGHT HELP TO KNOW WHAT YOU'RE CAPABLE OF.
WE HAVEN'T TIME. WE CAN ONLY TRY TO FIND--
--MY COMRADES?!
NOT LIKELY! THESE ARE-- WERE-- THE BAD GUYS.
GODS! THEY MUST HAVE BEEN TORTURED FOR DAYS BEFORE THEY DIED!
HOW COULD YOU HAVE LET IT COME TO THIS?
HOW DID YOU EVER CALL YOURSELVES HEROES?
WE MADE MISTAKES, WIZARD. ALL WE CAN DO NOW IS FIX THEM.
LET'S MOVE. IF MY FRIENDS ARE IN THE SAME SITUATION, WE HAVEN'T MUCH TIME.
NO "IFS," BLOODWYND. COUNT ON IT.

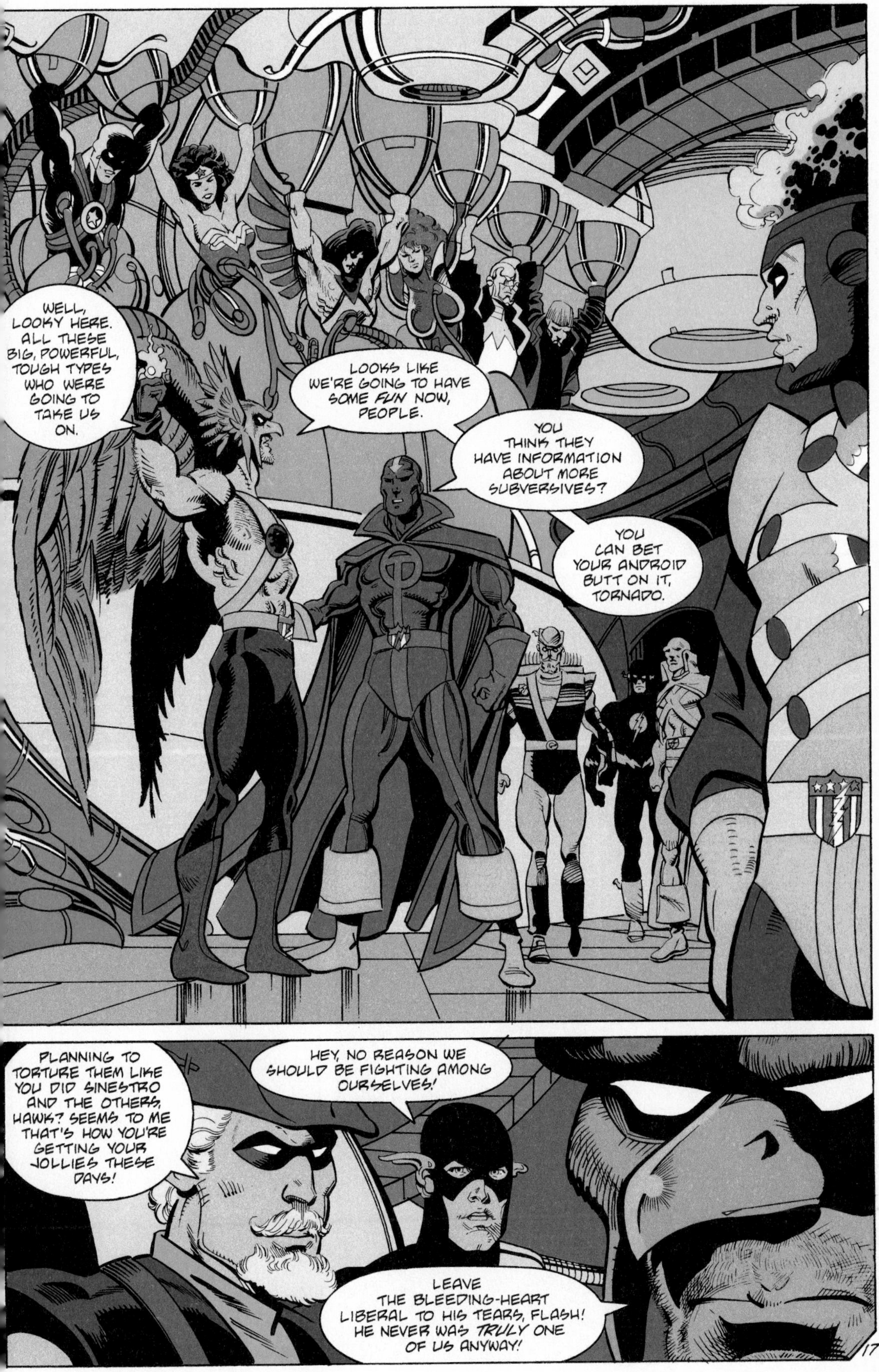
WELL, LOOKY HERE. ALL THESE BIG, POWERFUL, TOUGH TYPES WHO WERE GOING TO TAKE US ON.
LOOKS LIKE WE'RE GOING TO HAVE SOME FUN NOW, PEOPLE.
YOU THINK THEY HAVE INFORMATION ABOUT MORE SUBVERSIVES?
YOU CAN BET YOUR ANDROID BUTT ON IT, TORNADO.
PLANNING TO TORTURE THEM LIKE YOU DID SINESTRO AND THE OTHERS, HAWK? SEEMS TO ME THAT'S HOW YOU'RE GETTING YOUR JOLLIES THESE DAYS!
HEY, NO REASON WE SHOULD BE FIGHTING AMONG OURSELVES!
LEAVE THE BLEEDING-HEART LIBERAL TO HIS TEARS, FLASH! HE NEVER WAS TRULY ONE OF US ANYWAY!

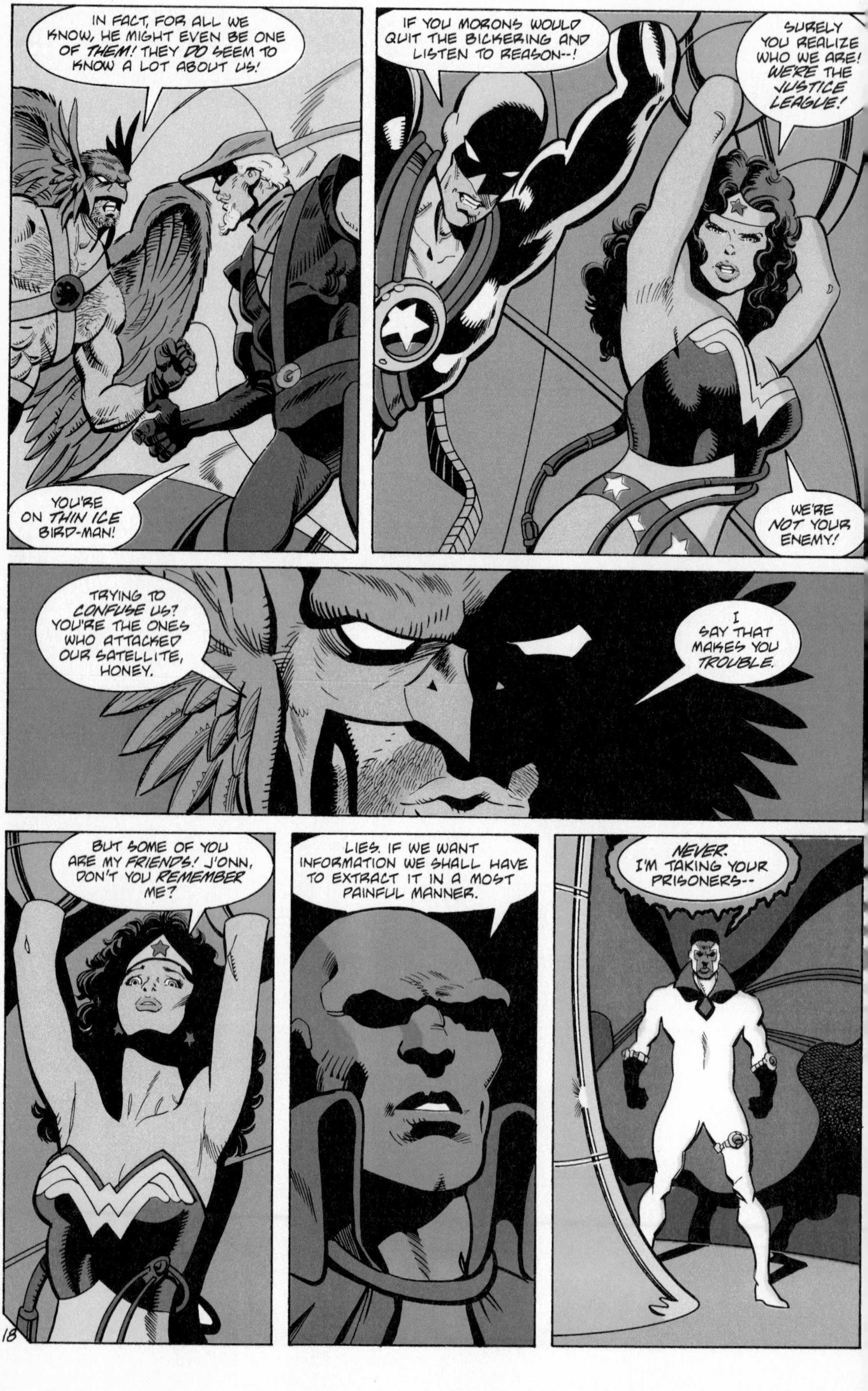

IN FACT, FOR ALL WE KNOW, HE MIGHT EVEN BE ONE OF *THEM!* THEY *DO* SEEM TO KNOW A LOT ABOUT US!
YOU'RE ON *THIN ICE* BIRD-MAN!
IF YOU MORONS WOULD QUIT THE BICKERING AND LISTEN TO REASON--!
SURELY YOU REALIZE WHO WE ARE! *WE'RE* THE *JUSTICE LEAGUE!*
WE'RE *NOT* YOUR ENEMY!
TRYING TO *CONFUSE* US? YOU'RE THE ONES WHO ATTACKED OUR SATELLITE, HONEY.
I SAY THAT MAKES YOU *TROUBLE.*
BUT SOME OF YOU ARE MY *FRIENDS!* J'ONN, DON'T YOU *REMEMBER* ME?
LIES. IF WE WANT INFORMATION WE SHALL HAVE TO EXTRACT IT IN A MOST PAINFUL MANNER.
NEVER. I'M TAKING YOUR PRISONERS--

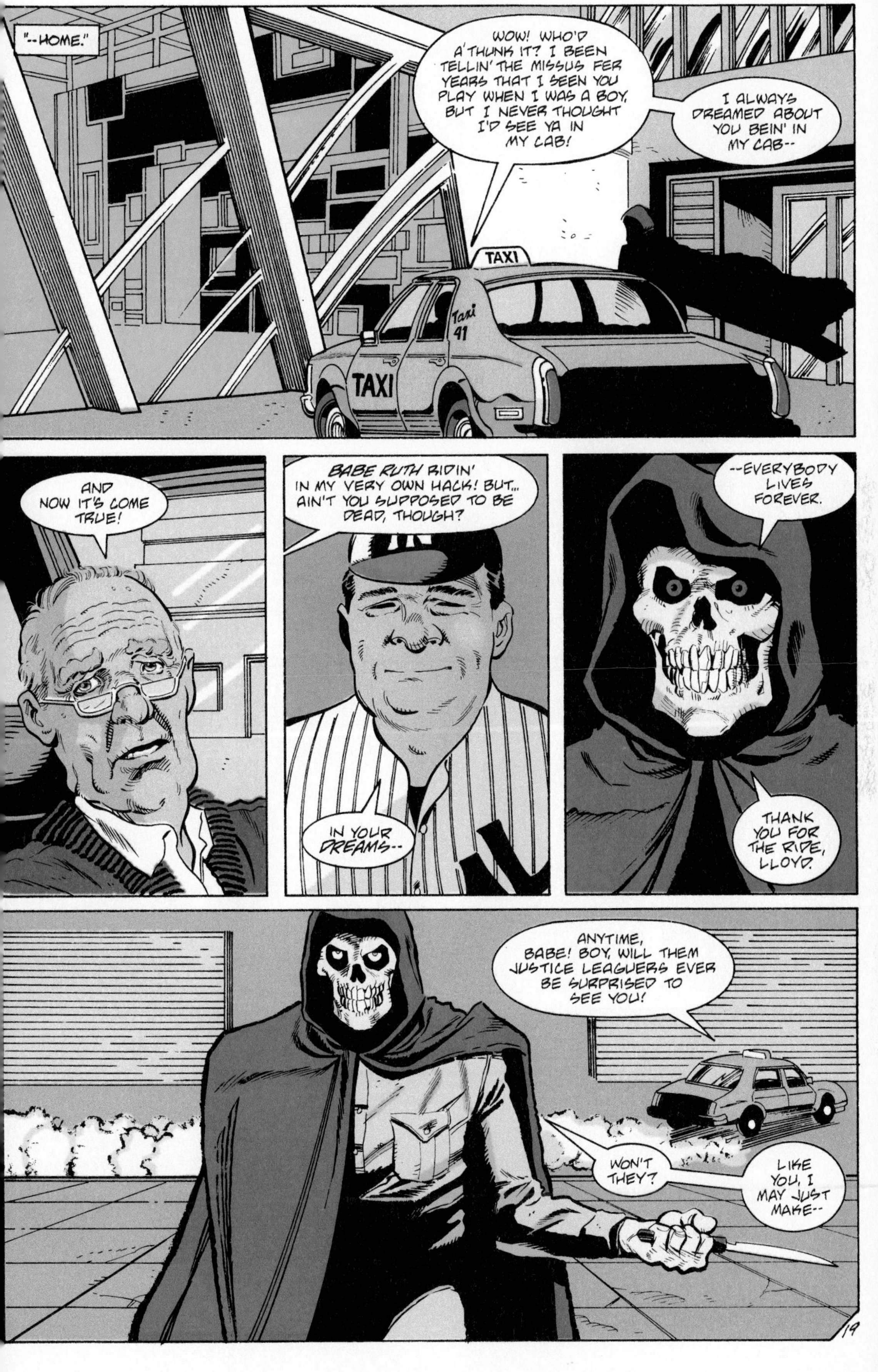
"--HOME."
WOW! WHO'D A'THUNK IT? I BEEN TELLIN' THE MISSUS FER YEARS THAT I SEEN YOU PLAY WHEN I WAS A BOY, BUT I NEVER THOUGHT I'D SEE YA IN MY CAB!
I ALWAYS DREAMED ABOUT YOU BEIN' IN MY CAB--
TAXI
Taxi 41
TAXI
AND NOW IT'S COME TRUE!
BABE RUTH RIDIN' IN MY VERY OWN HACK! BUT... AIN'T YOU SUPPOSED TO BE DEAD, THOUGH?
IN YOUR DREAMS--
--EVERYBODY LIVES FOREVER.
THANK YOU FOR THE RIDE, LLOYD.
ANYTIME, BABE! BOY, WILL THEM JUSTICE LEAGUERS EVER BE SURPRISED TO SEE YOU!
WON'T THEY?
LIKE YOU, I MAY JUST MAKE--

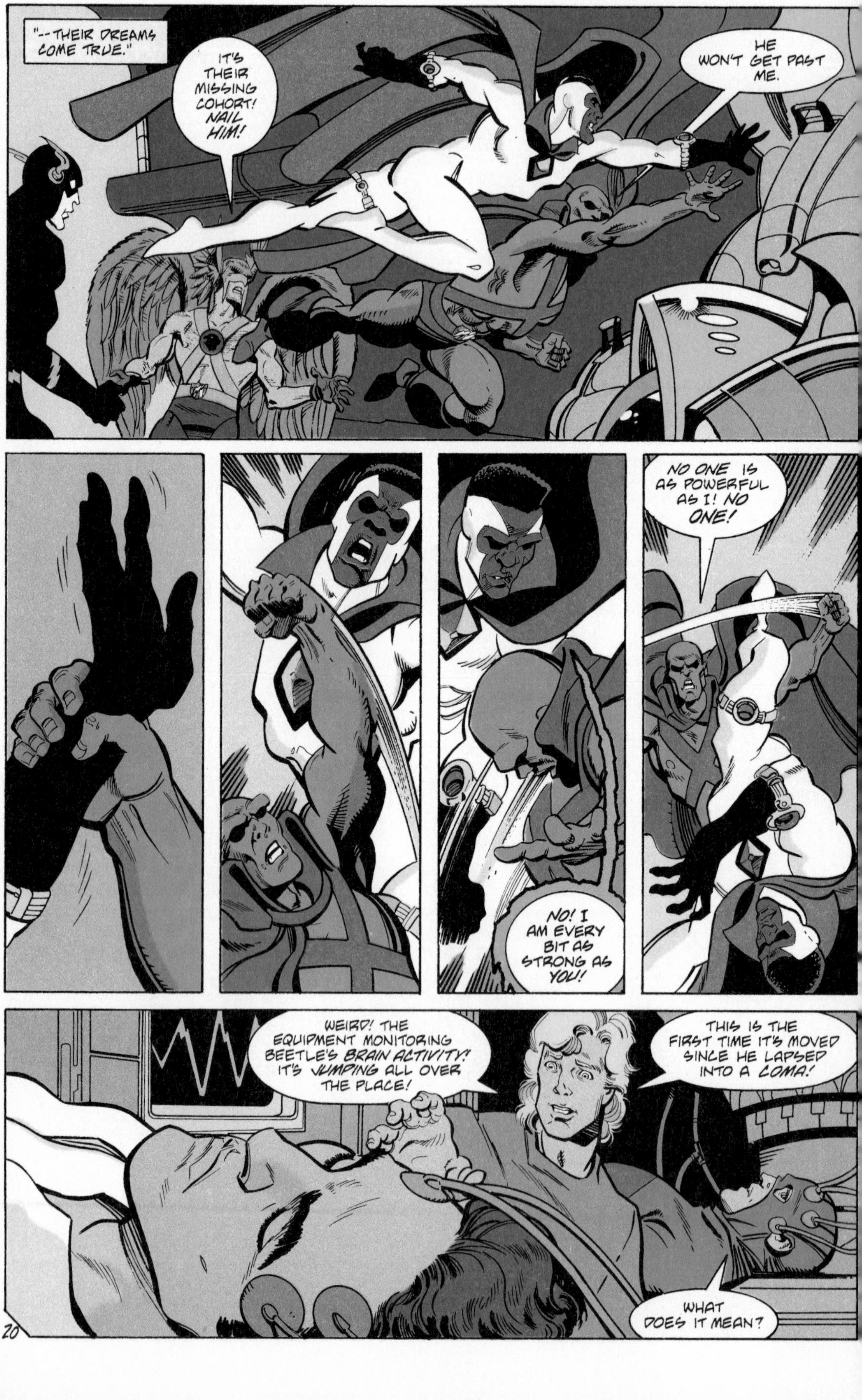
"--THEIR DREAMS COME TRUE."
IT'S THEIR MISSING COHORT! NAIL HIM!
HE WON'T GET PAST ME.
NO ONE IS AS POWERFUL AS I! NO ONE!
NO! I AM EVERY BIT AS STRONG AS YOU!
WEIRD! THE EQUIPMENT MONITORING BEETLE'S BRAIN ACTIVITY! IT'S JUMPING ALL OVER THE PLACE!
THIS IS THE FIRST TIME IT'S MOVED SINCE HE LAPSED INTO A COMA!
WHAT DOES IT MEAN?

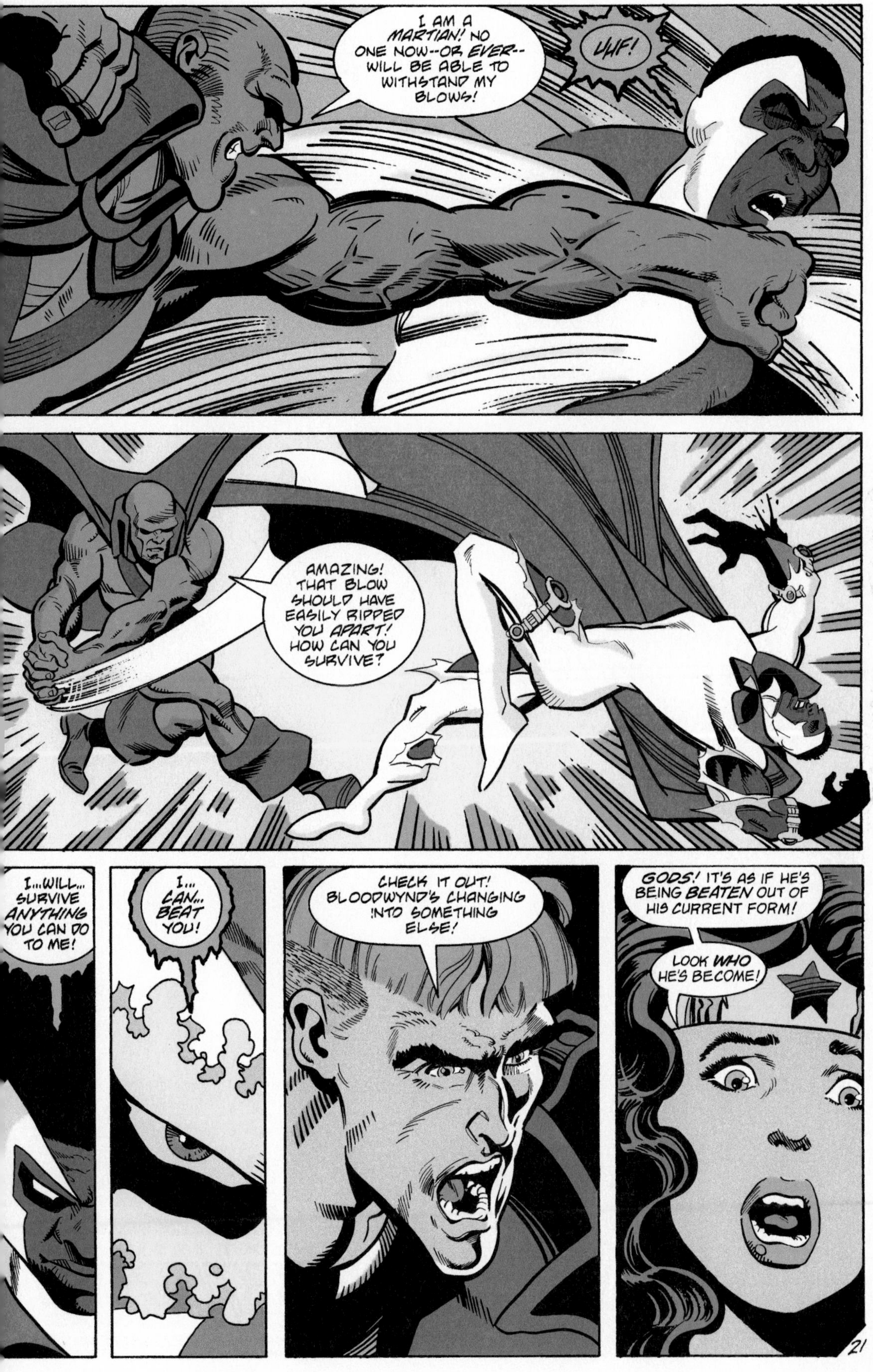

I AM A MARTIAN! NO ONE NOW--OR EVER--WILL BE ABLE TO WITHSTAND MY BLOWS!
UUF!
AMAZING! THAT BLOW SHOULD HAVE EASILY RIPPED YOU APART! HOW CAN YOU SURVIVE?
I...WILL... SURVIVE ANYTHING YOU CAN DO TO ME!
I... CAN... BEAT YOU!
CHECK IT OUT! BLOODWYND'S CHANGING INTO SOMETHING ELSE!
GODS! IT'S AS IF HE'S BEING BEATEN OUT OF HIS CURRENT FORM!
LOOK WHO HE'S BECOME!

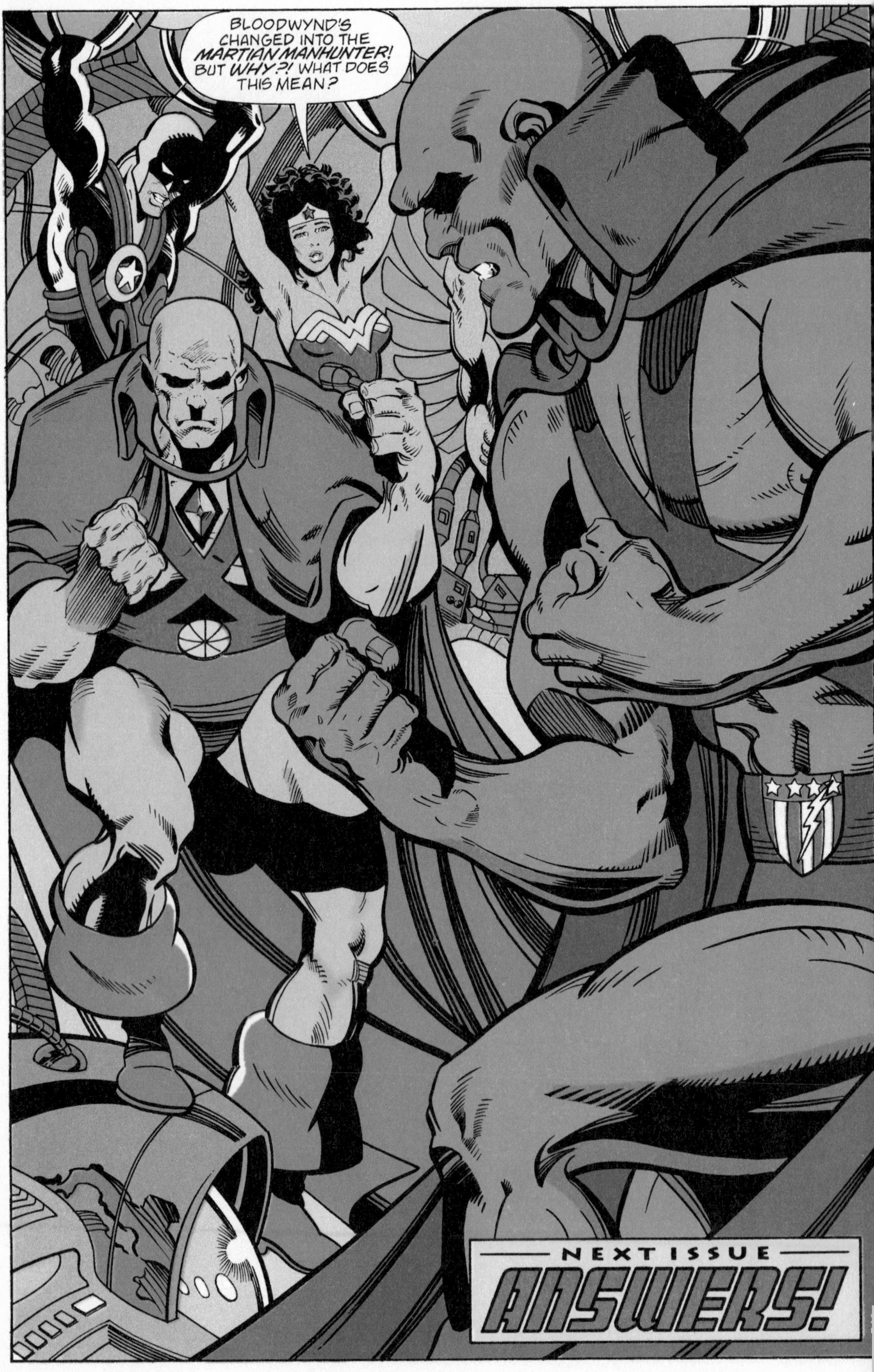
BLOODWYND'S CHANGED INTO THE MARTIAN MANHUNTER! BUT WHY?! WHAT DOES THIS MEAN?
NEXT ISSUE
ANSWERS!

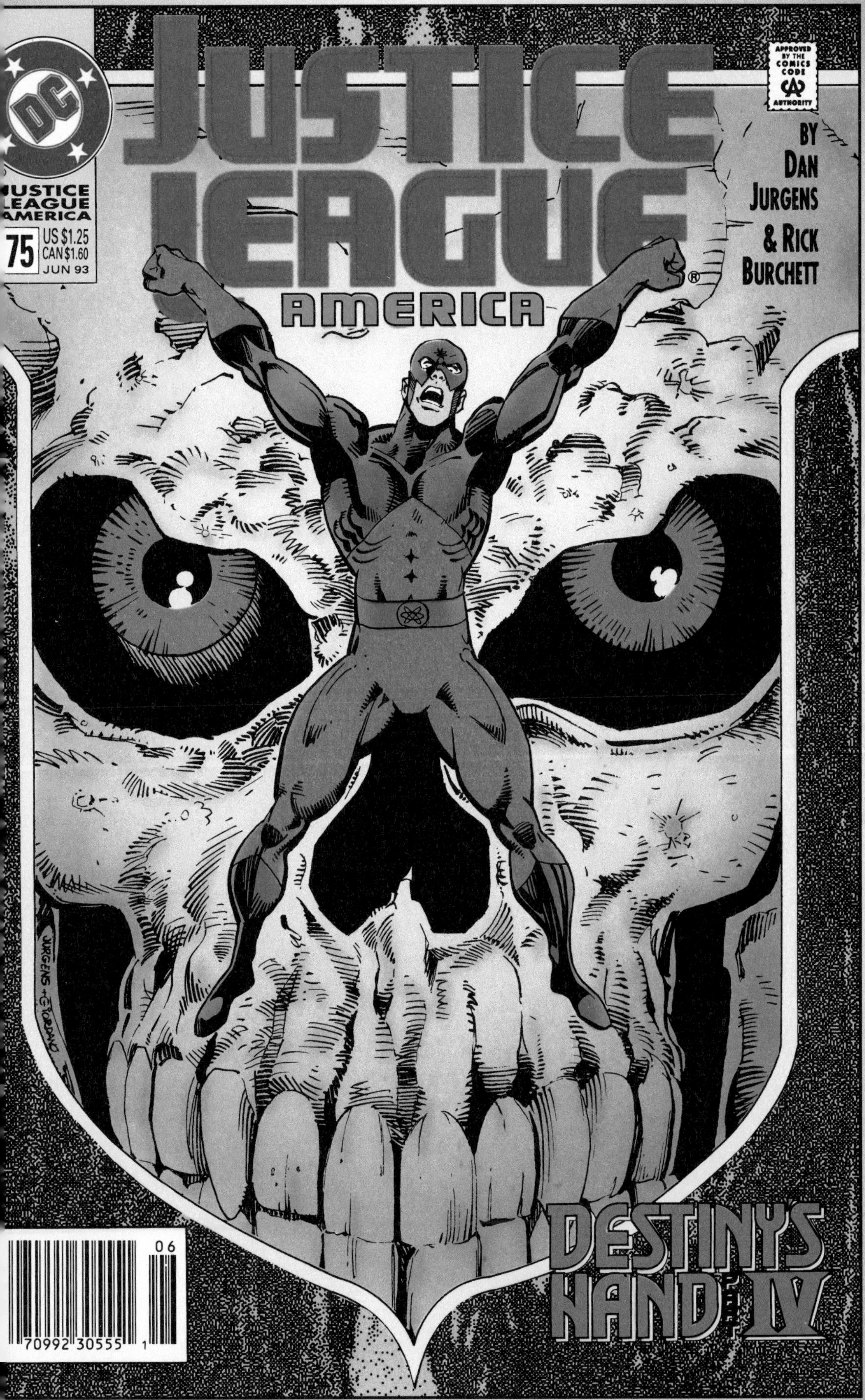
DC
JUSTICE LEAGUE AMERICA
75
US $1.25
CAN $1.60
JUN 93
JUSTICE LEAGUE AMERICA
APPROVED BY THE COMICS CODE AUTHORITY
BY DAN JURGENS & RICK BURCHETT
JURGENS + GIORDANO
DESTINY'S HAND PART IV
70992 30555 1
06

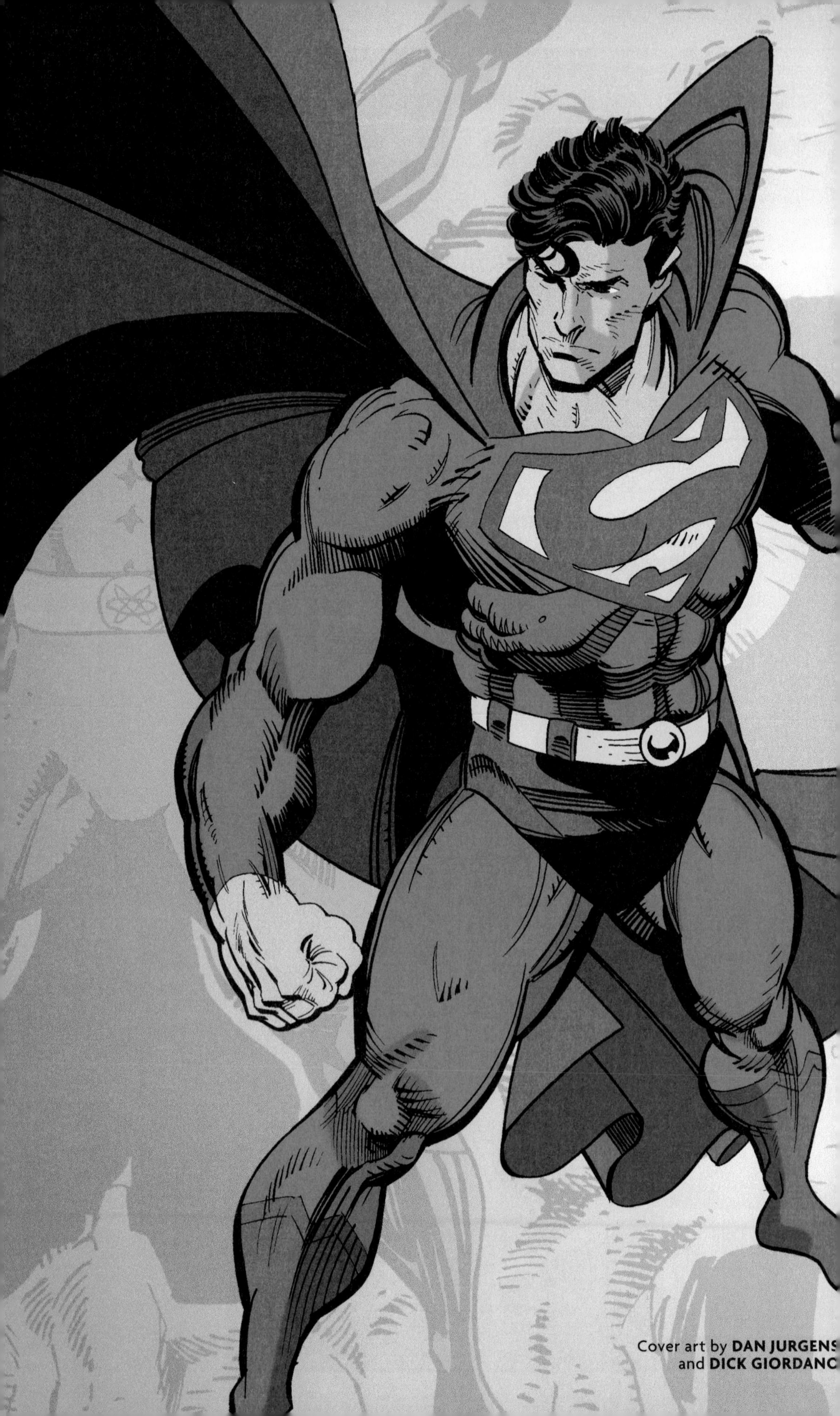

Cover art by **DAN JURGENS**
and **DICK GIORDANO**

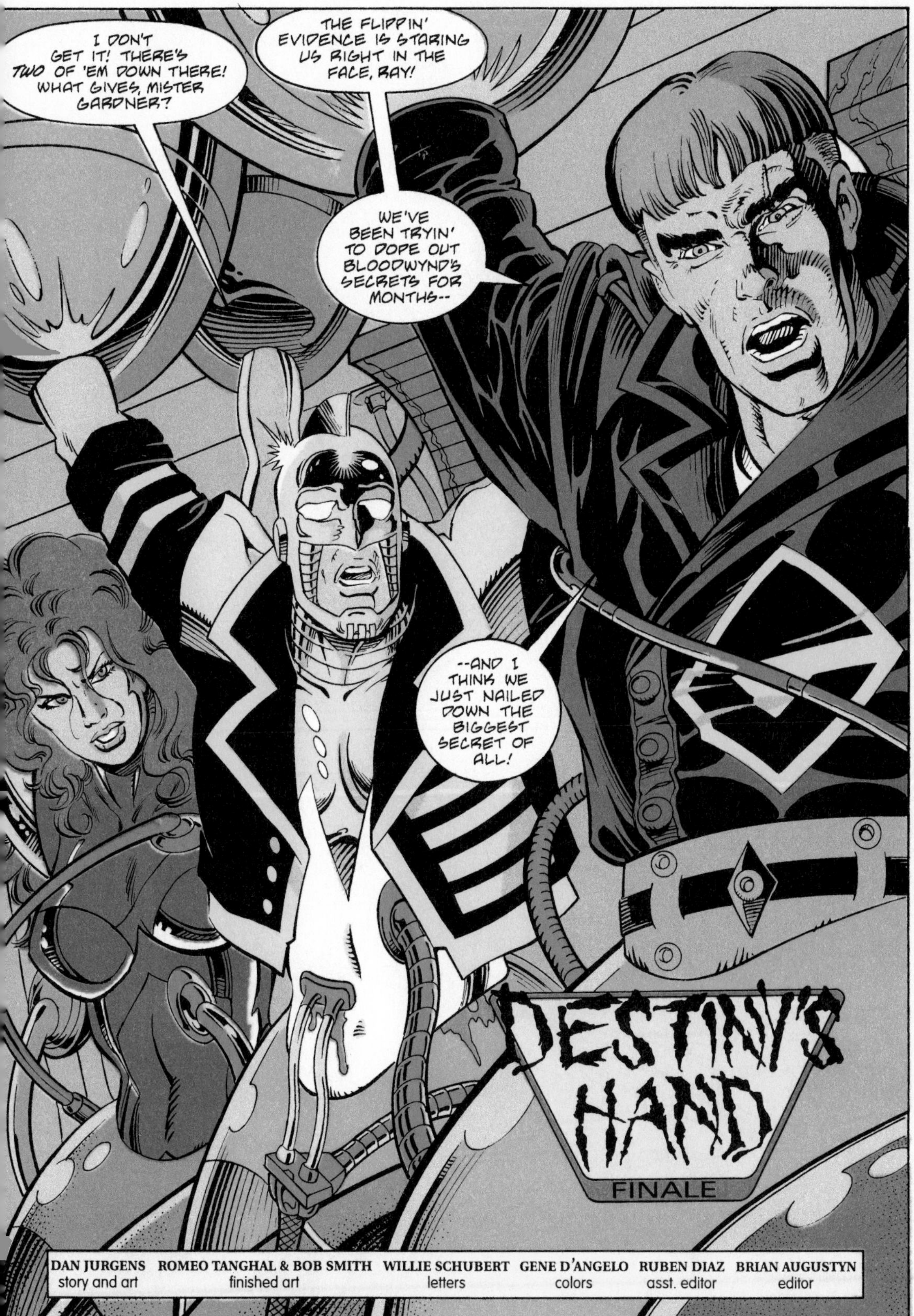
I DON'T GET IT! THERE'S TWO OF 'EM DOWN THERE! WHAT GIVES, MISTER GARDNER?
THE FLIPPIN' EVIDENCE IS STARING US RIGHT IN THE FACE, RAY!
WE'VE BEEN TRYIN' TO DOPE OUT BLOODWYND'S SECRETS FOR MONTHS--
--AND I THINK WE JUST NAILED DOWN THE BIGGEST SECRET OF ALL!
DESTINY'S HAND
FINALE
DAN JURGENS story and art
ROMEO TANGHAL & BOB SMITH finished art
WILLIE SCHUBERT letters
GENE D'ANGELO colors
RUBEN DIAZ asst. editor
BRIAN AUGUSTYN editor

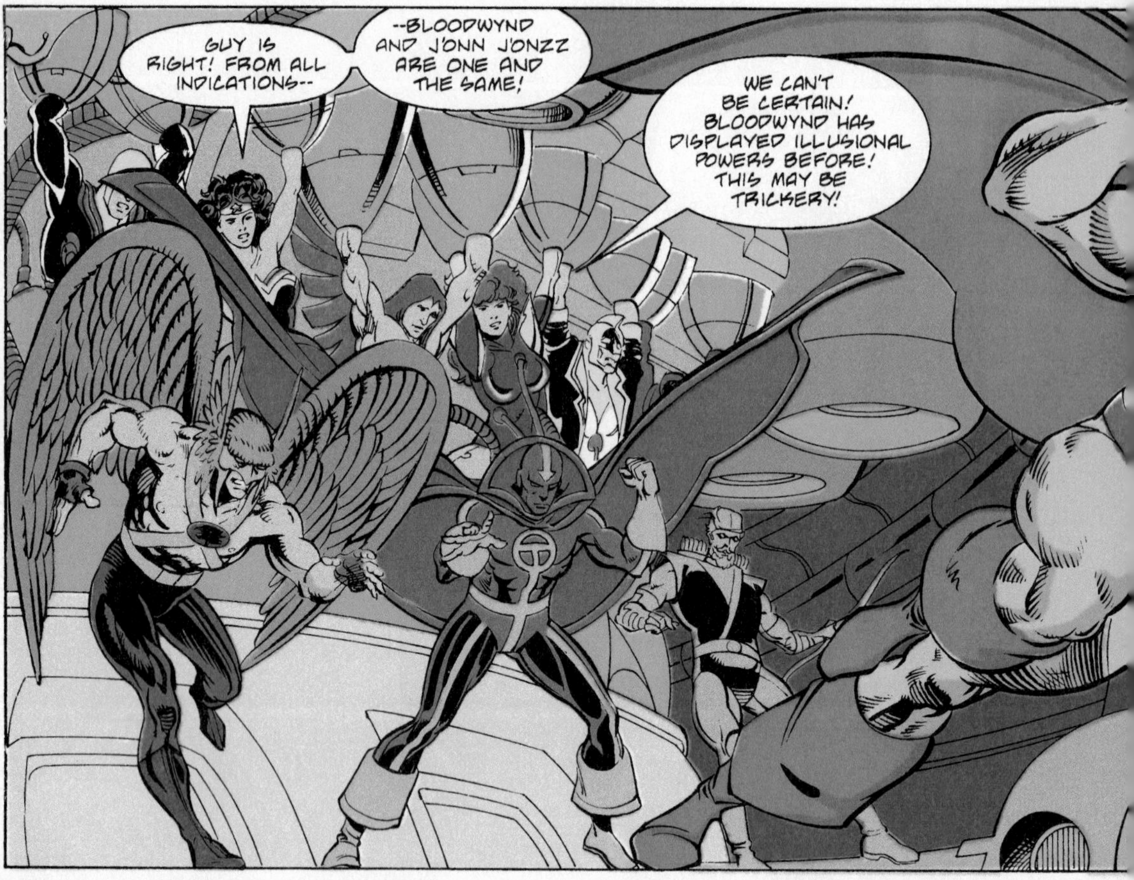
GUY IS RIGHT! FROM ALL INDICATIONS--
--BLOODWYND AND J'ONN J'ONZZ ARE ONE AND THE SAME!
WE CAN'T BE CERTAIN! BLOODWYND HAS DISPLAYED ILLUSIONAL POWERS BEFORE! THIS MAY BE TRICKERY!

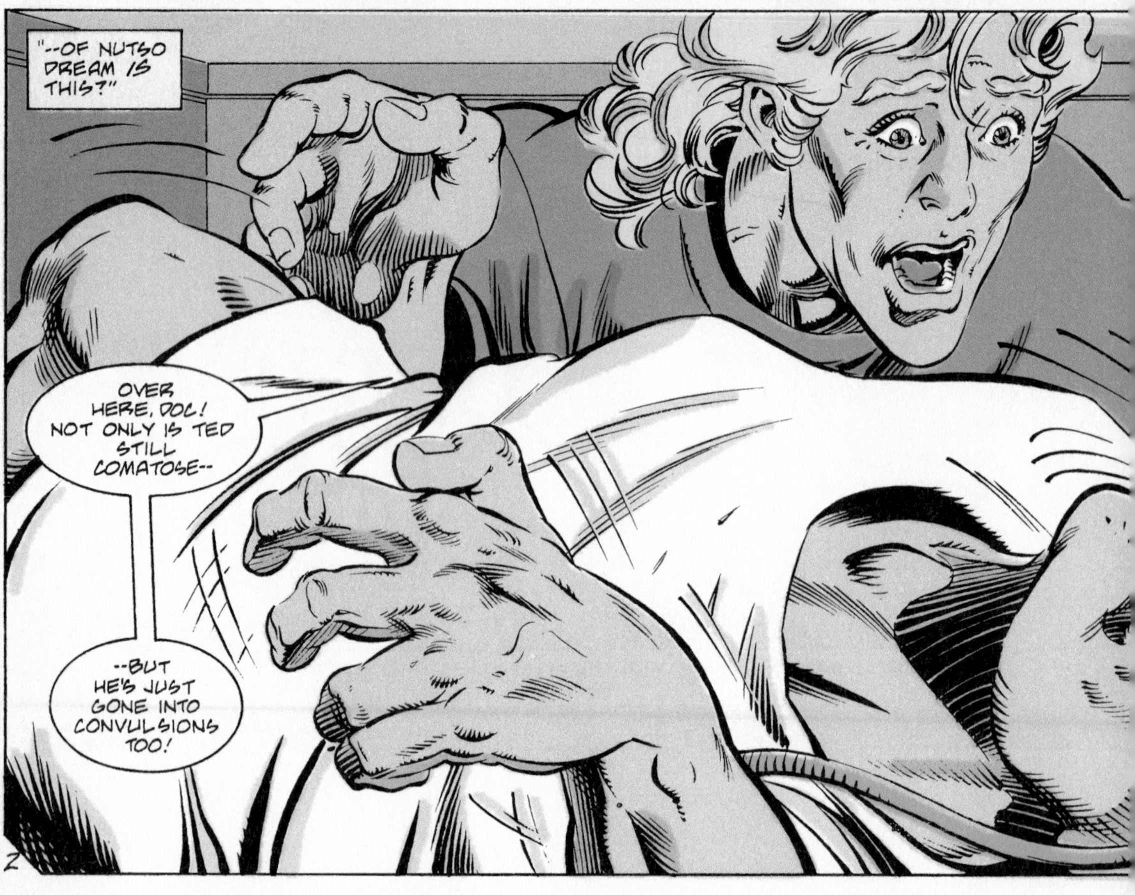
"--OF NUTSO DREAM IS THIS?"
OVER HERE, DOC! NOT ONLY IS TED STILL COMATOSE--
--BUT HE'S JUST GONE INTO CONVULSIONS TOO!

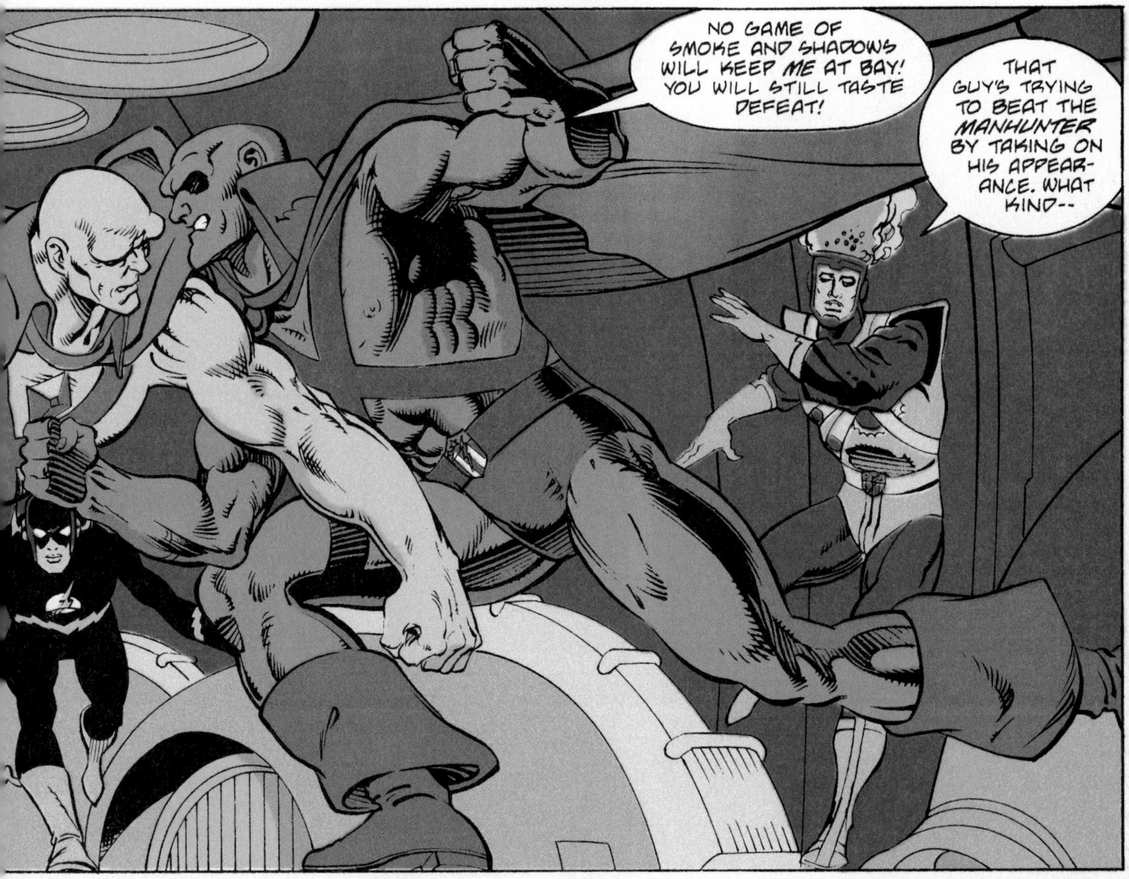
NO GAME OF SMOKE AND SHADOWS WILL KEEP *ME* AT BAY! YOU WILL STILL TASTE DEFEAT!
THAT GUY'S TRYING TO BEAT THE *MANHUNTER* BY TAKING ON HIS APPEARANCE. WHAT KIND--

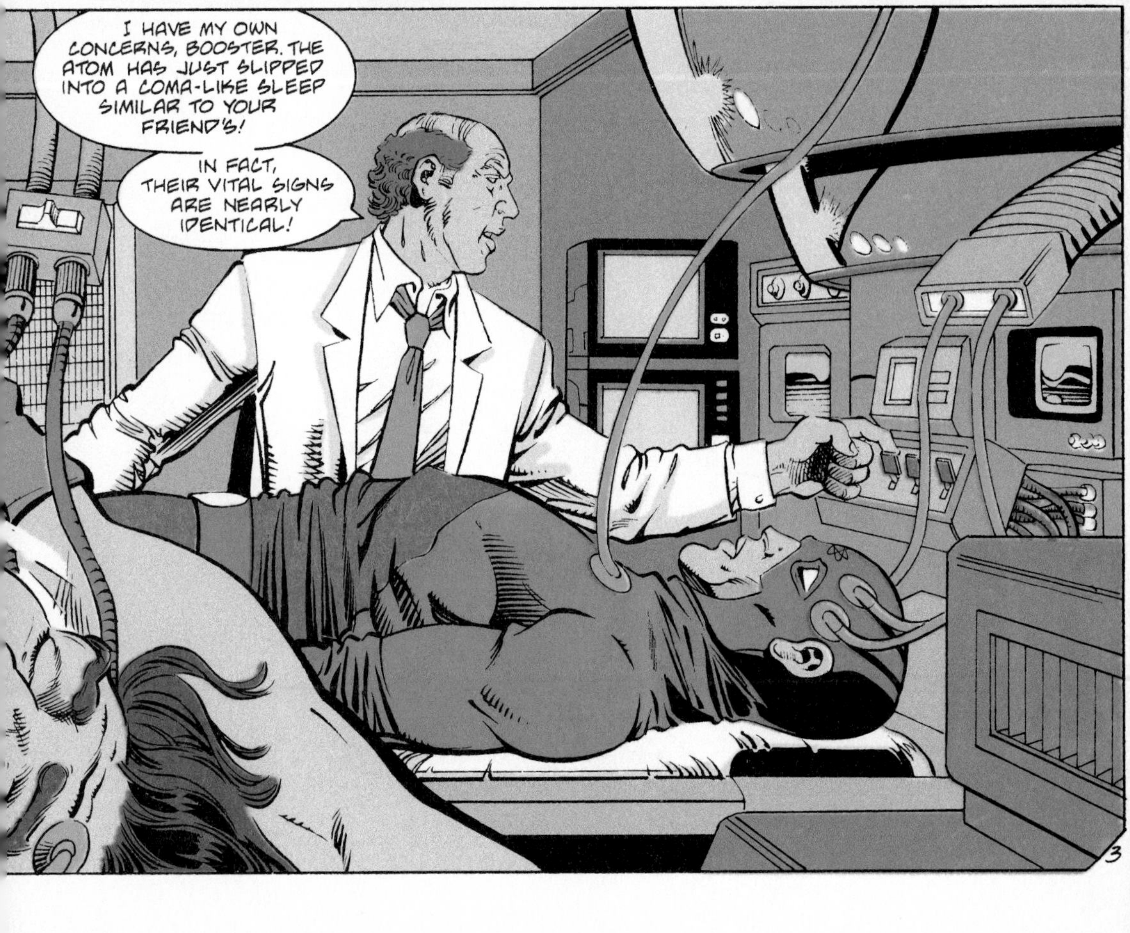
I HAVE MY OWN CONCERNS, BOOSTER. THE ATOM HAS JUST SLIPPED INTO A COMA-LIKE SLEEP SIMILAR TO YOUR FRIEND'S!
IN FACT, THEIR VITAL SIGNS ARE NEARLY IDENTICAL!

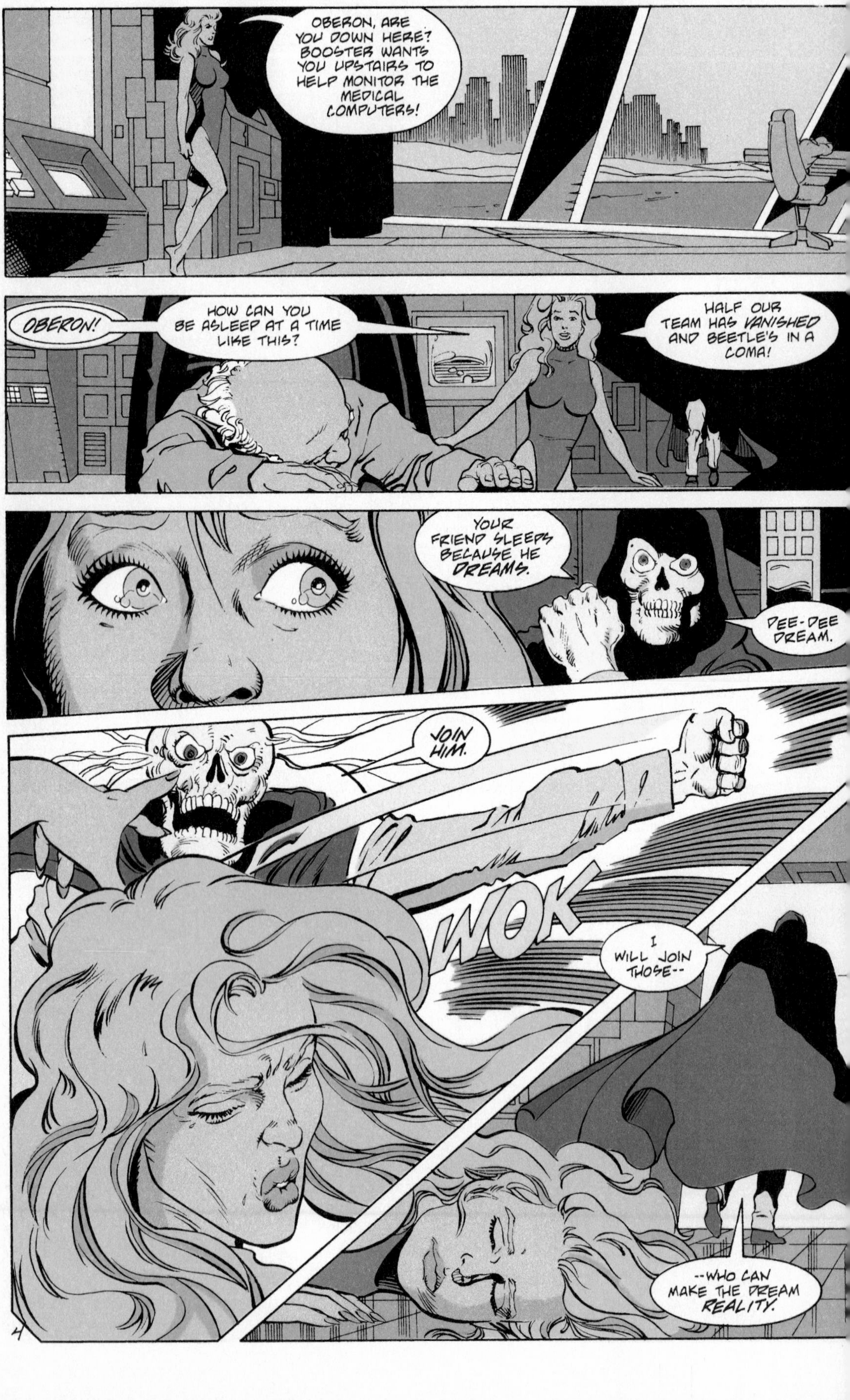
OBERON, ARE YOU DOWN HERE? BOOSTER WANTS YOU UPSTAIRS TO HELP MONITOR THE MEDICAL COMPUTERS!
OBERON!
HOW CAN YOU BE ASLEEP AT A TIME LIKE THIS?
HALF OUR TEAM HAS VANISHED AND BEETLE'S IN A COMA!
YOUR FRIEND SLEEPS BECAUSE HE DREAMS.
DEE-DEE DREAM.
JOIN HIM.
WOK
I WILL JOIN THOSE--
--WHO CAN MAKE THE DREAM REALITY.

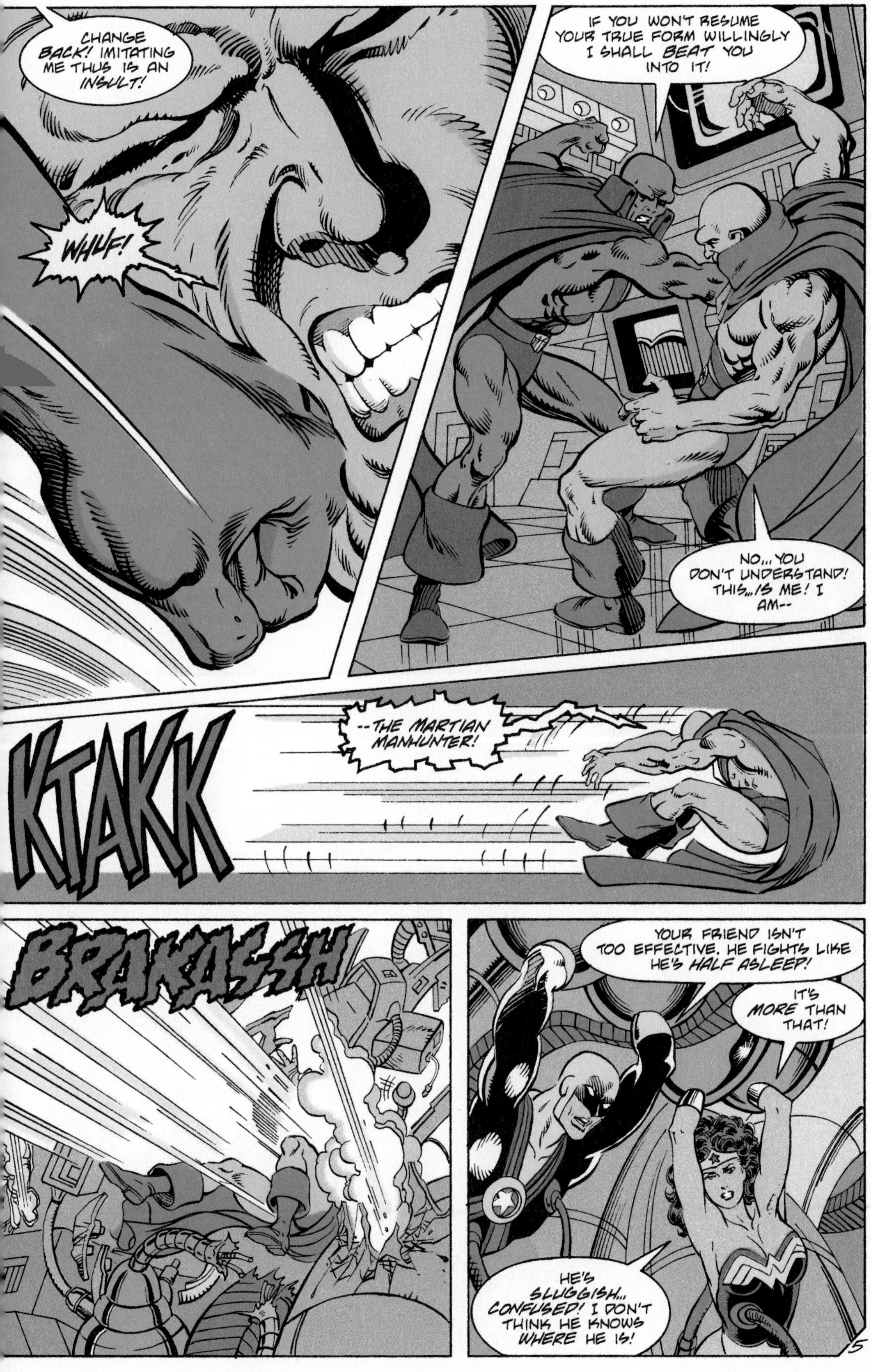
CHANGE BACK! IMITATING ME THUS IS AN INSULT!
WHUF!
IF YOU WON'T RESUME YOUR TRUE FORM WILLINGLY I SHALL BEAT YOU INTO IT!
NO... YOU DON'T UNDERSTAND! THIS... IS ME! I AM--
KTAKK
--THE MARTIAN MANHUNTER!
BRAKASSH
YOUR FRIEND ISN'T TOO EFFECTIVE. HE FIGHTS LIKE HE'S HALF ASLEEP!
IT'S MORE THAN THAT!
HE'S SLUGGISH... CONFUSED! I DON'T THINK HE KNOWS WHERE HE IS!

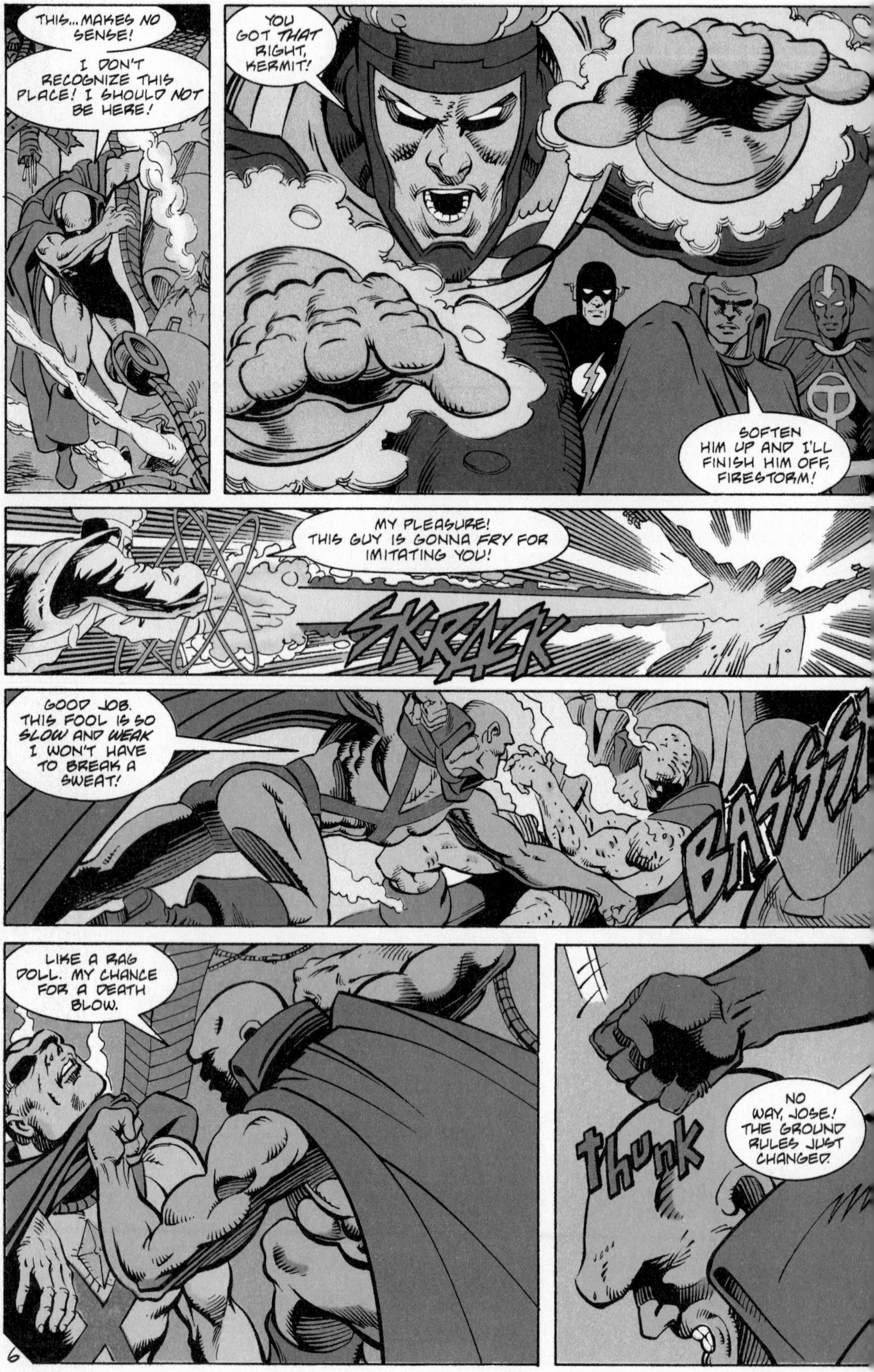
THIS...MAKES NO SENSE!
I DON'T RECOGNIZE THIS PLACE! I SHOULD NOT BE HERE!
YOU GOT THAT RIGHT, KERMIT!
SOFTEN HIM UP AND I'LL FINISH HIM OFF, FIRESTORM!
MY PLEASURE! THIS GUY IS GONNA FRY FOR IMITATING YOU!
SKRACK
GOOD JOB. THIS FOOL IS SO SLOW AND WEAK I WON'T HAVE TO BREAK A SWEAT!
LIKE A RAG DOLL. MY CHANCE FOR A DEATH BLOW.
thunk
NO WAY, JOSE! THE GROUND RULES JUST CHANGED.

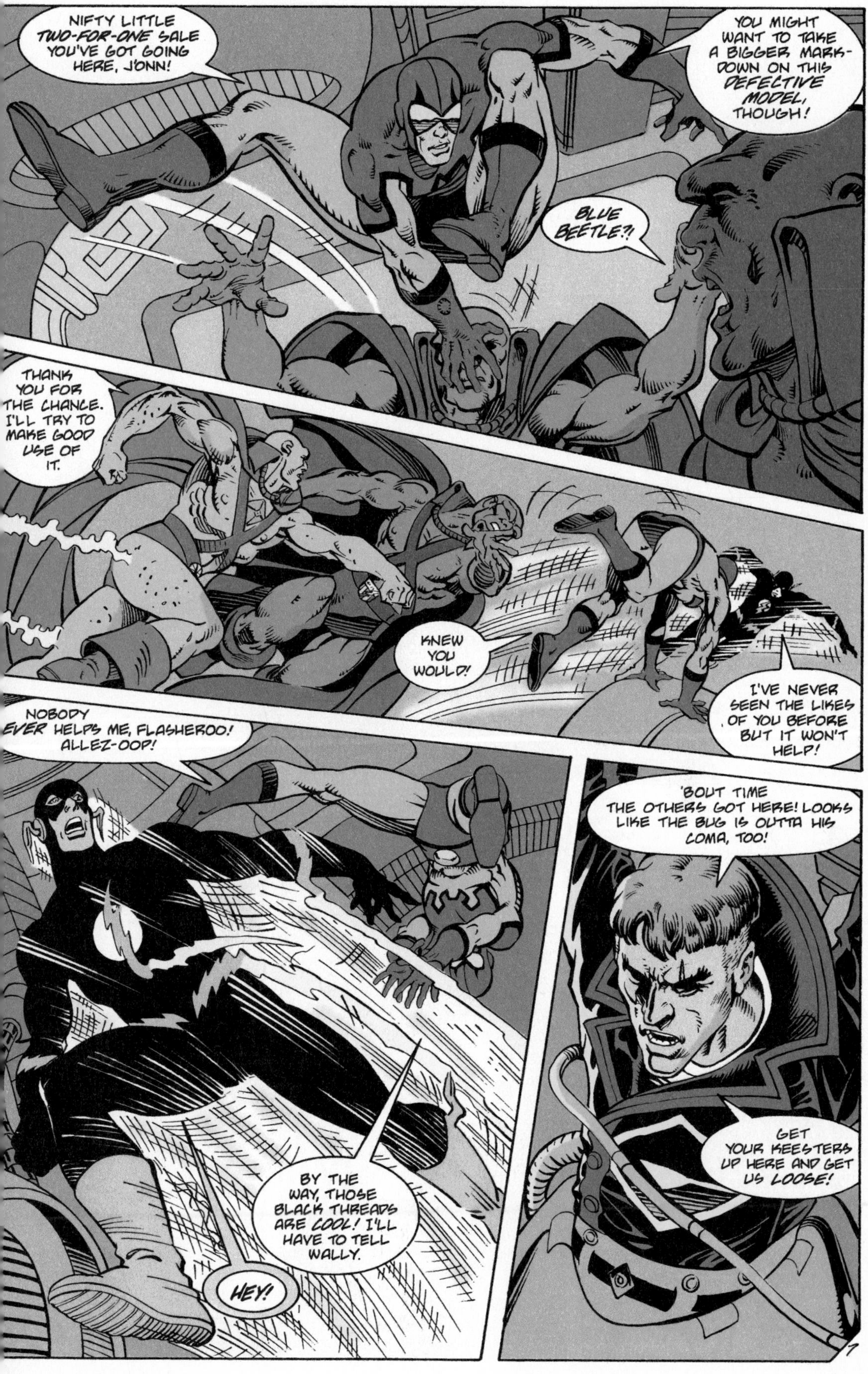

NIFTY LITTLE TWO-FOR-ONE SALE YOU'VE GOT GOING HERE, J'ONN!
YOU MIGHT WANT TO TAKE A BIGGER MARK-DOWN ON THIS DEFECTIVE MODEL, THOUGH!
BLUE BEETLE?!
THANK YOU FOR THE CHANCE. I'LL TRY TO MAKE GOOD USE OF IT.
KNEW YOU WOULD!
I'VE NEVER SEEN THE LIKES OF YOU BEFORE BUT IT WON'T HELP!
NOBODY EVER HELPS ME, FLASHEROO! ALLEZ-OOP!
BY THE WAY, THOSE BLACK THREADS ARE COOL! I'LL HAVE TO TELL WALLY.
HEY!
'BOUT TIME THE OTHERS GOT HERE! LOOKS LIKE THE BUG IS OUTTA HIS COMA, TOO!
GET YOUR KEESTERS UP HERE AND GET US LOOSE!

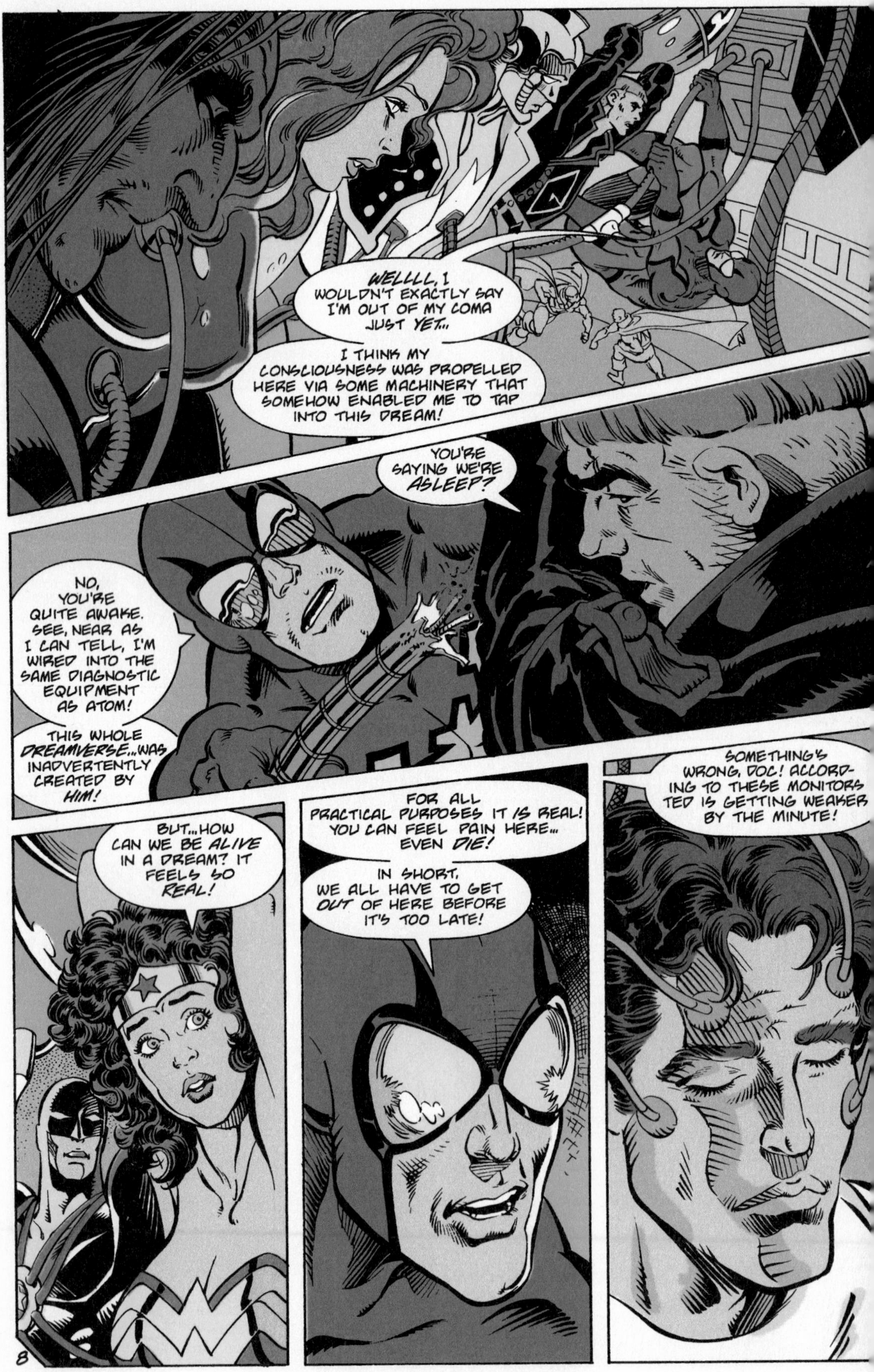

WELLLL, I WOULDN'T EXACTLY SAY I'M OUT OF MY COMA JUST YET...
I THINK MY CONSCIOUSNESS WAS PROPELLED HERE VIA SOME MACHINERY THAT SOMEHOW ENABLED ME TO TAP INTO THIS DREAM!
YOU'RE SAYING WE'RE ASLEEP?
NO, YOU'RE QUITE AWAKE. SEE, NEAR AS I CAN TELL, I'M WIRED INTO THE SAME DIAGNOSTIC EQUIPMENT AS ATOM!
THIS WHOLE DREAMVERSE...WAS INADVERTENTLY CREATED BY HIM!
BUT...HOW CAN WE BE ALIVE IN A DREAM? IT FEELS SO REAL!
FOR ALL PRACTICAL PURPOSES IT IS REAL! YOU CAN FEEL PAIN HERE... EVEN DIE!
IN SHORT, WE ALL HAVE TO GET OUT OF HERE BEFORE IT'S TOO LATE!
SOMETHING'S WRONG, DOC! ACCORDING TO THESE MONITORS TED IS GETTING WEAKER BY THE MINUTE!

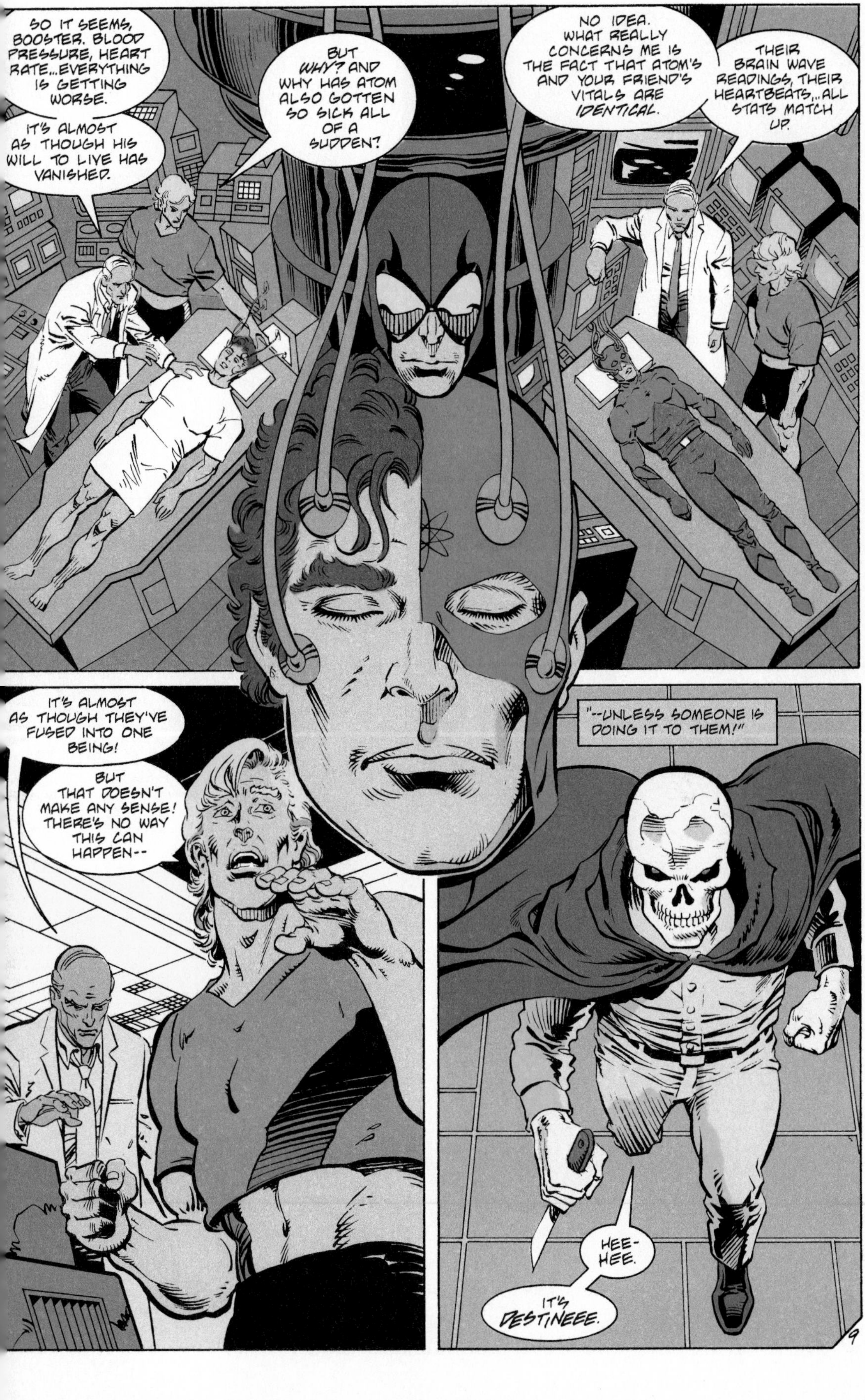
SO IT SEEMS, BOOSTER. BLOOD PRESSURE, HEART RATE...EVERYTHING IS GETTING WORSE.
IT'S ALMOST AS THOUGH HIS WILL TO LIVE HAS VANISHED.
BUT *WHY?* AND WHY HAS ATOM ALSO GOTTEN SO SICK ALL OF A SUDDEN?
NO IDEA. WHAT REALLY CONCERNS ME IS THE FACT THAT ATOM'S AND YOUR FRIEND'S VITALS ARE *IDENTICAL*.
THEIR BRAIN WAVE READINGS, THEIR HEARTBEATS...ALL STATS MATCH UP.
IT'S ALMOST AS THOUGH THEY'VE FUSED INTO ONE BEING!
BUT THAT DOESN'T MAKE ANY SENSE! THERE'S NO WAY THIS CAN HAPPEN--
"--UNLESS SOMEONE IS DOING IT TO THEM!"
HEE-HEE.
IT'S *DESTINEEE.*

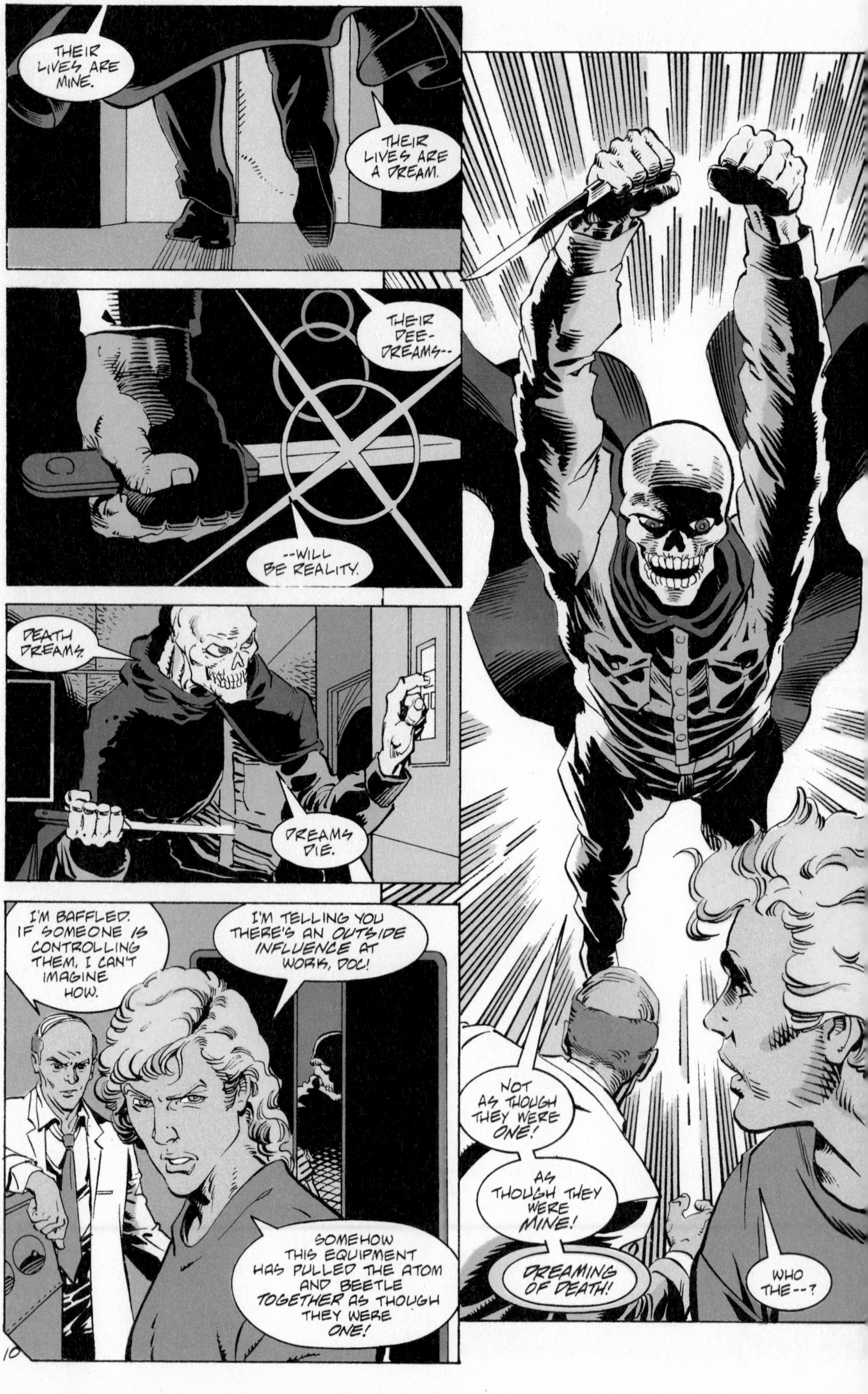
THEIR LIVES ARE MINE.
THEIR LIVES ARE A DREAM.
THEIR DEE-DREAMS--
--WILL BE REALITY.
DEATH DREAMS.
DREAMS DIE.
I'M BAFFLED. IF SOMEONE IS CONTROLLING THEM, I CAN'T IMAGINE HOW.
I'M TELLING YOU THERE'S AN OUTSIDE INFLUENCE AT WORK, DOC!
SOMEHOW THIS EQUIPMENT HAS PULLED THE ATOM AND BEETLE TOGETHER AS THOUGH THEY WERE ONE!
NOT AS THOUGH THEY WERE ONE!
AS THOUGH THEY WERE MINE!
DREAMING OF DEATH!
WHO THE--?

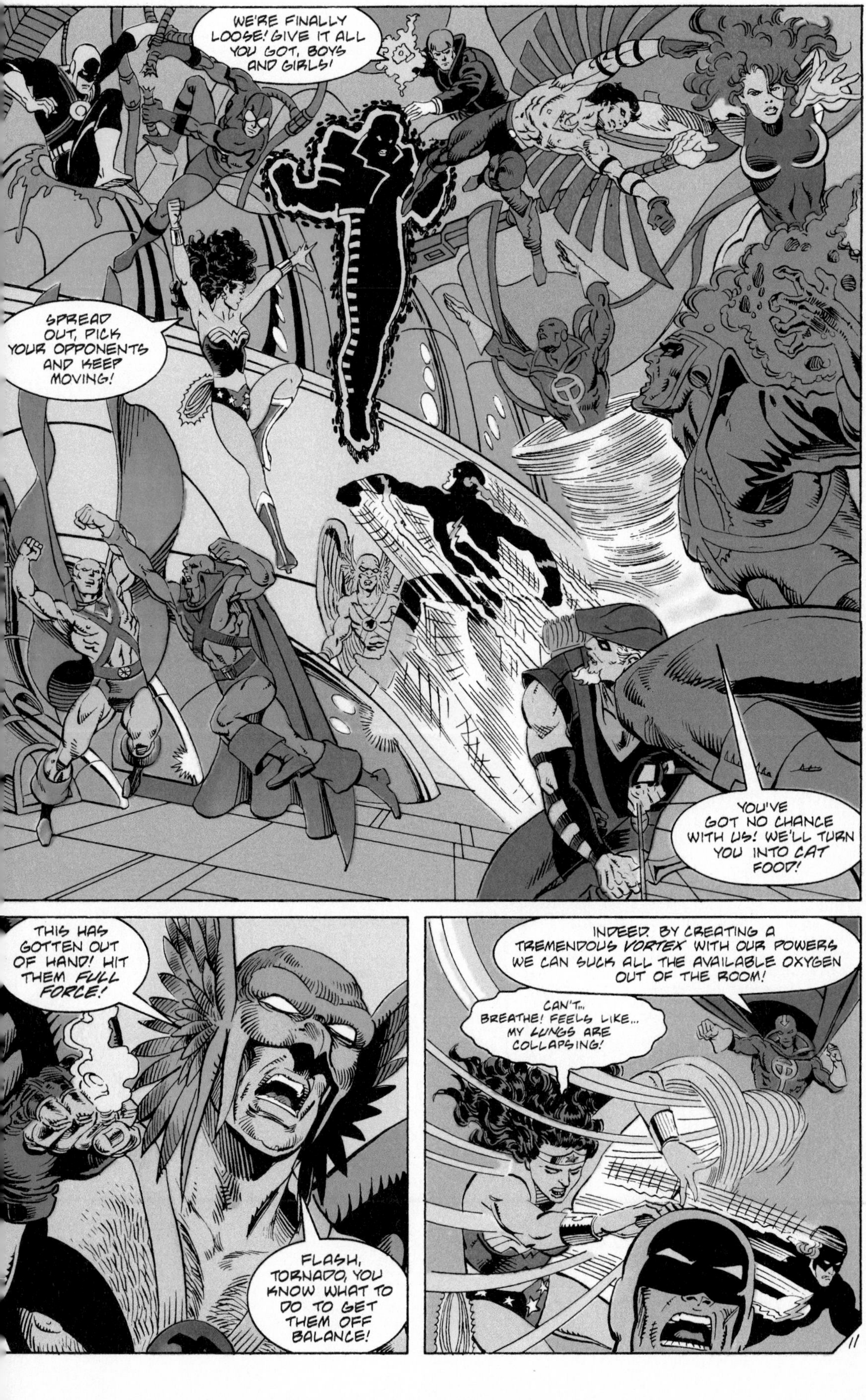
WE'RE FINALLY LOOSE! GIVE IT ALL YOU GOT, BOYS AND GIRLS!
SPREAD OUT, PICK YOUR OPPONENTS AND KEEP MOVING!
YOU'VE GOT NO CHANCE WITH US! WE'LL TURN YOU INTO CAT FOOD!
THIS HAS GOTTEN OUT OF HAND! HIT THEM FULL FORCE!
FLASH, TORNADO, YOU KNOW WHAT TO DO TO GET THEM OFF BALANCE!
INDEED. BY CREATING A TREMENDOUS VORTEX WITH OUR POWERS WE CAN SUCK ALL THE AVAILABLE OXYGEN OUT OF THE ROOM!
CAN'T... BREATHE! FEELS LIKE... MY LUNGS ARE COLLAPSING!

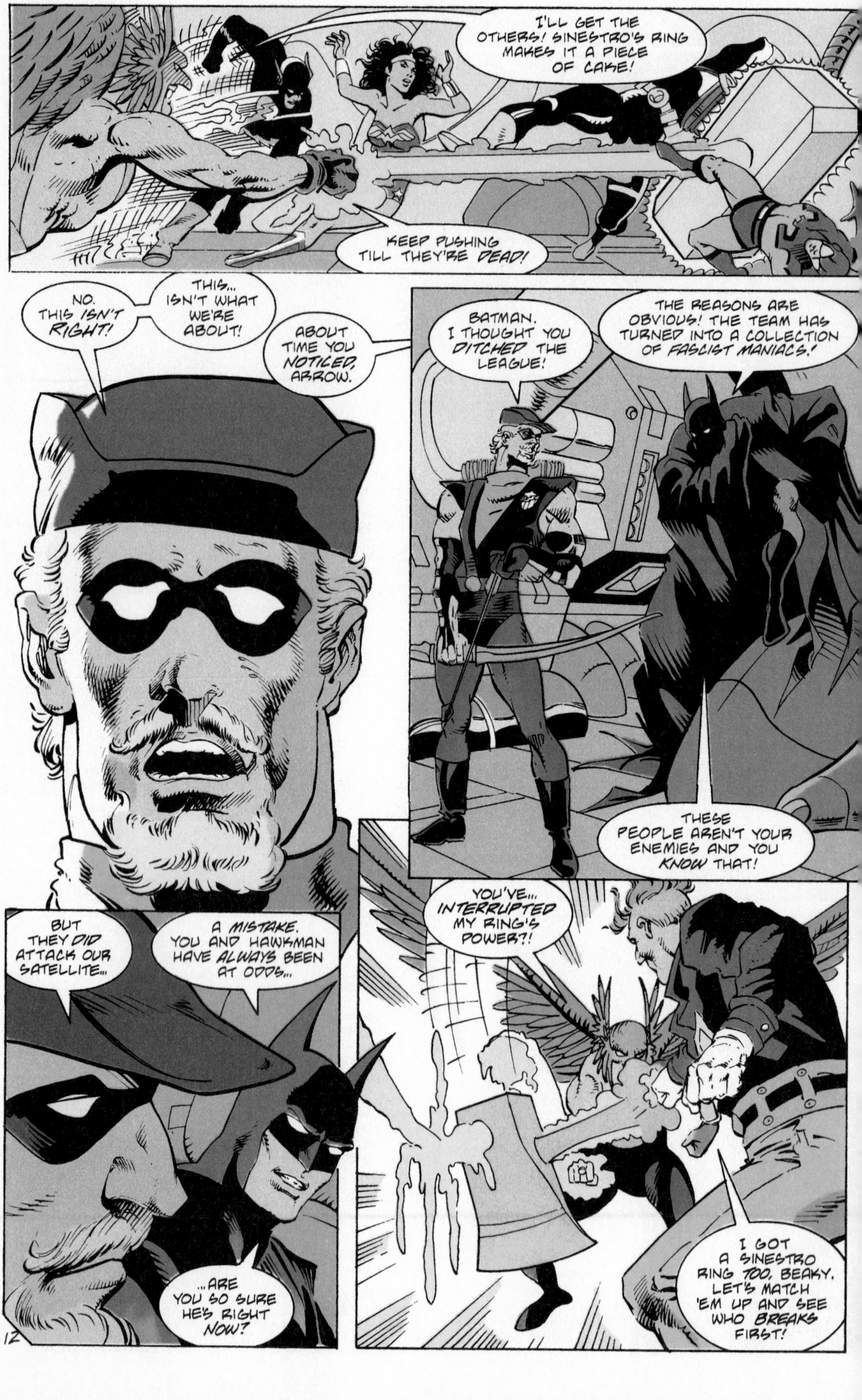

I'LL GET THE OTHERS! SINESTRO'S RING MAKES IT A PIECE OF CAKE!
KEEP PUSHING TILL THEY'RE DEAD!
NO. THIS ISN'T RIGHT!
THIS... ISN'T WHAT WE'RE ABOUT!
ABOUT TIME YOU NOTICED, ARROW.
BATMAN. I THOUGHT YOU DITCHED THE LEAGUE!
THE REASONS ARE OBVIOUS! THE TEAM HAS TURNED INTO A COLLECTION OF FASCIST MANIACS!
THESE PEOPLE AREN'T YOUR ENEMIES AND YOU KNOW THAT!
BUT THEY DID ATTACK OUR SATELLITE...
A MISTAKE. YOU AND HAWKMAN HAVE ALWAYS BEEN AT ODDS...
...ARE YOU SO SURE HE'S RIGHT NOW?
YOU'VE... INTERRUPTED MY RING'S POWER?!
I GOT A SINESTRO RING TOO, BEAKY. LET'S MATCH 'EM UP AND SEE WHO BREAKS FIRST!

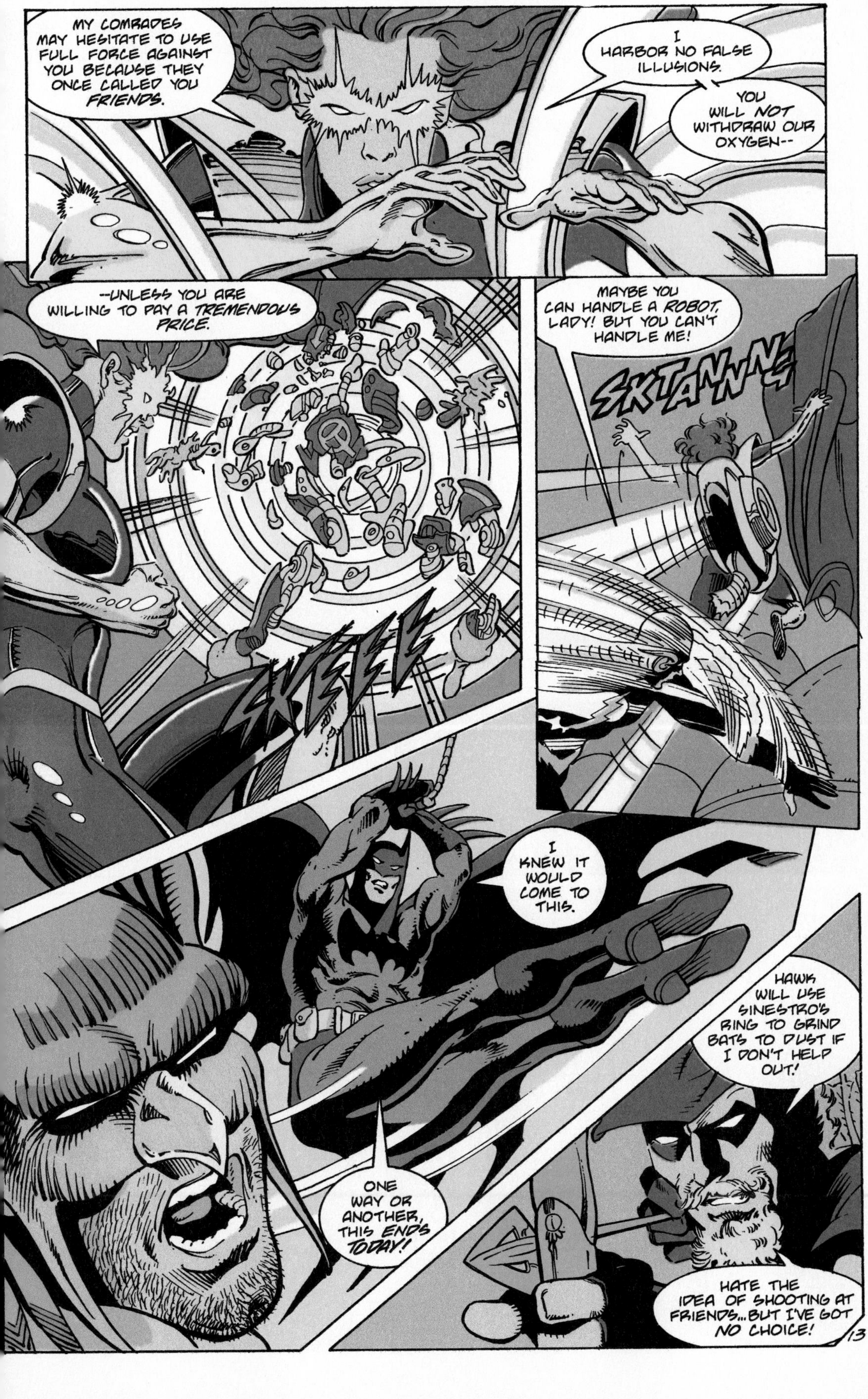

MY COMRADES MAY HESITATE TO USE FULL FORCE AGAINST YOU BECAUSE THEY ONCE CALLED YOU *FRIENDS*.
I HARBOR NO FALSE ILLUSIONS.
YOU WILL *NOT* WITHDRAW OUR OXYGEN--
--UNLESS YOU ARE WILLING TO PAY A *TREMENDOUS PRICE*.
SKEEEE
MAYBE YOU CAN HANDLE A *ROBOT*, LADY! BUT YOU CAN'T HANDLE ME!
SKTANNNG
I KNEW IT WOULD COME TO THIS.
ONE WAY OR ANOTHER, THIS *ENDS TODAY*!
HAWK WILL USE SINESTRO'S RING TO GRIND BATS TO DUST IF I DON'T HELP OUT!
HATE THE IDEA OF SHOOTING AT FRIENDS...BUT I'VE GOT *NO CHOICE*!

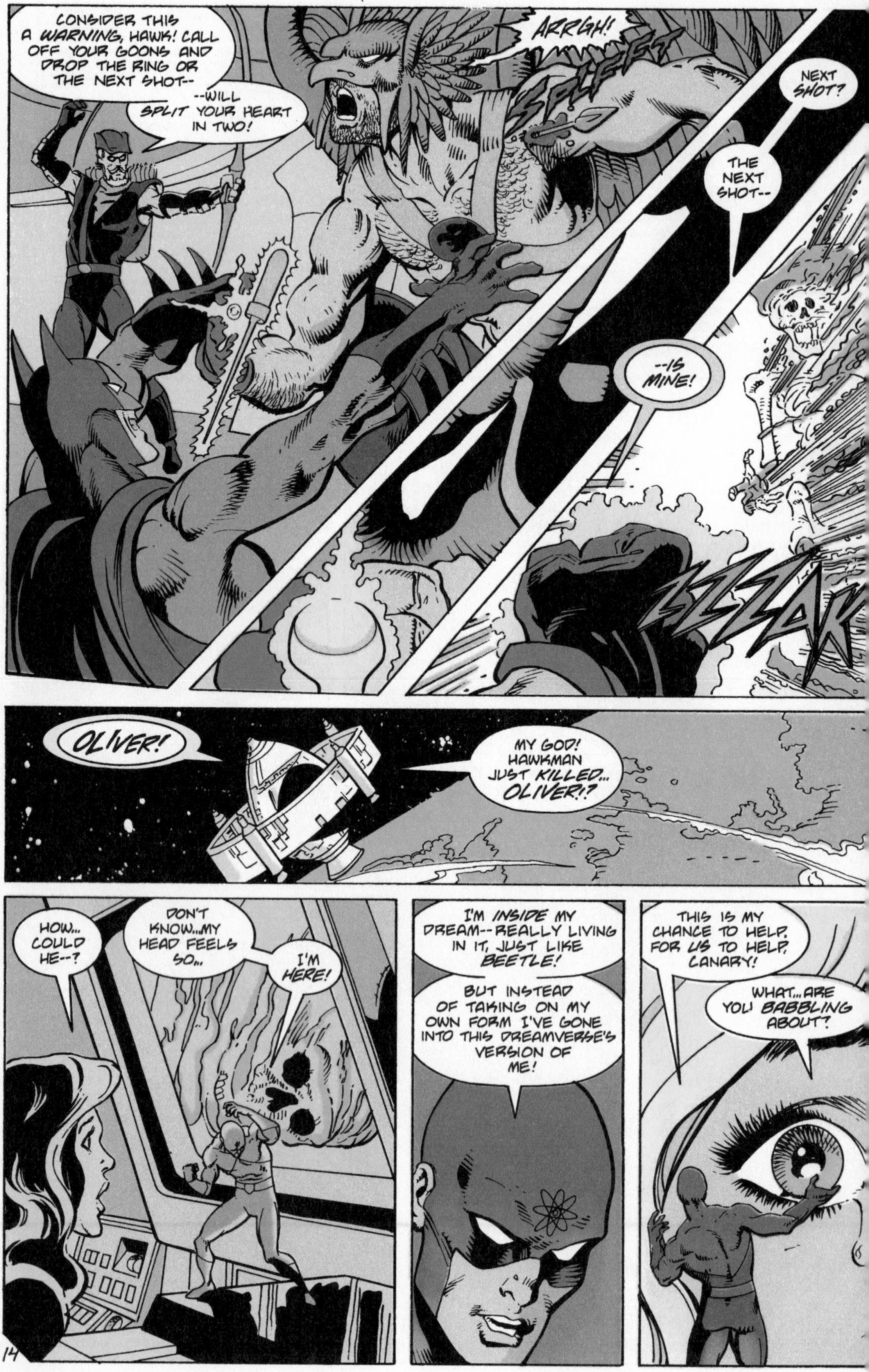
CONSIDER THIS A WARNING, HAWK! CALL OFF YOUR GOONS AND DROP THE RING OR THE NEXT SHOT--
--WILL SPLIT YOUR HEART IN TWO!
ARRGH!
SPLIFFT
NEXT SHOT?
THE NEXT SHOT--
--IS MINE!
OLIVER!
MY GOD! HAWKMAN JUST KILLED... OLIVER!?
HOW... COULD HE--?
DON'T KNOW...MY HEAD FEELS SO...
I'M HERE!
I'M INSIDE MY DREAM--REALLY LIVING IN IT, JUST LIKE BEETLE!
BUT INSTEAD OF TAKING ON MY OWN FORM I'VE GONE INTO THIS DREAMVERSE'S VERSION OF ME!
THIS IS MY CHANCE TO HELP, FOR US TO HELP, CANARY!
WHAT... ARE YOU BABBLING ABOUT?

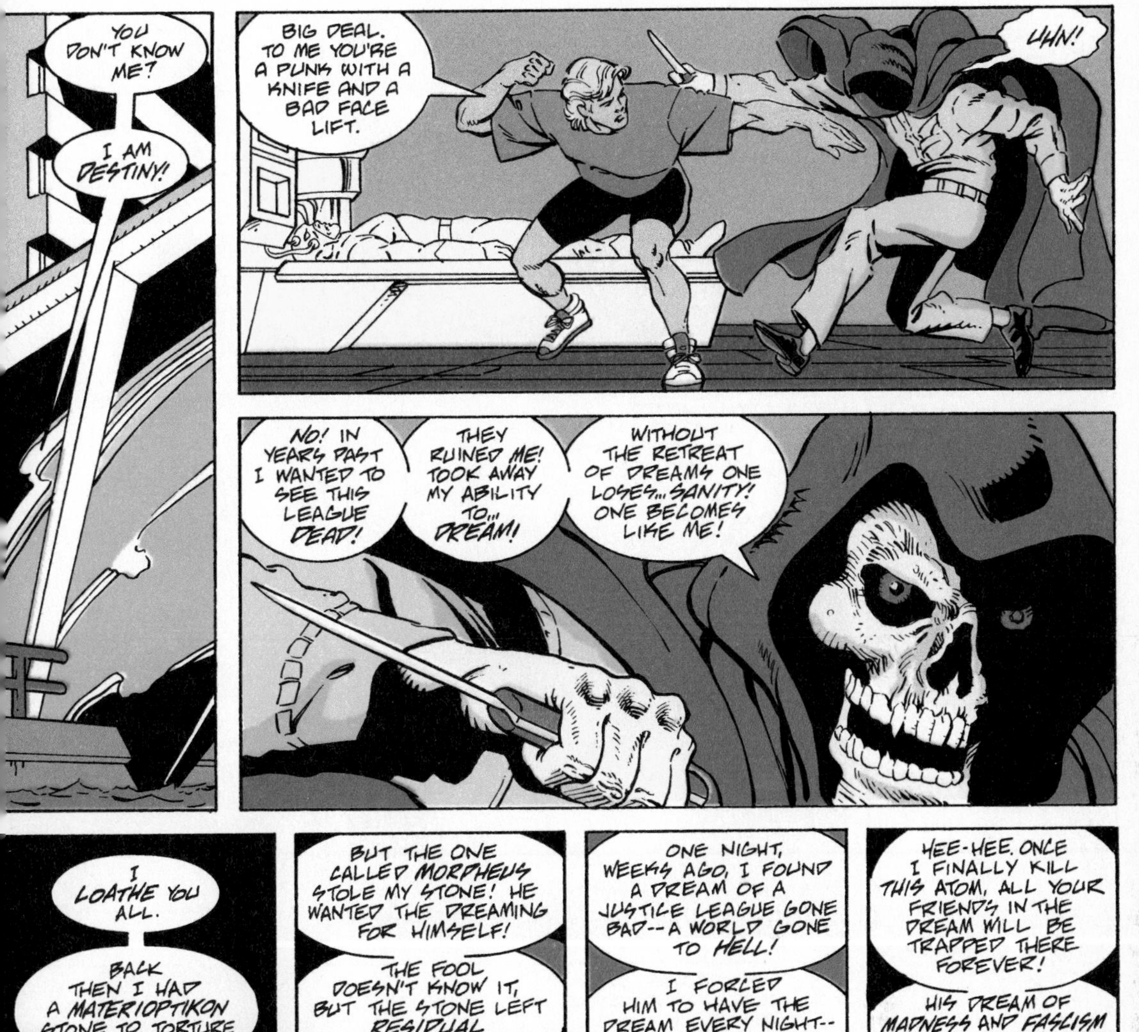
YOU DON'T KNOW ME?
I AM DESTINY!
BIG DEAL. TO ME YOU'RE A PUNK WITH A KNIFE AND A BAD FACE LIFT.
UHN!
NO! IN YEARS PAST I WANTED TO SEE THIS LEAGUE DEAD!
THEY RUINED ME! TOOK AWAY MY ABILITY TO... DREAM!
WITHOUT THE RETREAT OF DREAMS ONE LOSES... SANITY! ONE BECOMES LIKE ME!
I LOATHE YOU ALL.
BACK THEN I HAD A MATERIOPTIKON STONE TO TORTURE THEM!*
BUT THE ONE CALLED MORPHEUS STOLE MY STONE! HE WANTED THE DREAMING FOR HIMSELF!
THE FOOL DOESN'T KNOW IT, BUT THE STONE LEFT RESIDUAL ENERGIES!
ENERGIES I LEARNED TO USE TO WATCH THE DREAMS OF OTHERS!
ONE NIGHT, WEEKS AGO, I FOUND A DREAM OF A JUSTICE LEAGUE GONE BAD--A WORLD GONE TO HELL!
I FORCED HIM TO HAVE THE DREAM EVERY NIGHT--EVERY DAY--UNTIL AN ENTIRE UNIVERSE OF THAT LEAGUE WAS BUILT!
HEE-HEE. ONCE I FINALLY KILL THIS ATOM, ALL YOUR FRIENDS IN THE DREAM WILL BE TRAPPED THERE FOREVER!
HIS DREAM OF MADNESS AND FASCISM WILL BE ITS OWN CONCRETE REALITY THAT WILL EVENTUALLY PHASE INTO EXISTENCE WITH OUR WORLD!
*AS RECOUNTED IN MANY ADVENTURES OF THE JUSTICE LEAGUE OF AMERICA-- B.A.

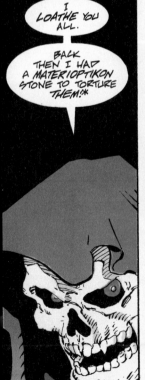

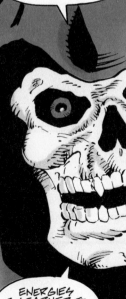

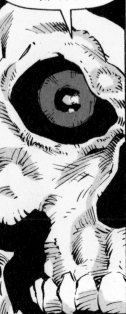

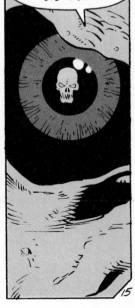

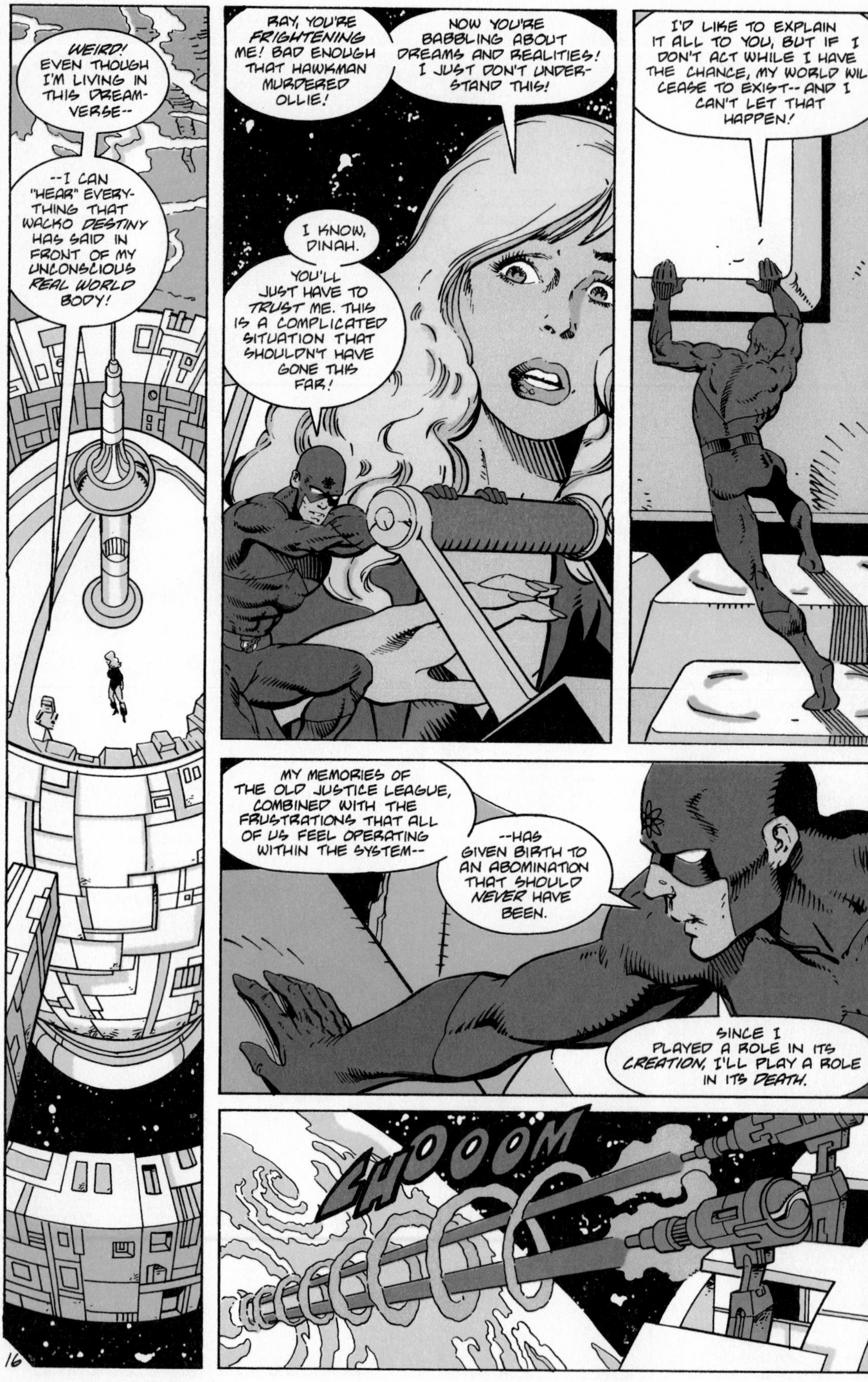

WEIRD! EVEN THOUGH I'M LIVING IN THIS DREAMVERSE--
--I CAN "HEAR" EVERYTHING THAT WACKO DESTINY HAS SAID IN FRONT OF MY UNCONSCIOUS REAL WORLD BODY!
RAY, YOU'RE FRIGHTENING ME! BAD ENOUGH THAT HAWKMAN MURDERED OLLIE!
NOW YOU'RE BABBLING ABOUT DREAMS AND REALITIES! I JUST DON'T UNDERSTAND THIS!
I KNOW, DINAH.
YOU'LL JUST HAVE TO TRUST ME. THIS IS A COMPLICATED SITUATION THAT SHOULDN'T HAVE GONE THIS FAR!
I'D LIKE TO EXPLAIN IT ALL TO YOU, BUT IF I DON'T ACT WHILE I HAVE THE CHANCE, MY WORLD WILL CEASE TO EXIST-- AND I CAN'T LET THAT HAPPEN!
MY MEMORIES OF THE OLD JUSTICE LEAGUE, COMBINED WITH THE FRUSTRATIONS THAT ALL OF US FEEL OPERATING WITHIN THE SYSTEM--
--HAS GIVEN BIRTH TO AN ABOMINATION THAT SHOULD NEVER HAVE BEEN.
SINCE I PLAYED A ROLE IN ITS CREATION, I'LL PLAY A ROLE IN ITS DEATH.
CHOOOM

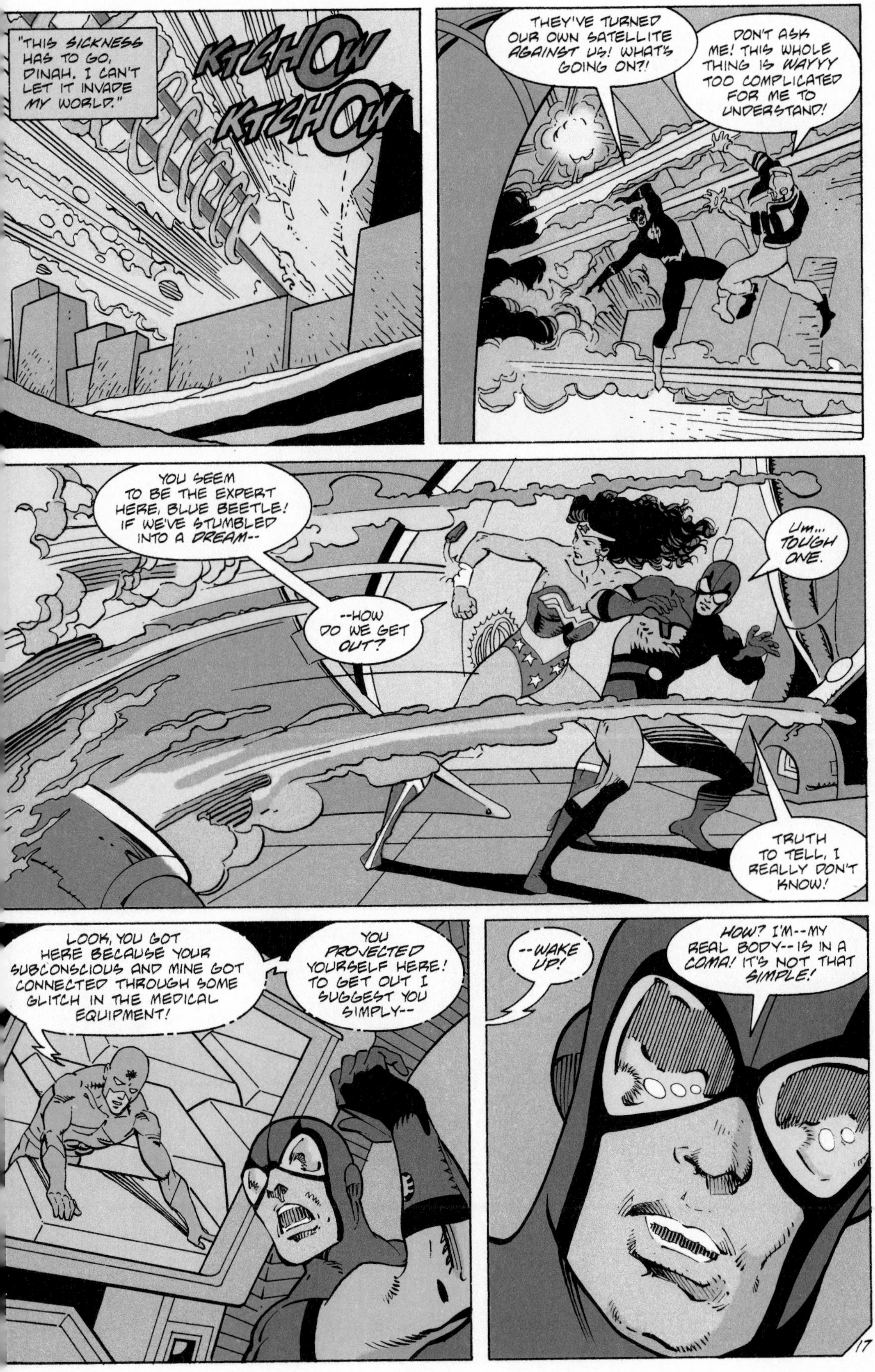
"THIS SICKNESS HAS TO GO, DINAH. I CAN'T LET IT INVADE MY WORLD."
KTCHOW
KTCHOW
THEY'VE TURNED OUR OWN SATELLITE AGAINST US! WHAT'S GOING ON?!
DON'T ASK ME! THIS WHOLE THING IS WAYYY TOO COMPLICATED FOR ME TO UNDERSTAND!
YOU SEEM TO BE THE EXPERT HERE, BLUE BEETLE! IF WE'VE STUMBLED INTO A DREAM--
--HOW DO WE GET OUT?
UM... TOUGH ONE.
TRUTH TO TELL, I REALLY DON'T KNOW!
LOOK, YOU GOT HERE BECAUSE YOUR SUBCONSCIOUS AND MINE GOT CONNECTED THROUGH SOME GLITCH IN THE MEDICAL EQUIPMENT!
YOU PROJECTED YOURSELF HERE! TO GET OUT I SUGGEST YOU SIMPLY--
--WAKE UP!
HOW? I'M--MY REAL BODY--IS IN A COMA! IT'S NOT THAT SIMPLE!

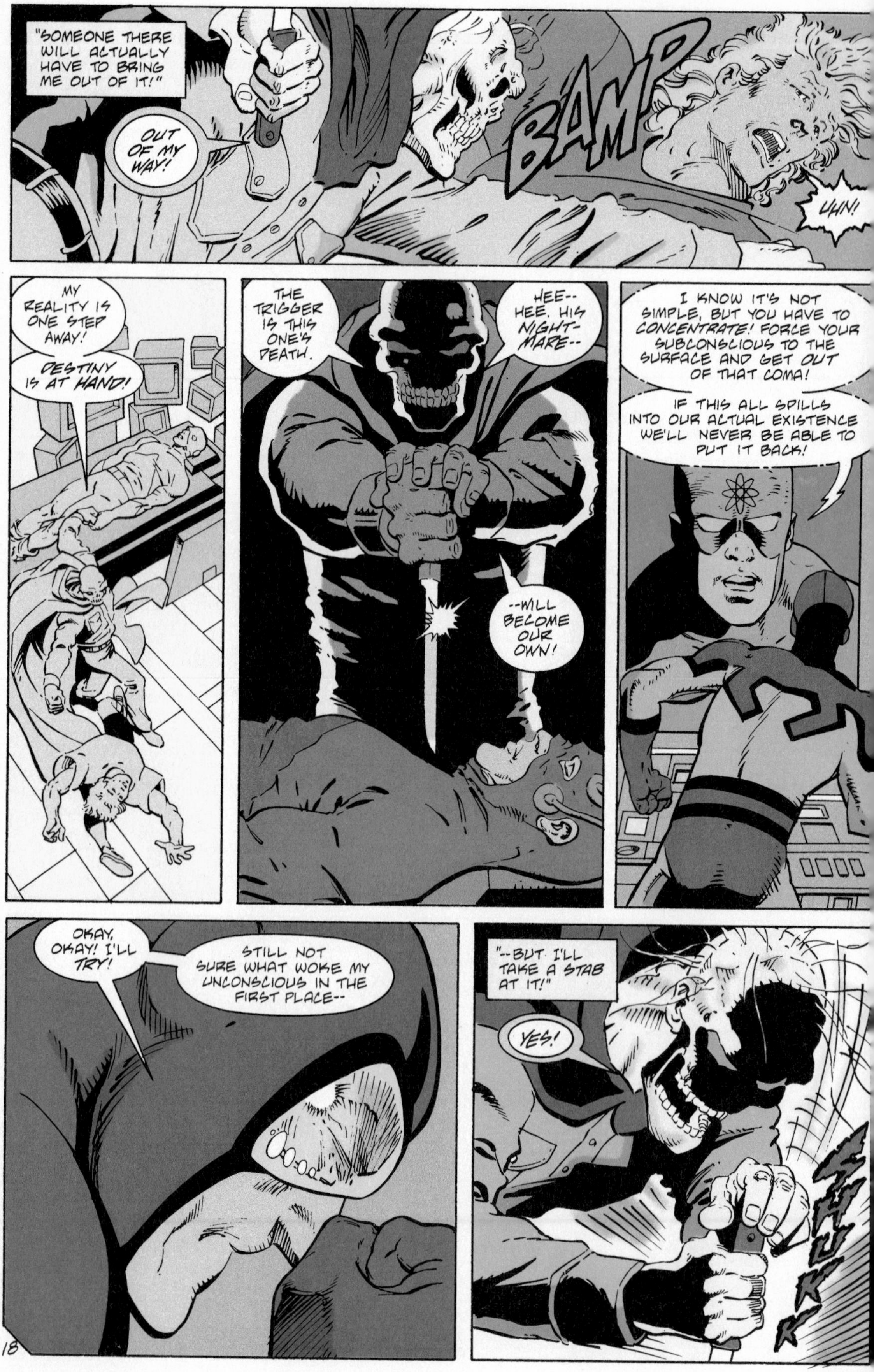
"SOMEONE THERE WILL ACTUALLY HAVE TO BRING ME OUT OF IT!"
OUT OF MY WAY!
BAMP
UHN!
MY REALITY IS ONE STEP AWAY!
DESTINY IS AT HAND!
THE TRIGGER IS THIS ONE'S DEATH.
HEE-- HEE. HIS NIGHT-MARE--
--WILL BECOME OUR OWN!
I KNOW IT'S NOT SIMPLE, BUT YOU HAVE TO CONCENTRATE! FORCE YOUR SUBCONSCIOUS TO THE SURFACE AND GET OUT OF THAT COMA!
IF THIS ALL SPILLS INTO OUR ACTUAL EXISTENCE WE'LL NEVER BE ABLE TO PUT IT BACK!
OKAY, OKAY! I'LL TRY!
STILL NOT SURE WHAT WOKE MY UNCONSCIOUS IN THE FIRST PLACE--
"--BUT I'LL TAKE A STAB AT IT!"
YES!

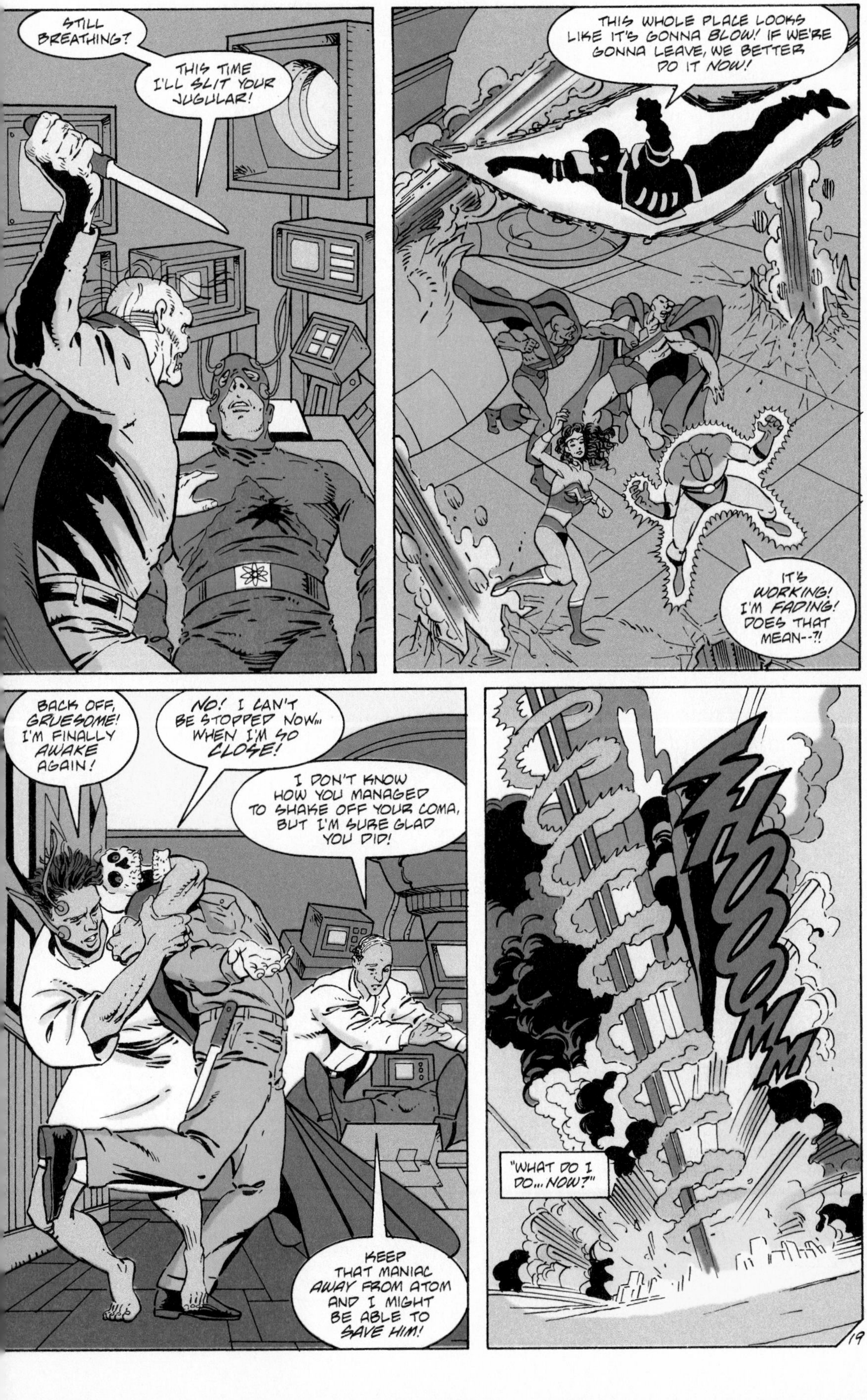

STILL BREATHING?
THIS TIME I'LL SLIT YOUR JUGULAR!
THIS WHOLE PLACE LOOKS LIKE IT'S GONNA BLOW! IF WE'RE GONNA LEAVE, WE BETTER DO IT NOW!
IT'S WORKING! I'M FADING! DOES THAT MEAN--?!
BACK OFF, GRUESOME! I'M FINALLY AWAKE AGAIN!
NO! I CAN'T BE STOPPED NOW... WHEN I'M SO CLOSE!
I DON'T KNOW HOW YOU MANAGED TO SHAKE OFF YOUR COMA, BUT I'M SURE GLAD YOU DID!
KEEP THAT MANIAC AWAY FROM ATOM AND I MIGHT BE ABLE TO SAVE HIM!
"WHAT DO I DO... NOW?"

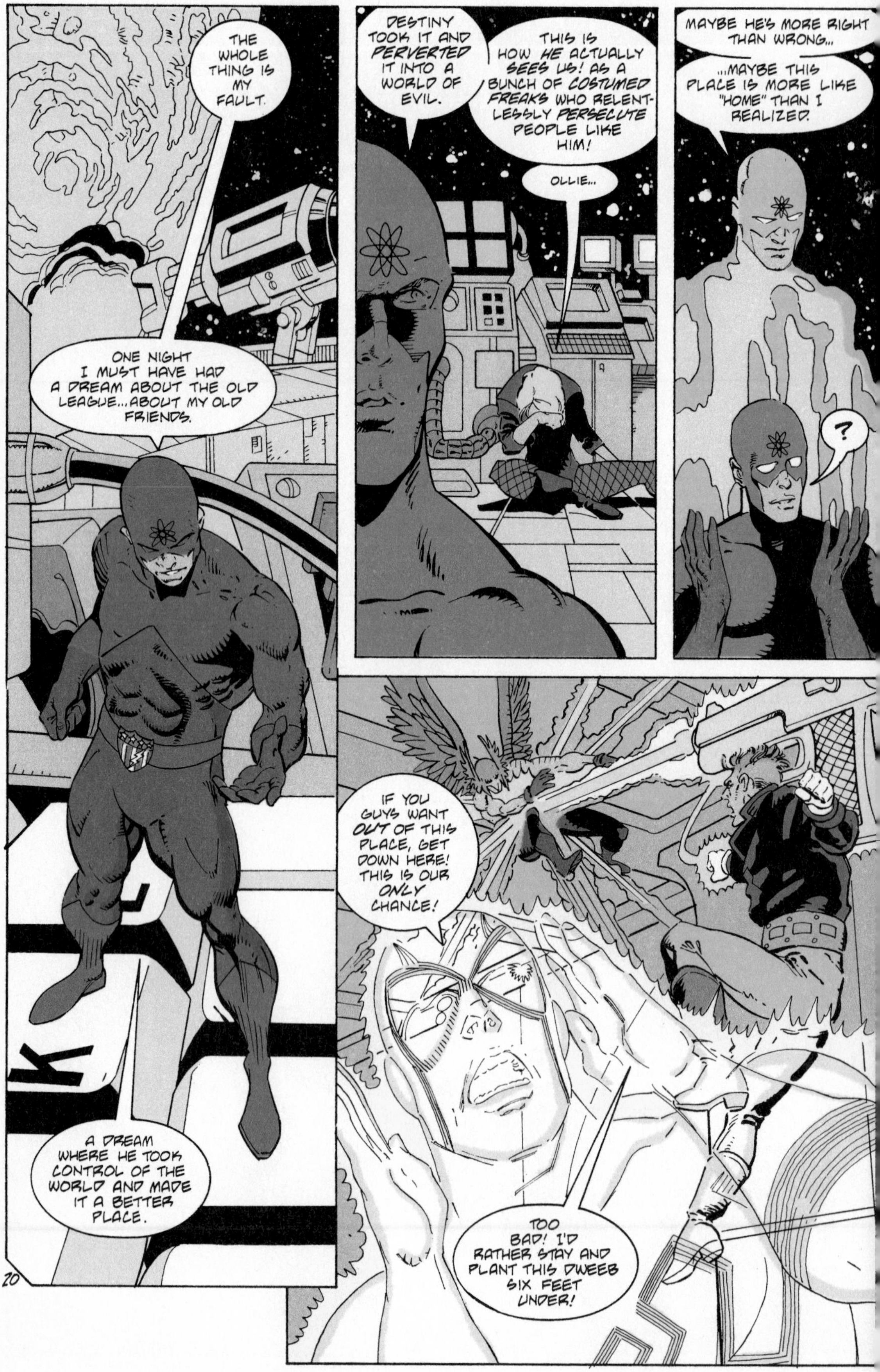
THE WHOLE THING IS MY FAULT.
ONE NIGHT I MUST HAVE HAD A DREAM ABOUT THE OLD LEAGUE...ABOUT MY OLD FRIENDS.
A DREAM WHERE HE TOOK CONTROL OF THE WORLD AND MADE IT A BETTER PLACE.
DESTINY TOOK IT AND PERVERTED IT INTO A WORLD OF EVIL.
THIS IS HOW HE ACTUALLY SEES US! AS A BUNCH OF COSTUMED FREAKS WHO RELENTLESSLY PERSECUTE PEOPLE LIKE HIM!
OLLIE...
MAYBE HE'S MORE RIGHT THAN WRONG...
...MAYBE THIS PLACE IS MORE LIKE "HOME" THAN I REALIZED.
?
IF YOU GUYS WANT OUT OF THIS PLACE, GET DOWN HERE! THIS IS OUR ONLY CHANCE!
TOO BAD! I'D RATHER STAY AND PLANT THIS DWEEB SIX FEET UNDER!

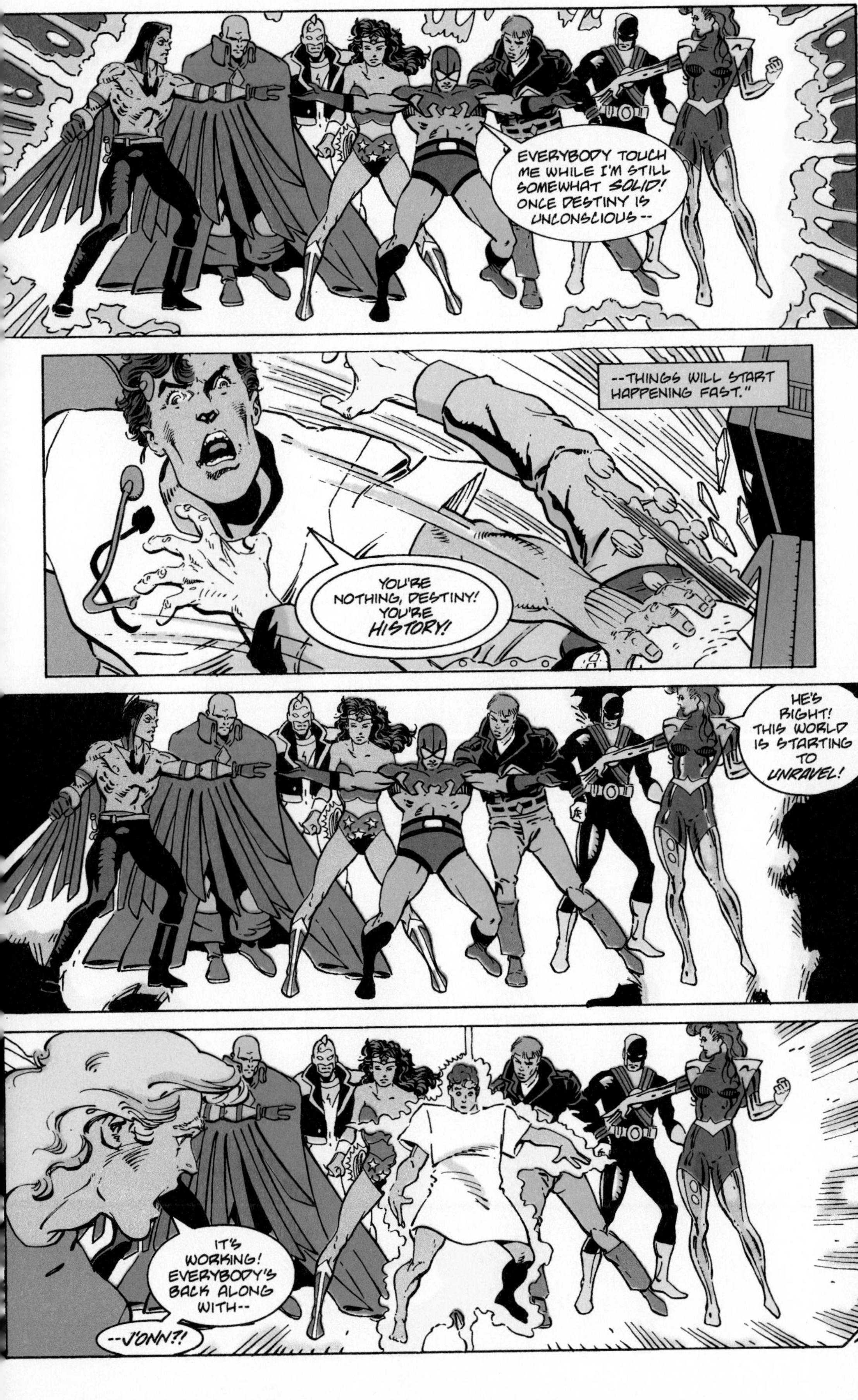

EVERYBODY TOUCH ME WHILE I'M STILL SOMEWHAT SOLID! ONCE DESTINY IS UNCONSCIOUS --
--THINGS WILL START HAPPENING FAST."
YOU'RE NOTHING, DESTINY! YOU'RE HISTORY!
HE'S RIGHT! THIS WORLD IS STARTING TO UNRAVEL!
IT'S WORKING! EVERYBODY'S BACK ALONG WITH--
--J'ONN?!

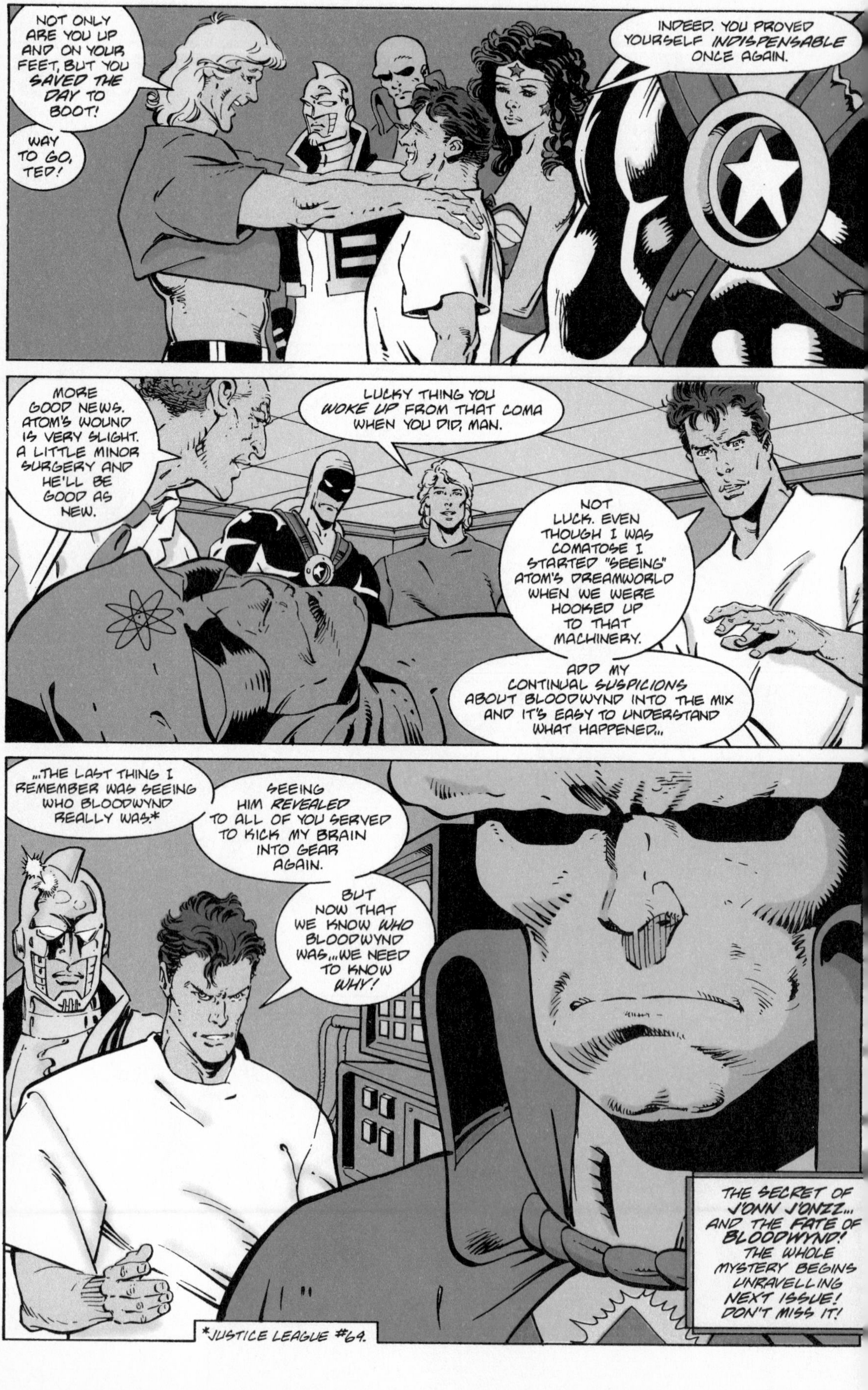
NOT ONLY ARE YOU UP AND ON YOUR FEET, BUT YOU SAVED THE DAY TO BOOT!
WAY TO GO, TED!
INDEED. YOU PROVED YOURSELF INDISPENSABLE ONCE AGAIN.
MORE GOOD NEWS. ATOM'S WOUND IS VERY SLIGHT. A LITTLE MINOR SURGERY AND HE'LL BE GOOD AS NEW.
LUCKY THING YOU WOKE UP FROM THAT COMA WHEN YOU DID, MAN.
NOT LUCK. EVEN THOUGH I WAS COMATOSE I STARTED "SEEING" ATOM'S DREAMWORLD WHEN WE WERE HOOKED UP TO THAT MACHINERY.
ADD MY CONTINUAL SUSPICIONS ABOUT BLOODWYND INTO THE MIX AND IT'S EASY TO UNDERSTAND WHAT HAPPENED...
...THE LAST THING I REMEMBER WAS SEEING WHO BLOODWYND REALLY WAS.*
SEEING HIM REVEALED TO ALL OF YOU SERVED TO KICK MY BRAIN INTO GEAR AGAIN.
BUT NOW THAT WE KNOW WHO BLOODWYND WAS...WE NEED TO KNOW WHY!
*JUSTICE LEAGUE #64.
THE SECRET OF J'ONN J'ONZZ... AND THE FATE OF BLOODWYND! THE WHOLE MYSTERY BEGINS UNRAVELLING NEXT ISSUE! DON'T MISS IT!

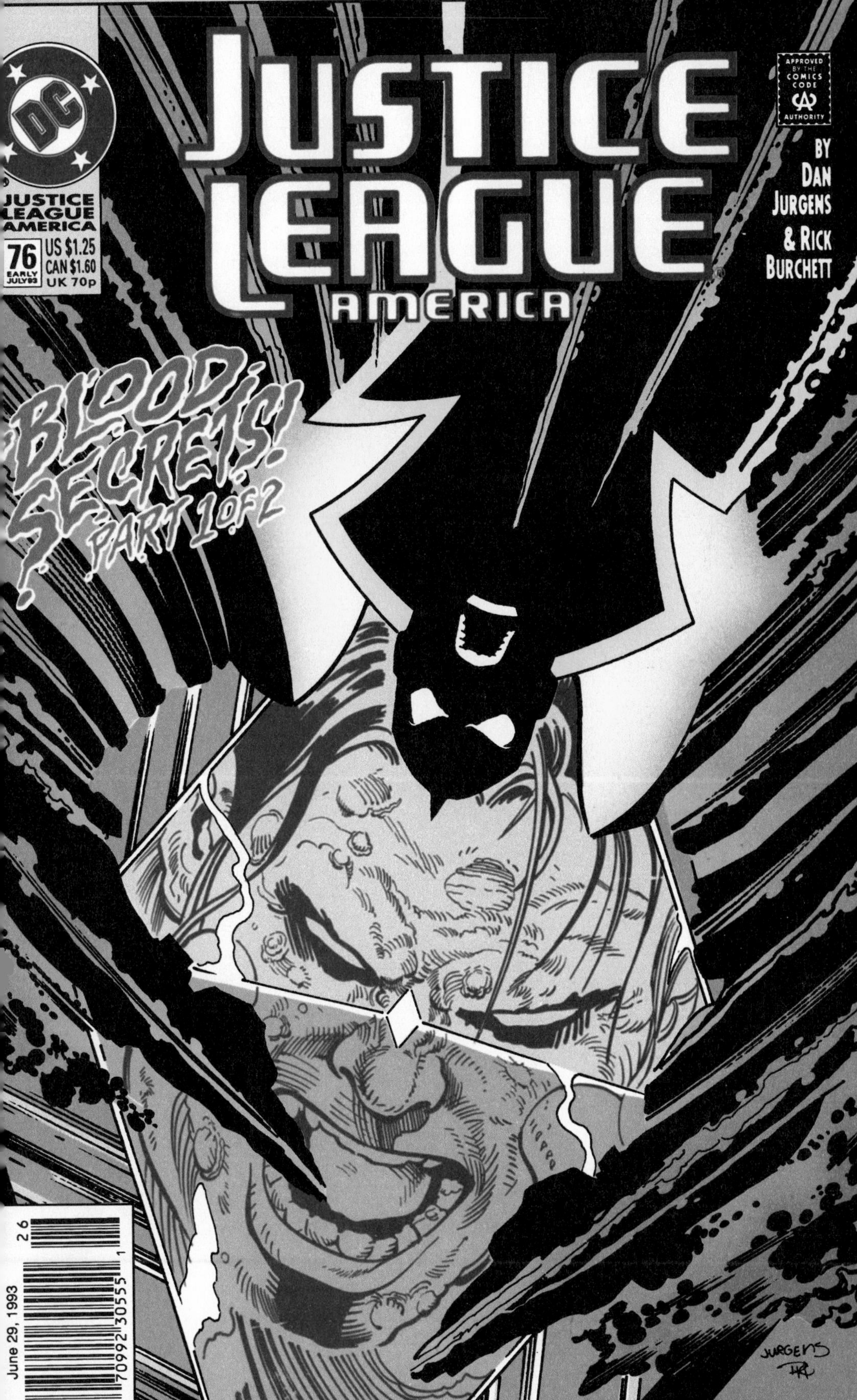

JUSTICE LEAGUE AMERICA
JUSTICE LEAGUE AMERICA
76
EARLY JULY 93
US $1.25
CAN $1.60
UK 70p
APPROVED BY THE COMICS CODE AUTHORITY
BY DAN JURGENS & RICK BURCHETT
BLOOD SECRETS! PART 1 OF 2
June 29, 1993
JURGENS

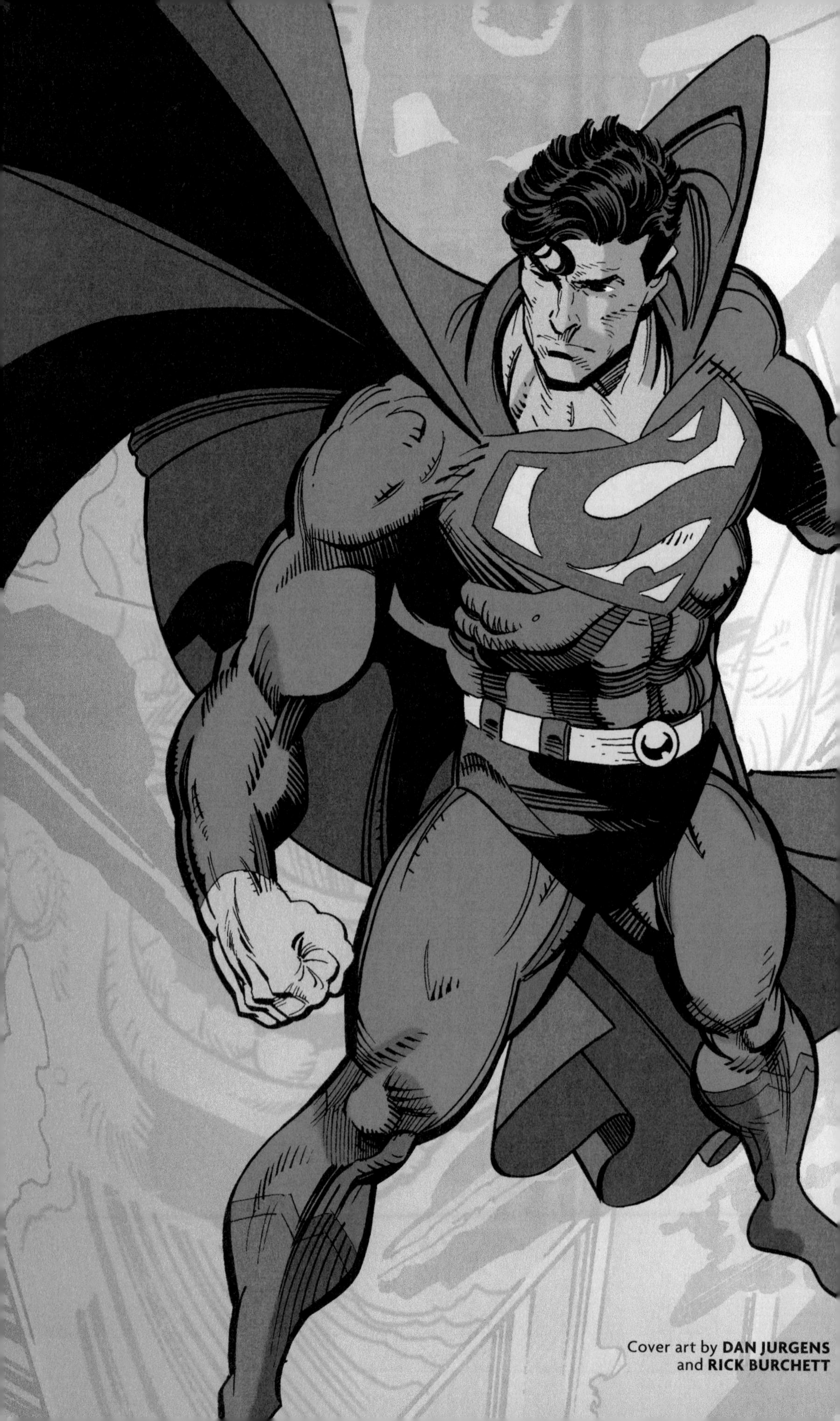

Cover art by **DAN JURGENS**
and **RICK BURCHETT**

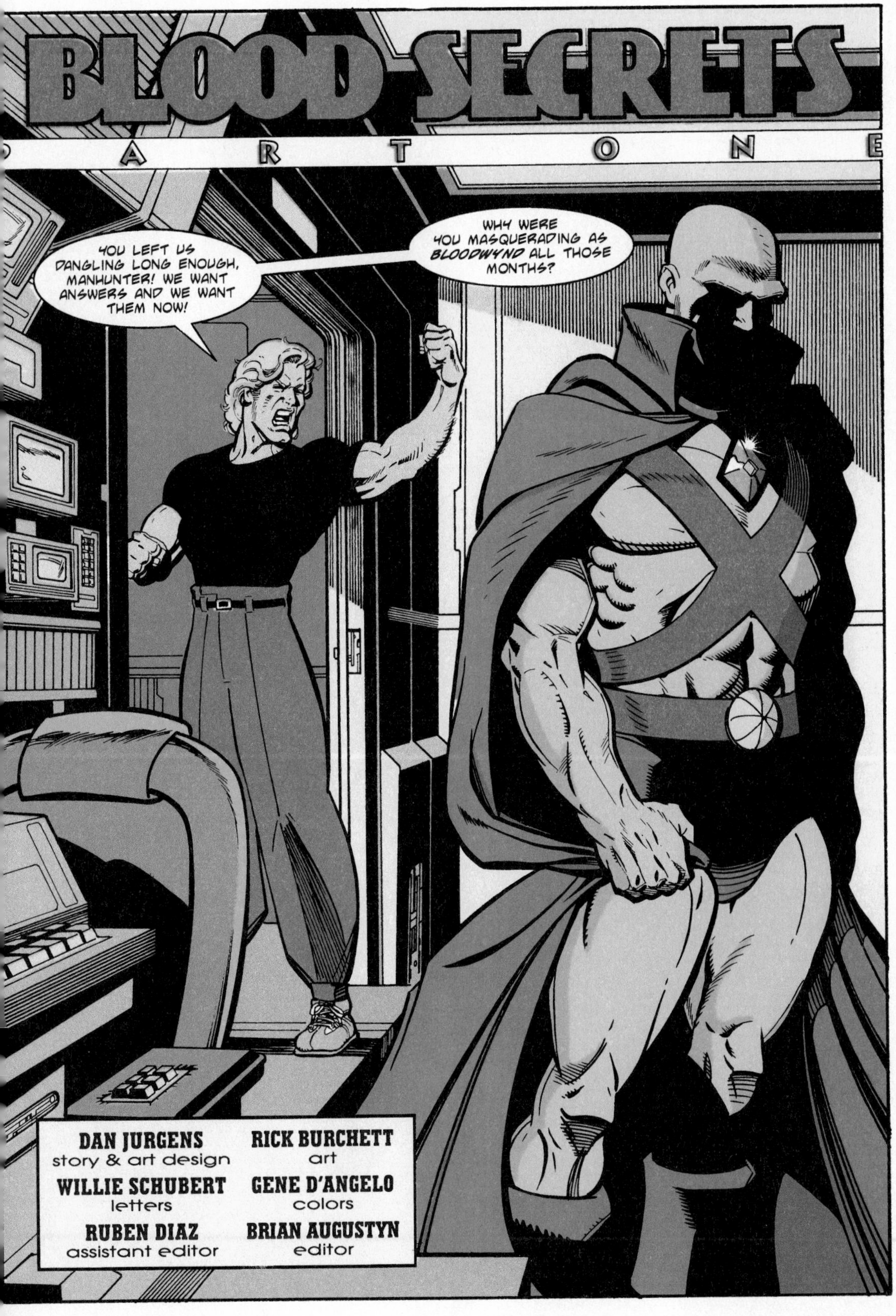
BLOOD SECRETS
PART ONE
YOU LEFT US DANGLING LONG ENOUGH, MANHUNTER! WE WANT ANSWERS AND WE WANT THEM NOW!
WHY WERE YOU MASQUERADING AS BLOODWYND ALL THOSE MONTHS?
DAN JURGENS story & art design
RICK BURCHETT art
WILLIE SCHUBERT letters
GENE D'ANGELO colors
RUBEN DIAZ assistant editor
BRIAN AUGUSTYN editor

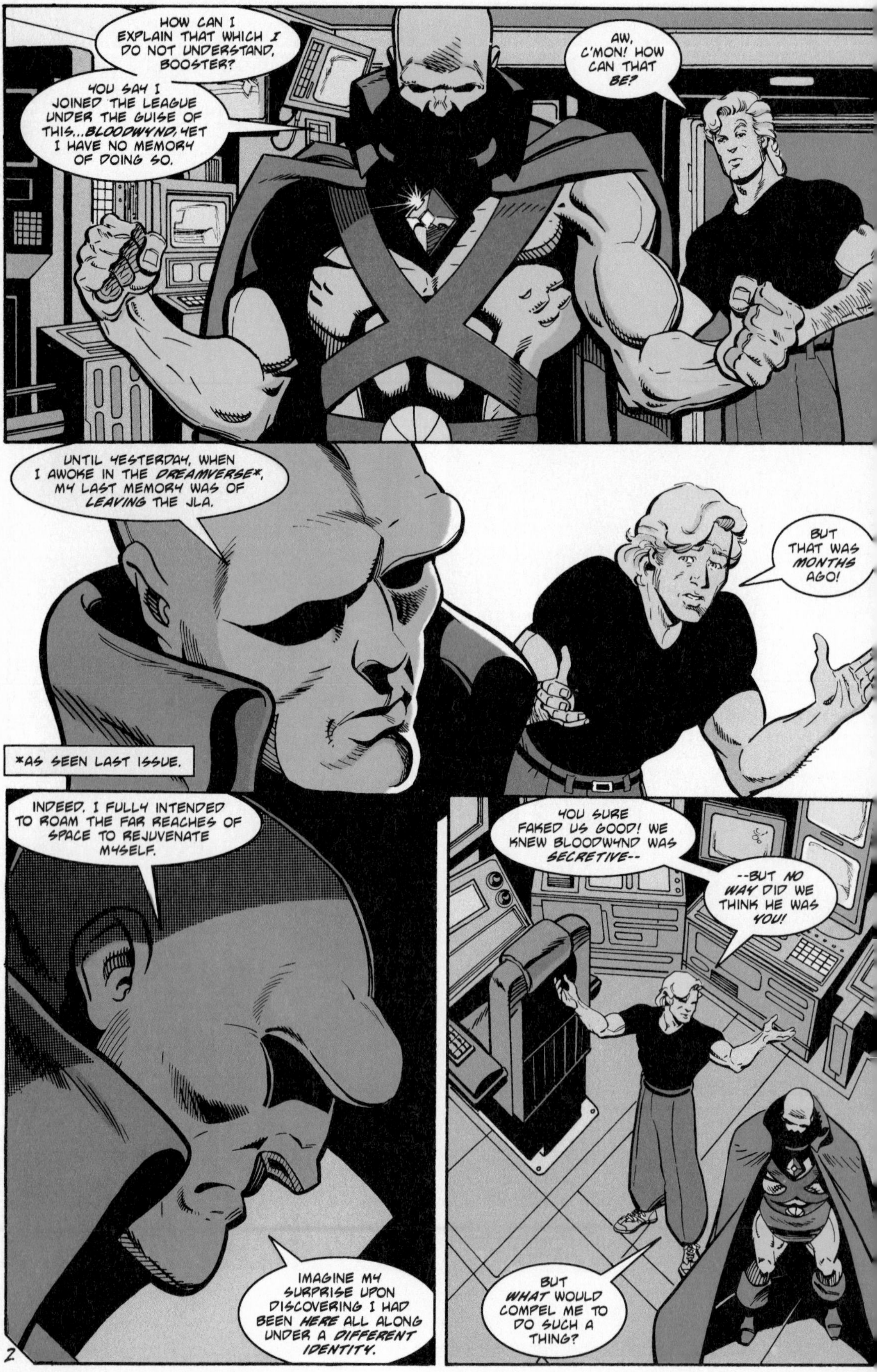
HOW CAN I EXPLAIN THAT WHICH *I* DO NOT UNDERSTAND, BOOSTER?
YOU SAY I JOINED THE LEAGUE UNDER THE GUISE OF THIS...*BLOODWYND*, YET I HAVE NO MEMORY OF DOING SO.
AW, C'MON! HOW CAN THAT *BE?*
UNTIL YESTERDAY, WHEN I AWOKE IN THE *DREAMVERSE**, MY LAST MEMORY WAS OF *LEAVING* THE JLA.
BUT THAT WAS *MONTHS* AGO!
*AS SEEN LAST ISSUE.
INDEED, I FULLY INTENDED TO ROAM THE FAR REACHES OF SPACE TO REJUVENATE MYSELF.
IMAGINE MY SURPRISE UPON DISCOVERING I HAD BEEN *HERE* ALL ALONG UNDER A *DIFFERENT IDENTITY*.
YOU SURE FAKED US GOOD! WE KNEW BLOODWYND WAS *SECRETIVE*--
--BUT *NO WAY* DID WE THINK HE WAS *YOU!*
BUT *WHAT* WOULD COMPEL ME TO DO SUCH A THING?

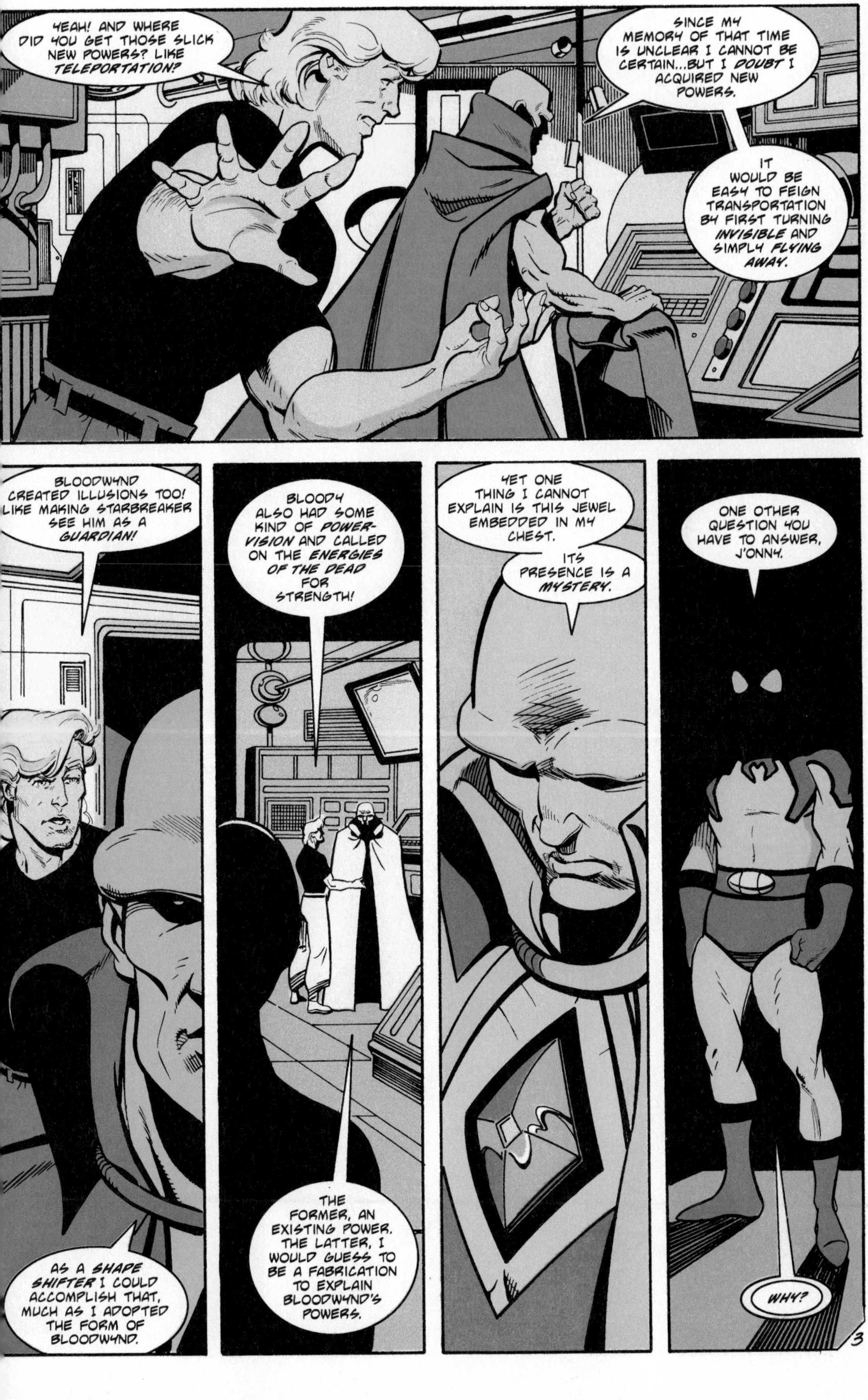
YEAH! AND WHERE DID YOU GET THOSE SLICK NEW POWERS? LIKE *TELEPORTATION?*
SINCE MY MEMORY OF THAT TIME IS UNCLEAR I CANNOT BE CERTAIN...BUT I *DOUBT* I ACQUIRED NEW POWERS.
IT WOULD BE EASY TO FEIGN TRANSPORTATION BY FIRST TURNING *INVISIBLE* AND SIMPLY *FLYING AWAY.*
BLOODWYND CREATED ILLUSIONS TOO! LIKE MAKING STARBREAKER SEE HIM AS A *GUARDIAN!*
AS A *SHAPE SHIFTER* I COULD ACCOMPLISH THAT, MUCH AS I ADOPTED THE FORM OF BLOODWYND.
BLOODY ALSO HAD SOME KIND OF *POWER-VISION* AND CALLED ON THE *ENERGIES OF THE DEAD* FOR STRENGTH!
THE FORMER, AN EXISTING POWER. THE LATTER, I WOULD GUESS TO BE A FABRICATION TO EXPLAIN BLOODWYND'S POWERS.
YET ONE THING I CANNOT EXPLAIN IS THIS JEWEL EMBEDDED IN MY CHEST.
ITS PRESENCE IS A *MYSTERY.*
ONE OTHER QUESTION YOU HAVE TO ANSWER, J'ONNY.
WHY?

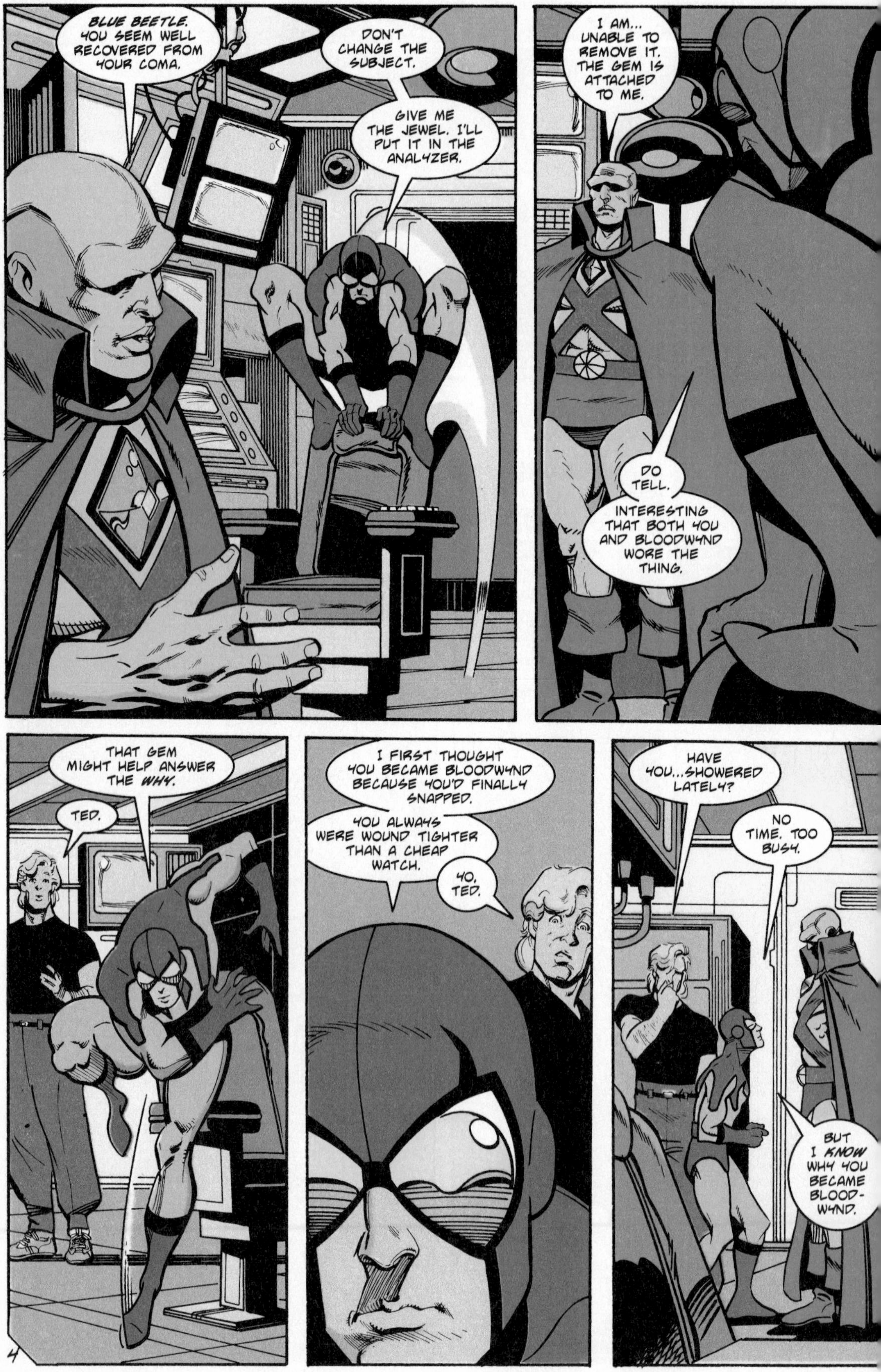
BLUE BEETLE. YOU SEEM WELL RECOVERED FROM YOUR COMA.
DON'T CHANGE THE SUBJECT.
GIVE ME THE JEWEL. I'LL PUT IT IN THE ANALYZER.
I AM... UNABLE TO REMOVE IT. THE GEM IS ATTACHED TO ME.
DO TELL.
INTERESTING THAT BOTH YOU AND BLOODWYND WORE THE THING.
THAT GEM MIGHT HELP ANSWER THE WHY.
TED.
I FIRST THOUGHT YOU BECAME BLOODWYND BECAUSE YOU'D FINALLY SNAPPED.
YOU ALWAYS WERE WOUND TIGHTER THAN A CHEAP WATCH.
YO, TED.
HAVE YOU...SHOWERED LATELY?
NO TIME. TOO BUSY.
BUT I KNOW WHY YOU BECAME BLOOD-WYND.

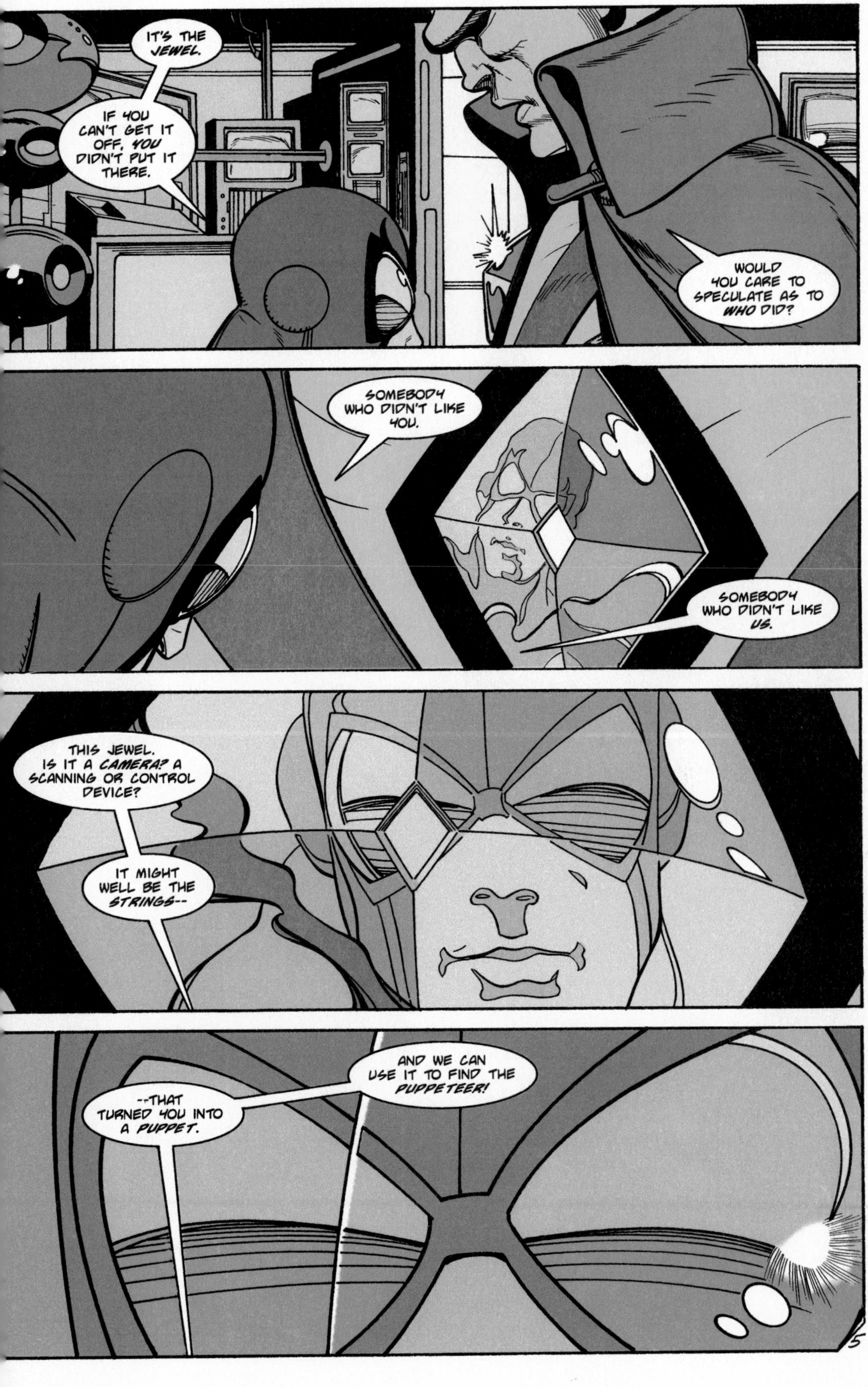
IT'S THE JEWEL.
IF YOU CAN'T GET IT OFF, YOU DIDN'T PUT IT THERE.
WOULD YOU CARE TO SPECULATE AS TO WHO DID?
SOMEBODY WHO DIDN'T LIKE YOU.
SOMEBODY WHO DIDN'T LIKE US.
THIS JEWEL. IS IT A CAMERA? A SCANNING OR CONTROL DEVICE?
IT MIGHT WELL BE THE STRINGS--
--THAT TURNED YOU INTO A PUPPET.
AND WE CAN USE IT TO FIND THE PUPPETEER!

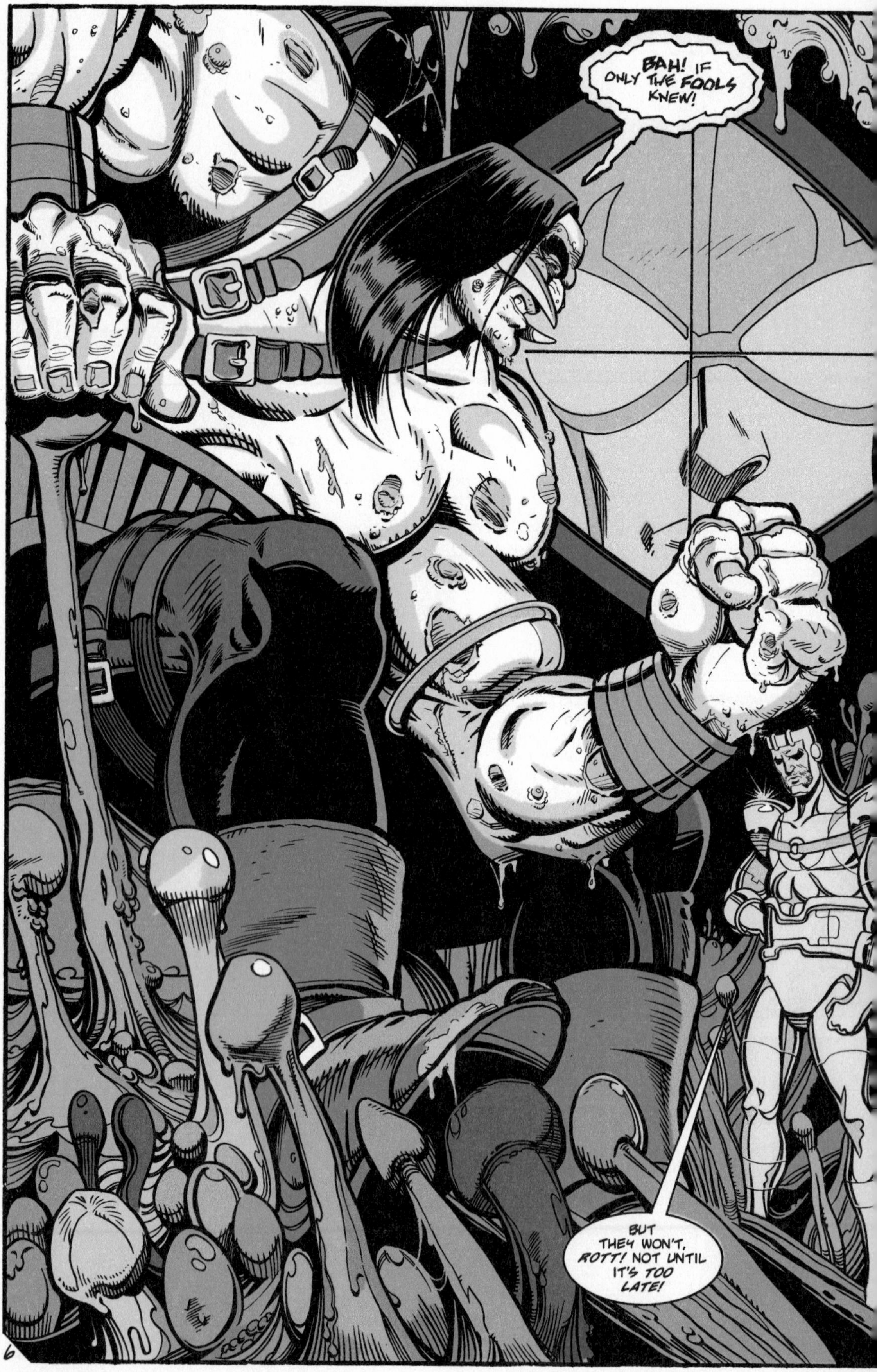
BAH! IF ONLY THE FOOLS KNEW!
BUT THEY WON'T, ROTT! NOT UNTIL IT'S TOO LATE!

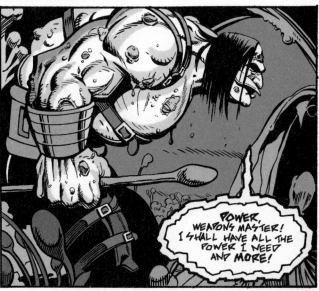

THEY *WILL* COME, THOUGH, ROTT. AND WHEN THEY DO--

--I'LL HAVE WHAT I WANT!

POWER, WEAPONS MASTER! I SHALL HAVE ALL THE POWER I NEED AND *MORE!*

YOU'VE BEEN *IMPRISONED* HERE A VERY LONG TIME, ROTT. IF I HADN'T STUMBLED ON THIS PLACE YOU'D *STILL* HAVE NO HOPE!

INFERNAL DIMENSION-HOPPER! IF YOU WERE HALF AS POWERFUL AS YOU THOUGHT--

--YOU WOULD FREE ME!

AH, BUT I *CAN'T!* THE FORCES THAT BIND THIS PLACE ARE FAR STRONGER THAN MINE.

YET I'LL DO ALL I CAN TO ASSIST YOU, ROTT. SO LONG AS THE JUSTICE LEAGUE PAYS THE PRICE IN THE PROCESS.

7

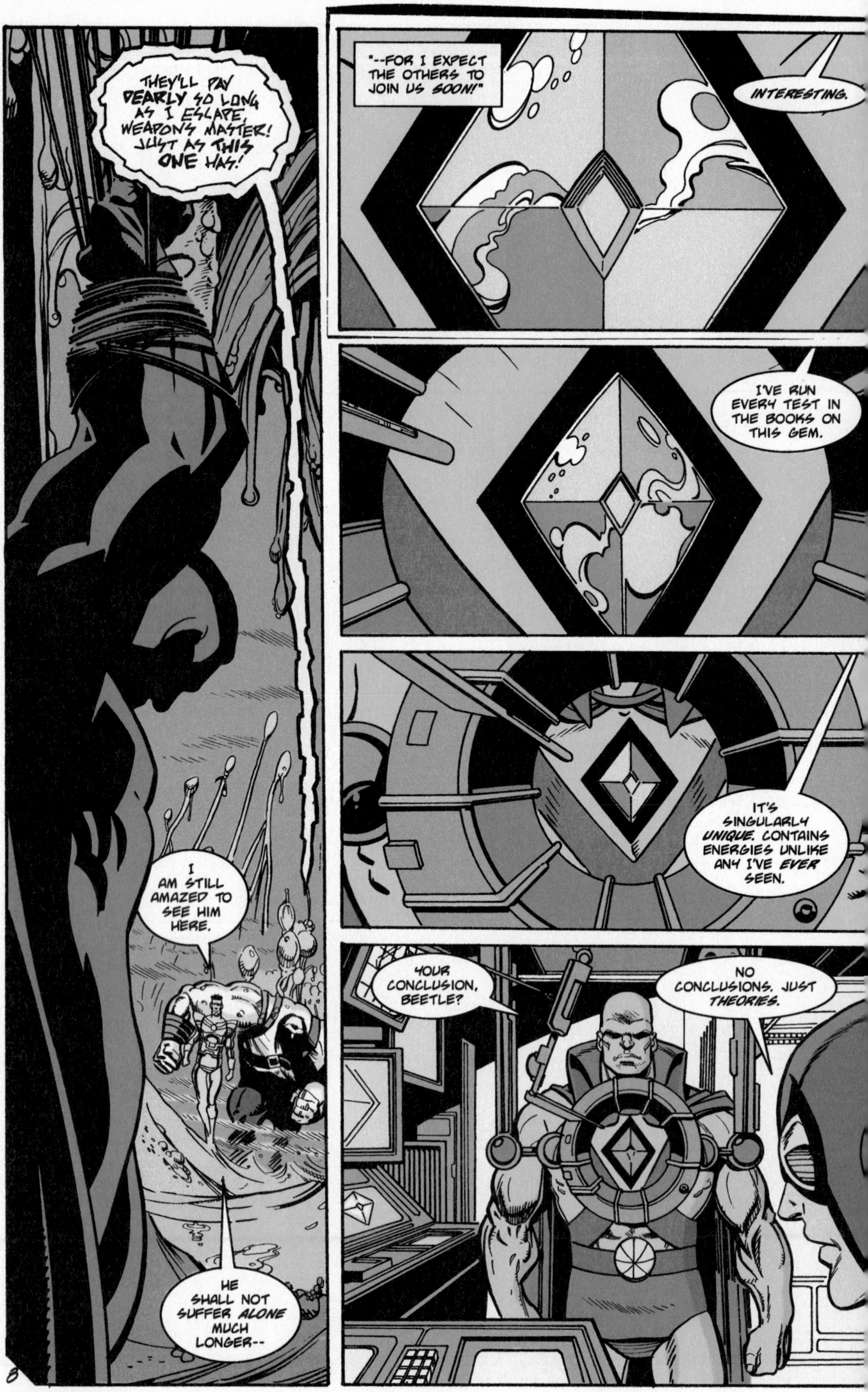
THEY'LL PAY DEARLY SO LONG AS I ESCAPE, WEAPONS MASTER! JUST AS THIS ONE HAS!
I AM STILL AMAZED TO SEE HIM HERE.
HE SHALL NOT SUFFER ALONE MUCH LONGER--
"--FOR I EXPECT THE OTHERS TO JOIN US SOON!"
INTERESTING.
I'VE RUN EVERY TEST IN THE BOOKS ON THIS GEM.
IT'S SINGULARLY UNIQUE. CONTAINS ENERGIES UNLIKE ANY I'VE EVER SEEN.
YOUR CONCLUSION, BEETLE?
NO CONCLUSIONS. JUST THEORIES.

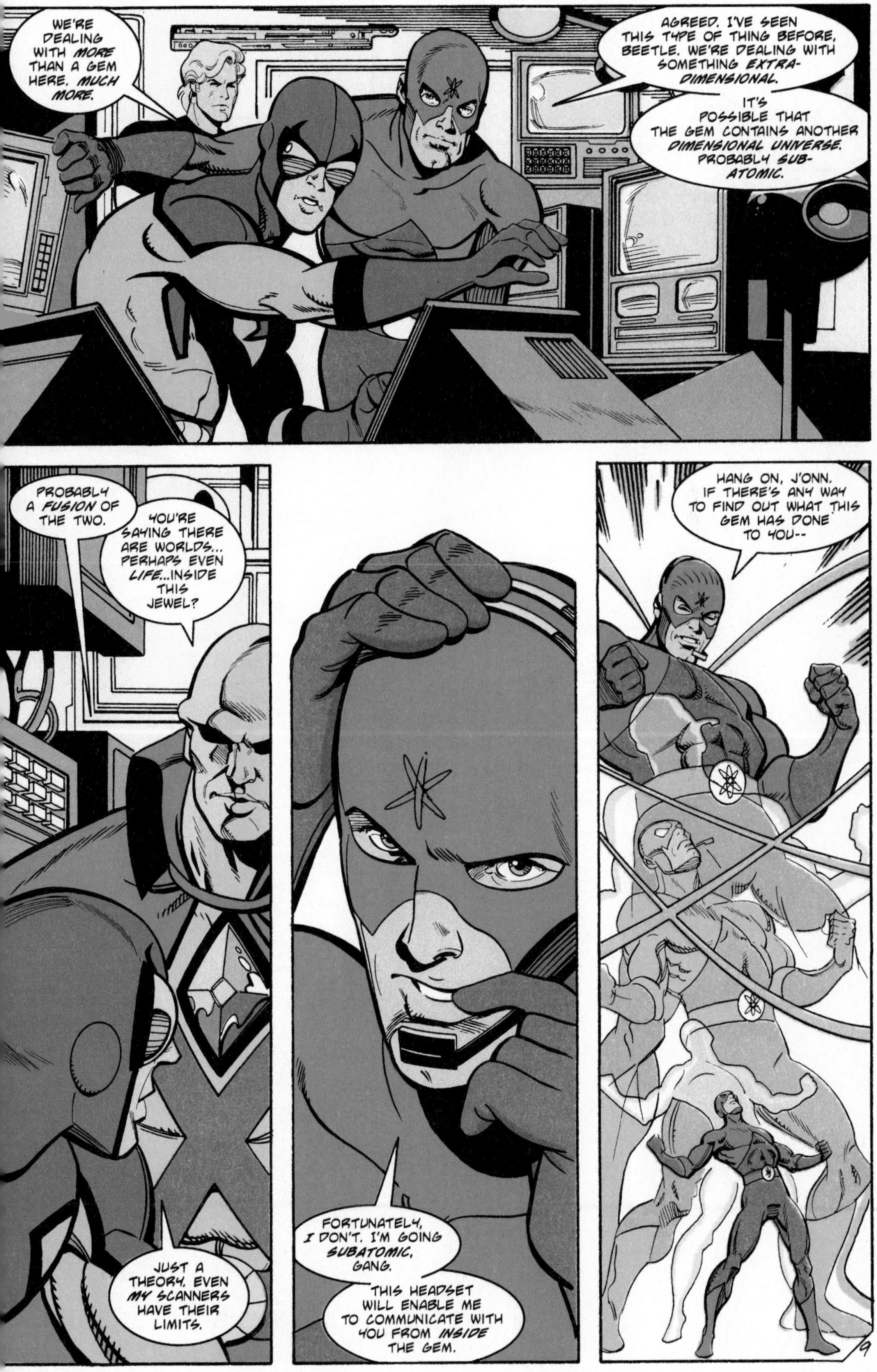
WE'RE DEALING WITH MORE THAN A GEM HERE. MUCH MORE.
AGREED. I'VE SEEN THIS TYPE OF THING BEFORE, BEETLE. WE'RE DEALING WITH SOMETHING EXTRA-DIMENSIONAL.
IT'S POSSIBLE THAT THE GEM CONTAINS ANOTHER DIMENSIONAL UNIVERSE. PROBABLY SUB-ATOMIC.
PROBABLY A FUSION OF THE TWO.
YOU'RE SAYING THERE ARE WORLDS... PERHAPS EVEN LIFE...INSIDE THIS JEWEL?
JUST A THEORY. EVEN MY SCANNERS HAVE THEIR LIMITS.
FORTUNATELY, I DON'T. I'M GOING SUBATOMIC, GANG.
THIS HEADSET WILL ENABLE ME TO COMMUNICATE WITH YOU FROM INSIDE THE GEM.
HANG ON, J'ONN. IF THERE'S ANY WAY TO FIND OUT WHAT THIS GEM HAS DONE TO YOU--
9

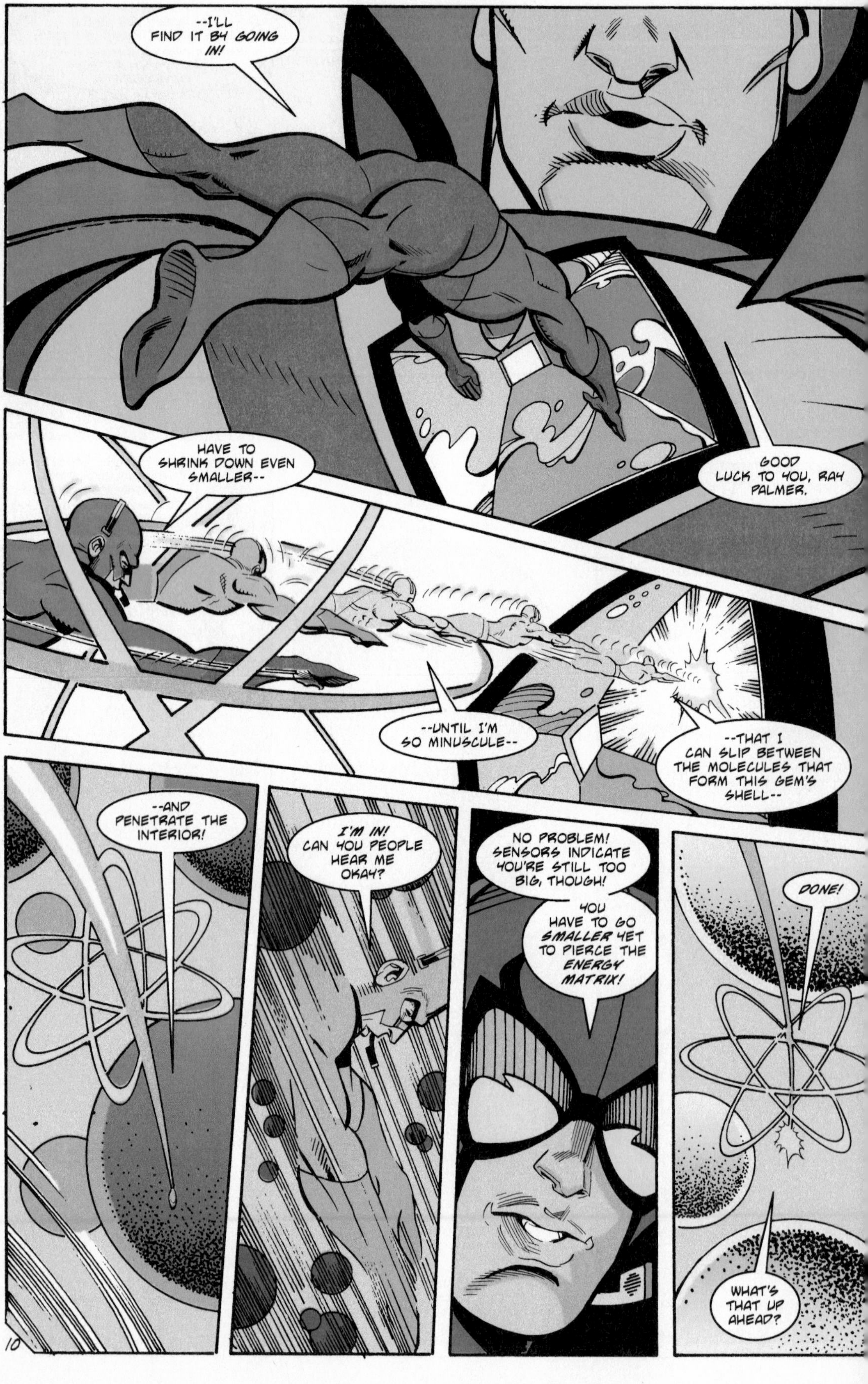
--I'LL FIND IT BY GOING IN!
HAVE TO SHRINK DOWN EVEN SMALLER--
GOOD LUCK TO YOU, RAY PALMER.
--UNTIL I'M SO MINUSCULE--
--THAT I CAN SLIP BETWEEN THE MOLECULES THAT FORM THIS GEM'S SHELL--
--AND PENETRATE THE INTERIOR!
I'M IN! CAN YOU PEOPLE HEAR ME OKAY?
NO PROBLEM! SENSORS INDICATE YOU'RE STILL TOO BIG, THOUGH!
YOU HAVE TO GO SMALLER YET TO PIERCE THE ENERGY MATRIX!
DONE!
WHAT'S THAT UP AHEAD?

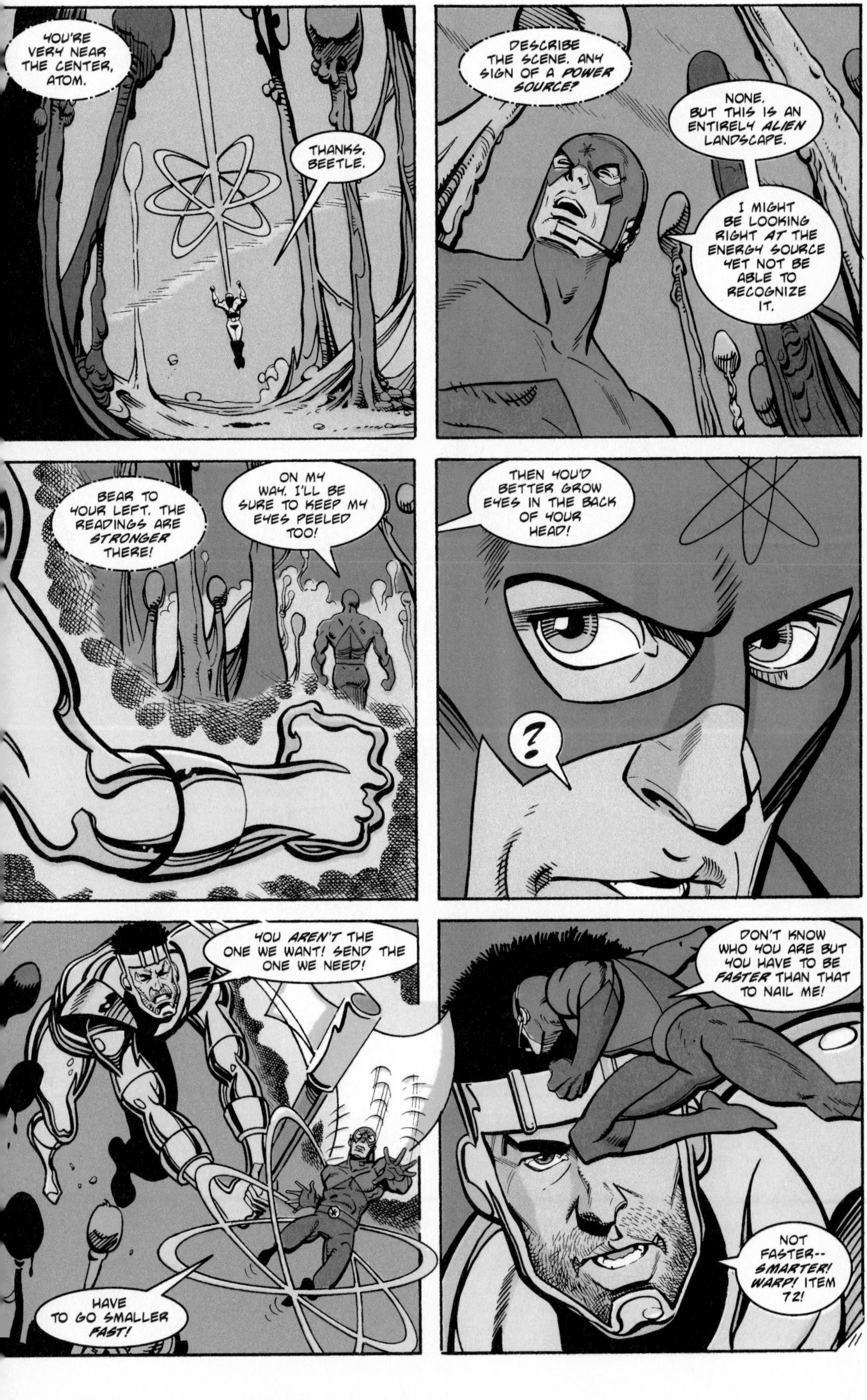
YOU'RE VERY NEAR THE CENTER, ATOM.
THANKS, BEETLE.
DESCRIBE THE SCENE. ANY SIGN OF A POWER SOURCE?
NONE. BUT THIS IS AN ENTIRELY ALIEN LANDSCAPE.
I MIGHT BE LOOKING RIGHT AT THE ENERGY SOURCE YET NOT BE ABLE TO RECOGNIZE IT.
BEAR TO YOUR LEFT. THE READINGS ARE STRONGER THERE!
ON MY WAY. I'LL BE SURE TO KEEP MY EYES PEELED TOO!
THEN YOU'D BETTER GROW EYES IN THE BACK OF YOUR HEAD!
?
YOU AREN'T THE ONE WE WANT! SEND THE ONE WE NEED!
HAVE TO GO SMALLER FAST!
DON'T KNOW WHO YOU ARE BUT YOU HAVE TO BE FASTER THAN THAT TO NAIL ME!
NOT FASTER-- SMARTER! WARP! ITEM 72!
11

THIS IS A *STASIS SQUARE*, HUMAN. I STOLE THIS FROM THE *WEAPONERS OF QWARD* QUITE SOME TIME AGO.

YAAH!

ATOM! WHAT'S HAPPENING THERE? *ATOM?!*

WHAT'S *THIS?* A *HEAD-SET?*

PAINFUL BUT EFFECTIVE AT HOLDING YOU *STILL.*

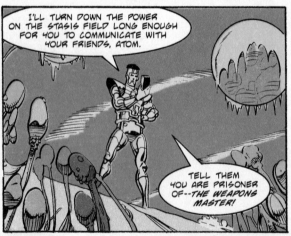

I'LL TURN DOWN THE POWER ON THE *STASIS FIELD* LONG ENOUGH FOR YOU TO COMMUNICATE WITH YOUR FRIENDS, ATOM.

TELL THEM YOU ARE PRISONER OF--*THE WEAPONS MASTER!*

YOU HEAR THAT, BEETLE? THIS GUY TALKS...LIKE HE *KNOWS* YOU!

HE OBVIOUSLY... EXPECTED SOMEONE OTHER THAN ME TO COME!

WE KNOW HIM ALL RIGHT. WE BEAT HIM BEFORE* AND WE CAN DO IT AGAIN.

I DON'T THINK SO, BLUE BEETLE. I'M SPEAKING INTO YOUR DIMINUTIVE FRIEND'S COMMUNICATOR TO LET YOU KNOW--

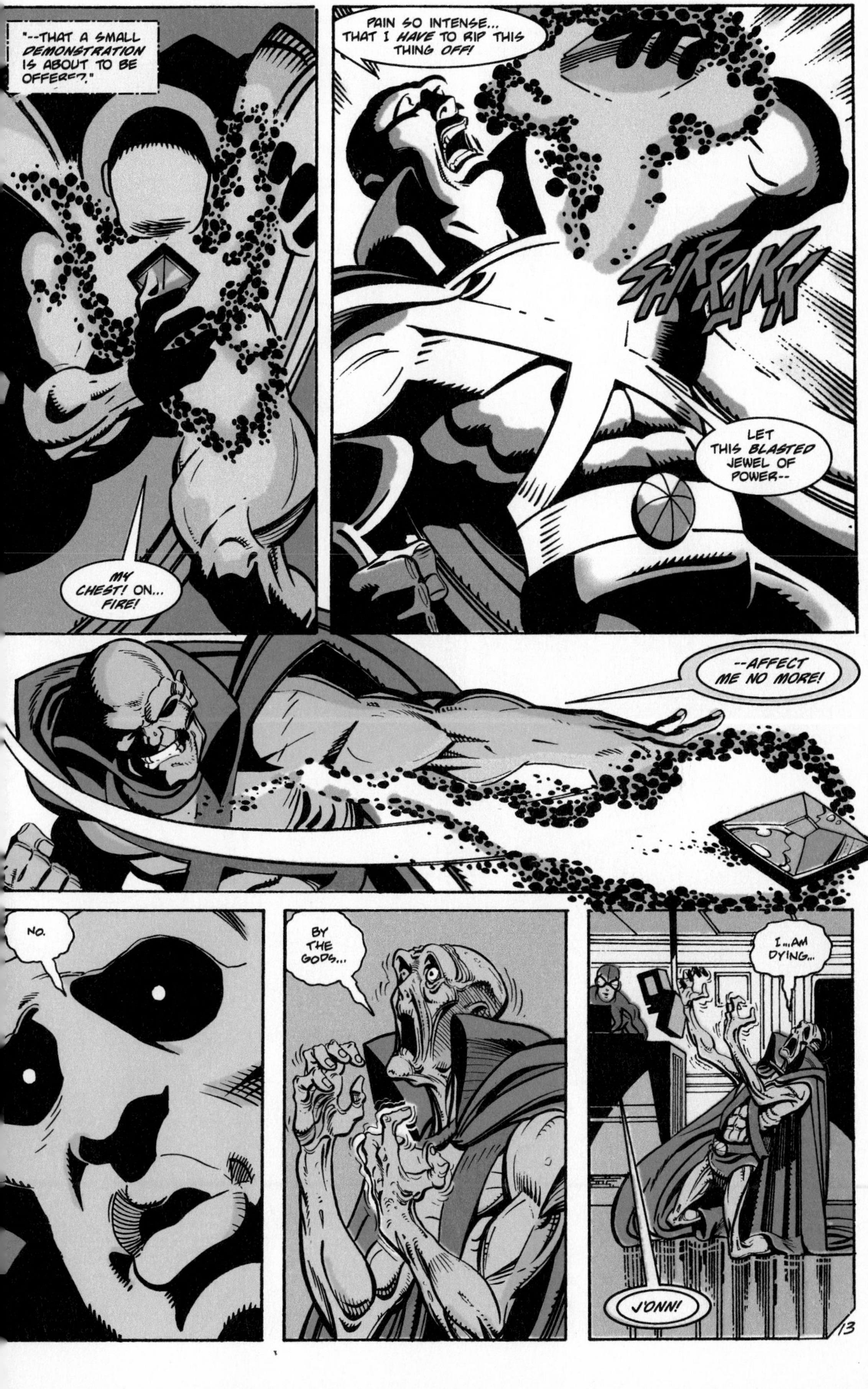
"--THAT A SMALL DEMONSTRATION IS ABOUT TO BE OFFERED?."
MY CHEST! ON... FIRE!
PAIN SO INTENSE... THAT I HAVE TO RIP THIS THING OFF!
SHRAAKK
LET THIS BLASTED JEWEL OF POWER--
--AFFECT ME NO MORE!
NO.
BY THE GODS...
I...AM DYING...
J'ONN!

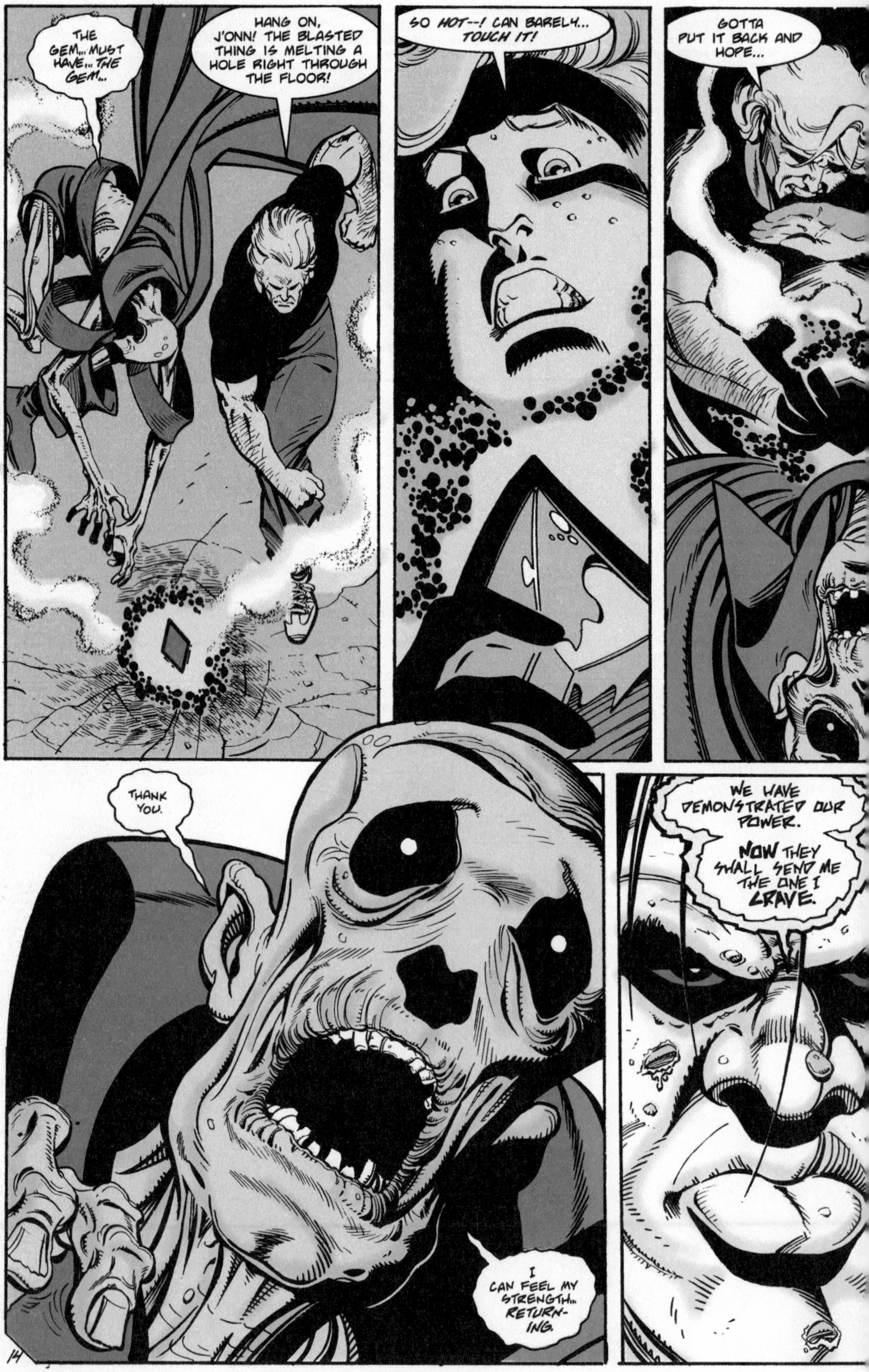

THE GEM... MUST HAVE... THE GEM...
HANG ON, J'ONN! THE BLASTED THING IS MELTING A HOLE RIGHT THROUGH THE FLOOR!
SO HOT--! CAN BARELY... TOUCH IT!
GOTTA PUT IT BACK AND HOPE...
THANK YOU.
I CAN FEEL MY STRENGTH... RETURN-ING.
WE HAVE DEMONSTRATED OUR POWER.
NOW THEY SHALL SEND ME THE ONE I CRAVE.

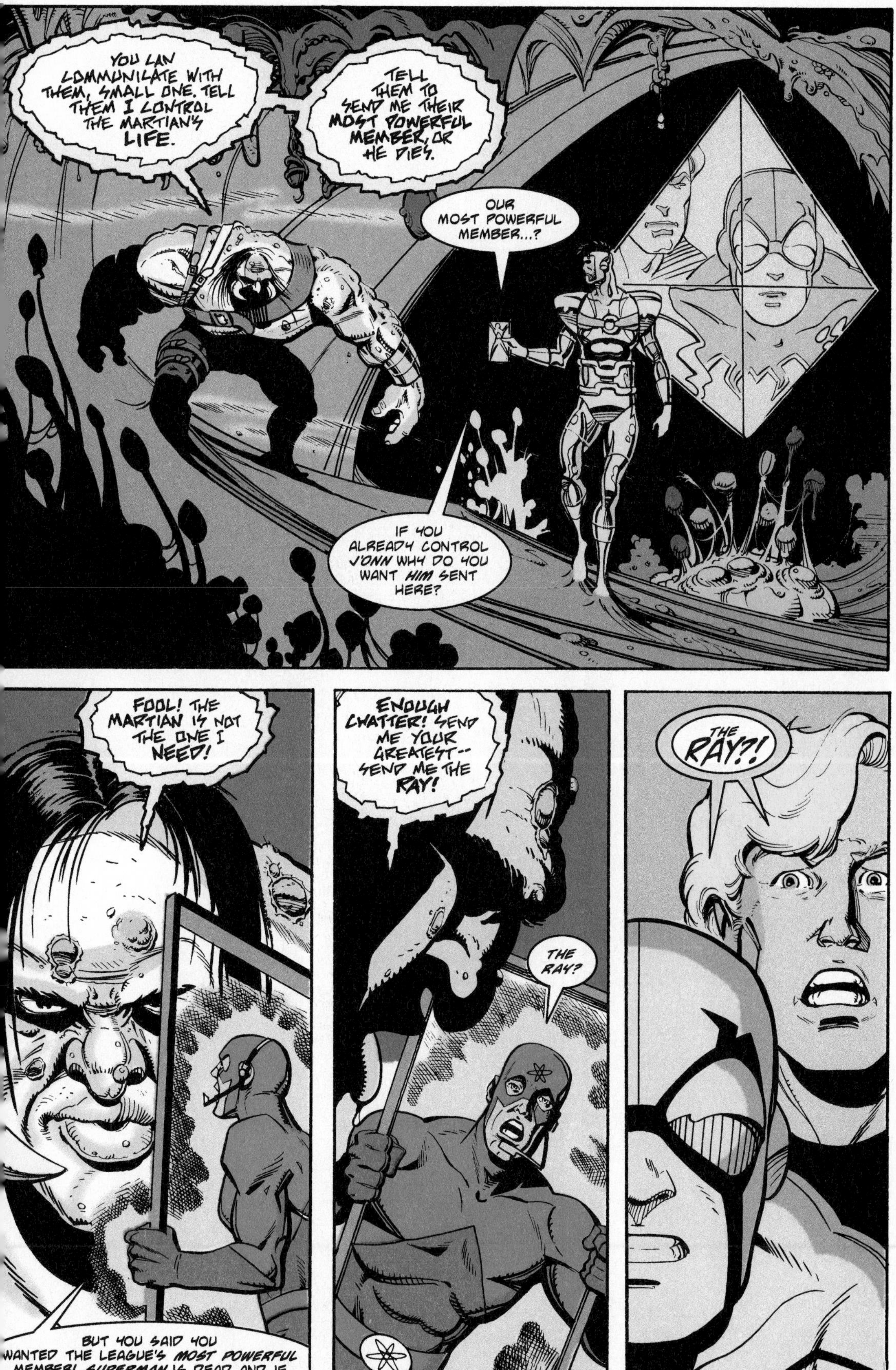
YOU CAN COMMUNICATE WITH THEM, SMALL ONE. TELL THEM I CONTROL THE MARTIAN'S LIFE.
TELL THEM TO SEND ME THEIR MOST POWERFUL MEMBER, OR HE DIES.
OUR MOST POWERFUL MEMBER...?
IF YOU ALREADY CONTROL J'ONN WHY DO YOU WANT HIM SENT HERE?
FOOL! THE MARTIAN IS NOT THE ONE I NEED!
BUT YOU SAID YOU WANTED THE LEAGUE'S MOST POWERFUL MEMBER! SUPERMAN IS DEAD AND IF YOU DON'T MEAN J'ONN...
ENOUGH CHATTER! SEND ME YOUR GREATEST-- SEND ME THE RAY!
THE RAY?
THE RAY?!

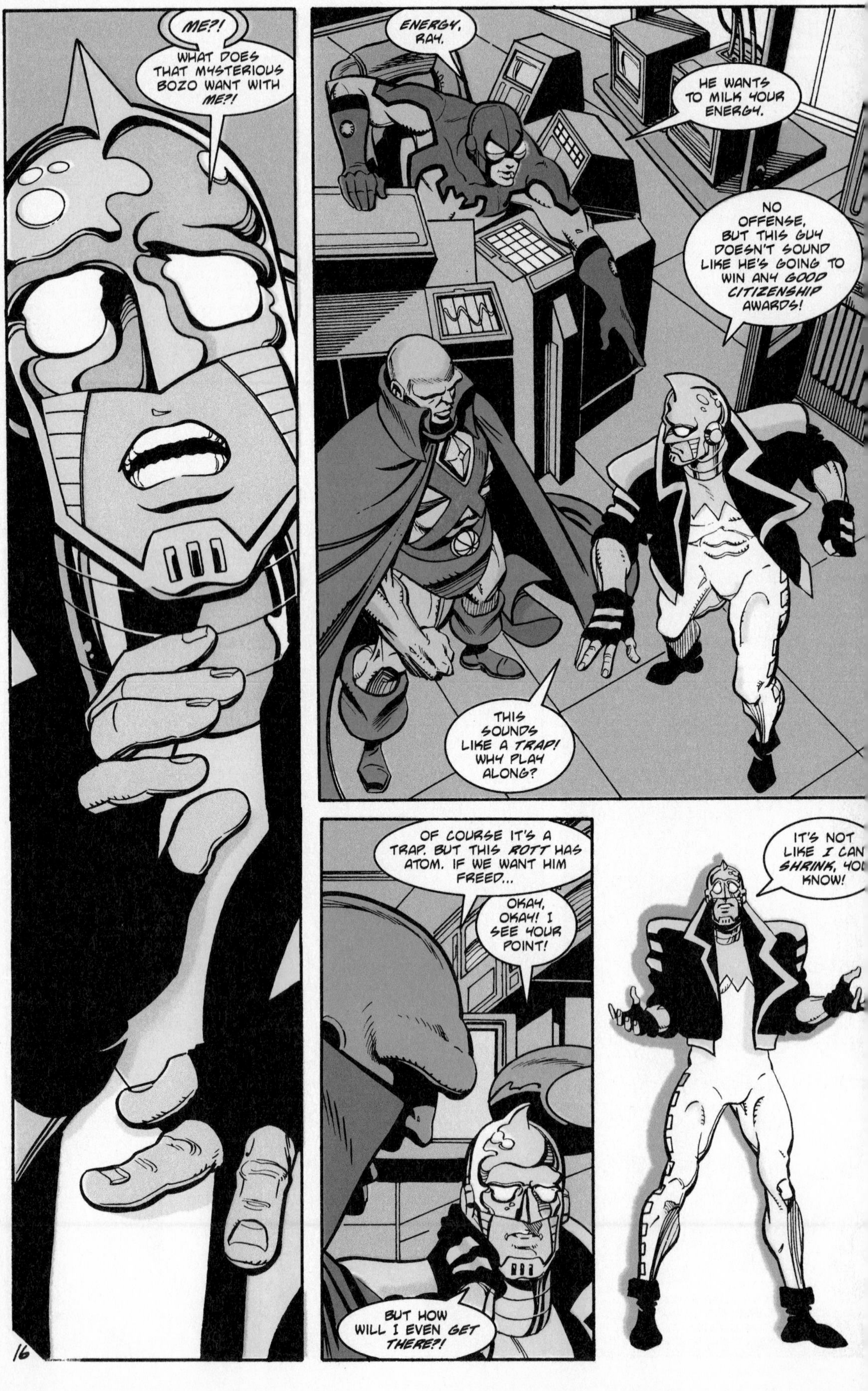
ME?! WHAT DOES THAT MYSTERIOUS BOZO WANT WITH ME?!
ENERGY, RAY.
HE WANTS TO MILK YOUR ENERGY.
NO OFFENSE, BUT THIS GUY DOESN'T SOUND LIKE HE'S GOING TO WIN ANY GOOD CITIZENSHIP AWARDS!
THIS SOUNDS LIKE A TRAP! WHY PLAY ALONG?
OF COURSE IT'S A TRAP. BUT THIS ROTT HAS ATOM. IF WE WANT HIM FREED...
OKAY, OKAY! I SEE YOUR POINT!
BUT HOW WILL I EVEN GET THERE?!
IT'S NOT LIKE I CAN SHRINK, YO KNOW!

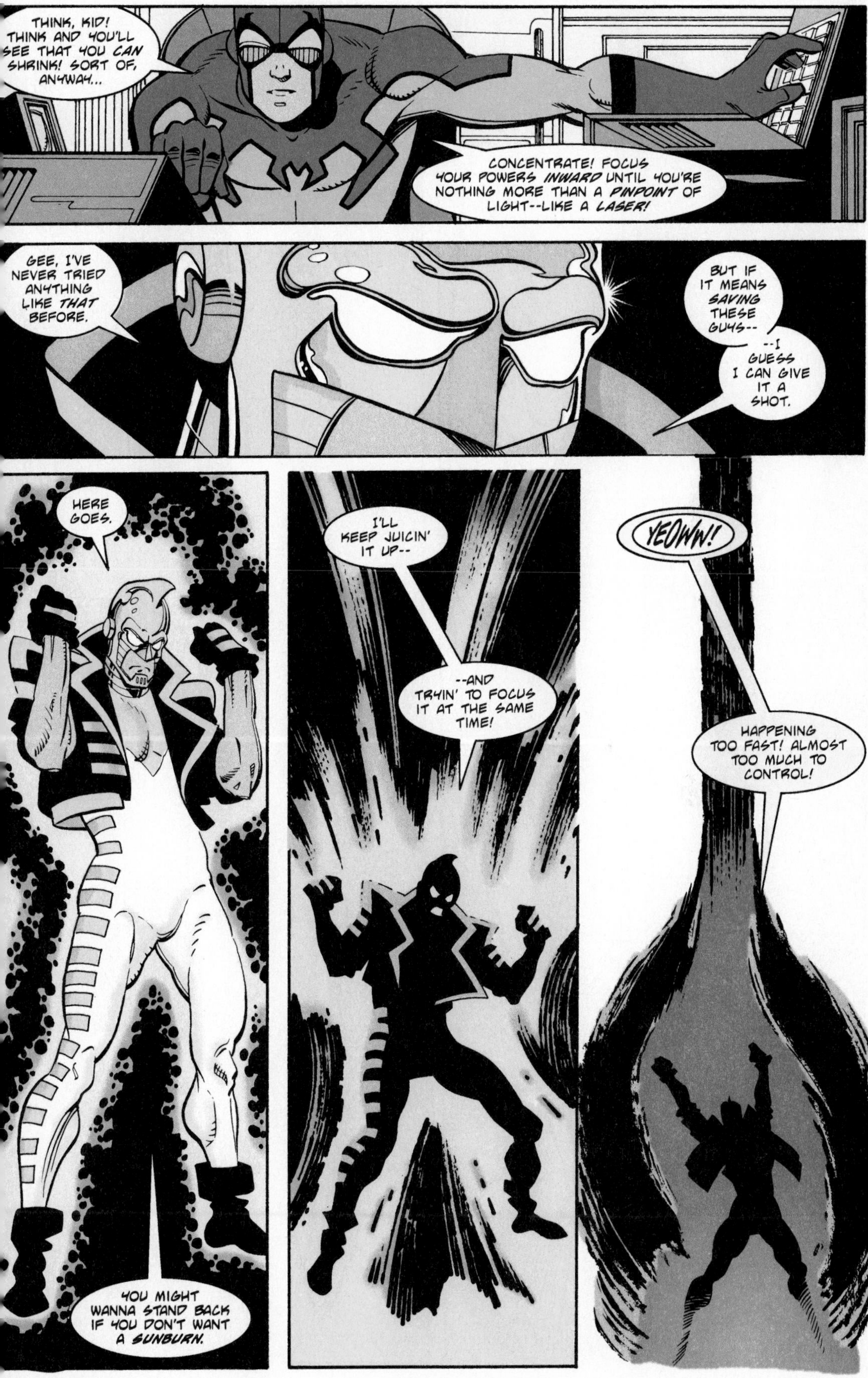

THINK, KID! THINK AND YOU'LL SEE THAT YOU CAN SHRINK! SORT OF, ANYWAY...
CONCENTRATE! FOCUS YOUR POWERS INWARD UNTIL YOU'RE NOTHING MORE THAN A PINPOINT OF LIGHT--LIKE A LASER!
GEE, I'VE NEVER TRIED ANYTHING LIKE THAT BEFORE.
BUT IF IT MEANS SAVING THESE GUYS--
--I GUESS I CAN GIVE IT A SHOT.
HERE GOES.
YOU MIGHT WANNA STAND BACK IF YOU DON'T WANT A SUNBURN.
I'LL KEEP JUICIN' IT UP--
--AND TRYIN' TO FOCUS IT AT THE SAME TIME!
YEOWW!
HAPPENING TOO FAST! ALMOST TOO MUCH TO CONTROL!

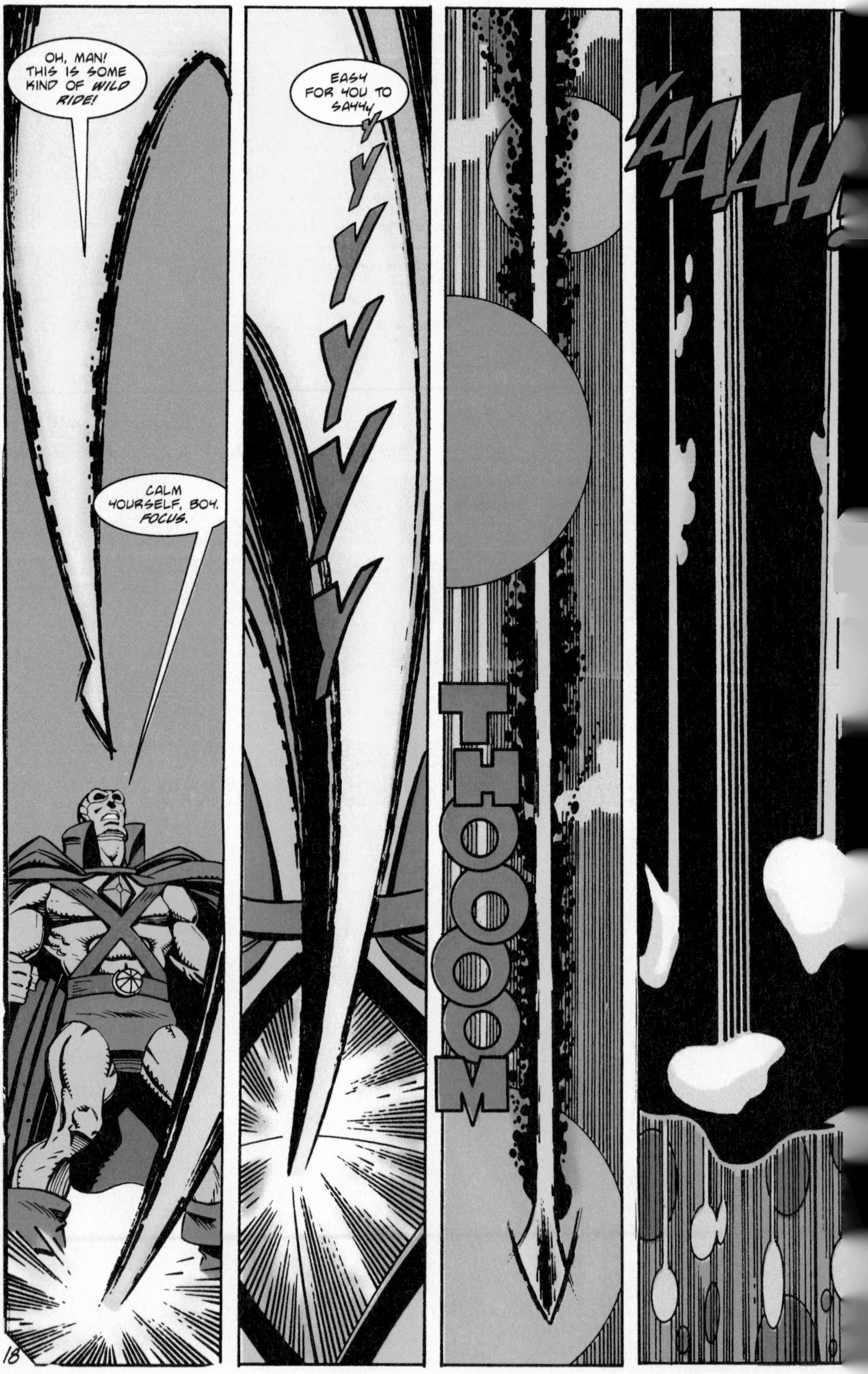
OH, MAN! THIS IS SOME KIND OF WILD RIDE!
CALM YOURSELF, BOY. FOCUS.
EASY FOR YOU TO SAYYY
THOOOOM
YAAAH

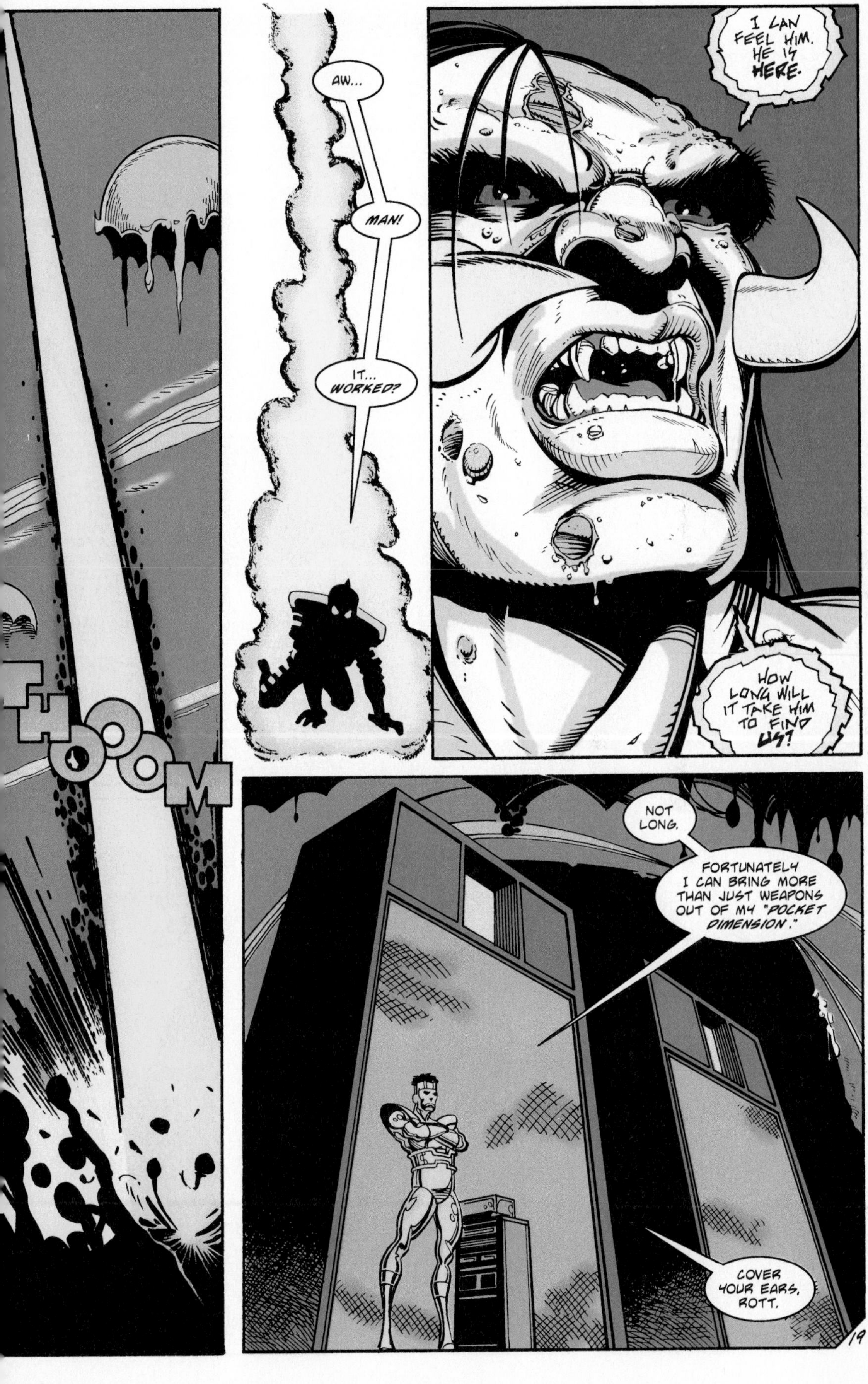
THOOOOM
AW...
MAN!
IT... WORKED?
I CAN FEEL HIM. HE IS HERE.
HOW LONG WILL IT TAKE HIM TO FIND US?
NOT LONG.
FORTUNATELY I CAN BRING MORE THAN JUST WEAPONS OUT OF MY "POCKET DIMENSION."
COVER YOUR EARS, ROTT.

PLAY

CLICK

SHUGGA-BOOM

SHUGGA SHUGGA-BOOOM

WHAT THE HECK IS *THAT?*

MUSIC? HERE?

SOUNDS LIKE THAT *N.I.N.* STUFF JENNIFER PLAYED FOR ME!

COOL.

IF SOMEBODY WANTED MY ATTEN- TION--

--THIS IS A PRETTY GOOD WAY TO GET IT!

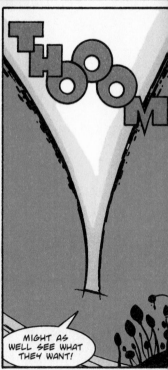

THOOOM

MIGHT AS WELL SEE WHAT THEY WANT!

20

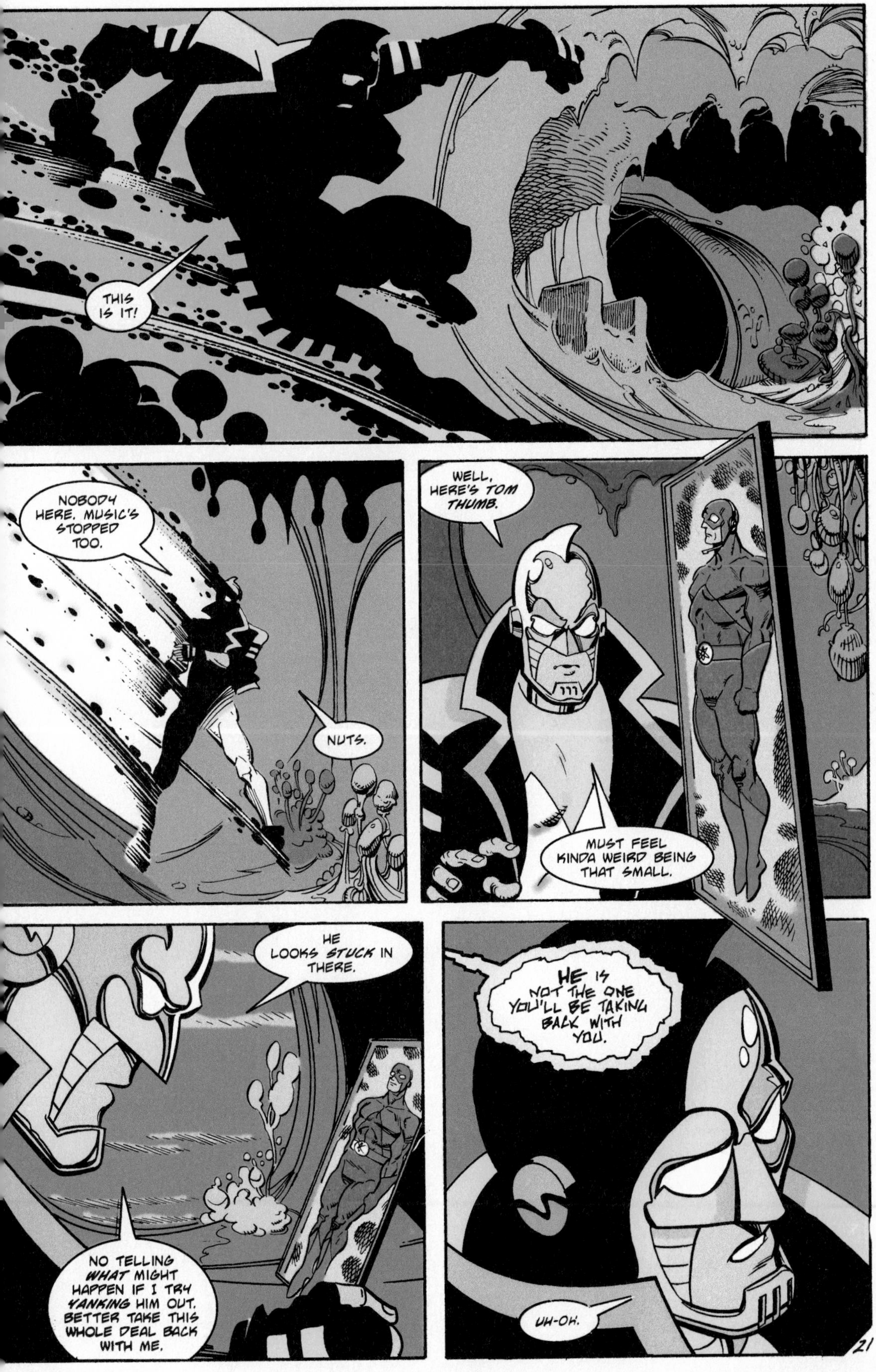
THIS IS IT!
NOBODY HERE. MUSIC'S STOPPED TOO.
NUTS.
WELL, HERE'S TOM THUMB.
MUST FEEL KINDA WEIRD BEING THAT SMALL.
HE LOOKS STUCK IN THERE.
NO TELLING WHAT MIGHT HAPPEN IF I TRY YANKING HIM OUT. BETTER TAKE THIS WHOLE DEAL BACK WITH ME.
HE IS NOT THE ONE YOU'LL BE TAKING BACK WITH YOU.
UH-OH.

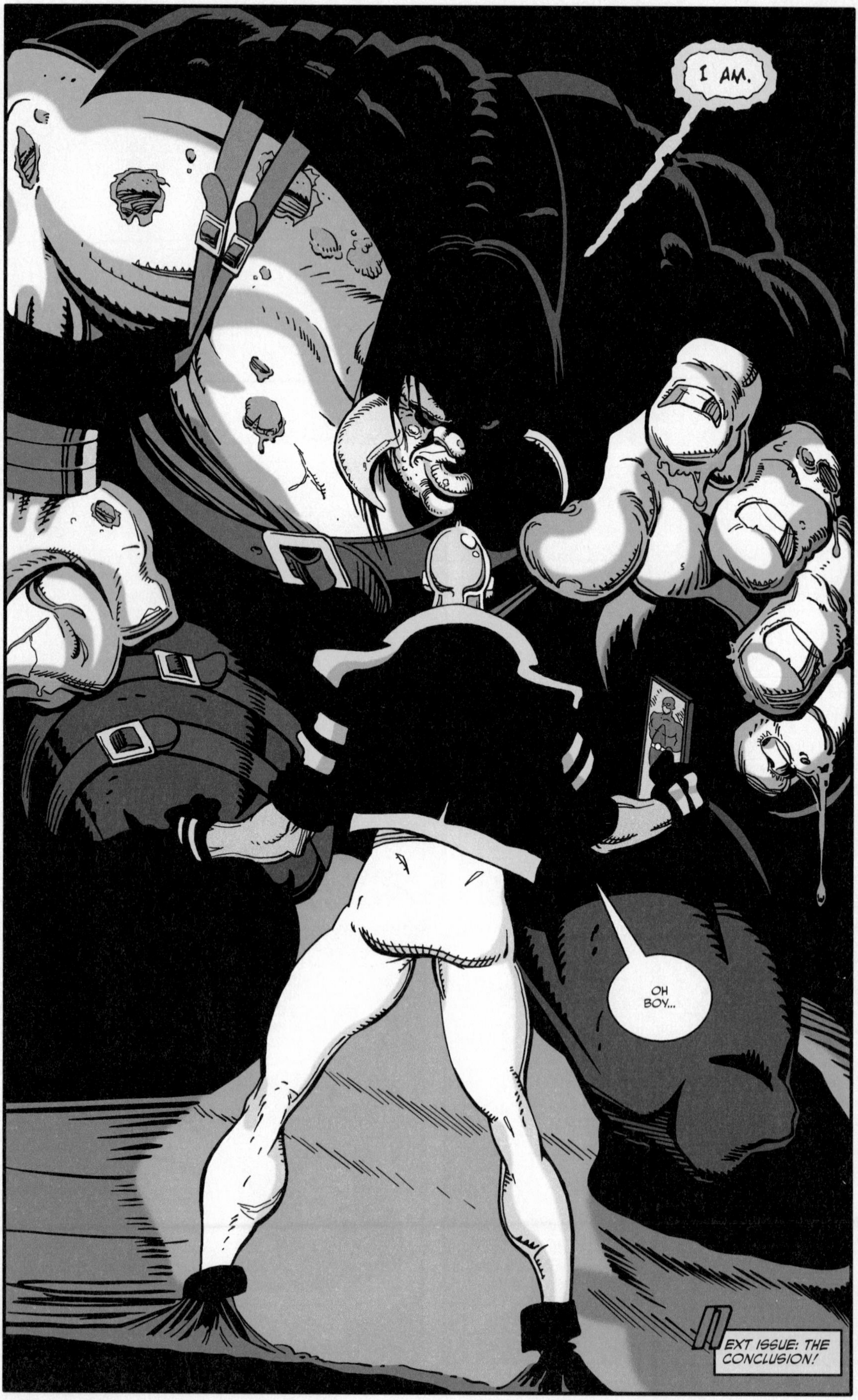
I AM.
OH BOY...
NEXT ISSUE: THE CONCLUSION!

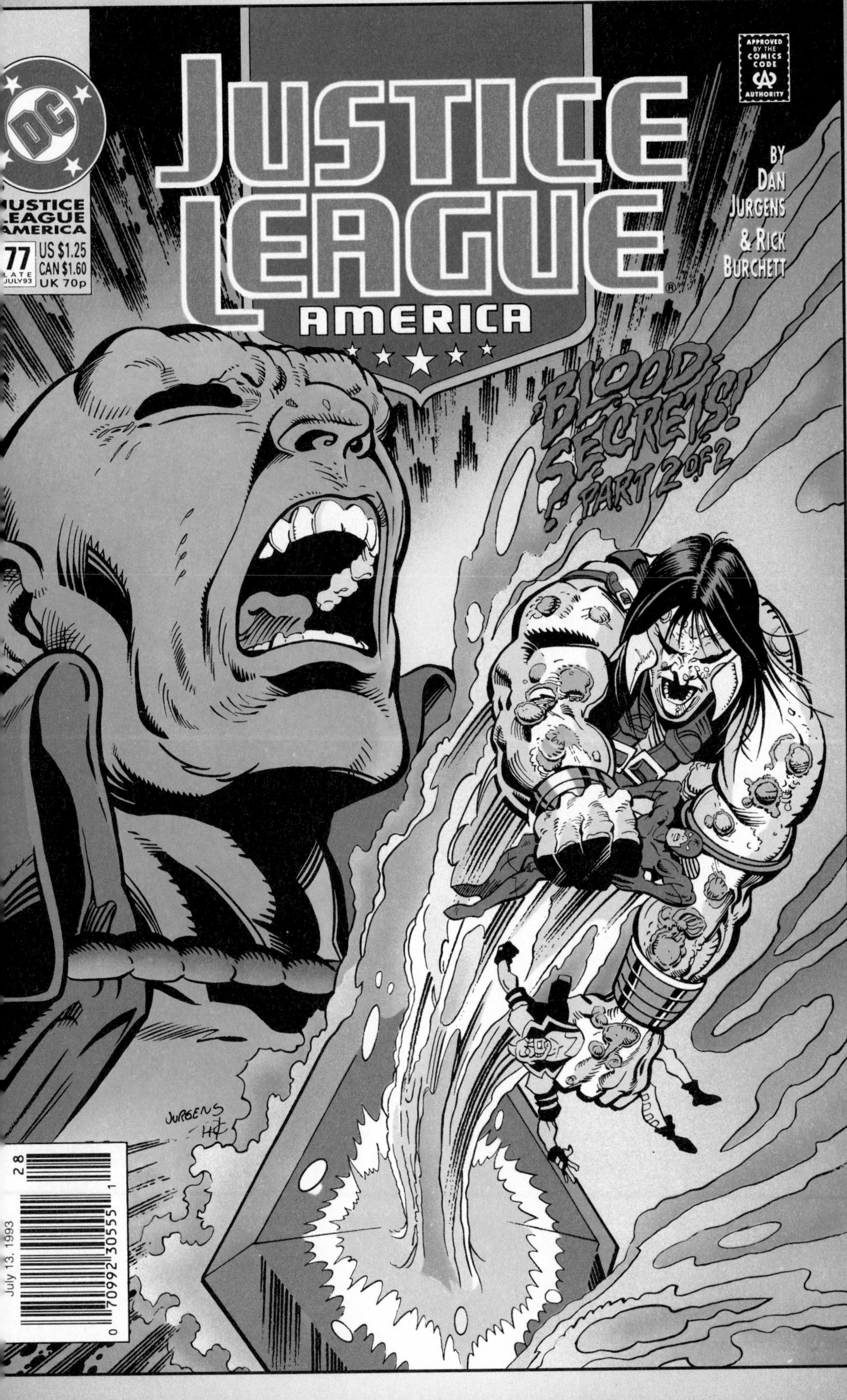

JUSTICE LEAGUE AMERICA
JUSTICE LEAGUE AMERICA
77
LATE JULY93
US $1.25
CAN $1.60
UK 70p
APPROVED BY THE COMICS CODE AUTHORITY
BY DAN JURGENS & RICK BURCHETT
"BLOOD SECRETS!" PART 2 OF 2
JURGENS
July 13, 1993

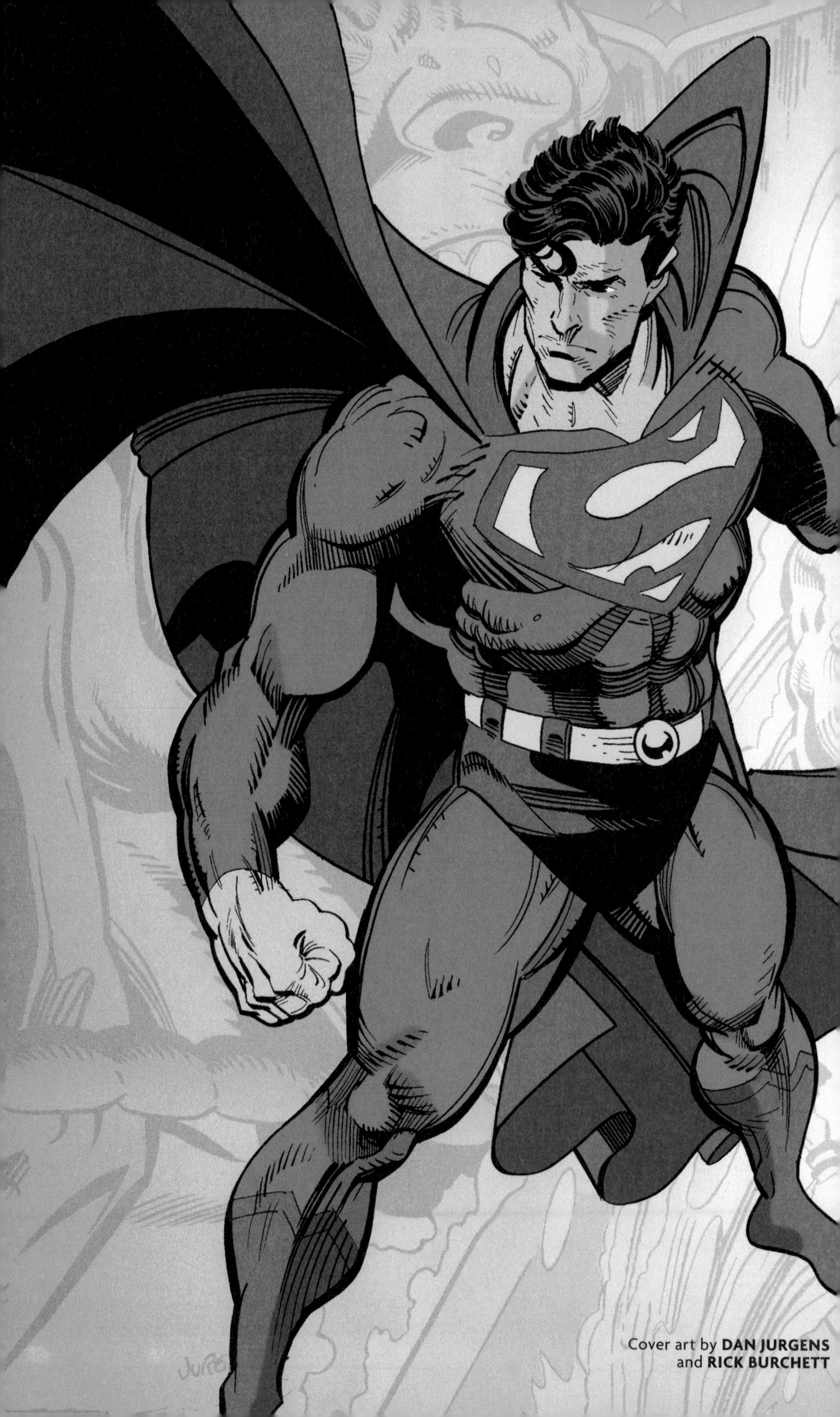

Cover art by **DAN JURGENS**
and **RICK BURCHETT**

BLOOD SECRETS
PART TWO
UNG!
THIS...IS NOT FUN!
DAN JURGENS
story & art design
RICK BURCHETT
art
WILLIE SCHUBERT
letters
GENE D'ANGELO
colors
RUBEN DIAZ
assistant editor
BRIAN AUGUSTYN
editor

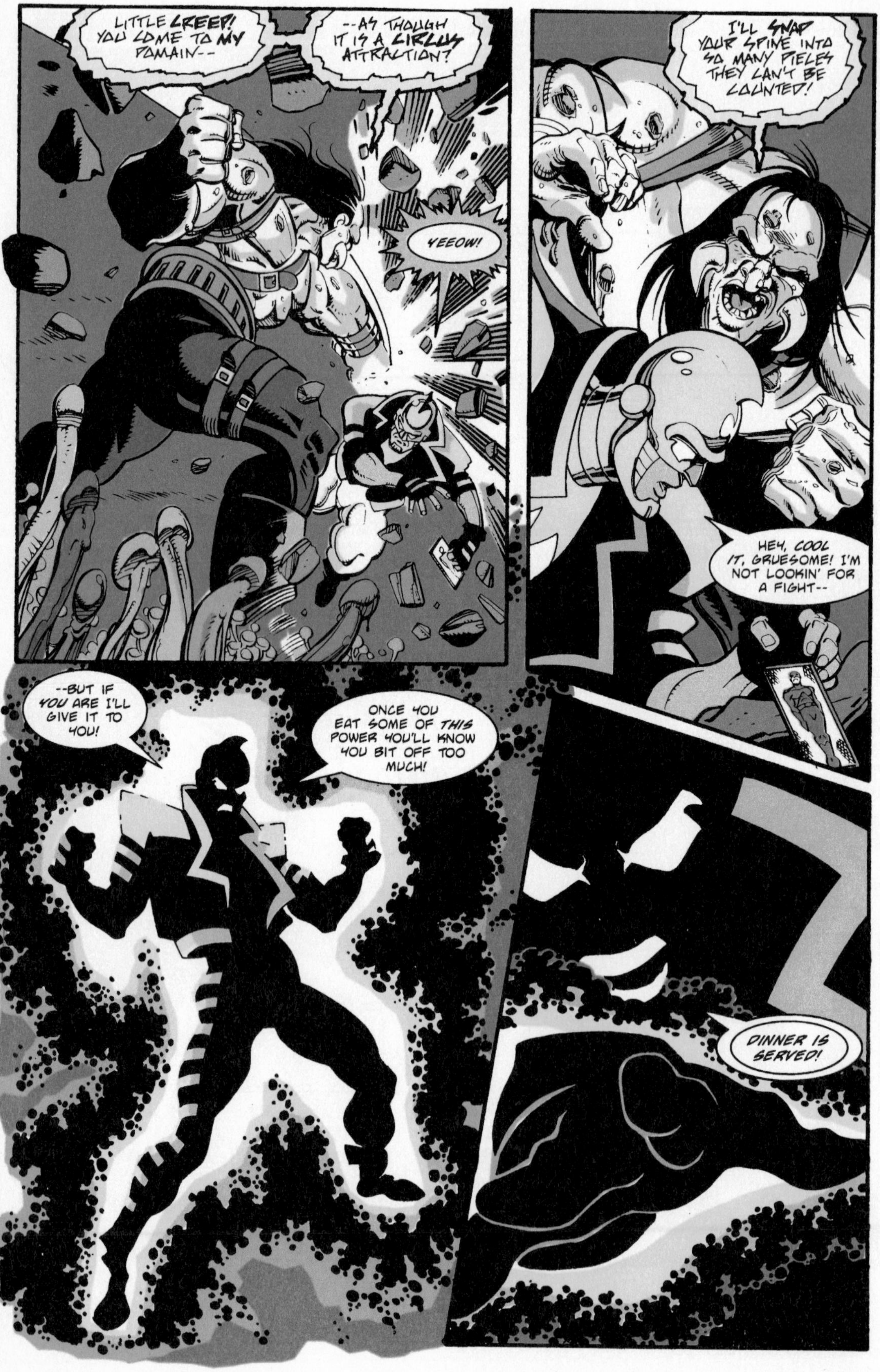
LITTLE CREEP! YOU COME TO MY DOMAIN--
--AS THOUGH IT IS A CIRCUS ATTRACTION?
YEEOW!
I'LL SNAP YOUR SPINE INTO SO MANY PIECES THEY CAN'T BE COUNTED!
HEY, COOL IT, GRUESOME! I'M NOT LOOKIN' FOR A FIGHT--
--BUT IF YOU ARE I'LL GIVE IT TO YOU!
ONCE YOU EAT SOME OF THIS POWER YOU'LL KNOW YOU BIT OFF TOO MUCH!
DINNER IS SERVED!

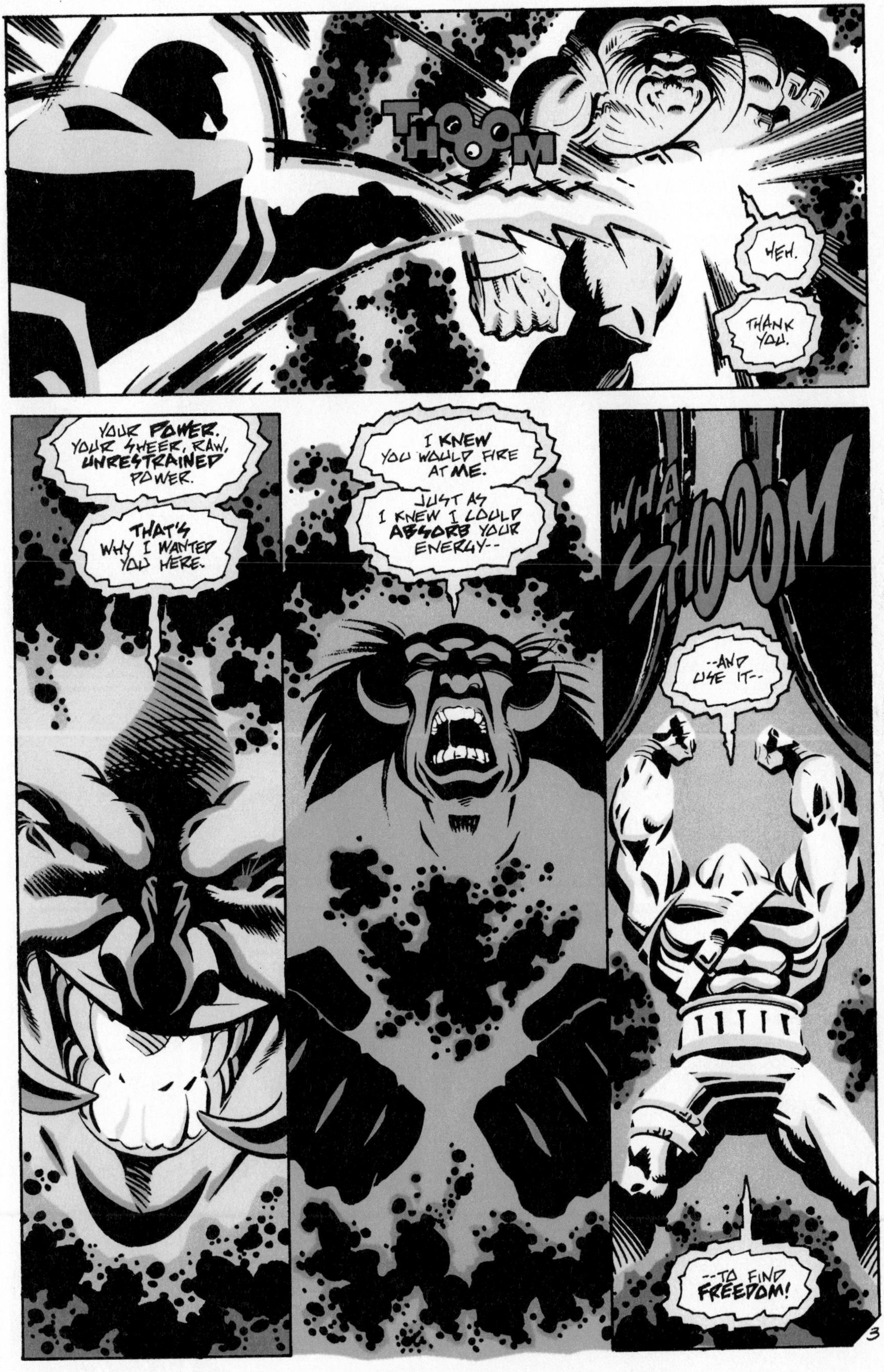
THOOOM
HEH.
THANK YOU.
YOUR POWER. YOUR SHEER, RAW, UNRESTRAINED POWER.
THAT'S WHY I WANTED YOU HERE.
I KNEW YOU WOULD FIRE AT ME.
JUST AS I KNEW I COULD ABSORB YOUR ENERGY--
WHA SHOOOM
--AND USE IT--
--TO FIND FREEDOM!

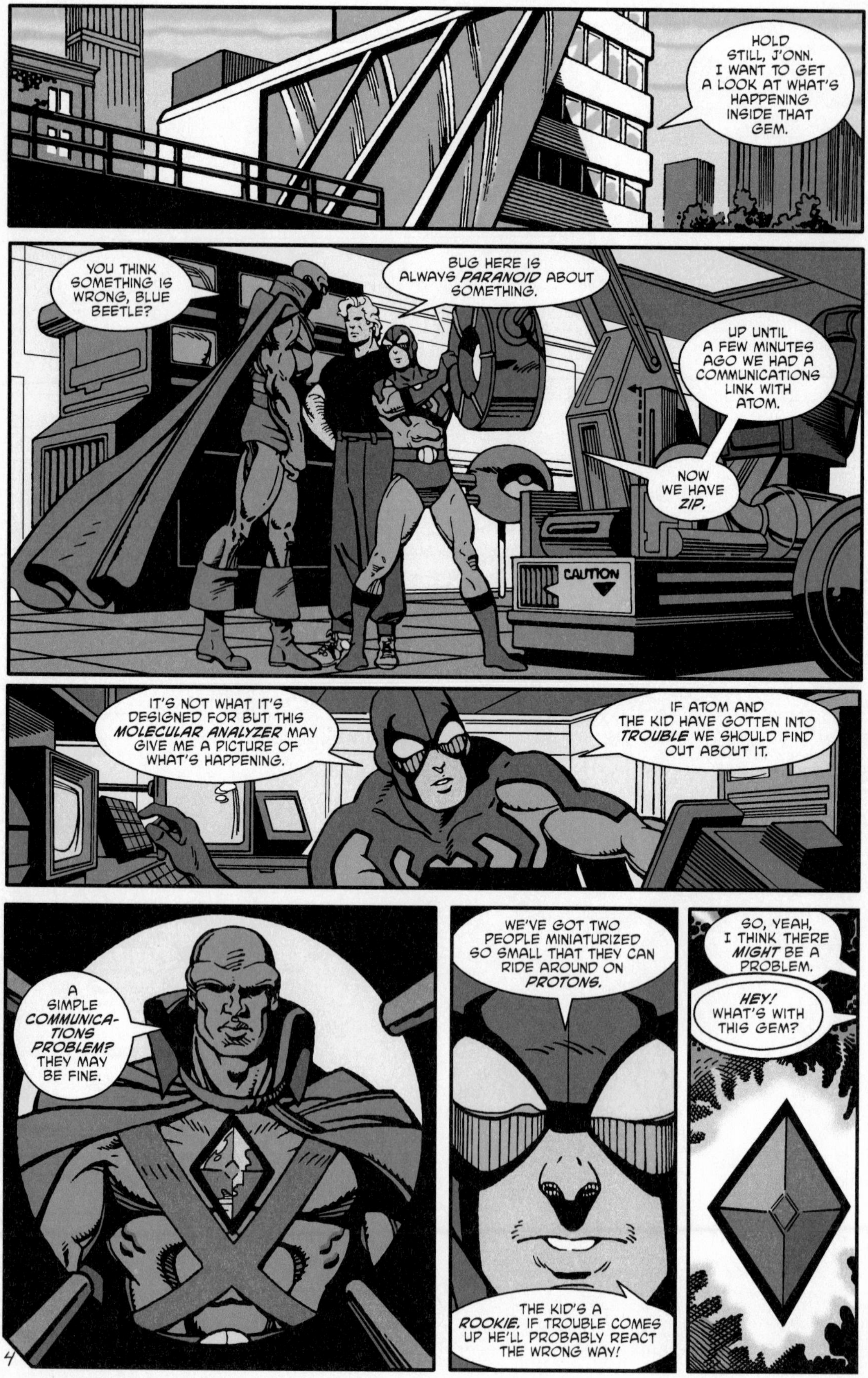
HOLD STILL, J'ONN. I WANT TO GET A LOOK AT WHAT'S HAPPENING INSIDE THAT GEM.
YOU THINK SOMETHING IS WRONG, BLUE BEETLE?
BUG HERE IS ALWAYS PARANOID ABOUT SOMETHING.
UP UNTIL A FEW MINUTES AGO WE HAD A COMMUNICATIONS LINK WITH ATOM.
NOW WE HAVE ZIP.
CAUTION
IT'S NOT WHAT IT'S DESIGNED FOR BUT THIS MOLECULAR ANALYZER MAY GIVE ME A PICTURE OF WHAT'S HAPPENING.
IF ATOM AND THE KID HAVE GOTTEN INTO TROUBLE WE SHOULD FIND OUT ABOUT IT.
A SIMPLE COMMUNICATIONS PROBLEM? THEY MAY BE FINE.
WE'VE GOT TWO PEOPLE MINIATURIZED SO SMALL THAT THEY CAN RIDE AROUND ON PROTONS.
THE KID'S A ROOKIE. IF TROUBLE COMES UP HE'LL PROBABLY REACT THE WRONG WAY!
SO, YEAH, I THINK THERE MIGHT BE A PROBLEM.
HEY! WHAT'S WITH THIS GEM?

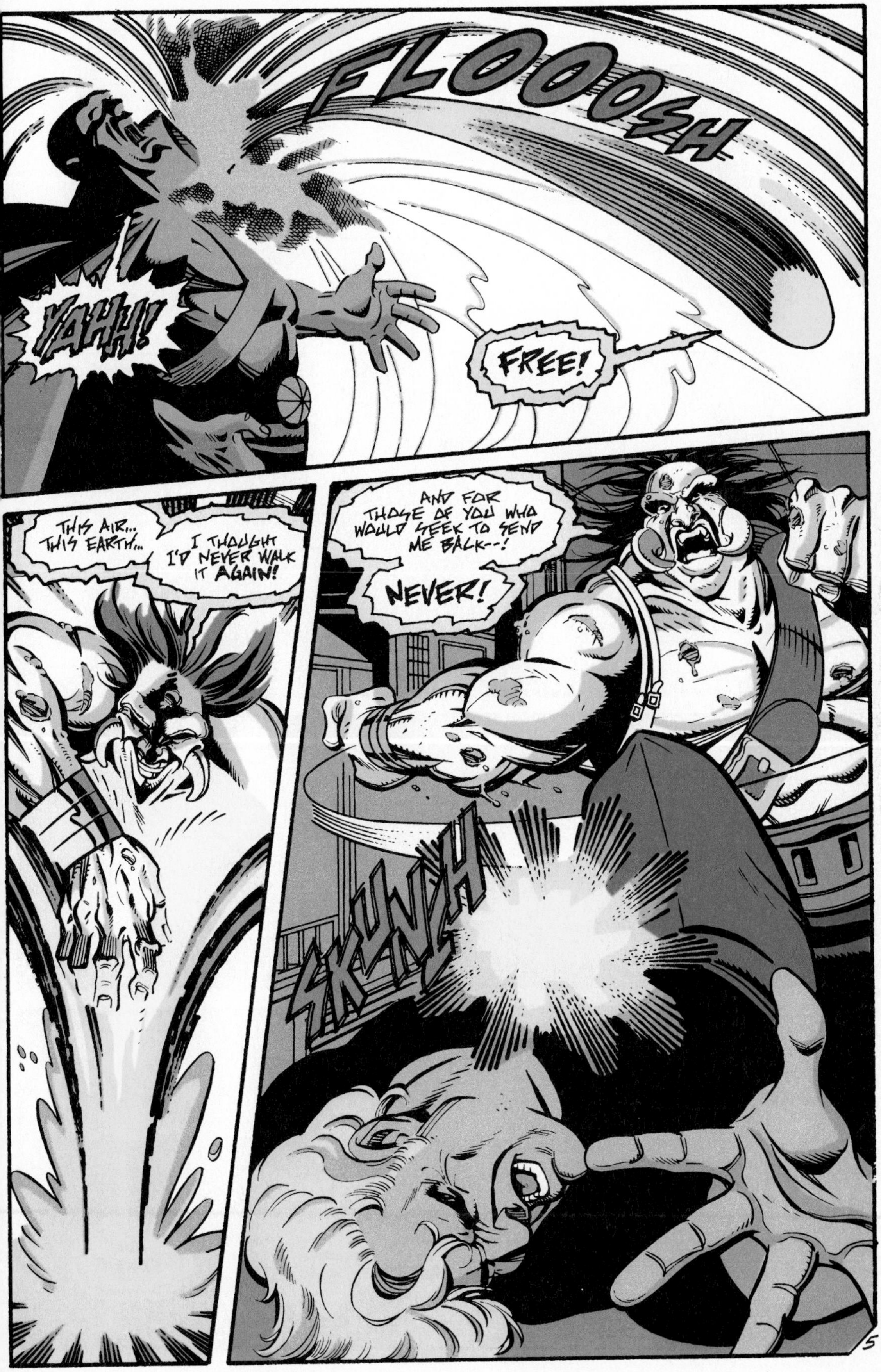
FLOOOSH
YAHH!
FREE!
THIS AIR... THIS EARTH...
I THOUGHT I'D NEVER WALK IT AGAIN!
AND FOR THOSE OF YOU WHO WOULD SEEK TO SEND ME BACK--!
NEVER!
SKUNCH

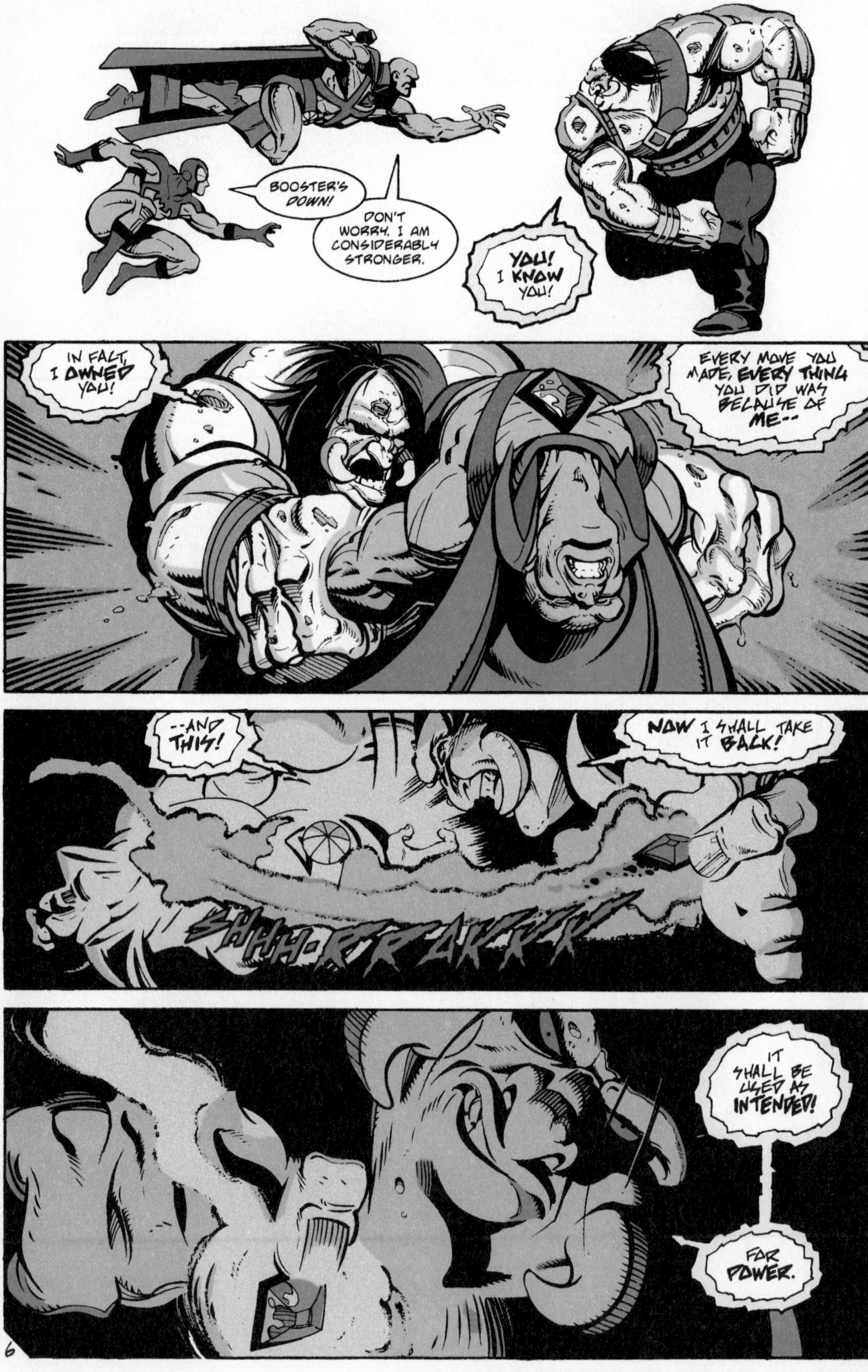
BOOSTER'S DOWN!
DON'T WORRY. I AM CONSIDERABLY STRONGER.
YOU! I KNOW YOU!
IN FACT, I OWNED YOU!
EVERY MOVE YOU MADE, EVERY THING YOU DID WAS BECAUSE OF ME--
--AND THIS!
NOW I SHALL TAKE IT BACK!
SHHH-RRAKRR
IT SHALL BE USED AS INTENDED!
FOR POWER.

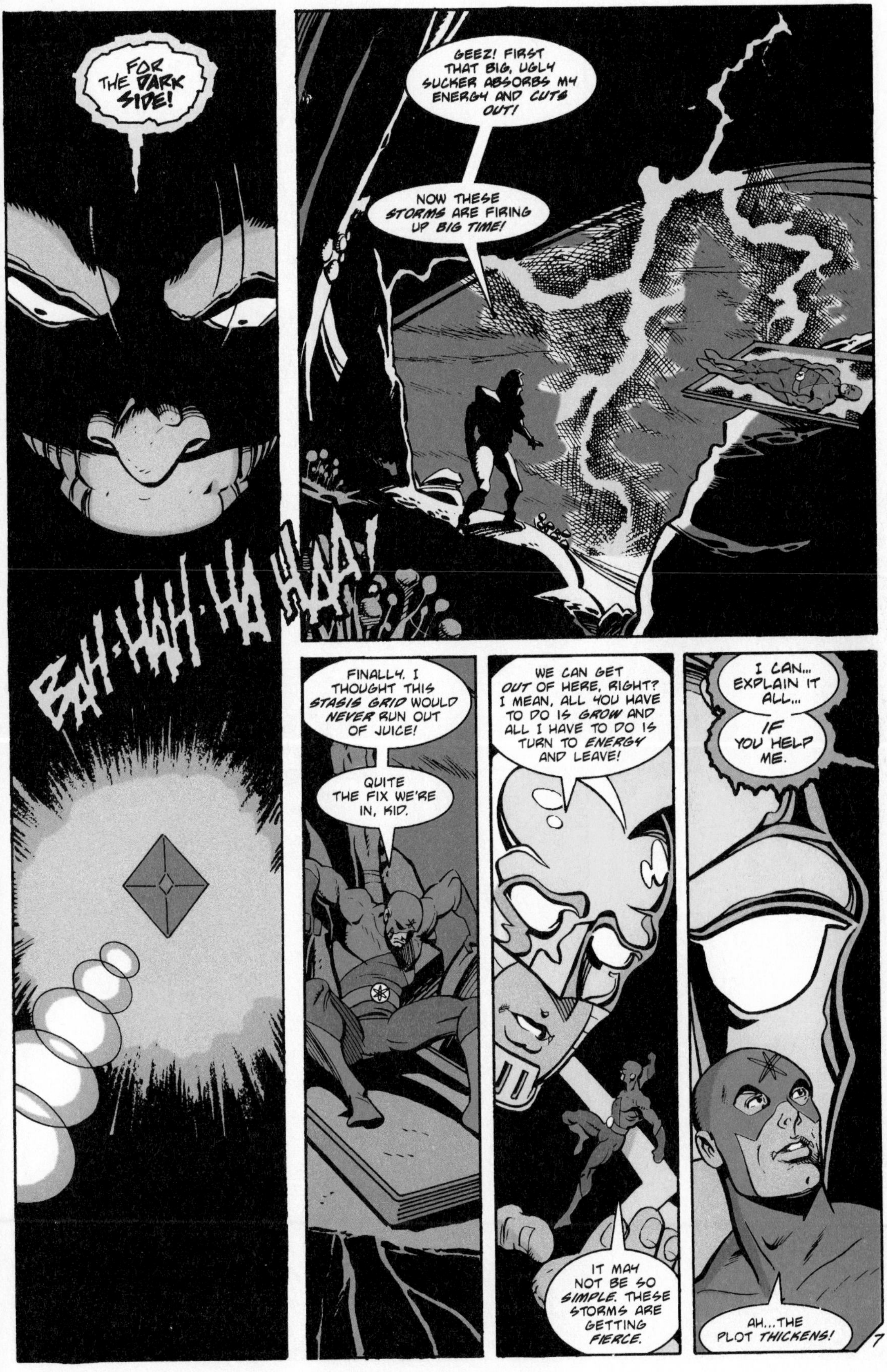
FOR THE DARK SIDE!
BAH-HAH-HA HAA!
GEEZ! FIRST THAT BIG, UGLY SUCKER ABSORBS MY ENERGY AND CUTS OUT!
NOW THESE STORMS ARE FIRING UP BIG TIME!
FINALLY. I THOUGHT THIS STASIS GRID WOULD NEVER RUN OUT OF JUICE!
QUITE THE FIX WE'RE IN, KID.
WE CAN GET OUT OF HERE, RIGHT? I MEAN, ALL YOU HAVE TO DO IS GROW AND ALL I HAVE TO DO IS TURN TO ENERGY AND LEAVE!
IT MAY NOT BE SO SIMPLE. THESE STORMS ARE GETTING FIERCE.
I CAN... EXPLAIN IT ALL...
IF YOU HELP ME.
AH...THE PLOT THICKENS!

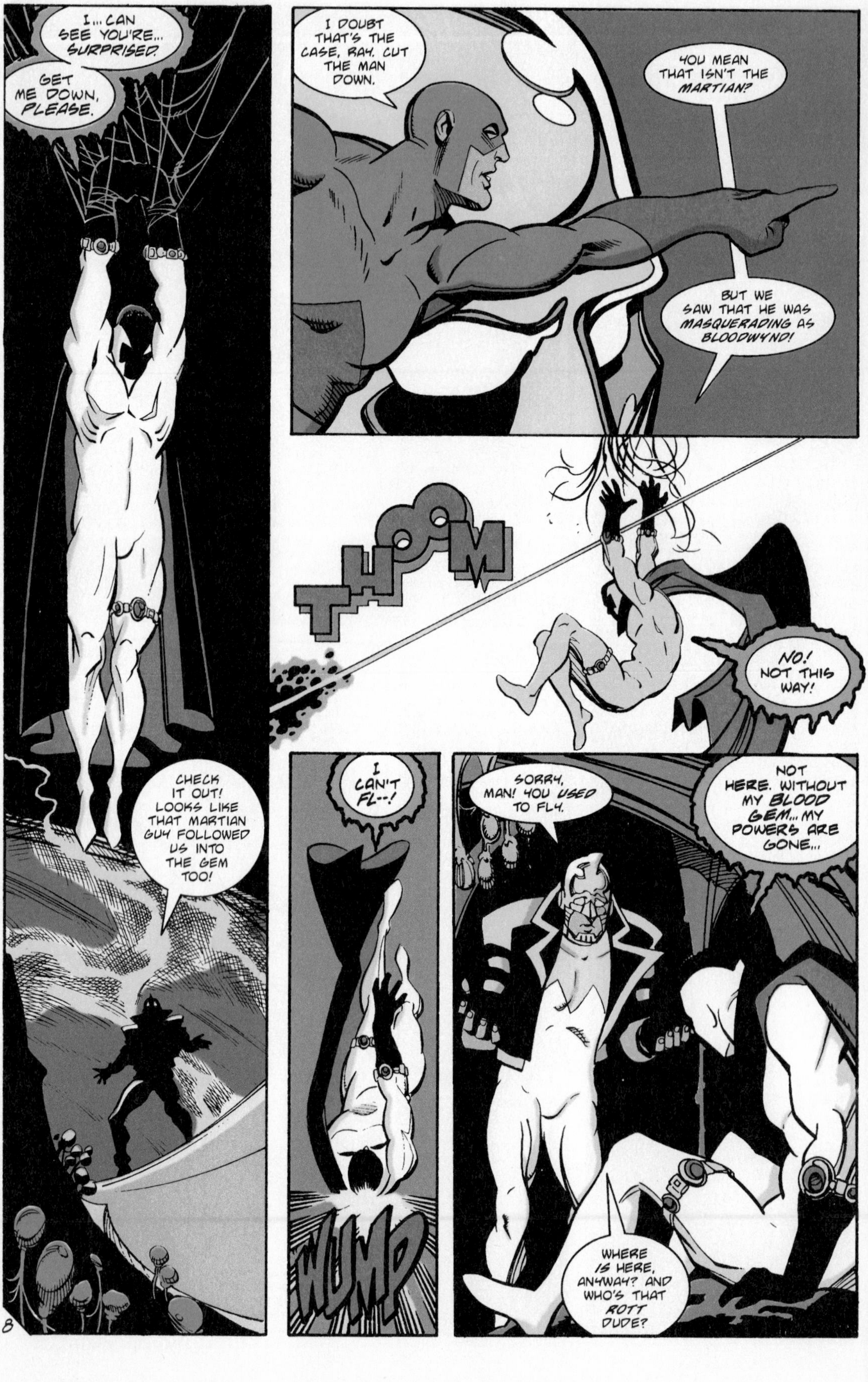

I... CAN SEE YOU'RE... SURPRISED.
GET ME DOWN, PLEASE.
I DOUBT THAT'S THE CASE, RAY. CUT THE MAN DOWN.
YOU MEAN THAT ISN'T THE MARTIAN?
BUT WE SAW THAT HE WAS MASQUERADING AS BLOODWYND!
THOOM
NO! NOT THIS WAY!
CHECK IT OUT! LOOKS LIKE THAT MARTIAN GUY FOLLOWED US INTO THE GEM TOO!
I CAN'T FL--!
WUMP
SORRY, MAN! YOU USED TO FLY.
NOT HERE. WITHOUT MY BLOOD GEM... MY POWERS ARE GONE...
WHERE IS HERE, ANYWAY? AND WHO'S THAT ROTT DUDE?

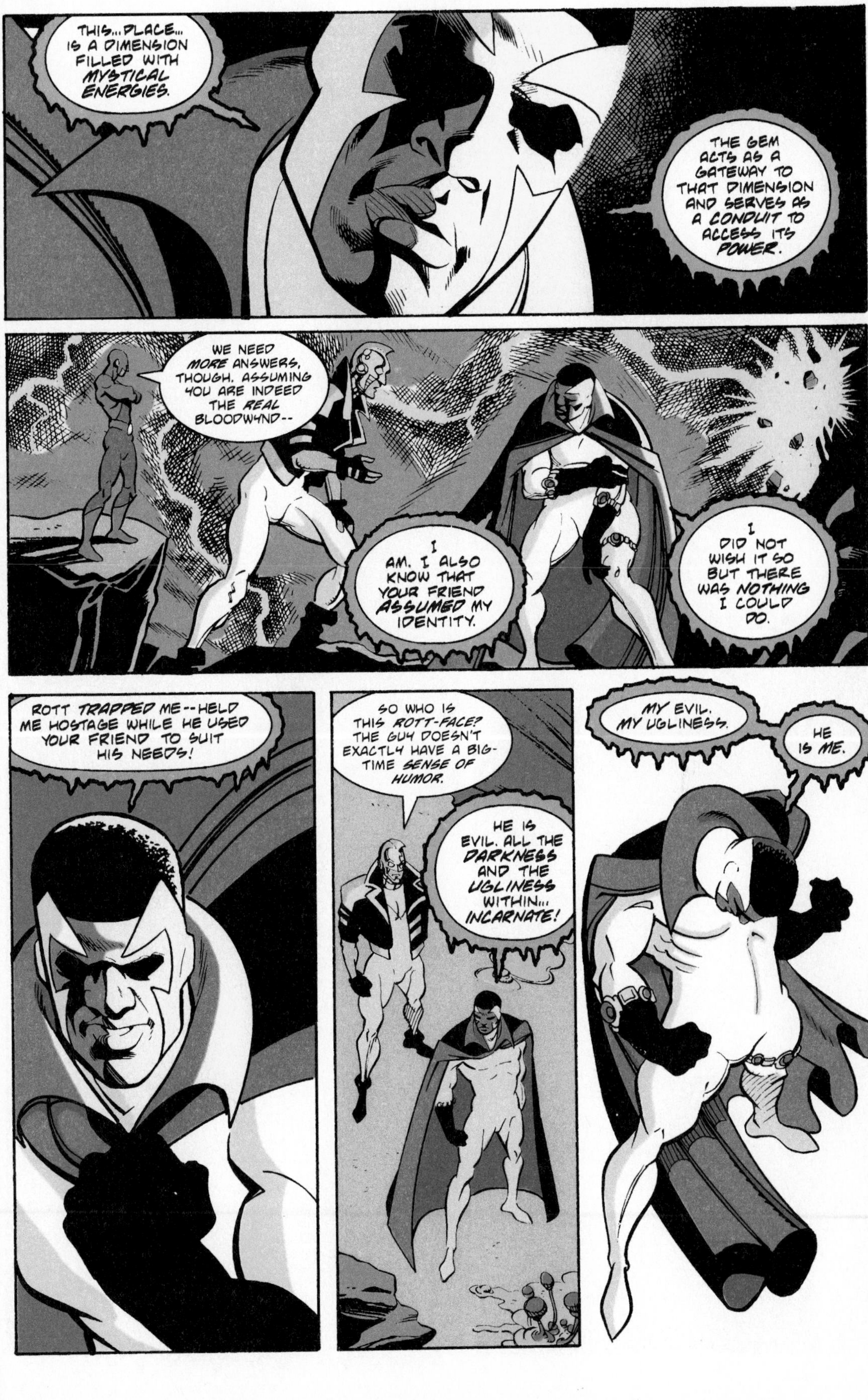
THIS... PLACE... IS A DIMENSION FILLED WITH MYSTICAL ENERGIES.
THE GEM ACTS AS A GATEWAY TO THAT DIMENSION AND SERVES AS A CONDUIT TO ACCESS ITS POWER.
WE NEED MORE ANSWERS, THOUGH. ASSUMING YOU ARE INDEED THE REAL BLOODWYND--
I AM. I ALSO KNOW THAT YOUR FRIEND ASSUMED MY IDENTITY.
I DID NOT WISH IT SO BUT THERE WAS NOTHING I COULD DO.
ROTT TRAPPED ME--HELD ME HOSTAGE WHILE HE USED YOUR FRIEND TO SUIT HIS NEEDS!
SO WHO IS THIS ROTT-FACE? THE GUY DOESN'T EXACTLY HAVE A BIG-TIME SENSE OF HUMOR.
HE IS EVIL. ALL THE DARKNESS AND THE UGLINESS WITHIN... INCARNATE!
MY EVIL. MY UGLINESS.
HE IS ME.

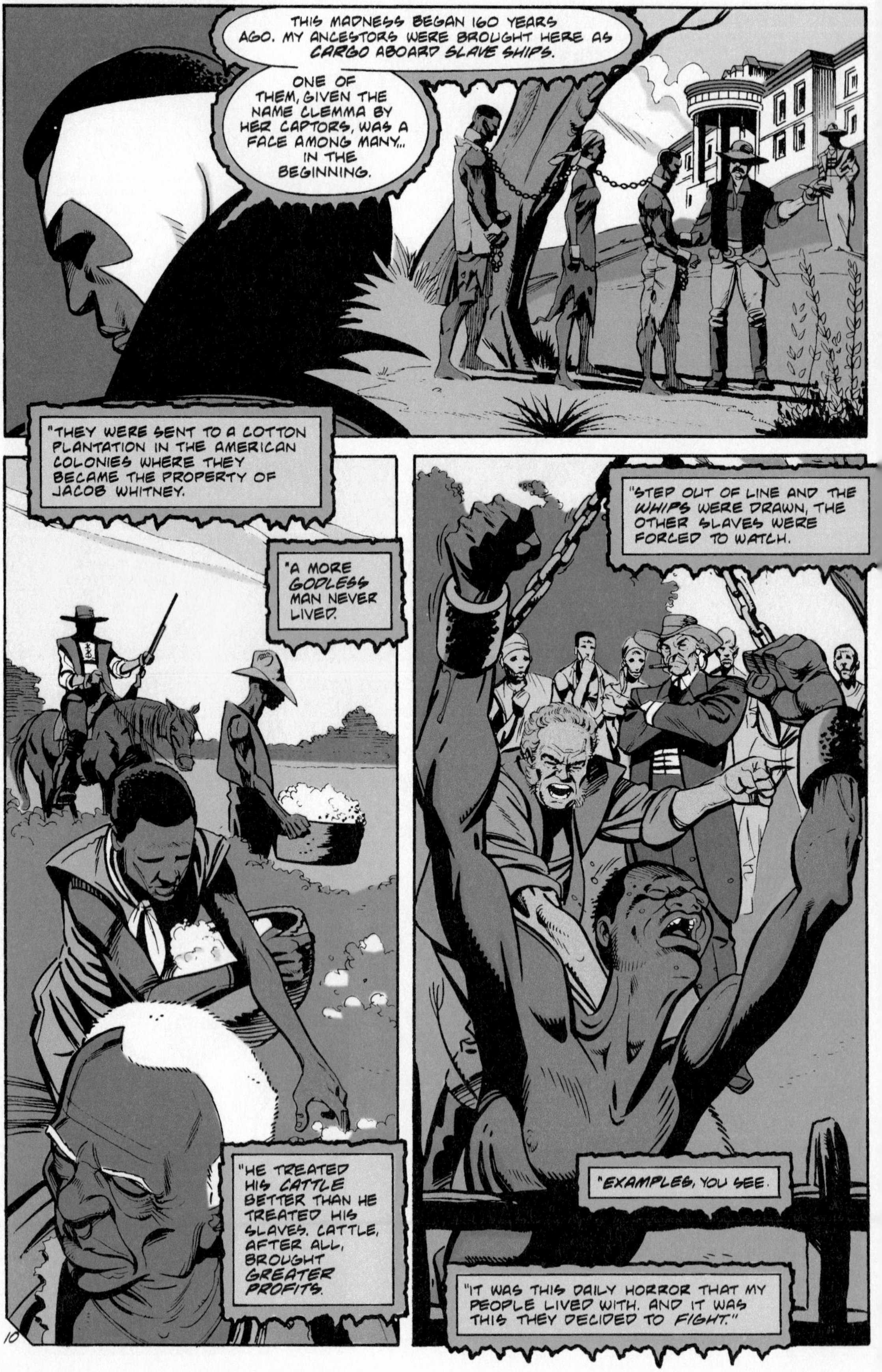
THIS MADNESS BEGAN 160 YEARS AGO. MY ANCESTORS WERE BROUGHT HERE AS CARGO ABOARD SLAVE SHIPS.
ONE OF THEM, GIVEN THE NAME CLEMMA BY HER CAPTORS, WAS A FACE AMONG MANY... IN THE BEGINNING.
"THEY WERE SENT TO A COTTON PLANTATION IN THE AMERICAN COLONIES WHERE THEY BECAME THE PROPERTY OF JACOB WHITNEY.
"A MORE GODLESS MAN NEVER LIVED.
"HE TREATED HIS CATTLE BETTER THAN HE TREATED HIS SLAVES. CATTLE, AFTER ALL, BROUGHT GREATER PROFITS.
"STEP OUT OF LINE AND THE WHIPS WERE DRAWN, THE OTHER SLAVES WERE FORCED TO WATCH.
"EXAMPLES, YOU SEE.
"IT WAS THIS DAILY HORROR THAT MY PEOPLE LIVED WITH. AND IT WAS THIS THEY DECIDED TO FIGHT."

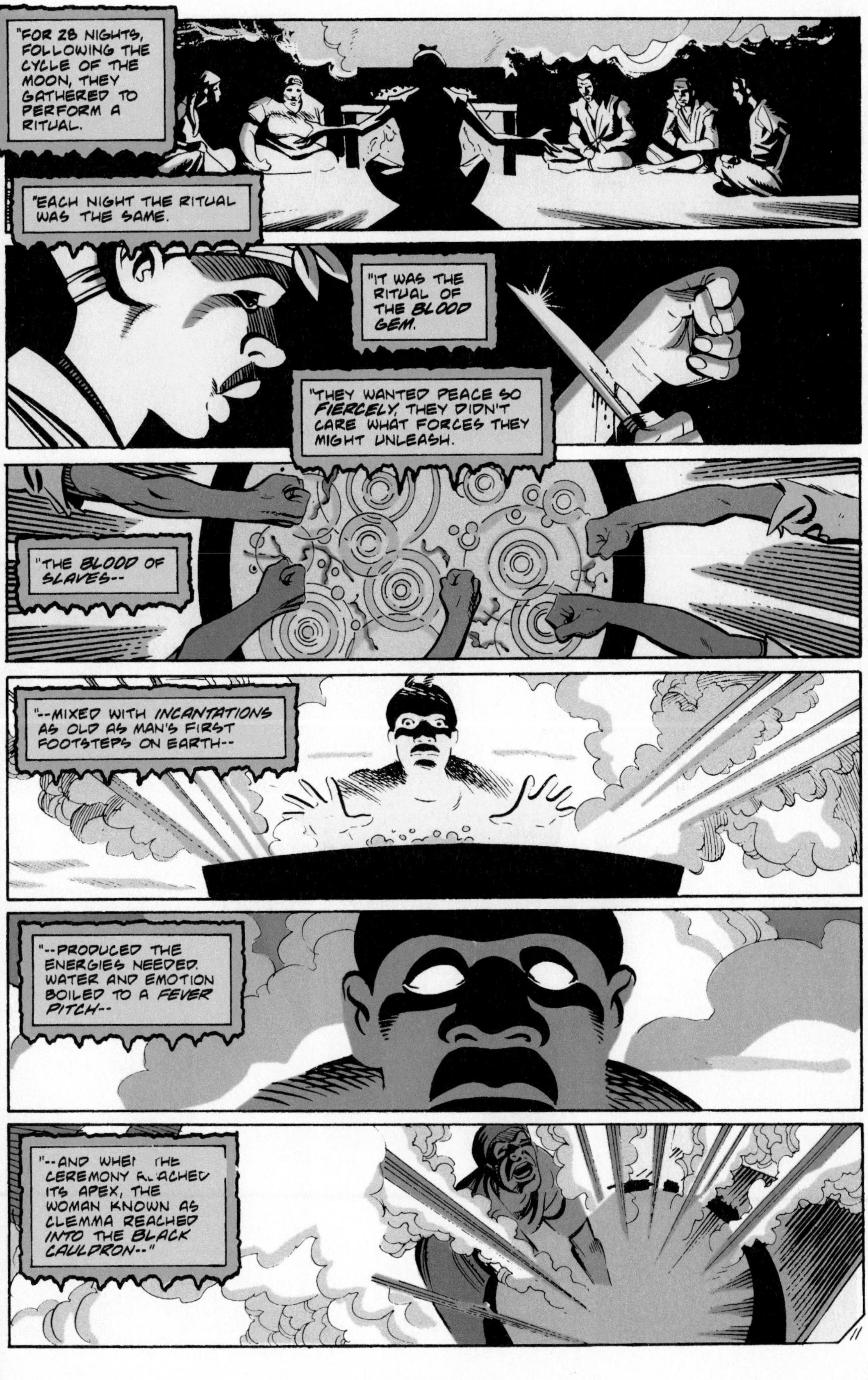
"FOR 28 NIGHTS, FOLLOWING THE CYCLE OF THE MOON, THEY GATHERED TO PERFORM A RITUAL.
"EACH NIGHT THE RITUAL WAS THE SAME.
"IT WAS THE RITUAL OF THE BLOOD GEM.
"THEY WANTED PEACE SO FIERCELY, THEY DIDN'T CARE WHAT FORCES THEY MIGHT UNLEASH.
"THE BLOOD OF SLAVES--
"--MIXED WITH INCANTATIONS AS OLD AS MAN'S FIRST FOOTSTEPS ON EARTH--
"--PRODUCED THE ENERGIES NEEDED. WATER AND EMOTION BOILED TO A FEVER PITCH--
"--AND WHEN THE CEREMONY REACHED ITS APEX, THE WOMAN KNOWN AS CLEMMA REACHED INTO THE BLACK CAULDRON--"

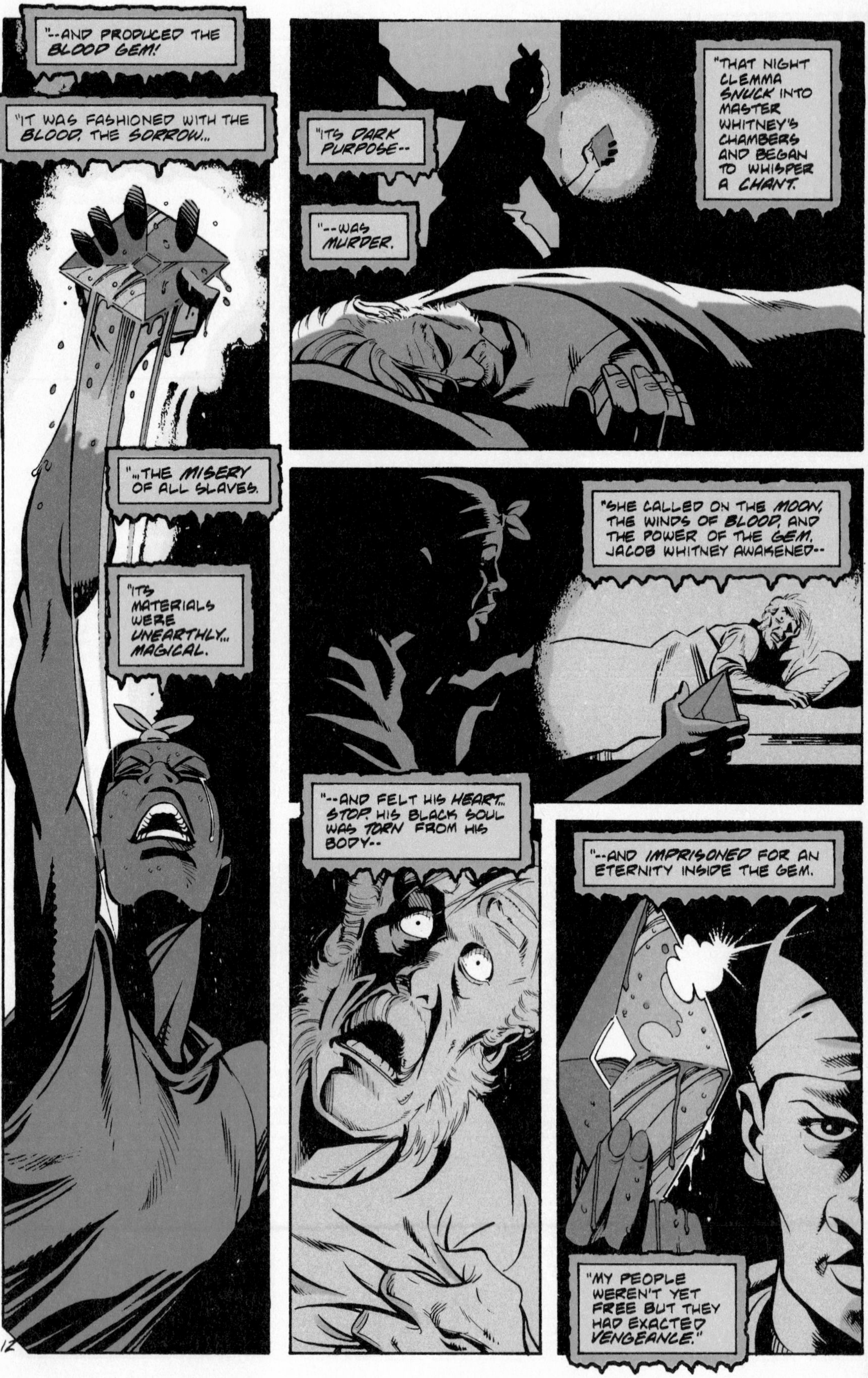
"--AND PRODUCED THE BLOOD GEM!
"IT WAS FASHIONED WITH THE BLOOD, THE SORROW...
"...THE MISERY OF ALL SLAVES.
"ITS MATERIALS WERE UNEARTHLY... MAGICAL.
"ITS DARK PURPOSE--
"--WAS MURDER.
"THAT NIGHT CLEMMA SNUCK INTO MASTER WHITNEY'S CHAMBERS AND BEGAN TO WHISPER A CHANT.
"SHE CALLED ON THE MOON, THE WINDS OF BLOOD, AND THE POWER OF THE GEM. JACOB WHITNEY AWAKENED--
"--AND FELT HIS HEART... STOP. HIS BLACK SOUL WAS TORN FROM HIS BODY--
"--AND IMPRISONED FOR AN ETERNITY INSIDE THE GEM.
"MY PEOPLE WEREN'T YET FREE BUT THEY HAD EXACTED VENGEANCE."

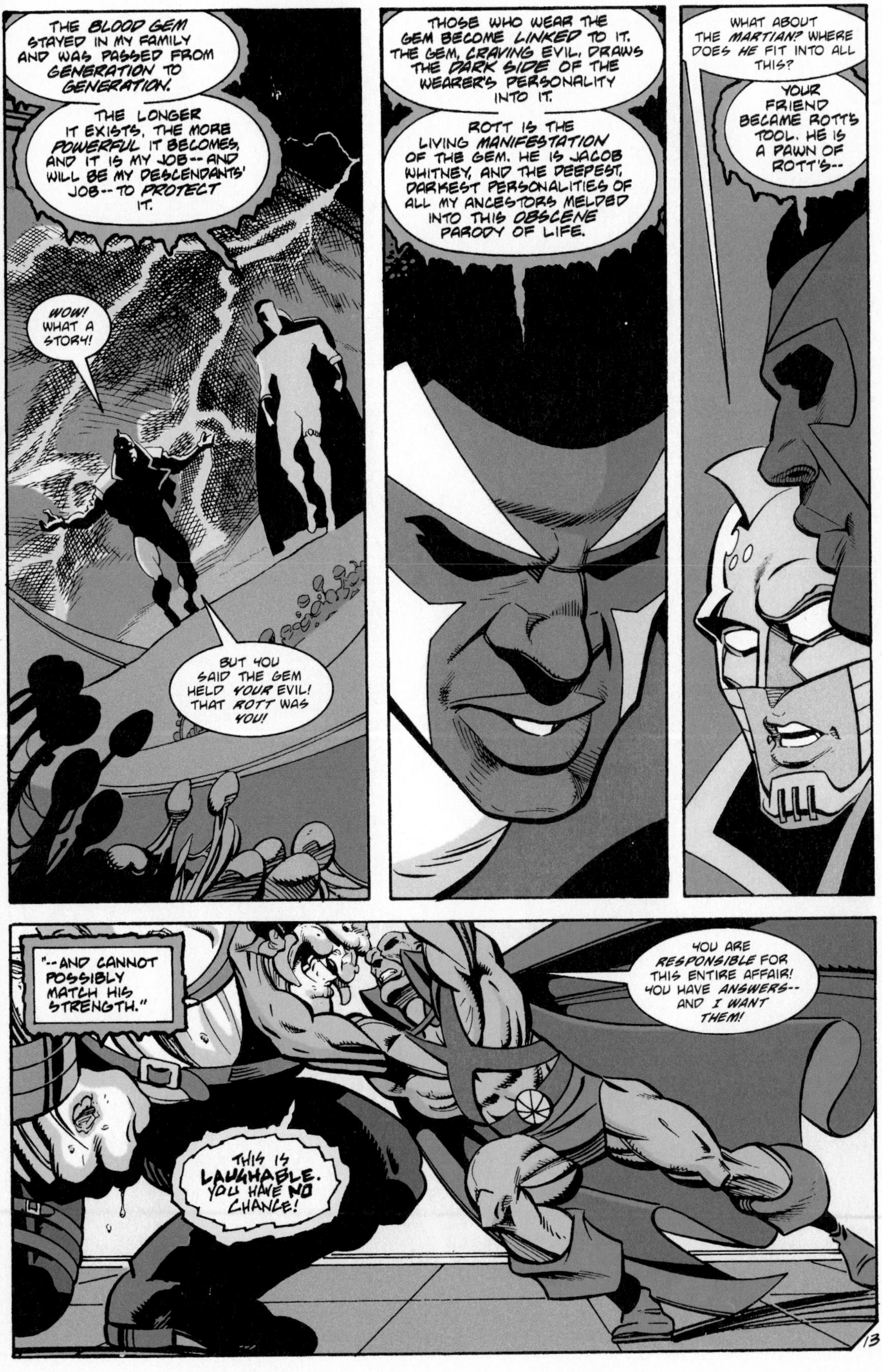
THE BLOOD GEM STAYED IN MY FAMILY AND WAS PASSED FROM GENERATION TO GENERATION.
THE LONGER IT EXISTS, THE MORE POWERFUL IT BECOMES, AND IT IS MY JOB-- AND WILL BE MY DESCENDANTS' JOB-- TO PROTECT IT.
WOW! WHAT A STORY!
BUT YOU SAID THE GEM HELD YOUR EVIL! THAT ROTT WAS YOU!
THOSE WHO WEAR THE GEM BECOME LINKED TO IT. THE GEM, CRAVING EVIL, DRAWS THE DARK SIDE OF THE WEARER'S PERSONALITY INTO IT.
ROTT IS THE LIVING MANIFESTATION OF THE GEM. HE IS JACOB WHITNEY, AND THE DEEPEST, DARKEST PERSONALITIES OF ALL MY ANCESTORS MELDED INTO THIS OBSCENE PARODY OF LIFE.
WHAT ABOUT THE MARTIAN? WHERE DOES HE FIT INTO ALL THIS?
YOUR FRIEND BECAME ROTT'S TOOL. HE IS A PAWN OF ROTT'S--
"--AND CANNOT POSSIBLY MATCH HIS STRENGTH."
YOU ARE RESPONSIBLE FOR THIS ENTIRE AFFAIR! YOU HAVE ANSWERS-- AND I WANT THEM!
THIS IS LAUGHABLE. YOU HAVE NO CHANCE!

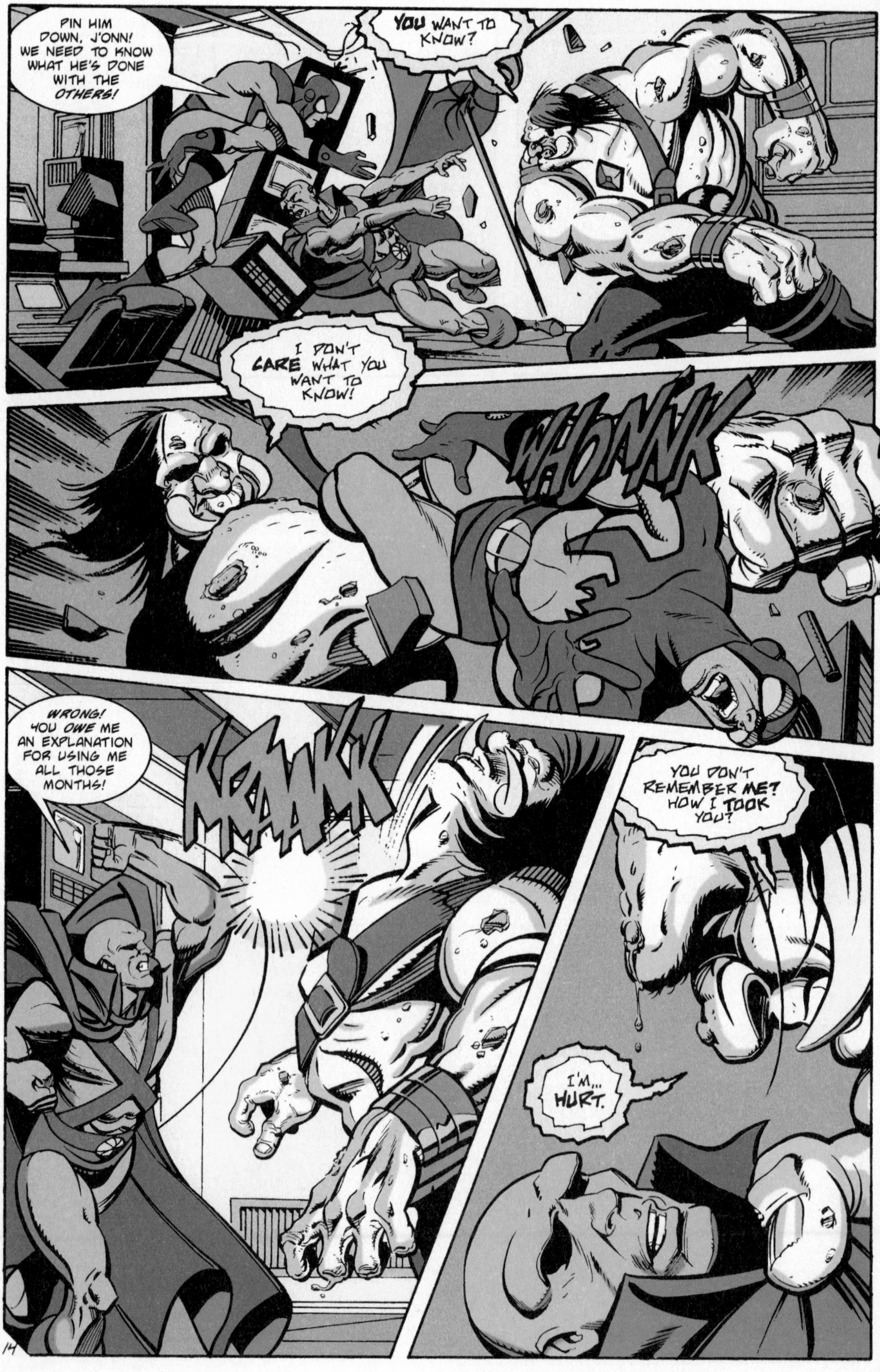

PIN HIM DOWN, J'ONN! WE NEED TO KNOW WHAT HE'S DONE WITH THE OTHERS!
YOU WANT TO KNOW?
I DON'T CARE WHAT YOU WANT TO KNOW!
WHONNK
WRONG! YOU OWE ME AN EXPLANATION FOR USING ME ALL THOSE MONTHS!
KRAAKK
YOU DON'T REMEMBER ME? HOW I TOOK YOU?
I'M... HURT.

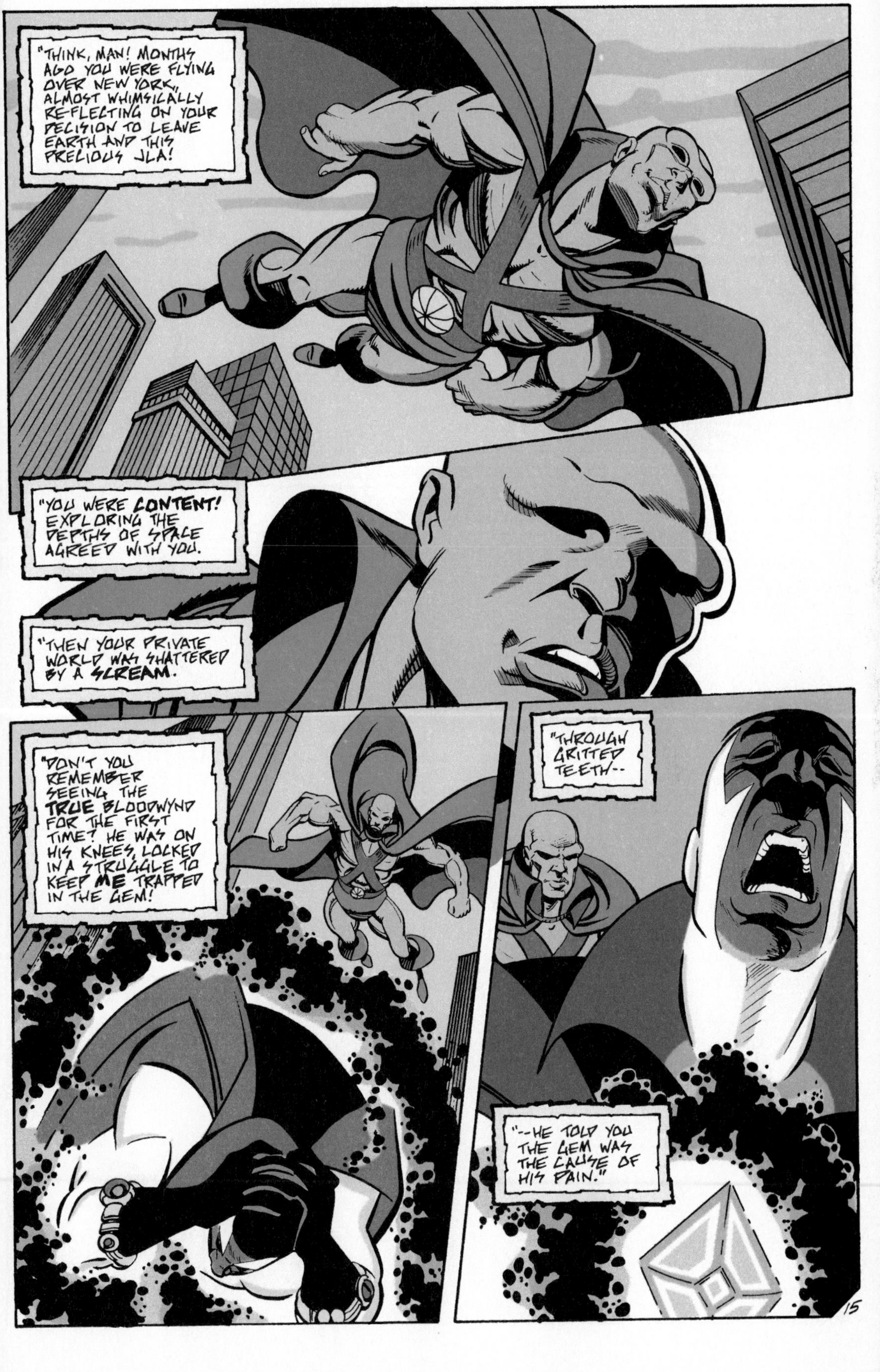
"THINK, MAN! MONTHS AGO YOU WERE FLYING OVER NEW YORK, ALMOST WHIMSICALLY RE-FLECTING ON YOUR DECISION TO LEAVE EARTH AND THIS PRECIOUS JLA!
"YOU WERE CONTENT! EXPLORING THE DEPTHS OF SPACE AGREED WITH YOU.
"THEN YOUR PRIVATE WORLD WAS SHATTERED BY A SCREAM.
"DON'T YOU REMEMBER SEEING THE TRUE BLOODWYND FOR THE FIRST TIME? HE WAS ON HIS KNEES, LOCKED IN A STRUGGLE TO KEEP ME TRAPPED IN THE GEM!
"THROUGH GRITTED TEETH--
"--HE TOLD YOU THE GEM WAS THE CAUSE OF HIS PAIN."

"BUT YOU WERE SO SILKENINGLY **GOOD** THAT YOU TRIED TO **HELP** HIM.

"BUT YOU KNEW NOTHING OF THIS MAGICIAN. YOU FOOLISHLY THOUGHT REMOVING THE GEM WOULD **EASE** HIS PAIN.

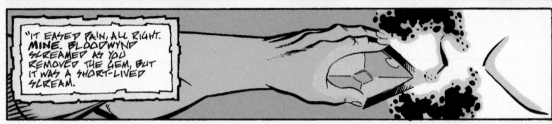

"IT EASED PAIN, ALL RIGHT. **MINE.** BLOODWYND **SCREAMED** AS YOU REMOVED THE GEM, BUT IT WAS A SHORT-LIVED SCREAM.

"BLOODWYND WAS SUCKED INTO THE GEM AT MY **COMMAND.** I WAS NOT YET POWERFUL ENOUGH TO ESCAPE.

"--BUT I WAS **STRONG** ENOUGH TO TAKE YOU AS MY PUPPET **HOST!**

"I COM-MANDED YOU TO WEAR THE GEM--

"--TO **CHANGE** YOUR IDENTITY--

"--AND ASSUME BLOODWYND'S ASPECT. YOU HAD ONE TASK--"

16

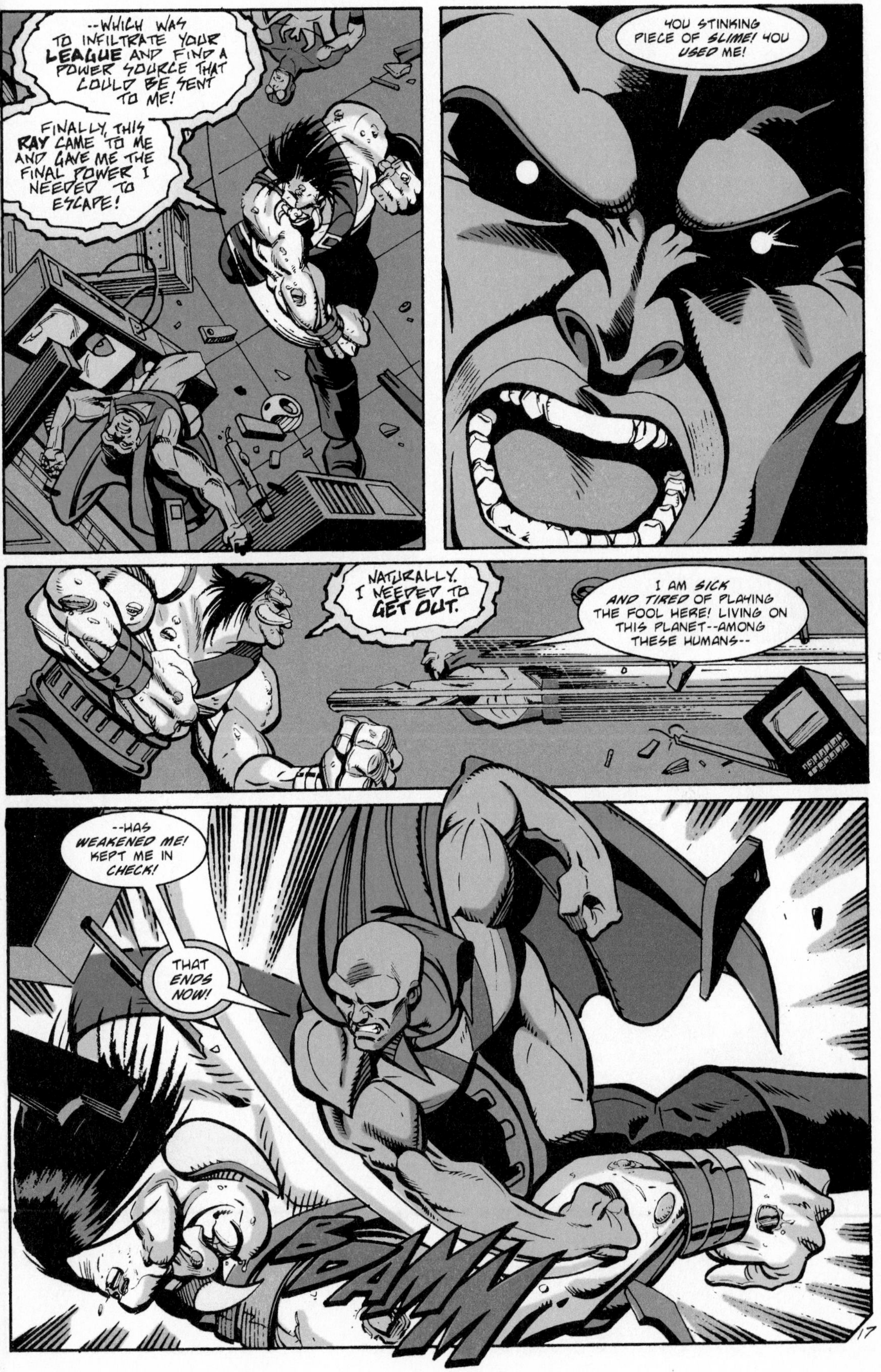
--WHICH WAS TO INFILTRATE YOUR LEAGUE AND FIND A POWER SOURCE THAT COULD BE SENT TO ME!
FINALLY, THIS RAY CAME TO ME AND GAVE ME THE FINAL POWER I NEEDED TO ESCAPE!
YOU STINKING PIECE OF SLIME! YOU USED ME!
NATURALLY. I NEEDED TO GET OUT.
I AM SICK AND TIRED OF PLAYING THE FOOL HERE! LIVING ON THIS PLANET--AMONG THESE HUMANS--
--HAS WEAKENED ME! KEPT ME IN CHECK!
THAT ENDS NOW!
BAMM

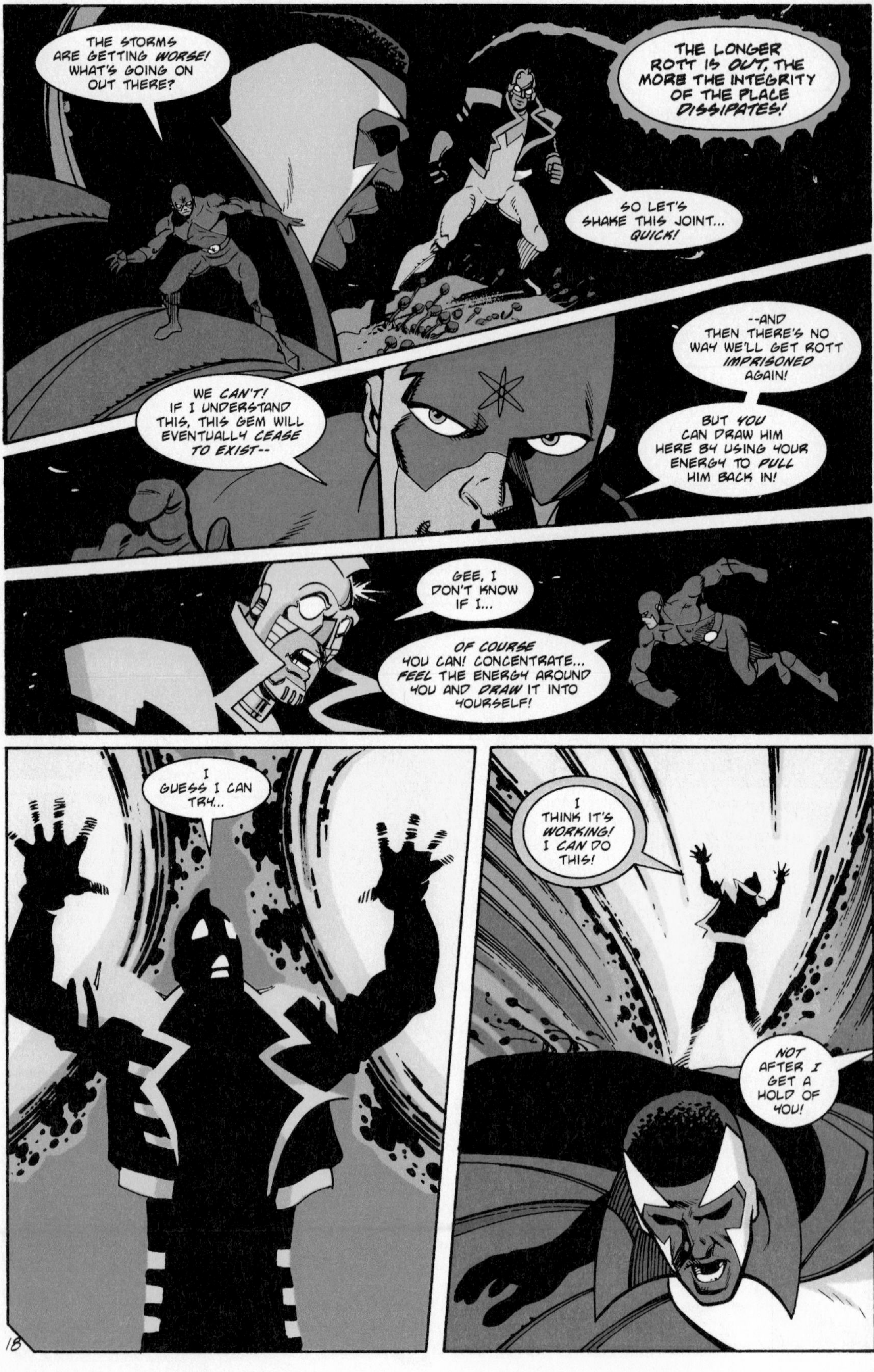
THE STORMS ARE GETTING WORSE! WHAT'S GOING ON OUT THERE?
THE LONGER ROTT IS OUT, THE MORE THE INTEGRITY OF THE PLACE DISSIPATES!
SO LET'S SHAKE THIS JOINT... QUICK!
WE CAN'T! IF I UNDERSTAND THIS, THIS GEM WILL EVENTUALLY CEASE TO EXIST--
--AND THEN THERE'S NO WAY WE'LL GET ROTT IMPRISONED AGAIN!
BUT YOU CAN DRAW HIM HERE BY USING YOUR ENERGY TO PULL HIM BACK IN!
GEE, I DON'T KNOW IF I...
OF COURSE YOU CAN! CONCENTRATE... FEEL THE ENERGY AROUND YOU AND DRAW IT INTO YOURSELF!
I GUESS I CAN TRY...
I THINK IT'S WORKING! I CAN DO THIS!
NOT AFTER I GET A HOLD OF YOU!

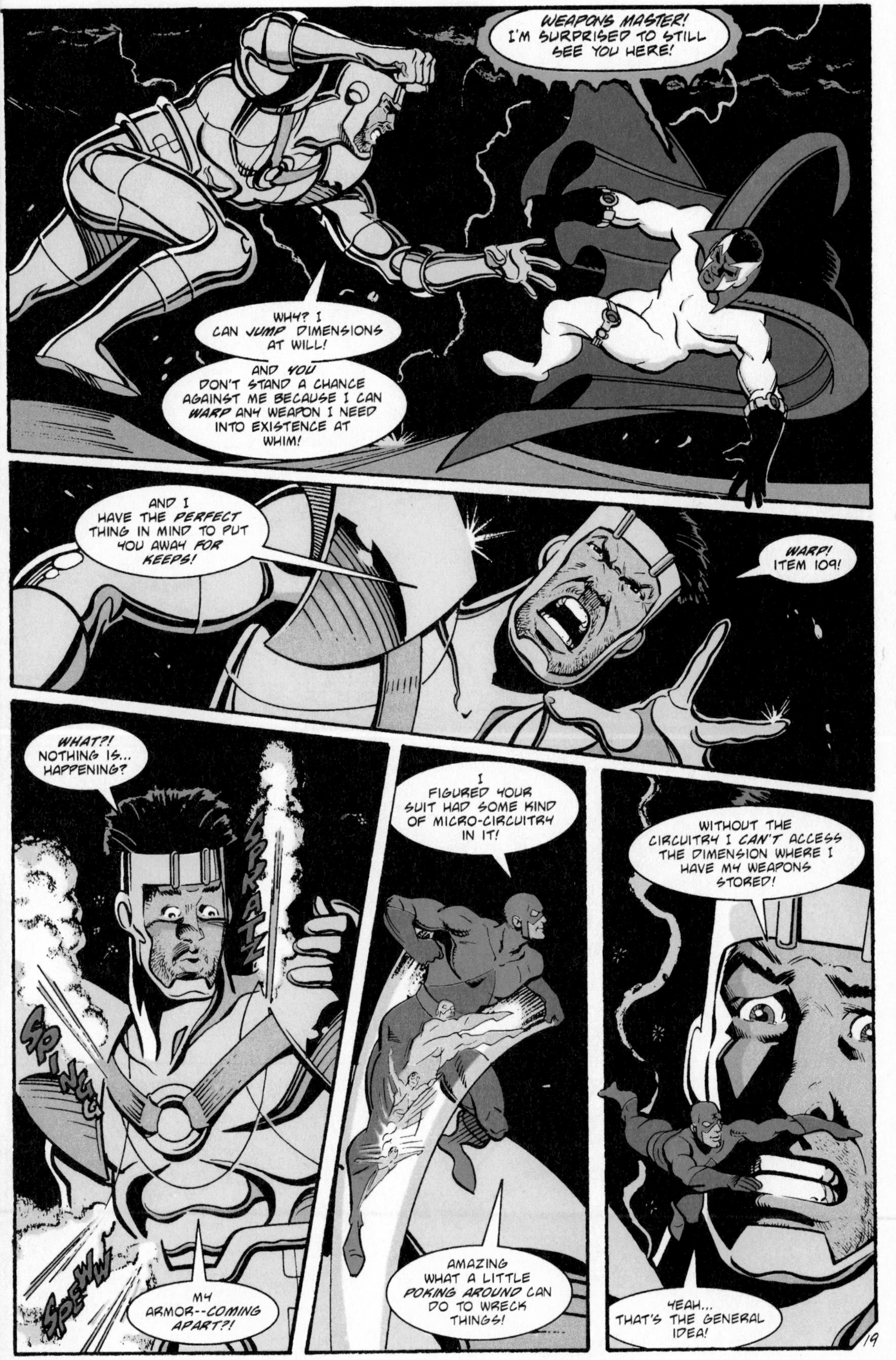
WEAPONS MASTER! I'M SURPRISED TO STILL SEE YOU HERE!
WHY? I CAN JUMP DIMENSIONS AT WILL!
AND YOU DON'T STAND A CHANCE AGAINST ME BECAUSE I CAN WARP ANY WEAPON I NEED INTO EXISTENCE AT WHIM!
AND I HAVE THE PERFECT THING IN MIND TO PUT YOU AWAY FOR KEEPS!
WARP! ITEM 109!
WHAT?! NOTHING IS... HAPPENING?
SPRATZ
SPRINGG
SPEWW
MY ARMOR--COMING APART?!
I FIGURED YOUR SUIT HAD SOME KIND OF MICRO-CIRCUITRY IN IT!
AMAZING WHAT A LITTLE POKING AROUND CAN DO TO WRECK THINGS!
WITHOUT THE CIRCUITRY I CAN'T ACCESS THE DIMENSION WHERE I HAVE MY WEAPONS STORED!
YEAH... THAT'S THE GENERAL IDEA!

SOMETHING'S...WRONG! FEELS LIKE... I'M BEING PULLED...INSIDE OUT!

IT'S WORKING! I CAN FEEL THE ENERGY RETURNING!

VROOOOOOOOOOOOOOOOOO

NO! NO! I'VE BEEN TRAPPED FOR SO LONG....

SOMETHING'S HAPPENING INSIDE THE GEM!

VROOOOOOOO

YOU GOT THAT RIGHT!

NOT NOW!

NOT WHILE I'M... FREE!

VROOOOOOOOOOOOOOOO...TAKZZET

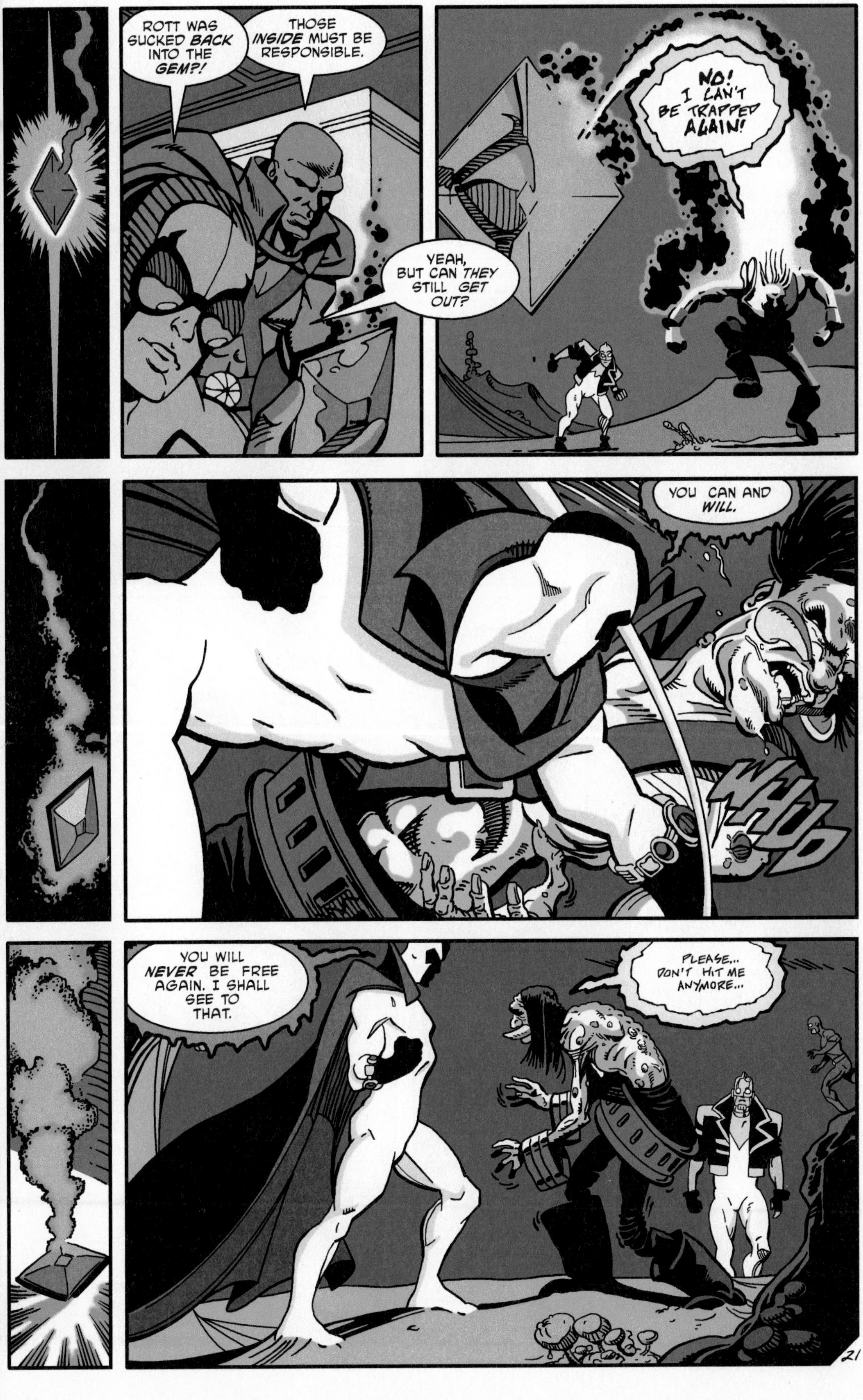
ROTT WAS SUCKED BACK INTO THE GEM?!
THOSE INSIDE MUST BE RESPONSIBLE.
YEAH, BUT CAN THEY STILL GET OUT?
NO! I CAN'T BE TRAPPED AGAIN!
YOU CAN AND WILL.
WHUD
YOU WILL NEVER BE FREE AGAIN. I SHALL SEE TO THAT.
PLEASE... DON'T HIT ME ANYMORE...

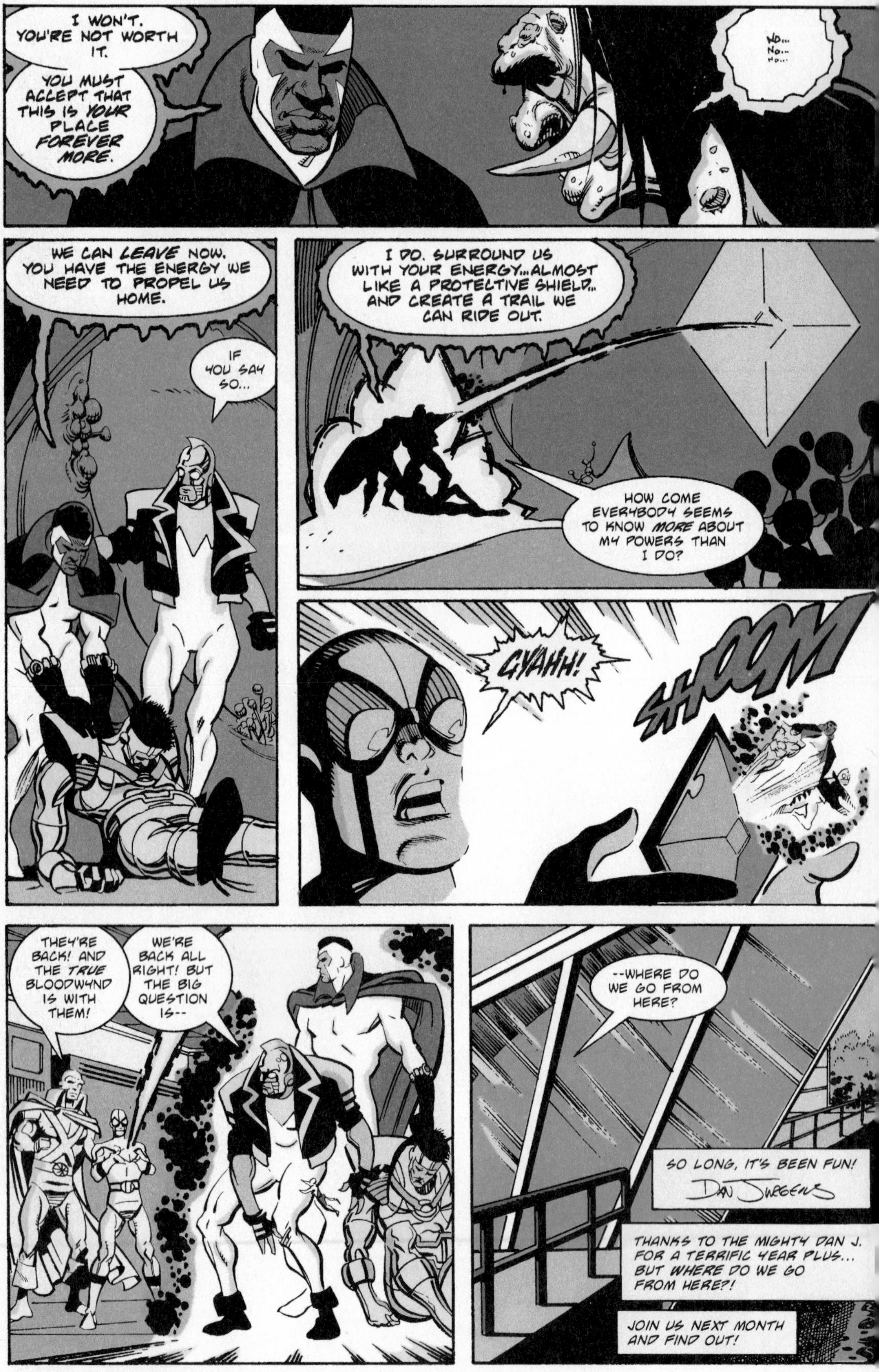
I WON'T. YOU'RE NOT WORTH IT.
YOU MUST ACCEPT THAT THIS IS YOUR PLACE FOREVER MORE.
NO... NO... NO...
WE CAN LEAVE NOW. YOU HAVE THE ENERGY WE NEED TO PROPEL US HOME.
IF YOU SAY SO...
I DO. SURROUND US WITH YOUR ENERGY...ALMOST LIKE A PROTECTIVE SHIELD... AND CREATE A TRAIL WE CAN RIDE OUT.
HOW COME EVERYBODY SEEMS TO KNOW MORE ABOUT MY POWERS THAN I DO?
GYAHH!
SHOOM
THEY'RE BACK! AND THE TRUE BLOODWYND IS WITH THEM!
WE'RE BACK ALL RIGHT! BUT THE BIG QUESTION IS--
--WHERE DO WE GO FROM HERE?
SO LONG, IT'S BEEN FUN!
DAN JURGENS
THANKS TO THE MIGHTY DAN J. FOR A TERRIFIC YEAR PLUS... BUT WHERE DO WE GO FROM HERE?!
JOIN US NEXT MONTH AND FIND OUT!